PAGE 38

ON THE ROAD

YOUR COMPLETE DESTINATION GUIDE
In-depth reviews, detailed listings
and insider tips

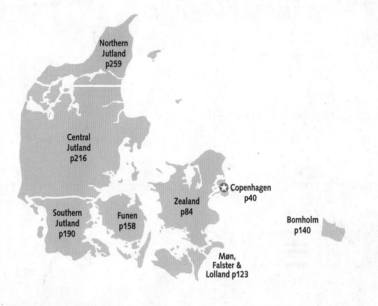

Northern
Jutland p259

Central
Jutland
p216

Copenhagen
p40

Zealand
p84

Southern
Jutland
p190

Funen
p158

Bornholm
p140

Møn,
Falster &
Lolland p123

PAGE 313

SURVIVAL GUIDE

VITAL PRACTICAL INFORMATION TO
HELP YOU HAVE A SMOOTH TRIP

Language

ACCOMMODATION

THIS EDITION WRITTEN AND RESEARCHED BY

Carolyn Bain

Cristian Bonetto, Andrew Stone

welcome to Denmark

Happiness & Hygge

It's heart-warming to know there's still a country where the term 'fairy tale' can be used freely – from its most enduring literary legacy to its fine textbook castles. In a nutshell, Denmark gets it right: old-fashioned charm embraces the most avowedly forward-looking design and social developments, and wins it a regular chart-topping place on lists of both the most liveable *and* the happiest nations on earth. You won't have to search hard to find some much-prized *hygge*, an untranslatable and uniquely Danish trait that has a profound influence on the locals' inestimable happiness. *Hygge* is social nirvana in Denmark: a sense of cosiness, camaraderie and contentment, when the worries of the world have been set aside.

Quality of Life

The world first took notice of Denmark more than a millennium ago, when Danish Vikings took to the seas and ravaged vast tracts of Europe. How things have changed! These days Denmark is regarded as the epitome of a civilised society, and it punches well above its weight on many fronts: progressive politics, urban planning, sustainability, design, architecture, film and literature – and now cuisine, thanks to the food world's latest crush, the New Nordic culinary movement.

Vikings, Hans Christian Andersen, Lego and now New Nordic cuisine – this is a small country with some big claims – a place that's perfected the art of living well.

(left) Country home near Egeskov Slot, Funen
(below) Colourful facades of Christianshavn, Copenhagen

While many other countries are noticeable for the ever-increasing gap between the 'haves' and 'have-nots', Denmark seems to be populated by the 'have enoughs', and the obviously rich and obviously poor are few and far between. This egalitarian spirit allows the best of the arts, architecture, eating and entertainment to be within easy reach of all. Indeed, the catchword for Denmark might well be 'inclusive' – everyone is welcome, everyone is catered to, be they young, old, gay, straight, male, female, and whether they travel with kids, pets or bikes in tow, or with a mobility issue or handicap. Cities are compact and user-friendly, infrastructure is clean and modern, and travel is a breeze.

The Danish Aesthetic

It's true, Denmark doesn't have the stop-you-in-your-tracks natural grandeur of its neighbours, but its landscapes are understated – pure and simple, often infused with an ethereal Nordic light. Such landscapes are reflected in the Danish design philosophy towards fashion, food, architecture, furniture and art. Simplicity of form and function come first, but not at the expense of beauty. And so you'll find moments of quintessential Danish loveliness on a long sandy beach, beside a lake, admiring a Renaissance castle, on the bike lanes of Bornholm, or in a candlelit cafe that has perfected the art of *hygge*.

› Denmark

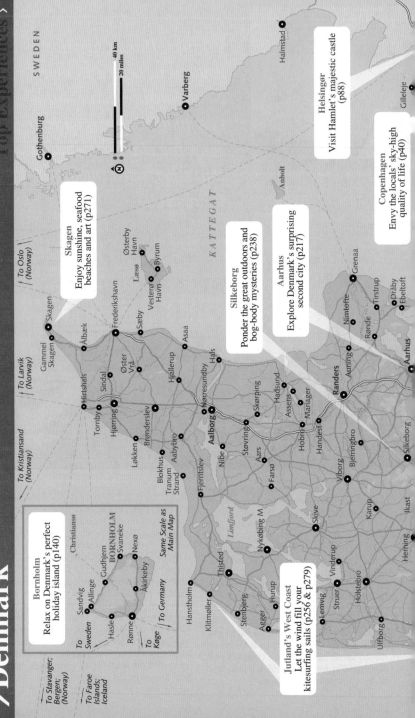

SWEDEN

To Stavanger;
Bergen;
(Norway)

To Faroe
Islands;
Iceland

Bornholm
Relax on Denmark's perfect
holiday island (p140)

To Kristiansand
(Norway)

To Larvik
(Norway)

To Oslo
(Norway)

Gothenburg

Varberg

Halmstad

Gilleleje

To
Sweden

Christiansø

BORNHOLM

Sandvig
Allinge
Gudhjem
Svaneke
Hasle
Nexø
Rønne
Åkirkeby

To Germany

To
Køge

Same Scale as
Main Map

Gammel
Skagen

Skagen

Skagen
Skagen
Enjoy sunshine, seafood
beaches and art (p271)

Hirtshals

Ålbæk

Frederikshavn

Sæby

Østerby
Havn

Læsø

Vesterø
Havn

Byrum

Anholt

KATTEGAT

Tornby

Hjørring

Sindal

Øster
Vrå

Hjallerup

Nørresundby

Hals

Asaa

Løkken

Brønderslev

Blokhus

Aabybro

Aalborg

Støvring

Skørping

Hadsund

Tranum
Strand

Fjerritslev

Nibe

Aars

Farsø

Hobro

Mariager

Assens

Handest

Silkeborg
Ponder the great outdoors and
bog-body mysteries (p238)

Aarhus
Explore Denmark's surprising
second city (p217)

Randers

Auning

Nimtofte

Tirstrup

Grenaa

Rønde

Dråby
Ebeltoft

Thisted

Nykøbing M

Limfjord

Skive

Viborg

Bjerringbro

Aarhus

Hanstholm

Klitmøller

Stenbjerg

Agger

Hurup

Struer

Vinderup

Holstebro

Karup

Silkeborg

Lemvig

Ulfborg

Herning

Ikast

Jutland's West Coast
Let the wind fill your
kitesurfing sails (p256 & p279)

Helsingør
Visit Hamlet's majestic castle
(p88)

Copenhagen
Envy the locals' sky-high
quality of life (p40)

40 km
20 miles

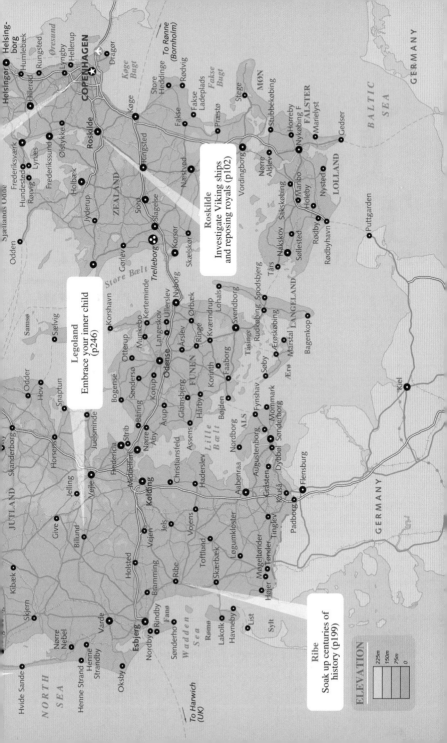

Legoland
Embrace your inner child (p246)

Roskilde
Investigate Viking ships and reposing royals (p102)

Ribe
Soak up centuries of history (p199)

ELEVATION

225m
150m
75m
0

15 TOP EXPERIENCES

Copenhagen

1 You may find it hard to suppress your envy for residents of Scandinavia's coolest capital. While this 850-year-old harbour town (p40) retains much of its historic good looks (think copper spires, cobbled squares and pastel-coloured gabled abodes), the focus here is on the innovative. Denmark's high-achieving capital is home to a thriving design scene, a futuristic metro system, and clean, green developments. Its streets are awash with effortlessly hip shops, cafes and bars; world-class museums and art collections; brave new architecture; and in 2011, no fewer than 10 Michelin-starred restaurants.
Cafes at Nyhavn

New Nordic Cuisine

2 The term 'New Nordic cuisine' is setting hearts aflutter on the international food scene, and gourmands are busy placing Copenhagen high on their food-fancying holiday itinerary. For two consecutive years (2010 and 2011), the Danish capital has been home to the world's number one restaurant, Noma (p70). Its owner-chef René Redzepi is the poster-boy for a movement (p301) that passionately embraces local and seasonal produce, and has taken Copenhagen (and, slowly, other parts of Denmark) from its humdrum pork-and-potatoes tradition to culinary dynamo.
Dish at Noma restaurant

NYHAVN

Nyhavn

Cycling

3 Is Denmark the best nation for bicycle touring in the world? Probably, thanks to its extensive national network of cycle routes (p296), terrain that is either flat or merely undulating, and a culture strongly committed to two wheels. But you needn't embark on lengthy tours of the country to enjoy cycle touring. The cities are a breeze to pedal around, and many have a public bike-sharing scheme with free bike usage. Nearly 40% of Copenhagen commuters travel by cycle – it's easy to follow their lead.

Bornholm

4 Bornholm (p140) is a Baltic beauty, lying some 200km east of the Danish mainland, located closer to Germany and Sweden than to the rest of Denmark. This magical island holds a special place in the hearts of most Danes, and is beloved for its plentiful sunshine, glorious sandy beaches, endless cycle paths, iconic *rundkirker* (round churches), artistic communities, fish smokehouses and idyllic thatched villages. If that's not enough to lure you, the island is developing a reputation for outstanding restaurants and local edibles. Lighthouse, Bornholm

CHRISTIAN ASLUND / LONELY PLANET IMAGES ©

Legoland

5 'The Happiest Place on Earth'? Disney-land may lay claim to the slogan, but Legoland (p246), though considerably smaller, could be a contender. This is, after all, a theme park celebrating the 'toy of the century' (as adjudged by *Fortune* magazine in 2000) in the country in which it was invented: Denmark, 'the world's happiest nation' (according to a Gallup World Poll). So you've got to believe Legoland will be something special – and it is. And it's just one of dozens of family-friendly amusement parks dotted around the country.

Copenhagen Jazz Festival

6 There's a fat calendar of summer festivals countrywide, from folk music in Tønder to rock at Roskilde, but the numbers suggest that Danes love their jazz fests above all else. The capital's largest music event (p63) invigorates the whole city with 10 days of music in early July, showcasing a wide range of Danish and international jazz, blues and fusion music in more than 500 indoor and outdoor venues, with music wafting out of practically every public square, park, pub and cafe from Strøget to Tivoli.

Sailing & Windsurfing

7 Denmark's long and varied coastline and abundance of islands, big and small, are made for exploration by sail. The mixture of lakes, placid fjords and calm inshore areas, combined with excellent marinas at old fishing ports, make Denmark a prime sailing destination. For more adrenalin, the wild winds of Jutland's west coast offer ideal conditions for windsurfers and kitesurfers, attracting enthusiasts of all skill levels to water-sport-heavy beach towns such as Hvide Sande (p256) and Klitmøller (aka Cold Hawaii; p279).

Sailing near Øresunds Bron bridge

Kronborg Slot

8 Something rotten in the state of Denmark? Not at this fabulous 16th-century castle in Helsingør (p88), made famous as the Elsinore Castle of Shakespeare's *Hamlet*. Kronborg's primary function was not as a royal residence, but rather as a grandiose toll house, wresting taxes for more than 400 years from ships passing through the narrow Øresund between Denmark and Sweden. The fact that Hamlet, Prince of Denmark, was a fictional character hasn't deterred legions of sightseers from visiting the site. It's the venue for summer performances of Shakespeare's play during the Hamlet festival.

Skagen

9 Skagen (p271) is an enchanting place, both bracing and beautiful. It lies at Denmark's northern tip and acts as a magnet for much of the population each summer, when the town is full to capacity yet still manages to charm. In the late 19th century artists flocked here, infatuated with the radiant light's impact on the rugged landscape. Now tourists flock to enjoy the output of the 'Skagen school' artists, soak up that luminous light, devour the plentiful seafood and laze on the fine sandy beaches. Tilsandede Kirke (Buried Church)

Bog Bodies

10 Relics and monuments from Denmark's illustrious past abound. Two stars of the early Iron Age are the intact bodies of the Tollund Man (p238) and the Grauballe Man (p223), who lived around 300 BC and were exhumed from Denmark's peat bogs after their two-millennia-long slumber. Their discoveries bring us tantalisingly close to ancient societies. Their bodies also provide compelling historical who- and why-dunnits: were they human sacrifices, executed prisoners, or victims of murder perhaps? Drop by the museums housing the bodies to investigate.
Tollund Man

Ribe

11 Compact, postcard-perfect Ribe (p199) is Denmark's oldest town, and it encapsulates the country's golden past in exquisite style, complete with imposing 12th-century cathedral, cobblestone streets, skewed half-timbered houses and lush water meadows. Stay overnight in atmospheric lodgings that exude history (low-beamed rooms in a wonky 1600s inn, or in converted jail cells), and take a free walking tour narrated by the town's nightwatchman – the perfect way to soak up the streetscapes as well as tall tales of local characters.
A house in Ribe

Viking History

12 The Vikings ensured that the Danes were known and feared throughout northern Europe from the 8th to 11th centuries, but battle and bloodlust is far from the whole story. The Vikings were not just plunderers but successful traders, extraordinary mariners and insatiable explorers. Getting a feel for the Viking era is easy, whether visiting the ship-burial ground of Ladby (p172), the Viking forts of Zealand (p116), the longship workshops at Roskilde (p102) or the museums that seek to re-create the era with live re-enactments. Viking Ship Museum, Roskilde

Danish Design

13 Denmark is a world leader in applied design (p293), characterised by cool clean lines, graceful shapes and streamlined functionality. These concepts have been applied to everything from concert halls to coffee pots to Lego blocks. The result has not just been great artistic acclaim but also big business. Iconic brands include Bang & Olufsen (sleek stereos), Bodum (kitchenware), Georg Jensen (silverware and jewellery) and Royal Copenhagen Porcelain. Then there's the furniture designers and fashion houses. Credit cards ready? Georg Jensen–designed bowl

Beaches

14 Having been cooped up for the winter, Denmark comes alive in summer, and the country's 7314km of coastline and its smorgasbord of islands (all 406 of them) draw the locals for wholesome pursuits and a dose of vitamin D. True, water temperatures may be a little unkind at times, but long sandy strands such as Bornholm's Dueodde (p146) or northern Jutland's Skagen (p271) easily fulfil any seaside-holiday fantasies. Other beachy favourites include Tisvildeleje (p100), summer cottages in Marielyst (p135) and the cafes and bars of Amager Strandpark (p60). Dueodde

Aarhus

15 Always the bridesmaid, never the bride, Aarhus (the second-largest city in Denmark) labours in the shadows of Copenhagen in terms of tourist appeal, but this is a terrific city (p217) in which to spend a couple of days. It has a superb dining scene, thriving nightlife (much of it catering to the large student population), picturesque woodland trails and beaches along the city outskirts, and one of the country's finest art museums, turning heads thanks to its new crowning glory, *Your Rainbow Panorama*. ARoS Aarhus Kunstmuseum

need to know

When to Go

Warm to hot summers, cool winters
Mild to hot summers, cold winters

Aalborg
GO May–Sep

Aarhus
GO May–Sep

Copenhagen
GO year–round

Odense
GO May–Sep

Bornholm
GO Jun–mid–Sep

High Season
(mid-Jun–mid-Aug)

» Long daylight hours, with A-list concerts, festivals and theme parks in full swing.

» Busy camping grounds, beaches, sights and transport.

» Accommodation prices peak.

Shoulder
(May–mid-Jun, mid-Aug–Sep)

» A good time to travel, with generally mild weather and fewer crowds.

» Spring offers local produce, flowers and a few festivals.

» Autumn has golden landscapes and cosy nights.

Low Season
(Oct–Apr)

» Cool and wet with short daylight hours, but *hygge* (cosiness) is in full swing.

» Big cities have Christmas lights, ice-skating rinks and *gløgg* (mulled wine).

» Reduced hours for sights; outdoor attractions closed.

Your Daily Budget

Budget less than
750kr

» Dorm bed or double in hostel: 150–600kr

» Bakeries and supermarkets for self-catering

» Cheap cafe meals: under 100kr

» Orange discounted train tickets; bike hire free-80kr per day

Midrange
750–1500kr

» Double in midrange hotel: 600–1500kr

» Main course in restaurant: 100–200kr

» Train ticket Aarhus–Copenhagen: 350kr

» Car rental: from 650kr per day

Top End over
1500kr

» Double in top-end hotel: 1500kr and up

» Main course in top-end restaurant: 200kr and up

Money

» ATMs widely available. Credit cards accepted in most hotels, restaurants and shops.

Visas

» Generally not required for stays of up to 90 days; not required for members of EU or Schengen countries.

Mobile Phones

» Local SIM cards widely available for use in most international mobile phones. Mobile coverage widespread.

Driving/ Transport

» Traffic drives on the right; steering wheel is on the left side of the car. Excellent train network.

Websites

» **Visit Denmark** (www.visitdenmark. com) Ranges from the practical to the inspirational.

» **Visit Copenhagen** (www.visitcopenhagen. com) All the capital's highlights.

» **Rejseplanen** (www. rejseplanen.dk) Great journey planner.

» **Denmark.dk** (www. denmark.dk) Hugely informative on diverse subjects.

» **Blogging Denmark** (http://blogs.denmark. dk) Great local blogs.

» **Lonely Planet** (www. lonelyplanet.com/ denmark) Info, hotel bookings, forums etc.

Exchange Rates

Australia	A$1	5.60kr
Canada	C$1	5.54kr
Euro zone	€1	7.45kr
Japan	¥100	7.07kr
New Zealand	NZ$1	4.49kr
UK	UK£1	8.55kr
USA	US$1	5.44kr

For current exchange rates see www.xe.com.

Important Numbers

There are no area codes in Denmark.

Denmark country code	☑45
International access code	☑00
Emergency (police, fire, ambulance)	☑112
Directory assistance (local)	☑118
Directory assistance (international)	☑113

Arriving in Denmark

» **Copenhagen Airport, Kastrup**

Trains – Connect the terminal to Copenhagen Central Station (København Hovedbanegården) every 20 minutes (36kr, 12 minutes duration). Taxis – It's about 20 minutes between the airport and city centre; cost is about 200/250kr (day/night). Metro – Line M2 runs from airport (station: Lufthavnen) to many neighbourhoods (eg Christianhavn, Kongens Nytorv, Nørreport, Frederiksberg) but doesn't run through Copenhagen Central Station.

Travelling Green

In Denmark, minimising your environmental impact has been made incredibly easy, not least by an excellent public-transport network, a bike-friendly culture and most businesses having a high regard for the environment.

The following resources will help you travel green to/from and within Denmark:

» **Blue Flag** (www.blueflag.org) Eco-label given to Danish beaches and marinas.

» **Green Key** (www.green-key.org) Eco-certification to tourism and leisure businesses.

» **Man in Seat 61** (http://seat61.com/Denmark) Reach Denmark by rail and sea.

» **Rejseplanen** (www.rejseplanen.dk) Travel planner that calculates carbon emissions.

» **Visit Copenhagen** (www.visitcopenhagen.com/ecopenhagen) Green travel in the capital.

» **Visit Denmark** (www.visitdenmark.com) Visit the 'Sustainable Holiday' pages.

first time

Everyone needs a helping hand when they visit a country for the first time. There are phrases to learn, customs to get used to and etiquette to understand. The following section will help demystify Denmark so your first trip goes as smoothly as your fifth.

Language

Danish is the local language, but most Danes speak English proficiently. Many also speak German. Note that the letters æ, ø and å, respectively, appear at the end of the Danish alphabet.

Booking Ahead

In keeping with the country's relaxed, informal vibe, a trip to Denmark requires little planning but a little organisation can help.

Consider buying online tickets to places such as Tivoli and Legoland, or to festivals, to avoid sometimes lengthy queues. If food's a priority, it's worth booking a table at Copenhagen's top restaurants at least a few weeks ahead.

Reserving a room, even if only for the first night of your stay, is the best way to ensure a smooth start to your trip. If you're travelling in popular coastal areas in July and August, be sure to book accommodation in advance, as this is the peak holiday period.

Hello.	Goddag.	go·da
I would like to book ...	Jeg vil gerne bestille ...	yai vil gir·ne bey·sti·le ...
a single room	et enkelt værelse	it eng·kelt verl·se
a double room	et dobbelt værelse	it do·belt verl·se
My name is ...	Mit navn er ...	mit nown ir ...
from ... to ... (date)	fra ... til ...	fraa ... til ...
How much is it ...?	Hvor meget koster det ...?	vor maa·yet kos·ta dey ...
per night/person	per nat/person	peyr nat/per·sohn
Thank you (very much).	(Mange) Tak.	(mang·e) taak

What to Wear

The Danes are an effortlessly stylish bunch. In general, casual jeans, trousers and shirts or T-shirts for guys; dresses, skirts or jeans/trousers for women, will serve you well. For evening wear, smart casual is the norm. Shorts are fine in summer, but warm weather is never a guarantee, so pack layers. Year-round, a waterproof coat and comfy walking shoes are a must. As an expat blog states: 'Danes do not sacrifice comfort to vanity in winter, so there's no reason you should.'

What to Pack

» Passport
» Credit card
» Driving licence
» Mobile (cell) phone and charger
» Camera and charger
» Electric-plug adapter
» Phrasebook
» Earplugs
» Eyemask
» Inflatable pillow
» Clothes
» Toiletries
» Medications
» Sunscreen
» Sunhat and shades
» Swimsuit
» Waterproof clothing
» Umbrella
» Padlock
» Torch
» Pocketknife

Checklist

» Check the validity of your passport

» Make necessary bookings (sights, accommodation etc)

» Inform your credit/ debit card company

» Organise travel insurance (p318)

» Check if you can use your mobile phone (and whether you need to get a local SIM card; p320)

» Find out car-hire requirements (see p327)

Etiquette

» **Road Rules**
If you'll be driving or cycling, brush up on the rules of the road. Cyclists often have the right of way, and for drivers it's particularly important to check cycle lanes before turning right.

» **Punctuality**
Trains and tours run on time and aren't a minute late. Danes operate similarly in social situations and don't wait for the disorganised.

» **Queuing**
When you go to a Danish bakery, or tourist office – just about any place there can be a queue – there's invariably a machine dispensing numbered tickets. Grab a ticket as you enter.

» **Toasts**
As you raise your glass and say 'skål' (cheers!), make eye contact with everyone.

Tipping

» **Hotels & restaurants**
Hotel and restaurant bills include service charges. Further tipping is unnecessary, although rounding up the bill in restaurants is not uncommon when service has been good.

» **Taxis**
Taxi fares include service charges so there is no need to tip (although you may consider rounding up the bill).

Money

The currency in Denmark is the Danish krone (written DKK in money markets, kr in this book), which is divided into 100 øre. You can withdraw Danish kroner with a Euro, Visa, Cirrus or MasterCard from most ATMs, widespread around the country. Credit and debit cards can be used almost everywhere, though there may be a mini-mum purchase (eg 50kr). Visa and MasterCard are the most popular options; American Express is only accepted by major chains, and few places take Diners Club. Ask if bars, cafes and restaurants take cards before you order.

In many places (hotels, restaurants, stores) a surcharge may be imposed on foreign cards (up to 3.75%). If there is a surcharge, it must be advertised (eg on the menu, at reception). Cash and travellers cheques are changed at banks.

what's new

For this new edition of Denmark, our authors have hunted down the fresh, the transformed, the hot and the happening. These are some of our favourites. For up-to-the-minute recommendations, see lonelyplanet.com/denmark.

New Nordic Cuisine

1 The gastronomic world has put Copenhagen and New Nordic cuisine (p301) in the spotlight, and the capital's restaurants are garnering acclaim – including the world's best restaurant (2010 and 2011), bestowed on Noma (p70). Added to that are Copenhagen's 10 Michelin-starred restaurants, plus Geranium (p71), the restaurant of young Rasmus Kofoed, the 2011 gold medallist at the prestigious Bocuse d'Or.

Meatpacking District

2 The one-time slaughterhouse complex of Kødbyen (p59) in Copenhagen has developed into one of the city's coolest districts, with an ever-increasing army of restaurants, bars and galleries.

Your Rainbow Panorama, Aarhus

3 The new and spectacular 360-degree rooftop walkway atop ARoS art museum is the brainchild of Danish-Icelandic artist Olafur Eliasson (p217).

Aalborg Waterfront

4 Not to be left out, Aalborg (p260) has a rejuvenated waterfront area, a flash new design and architecture space (from Jørn Utzon), and a new cultural centre in a disused power station.

Food, Glorious Food

5 The islands of Bornholm (p140) and Møn (p125) are getting in on the gourmet act, with an expanding league of food artisans, hot new dining options and (in the case of Bornholm), a new annual chef event.

Graceland Randers

6 You don't expect to find a shrine to Elvis Presley in this designer-clad land, but one superfan has built a replica of the King's Memphis mansion (p250).

Water Activities

7 There's a new waterskiing course in Hvide Sande (p256), a new surf school in Klitmøller (p280), new kayaking tours of Copenhagen's canals (p62), and a new branch of mega-waterpark Lalandia (p247) neighbouring Legoland in Billund.

National Parks

8 Some newly designated parks recognise Denmark's natural heritage: Mols Bjerge in Djursland (p236), Thy in northern Jutland (p280) and Wadden Sea National Park in west-coast Jutland (p206).

New Museums

9 Herning has HEART, which is filled with modern art (p242), Funen has a new Viking-ship museum at Ladby (p172), and Lolland has upped its cultural cred with a new gallery (p138).

Royal Progeny

10 There's a royal baby boom! Crown Prince Frederik and Crown Princess Mary have added to their brood with twins, Vincent and Josephine, and Prince Joachim and Princess Marie welcomed the birth of a daughter in January 2012.

if you like...

Islands

Denmark has been likened to a china plate that's been dropped and smashed into pieces, and those pieces are all islands – Denmark has 406 of them. The midsized islands, each with their own character, are the most fun to explore.

Bornholm Lose yourself in nature and nosh on this Baltic summer playground (p140)

Møn Tackle the brilliant-white cliffs of Møns Klint (p125)

Falster Kick back at Marielyst, Falster's premier summer beach resort (p133)

Lolland Explore Maribo's small-town charm, as well as blockbuster family attractions (p137)

Langeland Descend into the bunkers and battleships at Cold War–era Langelandsfort (p181)

Ærø Cycle between character-filled towns rich in seafaring tradition (p185)

Læsø Check out salt-flavoured traditions and unwind in a restorative salt bath (p269)

Fanø Observe the metaphorical distance between industrial Esbjerg and beguiling Fanø (p198)

Rømø Choose your pace – gentle (horse riding) or wind-whipped (blokarts and kitebuggies) (p206)

Viking History

The bloodlust, bravery and globe-trotting prowess of the Vikings, who spent centuries at the pinnacle of European power, is celebrated and re-created at sites around the country.

Roskilde Five Viking ships discovered at the bottom of Roskilde Fjord, displayed at the Viking Ship Museum (p102)

Lejre The fascinating experimental archaeology centre 'Land of Legends' (p106)

Ladby An unearthed ship grave, where a chieftain was laid to rest in a splendid warship (p172)

Trelleborg An enigmatic circular fortress constructed in the 10th century and built to a precise mathematical plan (p116)

Ribe A sober museum as well as a fun village re-creation – with warrior training! (p202)

Jelling The royal seat of King Gorm during the Vikings' most dominant era (p244)

Aalborg The atmospheric Viking burial ground at Lindholm Høje (p260)

Copenhagen Rune stones and unearthed Viking loot on show at Nationalmuseet (p43)

Hobro A ring fortress to match Trelleborg's, plus a re-created Viking-era farmstead (p252)

Fabulous Food

Interesting things are afoot in Danish kitchens, not least the culinary movement that's got the world raving: New Nordic cuisine. But we love Denmark just as much for its pork-and-potatoes heartiness, pastries, sublime seafood and sculptural smørrebrød.

Copenhagen For any Scandi-related edible your appetite may desire – old-school, new-school, Michelin-starred or waistband-stretching (p67)

Lammefjorden Denmark's famous 'vegetable garden' has made Dragsholm Slot a destination dining favourite (p107)

Bornholm True to its roots with smokin'-hot fish smokehouses, but adding to its arsenal with an ever-expanding league of food artisans (p140)

Skagen Feisty fish auctions, peel-your-own prawns fresh off the boats, or fancy-pants dining (p278)

Aarhus Denmark's second-largest city is no slouch, with an ever-growing dining scene full of must-tries, plus awesome meals on a budget (p228)

Møn A burgeoning food scene and some great foodie haunts are putting this island on the map (p125)

» Cycling through flowers in Bornholm (p140)

Family Attractions

Denmark is very child-friendly; theme parks, amusement parks, zoos and child-friendly beaches are just part of the story. Businesses go out of their way to woo families, and children are made to feel welcome.

Copenhagen Let's start with Tivoli, shall we? it's Denmark's number-one tourist destination. There's plenty more (p43)

Legoland Move on to the plastic-fantastic world built of coloured bricks, now with a Lalandia mega-waterpark as its neighbour (p246)

Odense The city that gave birth to children's literature by way of Hans Christian Andersen (p160)

Randers Home to a magnificent manmade rainforest with critters (p249)

Djursland A family mecca overflowing with amusement parks, theme parks, safari parks and beaches (p234)

Lolland More waterparks and safari parks to explore, and more beaches (p137)

Als Your kids will learn stuff at Danfoss Universe, an 'exploration park for the curious' (p215)

Hirtshals A huge aquarium full of seals and a smorgasbord of sea life (p275)

Outdoor Activities

Food, museums – sometimes all a person wants is to get outside and stretch their legs, or feel the wind in their hair. Flat-as-a-pancake Denmark is perfect for cycling, but there's plenty more.

Copenhagen City jogging tours, cycling tours and kayaking tours, and an architect-designed (natch) swimming spot on the main canal (p60)

Lake District Rolling hills, beech forest, lakes and rivers – and canoe-hire places itching to build you a paddling itinerary (p238)

Bornholm An island full of cycling trails and worthy destinations to cycle between (p140)

Hvide Sande Learn to coach those wild winds into windsurf sails and kites, or waterski a fun course (p256)

Rebild Bakker Walking trails and mountain-bike tracks in rolling rural forests (p253)

Klitmøller Waves to conquer and winds to tame thanks to surfing and windsurfing schools (p280)

Rømø Horse rides along the island's shoreline, or kitebuggies and blokarts zipping across the sand (p207)

Architecture & Design

Along with its Scandinavian neighbours, Denmark has had a massive influence on the way the world builds its public and private spaces, and on the way it designs interiors, furniture and homewares.

Copenhagen The architecture and design mother lode. Modern architectural marvels such as the Black Diamond library extension and Operaen; contemporary art museums such as Arken, Louisiana and Ordrupgaard; and museums dedicated to design icons (p43)

Aalborg A striking new waterfront centre designed by and dedicated to Jørn Utzon, plus an art museum designed by Finnish great Alvar Aalto (p267)

Kolding The Trapholt museum of modern art, applied art and furniture design is a gem, and incorporates Arne Jacobsen's one-of-a-kind prototype summerhouse (p192)

Tønder A converted water tower now showcases the fabulous chairs of homegrown design hero Hans Wegner (p209)

Aarhus A distinctly modernist, Jacobsen-designed town hall, plus an arresting art museum topped by a rainbow walkway (p217)

Top Events

1 **Riverboat Jazz Festival**, June

2 **Roskilde Festival**, July

3 **Copenhagen Jazz Festival**, July

4 **Aarhus Festival**, August

5 **Christmas lead-up**, December

month by month

January

After the festivities of Christmas and New Year's Eve the first few weeks of the year can feel like a bit of an anticlimax – not helped by the short daylight hours and inclement weather.

 Winter Jazz Festival

Danes love their summer jazz festivals; from late January to early February, those suffering from jazz withdrawal can get a fix from this smaller-scale event (www.jazz.dk/en/vinter-jazz) held at cosy venues countrywide.

February

Midwinter in Denmark may be scenic under snow and in sunshine, but more likely grey and gloomy, with few events to brighten the mood. A midterm school holiday sees many locals head north to ski.

Copenhagen Fashion Week

Models and style connoisseurs make Copenhagen shine during the twice-yearly Fashion Week (early February and early August). The associated Fashion Festival (www.copenhagenfashionfestival.com) brings the finery to a more accessible level – lots of shopping, sales, shows and parties.

April

Spring has sprung! Warmer, drier days bring out the blossoms, and attractions that were closed for the winter reopen: Legoland at the start of April, Tivoli midmonth.

CPH PIX

Held over two weeks from mid-April, this is Copenhagen's feature-film festival (www.cphpix.dk). Expect more than 170 flicks from Denmark and abroad, as well as a busy program of film-related events.

Sort Sol

The marshlands of the west-coast Wadden Sea provide food and rest for millions of migratory birds, and in late March and April (and again in September/October) huge formations of starlings put on a brilliant natural show known as the 'Sort Sol' (Black Sun); see p206.

May

The sun comes out on a semipermanent basis, more warm-weather attractions open, and the events calendar starts filling as Danes throw off winter's gloom. Tourists have yet to arrive in great numbers.

Aalborg Carnival

In late May, Aalborg kicks up its heels hosting the biggest Carnival celebrations (www.karnevaliaalborg.dk) in northern Europe, when up to 100,000 participants and spectators shake their maracas and paint the town red.

 Ølfestival

Specialist beer and microbrewing are booming in Denmark. This is the country's largest beer festival (http://beerfestival.dk, in Danish), held around mid-May in the capital and drawing over 13,000 thirsty attendees.

June

Hello summer! Denmark's festival pace quickens alongside a rising temperature gauge and longer daylight hours. The main tourist season begins in earnest in late June, when schools break for a seven-week vacation.

Copenhagen Distortion

Known to get a little crazy, Distortion (www.cphdistortion.dk) is a celebration of the capital's nightlife, with the emphasis on clubs and DJs. It's a five-day mobile street party, rolling through one Copenhagen neighbourhood each day.

Sculpture by the Sea

Aarhus' southern beachfront is transformed into an outdoor gallery courtesy of this month-long event (www.sculpturebythesea.dk), with dozens of sculptures from Danish and foreign artists displayed beside (and in) the water. It's held biennially (odd-numbered years).

Riverboat Jazz Festival

Jutland's bucolic Lake District, centred on Silkeborg, comes alive with five days of jazz (www.riverboat.dk). It's not quite New Orleans but you can buy a ticket and take a cruise down the river, or stroll the streets and enjoy the free performances.

Midsummer Eve

The Danes let rip on the longest night of the year (23 June), known as Sankt Hans Aften (St Hans Evening), with bonfires in parks, gardens and, most popular of all, on the beaches. They burn an effigy of a witch on the pyre, sing songs and get merry.

Sol over Gudhjem

Bornholm is home to Denmark's biggest one-day cook-off (the name translates as 'Sun over Gudhjem'). It sees some of the country's best chefs battle it out using the fine local produce. It's a growing hit with visitors and is broadcast on TV; see the boxed text, p152.

July

Many Danes take their main work holiday during the first three weeks of July, so expect busy seaside resorts, chock-a-block camping grounds and near-full coastal hotels – book ahead to join in on the beachy summer-holiday vibe.

Skagen Festival

Skagen acts as a magnet in summer, drawing well-heeled holidaymakers to Jutland's far-northern tip. Held over four days in late June/early July, this festival (www.skagenfestival.dk) entertains with quality folk and world music.

Roskilde Festival

Roskilde is rocked by Scandinavia's largest music festival (www.roskilde-festival.dk) for four days in early July, with major international acts and some 75,000 music fans (most camping on-site). It's renowned for its relaxed, friendly atmosphere; see the boxed text, p104.

Copenhagen Jazz Festival

This swingin' party (www.jazzfestival.dk) is the biggest annual entertainment event in the capital. For your sensory pleasure there's 10 days of Danish and international jazz, blues and fusion music, with 500 indoor and outdoor concerts.

August

Summer continues unabated, with beaches and theme parks packed to the gills, and the populace determined to wring every last ray of sunshine out of the summer. Schools resume around midmonth.

Hamlet Summer Plays

Helsingør's grand Kronborg Slot was made famous as the Elsinore Castle of Shakespeare's *Hamlet*. Every summer it hosts an outdoor production of the play – Laurence Olivier, Richard Burton and Kenneth Branagh have all 'played the Dane' here.

Copenhagen Pride

Out and proud since 1996, this five-day festival (www.copenhagenpride.dk) brings Carnival-like colour to the capital, culminating in a gay-pride march. Needless to say, there's lots of dancing and flirting.

Tønder Festival

Regarded as one of Europe's best folk-music festivals, this south-Jutland shindig (www.tf.dk) draws some 20,000 attendees to its celebration of folk and roots

music, renowned for its friendly, fun atmosphere.

✦ Skanderborg Festival

This midmonth music marvel bills itself as Denmark's most beautiful festival (www.smukfest.dk), and is second only to Roskilde in terms of scale. It takes place in lush parkland in the scenic Lake District and attracts up to 40,000 music fans; see the boxed text, p244.

✦ Aarhus Festival

Denmark's second city dons its shiniest party gear at the end of August, when this festival (www.aarhusfestival.com) transforms the town for 10 days, celebrating music, food, short film, theatre, visual arts and outdoor events for all ages (many of which are free).

◉ Copenhagen Design Week

As befits one of the great design cities of the world, Copenhagen stages a biennial design event (www.copenhagendesignweek.com) in late August/early September in odd-numbered years. The event incorporates the INDEX: Award, the world's most lucrative design prize.

🍴 Copenhagen Cooking

The world's foodie lens seems trained on Copenhagen of late, and this food festival (Scandinavia's largest) focuses on the gourmet end of the food spectrum and is held in venues and restaurants throughout the city. See www.copenhagencooking.dk.

(Above) The exhibition area at Copenhagen Design Week, Copenhagen
(Below) Prince performs on stage at the Roskilde Festival (p22)

September

The summer madness drops off as abruptly as it began, and crowds have largely disappeared. Good weather is still a chance, but by month's end many big outdoor attractions have wrapped things up for another year.

⭐ Copenhagen Blues Festival

If the shorter days have you feeling blue, this five-day international event (www.copenhagenbluesfestival.dk) should suit, with more than 50 toe-tapping concerts staged at venues around the capital.

October

Summer is a distant memory, with the weather crisp and cool and the countryside taking on a golden tinge. Business travellers outnumber those travelling for pleasure.

👁 Kulturnatten (Culture Night)

Usually held on the second Friday in October, this wonderful, atmospheric event (www.kulturnatten.dk) sees Copenhagen's museums, theatres, galleries, libraries and even Rosenborg Slot throw open their doors through the night with a wide range of special events.

⭐ Halloween

Historically Halloween hasn't been a big Danish tradition, but it coincides with the midterm break, so the country's big theme parks fire up for the week and highlight the fright factor (in a family-friendly way, of course). Tivoli and Djurs Sommerland both come to the party.

December

Sure, the weather is cold and damp, but Denmark cranks up the hygge (cosiness) and celebrates Christmas in style: twinkling lights, ice-skating rinks, and gallons of warming gløgg (mulled wine).

🔒 Christmas Fairs

Fairs are held countrywide throughout December, with booths selling sometimes-kitschy arts and crafts and traditional Yuletide foodie treats. For an idyllic, olden-days atmosphere, visit somewhere with a strong connection to the past: Den Gamle By in Aarhus, or historic Ribe in southern Jutland.

👁 Tivoli

Copenhagen's Tivoli reopens for Christmas with a large market and buckets of schmaltz. Attractions include special Christmas tableaux, costumed staff and theatre shows. Fewer rides are operational but the traditional *gløgg* and *æbleskiver* (spherical pancakes) ought to be ample compensation.

itineraries

Whether you've got six days or 60, these itineraries provide a starting point for the trip of a lifetime. Want more inspiration? Head online to lonelyplanet. com/thorntree to chat with other travellers.

Two Weeks
Denmark's Classic Hits

> The beauty of Denmark's compact size is that it never takes too long to get from point A to B. To cover the classic sites, start in **Copenhagen** and soak up the riches (cultural, culinary, retail) of the capital. From there, it's a short hop west to **Roskilde** to investigate Denmark's royal and Viking heritage. Further west, **Odense** offers up fairy-tale charm in abundance and plenty of ways to connect with the city's famous native son, Hans Christian Andersen. Stop in **Kolding** for a polished mix of the old and cutting-edge before you reach history-soaked **Ribe**, Denmark's oldest town, oozing chocolate-box appeal. From here, you can pause on the history lessons for a hefty dose of childhood nostalgia at **Legoland**, then some lakeside R&R in **Silkeborg** (go canoeing or do a cruise through the picturesque lakes of the area). Finally, stop by cosmopolitan **Aarhus**, the country's second city. It holds a few surprises – not least its rainbow-topped art museum – and from here, you can take a ferry to northern Zealand for an easy and scenic return to Copenhagen.

Three to Four Weeks

Denmark in Detail

Got some time up your sleeve and a desire to delve deep into Denmark? Designate **Copenhagen** some quality time in your itinerary, and make a couple of day trips outside the capital to check out the superb modern art at the Louisiana Museum in **Humlebæk** and magnificent castles such as Kronborg Slot at **Helsingør**. Head south to potter about pretty, historic **Køge**, then catch a ferry out to the Baltic bombshell of **Bornholm** – spend a few days exploring the island's bike trails, sandy beaches and gastronomic treats. Once you're back on Zealand, head further south to **Møn**, an enchanting island with some of the country's most dramatic scenery – for such a flat country that's not saying much, but the white-chalk cliffs of Møn rise sharply over a jade-green sea and are as pretty as a picture.

Head back across southern Zealand to reach the island of Funen. **Odense** is a must-see for its various tributes to hometown-hero Hans Christian Andersen, but take time to visit the Viking ship grave at **Ladby**, and the marvellous Renaissance treats at **Egeskov Slot**. A day or two on the friendly old seafaring island of **Ærø** will recharge your batteries.

Onward west – a ferry can take you from Ærø to easygoing **Als**, and on to southern Jutland, where you can reach **Ribe** for history lessons with a decidedly friendly face (mock Viking settlements, a nightwatchman's tour of the cobbled streets), plus some outstanding bird-watching nearby. Jump on a boat out of Esbjerg for the 12-minute trip to idyllic **Fanø**, and take a pause in Sønderho.

A detour to **Legoland** is essential – this place will blow your mind with its astounding creations made from the humble plastic brick. Then it's back to the west coast for more mind-blowing activity – this time courtesy of North Sea winds, just perfect for kitesurfing in **Hvide Sande**.

From here, wend your way east to leafy, lakeside **Silkeborg**, then on to **Aarhus** for top-notch museum-mooching and noshing. The rejuvenated northern city of **Aalborg** warrants a stop for its Utzon architecture and a Viking burial ground, but the best comes last at cinematic **Skagen**, hugging Denmark's northernmost tip. Make time to admire the artwork, indulge in fine seafood, soak in the incredible northern light and dip a toe in the angry seas.

Two Weeks
Northern Exposure

> For some seaside R&R, northern Jutland delivers, with some quirky treats alongside the expected sun, sea, sand and seafood. Start from **Aarhus** , which has some fine museums, including the ARoS art museum, and head north, stopping in **Randers** for a man-made rainforest and a left-field dose of Elvis kitsch. Sleepy **Hobro** offers history in the shape of a 10th-century Viking ring fortress, before **Aalborg** puts on her best face to impress you with a rejuvenated waterfront and the final design from revered architect Jørn Utzon. At sweet **Sæby** you can connect with Danish literature and go back for seconds at bounteous seafood buffets.

From **Frederikshavn**, catch a ferry to the island of **Læsø** to take a step back in time (salt baths optional). Next is **Skagen**, a delightful slice of seaside life with a winning art museum, boutique hotels and alfresco dockside dining. Southwest of Skagen, the walkabout sand dunes of **Råbjerg Mile** let you know mother nature is still in charge here, while in **Hirtshals** you can admire more of her handiwork at northern Europe's largest aquarium. Relax in **Løkken** – but not too much. Nearby **Fårup Sommerland** can get your heart pumping with amusement rides and a waterpark. You'll return to Aarhus with the cobwebs well and truly blown away.

HOLGER LEUE / LONELY PLANET IMAGES ©

» (above) *Slender Ribs* sculpture by
Alexander Calder at Louisiana art
museum (p81)
» (left) Denmark's northern tip, near
Skagen (p271)

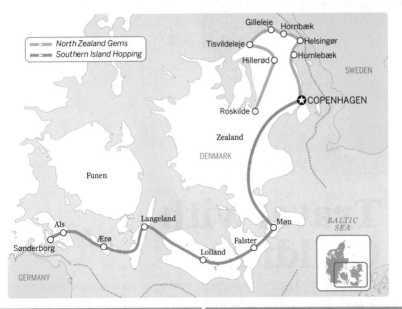

One Week
North Zealand Gems

An easy and accessible circuit of north Zealand offers glam beaches, royal remains, fairytale castles, Viking ships and cutting-edge architecture.

Start in fjord-side **Roskilde**, where you can check out Viking longships and pay your respects to a millennia's worth of Danish kings and queens at the country's finest cathedral. North from here is magnificent Frederiksborg Slot, dominating the unassuming town of **Hillerød**. It's hard to decide which is more impressive, the baroque interiors or the regal grounds.

For northern light and sunbathing Scandi-style, head to the northern beaches: the chic bathing hotels of **Tisvildeleje** are worth a stop, as are the sculptures between **Gilleleje** and Hornbæk. **Hornbæk** is where the young and gorgeous go to appreciate both the natural beauty and their own.

Further along the coast stands historic Kronborg Slot in **Helsingør**, much more than simply the home of the existential ditherer Hamlet. Be sure to take the scenic coastal road south to **Humlebæk** and the Louisiana Museum – its splendid architecture rivals its collection of contemporary art. A short but picturesque drive along the 'Danish Riviera' leads to **Copenhagen**.

One Week
Southern Island Hopping

Most travellers between Copenhagen and Jutland take the quickest, direct route across Funen, but this meandering option is for those after rural retreats and quiet villages, with small ferries providing island-hopping potential.

From the capital make a beeline south to **Møn**, then across to **Falster** and on to **Lolland**. This trio is known as Denmark's 'South Sea Islands'. While they may lack the coconut palms and hula hoops normally associated with that label, they do offer a fine glimpse of rural Scandinavian island life: rolling fields, sandy beaches and rustic manor houses. Allocate time to Møn's chalky cliffs, Marielyst's glorious beach (on Falster), and Lolland's theme parks.

Western Lolland connects to **Langeland** by ferry – and now you're in the South Funen Archipelago. This sleepy stretch of green in turn connects to **Ærø**, an enchanting island well worth exploring. Villages here drip with maritime history and are home to crooked old houses. When you've had your fill, there's a ferry on to **Als**, connected by road to Jutland proper at the larger town of **Sønderborg**. And now you're in the southeast corner of Jutland, with a whole peninsula to explore...

Travel with Children

Best Regions for Kids

Copenhagen

Capital attractions: Tivoli – where funpark meets fairy tale – is beguiling, while the Experimentarium happily boggles young minds.

Møn, Falster & Lolland

Natural and man-made: chalk cliffs and a mind-bending geology centre on Møn, beaches and a medieval village on Falster, and a safari park and waterpark on Lolland.

Funen

Literary legend: Odense pays homage to the tales of Hans Christian Andersen. Also there's a moat-encircled castle with mazes and marvels, and bunkers and battleships at a 1950s fort.

Central Jutland

Plastic fantastic: Legoland – need we say more? Close by are a huge waterpark and a safari park, plus family canoeing opportunities, beaches and loads of other amusement parks.

Northern Jutland

Beach babes: endless sandy strands and shifting sand dunes that will put your sandcastles to shame, plus a mega-aquarium that reveals just what lies beneath.

Denmark is prime family-holiday territory, especially in high season when family-filled camper vans hit the road to celebrate the long summer break. Domestic tourism is organised around the assumption that many Danes will be travelling as a family. Theme parks, amusement parks, zoos and child-friendly beaches are just part of the story – businesses go out of their way to woo families, and children are rarely made to feel unwelcome.

Denmark for Kids

Travellers with kids looking to be entertained should enquire at local tourist offices – all regions have places where kids are king, from huge indoor swim centres to play centres and petting farms.

Culture Vultures

Entry to most museums is free for kids, and you won't have to minimise your time in cultural attractions lest your offspring start climbing the walls – almost everywhere has displays and activities designed especially to keep kids entertained.

Copenhagen Nationalmuseet has a brilliant hands-on children's section, while kids are spoiled at Louisiana with a wing of their own, where they can create artistic masterpieces.

Zealand The superb Viking Ship Museum displays five Viking ships; there's also Viking shipbuilding and the chance to go on a longboat cruise.

Funen At Fyrtøjet (Tinderbox) in Odense, kids get to explore the world of Hans Christian Andersen

» (above) Ferris wheel at Tivoli (p43), Copenhagen
» (left) An image of Hans Christian Andersen in Odense (p160)

» (above) A toddler and large Lego friend, Legoland (p246)
» (left) Building sandcastles on the shore of the Wadden Sea (p206)

through storytelling and music. Egeskov Slot is a must – the summer program includes evening concerts, falconry displays, ghost hunts and fireworks.

Central Jutland Aarhus' art museum will wow kids with its giant *Boy* sculpture and awesome rooftop rainbow walkway. Kvindemuseet has hands-on kids' exhibits in its 'History of Childhood' section.

Funparks & Theme Parks

Copenhagen Tivoli is a charming combination of amusement rides, flower gardens, food pavilions, carnival games and open-air stage shows. Bakken is its poor relation but still provides loads of old-fashioned fun.

Zealand BonBon-Land's biggest ride is the bonkers-looking Wild Boar roller coaster.

Møn, Falster & Lolland Lalandia on Lolland really undersells itself with the label 'waterpark'.

Southern Jutland Danfoss Universe is an 'exploration park for the curious' and has loads of interactive science fun.

Central Jutland Legoland is the big daddy of Danish theme parks, joined by a new Lalandia as its neighbour. Aarhus has Tivoli Friheden for rides and games, and Djurs Sommerland has the blockbuster combo of waterpark and amusement park in one superpopular attraction.

Northern Jutland Djurs Sommerland's northern sister is Fårup Sommerland, equally popular and home to a waterpark and amusement rides.

Animal Encounters

Copenhagen Zoologisk Have houses a multitude of critters, and some lovely new architect-designed homes for them. Danmarks Akvarium takes its fishy business seriously.

Møn, Falster & Lolland Knuthenborg Safari Park on Lolland has a drive-through savannah area for a taste of Africa (but with crappier weather).

Bornholm Sommerfugle og Tropeland showcases jungle climates and has 1000 butterflies.

Funen Odense Zoo has a new African area. Kertimende's aquarium is home to seals, porpoises and fine-finned fish.

Central Jutland Randers Regnskov is a sultry, dome-enclosed tropical zoo taking you to Africa, Asia and South America. At Skandinavisk Dyrepark you can assess a full collection of Scandi species, including polar bears and brown bears. Ree Park has animals from all corner of the globe. Silkeborg's Aqua has an abundance of fish and cute otters.

Northern Jutland Aalborg has a quality zoo, while Hirtshals is home to the largest aquarium in northern Europe.

Time Travel

The Danes have a seemingly limitless enthusiasm for dressing up and re-creating history, and they do it well in countless open-air museums and re-created Viking camps and medieval villages, all with activities for youngsters.

Zealand The experimental archaeology centre of Sagnlandet Lejre, 'Land of Legends', is fascinating.

Møn, Falster & Lolland Falster's Middelaldercentret re-creates an early-15th-century medieval village.

Bornholm Oh look, it's another ye-olde village: Bornholms Middelaldercenter re-creates a medieval fort and village.

Funen Den Fynske Landsby is a re-created olden-days country village with the requisite costumes and farmyard animals.

Southern Jutland Ribe VikingeCenter re-creates the Viking era in Denmark's oldest town; finish the day with a walk alongside the town's night watchman.

Central Jutland Den Gamle By (The Old Town) in Aarhus is a photogenic open-air museum. Hobro has a Viking-era farmstead to complement its Viking fortress.

Planning
When to Go

The best time for families to visit Denmark is the best time for any traveller – between May and September. Local school holidays run from late June to mid-August. On the plus side, at this time, good weather is likely (though never assured), all attractions and activities are in full swing and your kids are likely to meet other kids. On the downside, beaches and attractions are busy, and camping grounds and hostels are heavily in demand (and also charge peak prices).

Where to Stay

In high season (mid-June to mid-August) camping grounds are hives of activity, and many put on entertainment and activity programs for junior guests.

Hostels are exceedingly well set up for, and welcoming to, families. Rooms often sleep up to six (in bunks); there will invariably be a guest kitchen and lounge facilities.

BEST FRESH-AIR FUN

Copenhagen Amager Strandpark is a sand-sational artificial lagoon, with acres of sandy beach. Playground facilities and shallow water make it ideal for children. Plus, you can't visit Copenhagen and *not* take a canal boat trip.

Zealand The Jungle Path at Ledreborg Slot is a series of suspended walkways, ropes, ladders and installations.

Møn, Falster & Lolland The Falster beach resort of Marielyst is marketed as a family-oriented 'activity town'; take a boat trip to see the white cliffs of Møns Klint.

Bornholm The calm and shallow waters of the sweeping beach at Dueodde suit families to a T.

Funen Release your inner primate at Gorilla Park, an adrenaline-fuelled high-ropes adventure park. Maritimt Center Danmark offers sailing trips and pirate-related fun.

Southern Jutland For older kids, Rømø's southern beach is full of wind-blown speed treats: land-yachts or blokarts – buggies with attached parachutelike kites.

Central Jutland Canoeing and camping in the picturesque Lake District is an undeniably wholesome family pursuit.

Northern Jutland Loads of beaches, mega-sand dunes at Rubjerg Knude and Råbjerg Mile, and a tractor-pulled bus ride to Denmark's northernmost tip.

Farm stays may offer a rural idyll and/or the chance to get your hands dirty.

In resorts, summer houses are available at a reasonable price (usually by the week). In cities that are emptier due to the summer exodus, business hotels may drop their rates and add bunks to rooms to woo family business.

Where to Eat

On the whole, Danish restaurants welcome children with open arms. Virtually all offer high chairs, many have a *børnemenu* (children's menu) or will at least provide children's portions, and some have play areas. Two family-focused chains to look for are the steak chain Jensen's Bøfhus (www.jensens. com, in Danish), and the US-influenced Bone's (www.bones.dk, in Danish), with a menu of spare ribs, burgers and barbecued chicken (found in Jutland and Funen). Both chains offer extensive kids menus and all-you-can-eat ice-cream bars – bonus!

Self-catering will be a breeze if you are staying somewhere with kitchen facilities – larger supermarkets will stock all you'll need (including baby items), but may have shorter hours than you might expect. There are oodles of prime picnic spots.

Transport

Naturally, having your own set of wheels will make life easier, but public transport shouldn't be dismissed – on trains, children under 12 years travel free if they are with an adult travelling on a standard ticket (each adult can take two children free).

A cycling holiday may be doable with slightly older kids, as the terrain is flat and distances between towns are not vast.

regions at a glance

Copenhagen

Food ✓✓✓
Design ✓✓✓
Museum & Galleries ✓✓✓

New Nordic or Old Danish

Copenhagen has been transformed into one of the world's hottest culinary destinations, home to a league of young, visionary chefs concocting uniquely Nordic dishes that showcase intriguing regional ingredients – and isn't the food world taking notice? At the other end of the spectrum, old-school cafes excel at prized Danish *hygge* (cosiness), and historic restaurants allow you to discover traditional favourites such as smørrebrød (open sandwiches), herring and akvavit (an alcoholic beverage).

Top Marks for Design

Everything's easy on the eye here. Check out architectural show-stealers like the Black Diamond library extension and Operaen; admire town planning that makes this city so damn user-friendly; and browse museums dedicated to local output that changed the way the world designs and decorates. Then shop to your heart's content in high-quality flagship and department stores, and brilliant boutiques showcasing local fashion and homewares.

Calling Culture Vultures

There's an abundance of Danish history and art to investigate, plus churches, castles and theatres. For a whistle-stop tour through the country's history, nothing beats the Nationalmuseet; fine art excels at Statens Museum for Kunst and Ny Carlsberg Glyptotek. Out of town you can ogle modern art in modern architectural marvels, then take the pulse of the current art scene in fab city galleries such as V1 and Ny Carlsberg Vej 68.

p40

Zealand

Castles ✓✓✓
Viking History ✓✓✓
Beaches ✓✓

Crowning Glories

Most visitors gravitate to Helsingør's magnificent Kronborg Slot, otherwise known as Elsinore, home of Shakespeare's indecisive antihero, Hamlet. But don't ignore Frederiksborg Slot, a glorious Dutch Renaissance–style confection. Divine Dragsholm Slot combines food and finery with aplomb.

Investigate the Viking Era

Got a thing for rugged, hirsute marauders? Be wowed by Viking ships at Roskilde, ponder the enigmatic ring fortress at Trelleborg, and get swept into the Iron Age lifestyle at the superb experimental archaeology centre outside Lejre.

Coastal Capers

Gorgeous white-sand beaches with shallow water and gentle waves line the northern coast, and summer beach goers create a salubrious sunshine-and-ice-cream atmosphere in favourite spots such as Hornbæk and Tisvildeleje.

p84

Møn, Falster & Lolland

Landscapes ✓✓
Family Attractions ✓✓
Arts & Crafts ✓✓

Elevated Heights

You may notice Denmark is rather flat. So Møn's striking white chalk cliffs, rising 128m above a jade-green sea, are beloved of scenery-seekers. The cliffs are one of Denmark's most famous landmarks – take a boat trip to check them out.

Fun for the Whole Family

This island trio attracts summer-sun-seeking families, and there are oodles of attractions aiming to enrich the holiday experience: interactive museums, a mega-waterpark, zoo, safari park and re-created medieval village.

Møn Artistry

Møn is a magnet for artists and potters, keen to tap into the inspiration offered by cliffs, coastline and clay soils. Their works are on display in various studios and galleries, but you can admire wondrous art from an altogether different era in ancient, fresco-adorned churches.

p123

Bornholm

Beaches ✓✓✓
Food ✓✓✓
Cycling ✓✓✓

Bathing Beauties

This Baltic outpost is encircled by beaches, but Dueodde justifiably hogs the limelight: a vast stretch backed by pine trees and expansive dunes. Its soft sand is so fine-grained it was once used in hourglasses and ink blotters.

Culinary Offerings

The productive island is home to historic fish smokehouses, first-class organic produce, a brace of fine-dining restaurants (Kadeau is a New Nordic star), and an ever-expanding league of food artisans, creating treats from ice creams to caramels, hams to microbrews.

Cycling Bliss

More than 230km of bike trails cover main roads, forests, former train routes and beaches. There's a multitude of picturesque coastal hamlets and medieval round churches, and the excellent local food and drink are your reward for pedalling some gently undulating landscape.

p140

Funen

Castles ✓✓
Fairy Tales ✓✓✓
Islands ✓✓

To the Manor Born

Dozens of castles and manor houses dot Funen. The big daddy of them all is splendid Egeskov Slot, complete with moat and drawbridge, a doll's house beyond compare and summertime evening fireworks.

Once upon a Time...

A baby was born to a cobbler and a washerwoman, in 1805 in Odense. That baby went on to write fairy tales known and loved the world over. Odense honours home-grown Hans Christian Andersen in all manner of ways, including museums dedicated to the man and sculptures of his most famous stories.

Island-Hopping

This region includes a bevy of islands (90 of 'em!), some home to people, some just to birds, rabbits and deer. Island-hopping by ferry or yacht is a salt-sprayed pleasure, as is exploring nautical-but-nice Ærø.

p158

Southern Jutland

Historic Villages ✓✓✓
Nature ✓✓
Design ✓✓

Picturebook Destinations

You want thatch-roofed houses, blooming gardens and cobblestone streets lined with boutiques, galleries and cafes? You need Ribe (Denmark's oldest town), Møgeltønder and the island of Fanø on your itinerary. Careful, you might overdose on quaintness.

Bird-Watching Bliss

Stretching along Jutland's west coast is the marshy Wadden Sea National Park, ripe for exploration. Its tidal rhythms provide opportunities for seal-spotting, winter oyster-collecting and bountiful bird-watching.

Unlikely Designer Destinations

Admire Utzon architecture in modern Esbjerg, a brilliant design museum in suburban Kolding and, in a converted water tower in Tønder, a Wegner chair collection that will have design buffs drooling.

p190

Central Jutland

Activities ✓✓✓
Family Attractions ✓✓✓
Art ✓✓

The Great Outdoors

Truly something for everyone: the Lake District has canoeing and rambling; the wild west coast offers first-class wind- and kitesurfing; and Rold Skov has excellent mountain biking. Aarhus is perfect for city cycling, while Djursland has long, pristine beaches.

Legoland & Loads More

Did someone say Lego? Yes, this is the spiritual home of the wondrous plastic brick. There's also some cool kid-oriented stuff in Aarhus, Randers has a brilliant man-made rainforest, and Djursland is prime holiday turf, brimming with amusement and safari parks.

Modern Art Marvels

Modern art struts its stuff in this region – prime viewing is *Your Rainbow Panorama* atop Aarhus' outstanding ARoS. You can admire (don't touch!) gobsmacking glassworks in Ebeltoft, appreciate Asger Jorn's repertoire in Silkeborg and ponder conceptual art in Herning.

p216

Northern Jutland

Landscapes ✓✓✓
Beaches ✓✓✓
Food ✓✓

Mother Nature's Finest

Visitors can witness the region's natural beauty without needing to rough it: the shifting sands, the luminous light, the raging winds, the clashing waters. You'll understand why artists and writers have felt inspired here.

Beachy Keen

Both the east and west coasts draw holidaymakers to long sandy stretches – sometimes windy and woolly on the west, more sheltered on the east. Northernmost Skagen combines the best of both worlds, but Løkken, Tornby Strand and Frederikshavn have shore appeal.

Fresh Catch

At the traditional *røgeri* (smokehouse) in Klitmøller, harbourside buffets of Sæby, chic restaurants of Skagen and the smart menus around Aalborg, you're left in little doubt – seafood is king here. And it's a worthy monarch, fresh as can be.

p259

Every listing is recommended by our authors, and their favourite places are listed first

Look out for these icons:

TOP CHOICE Our author's top recommendation

A green or sustainable option

FREE No payment required

See the Index for a full list of destinations covered in this book.

On the Road

Copenhagen

Best Places to Eat

» Noma (p70)

» Geranium (p71)

» Relæ (p71)

» Kødbyens Fiskebar (p70)

» Fischer (p71)

Best Places to Stay

» Hotel Nimb (p64)

» Hotel Guldsmeden (p66)

» WakeUp Copenhagen (p67)

» CPH Living (p66)

» Hotel Fox (p64)

Why Go?

Copenhagen is the coolest kid on the Nordic block. Edgier than Stockholm and worldlier than Oslo, the Danish capital gives Scandinavia the X factor. Just ask style bibles *Monocle* and *Wallpaper* magazines, which fawn over its industrial-chic bar, design and fashion scenes, and culinary revolution. This is where you'll find New Nordic pioneer Noma, voted the world's best restaurant in 2010 and 2011, and one of 10 Michelin-starred restaurants in town – not bad for a city of 1.2 million.

Yet Copenhagen is more than just seasonal cocktails and geometric threads. A royal capital with almost nine centuries under its svelte belt, it's equally well versed when it comes to world-class museums and storybook streetscapes. Its cobbled, bike-loving streets are a *hyggelig* (cosy) concoction of sherbet-hued town houses, craft studios and candle-lit cafes. Add to this its compact size, and you have what is possibly Europe's most seamless urban experience.

When to Go

Arguably, the best time to drop by is from May to August, when the days are long and the mood upbeat. Events such as Distortion in June, Copenhagen Jazz Festival in July and Copenhagen Pride in August give the city a fabulous vibe, though many of Copenhagen's top restaurants close for several weeks in July and August.

Golden foliage and top cultural events such as Kopenhagen Contemporary and Kulturnatten make autumn appealing, while late November and December counter the chill with Yuletide markets, twinkling lights and *gløgg* (mulled wine).

History

Copenhagen was founded in 1167 by tough-as-nails Bishop Absalon, who erected a fortress on Slotsholmen Island, fortifying a small and previously unprotected harbour-side village.

After the fortification was built, the harbourside village grew in importance and took on the name Kømandshavn (Merchant's Port), which was later condensed to København. Absalon's fortress stood until 1369, when it was destroyed in an attack on the town by the powerful Hanseatic states.

In 1376 construction began on a new Slotsholmen fortification, Copenhagen Castle, and in 1416 King Erik of Pomerania took up residence at the site, marking the beginning of Copenhagen's role as the capital of Denmark.

Still, it wasn't until the reign of Christian IV, in the first half of the 17th century, that the city was endowed with much of its splendour. A lofty Renaissance designer, Christian IV began an ambitious construction scheme, building two new castles and many other grand edifices, including the Rundetårn observatory and the glorious Børsen, Europe's first stock exchange.

In 1711 the bubonic plague reduced Copenhagen's population of 60,000 by one-third. Tragic fires, one in 1728 and the other in 1795, wiped out large tracts of the city, including most of its timber buildings. However, the worst scourge in the city's history is generally regarded as the unprovoked British bombardment of Copenhagen in 1807, during the Napoleonic Wars. The attack targeted the heart of the city, inflicting numerous civilian casualties and setting hundreds of homes, churches and public buildings on fire.

Copenhagen flourished once again in the 19th and 20th centuries, expanding beyond its old city walls and establishing a reputation as a centre for culture, liberal politics and the arts. Dark times were experienced with the Nazi occupation during WWII, although the city managed to emerge relatively unscathed.

During the war and in the economic depression that had preceded it, many Copenhagen neighbourhoods had deteriorated into slums. In 1948 an ambitious urban renewal policy called the 'Finger Plan' was adopted; this redeveloped much of the city, creating new housing projects interspaced with green areas of parks and recreational facilities that spread out like fingers from the city centre.

A rebellion by young people disillusioned with growing materialism, the nuclear arms race and the authoritarian educational system took hold in Copenhagen in the 1960s. Student protests broke out on the university campus and squatters occupied vacant buildings around the city. It came to a head in 1971 when protesters tore down the fence of an abandoned military camp at the east side of Christianshavn and began an occupation of the 41-hectare site, naming this settlement Christiania (see p55).

While the Global Financial Crisis has created undercurrents of unease, there's no doubt that Copenhagen is currently basking

COPENHAGEN IN...

Two Days

Start with a canal and harbour tour, then soak up the salty atmosphere of Nyhavn on your way to **Designmuseum Danmark**. Lunch on fabulous smørrebrød at **Schønnemann** before heading up the historic **Rundetårn** for a bird's-eye view of the city. Done, take in bohemian **Christiania** before an evening of shameless fun at **Tivoli**. On day two, brush up on your Danish history at **Nationalmuseet**, lunch at New Nordic up-and-comer **Marv & Ben** and take in a museum or two on **Slotsholmen**. Assuming you've booked ahead, end on a culinary high with dinner at **Noma**, **Alberto K** or **Mielcke & Hurtigkarl**.

Four Days

If you have a third day, escape the city with a trip to art museum **Louisiana**. Lunch there before heading back into the city for a retail rush at design meccas **Hay** and **Illums Bolighus**. Come evening, hit Vesterbro's trendy Kødbyen district, supping at **Kødbyens Fiskebar** and sipping at **Mesteren & Lærlingen**. Kick-start day four with centuries of art at **Statens Museum for Kunst**, then spend the rest of the day treading the grit-hip streets of **Nørrebro**, stopping for coffee at **The Coffee Collective**, vino at **Malbeck** and contemporary Danish grub at **Relæ**.

Copenhagen Highlights

1 Hunt down Danish design and fashion at trend-setting Hay (p77), Henrik Vibskov (p77) and Wood Wood (p77) in the city's **historic centre**

2 Cruise the city on a **canal and harbour tour** (p62)

3 Be inspired by art and the views at modern art heavyweight **Louisiana** (p81)

4 Taste test Nordic culinary innovation at restaurant hot spots in the city.

5 Indulge in an evening of thrills, spills and fairy floss at ever-enchanting **Tivoli** (p43)

6 Let your hair down in Europe's capital of free-spirited living, the **Christiania** (p55) neighbourhood

7 Learn the truth about the Vikings at **Nationalmuseet** (p43)

8 Hit the cafes, bars, boutiques and galleries of Copenhagen's coolest quarters, **Nørrebro** (p57) and **Vesterbro** (p59)

9 Savour seasonal cocktails at in-the-know bars such as Ruby (p72), 1105 (p72) and Union Bar (p72) in the city's **historic centre**

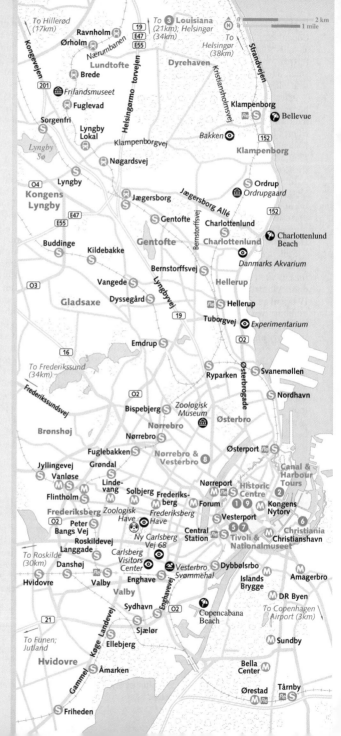

in a confident glow. In 2008 influential magazine *Monocle* proclaimed it the world's most liveable city. Two years later (and again in the following year), one of its Michelin-starred restaurants, Noma (p70), topped the coveted S.Pellegrino World's Best Restaurant list, sealing the city's status as a new-school culinary hot spot. Add to this a new wave of bold architectural statements such as the 'Black Diamond' extension at Det Kongelige Bibliotek (p52), and the city's status as the world's top bike city according to the Union Cycliste Internationale, and Copenhagen's pull makes perfect sense.

⊙ Sights

One of the great things about Copenhagen is its size. Virtually all of Copenhagen's major sightseeing attractions – Tivoli, Nationalmuseet, Statens Museum for Kunst, Marmorkirken, Nyhavn, Rosenborg, Christiansborg, Christiania and Amalienborg – are in or close to the medieval city centre. Only the perennially disappointing Little Mermaid lies outside of the city proper on the harbourfront.

RÅDHUSPLADSEN & TIVOLI

The large central square of Rådhuspladsen (Map p48), flanked on one side by the city hall (or rådhus) and on another by Copenhagen's municipal bus terminus, marks the heart of Copenhagen. The bustling pedestrian shopping street Strøget begins at the northeast side of Rådhuspladsen, while the historic pleasure garden, Tivoli, glitters to the southwest.

Tivoli AMUSEMENT PARK
(Map p48; www.tivoli.dk; Vesterbrogade 3; adult/under 8yr 95kr/free, after 8pm Fri 125kr/free; ⊙11am-11pm Sun-Thu, to 12.30am Fri, to midnight Sat mid-Jun–mid-Aug, earlier close Sun-Thu mid-Apr–mid-Jun & mid-Aug–late Sep) Situated in the heart of the city, Tivoli is a shamelessly charming combination of amusement rides, flower gardens, food pavilions, carnival games and open-air stage shows. Dating from 1843, the entertainment park is Denmark's most popular attraction. Visitors can ride the roller coaster (named 'The Demon'), take in the famous fireworks display at night or just soak up the timeless, storybook atmosphere in what is the city's best-loved drawcard.

Tivoli is fun by day but in the evening it takes on a more romantic mood as the thousands of specially made fairy lights are switched on and a wide range of cultural ac-

tivities unfold, from theatrical performances to pantomime to live rock and pop acts, some of them major international names.

Each of Tivoli's numerous entertainment venues has a different character. Perhaps best known is the open-air pantomime theatre, which features mime and ballet, and was built in 1874 by Vilhelm Dahlerup, the Copenhagen architect who also designed the royal theatre. Tivoli also has an indoor cabaret theatre and a large concert hall that features performances by international symphony orchestras and ballet troupes.

Between all the nightlights and glorious flowerbeds, Tivoli is an enchanting place to stroll around, and if you feel like eating there are some decent (and even some very good) restaurants that make for a satisfying dining experience.

A good tip is to go on Fridays during the summer season, when the open-air Plænen stage hosts free rock concerts from Danish bands (and the occasional international superstar) from 10pm.

Amusement ride tickets cost 25kr (some rides require up to three tickets), making the multiride ticket (195kr) better value in most cases.

The numerous open-air performances are free of charge, but there's usually an admission fee for the indoor performances – check the website for venue details, line-ups and prices.

Outside the main summer season, Tivoli also opens for around 10 days at Halloween and from mid-November to late December for Christmas. For up-to-date opening times, see the Tivoli website.

FREE Nationalmuseet MUSEUM
(National Museum; Map p48; www.natmus.dk; Ny Vestergade 10; ⊙10am-5pm Tue-Sun) For a crash course in Danish history and culture, you couldn't do better than spending an afternoon at Nationalmuseet, opposite the western entrance to Slotsholmen.

The National Museum has first claims on virtually every antiquity found on Danish soil. These range from the Upper Palaeolithic period to the 1840s and include Stone Age tools, Viking weaponry and impressive Bronze Age, Iron Age and rune-stone collections. Don't miss the exhibition of bronze lurs, some of which date back 3000 years and are still capable of blowing a tune, and the finely crafted 3500-year-old Sun Chariot, unearthed in a Zealand field a century ago.

COPENHAGEN SIGHTS

Copenhagen

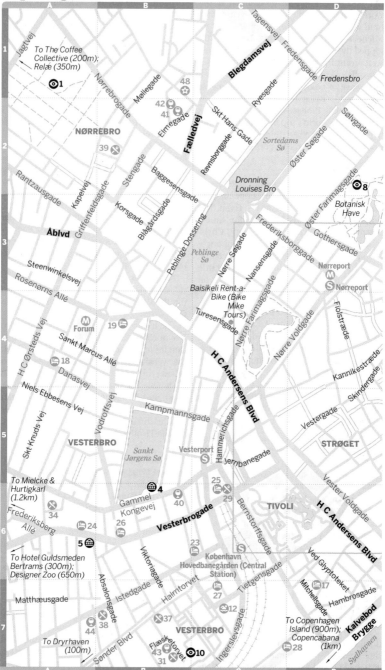

To The Coffee
Collective (200m);
Relæ (350m)

Jagtvej

Tagensvej

Fredensgade

Blegdamsvej

Fredensbro

Nørrebrogade

Møllegade

48

Ryesgade

42
41
Elmegade

Fælledvej

Skt Hans Gade

Sortedams
Sø

Øster Søgade

Sølvgade

NØRREBRO

39

Stengade

Baggesensgade

Ravnsborggade

Dronning
Louises Bro

8

Rantzausgade

Kapelvej

Griffenfeldsgade

Korsgade

Blågårdsgade

Peblinge Dossering

Frederiksborggade

Øster Farimagsgade

Botanisk
Have

Gothersgade

Åblvd

Steenwinkelsvej

Peblinge
Sø

Nørre Søgade

Nansensgade

Nørreport

Nørreport

Rosenørns Allé

Baisikeli Rent-a-
Bike (Bike
Mike
Tours)

Turesensgade

Nørre Farimagsgade

Forum

19

H C Ørsteds Vej

Sankt Marcus Allé

18

Danasvej

Nørre Voldgade

Flolstræde

Niels Ebbesens Vej

Vodroffsvej

Kampmannsgade

H C Andersens Blvd

Kannikestræde

Skindergade

Skt Knuds Vej

VESTERBRO

Sankt
Jørgens Sø

Vesterport

Hammerichsgade

Jernbanegade

Vestergade

STRØGET

To Mielcke &
Hurtigkarl
(1.2km)

34

Gammel
Kongevej

4

40

25
29

TIVOLI

Bernstorffsgade

Vester Voldgade

H C Andersens Blvd

Frederiksberg
Allé

24

26

Vesterbrogade

5

23

København
Hovedbanegården (Central
Station)

Ved Glyptoteket

17

To Hotel Guldsmeden
Bertrams (300m);
Designer Zoo (650m)

Absalonsgade

Istedgade

Viktoriagade

Halmtorvet

27

Tietgensgade

Mitchellsgade

Hambrosgade

Matthæusgade

12

To Copenhagen
Island (900m);
Copencabana
(1km)

Kalvebod
Brygge

44
38

37

VESTERBRO

Ingerslevsgade

28

Sydhavnen

To Dryrhaven
(100m)

Sønder Blvd

Flæsketorvet

43
31

10

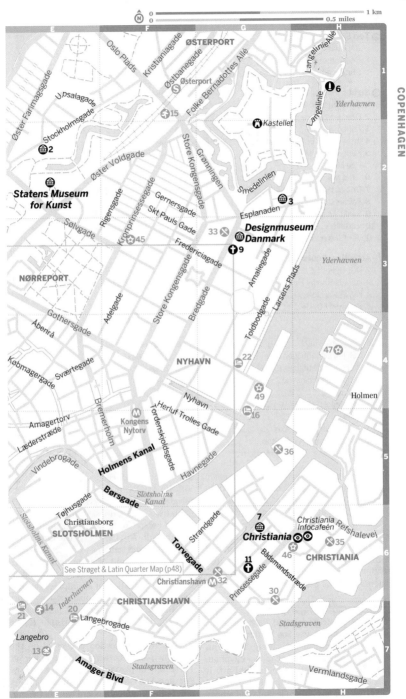

0
0

1 km
0.5 miles

ØSTERPORT

Oslo Plads

Kristaniagade

Østbanegade

Ⓢ Østerport

Upsalagade

Folke Bernadottes Allé

Langelinie Allé

❶ 6

Langelinie

Yderhavnen

✪ 15

Stockholmsgade

Øster Farimagsgade

🏛 2

Øster Voldgade

🏛

**Statens Museum
for Kunst**

Store Kongensgade

Grønningen

🏛 Kastellet

Smedelinien

🏛 3

Esplanaden

Rigensgade

Kronprinsessegade

Gernersgade

Skt Pauls Gade

Sølvgade

Fredericiagade

33 ✕

🏛 **Designmuseum
Danmark**

✪ 45

NØRREPORT

❶ 9

Amaliegade

Yderhavnen

Gothersgade

Adelgade

Store Kongensgade

Bredgade

Abenrå

Totboldgade

Larsens Plads

Købmagergade

Sværtegade

Bremerholm

NYHAVN

Nyhavn

🅜 **Kongens
Nytorv**

Herluf Trolles Gade

Tordenskjoldsgade

47 ✪

🅓 22

✪ 49

Holmen

🅓 16

Amagertorv

Læderstræde

Vindebrogade

Holmens Kanal

Havnegade

✪ 36

Børsgade

*Slotsholms
Kanal*

Strandgade

7
🏛
Christiania ◎ ◎

*Christiania
Infocaféen*

Refshalevej

Tøjhusgade

Christiansborg

SLOTSHOLMEN

Torvegade

✕ 35

46

CHRISTIANIA

Slotsholms Kanal

See Strøget & Latin Quarter Map (p48)

11
❶

Bådsmandsstræde

Christianshavn 🅜 32

Prinsessegade

Inderhavnen

CHRISTIANSHAVN

30
✕

🅓
21

✪ 14

20

🅓 Langebrogade

Stadsgraven

Langebro

13 ✕

Stadsgraven

Amager Blvd

Vermlandsgade

Copenhagen

There are sections devoted to the Norsemen and Inuit of Greenland, collections of 18th-century Danish furniture and a 'Please Touch' exhibition for sight-impaired visitors.

The museum also has an excellent toy museum, a brilliant hands-on children's section, a fine collection of Greek, Roman and medieval coins, and a Classical Antiquities section complete with Egyptian mummies. There's a cafe as well as a gift shop to boot.

TOP CHOICE Ny Carlsberg Glyptotek   ART MUSEUM
(Map p48; www.glyptoteket.dk; Tietgensgade 25; adult/child 75kr/free, free Sun; ⊙11am-5pm Tue-Sun) This whimsical art gallery houses an excellent collection of Greek, Egyptian, Etruscan and Roman sculpture and art. It was built a century ago by beer baron Carl Jacobsen, an ardent collector. The muse-

um's main building, designed by architect Vilhelm Dahlerup, is set around a delightful glass-domed conservatory, replete with palm trees, which houses a lovely cafe – the perfect escape from the Danish winter.

Although Ny Carlsberg Glyptotek was originally – and remains – dedicated to classical art, a later gift of more than 20 works by Paul Gauguin (whose wife was Danish) led to the formation of an impressive 19th-century French and Danish art collection. The Danish collection includes paintings by JC Dahl, CW Eckersberg, Christian Købke and Jens Juel.

The French collection is centred on the Gauguin paintings, which now number 47. These are displayed along with works by Cézanne, Van Gogh, Pissarro, Monet and Renoir in the stunning modern wing of the museum. This 'French Wing' also boasts one of only three complete series of Degas bronzes.

An added treat for visitors are the concerts of classical and choral music, usually held once a month on Sunday (August to May). Performances take place in the museum's concert hall, evocatively lined by life-size statues of Roman patricians. Aside from the August/September Summer Concert Series (admission around 100kr), the performances, like Sunday admission, are free.

Dansk Design Center — DESIGN MUSEUM
(Map p48; www.ddc.dk; HC Andersens Blvd 27; adult/child 55/30kr; ☺10am-6pm Mon-Wed & Fri, 10am-9pm Wed, 11am-5pm Sat & Sun; ☎) Housed in a building by senior Danish architect Henning Larsen, the Dansk Design Center showcases Danish design classics in the basement and imaginative changing exhibits on a variety of design-related topics on the ground and 1st floors. Admittedly, the collection of design pieces is relatively small, so Danish design buffs with limited time are better off exploring the more extensive collection at Designmuseum Danmark (p54). The centre also houses a suitably slick cafe, free wi-fi, and a gift shop for a little design-themed retail therapy.

FREE **Rådhus** — HISTORIC BUILDING
(City Hall; Map p48; admission free; ☺7.45am-5pm Mon-Fri, 10am-1pm Sat) Designed by the Danish architect Martin Nyrop and completed in 1905, Copenhagen's show-off town hall is an architectural fusion of 19th-century national Romanticism, medieval Danish design and northern Italian architecture, the last-mentioned most notable in the central courtyard.

Adorning the facade above the main entrance is a golden statue of Bishop Absalon, who founded the city in 1167. The entrance leads to the main hall, a grand room that serves as a polling station during municipal elections.

You can poke around the main hall on your own but it's more interesting to climb up the 105m **clock tower** (admission 20kr; ☺tour 11am & 2pm Mon-Fri, noon Sat, min 4 people) for a view that could rival Google Earth (well, almost). An altogether more curious drawcard is the town hall's **Jens Olsens Clock** (adult/child 10/5kr; ☺8.30am-4.30pm Mon-Fri, 9.30am-1pm Sat), designed by Danish astromechanic Jens Olsen (1872–1945) and built at a cost of one million kroner. Not only does it display local time, but also solar time, sidereal time, sunrises and sunsets, firmament and celestial pole migration, planet revolutions, the Gregorian calendar and even changing holidays!

STRØGET & THE LATIN QUARTER

Stretching from Rådhuspladsen to Kongens Nytorv, pedestrian shopping street Strøget (Map p48) – pronounced 'stroll' – weaves its way through Copenhagen's historical core. Technically consisting of five continuous streets, this is the city's 'Main Street' – a veritable catwalk buzzing with shoppers, camera-toting tourists and street performers of varying talent. At its western end, it's a somewhat tacky medley of souvenir stores, mediocre fashion brands and kebab shops. The scene improves further east towards Kongens Nytorv. Here, 'I Bike CPH' T-shirts give way to flagship design and department stores, as well as luxury fashion boutiques. This said, many of these retail stores peddle ubiquitous global brands, broken up by average, over-priced cafes and restaurants. Our suggestion? Walk down it once, then slip into the side streets for an altogether more inspiring and intimate vibe.

Especially appealing is the so-called 'Latin Quarter'. Located north of Strøget (around the old campus of Københavns Universitet, or Copenhagen University), its collection of snug cafes and bars, secondhand bookshops and offbeat boutiques make it a great area for some lazy ambling. The university, which was founded in 1479, has largely outgrown its original quarters and moved to a new campus on Amager, but parts of the old campus, including the law department, remain here.

In the north of the Latin Quarter is **Kultorvet**, a somewhat soulless pedestrian plaza and summer hang-out laced with beer bars, flower stalls and produce stands. On sunny days you'll usually find impromptu entertainment here, which can range from the ever-present sounds of the Andean flute to mime artists. Consider yourself warned...

Rundetårn — HISTORIC BUILDING, OBSERVATION TOWER
(Round Tower; Map p48; ☎33 73 03 73; www.rundetaarn.dk; Købmagergade 52A; adult/child 25/5kr; ☺10am-8pm late May-late Sep, 10am-5pm rest of the year) Haul yourself to the top of the 34.8m-high, red-brick 'Round Tower' and you will be following in the footsteps of such luminaries as King Christian IV, who built it in 1642 as an observatory for the famous astronomer Tycho Brahe (see p93). You'll

Strøget & Latin Quarter

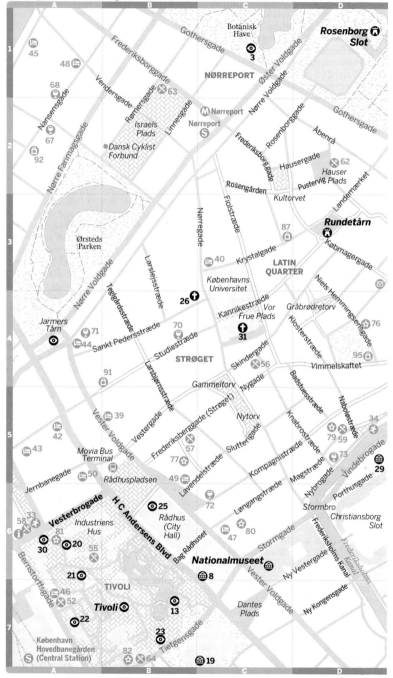

COPENHAGEN

Gothersgade

Botanisk
Have
3

Rosenborg
Slot

45

48

Frederiksborggade

NØRREPORT

Øster Voldgade

68

Vendersgade

Rømersgade

63

Nørre Voldgade

Nørre Voldgade

Gothersgade

Nansensgade

Israels
Plads

Limesgade

M Nørreport

Nørreport
S

Rosenborggade

Åbenrå

67

Dansk Cyklist
Forbund

Frederiksborggade

Hausergade

62

92

Nørre Farimagsgade

Rosengården

Pustervig Plads

Hauser
Plads

Landemærket

Kultorvet

Fiolstræde

Rundetårn

Nørregade

87

Rundetårn

Ørsteds
Parken

Larslejsstræde

40

Krystalgade

LATIN
QUARTER

Købmagergade

Nørre Voldgade

Teglgårdstræde

Københavns
Universitet

26

Niels Hemmingsensgade

76

Jarmers
Tårn

71

Sankt Pedersstræde

Studiestræde

70

Kannikestræde

Vor
Frue Plads

Gråbrødretorv

Klosterstræde

95

44

STRØGET

Skindergade

56

Vimmelskaftet

91

Larsbjørnsstræde

Gammeltorv

Nygade

Badstuestræde

Nabolostræde

34

39

Vester Voldgade

Vestergade

Frederiksberggade (Strøget)

Nytorv

Nytorv

Knabrostræde

Slutterigade

79

59

42

Movia Bus
Terminal

77

57

Kompagnistræde

Magstræde

73

Vindebrogade

43

Jernbanegade

50

Rådhuspladsen

49

Lavendelstræde

Løngangstræde

Nybrogade

Porthusgade

29

58

33

Vesterbrogade

H C Andersens Blvd

25

72

Rådhus
(City
Hall)

80

Stormbro

Stormgade

Christiansborg
Slot

Bernstorffsgade

81

30

20

55

Industriens
Hus

47

Bag Rådhuset

Frederiksholms Kanal

Ny Vestergade

Nationalmuseet

8

Ny Kongensgade

21

TIVOLI

46

52

Tivoli

13

Dantes
Plads

22

23

København
Hovedbanegården
(Central Station)

S

82

64

Tietgensgade

19

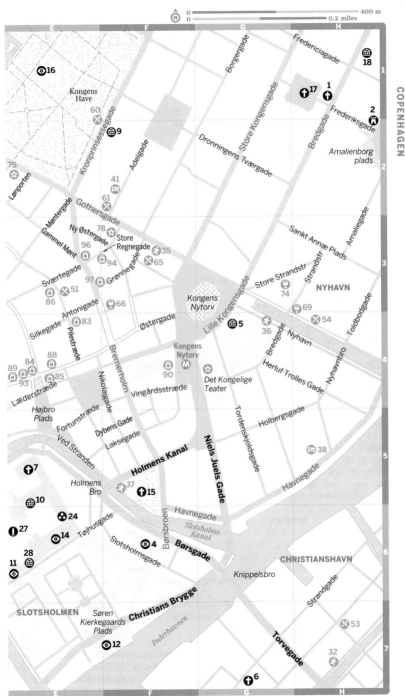

0   0
400 m
0.2 miles

E   F   G   H

⊙16

Kongens Have

60

9

75

Lønporten

Kronprinsessegade

Adelgade

Borgergade

Fredericiagade

18

17 1

2

Bredgade

Frederiksgade

Amalienborg plads

Store Kongensgade

Dronningens Tværgade

41

61

Gothersgade

Møntergade

Ny Østergade   78
Store Regnegade

Gammel Mønt   96
94   35
65

Svæertegade   97   Grønnegade
51
86

Antonigade   66

Silkegade   83   Østergade

Pilestræde   88
89   84
93   85

Læderstræde

Bremerholm

Nikolajgade

Vingårdsstræde

Sankt Annæ Plads

Amaliegade

Store Strandst

Strandstr
74

NYHAVN

Kongens Nytorv

Lille Kongensgade

5   36   69
54

Bredgade   Nyhavn

Toldbodgade

Nyhavnbro

Herluf Trolles Gade

Kongens Nytorv   M
90

Det Kongelige Teater

Tordenskjoldsgade

Holbergsgade

Havnegade

38

Højbro Plads

Fortunstræde

Dybens Gade

Ved Stranden   Laksegade

Holmens Kanal

Niels Juels Gade

7

10

24

27

14

Holmens Bro   37   15

Tøjhusgade

Slotsholmsgade

Havnegade

Børsbroen

Slotsholms Kanal

Børsgade   4

CHRISTIANSHAVN

Knippelsbro

Strandgade

11   28

SLOTSHOLMEN   Søren Kierkegaards Plads

Christians Brygge

Inderhavnen

Torvegade

53

32

12

6

Strøget & Latin Quarter

also be following in the hoofsteps of Tsar Peter the Great's horse and, according to legend, the track marks of a car that made its way up the tower's spiral ramp in 1902. While we can't verify the latter claim, we can attest that the panorama of rooftops and spires from the top is nothing short of inspiring.

The tower still functions as an excellent stargazing platform, making it the oldest functioning observatory in Europe. Visitors wanting to view the night sky from the 3m-long telescope mounted within the rooftop dome should call ahead to confirm opening times and days.

Halfway up the tower is an exhibition space featuring engaging, temporary displays of art and architecture.

FREE Vor Frue Kirke CHURCH
(Map p48; www.koebenhavnsdomkirke.dk; Nørregade 8; ◎8am-5pm) Opposite the university is Vor Frue Kirke, Copenhagen's cathedral,

which was founded in 1191 and rebuilt three times after devastating fires. The current structure dates from 1829 and was designed in neoclassical style by CF Hansen. With its high-vaulted ceilings and columns, Vor Frue Kirke seems as much museum as church – quite apropos because it's also the showcase for sculptor Bertel Thorvaldsen's statues of Christ and the 12 apostles, his most acclaimed works, which were completed in 1839. Thorvaldsen's depiction of Christ, with comforting open arms, became the most popular worldwide model for statues of Christ and remains so today. In May 2004, Vor Frue Kirke was the site of Denmark's biggest wedding – that of Crown Prince Frederik to Mary Donaldson.

FREE Sankt Petri Kirke CHURCH
(Map p48; www.sankt-petri.dk; Sankt Pedersstræde 2; ◎11am-3pm Tue-Sat) Another handsome place of worship in the Latin Quarter is Sankt Petri Kirke, a German church that dates from the

COPENHAGEN SIGHTS

15th century, making it the oldest church building in the city.

SLOTSHOLMEN
Slotsholmen is the seat of national government and a veritable repository of historical sites. Located on a small island and separated from the city centre by a moat-like canal, Slotsholmen's centrepiece is **Christiansborg Slot** (Map p48), a large palace that is home to Folketinget (the Danish parliament) and various government offices.

Several short bridges link Slotsholmen to the rest of Copenhagen. If you walk into Slotsholmen from Ny Vestergade, you'll cross the western part of the canal and enter Christiansborg's large main courtyard, which was once used as royal riding grounds. The courtyard maintains a distinctively equestrian feel, overseen by a **statue of Christian IX** (1863–1906) on horseback and flanked to the north by stables and to the south by carriage buildings.

The stables and buildings surrounding the main courtyard date back to the 1730s when the original Christiansborg palace was built by Christian VI to replace the more modest Copenhagen Castle that previously stood there.

The grander west wing of Christian VI's palace went up in flames in 1794, was rebuilt in the early 19th century and was once again destroyed by fire in 1884. In 1907 the cornerstone for the third (and current) Christiansborg palace was laid by Frederik VIII and, upon completion, the national parliament and the Supreme Court moved into new chambers there.

In addition to the sights listed here, visitors can enter **Christiansborg Slotskirke** (Map p48; admission free; ◷noon-4pm Sun Aug-Jun, noon-4pm daily Jul), the castle's domed church, which was set ablaze by stray fireworks in 1996 and has since been painstakingly restored.

COPENHAGEN FOR FREE

Copenhagen has a reputation for being heavy on the budget, but many of its top sights are free for at least one day of the week. So zip up that wallet and head to these spots, all of which are free all week unless a particular day is specified.

» Assistens Kirkegård (p58)
» Christiania (p55)
» Churches, including Marmorkirken (p54)
» Davids Samling (p57)
» Den Hirschsprungske Samling (free on Wednesday only; p58)
» Folketinget (p53)
» Frihedsmuseet (p55)
» Københavns Museum (free on Friday only; p60)
» Nationalmuseet (p43)
» Ny Carlsberg Glyptotek (free on Sunday only; p46)
» Ny Carlsberg Vej 68 (p59)
» Statens Museum for Kunst (p57)
» Thorvaldsens Museum (free on Wednesday only; p52)
» V1 Gallery (p59)

De Kongelige Repræsentationslokaler   RENAISSANCE HALL

(The Royal Reception Chambers; Map p48; www.ses.dk; adult/child 70/35kr; ⊗10am-5pm May-Sep, closed Mon Oct-Apr, English guided tours 3pm) The grandest part of Christiansborg is De Kongelige Repræsentationslokaler, an ornate Renaissance hall where the queen holds royal banquets and entertains heads of state.

Of particular note are the very colourful (almost cartoonish) wall tapestries depicting the history of Denmark from Viking times to the present day. Created by tapestry designer Bjørn Nørgaard, the tapestries took a full 10 years (until 2000) to complete. Tapestries to pay particular attention to include the Adam and Eve–style representation of the queen and her husband (albeit clothed) in a Danish Garden of Eden.

Thorvaldsens Museum   ART MUSEUM

(Map p48; www.thorvaldsensmuseum.dk; Bertel Thorvaldsens Plads 2; adult/child 40kr/free, free Wed; ⊗10am-5pm Tue-Sun) This museum exhibits the works of famed Danish sculptor Bertel Thorvaldsen (1770–1844). Heavily influenced by mythology, after four decades in Rome, Thorvaldsen returned to Copenhagen and donated his private collection to the Danish public. In return the royal family provided this site for the construction of a remarkable, frescoed museum to house Thorvaldsen's drawings, plaster moulds and beautiful statues. The museum also contains antique art from the Mediterranean region that Thorvaldsen collected during his lifetime.

FREE Det Kongelige Bibliotek   LIBRARY

(The Royal Library; Map p48; www.kb.dk; Søren Kierkegaards Plads; ⊗9am-9pm Mon-Fri, 10am-5pm Sat) The largest library in Scandinavia, Det Kongelige Bibliotek has two very distinct parts: the original, 19th-century red-brick building and the head-turning 'Black Diamond' extension, completed in 1999. Sporting a sleek black granite facade, smoked black windows and a leaning parallelogram design, the extension is one of Copenhagen's most striking examples of contemporary architecture.

Inside, Denmark's national library contains a complete collection of all Danish printed works produced since 1482 and houses some 21 million items in all.

In the lobby (which comes complete with canal views), be sure you don't miss the 210-sq-metre ceiling mural by the celebrated Danish artist Per Kirkeby, as well as the library's fascinating, temporary art and history exhibitions.

There's also a bookshop and a light-filled restaurant serving contemporary Danish dishes.

Teatermuseet   MUSEUM

(Theatre Museum; Map p48; www.teatermuseet. dk; Christiansborg Ridebane 18; adult/child 50kr/ free; ☺11am-3pm Tue-Thu, 1-5pm Wed, 1-4pm Sat & Sun) Occupying the Hofteater (Old Court Theatre), which dates from 1767 and drips with historic character, is Teatermuseet. Performances here have ranged from Italian opera and pantomime to shows by local ballet troupes, one of which included fledgling ballet student Hans Christian Andersen. The theatre, which took on its current appearance in 1842, drew its final curtain in 1881 but was reopened as a museum in 1922. Explore the stage, boxes and dressing rooms, along with displays of set models, drawings, costumes and period posters tracing the history of Danish theatre. Royal-watchers will enjoy peeking into the royal boxes – Christian VIII's entertainment area is even equipped with its own commode!

Ruinerne under Christiansborg   RUINS

(Ruins under Christiansborg; Map p48; www.ses. dk; adult/child 40/20kr; ☺10am-5pm, closed Mon Oct-Apr) A walk through the crypt-like bowels of Slotsholmen, known as Ruinerne under Christiansborg, offers a unique perspective on Copenhagen's well-seasoned history. In the basement of the current palace, beneath the tower, are the remains of two earlier castles. The most notable are the ruins of Absalon's fortress, Slotsholmen's original castle, built by Bishop Absalon in 1167.

De Kongelige Stalde & Kareter   MUSEUM

(The Royal Stables & Coaches; Map p48; www.kongehuset.dk; adult/child 20/10kr; ☺2-4pm Fri-Sun May-Sep, 2-4pm Sat & Sun Oct-Apr) Here visitors can view a collection of antique coaches, uniforms and riding paraphernalia, some of which are still used for royal receptions. You can also eye-up the royal family's carriage and saddle horses.

FREE **Folketinget**   PARLIAMENT

(Map p48; www.ft.dk; Rigsdagsgården; ☺guided tours in English 1pm Sun & public holidays, also noon & 2pm Mon-Fri Jul-early Aug) Folketinget is where the 179 members of the Danish parliament debate national legislation. Guided tours also take in Wanderer's Hall, which contains the original copy of the Constitution of the Kingdom of Denmark, enacted in 1849. Tickets for the free guided tour are available at the front desk from 9am on tour days.

FREE **Holmens Kirke**   CHURCH

(Church of the Royal Danish Navy; Map p48; www. holmenskirke.dk; Holmens Kanal 21; admission free; ☺10am-4pm Mon-Fri, 9am-noon Sat) Just across the canal to the northeast of Slotsholmen is Holmens Kirke. This historic brick structure, with a nave that was originally built in 1562 to be used as an anchor forge, was converted into a church for the Royal Navy in 1619. Most of the present structure, which is predominantly in Dutch Renaissance style, dates from 1641. The church's burial chapel contains the remains of some important naval figures, including Admiral Niels Juel, who beat back the Swedes in the crucial 1677 Battle of Køge Bay.

It was at Holmens Kirke that Queen Margrethe II took her marriage vows in 1967. The interior of the church has an intricately carved 17th-century oak altarpiece and pulpit.

Børsen   HISTORIC BUILDING

(Map p48; Børsgade) Another striking Renaissance building is Børsen, the city's stock exchange, at the eastern corner of Slotsholmen. Constructed in the 1620s, it's of note for its ornate spire, formed from the entwined tails of four dragons, and for its richly embellished gables. This still-functioning chamber of commerce, which first opened during the bustling reign of Christian IV, is the oldest in Europe but is not open to the public.

NYHAVN TO THE LITTLE MERMAID
When the sun pours over Copenhagen, you can do a lot worse than killing a beer by the Nyhavn canal. Built to connect Kongens Nytorv to the harbour, the canal was long a haunt for sailors and writers, including Hans Christian Andersen, who lived there for most of his life at, variously, numbers 20, 18 and 67. These days Nyhavn is the city's default postcard image, defined by smitten tourists, brightly coloured gabled town houses, herring buffets and foaming ale. Behind the bustle is the blue-blooded quarter of Frederiksstaden, home to Denmark's much-loved royal family, the Vatican-esque pomp of Marmorkirken, a string of fascinating museums, as well as the A-list art galleries and antique shops in the streets of Bredgade and Store Kongensgade. At its northern end sits the ancient city fortress of Kastellet, kept company by one of Copenhagen's most anticlimactic sights, the Little Mermaid.

COPENHAGEN SIGHTS

TOP CHOICE **Designmuseum Danmark** MUSEUM
(Map p44; www.designmuseum.dk; Bredgade 68; adult/child 60kr/free; ⊙11am-5pm Tue-Sun) The Denmark Design Museum, south of Kastellet, is based in the former Frederiks Hospital (c 1752). Boasting an extraordinary, eclectic collection of nearly 300,000 items from Europe and Asia, dating from the Middle Ages, it's a particular treat for those interested in the applied arts and industrial design.

The displays include a fairly extensive collection of Danish silver and porcelain and healthy coverage of innovations in contemporary Danish design. One exhibit, for example, shows Denmark's contribution to chair design, showcasing chairs by influential 20th-century designers Kaare Klint, Poul Henningsen and Arne Jacobsen. There's a cafe on-site with a gorgeous, grassy alfresco area for sunny days.

Amalienborg Slot PALACE
(Map p48; www.dkks.dk/amalienborgmuseet; Amalienborg Plads; adult/child 60kr/free; ⊙10am-4pm May-Oct, reduced hrs rest of year) Visitors can enter one wing of the Amalienborg Slot, which features exhibits of the royal apartments used by three generations of the monarchy from 1863 to 1947.

The reconstructed rooms have heavy oak furnishings, gilt-leather tapestries, family photographs and old knick-knacks. They include the study and drawing room of Christian IX (1863–1906) and Queen Louise, whose six children wedded into nearly as many royal families – one ascending the throne in Greece and another marrying Russian Tsar Alexander III. The changing of the guard takes place – entirely for the benefit of tourists, one suspects – outside Amalienborg at noon daily, the new guard having marched through the city centre from the barracks on Gothersgade at 11.30am.

Marmorkirken CHURCH, OBSERVATION DOME
(Marble Church; Map p44; www.marmorkirken.dk; Frederiksgade 4; church admission free, dome adult/child 25/10kr; ⊙church10am-5pm Mon-Thu,

DANISH DESIGN MUSTS

» Designmuseum Danmark (p54)

» Dansk Design Center (p47)

» Illums Bolighus (p77)

» Hay (p77)

» Designer Zoo (p78)

noon-5pm Fri-Sun, dome 1pm & 3pm Sat & Sun Jul & Aug) Also called Frederikskirken, Marmorkirken is a stately neobaroque church located a block west of Amalienborg Slot. The church's massive dome, which was inspired by St Peter's in Rome and measures more than 30m in diameter, is one of Copenhagen's most impressive landmarks.

The plans for the church were ordered by Frederik V and drawn up by Nicolai Eigtved as part of a grand design that included the Amalienborg mansions. Although church construction began in 1749, it encountered problems as costs overran, due in part to the prohibitively high price of Norwegian marble, and the project was soon shelved.

It wasn't until Denmark's wealthiest 19th-century financier CF Tietgen bankrolled the project's revival that it was finally taken to completion. It was consecrated as a church in 1894.

The church's exterior is ringed by statues of Danish theologians and saints. In addition to viewing the interior, with its huge circular nave, you can tour the dome and catch a broad view of the city from its rim.

Charlottenborg ART MUSEUM
(Map p48; www.kunsthalcharlottenborg.dk; Nyhavn 2; adult/child 60kr/free, free after 6pm Wed; ⊙11am-6pm Tue & Thu-Sun, to 9pm Wed) Fronting Kongens Nytorv is Charlottenborg, built in 1683 as a palace for the royal family. Since 1754 Charlottenborg has housed Det Kongelige Kunstakademi. The academy's exhibition hall, on the eastern side of the central courtyard, features highly recommended changing exhibitions of modern art by Danish and international artists. The in-house cafe features Danish-inspired furniture by Italian designer Martino Gamper.

Alexander Newsky Kirke CHURCH
(Map p48; Bredgade 53; admission free; ⊙only for services) There is a cluster of sights along the upmarket street known as Bredgade, home to many of the city's top antique dealers and auction houses. Alexander Newsky Kirke was built in Russian Byzantine style in 1883 by Tsar Alexander III.

Medicinsk-Historisk Museum MUSEUM
(Map p48; www.museion.ku.dk; Bredgade 62; adult/concession 50/30kr; ⊙guided tours in English 2.30pm daily Jul & Aug, in Danish 1.30pm, 2.30pm & 3.30pm Wed, Thu, Fri & Sun all year) Adjacent to Alexander Newsky Kirke is the Medicinsk-Historisk Museum, housed in a former surgical academy dating from 1786 and deal-

THAT LITTLE MERMAID

New York has its Lady Liberty, Sydney its (Danish-designed) Opera House. When the world thinks of Copenhagen, chances are they're thinking Little Mermaid (Den Lille Havfrue; Map p44). Love her or loathe her (watch Copenhagers cringe at the very mention of her), this small, underwhelming statue is arguably the most photographed sight in the country, as well as the cause of countless 'is that it?' shrugs from tourists who have trudged the kilometre or so along an often windswept harbourfront to see her.

In 1909 the Danish beer baron Carl Jacobsen was so moved after attending a ballet performance based on the Hans Christian Andersen fairy tale 'The Little Mermaid' that he commissioned sculptor Edvard Eriksen to create a statue of the eponymous lady-fish to grace Copenhagen's harbourfront.

The face of the famous statue was modelled after the ballerina Ellen Price, while Eline Eriksen, the sculptor's wife, modelled for the body.

The Little Mermaid survived the Great Depression and the WWII occupation unscathed, but modern times haven't been so kind to Denmark's leading lady, with several decapitations and lost limbs at the hands of vandals and protesters trying to make various political points.

Partly in response to this, Carlsberg commissioned Danish artist Bjørn Nørgaard to create a new Little Mermaid in 2006. The result is a 'genetically altered' mermaid, sitting only a few hundred metres from the original. While there's no doubt that Eriksen's creation may be the prettier sibling, Nørgaard's misshapen creation is arguably truer in spirit to Andersen's rather bleak, twisted fairy tale, in which the fish-tailed protagonist is physically and emotionally tormented...and never gets her man.

---

ing with the history of medicine, pharmacy and dentistry over the past three centuries. While English-language tours only take place in July and August, an information sheet in English is always available.

Sankt Ansgars Kirke CHURCH
(Map p44; Bredgade 64; admission free; ⊙10am-4pm Tue-Fri) Sankt Ansgars Kirke, next door to the Medicinsk-Historisk Museum, is Copenhagen's Roman Catholic cathedral. It was built in 1841 in the neo-Romanesque style and has a colourfully painted apse.

FREE **Frihedsmuseet** MUSEUM
(Museum of Danish Resistance; Map p44; www.nat mus.dk; Churchillparken; ⊙10am-3pm Tue-Sun Oct-Apr, 10am-5pm Tue-Sun May-Sep) This museum features exhibits on the Danish resistance movement from the time of the German occupation in 1940 to liberation in 1945. There are displays on the Danish underground press, the clandestine radio operations that maintained links with England and the smuggling operations that saved 7200 Danish Jews from capture by the occupying Nazis.

CHRISTIANSHAVN
Christianshavn lays on the charm with its glittering canals, outdoor cafes and easygoing attitude. Located on the city's eastern

flank, the quarter was established by Christian IV in the early 17th century as a commercial centre and also a military buffer for the expanding city. That it may remind you of Amsterdam is no coincidence, its network of boat-lined waterways having been modelled after those in Holland. Equally reminiscent of free-minded Amsterdam is the area's most famous attraction, the alternative, pot-scented neighbourhood of Christiania.

Still surrounded by its old ramparts, contemporary Christianshavn is an altogether appealing combo of standard-issue public housing complexes and elegant period warehouses that have found second lives as upmarket housing and restored government offices. The neighbourhood attracts an interesting mix of boho-chic artists, yuppies, anarchist dropouts and a sizable Greenlandic community. It was the setting for parts of the novel and movie *Miss Smilla's Feeling for Snow*. To get to Christianshavn, you can walk over the copper-toned Knippelsbro from the southeastern part of Slotsholmen, catch bus 2A, 40, 66 or 350S, or take the metro to the stop of the same name.

Christiania NEIGHBOURHOOD
(Map p44; www.christiania.org; Prinsessegade) In 1971 an abandoned 41-hectare military camp on the eastern side of Christianshavn

was taken over by squatters who proclaimed it the 'free state' of Christiania, subject to their own laws. The police tried to clear the area but it was the height of the hippie revolution and an increasing number of alternative folk from throughout Denmark continued to pour in, attracted by the concept of communal living and the prospect of reclaiming military land for peaceful purposes.

Bowing to public pressure, the government allowed the community to continue as a social experiment. About 1000 people settled into Christiania, turning the old barracks into schools and housing, and starting their own collective businesses, workshops and recycling programmes.

Christiania residents, self-governing, ecology-oriented and generally tolerant, did, in time, find it necessary to modify their free-law/anything goes approach. A new policy was established that outlawed hard drugs, and the heroin and cocaine pushers were expelled, although for many years a blind eye was turned to the sale of marijuana and hash on 'Pusher Street'.

The sheer size and incredible location of the land means that the pressure for the government to take back the space it's been 'lending' to the Christiania locals for the last 30-odd years has greatly increased. In a real estate deal made with the government in April 2011, Christiania's residents have until 2018 to officially 'buy' the land...for a sobering 76 million kroner. Needless to say, this decade will be a challenging one for the neighbourhood, whose residents plan on raising the funds through bank loans and events.

Despite the pressure, Christiania hasn't lost its free-spirited soul, and visitors are welcome to stroll or cycle through to share the love. The commune itself has a small market, a couple of craft shops and a few eateries; the open sale of soft drugs is now banned. For a truly rewarding experience, however, explore the commune's quieter parts, where rambling paths lead past DIY abodes and cosy little gardens.

The main entrance into Christiania is on Prinsessegade, 200m northeast of its intersection with Bådsmandsstræde. You can take a **guided tour** (☏32 57 96 70; www.rund visergruppen.dk; per person 40kr; ☺3pm daily late Jun-Aug, 3pm Sat & Sun Sep-Jun) of Christiania. Meet just inside the main entrance. There's a Pusher Street **Infocaféen** (☏32 95 65 07;

nytforum@christiania.org; ☺noon-6pm) of sorts, where you can pick up the useful *Christiania Guide* (10kr). You'll find the office just next to the Oasen cafe.

Vor Frelsers Kirke   CHURCH, OBSERVATION TOWER
(Our Saviour's Church; Map p44; Sankt Annæ Gade 29; church admission free, tower adult/child 30/10kr; ☺church 11am-3.30pm, tower 10am-4pm Jun, 10am-7pm Mon-Sat, 10.30am-7pm Sun Jul–mid-Sep, reduced hrs rest of year) A few minutes' stroll southwest of Christiania is the 17th-century Vor Frelsers Kirke. The church has a grand interior that includes an elaborately carved pipe organ dating from 1698 and an ornate baroque altar with marble cherubs and angels.

For a soul-stirring panoramic city views make the head-spinning 400-step ascent up the church's 95m-high spiral tower – the last 150 steps run along the outside rim of the tower, narrowing to the point where they literally disappear at the top. The colourful spire was added to the church in 1752 by Lauritz de Thurah, who took his inspiration from Boromini's tower of St Ivo in Rome. It was climbed in 1752 by King Frederik V on inauguration day.

Orlogsmuseet   MUSEUM
(Royal Danish Naval Museum; Map p44; www. orlogsmuseet.dk; Overgaden Oven Vandet 58; adult/child 40kr/free; ☺noon-4pm Tue-Sun) If you, or someone you know, gets high from tooling around with hobby glue, then you have stumbled upon the mother lode. Occupying a former naval hospital on Christianshavn Kanal, Denmark's naval museum has more than 400 model ships, many dating from the 16th to the 19th century. Its booty also includes a collection of figureheads, navigational instruments, ship lanterns and the propeller from the German U-boat that sank the *Lusitania*.

Lille Molle   HISTORIC BUILDING
(Map p44; www.natmus.dk; Christianshavns Voldgade 54; adult/child 50kr/free; ☺guided tours 1pm, 2pm & 3pm Sat & Sun Jun-Sep) This 17th-century windmill, turned over to the National Museum in the 1970s, has been preserved as its last owners left it – and they left it in a very interesting state. If you time your visit just right, it's perfect for a guided tour preceded or followed by a fabulous feed at Bastionen & Løven, the attached restaurant-cafe (see p70).

Christians Kirke CHURCH
(Map p48; Strandgade 1; admission free; ⏰10am-4pm Tue-Fri) Designed by the Danish architect Nicolai Eigtved and completed in 1759, Christians Kirke features a theatrical, rococo interior. The church once served Copenhagen's German congregation.

NØRREPORT TO NØRREBRO

Straddling the city's shallow lakes, with Nørreport to the south and Nørrebro to the northwest, these are two of Copenhagen's most intriguing areas. Nørreport's star strip is Nansensgade, a low-key street studded with a handful of atmospheric cafes, bars and independent boutiques. Across the water, livelier Nørrebro subverts the pristine Nordic stereotype with its dense, sexy funk of art-clad 19th-century tenements; multicultural crowds; thronging cafes, bars and clubs; and independent fashion boutiques. While streets such as Elmegade, Blågårdsgade, Ravnsborggade and Sankt Hans Torv have long offered a fix of Nørrebro cool, Nørrebro's lastest up-and-comer street is Jægersborggade.

At the western edge of the strangely enchanting cemetery Assistens Kirkegård – the final resting place of numerous Danish luminaries, including Hans Christian Andersen – this one-time notorious drug strip is quickly reinventing itself as a hot spot for top-notch dining, coffee and good old-fashioned hanging out.

TOP CHOICE Statens Museum for Kunst ART MUSEUM
(National Gallery of Denmark; Map p44; www.smk.dk; Sølvgade 48-50; admission free; ⏰10am-8pm Wed, to 5pm Tue & Thu-Sun) Denmark's national gallery was founded in 1824 to house art collections belonging to the royal family. Originally sited at Christiansborg Slot, the museum opened in its current location in 1896. Statens Museum is the largest art museum in the country, thanks to an enormous, light-filled modern extension constructed in recent times.

Its collection covers seven centuries of European art, ranging from medieval works with stylised religious themes to free-form modern art. There's an interesting collection of old masters by Dutch and Flemish artists, including Rubens and Frans Hals, as well as more contemporary European paintings by Matisse, Picasso and Munch. The museum also has an extensive collection of drawings, engravings and lithographs representing the works of such prominent artists as Degas and Toulouse-Lautrec.

As might be expected, the museum has a wonderful collection of Danish fine art, including works by CW Eckersberg, Jens Juel, Christen Købke, PS Krøyer and Per Kirkeby. There's plenty to keep children amused too, with special programmes year-round. There's a fabulous light-filled cafe, and accessibility to people in wheelchairs is generally very good.

Rosenborg Slot CASTLE
(Map p48; www.dkks.dk; Øster Voldgade 4A; adult/child 75kr/free; ⏰10am-5pm Jun-Aug, 11am-4pm Sep & Oct, reduced hrs rest of year) To the east of Nørreport proper is the beautiful early-17th-century Rosenborg Slot with its fairytale moat-and-garden setting. It was built between 1606 and 1633 by King Christian IV in Dutch Renaissance style to serve as his summer home. A century later King Frederik IV, who felt cramped at Rosenborg, built a roomier palace north of the city in the town of Fredensborg. In the years that followed, Rosenborg was used mainly for official functions and as a place in which to safeguard the monarchy's heirlooms.

In the 1830s the royal family decided to open the castle to visitors as a museum, while still using it as a treasury for royal regalia and jewels. It continues to serve both functions today.

The 24 rooms in the castle's upper levels are chronologically arranged, housing the furnishings and portraits of each monarch from Christian IV to Frederik VII. In the basement is the dazzling collection of crown jewels. There's Christian IV's ornately designed crown, the jewel-studded sword of Christian III and Queen Margrethe II's emeralds and pearls.

Kongens Have (King's Gardens; Map p48), the expansive green space behind Rosenborg Slot, is the city's oldest public park. It has manicured box hedges, lovely rose beds and plenty of shaded areas. Kongens Have is a very popular picnic spot on sunny days and the site of a free marionette theatre that performs on summer afternoons.

FREE Davids Samling ART MUSEUM
(Map p48; www.davidmus.dk; Kronprinsessegade 30-32; admission free; ⏰1-5pm Tue & Fri, 10am-9pm Wed, 10am-5pm Thu, 11am-5pm Sat & Sun) East of Kongens Have, Davids Samling is a wonderful curiosity of a gallery housing Scandinavia's largest collections of

Islamic art, including jewellery, ceramics and silk, and exquisite works such as an Egyptian rock crystal jug from AD 1000 a 500-year-old Indian dagger inlaid with rubies. That's all up on the 4th floor and worth a visit in itself, but on your way up you can spend a fruitful couple of hours taking in the museum's fine Danish, English and French furniture and art from the 18th and 19th centuries. All of this was bequeathed to the museum by the barrister Christian Ludvig David, who died in 1960, and is maintained by the foundation he founded. The museum is housed in his former home, a neoclassical mansion dating from 1806.

Botanisk Have GARDEN

(Botanical Garden; Map p48; www.botanik.snm. ku.dk; Gothersgade 128; admission free; ☉8.30am-6pm May-Sep, to 4pm Tue-Sun Oct-Apr) In the 10-hectare Botanisk Have you can wander along fragrant paths amid arbours, terraces, rock gardens and ponds. Within the gardens is the Palmehus (Palm House; ☉10am-3pm, closed Mon Oct-Apr), a large walk-through glasshouse containing a lush collection of tropical plants. There's also a cactus house (☉1-2pm Wed, Sat & Sun), an orchid greenhouse (☉2-3pm Wed, Sat & Sun) and an endangered species greenhouse (☉1-3pm Wed, Sat & Sun). One entrance to the Botanisk Have is at the intersection of Gothersgade

and Øster Voldgade, while the other is off Øster Farimagsgade.

You can get to the gardens and Rosenborg Slot by taking the S-train or metro to Nørreport station and then walk or take a frequent bus.

Den Hirschsprungske Samling ART MUSEUM

(The Hirschsprung Collection; Map p44; www. hirschsprung.dk; Stockholmsgade 20; adult/child 50kr/free, free Wed; ☉11am-4pm Wed-Mon) Dedicated to Danish art of the 19th and early 20th centuries, Den Hirschsprungske Samling is an enchanting little gallery, full of wonderful surprises for art lovers unfamiliar with the classic era of Danish oil painting from the early 19th century. Originally the private holdings of tobacco magnate Heinrich Hirschsprung, it contains works by 'Golden Age' painters such as Christen Købke and CW Eckersberg, a notable selection by Skagen painters PS Krøyer and Anna and Michael Ancher, and also works by the Danish symbolists and the Funen painters.

Assistens Kirkegård CEMETERY

(Map p44; www.assistens.dk; Kapelvej 4; admission free; ☉7am-10pm Apr-Sep, to 7pm Oct-Mar) The serene Assistens Kirkegård in the heart of Nørrebro is the final resting place of some of Denmark's most celebrated citizens, including philosopher Søren Kierkegaard, physicist Niels Bohr, author Hans Christian

---

LOCAL KNOWLEDGE

TUE HESSELBERG FOGED, ARCHITECT

My favourite neighbourhood...

...is Islands Brygge. It used to be a working-class area, with industry along the harbour. Now it's like the Copacabana of Copenhagen. During summer, it's packed with near-naked people jumping into the harbour. The water is clean and you can swim in the centre of the city. It's a symbol of Copenhagen and what it can do. It's free and accessible to all. Just hanging out here in July and August is a must-do.

A perfect day in Copenhagen...

...would start in my favourite park, Kongens Have. There are always loads of people hanging out there on beautiful days. Across the street, I'd stop at Cinemateket, run by the Danish Film Institute. They only show good-quality classics and art-house films. Further out, I'd head to the Ny Carlsberg Vej 68 art precinct. It's home to Galleri Nicolai Wallner, one of the coolest galleries in Copenhagen.

The coolest things about Copenhagen...

...are festivals such as CPH Distortion, which turns the city into one big block party. It's getting bigger and bigger each year and it's worth coming to Copenhagen just to experience it. It's what I love most about the city – the best parts are the temporary parties.

As told to Cristian Bonetto

Andersen, and artists Jens Juel, Christen Købke and CW Eckersberg. It's a wonderfully atmospheric place to wander around – as much a park and garden as it is a graveyard.

A good place to start is at the main entrance on Kapelvej, which has an office where you can pick up a brochure mapping famous grave sites.

Zoologisk Museum
MUSEUM

(Map p42; www.zoologi.snm.ku.dk; Universitetsparken 15; adult/child 75/40kr; ☺10am-5pm Tue-Sun) The Zoologisk Museum, 1km north of Assistens Kirkegård, is the sort of place where once magnificent wild creatures, from north Zealand deer to Greenlandic polar bears, get well and truly stuffed. There are also interesting dioramas, recorded animal sounds, a whale skeleton and insect displays. To get here, take bus 18, 42, 43, 184, 185 or 150S.

Experimentarium
SCIENCE CENTRE

(Map p42; www.experimentarium.dk; Tuborg Havnevej 7, Hellerup; adult/child 160/100kr; ☺9.30am-5pm Mon & Wed-Fri, 9.30am-9pm Tue, 11am-5pm Sat & Sun) The extensive hands-on technology and natural-world exhibits at Experimentarium are housed in a former bottling hall of Tuborg Breweries in Hellerup, 7km north of the city centre. Containing some 300 exhibits, it's a fun place for kids, featuring such time-honoured standards as the hall of mirrors, as well as computer-enhanced activities that make it possible to compose music on a hopscotch board, fly on a magic carpet and experience a 5.5 Richter-scale earthquake. To get here take the S-train to Hellerup.

VESTERBRO TO FREDERIKSBERG

It is hard to imagine two more disparate neighbours than leafy, middle-class Frederiksberg and gritty, urban Vesterbro, but both promise an intriguing handful of sights, not to mention some must-try restaurants, bars and cafes.

Vesterbro begins at the western side of Central Station with the city's most infamous thoroughfare, Istedgade. At its 'station end', the strip is Copenhagen's seedy red light district, littered with sex shops, massage parlours, stiletto-strapped prostitutes and lower range hotels. Since the police clamped down on official drug facilities, the junkies have taken to the streets here, which makes for a fairly shaming spectacle in a city so supposedly advanced in its social provision. Further west, however, Isted-

gade transforms into one of the city's most interesting streets, lined with independent boutiques, Middle Eastern grocery shops, as well as cafes and bars filled with Vesterbro creative types.

South of Istedgade awaits Kødbyen (literally 'Meat City'). Dubbed Copenhagen's 'Meatpacking District', this one-time industrial site has developed into one of the city's trendiest districts, with an ever-increasing army of grit-chic restaurants and bars. It's also home to one of the city's coolest art galleries, V1.

North of Istedgade lies Vesterbrogade, a mainstream shopping street with supermarkets and midrange fashion stores. Turn right where Vesterbrogade meets Frederiksberg Allé, and you'll hit atmospheric Værndamsvej. Known locally as Copenhagen's 'Little Paris', it's a gorgeous little strip with a handful of buzzing cafes, wine bars, restaurants and fashion boutiques.

Further west, respectable Frederiksberg is where you'll find two of the city's most popular tourist attractions – the zoo (p60) and the Carlsberg Visitors Center (p60). It's also home to contemporary-art hot spot Ny Carlsberg Vej 68 (following), not to mention Copenhagen's most romantic park, Frederiksberg Have – where you'll find culinary gem Mielcke & Hurtigkarl (p70).

Ny Carlsberg Vej 68
ART MUSEUMS

(Map p42; www.nycarlsbergvej68.dk; Ny Carlsberg Vej 68; ☺noon-5pm Tue-Fri, to 3pm during exhibitions) What was once a garage for the Carlsberg brewery is now one of Copenhagen's hottest art precincts, with three leading galleries under the one roof. Top of the heap is **Galleri Nicolai Wallner**, considered a major player on the contemporary Danish art scene (artists represented here include Jeppe Hein and Berlin-based Nordic duo Michael Elmgreen and Ingar Dragset). Neighbouring gallery **Nils Stærk** is equally established and renowned, while **IMO** mixes cutting-edge art with broader cultural events such as retro film screenings and performances. Buses 10 and 3A stop nearby.

V1 Gallery
ART MUSEUM

(Map p44; www.v1gallery.com; Flæsketorvet 69-71; ☺noon-6pm Wed-Fri, to 4pm Sat during exhibitions) Part of the Kødbyen (Vesterbro's 'Meatpacking District'), V1 is one of Copenhagen's most progressive art galleries. Cast your eye on fresh work from both emerging and established local and foreign artists. Some of

WHEN IN ROME

Want to blend in with the locals? Then follow our essential 10-point plan:

» Smoke like a kipper
» Men – throw away your ties
» Women – throw away your bras
» Everyone – get on your bikes
» Throw away that extraneous top layer of bread; have smørrebrød for lunch
» Wait for the green man before crossing
» Snicker at the Swedes
» Never serve salmon on brown bread
» Spend big on lampshades
» Don't queue for the bus – it's everyone for themselves

the world's hottest names in street- and graffiti art have exhibited here, from Britain's Banksy to the USA's Todd James and Lydia Fong (aka Barry McGee).

Carlsberg Visitors Center BREWERY
(Map p42; www.visitcarlsberg.dk; Gamle Carlsberg Vej 11; adult/concession 40/25kr; ⊙10am-4pm Tue-Sun) Adjacent to the famed Carlsberg brewery, the Carlsberg Visitors Center has an evocative exhibition on the history of Danish beer from 1370 BC (yes, they carbon-dated a bog girl who was found in a peat bog caressing a jug of well-aged brew). Dioramas give the lowdown on the brewing process and en route to your final destination you'll pass antique copper vats and the stables with a dozen Jutland dray horses. The self-guided tour ends at the inhouse bar where you can knock back two free beers.

Københavns Museum MUSEUM
(Copenhagen Museum; Map p44; www.copen hagen.dk; Vesterbrogade 59; adult/child 20kr/ free, free Fri; ⊙10am-5pm) True to its name, Københavns Museum in Vesterbro has displays about the history and development of Copenhagen – mainly paintings and scale models of the old city. There is a small room dedicated to 19th-century, Copenhagenborn philosopher Søren Kierkegaard, as well as eclectic temporary exhibitions spanning anything from recent archaeological finds to garbage in the city.

Imax Tycho Brahe Planetarium PLANETARIUM
(Map p44; www.tycho.dk; Gammel Kongevej 10; adult/child 135/85kr; ⊙11.30am-8.30pm Mon, 10.30am-8.30pm Tue-Fri, 9.30am-8.30pm Sat & Sun) Copenhagen's Planetarium, located 750m northwest of Central Station, has a domed space theatre that offers shows of the night sky using state-of-the-art equipment capable of projecting more than 7500 stars, planets and galaxies. The planetarium's 1000-sq-metre screen also shows Imax and digital 3-D films on subjects ranging from sea monsters to Irish rockers U2.

The planetarium was named after the famed Danish astronomer Tycho Brahe (1546–1601; see p93), whose creation of precision astronomical instruments allowed him to make exact observations of planets and stars, and paved the way for the discoveries made by later astronomers.

Zoologisk Have ZOO
(Zoo; Map p42; www.zoo.dk; Roskildevej 32, Frederiksberg; adult/child 140/80kr; ⊙10am-6pm early-late Jun & early-late Aug, 10am-9pm late Jun-early Aug, reduced hrs rest of year) Copenhagen's Zoologisk Have, located up on Frederiksberg (Frederik's Hill), has a large collection (over 2500 critters) of nature's lovelies, including lions, elephants, zebras, hippos, gorillas and polar bears. Both the giraffes and the elephants have new, state-of-the-art homes, the latter courtesy of English architect, Sir Norman Foster.

Activities

You'll be forgiven for wanting to damn the Danes. Despite their high-level intake of tobacco, alcohol and fat, svelte bodies are the norm on Copenhagen streets. So what's their secret? A passion for physical activity. Top of the list is cycling, which combines ecofriendly transport with a decent workout. Beyond the pedal are a number of fine swimming options...allowing the locals to flaunt those frustratingly fine figures.

Swimming
BEACHES
If brisk water doesn't deter you, the greater Copenhagen area has several bathing spots. The water is tested regularly and if sewage spills or other serious pollution occur, the beaches affected are closed and signposted.

Amager Strandpark BEACH
This is a sand-sational artificial lagoon to the southeast of the city centre, with acres of sandy beach and, during summer, a fes-

tival atmosphere most days with cafes and bars. Playground facilities and shallow water make it ideal for children. Take the Metro to Amager Strand.

Bellevue
BEACH
(Map p42) An attractive and popular beach at Klampenborg on the so-called Danish Riviera. To get there take S-train C to Klampenborg.

Charlottenlund
BEACH
(Map p42) This is an accessible beach north of central Copenhagen. Take S-train C to Charlottenlund.

SWIMMING POOLS
Whether you're after indoor laps or a harbour splash, Copenhagen has you covered; the following are Copenhagen's most central swimming options.

FREE Copencabana
POOL
(Map p42; ☺11am-7pm Jun-Aug) With diving, children's and swimming pools, this harbour-based, open-air venue to the south of the city centre is popular during summer with swimmers and sunbathers alike. It's at Havneholmen, in front of the cinema in Fisketorvet shopping centre.

DGI-byen
POOL
(Map p44; www.dgibyen.dk; Tietgensgade 65; adult 42-60kr, child 26-40kr; ☺6.30am-10pm Mon-Thu, 6.30am-8pm Fri, 9am-7pm Sat, 9am-6pm Sun, last entry 1hr before close) An extravagant swim centre with several pools, including a grand ellipse-shaped affair with 100m lanes, a deep 'mountain pool' with a climbing wall, a hot-water pool and a children's pool. If you've forgotten your togs or towels, they can be hired for 25kr each (assuming you have photo ID as a deposit). There's also a small gym on the premises.

FREE Islands Brygge Havnebadet
POOL
(Map p44; Islands Brygge; ☺7am-7pm Mon-Fri, 11am-7pm Sat & Sun Jun-Aug) Copenhagen's funkiest outdoor pool complex (designed by trendy architects Plot) sits right in the central city's main canal. Green flags mean good quality water, so don't worry about pollution. If you don't fancy a swim, the lawns, skateboarding parks, basketball courts and eateries here are a top spot to see and be seen on a warm summer day.

Boating
If you want to explore Christianshavn's historic canals, **Christianshavns Bådudlejn-**

ing og Café (Map p48; ☎32 96 53 53; Overgaden neden Vandet 29; boats per hr 100kr; ☺10am-sunset May–mid-Sep) rents out rowing boats on the canal just beside Christianshavns Torv. An added bonus is the buzzing waterside cafe on the premises.

Kayaking tours in Copenhagen are also available; see p62.

Cycling
Hiring a bike is easy in Copenhagen. In addition to the rental rates, expect to pay a refundable deposit of around 500kr for a regular bike, 1000kr for a mountain bike or tandem. Tours are also available; see p62.

Københavns Cyklerbørs
CYCLING
(Map p44; ☎33 14 07 17; www.cykelboersen. dk; Gothersgade 157; bicycle hire per day/week 75/285kr; ☺9am-5.30pm Mon-Fri, 10am-1.30pm Sat) Close to the Botanisk Have (Botanical Gardens) on the northwest edge of the city centre.

Østerport Cykler
CYCLING
(Map p44; ☎33 33 85 13; www.oesterport-cykler. dk; Oslo Plads 9; bicycle hire per day/week from 85/375kr; ☺8am-6pm Mon-Fri, 9am-1pm Sat) At Østerport S-train station near track 13.

☞ Tours

Bus Tours

Copenhagen City Sightseeing
TOURS
(www.citysightseeing.dk; departs from Axeltorv, beside the tourist office; tickets adult/child from 125/62.50kr; ☺departures every 30min May–mid-Dec) A hop-on/hop-off red double-decker bus tour, with three themed tours: Mermaid, Carlsberg and Christiania. Multilingual tape recordings make sure everyone gets the picture. A two-day 'Freedom Ticket' (adult/child 3-11 years 220/110kr) also covers the DFDS Canal Tours (see p62).

COPENHAGEN ACTIVITIES

TOP EXPERIENCES FOR KIDS

» Tivoli (p43)
» DGI-byen (p61)
» Nationalmuseet (p43)
» Canal Boat Tour (p62)
» Planetarium (p60)

For more on travelling with children in Denmark, see p30.

Boat Tours

You can't visit Copenhagen and *not* take a canal boat trip. Not only is it a fantastic way to see the city, but you see a side of it land-lubbers never see. There are two companies that operate guided canal tours during summer – DFDS and Netto-Bådene. Be aware that, in most boats, you are totally exposed to the elements (which can be quite elemental in Copenhagen harbour, even during summer). Both operators offer tours in covered, heated boats from October to March.

DFDS Canal Tours   BOAT TOURS

(Map p48; ☎32 96 30 00; www.canaltours.com; adult/3-11yr/family 70/40/180kr; ⊘every 30min 10am-5pm Apr-Oct, reduced services rest of year) Has embarking points at Nyhavn and Gammel Strand, with extra departures also from the Marriott Hotel from mid-March to October. Sights include the Little Mermaid, the Opera House, Amalienborg Palace and Slotsholmen. A two-day unlimited-use 'Freedom Ticket' (adult/child 3-11 years 220/110kr) also includes the Copenhagen City Sightseeing bus.

Netto-Bådene   BOAT TOURS

(Map p48; ☎32 54 41 02; www.havnerundfart.dk; adult/child 40/15kr; ⊘2-5 times per hr, 10am-7pm Jul & Aug, to 5pm Apr-Jun & Sep–mid-Oct) Better value than the DFDS Canal Tours, Netto-Bådene covers the same route. Embarkation points are at Holmens Kirke and Nyhavn. From mid-July to August, boats also depart from the Little Mermaid. Check the website for timetable updates.

Kayak Tours

Kayak Republic   KAYAK TOURS

(Map p44; ☎30 49 86 20; www.mykayak.dk; per person 325-495kr) Based beside Langebro bridge, this outfit runs two-hour and full-day kayak tours along the city's canals. It also rents out kayaks for self-exploration (single kayak per one/two/three hours 150/250/325kr).

Walking & Cycle Tours

Jogging Tours   JOGGING TOURS

(☎61 60 69 67; www.joggingtours.dk; per person 200kr) Students from the University of Copenhagen offer jogging tours following three routes – a Royal Tour, a Nørrebro Tour and a Frederiksberg Tour.

Copenhagen Walking Tours   WALKING TOURS

(☎40 81 12 17; www.copenhagen-walkingtours.dk) Organises a range of themed tours of the city for, typically, around 100kr per person.

History Tours   WALKING TOURS

(☎28 49 44 35; www.historytours.dk; prices vary) History Tours leads historically themed walking tours of the city centre, leaving from Højbro Plads, which is north of Christiansborg Slotskirke.

Bike Copenhagen With Mike   CYCLING TOURS

(☎26 39 56 88; www.bikecopenhagenwithmike.dk) If you don't fancy walking, Bike Mike offers daily three-hour cycling tours of the city, departing from outside the Baisikeli Rent-a-Bike shop (Turesensgade 10), just west of Ørstedsparken (which is southwest of Nørreport station). The tour costs 260kr, and includes bike rental. In the summer, themed options are also offered, including a contemporary architecture tour.

CPH:cool   WALKING TOURS

(☎29 80 10 40; www.cphcool.dk) It offers tours that trade the beaten-track tourist sights for the city's in-the-know hot spots, with themes including gastronomy, shopping, architecture and design. Prices vary according to the number of participants.

✪ Festivals & Events

Winter Jazz Festival   MUSIC

(www.jazz.dk/en/vinter-jazz) Toe-tap your blues away at this smaller scale version of Copenhagen's summertime jazz festival. Usually spanning around 17 days in late January and February, events are held in venues across the city.

CPH:PIX   FILM

(www.cphpix.dk) Held over 18 days in April, this is Copenhagen's feature film festival. Expect over 160 flicks from Denmark and abroad, as well as a busy programme of film-related events, including director and actor Q&As.

Dronning Margrethe II's Birthday   ROYAL

On 16 April the much-loved Danish queen greets the crowds from the balcony of Amalienborg Slot at noon as soldiers in full ceremonial dress salute her. Thousands flock to pay their respects and even the city buses fly flags in honour.

Copenhagen Carnival   CULTURE

(www.copenhagencarnival.dk) Held over three days at Whitsun (50 days after Easter), this is the Danes' take on the Brazilian-style shebang with colourful floats, musicians, workshops and sequin-happy, booty-shaking dancers.

Copenhagen Distortion   MUSIC

(www.cphdistortion.dk) Taking place over five heady days in early June, Copenhagen Distortion celebrates the city's street life and club culture. Expect raucous block parties and top-name DJs spinning dance tracks in bars and clubs across town.

Skt Hans Aften (St Hans Evening)   CULTURE

The Danes let rip on the evening of 23 June – the longest night of the year – with bonfires in parks, gardens and, most popular of all, on the beaches. Join them in burning an effigy of a witch on a pyre, singing songs and getting merry.

Copenhagen Jazz Festival   MUSIC

(www.jazz.dk) Copenhagen's single largest event, and the largest jazz festival in northern Europe, hits the city over 10 days in early July. The programme spans jazz in all its forms, with an impressive line-up of local and international talent. For more, see p76.

Kulturhavn   CULTURE

(www.kulturhavn.dk) For three days in early August, Copenhagen takes culture to the harbour and waterways with a wide programme of theatre, dance, music, sports and parades on the 'beach' at Islands Brygge, as well as at Sydhavnen and Refshaleøen. Most events are free.

Copenhagen Pride   GAY & LESBIAN

(www.copenhagenpride.dk) Rainbow flags fly high during the city's five-day queer fest in August. Expect live music and merry revellers in Rådhuspladsen, fabulous club parties, cultural events and the razzle dazzle of the Pride parade, the latter taking place on the Saturday afternoon.

Copenhagen Cooking   FOOD

(www.copenhagencooking.dk) All of Scandinavia's largest food festival serves up a truly drool-worthy events list spanning cooking demonstrations from A-list chefs, to tastings and foodie tours of the city. Events are held in venues and restaurants across town, usually from mid-August to early September.

Art Copenhagen   ART

(www.artcopenhagen.dk) Taking place over three days in September, this major art fair sees the participation of 80 art galleries from across Nordic Europe. The art itself focuses on contemporary artists from Denmark, Sweden, Norway, Finland, Iceland and the Faroe Islands. The fair usually takes place at Forum Copenhagen.

Copenhagen Design Week   DESIGN

(www.copenhagendesignweek.dk) This major biennial event features six days of design-related seminars, screenings, exhibitions and themed walks in late August or early September. The event also showcases the work of 60 designers competing for the INDEX Award (www.indexaward.dk), the world's most lucrative design prize. The next events will take place in 2013 and 2015.

Kopenhagen Contemporary   ART

(www.kopenhagencontemporary.com) This four-day festival in early September celebrates Copenhagen's thriving contemporary-art scene, with both local and foreign talent on display. Events include openings, performances, debates and free guided tours.

Copenhagen Blues Festival   MUSIC

(www.copenhagenbluesfestival.dk) For five days in late September or early October, Copenhagen celebrates the moody sounds of the blues with this international music festival. The line-up includes both Danish and international acts.

Kulturnatten (Culture Night)   CULTURE

(www.kulturnatten.dk) Usually held on the second Friday in October, this wonderfully atmospheric event sees the city's museums, galleries, theatres and libraries throw open their doors from 6pm to midnight (or beyond) to those with a Kulturpas (Culture Pass; 90kr), and there are a wide range of special events. Public transport is also free with the Kulturpas; see the website for more details of the pass.

CPH:Dox   FILM

(www.cphdox.dk) CPH:Dox is an acclaimed international documentary film festival. The largest of its kind in Scandinavia, it screens films in several cinemas throughout the city. The festival takes place over 11 days from early to mid-November.

Tivoli   ART

(www.tivoli.dk) Copenhageners really know how to go to town at Christmas, with extravagant decorations, church concerts and Christmas markets. Tivoli gets in on the act too, reopening from mid-November to late December with a large market, Yuletide tableaux, costumed staff and theatre shows. Fewer rides are operational but the mulled wine and æbleskiver (small doughnuts) are ample compensation.

ACCOMMODATION PRICE RANGES

Our listings in this chapter are for prices for doubles with bathrooms (or dorm beds for hostels), as follows:

€ (budget)	Under 600kr per night
€€ (midrange)	From 600kr to 1500kr
€€€ (top end)	More than 1500kr

Sleeping

Copenhagen has enjoyed a hotel boom in recent years. While the main growth area has been in the midprice range, particularly noteworthy has been the arrival of seriously sleek, design-savvy budget options WakeUp Copenhagen and Generator Hostel. Thankfully, sleeping in Copenhagen is no longer the dauntingly expensive exercise it used to be.

With both WakeUp Copenhagen and Generator Hostel being exceptions, most of the city's main budget hotels are centred on the western side of the Central Station, around Vesterbrogade and the fruitier parts of Istedgade. Ironically, what was once a relatively downtrodden part of town is now home to one of its trendiest districts, Kødbyen, now filling up with some of Copenhagen's hottest eateries and bars.

Across the city you'll find a wide range of accommodation options, from the outrageous, artist-designed rooms of Hotel Fox, to chic floating hotel CPH Living, to the classic Danish design aesthetics of the Radisson Blu Royal Hotel.

The hotel rates quoted in this section include service charge and value-added tax (VAT). It's a good idea to book in advance – rooms in many of the most popular midrange hotels fill quickly, particularly during the convention season, typically from August to October, when prices increase significantly too. At other times, prices for rooms fluctuate greatly, depending on the time of year or even the time of week, with most hotels tempting guests with special offers throughout the year. Copenhagen's hostels often fill early in summer so it's best to make reservations in advance. You will need a hostelling card to get the advertised rates at hostels belonging to the Danhostel (www.danhostel.dk) organisation.

The Copenhagen Visitor Centre (p79) can book rooms in private homes (350/500kr for singles/doubles); there is a 100kr booking fee if you do it via the tourist office when you arrive, otherwise it is free online. This office also books unfilled hotel rooms, typically at discounted rates that vary from around 100kr off for budget hotels to as much as 50% off for top-end hotels. These discounts, however, are based on supply and demand, and are not always available during busy periods.

RÅDHUSPLADSEN, TIVOLI & AROUND

TOP CHOICE / Hotel Nimb BOUTIQUE HOTEL €€€
(Map p48; ☑88 70 00 00; www.nimb.dk; Bernstorffsgade 5; r 2800-4900kr, ste 6900-9000kr; @⊙) Located at Tivoli Gardens, this boutique belle is the darling of international travel magazines with good reason. Its 14 individually styled rooms and suites are a soothing fusion of clean Scandi lines, beautiful art and antiques, luxury fabrics and high-tech perks such as Bang & Olufsen TVs and sound systems. All rooms except one also feature a fireplace and views over Tivoli. And did we mention the three fabulous restaurants and cocktail bar?

Hotel Fox DESIGN HOTEL €€
(Map p48; ☑33 13 30 00; www.foxhotel.dk; Jarmers Plads 3; s 700-1495kr, d 850-2095kr; @⊙) With every room designed by a different artist/designer/totally crazy person, a room at Hotel Fox adds just a little more to your visit to the city than a trouser press and some nice prints of the canals. Standouts include room 302 (Moroccan bathhouse meets Stanley Kubrick), room 409 (Swiss chalet kitsch) and room 510 (regal fairy tale).

Radisson BLU Royal Hotel HOTEL €€€
(Map p44; ☑33 42 60 00; www.radissonblu.com; Hammerichsgade 1; d 1500-2300kr; P✱@⊙) Centrally located and famous among the design cognoscenti (Arne Jacobsen designed it and room 606 – a tidy 5000kr per night – has been left intact), this multistorey hotel of 260 rooms is popular with well-to-do business travellers and visiting dignitaries. Service is peerless, there's a full-service gym, and the excellent Alberto K restaurant (p68) on the top (20th) floor is a culinary must.

Hotel Twentyseven HOTEL €€€
(Map p48; ☑70 27 56 27; www.hotel27.dk; Løngangstræde 27; s 820-2080kr, d 1020-2280kr; ✱@⊙) The rooms might be a little small, but their minimalist styling and cool furniture fit the

hipster bill at this super-cool Scandi number. Perks include organic products in the black-slate bathrooms, friendly staff, and decent cocktails in the popular ground-floor bar (request a room away from the bar if you're a light sleeper). Even cooler (literally) is the Absolut Ice Bar in the basement. Rooms on the 5th floor have air-con.

The Square
HOTEL €€

(Map p48; ☑33 38 12 00; www.thesquare.dk; Rådhuspladsen 14; s 1000-2200kr, d 1100-2600kr; ✴@) Pimped with Jacobsen chairs and red leather, The Square is an excellent three-star hotel with design touches and amenities generally associated with greater expense and more stiffness. Standard rooms are a little small but well equipped, and some have sterling views of the main square – plus all the city's main sights are within walking distance.

First Hotel Kong Frederik
HOTEL €€€

(Map p48; ☑33 12 59 02; www.firsthotels.com; Vester Voldgade 25; s 895-2295kr, d 1095-2495kr; @) Recently renovated, black-and-gold Kong Frederik oozes a classic baronial vibe – think dark woods, antique furnishings and paintings of Danish royalty and hunting scenes. The well-appointed rooms come in three themes: Classic, Romantic and Library (the latter featuring silvery 'bookshelf' wallpaper). The staff are genuinely friendly and there's a Nespresso machine in the communal reading room.

Hotel Alexandra
HOTEL €€

(Map p48; ☑33 74 44 44; www.hotelalexandra.dk; HC Andersens Blvd 8; s/d from 1445/1745kr; P@) The furniture of Danish design greats such as Arne Jacobsen, Ole Wanscher and Kaare Klint grace the interiors of the refined yet homely Alexandra. The rooms are effortlessly cosy, and each features modern art and flat-screen TVs. Staff are attentive, and the hotel's vintage air makes a refreshing change from all that sleek Nordic minimalism.

Danhostel Copenhagen City
HOSTEL €

(Map p44; ☑33 11 85 85; www.danhostel.dk/copenhagencity; HC Andersens Blvd; dm 135-185kr, s/d 520-720kr; @) Featuring interiors by design company Gubi and a cafe-bar in the lobby, this friendly, ever-popular hostel is set in a tower block overlooking the harbour just south of Tivoli Gardens (did we mention the views?). Both the dorms and private rooms are bright, light and modern, each with bathroom. Book ahead.

Palace Hotel
HOTEL €€€

(Map p48; ☑33 14 40 50; www.scandichotels.com; Rådhuspladsen 57; s/d 2660/2860kr; ✴@) Bang on Rådhuspladsen and housed in a 1920s building – by architect Anton Rosen – whose tower is a city landmark itself, the Palace skilfully balances historic architecture with contemporary detailing. Rooms are elegant and minimalist, with sleek bathrooms and shades of pastel or grey breaking up the Nordic white.

Cab Inn
BUDGET HOTEL €

(www.cabinn.dk; s/d from 485/615kr; @) Well managed, functional and cheap, the Cab Inn chain has four hotels in Copenhagen, the most central being **Cab Inn Copenhagen City** (Map p44; ☑33 46 16 16; Mitchellsgade 14), which lies just to the south of Tivoli. Although small and anonymous, the rooms are comfortable and have cable TV, phone, complimentary tea, and bathroom. Reception is open 24 hours and all rooms have free wi-fi connection. Both **Cab Inn Scandinavia** (Map p44; ☑35 36 11 11; Vodroffsvej 57, Frederiksberg) and **Cab Inn Copenhagen Express** (Map p44; ☑33 21 04 00; Danasvej 32, Frederiksberg) are less than 2km west of Tivoli, while the newer **Cab Inn Metro** (☑32 46 57 00; Arne Jakobsens Allé 2) is a short walk from Ørestad metro station, and close to the airport.

Hotel Ascot
HOTEL €€€

(Map p48; ☑33 12 60 00; www.ascothotel.dk; Studiestræde 61; s 1390-1490kr, d 1590-1690kr; @) The friendly Ascot occupies a former bathhouse erected a century ago by the same architect (Martin Nyrop) who designed Copenhagen's city hall. Most of the 190 rooms are large and decorated in classic Danish style. Each has a deep soaking tub in the bathroom, and some have a kitchen. Guests also have free access to the hotel's fitness room. On the downside, the hotel is not particularly wheelchair friendly.

STRØGET & THE LATIN QUARTER

Generator Hostel
HOSTEL €

(Map p48; ☑78 77 54 00; www.generatorhostels.com; Adelgade 5-7; dm 209-312kr, s 744-790kr, d 798-845kr, tr 768-900kr; @) Copenhagen's latest 'cheap chic' option is this upbeat, design-literate hostel, located on the very edge of the city's medieval core. It's pimped with designer furniture, slick communal areas (including a bar and outdoor terrace) and upbeat young staff. While the rooms can be a little small, all are bright and modern, with bathroom in both private rooms and dorms.

First Hotel Sankt Petri
HOTEL €€

(Map p48; ☎33 45 91 00; www.hotelsktpetri.com; Krystalgade 22; r 995-2895kr; ✳@🛜) The Technicolor sea of Arne Jacobsen Egg chairs in the atrium lobby attests to Sankt Petri's designer tendencies. The comfortable rooms feature contemporary interiors and art, with many offering views over the Latin Quarter's rooftops. Redesign your body at the gym next door (free for hotel guests) or simply sip and pose in the lobby bar.

NYHAVN

71 Nyhavn Hotel
HOTEL €€

(Map p44; ☎33 43 62 00; www.71nyhavnhotel.dk; Nyhavn 71; s 1125-1750kr, d 1325-2050kr; @🛜) Housed in a stunning 200-year-old canalside warehouse, this atmospheric slumber spot has incorporated some of the building's period features and great views of both the harbour and Nyhavn canal. Rooms facing Nyhavn are quite small, while those without the magical view compensate with more space. The hotel is popular with business travellers, and therefore can be a bargain on weekends. Breakfast (optional) is an extra 150kr.

Copenhagen Strand
HOTEL €€

(Map p48; ☎33 48 99 00; www.copenhagenstrand. dk; Havnegade 37; s/d from 990/1285kr; @🛜) Set in a converted 19th-century warehouse, the appealing Strand hotel overlooks Copenhagen Harbour. Its 174 rooms are equipped with cable TV, minibar and phone. The standard rooms are smallish but cosy, and only the suites have harbour views. There's an on-site business centre, and a lobby bar, making this a good choice for the business traveller.

Front
HOTEL €€

(Map p44; ☎33 13 34 00; www.front.dk; Sankt Annæ Plads 21; s 890-1890kr, d 1190-2190kr; ✳@🛜) Conveniently plonked to the rear of Nyhavn and overlooking the harbour, Front is light, bright and sexed-up with a bold colour scheme (although the orange carpets that grace some rooms are probably best avoided). Admittedly, the rooms are looking a little worn these days, though we do love the pebble-floored bathrooms, amiable staff and handy little on-site gym.

CHRISTIANSHAVN

TOP CHOICE CPH Living
FLOATING HOTEL €€

(Map p44; ☎61 60 85 46; www.cphliving.com; Langebrogade 1C; r from 1000kr; 🛜) Located on a converted freight boat, this simple, savvy floating hotel features 12 stylish rooms, each with harbour and city views. Perks include flat-screen TVs, modern bathrooms with rainforest shower, and a communal sundeck for summertime lounging. Breakfast is a simple continental affair, while the central location makes it an easy walk to the city centre, Christianshavn and the harbour beach at Islands Brygge.

NØRREPORT

Hotel Kong Arthur
HOTEL €€

(Map p48; ☎33 11 12 12; www.kongarthur.dk; Nørre Søgade 11; s 895-1895kr, d 1095-2095kr; @🛜) Sprawling over four historic buildings, the 107-room Kong Arthur fuses understated elegance with quirky period details such as suits of armour. Rooms are a soothing white, splashed with contemporary art and including TV, minibar, trouser press and attractive bathroom. Some overlook the waters of Peblinge Sø. The hotel also features a stylish inner courtyard, a lovely glassed-in atrium for breakfast in inclement weather, and complimentary use of iPads.

Ibsens Hotel
BOUTIQUE HOTEL €€

(Map p48; ☎33 13 19 13; www.ibsenshotel.dk; Vendersgade 23; s 745-1745kr, d 945-1945kr; @🛜) Part of the Brøchner Group (which also includes Hotel Fox and Hotel Kong Arthur), the recently revamped Ibsens is a three-star hotel with boutique finesse. Local creativity defines everything, from the textiles and artwork, to the leather key tags by Piet Breinholm (see p77). Rooms are minimalist yet plush, with muted tones, designer fixtures and blissful beds. The upbeat, design-savvy breakfast room morphs into a cafe and a bar as the day progresses.

VESTERBRO

TOP CHOICE Hotel Guldsmeden
BOUTIQUE HOTEL €€

(www.hotelguldsmeden.dk) The gorgeous Guldsmeden hotels include Bertrams (off Map p44; ☎33 25 04 05; Vesterbrogade 107; s 930-1595kr, d 1190-1995kr), Carlton (Map p44; ☎33 22 15 00; Vesterbrogade 66; s 695-895kr, d 845-1095kr) and the equally alluring Axel (Map p44; ☎33 31 32 66; Helgolandsgade 7-11; s 765-1250kr, d 895-1470kr), just off Istedgade.

Axel features more of the same raw stone, bare wood, crisp white linen, spectacular bathtubs and colonial style that have made these hotels *the* place to stay for savvy, style-conscious travellers.

WakeUp Copenhagen BUDGET HOTEL €
(☑44 80 00 00; www.wakeupcopenhagen.com; Carsten Niebuhrs Gade 11; r 500-800kr; @ 🐨) Travellers with more cool than krone will appreciate this cheap-chic slumber number, an easy walk from Tivoli and Central Station. While the foyer is an impressive combo of concrete, glass and Arne Jacobsen chairs, the 500-plus rooms are compact, fresh and stylish, complete with flat-screen TV and funky capsule-like showers. Book online for the cheapest rates.

Tiffany HOTEL €€
(Map p44; ☑33 21 80 50; www.hoteltiffany.dk; Colbjørnsensgade 28; s 795-1695kr; d 895-1995kr; @ 🐨) The Tiffany, which proudly bills itself as a 'Sweet Hotel', is a pleasant little place filled with character. The 30 rooms each have TV, phone, trouser press, bathroom, and kitchenette with refrigerator, microwave oven and toaster. Service is kind and considerate, and it's an easy walk from Central Station and the hip cafes, bars and restaurants of the Vesterbro neighbourhood.

Savoy Hotel HOTEL €€
(Map p44; ☑33 26 75 00; www.savoyhotel.dk; Vesterbrogade 34; s 695-1095kr; d 795-1475kr; @ 🐨) Located in the hip Vesterbro district, this century-old hotel still retains some of its period character and art-nouveau decor, though its 66 rooms were set for a revamp in 2012. Although the hotel fronts a busy road, all rooms face a quiet courtyard, and each has cable TV, a minibar and coffee maker. Best of all, the service is some of the sweetest and most efficient in town.

GREATER COPENHAGEN
Copenhagen Island HOTEL €€
(☑33 38 96 00; www.copenhagenisland.dk; Kalvebod Brygge; s/d 1090/1190kr; ✼@ 🐨) Built on an island in the redeveloped South Harbour district, this sleek 325-room hotel is the work of Utzon's team of architects. Although some rooms are seriously small, they're all expectantly svelte, complete with sexy Danish-designed furniture. Harbour-view rooms are particularly appealing, as is the fitness centre and restaurant. On the down side, it's a little out of the way.

Charlottenlund Fort CAMPING GROUND €
(☑39 62 36 88; www.campingcopenhagen.dk; Strandvejen 144B; camping per adult 95kr; ☺mid-Apr–late Sep) Eight kilometres north of central Copenhagen, this friendly camping ground, on Charlottenlund beach, is set in the tree-lined grounds of an old moat-encircled coastal fortification. Space is limited so advance bookings are recommended. There's a snack kiosk, showers and a coin laundry on-site; a bakery and a supermarket are just a few hundred metres away. To get here, take S-train line A, B or C to Svanemøllen station and switch to bus 14 (ask the driver to let you off at the camping ground).

Danhostel Copenhagen Bellahøj HOSTEL €
(☑38 28 97 15; www.copenhagenhostel.dk; Herbergvejen 8, Brønshøj; dm/d/tr 145/430/515kr; ☺1 Feb-2 Jan; Ⓟ@ 🐨) This place is in a quiet suburban neighbourhood 4km northwest of the city centre. Although it has 250 beds, it's quite cosy for its size. Facilities include a laundry room, guest kitchen, TV room and table tennis. To get here, take bus 2A.

Danhostel Copenhagen Amager HOSTEL €
(☑32 52 29 08; www.copenhagenyouthhostel.dk; Vejlands Allé 200, Amager; dm 145kr, s/d 460/490kr; Ⓟ@) In an isolated part of Amager just off the E20, about 5km southeast of the city centre, this is one of Europe's largest hostels, with 528 beds in a series of low-rise wings containing cells of two-bed and five-bed rooms. There's a laundry room and a cafeteria. It's also wheelchair friendly. To get here, take the metro to Bella Center.

✕ Eating

Copenhagen is one of the hottest culinary destinations in Europe right now. The city has more Michelin stars than any other Scandinavian city. So what has turned this one-time dining dowager into a burgeoning culinary destination? The answer: a league of young, visionary chefs including Noma's René Redzepi and Geranium's Rasmus Kofoed, fuelled by a passion for Scandinavia's raw ingredients – from excellent seafood to wild herbs – and an obsession with seasonality. The end result is a new style of regional cooking that is light, playful and unmistakably Scandinavian.

Until recently the exclusive domain of fine dining, wallet-draining restaurants, this New Nordic innovation is now defining a growing number of more casual, affordable, bistro-style eateries, among them Marv &

Ben, Kødbyens Fiskebar and Relæ. The latter two are actually headed by ex-Noma chefs, determined to bring top produce and local innovation to a wider range of gastronomes.

But it's not all sea buckthorn, *skyr* (strained yoghurt) curd and pickled quail eggs, with old-school Danish fare still a major player on the city's tables. Indeed, tucking into classics such as *frikadeller* (meatballs), *sild* (pickled herring) and the iconic Danish open sandwich (smørrebrød) at institutions such as Schønnemann and Cap Horn is an integral part of the Copenhagen experience...and always best washed down with a cold local beer.

Geographically speaking, Vesterbro and Nørrebro are especially good for trendy new bistros, buzzing cafes and ethnic food; Nyhavn is a good bet for beer and a sandwich; and Christianshavn is a choice spot to enjoy lunch by the canals away from the crowds.

There are a couple of things to note when eating out in Copenhagen. Firstly, a few of the city's A-list restaurants, including Mielcke & Hurtigkarl, offer pared-back lunch menus, which is good news for krone-economising foodies. Secondly, the Danes are not Mediterraneans, meaning that if you like to eat late, you'll have trouble finding a place to accommodate you after about 10pm.

Restaurants that open during the day will commence business at 11am or noon, and keep the kitchen serving lunch until about 3pm, before opening again at about 6pm. Many of the top restaurants close for some weeks in July and August, so be sure to book ahead to avoid culinary heartbreak.

RÅDHUSPLADSEN & TIVOLI

Tivoli boasts nearly 30 places to eat, from simple stalls offering typical amusement-park fare such as hot dogs, to some of the most respected eating establishments in the city. You need to pay Tivoli admission to eat at its restaurants – and they only open during the Tivoli season.

Alberto K   MODERN DANISH €€€

(Map p44; ☎33 42 61 61; www.alberto-k.dk; Hammerichsgade 1; 5/7 courses 675/800kr; ☉dinner Mon-Sat) Suitably perched on the 20th floor of the Radisson Blu Royal Hotel, Alberto K is one of Copenhagen's top choices for a culinary high. Merging local produce, Nordic innovation and Italian influences, its flavours are clean, arresting and nothing short of sublime. Arne Jacobsen cutlery and furniture pay tribute to the hotel's celebrated designer, while the restaurant's wine cellar will please picky oenophiles. Book ahead.

Grøften   DANISH €€

(Map p48; open sandwiches 59-125kr, mains 135-310kr; ☉lunch & dinner) If you're getting your thrills at Tivoli, jolly Grøften is a handy place to refuel. Since 1974, the speciality here is a type of smørrebrød that comes with lip-smacking tiny fjord shrimps spiced with lime and fresh pepper. For something a little more warming, scan the mains, which include a hefty selection of meats and a handful of fish dishes.

Andersen Bakery Hot
Dog Kiosk   HOT DOGS €

(Map p48; Bernstorffsgade 5; gourmet hot dog 50kr; ☉11am-6.30pm) Made with organic pork sausage, Bornholm mustard and a to-die-for chanterelle sauce, Andersen's Grand Danois is the Rolls Royce of Danish hot dogs. The kiosk is just to the left of Andersen Bakery's main entrance, and customers are welcome to grab a seat inside the bakery if you prefer to tackle your dog sitting down.

Wagamama   ASIAN €€

(Map p48; www.wagamama.dk; Tietgensgade 20; mains 95-135kr; ☉noon-10pm) It might be a ubiquitous UK chain, but trendy Wagamama is a safe bet for fresh, flavoursome Asian soups, noodles and curries (and it's open every day!). Drink options include freshly squeezed fruit and vegetable juices, and the menu doesn't snub vegetarians. Although it's part of the Tivoli complex, it's accessible to all from Tietgensgade.

STRØGET & THE LATIN QUARTER

Strøget and, more particularly, the grid of streets to its north and south are a fertile hunting ground for restaurants and cafes, with everything from hole-in-the-wall kebab kiosks to old-school Danish lunch restaurants, cafes and the odd Mod-Danish culinary darling.

Marv & Ben   MODERN DANISH €€

(Map p48; ☎33 91 01 91; www.marvogben.dk; Snaregade 4; 2-/3-course lunch 255/275kr, 3-/5-course dinner 315/375kr; ☉lunch Tue-Sat, dinner Mon-Sat, closed Jul) For krone-conscious foodies, salvation comes in the form of this simple yet elegant hot spot. Behind a glass wall, young-gun chefs let regional produce (some from a chef's own parents' farm in north Zealand) shine in dishes such as tartar of veal topside with poached egg, hazelnut and celery. While not in the Noma league just yet, the beautifully presented dishes are more hit than miss, with clean flavours and surprising combinations. The waitstaff are knowledgeable and attentive, and the vibe is refreshingly relaxed. Book ahead.

Schønnemann DANISH €€
(Map p48; www.restaurantschonnemann.dk; Hauser Plads 16; smørrebrød 59-158kr; ☺lunch Mon-Sat) Schønnemann has been lining local bellies with smørrebrød and schnapps since 1877. Originally a hit with farmers in town peddling their produce, its current fan base includes Michelin-lauded chefs such as Noma's (p70) René Redzepi. We're talking 'local institution' so book ahead if possible.

Torvehallerne KPH FOOD MARKET €
(Map p44; Israels Plads; ☺bread, cake & coffee 7am-9pm daily, fresh produce 10am-7pm Tue-Thu, 10am-8pm Fri, 9am-5pm Sat, 10am-3pm Sun) A quick walk west of the Nørreport S-train station, Copenhagen's brand-new indoor food market is the latest destination for peckish gastronomes. A feast for both eyes and taste buds, its beautiful stalls peddle everything from seasonal fruit and vegetables to meats, seafood, cheeses and other specialities from Denmark and beyond. Taste test, stock the larder, and stop for Copenhagen's best cup of Joe at The Coffee Collective.

Pastis FRENCH €€
(Map p48; Gothersgade 52; mains 185-245kr; ☺lunch & dinner Mon-Sat) Channelling both Paris and NYC with its lipstick-red banquettes and white subway tiles, this upbeat bistro is perfect for a post-shopping bite or a more substantial dinner date. Tuck into a light *salade chévre chaud* (grilled goat's cheese salad with pickled walnuts and raisins) or delve into warming, delicate classics such as bouillabaisse (fish soup with gruyere cheese).

42° Raw HEALTH FOOD €€
(Map p48; www.42raw.com; Pilestræde 32; meals 88-128kr; ☺10am-8pm Mon-Fri, to 6pm Sat, 11am-5pm Sun) The focus at this hip and healthy eat-in or takeaway is raw food, served in dishes such as 'raw' lasagne, tapas, pizza and sexed-up salads (think tomato and avocado with parsley, garlic, chilli, red quinoa and a trout oil and vinegar dressing). The libations are just as virtuous, with smoothies and freshly squeezed juices – try the refreshing spinach, apple and basil combo.

La Glace BAKERY €
(Map p48; www.laglace.com; Skoubogade 3; pastries from 40kr; ☺8.30am-5.30pm Mon-Thu, to 6pm Fri, 9am-5pm Sat, also 10am-5pm Sun late-Sep-Easter) This is *the* classic *konditori* (bakery-cafe) in town and it has been serving tea and fancy cakes for more than a century. A rite of passage if you have a sweet tooth, or are looking to develop one.

NYHAVN TO THE LITTLE MERMAID

Orangeriet FRANCO-DANISH €€
(Map p48; ☑33 11 13 07; www.restaurant-orangeriet.dk; Kronprinsessegade 13; open sandwiches 70-75kr, 3-/5-course dinner 345/465kr; ☺lunch daily, dinner Mon-Sat) Enchantingly set in a vintage conservatory in Kongens Have, Orangeriet has quickly become one of Copenhagen's culinary highlights. At the helm is award-winning chef Jasper Kure, whose contemporary Franco-Danish creations focus on simplicity and premium seasonal produce. Savour the brilliance in dishes such as salt-baked artichokes with jellied mushroom bouillon, pickled mushrooms and salted lemons. Sunday lunch is a simple affair of smørrebrød and cake. Book ahead.

Le Sommelier FRENCH €€
(Map p44; ☑33 11 45 15; www.lesommelier.dk; Bredgade 63; 3 courses 395kr; ☺dinner daily, also lunch Mon-Fri mid-Aug–Jun) A chic, pared-back combo of white linen tables, wooden floorboards and vintage French and Italian posters, Le Sommelier fuses French traditions with seasonal Nordic produce. Dishes are delicate and memorable, with gems like chicken consommé with shellfish ravioli, mushrooms and ginger. The wine list has a particularly impressive French selection and service is smooth and attentive.

Cap Horn DANISH €€
(Map p48; www.caphorn.dk; Nyhavn 21; mains 189-199kr; ☺lunch & dinner) A deservedly popular spot, this canal favourite specialises in Danish fare and laces its menu with organic ingredients. Grab a lunch plate of three open-faced sandwiches, or tackle heartier grub such as fried plaice with sautéed capers, tomatoes and spinach. Either way, wash it all down with a river of beer. Open until the crowds die down (it's popular with cruise passengers), which is usually late.

Wokshop Cantina ASIAN €€
(Map p48; Ny Adelgade 6; mains 119-145kr; ☺lunch & dinner Mon-Fri, dinner Sat) This good-value, Wagamama-style modern Thai/Asian place

is close to Kongens Nytorv to the rear of Hotel d'Angleterre.

CHRISTIANSHAVN

TOP CHOICE Noma MODERN DANISH €€€
(Map p44; ☑32 96 32 97; www.noma.dk; Strandgade 93; 7-course menu 1095kr; ☺lunch & dinner Tue-Sat) Topping the S.Pellegrino 'World's Best Restaurants' list in 2010 and 2011, this Michelin-starred restaurant has become a Holy Grail for gastronomes across the globe. At the helm is groundbreaking chef René Redzepi (formerly of elBulli and the French Laundry), who continues to push New Nordic cuisine to breathtaking highs. Noma's name is an abbreviation of *nordisk mad,* or Nordic food. The menu features only Scandinavian-sourced produce such as musk ox, *skyr* curd and locally caught seafood, transformed into extraordinary symphonies of flavour and texture. Book three months ahead.

Bastionen & Løven DANISH €€
(Map p44; www.bastionen-loven.dk; Lille Molle, Christianshavns Voldgade 50; lunch meals 65-105kr, dinner mains 170-185kr; ☺lunch daily, dinner Mon-Sat) While the elegant bare wood interior and storybook garden of this old miller's cottage will induce bucolic Nordic fantasies, the real reason to head here is the menu. Seasonal, and often creative, dishes might include pearl barley risotto with mushrooms, white beer, bacon and wild boar. The whole place feels like a wonderful secret – although the weekend brunch sessions can get mighty packed with faithful regulars.

Spiseloppen INTERNATIONAL €€
(☑32 57 95 58; Bådmandsstræde 43; mains 165-225kr; ☺dinner Tue-Sun) Christiania's evening offering is a little more ambitious than Morgenstedet (see following). Located upstairs in the Loppen building, its daily changing menu reflects not only the morning's best market produce, but also the nationality of the chef working that day. Whether it's Danish, Italian or Thai, expect vibrant, salubrious flavours. It's a hit, so book ahead.

Lagkagehuset BAKERY €
(Map p44; www.lagkagehuset.dk; Torvegade 45; sandwiches 55kr, pastries from 14.50kr; ☺6am-7pm) This much-loved bakery – invariably voted the best in the city – sells excellent sandwiches as well as the usual sticky, sweet pastries and heavyweight rye bread. You'll find other branches on pedestrianised Strøget (Frederiksberggade 21; open 7.30am to 8pm) and at the Copenhagen Visitor Centre (p79; open 7.30am to 6.30pm, to 8pm July and August).

Morgenstedet VEGETARIAN €
(Map p44; Langgade Christiania; soup 45kr, mains 75kr; ☺lunch & dinner Tue-Sun; ☑) A homely, hippy bolthole in the heart of the alternative commune of Christiania, Morgenstedet offers but two dishes of the day, one of which is usually a soup. Choices are always vegetarian, organic, and always at a bargain price.

Cafe Wilder INTERNATIONAL €€
(Map p44; www.cafewilder.dk; Wildersgade 56; lunch 89-129kr, dinner mains 129-185kr; ☺lunch & dinner; ☎) This friendly corner cafe-cum-bistro in the heart of Christianshavn serves simple, beautiful lunch options such as soy-grilled tuna salad with pickled onions, baked tomatoes, new potatoes and haricot vert. Evening options are heartier (think roasted plaice with oven-roasted potatoes, pointed cabbage, spring onion, lemon, dill and butter sauce). One of Copenhagen's oldest cafes, it's popular with local bohemians.

VESTERBRO TO FREDERIKSBERG

TOP CHOICE Kødbyens Fiskebar SEAFOOD €€
(Map p44; ☑32 15 56 56; www.fiskebaren.dk; Flæsketorvet 100, Vesterbro; mains 195-235kr; ☺dinner Tue-Sat) Postindustrial cool (concrete floors, tiled walls and a 1000-litre aquarium) meets sterling seafood at this Michelin-listed must. Occupying a former factory in trendy Kødbyen, its seasonal menu keeps it simple and fresh with dishes such as Limfjorden blue mussels with steamed apple cider and herbs. There's usually a meat and vegetarian option, and delectable desserts such as English liquorice with sea buckthorn and white chocolate ice cream.

Mielcke & Hurtigkarl MODERN DANISH €€€
(☑38 34 84 36; www.mielcke-hurtigkarl.dk; Frederiksberg Runddel 1, Frederiksberg; 4-course lunch/dinner degustation menu 425/850kr; ☺lunch & dinner Tue-Sat Apr-Sep, dinner Thu-Sat Oct-Mar) If you plan on seducing someone (or just your own taste buds), book a table at this culinary charmer. Set in a former royal summer house adorned with contemporary murals and a forest soundscape, it's as dreamy as its menu is heavenly. While the set lunch menu offers simpler, cheaper fare, the highlight here is the dinner degustation menu, showcasing head chef Jakob Mielcke's inspired

approach to local and global ingredients (think Norwegian lobster jelly with salty plum ice cream).

Paté Paté
INTERNATIONAL €€

(Map p44; ☑39 69 55 57; www.patepate.dk; Slagterboderne 1; mains 145-195kr; ⊘lunch & dinner) Another Kødbyen must, this pâté factory-turned-restaurant/wine bar is run by the brilliant team behind Bibendum (p72). Here, Euro classics get modern, seasonal twists in dishes such as poussin with liver crostini, pickled cherries and summer truffle. Hip yet warm and convivial, bonus extras include clued-up staff, a well-versed wine list and close proximity to late-night drinking hot spot Mesteren & Lærlingen (p72).

Cofoco
FRANCO-DANISH €€

(☑33 13 60 60; Abel Cathrines Gade 7; 4 courses 275kr; ⊘dinner Mon-Sat) One of several top-quality, fixed-menu places owned by the same team, Cofoco offers a glamorous setting and refined Franco-Danish food (foie gras, pear and pork terrine, for instance, or duck leg with Jerusalem artichoke and mushrooms), on a budget. **Les Trois Cochons** (Map p44; ☑33 31 70 55; Værndamsvej 10, Vesterbro; ⊘lunch Mon-Sat, dinner daily) is another great-value restaurant from the same people, which we also heartily recommend.

Siciliansk Is
ICE CREAM €

(Map p44; Skydebanegade 3, Vesterbro; medium cup 30kr; ⊘noon-9pm May-Aug, 1-6pm Apr & Sep) Honing their skills in Sicily, gelato meisters Michael and David churn out Copenhagen's (dare we say Denmark's) best gelato. Lick yourself out on smooth, seasonal flavours such as *havtorn* (sea buckthorn) and *koldskål* (a frozen take on the classic Danish buttermilk and lemon dessert). For an unforgettable combo, try *lakrids* (liquorice) with Sicilian mandarin.

Dyrehaven
DANISH €

(www.dyrehavenkbh.dk; Sønder Blvd 72, Vesterbro; lunch 55-90kr, dinner mains 135-145kr; ⊘9am-midnight Mon-Wed, 9am-2am Thu & Fri, 10am-2am Sat, 10am-midnight Sun) Once a spit-and-sawdust working-class bar (the vinyl booths and easy-wipe floors tell the story), Dyrehaven is now a second home for Vesterbro's cool, young bohemians. Squeeze into your skinny jeans and join them for cheap drinks, simple tasty grub (the 'Kartoffelmad' egg open sandwich is a classic, made with homemade mayo and fried shallots) and some late-night camaraderie.

NØRREBRO & ØSTERBRO

Geranium
MODERN DANISH €€€

(☑69 96 00 20; www.geranium.dk; Per Henrik Lings Allé 4, Østerbro; tasting menus 848-1048kr; ⊘dinner Wed-Sat; ☑) Geranium is giving Noma some serious competition: in 2011 its chef Rasmus Kofoed bagged the coveted Bocuse d'Or prize (the unofficial Olympic Games for chefs), while Geranium itself was nominated world's best restaurant. Perched on the 8th floor of Parken football stadium in Østerbro, its menu is a sublime fusion of French techniques and Danish produce and ingenuity. There's a 'Green Tasting Menu' for herbivores, and enlightened juice pairings for those not wanting to sample the (fabulous) wines. Book a good month ahead.

Relæ
MODERN DANISH €€

(☑36 96 66 09; www.restaurant-relae.dk, in Danish; Jægersborggade 41, Nørrebro; 4 courses 345kr; ⊘dinner Wed-Sat; ☑) Another 'It Kid' of the New Nordic scene, this pared-back, bistro-style hot spot is the domain of ex-Noma chef Christian Puglisi. Seasonal ingredients are the starting point for often knockout (occasionally 'miss') creations such as celeriac and seaweed rolls or lumpfish roe with hazelnut milk. The wine list is expectantly well versed and there's a vegetarian set menu for herbivorous gastronomes.

[TOP CHOICE] Fischer
ITALIAN €€

(www.hosfischer.dk, in Danish; Victor Borges Plads 12, Østerbro; mains 175-185kr; ⊘lunch & dinner Mon-Sat) Set in a converted workingman's bar, neighbourly Fischer serves Italian soul food such as freshly made linguini with *aglio e olio* (pasta with garlic, olive oil and chilli), or tender pork with cherries and celery purée. That it's all seriously good isn't surprising considering owner and head chef David Fischer worked the kitchen at Rome's Michelin-starred La Pergola. Undoubtedly one of Copenhagen's best-value nosh spots.

Spiseri
ITALIAN €€

(Map p44; ☑42 36 02 22; www.spiseri.dk; Griffenfeldsgade 28, Nørrebro; mains 110-140kr; ⊘dinner Wed-Sat) Seasonal produce and simple, honest Italian flavours dictate the chalkboard menu at Spiseri, a convivial hot spot run by four young women with a passion for good, affordable food. Choices, which span two starters, two mains and two desserts, might include soul-coaxing gnocchi with a delicate rabbit ragù, served on vintage crockery with love. Book ahead or prepare for a long wait.

🍷 Drinking

Copenhagen is packed with a diverse range of drinking options, from nicotine-stained *bodegas* (pubs) to luxe cocktail bars. Several venues change role from cafe to restaurant to DJ bar as the day progresses. Top areas to head to for a night out include Kødbyen (the 'Meatpacking District') and Istedgade in Vesterbro, Elmegade and Sankt Hans Torv in Nørrebro, Nansensgade close to Nørreport and the maze of streets to the north of Strøget, including Pilestræde, around Gråbrødretorv and especially gay-friendly Studiestræde. And, of course, on a sunny day there is always Nyhavn, although there can be a serious risk of encountering a Dixieland jazz band.

Ruby   COCKTAIL BAR
(Map p48; www.rby.dk; Nybrogade 10; ☺4pm-2am Mon-Sat, 6pm-midnight Sun) Cocktail connoisseurs raise their glasses to high-achieving Ruby. Here, hipster-geek mixologists whip-up near-flawless libations such as Prickly Thistle Martini, and a lively crowd spill into a labyrinth of cosy, decadent rooms. For a gentlemen's club vibe, head downstairs into a world of Chesterfields, oil paintings, and wooden cabinets lined with spirits.

The Coffee Collective   CAFE
(www.thecoffeecollective.dk; Jægersborggade 10, Nørrebro; ☺7am-9pm Mon-Fri, 8am-6pm Sat-Sun) In a city where lacklustre coffee is as common as perfect cheekbones, this micro roastery peddles the good stuff – we're talking rich, complex cups of caffeinated magic. The baristas are passionate about their beans and the cafe itself sits on up-and-coming Jægersborggade, located near the southwest corner of Assistens Kirkegård. There's a second branch at Torvehallerne KPH (Map p44; same opening hours).

Mesteren & Lærlingen   BAR
(Map p44; Flæsketorvet 86, Vesterbro; ☺8pm-3am Wed-Sat) Occupying a former slaughterhouse bodega in Vesterbro's gritty Meatpacking District, this is one of Copenhagen's newer in-the-know hang-outs. A suitable combo of tiled walls, concrete floors and wax-splashed tables, it packs a friendly, hipster crowd of trucker caps and skinny jeans, knocking back rum and ginger (the house speciality) to DJ-spun retro, soul, reggae and country.

1105   COCKTAIL BAR
(Map p48; Kristen Bernikows Gade 4; ☺8pm-2am Wed, Thu & Sat, 4pm-2am Fri) Head in before 11pm for a bar seat at this dark, luxe cocktail lounge. The domain of legendary barman Gromit Eduardsen, its perfect libations include both classic cocktails and classics with a twist. If you're undecided, consider the smashing No 4 (Tanqueray gin, cardamom seeds, pepper, lime and honey). Whisky connoisseurs will be equally enthralled.

Bibendum   WINE BAR
(Map p48; Nansensgade 45; ☺4pm-midnight Mon-Sat) You'll find Copenhagen's best wine bar in a cosy, rustic cellar on trendy Nansensgade. Slip in and drool over a savvy list that offers over 30 wines – including drops from Australia, New Zealand, Spain, France and Italy – by the glass. The vibe is intimate but relaxed, with extremely knowledgeable staff and a refreshing lack of wine snobs.

Malbeck   WINE BAR
(Map p44; Birkegade 2, Nørrebro; ☺4pm-midnight Wed & Thu, to 1am Fri & Sat) Giant industrial lamps, découpage table tops and a convivial buzz set the scene at this new Nørrebro's favourite. The well-versed wine list leans heavily towards Argentine and French drops, with plenty of well-priced wines by the glass. Graze on tapas or more substantial Franco-Spanish grub, or simply while away the night scanning Elmegade's fashion-forward locals.

Union Bar   COCKTAIL BAR
(Map p48; Store Strandstræde 19; ☺8pm-2am Wed & Thu, 8pm-late Fri & Sat) Inspired by the speakeasy bars of old New York (even the cocktails are named after 1920s slang), the sneaky Union lies behind an unmarked black door. Ring the buzzer and head down the steps to a suitably dim, decadent scene of handsome bartenders, in-the-know revellers and silky tunes.

Halvandet   BEACH BAR
(www.halvandet.dk; Refshalevej 325, Refshaleøen; ☺10am-midnight Jun-Aug) Copenhagen meets Ibiza at this glam, waterside bar/lounge. Book a cabana, grab a mojito and tan away to sexy lounge tunes. Edibles include nachos, grilled meats, seafood and salads, but the real reason to head in is the vibe and music. It's located north of Operaen, out in the old docklands (Holmen).

Bankeråt   BAR
(Map p48; www.bankeraat.dk; Ahlefeldtsgade 27; ☺9.30am-midnight Mon-Fri, 10.30am-midnight Sat & Sun) A top spot to get stuffed, literally, this

cultish bar is dotted with taxidermic animals in outlandish get-ups – yes, there's even a ram in period costume. The man behind it all is local artist Phillip Jensen. But is it art? Debate this, and the porn-adorned loos, over a beer or three.

Estate Coffee
CAFE

(Map p44; www.estatecoffee.dk; Gammel Kongevej 1; ⊙7.30am-9pm Mon-Fri, 10am-9pm Sat & Sun) Coffee snobs in the vicinity of Central Station and the tourist office can get their caffeine fix at this brilliant micro roaster. The coffee is fruity and complex and perfectly paired with a pain au chocolat. Tea lovers are also spoilt with a choice of boutique loose-leaf varieties.

Fisken
PUB

(Map p48; Nyhavn 27; ⊙8.30am-2am Sun-Thu, to 3am Fri & Sat) This open-all-hours cellar pub beneath the atmospheric Skipper Kroen restaurant distils the essence of everything great about Nyhavn's salty sea-dog atmosphere. Tap your fingers and toes to live folk music on Friday and Saturday nights.

Laundromat Cafe
CAFE

(Map p44; Elmegade 15, Nørrebro; ⊙8am-midnight Mon-Fri, 10am-midnight Sat & Sun) This playful corner cafe was the brainchild of Icelander Fridrik Weisshappel who decided to turn the old Morgans juice bar into a cafe-cum-laundrette, with washing machines just around the corner from the bar. Throw in 4000 secondhand books (for sale) and a regular crowd of creative types and you have one of Copenhagen's quirkiest, best-loved hang-outs.

Nimb Bar
COCKTAIL BAR

(Map p48; www.tivoli.dk/nimb; Bernstorffsgade 5; ⊙10am-midnight Mon-Thu, to 1am Fri & Sat, 11am-midnight Sun) If you fancy chandeliers, whimsical murals and an open fire with your well-mixed drink, make sure this ballroom bar is on your list. Located inside super chic Hotel Nimb, it was kick-started by legendary bartender Angus Winchester. The cocktails are seasonal, classically styled and rather fabulous.

Oscar Bar & Cafe
GAY & LESBIAN

(Map p48; www.oscarbarcafe.dk; Rådhuspladsen 77; ⊙noon-midnight Sun-Wed, noon-2am Thu-Sat) A corner cafe-bar by Rådhuspladsen, and especially popular with local and visiting eye-candy men, this is a good place to get up to speed with what's happening on the Copenhagen gay scene. On warm nights, the crowd spills out onto the street, with plenty of smiles and fleeting glances.

Jailhouse
GAY & LESBIAN

(Map p48; www.jailhousecph.dk; Studiestræde 12; ⊙bar 3pm-2am Sun-Thu, to 5am Fri & Sat) Popular, attitude-free and particularly popular with an older male crowd, this themed bar promises plenty of penal action, with uniformed 'guards' and willing guests. The theme in its tasteful upstairs restaurant (open from dinner Thursday to Saturday) is 'soup', from the entrees right through to desserts.

Sort Kaffe & Vinyl
CAFE

(Map p44; Syydebanegade 4, Vesterbro; ⊙8am-9pm Mon-Fri, 9am-9pm Sat, 9am-7pm Sun) This skinny little cafe–record store combo is a second home for Vesterbro's coffee cognoscenti. Join them for velvety espresso, hunt down that limited edition Blaxploitation LP, or score a prized pavement seat and eye-up the eye-candy regulars.

Never Mind
GAY & LESBIAN

(Map p48; www.nevermindbar.dk; Nørre Voldgade 2; ⊙10pm-6am) Tiny, smoky and often packed to the rafters, Never Mind is a seriously fun spot for shameless pop and late-night flirtation.

☆ Entertainment

Copenhagen's 'X factor' fuels its entertainment options. Its live-music and club scenes are equally kicking, with choices spanning from intimate jazz and blues clubs, to mega rock venues and secret clubs dropping experimental beats. A string of arresting new cultural venues, including Operaen (Copenhagen Opera House) and Skuespilhuset (Royal Danish Playhouse), have injected the city's high-end cultural scene with new verve, while its score of cinemas keep film buffs busy with both mainstream and arthouse flicks. Keep in mind that Danes tend to be late-nighters and, unlike the restaurants, many nightspots don't get the party started until 11pm or midnight.

Most events can be booked through **BilletNet** (☑70 15 65 65; www.billetnet.dk), a service that's also available at all post offices. You can also try www.billetlugen.dk or call them on ☑70 26 32 67.

For listings, scan www.aok.dk (mostly in Danish) and www.hellocopenhagen.dk.

HYGGE HOT SPOTS

The Danes love all things *hygge*, loosely translated as 'cosy' but encompassing everything from flickering candles to bonhomie. So when the sky is dark and grey, get that *hygge* vibe at these seriously snug hang-outs:

» Bationen & Løven (p70)
» Fischer (p71)
» Fisken (p73)
» Bankeråt (p72)
» La Glace (p69)

Nightclubs

Simons
NIGHTCLUB

(Map p48; www.simonscopenhagen.dk; Store Strandstræde 14; ⊙11.30pm-5am Fri & Sat) Brainchild of promoters Simon Frank and Simon Lennet, this is Copenhagen's 'It' club. Occupying a former art gallery, its biggest and smallest claims to fame are A-list DJs and dwarves behind the bar. Expect selective electronica and an even more selective door policy (you will need a Danish sim card to register online and get on the door list).

Rust
NIGHTCLUB

(Map p44; www.rust.dk; Guldbergsgade 8; admission 40-60kr; ⊙9pm-5am Wed-Sat) A thriving, smashing place that attracts one of the largest and coolest club crowds in Copenhagen. There's a choice of spaces here from nightclub to stage and cocktail lounge, with tunes ranging from edgy electronica to house and hip hop. Weekends see some earnest queuing. You'll need to be aged over 21 to enter the nightclub.

Culture Box
NIGHTCLUB

(Map p44; www.culture-box.com; Kronprinsessegade 54; admission 70kr; ⊙midnight-6am Fri & Sat) Spread over two levels, Culture Box ditches cheesy commercial hits for innovative beats spanning anything (and everything) from electro, techno and house to drum'n'bass, dubstep and electronic jazz. Local talent aside, guest DJs have included Chicago's Billy Dalessandro. Next door, Cocktail Box (⊙8pm-late Fri and Sat) is handy for a pre-club swill.

Vega
LIVE MUSIC, NIGHTCLUB

(www.vega.dk; Enghavevej 40; ⊙varies) A big gun of the live music and clubbing scenes, Vega hosts everyone from big-name rock, pop, blues and jazz acts to underground indie, hip hop and electro up-and-comers. Gigs take place on either the main stage (Store Vega), small stage (Lille Vega) or the ground floor Ideal Bar (⊙8pm-1am Wed, 9pm-2am Thu, 10pm-5am Fri & Sat).

Cinemas

First-release movies are shown on about 20 screens in the group of cinemas along Vesterbrogade between Rådhuspladsen and Central Station. Tickets for movies range from around 70kr for weekday matinees to 90kr for weekend evenings. As in the rest of Denmark, movies are generally shown in their original language with Danish subtitles.

Cinemateket
FILM CENTRE

(Map p48; www.dfi.dk; Gothersgade 55; admission 65kr; ⊙10am-10pm Tue-Fri, noon-10pm Sat & Sun) Fresh from a revamp, the Danish Film Institute's clued-up cinema plays classic Danish and foreign films. There's also a well-stocked shop and stylish restaurant on-site.

Grand Teatret
CINEMA

(Map p48; www.grandteatret.dk; Mikkel Bryggersgade 8; admission 60-80kr; ⊙11.30am-9.30pm) Just off Strøget, this historic, award-winning theatre screens international art-house and some mainstream films.

Dance, Opera, Theatre & Classical Music

Tivoli Billetcenter (Map p48; ☑33 15 10 12; www.tivoli.dk; Vesterbrogade 3; ⊙10am-midnight Sun-Thu, to 12.30am Fri & Sat mid-Jun–mid-Aug, reduced hrs rest of year), at the main Tivoli entrance, is good for tickets of any kind. Not only does it sell Tivoli performance tickets, but it's also an agent for BilletNet, which sells tickets for concerts and music festivals nationwide.

Operaen
OPERA

(Copenhagen Opera House; Map p44; ☑box office 33 69 69 69; www.kglteater.dk; Ekvipagemestervej 10; tickets 95-895kr, standing 'seats' 95kr, under 25 yrs & over 65 yrs 50% discount; ⊙varies) Copenhagen's state-of-the-art opera house features two stages: the Main Stage and the smaller Takkeløftet. The repertoire runs the gamut from classic to contemporary opera, as well as the odd curve ball such as a performance by Elvis Costello or something from the Jazz Festival (see p63). Productions usually sell out in advance but any unsold tickets are offered at half-price at the Opera House box office one hour before the performance (two hours before if performances start before 7pm or on Sunday). General tickets are available through the opera house's website. Alternatively, many come just to eat in the panoramic New Nordic restaurant or to explore the building on a guided tour. The tours (in English during summer only) run at 9.30am and 4.30pm on Saturday and Sunday (100kr), with extra weekday tours in summer. Book tours in advance, either online or by calling the box office between 10am and 2pm on weekdays.

Dansescenen CONTEMPORARY DANCE
(☑box office 33 29 10 29; www.dansehallerne. dk; Pasteursvej 20, Vesterbro) Set in a disused Carlsberg mineral water factory, Dansescenen remains Copenhagen's leading contemporary-dance venue. Its two stages showcase over 20 works each year, from both Danish artists and international ensembles. Tickets can be purchased by calling the box office between 2pm and 4pm on weekdays, or online at www.billetten.dk (in Danish).

Skuespilhuset THEATRE
(Royal Danish Playhouse; Map p44; ☑box office 33 69 69 69; www.kglteater.dk; Sankt Annæ Plads 36; tickets 75-495kr, under 25 yrs & over 65 yrs 50% discount; ☺varies) Copenhagen's striking playhouse is home to the Royal Danish Theatre and a world-class repertoire of both homegrown and foreign plays. Productions range from classic Shakespeare to fresh, provocative contemporary works. Tickets often sell out well in advance but any unsold tickets are sold at half-price at the box office one hour before the performance (two hours before for performances starting before 7pm and on Sunday).

Tivoli Koncertsal CONCERT HALL
(Concert Hall; Map p48; www.tivoli.dk; Tietgensgade 30) Tivoli's revamped concert hall serves up symphony orchestras, string quartets and other classical-music performances by Danish and international musicians. It also hosts the occasional contemporary music artist, musical and comedy act. Tickets are sold at the Tivoli Billetcenter (p74).

Live Music

Copenhagen Jazz House JAZZ
(Map p48; www.jazzhouse.dk; Niels Hemmingsensgade 10; ☺6pm-midnight Sun-Thu, to 5am Fri & Sat) Copenhagen's leading jazz joint features top Danish musicians and international performers. The music runs the gamut from be-bop to fusion jazz, and there's a large dance floor that usually fills after live gigs on Friday and Saturday.

La Fontaine JAZZ
(Map p48; www.lafontaine.dk; Kompagnistræde 11, Strædet; admission varies; ☺7pm-5am, live jazz 10.30pm-2.30am Fri & Sat, 9pm-1am Sun) Cosy and intimate, Copenhagen's jazz club veteran is a great spot to catch emerging homegrown talent and the occasional big name. If you're an aspiring jazz star, hang around until late, when the stage is thrown open to songbirds in the audience.

Jazzhus Montmartre JAZZ
(Map p48; www.jazzhusmontmartre.dk; Store Regnegade 19A; admission varies; ☺5.30-11.30pm Wed-Sat) The reopening of Jazzhus Montmartre in 2010 signalled the rebirth of one of Scandinavia's great jazz venues. Going back to its roots, the place dishes out live jams from both local and international talent. On concert nights, you can also tuck into dinner at its cafe-style restaurant. Check the website for upcoming performances.

Loppen MUSIC
(Map p44; www.loppen.dk; Bådsmandsstræde 43; admission free-150kr; ☺varies) Housed in an atmospheric, wooden-beamed warehouse in free-spirited Christiania, Loppen showcases both established and emerging acts playing anything from rock and funk to post-punk and jazz. Gigs take place most nights.

Mojo BLUES
(Map p48; www.mojo.dk; Løngangstræde 21; admission free-60kr; ☺8pm-5am) East of Tivoli, this is a great spot for blues, with live entertainment nightly and draught beer aplenty.

🛍 Shopping

Strøget is usually people's first experience of shopping in Copenhagen, and it's here that you'll find the flagship stores of homegrown heavyweights Georg Jensen and Royal Copenhagen Porcelain, as well as the sprawling design store Illums Bolighus.

Running parallel to the south of Strøget is another pedestrian shopping street, Strædet (made up of two streets, Kompagnistræde and Læderstræde), dotted with interesting jewellery, clothing, interior design and antique shops. To the north of Strøget, the area of Pisserenden (centred on Studiestræde, Larsbjørnstræde and Vestergade) is good for street style and CDs, while the so-called Latin Quarter (from Vor Frue

ALL THAT JAZZ

Copenhagen's **Jazz Festival** (www.jazz.dk) is *the* biggest entertainment event in the city's calendar, with 10 days of toe-tapping, hip-swinging tunes beginning on the first Friday in July. The festival energises the Danish capital like nothing else, bringing not just live music to its streets, canalsides and an eclectic mix of venues, but creating a tangible buzz of excitement in the air.

There are usually over 1000 different concerts held in every available space, from cafes and street corners to the Operaen (Opera House) and Tivoli's Koncertsal – in fact, the city itself becomes one big sound stage. Amble through the city centre on a summer night during the festival and the party mood is nothing short of infectious. Even if you have an instinctive aversion to men in black turtlenecks, expect to be won over by the incredible line-up each year. You'll even find special children's jazz events in Kongens Have, ready to hook the next generation of sax and bass fiends early.

Copenhagen has been the jazz capital of Scandinavia since the 1920s, when the Montmartre Club was one of the most famous in Europe. Revived in 2010 after a long hiatus, the new Jazzhus Montmartre (p75) is in good company, with top venues such as La Fontaine (p75), the city's most 'hard-core' jazz club, and Copenhagen Jazz House (p75), the largest and most popular, ensuring that legacy remains alive and kicking. The fact that the city is also home to a disproportionately large population of both home-grown and international jazz musicians doesn't hurt either.

Copenhagen's first jazz festival took place in 1978. Since then it has mushroomed into one of Europe's leading jazz events. Over the years, performers have included such renowned names as Dizzy Gillespie, Miles Davis, Sonny Rollins, Oscar Peterson, Ray Charles and Wynton Marsalis. Tony Bennett, Herbie Hancock and Keith Jarrett are regulars, as are Denmark's own Cecilie Norby and David Sanborn.

It's a fun, slightly haphazard scene that brings everyone in the city out to party. Most of the open-air events are free, but you have to buy tickets to the big names in big venues. The music at the Copenhagen Jazz Festival is as varied as the venues. Traditional sounds range from old-fashioned Dixieland jazz and Satchmo-style solo improvisation to the WWII-era swing music that reigned in Duke Ellington and Benny Goodman's day – the Danish free jazz scene also gets a look-in. There's plenty of modern jazz along the lines of that inspired by legendary trumpeter Miles Davis, and you can also find lots of contemporary hybrid sounds: free-jazz, acid jazz, soul jazz, nu-jazz, jazz vocals and rhythm and blues. The festival programme is usually published in May.

If you can't make it to Copenhagen in summer for the main jazz festival, you can take heart that a smaller festival takes place in winter. It's called, not surprisingly, Vinter Jazz (it shares a website with the July festival). Also, not surprisingly, the winter version has a mellower, less-harried vibe.

Kirke to Købmagergade) is worth a wander for books and clothing.

Serious fashionistas flock to the area roughly bordered by Strøget, Købmagergade, Kronprinsensgade and Gothersgade, crammed with high-end Nordic labels, trendsetting concept stores and cutting-edge jewellery shops.

North of Nyhavn, exclusive Bredgade and Store Kongensgade are lined with private art galleries and high-end antique stores selling classic, collectable Danish furniture.

For more affordable bric-a-brac, vintage jewellery and kitschy furniture, scour the shops on Ravnsborggade in Nørrebro. Arty Nørrebro is also home to Elmegade, a street lined with some of the city's hippest fashion boutiques. West of Nørrebro's Assistens Kirkegård, up-and-coming strip Jægersborggade is home to a growing number of independent art and craft studios.

Further south, the equally fashionable Vesterbro district is another good bet for independent fashion designers and homewares, with most of the offerings on and around Istedgade and Værndamsvej.

Fashion & Accessories

Day Birger Mikkelsen　　　FASHION
(Map p48; www.day.dk; Pilestræde 16; ⊙10am-6pm Mon-Thu, to 7pm Fri, to 4pm Sat) Understated elegance with a hippy-chic twist defines

this Danish fashion heavyweight. Here you can bag sophisticated men's and women's threads, and accessories such as jewellery, bags and homewares. Designer Malene Birger's own shop (she is no longer part of the Day group) is just around the corner (www.bymalenebirger.dk; Antonigade 10; same opening hours).

Rützou
FASHION

(Map p48; www.rutzou.com; Store Regnegade 3; ☺11am-5.30pm Mon-Thu, to 6pm Fri, 10am-4pm Sat) Another stalwart of the Danish fashion scene, designer Susanne Rützou is celebrated for her women's threads. The style is in equal parts glam, kooky and überfeminine – think printed silk blouses, polka-dot jackets and little gold shorts.

Storm
FASHION, ACCESSORIES

(Map p48; www.stormfashion.dk; Store Regnegade 1; ☺11am-5.30pm Mon-Thu, to 7pm Fri, to 5pm Sat) Storm is one of Copenhagen's coolest fashion pit stops, with trendsetting men's and women's labels such as Billionaire Boys Club, Visvin and Anne Demeulemeester on the racks. The vibe is youthful and extras include shoes, boutique fragrances, art and design coffee-table tomes, fashion mags and jewellery. A must for cashed-up hipsters.

Wood Wood
FASHION, ACCESSORIES

(Map p48; www.woodwood.dk; Grønnegade 1; ☺10.30am-6pm Mon-Thu, to 7pm Fri, to 4pm Sat) Like Storm, Wood Wood is another 'It kid' of the fashion scene and its beautiful new flagship store (complete with the scent of freshly chopped – you guessed it – wood) is a veritable who's who of in-the-know labels. Top of the heap is Wood Wood's own hipster-chic creations, made with superlative fabrics and attention to detail. The supporting cast includes solid knits from classic Danish brand Herning, graphic tees from Cool Cats, and fragrances from Monocle and Dover Street Market.

Henrik Vibskov
FASHION, ACCESSORIES

(Map p48; www.henrikvibskov.com; Krystalgade 6; ☺11am-6pm Mon-Thu, to 7pm Fri, to 5pm Sat) Not just a drummer and prolific artist, Danish enfant terrible Henrik Vibskov is pushing the fashion envelope too. Break free with his bold, bright, creatively silhouetted threads for progressive guys and girls, as well as other fashion-forward labels such as Comme des Garçons, Walter Van Beirendonck and Denmark's own Stine Goya.

Piet Breinholm – The Last Bag
LEATHER GOODS

(Map p44; www.pietbreinholm.dk; Nansensgade 48; ☺11am-7pm Fri, by appointment rest of week) Musician-turned-designer Piet Breinholm is famous for his classic leather satchels, available in small or large, and in colours ranging from sensible black to outrageous canary yellow. A handful of other styles are also available, all using high-quality leather sourced from an ecofriendly Brazilian tannery.

Other Shopping Options

Stilleben
DESIGN

(Map p48; www.stilleben.dk; Niels Hemmingsensgade 3; ☺10am-6pm Mon-Fri, to 4pm Sat) Formerly on Strædet, beautiful Stilleben has moved to larger premises. Owners Ditte and Jelena are graduates of the Danish Design School's ceramic and glass course, and stock a contemporary and stunningly beautiful range of ceramic, glassware, jewellery and textiles from mostly emerging Danish and foreign designers.

Hay
DESIGN

(Map p48; www.hay.dk; Østergade 61, Strøget; ☺11am-6pm Mon-Fri, to 4pm Sat) Rolf Hay's fabulous interior design store sells well-chosen Danish furniture as well as irresistible design gifts such as ceramic cups, funky textiles, art books and Andreas Lintzer's cuddly towelling toys. There's a second branch at Pilestræde 29-31 (same opening hours).

Illum
DEPARTMENT STORE

(Map p48; ☑33 14 40 02; www.illum.dk; Østergade 52; ☺10am-7pm Mon-Thu, 10am-8pm Fri, 9am-5pm Sat) Copenhagen's answer to Selfridges or Bloomingdales, this style-savvy department store is a good spot to hunt for top Danish and international fashion under the one roof.

Magasin du Nord
DEPARTMENT STORE

(Map p48; www.magasin.dk; Kongens Nytorv 13; ☺10am-7pm Mon-Thu, to 8pm Fri, to 6pm Sat) The city's largest (and oldest) department store, this place covers an entire block on the southwestern side of Kongens Nytorv and stocks everything from clothing and luggage to books and groceries.

Illums Bolighus
DEPARTMENT STORE

(Map p48; www.illumsbolighus.dk; Amagertorv 10; ☺10am-7pm Mon-Fri, to 6pm Sat, 11am-4pm Sun) Revamp everything from your wardrobe to your living room at this multilevel department store, dedicated to the best of Danish and international design. Stock up on everything (and anything) from svelte fashion, jewellery and silverware, to classic Danish furniture pieces, textiles and playful office accessories.

Royal Copenhagen Porcelain   PORCELAIN

(Map p48; Amagertorv 6; ☺10am-7pm Mon-Fri, to 5pm Sat, noon-5pm Sun) This is the main showroom for the historic Royal Danish Porcelain, famed the world over for its 'blue fluted' pattern. Its refined dinnerware, figurines and vases make for exquisite souvenirs (legend has it that Nelson took some home after bombarding the city in 1807).

Georg Jensen   DESIGN

(Map p48; www.georgejensen.com; Amagertorv 4; ☺10am-6pm Mon-Thu, to 7pm Fri, to 5pm Sat) The world famous Georg Jensen silverware store is near Illums Bolighus, which is next door to another Copenhagen design stalwart: Royal Copenhagen Porcelain, incorporating the former Holmegaard Glass store.

Designer Zoo   DESIGN

(www.dzoo.dk; Vesterbrogade 137, Vesterbro; ☺10am-5.30pm Mon-Thu, to 7pm Fri, to 3pm Sat) If you find yourself in Vesterbro – and you should – make sure to drop into this supercool interior and fashion complex at the 'unfashionable' end of Vesterbrogade. Here, fashion, jewellery and furniture designers, as well as ceramic artists and glass blowers, work and sell their limited edition, must-have creations.

Nordisk Korthandel   BOOKS

(Map p48; Studiestræde 26; ☺10am-6pm Mon-Fri, 9.30am-3pm Sat) Sells guidebooks as well as an extensive range of cycling and hiking trail maps of Denmark and elsewhere in Europe.

❶ Information

Emergency

Dial ☎112 to contact police, ambulance or fire services; the call can be made without coins from public phones.

Politigården (Map p44; ☎33 14 14 48; Polititorvet; ☺24hr) Police headquarters; south of Tivoli.

Internet Access

Hovedbiblioteket (Map p48; Krystalgade 15; ☺10am-7pm Mon-Fri, to 2pm Sat) The main public library – computers on all floors provide free internet access. There is a 20-minute time limit.

Internet Resources

Four websites that will link you to a wealth of information in English:

www.aok.dk An online listings guide to Copenhagen with some English content.

www.cphpost.dk The online edition of the *Copenhagen Post*, with plenty of news and cultural insight.

www.kopenhagen.dk The top website for Copenhagen's art scene, with exhibition listings, news and artist interviews.

www.visitcopenhagen.com Run by Wonderful Copenhagen, the tourism office.

Left Luggage

Central Station (Map p48; ☺5.30am-1am Mon-Sat, 6am-1am Sun) Left-luggage office (☎24 68 31 77; per 24hr, max 10 days luggage per piece 45-55kr, pram, bike per piece 55kr); Luggage lockers (per 24hr, max 72hr small/large 40/50kr)

Copenhagen airport Left-luggage room (☎32 31 23 60; per piece per day 50kr; ☺5am-10pm); Luggage lockers (small/large 30/60kr per 24hr) In car park 4.

Medical Services

Hospitals with 24-hour emergency wards:

Amager Hospital (☎32 34 32 34; Italiensvej 1) Southeast of the city centre.

Bispebjerg Hospital (☎35 31 35 31; Bispebjerg Bakke 23) Northwest of the city centre.

Frederiksberg Hospital (☎38 16 38 16; Nordre Fasanvej 57)

Private doctor and dentist visits vary but usually cost from around 700kr. To contact a doctor, call ☎60 75 40 70.

Tandlægevagten (☎35 38 02 51; Oslo Plads 14) Emergency dental service near Østerport station.

There are numerous pharmacies around the city; look for the sign *apotek*.

Steno Apotek (Vesterbrogade 6; ☺24hr) Opposite Central Station.

Money

Banks are plentiful and can be found on nearly every second corner in central Copenhagen. Most are open from 10am to 4pm weekdays (to 6pm on Thursday). Most banks in Copenhagen have ATMs accessible 24 hours per day.

Danske Bank (Arrival & Transit Halls, Copenhagen airport; ☺6am-10pm)

Forex Central Station (Map p48; ☺8am-9pm); Gothersgade (Gothersgade 8; ☺9am-7pm Mon-Fri, to 4pm Sat); Nørreport (Nørre Voldgade 90; ☺9am-7pm Mon-Fri, 10am-4pm Sat)

Post

Post office (Map p48; Købmagergade 33; ⊘10am-6pm Mon-Fri, to 2pm Sat) A handy post office near Strøget and the Latin Quarter.

Post office in Central Station (Map p48; ⊘8am-9pm Mon-Fri, 10am-4pm Sat & Sun)

Tourist Information

Copenhagen Visitor Centre (Map p48; ☑70 22 24 42; www.visitcopenhagen.dk; Vesterbrogade 4A; ⊘9am-6pm Mon-Sat, 10am-4pm Sun May & Jun, 9am-8pm Mon-Sat, 10am-6pm Sun Jul & Aug, 9am-4pm Mon-Fri, 9am-2pm Sat rest of year) Copenhagen's excellent information centre also has a cafe, gift shop and multilingual staff. It's the best source of information in town – free maps, masses of brochures and guides to take away, and booking services and hotel reservations available for a fee. It also sells the Copenhagen Card (see p81).

ℹ Getting There & Away

Air

Copenhagen's user-friendly international airport is Scandinavia's busiest hub, with flights from over 100 cities across the world. There are direct flights to Copenhagen from Europe, Asia and North America, as well as a handful of Danish cities.

Located in Kastrup, 9km southeast of Copenhagen's city centre, the airport has good eating, retail and information facilities.

If you're waiting for a flight, note that this is a 'silent' airport and there are no boarding calls, although there are numerous monitor screens throughout the terminal.

Boat

Copenhagen offers regular direct ferry services to/from Norway. There is also a combined bus-ferry service to Poland and a train-ferry service to Germany.

DB (www.bahn.de) Runs direct ICE trains from Copenhagen Central Station to Hamburg several times daily, with a ferry crossing between Puttgarden and Rødby. Journey time is 4½ hours.

DFDS Seaways (www.dfdsseaways.com) One daily service to/from Oslo leaves from Søndre Frihavn, just north of Kastellet. Journey time is around 16½ hours.

Polferries (www.polferries.pl) Offers one daily bus-ferry combo to/from Poland. Bus 866 connects Copenhagen to Ystad in Sweden (1¼ hours), from where ferries travel to/from Swinoujscie, Poland. Journey time is around nine to 11 hours.

Bus

Eurolines (www.eurolines-travel.com; Reventlowsgade 8) Operates buses to several European cities. The ticket office is behind Central Station. Long-distance buses leave from opposite the DGI-byen sports complex on Ingerslevsgade, just southwest of Central Station. For some more bus information see p327.

Car & Motorcycle

The main highways into Copenhagen are the E20 from Jutland and Funen (and continuing towards Malmö in Sweden) and the E47 from Helsingør and Sweden. If you're coming from the north on the E47, exit onto Lyngbyvej (Rte 19) and continue south to reach the heart of the city.

Train

All long-distance trains arrive at and depart from Central Station, an elegant, 19th-century wooden-beamed hall with numerous facilities, including currency exchange, a post office, lockers and left-luggage facilities, and food outlets. There are showers at the underground toilets opposite the police office.

ℹ Getting Around

To/From the Airport

Metro The 24-hour **metro** (www.m.dk) runs every four to 20 minutes between the airport arrival terminal (the station is called Lufthavnen) and the eastern side of the central city. It does not stop at Central Station but is handy for Christianshavn and Nyhavn (get off at Kongens Nytorv for Nyhavn). Journey time to Kongens Nytorv is 14 minutes (36kr).

Taxi By taxi, it's about 20 minutes between the airport and the city centre, depending on traffic. Expect to pay about 200kr (day) or 250kr (night and weekends).

Train Trains (www.dsb.dk) connect the airport arrival terminal to Copenhagen Central Station (København Hovedbanegården) every 20 minutes. Journey time is 12 minutes (36kr). Check schedules at www.rejseplanen.dk.

Bicycle

Copenhagen is quite possibly the world's most bike-friendly city. Most streets have cycle lanes and, more importantly, motorists tend to respect them. The following guidelines will help you cycle happily:

» Bikes can be carried free on S-trains. Enter carriages through the middle door and keep your bike behind the red line in the designated bicycle area. Stay with the bike at all times. Bikes can be carried on the metro (except from 7am to 9am, and from 3.30pm to 5.30pm, on weekdays from September to May). Bike tickets cost 12kr.

» Virtually all of Copenhagen can be toured by bicycle, except for pedestrian-only streets such as Strøget. Bicycles are allowed to cross Strøget at Gammel Torv and Kongens Nytorv.

FREE CITY BIKES

Long before Paris got in on the act of free bikes, Copenhagen had its famous **Bycykler** (City Bikes; www.bycyklen.dk), allowing anyone to borrow a bicycle for free. In all there are over 1000 bikes available from mid-April to November.

These gearless bicycles are rudimentary and are certainly not practical for long-distance cycling, but that's part of the plan – use of the cycles is limited to the city centre. To deter theft and minimise maintenance, the bicycles have a distinctive design that includes solid spokeless wheels with puncture-resistant tyres. The bikes can be found at 110 widely scattered street stands in public places, including S-train stations.

The way it works is that if you're able to find a free bicycle, you deposit a 20kr coin in the stand to release the bike. When you're done using the bicycle, you can return it to any stand and get your 20kr back.

» Cyclists should give way to bus passengers traversing cycle lanes to reach the pavement, and to pedestrians (particularly tourists) who sometimes absent-mindedly step off the kerb and into the path of oncoming cyclists.

» Cycling maps, including a 1:100,000-scale map of North Zealand (which includes the Greater Copenhagen area) called *Nordsjælland kortbog* (129kr), are produced by the Danish cycling federation, **Dansk Cyklist Forbund** (Map p48; www.dcf.dk; Rømersgade 5-7), near Israels Plads. For information on bicycle hire, see p61.

Car & Motorcycle

Except for the weekday-morning rush hour, when traffic can bottleneck coming into the city (and vice versa around 5pm), traffic in Copenhagen is generally manageable. Getting around by car is not problematic, except for the usual challenge of finding an empty parking space in the most popular places.

To explore sights in the centre of the city, you're best off on foot or using public transport, but a car is convenient for getting to the suburban sights.

PARKING

» For street parking, buy a ticket from a kerbside *billetautomat* (automated ticket machine) and place it inside the windscreen. Ticket machines accept credit cards.

» Copenhagen parking is zoned (red, green and blue). Those in the central commercial area (red zone) are the most costly (29kr per hour). Blue zone parking, located on the fringe of the city centre, is the cheapest, costing 10kr per hour. Closer to the centre, green zone parking costs 17kr per hour. These rates are valid between 8am and 6pm, with reduced rates at other times.

» If you can't find street parking, there are car parks at the main department stores, at the Radisson Blu Royal Hotel and on Jerbanegade, east of Axeltorv.

» *Parkering forbudt* means 'no parking' and is generally accompanied by a round sign with a red diagonal slash. You can stop for up to three minutes to unload bags and passengers. A round sign with a red 'X', or a sign saying *Stopforbud*, means that no stopping at all is allowed.

RENTAL

The following car hire companies have booths at the airport in the international terminal. Each also has an office in central Copenhagen.

Avis (☎70 24 77 07; www.avis.com; Kampmannsgade 1)

Budget (☎33 55 05 00; www.budget.dk; Kampmannsgade 1)

Europcar (☎33 55 99 00; www.europcar.com; Gammel Kongevej 13)

Hertz (☎33 17 90 20; www.hertzdk.dk; Ved Vesterport 3)

On Foot

We can't stress enough that by far the best way to see Copenhagen is on foot. This has to be the most eminently walkable capital in Europe, with much of the city centre pedestrianised and few main sights or shopping quarters more than a 20-minute walk from the city centre.

Public Transport

Copenhagen has an extensive public transit system consisting of a metro, rail and bus network.

The driverless **metro** (www.m.dk) system runs through the eastern side of the city centre connecting Nørreport with Kongens Nytorv and Christianshavn. The system also runs to the airport.

The **S-train** (www.dsb.dk/s-tog) network has seven lines passing through Central Station (København H), and there's also a vast bus system run by **Movia** (www.moviatrafik.dk, in Danish), the main terminus of which is at Rådhuspladsen (Map p48), a couple of blocks northeast of Central Station.

COPENHAGEN CARD

The **Copenhagen Card** (www.cphcard.com; 24hr adult/child 10-15 249/135kr, 72hr 479/245kr), available at the Copenhagen Visitor Centre (p79) or online, gives you free access to around 60 museums and attractions in the city and surrounding area, as well as free travel for all S-train, metro and bus journeys within the seven travel zones.

BUSES & TRAINS

Copenhagen's bus and train network has an integrated ticket system based on seven geographical zones. Most of your travel within the city will be within two zones. Travel between the city and airport covers three zones.

The cheapest ticket *(billet)* covers two zones, offers unlimited transfers, and is valid for one hour (adult/12 to 15 years 24/12kr). Children under 12 travel free if accompanied by an adult. Another option is the discount 10-ticket card *(klippekort;* two zones adult/12 to 15 years 140/70kr; three zones 180/90kr). Stamp the ticket in the yellow machines when boarding buses or on the train/metro platforms.

If you plan on exploring sights outside the city, including Helsingør, the north coast of Zealand and Roskilde, you're better off buying a 24-hour ticket (all zones adult/12 to 15 years 130/65kr) or a seven-day FlexCard (all zones 590kr).

Tickets are valid for travel on the metro, buses and S-tog (S-train or local train) even though they look slightly different, depending on where you buy them. S-trains are free on the first Sunday of the month.

The free Copenhagen city maps that are distributed by the tourist office show bus routes (with numbers) and are very useful for finding your way around the city.

Online, click onto the very handy www.rejseplanen.dk for all routes and schedules.

Taxi

Taxis can be flagged on the street and there are ranks at various points around the city centre. If the yellow *taxa* (taxi) sign is lit, the taxi is available for hire. The fare will start at 24kr and costs 13.30kr per kilometre from 7am to 4pm Monday to Friday, and 16.80kr from 11pm to 7am Friday and Saturday. The rate at all other times is 14.20kr. Most taxis accept major credit cards. Three of the main companies are **DanTaxi** (☏70 25 25 25), **Taxa** (☏35 35 35 35) and **Taxamotor** (☏38 10 10 10).

AROUND COPENHAGEN

Many places in the greater Copenhagen area make for quick and easy excursions from the city. If you're hankering for woodlands, lakes, beaches, historic areas or A-list art museums, the mix of destinations that follows should satisfy. For other day-trip possibilities a bit further afield, see the Zealand chapter (p84).

LOUISIANA: A MODERN ART MUST

Even if you don't have a consuming passion for modern art, Denmark's outstanding **Louisiana** (www.louisiana.dk; Gammel Strandvej 13, Humlebæk; adult/under 18 yr 95kr/free; ⊘11am-10pm Tue-Fri, to 6pm Sat & Sun; ☏) should be high on your 'To Do' list. It's a striking modernist gallery, made up of four huge wings, which sprawl across a sculpture-filled park, burrowing down into the hillside and nosing out again to wink at the sea (and Sweden).

The museum's permanent collection, mainly postwar paintings and graphic art, covers everything from constructivism, CoBrA movement artists and minimalist art, to abstract expressionism, pop art and staged photography. Pablo Picasso, Francis Bacon and Alberto Giacometti are some of the international luminaries you'll come across inside, while Henry Moore's monumental bronzes and Max Ernst's owl-eyed animals lurk between the hillocks of the garden. Prominent Danish artists include Asger Jorn, Carl-Henning Pedersen, Robert Jacobsen and Richard Mortensen. Six to eight temporary exhibitions take place each year, often with supporting films and concerts.

Kids are spoiled with an entire wing of their own, where they can create masterpieces inspired by the gallery's exhibitions, using everything from crayons to interactive computers. Louisiana's artsy cafe, with its large sunny terrace and sea views, is a great place for a reviving coffee. A two-storey shop offers art books, prints and Scandinavian design.

Louisiana is in the leafy town of **Humlebæk**, 30km north of Copenhagen. From Humlebæk train station, the museum is a 1.5km signposted walk along Gammel Strandvej. Trains to Humlebæk run roughly every 30 minutes from Copenhagen (108kr, 40 minutes) and Helsingør (36kr, 12 minutes). If day-tripping it from Copenhagen, the 24-hour ticket (130kr) is much better value.

WORTH A TRIP

SØLLERØD KRO

Not all of Copenhagen's Michelin stars are inner-city dwellers. One of them lives in Holte, an unassuming outer suburb 19km north of the city centre. We're talking about **Søllerød Kro** (☎45 80 25 05; www.soelleroed-kro.dk; Søllerødvej 35, Holte; 3-/5-course lunch 495/650kr, 4-/6-course dinner 740/950kr; ⊙lunch & dinner Wed-Sun), a one-star Michelin restaurant set in a beautiful 17th-century thatched-roof inn. The kitchen's creations are nothing short of extraordinary, pushing the Franco-Danish tradition to new, enlightened heights. Here, silky Læsø langoustines might be paired with pink grapefruit and coral butter sauce, while the roasted foie gras could come with beets and an elderberry jus. The balancing of flavours and textures is quite often breathtaking, as are the wine pairings for each course.

Yet, despite the fame, adulation and classically chic interiors, Søllerød Kro keeps its feet firmly on the ground, ditching pomp and attitude for a genuine hospitality that's as much a highlight as its degustation menus (which include a 'Green Menu' for the herbivorous). Book your table at least one week in advance.

To get here from Copenhagen, catch S-train (Line E) north to Holte station, from where bus 105 will drop you off 150m from the restaurant (tell the driver you're going to Søllerød Kro). Journey time is about 35 minutes.

Alternatively, for those who want to tick off two countries in one visit, Sweden's third largest city, Malmö, is just 35 minutes away by train from Copenhagen Central Station via the majestic Øresund Fixed Link bridge and tunnel.

Arken Museum of Modern Art

Modern art fans won't regret making the trip out to the outstanding **Ark** (www.arken.dk; Skovvej 100, Ishøj; adult/child 85kr/free; ⊙10am-5pm Tue & Thu-Sun, to 9pm Wed). The art museum's fine collection of post-1945 art includes several Warhols, works by Jeff Koons and Damien Hirst, as well as creations by celebrated contemporary Danish artists such as Per Kirkeby, Asger Jorn, Jesper Just and Olafur Eliasson. There's plenty to keep children intrigued too, including the wonderful sandy beach outside.

To get here from Copenhagen, take the S-train southwest to Ishøj station, then bus 128 from there.

Charlottenlund

Charlottenlund is a well-to-do coastal suburb just beyond the northern outskirts of Copenhagen. Despite being so close to the city, it has a decent **sandy beach**. Its other attractions are a fine art gallery and an aquarium.

◉ Sights

Ordrupgaard ART GALLERY

(Map p42; www.ordrupgaard.dk; Vilvordevej 110, Charlottenlund; adult/child 85kr/free; ⊙1-5pm Tue, Thu & Fri, 1-7pm Wed, 11am-5pm Sat & Sun, Finn Juhl house 11am-5pm Sat & Sun, also 3-5pm Mon-Fri Jul & Aug) Architect Zaha Hadid's sexy, slinky glass-and-stone extension put Ordrupgaard, a charming small art museum, on the international map when it opened in 2005. But the museum, housed in a pretty, early-20th-century manor house to the north of Copenhagen, has always had an enviable collection of 19th- and 20th-century art, including works by Gauguin (who lived in Copenhagen for many years), Renoir and Matisse, as well as notable Danish artists of that period such as JT Lundbye and Vilhelm Hammershøj. The museum also incorporates the former home of pioneering 20th-century Danish designer Finn Juhl, as well as a lovely cafe. To get here, take the S-train to Klampenborg, then bus 388.

Danmarks Akvarium AQUARIUM

(Map p42; www.akvarium.dk; Kavalergården 1; adult/child 100/55kr; ⊙10am-6pm Jul & Aug, to 5pm Feb-May, Sep & Oct, to 4pm Nov-Jan) Danmarks Akvarium is 500m north of the beach on the inland side of the road. By Scandinavian standards it's a fairly large aquarium. The collection is well presented and includes both cold-water and tropical fish, colourful live corals, nurse sharks, sea turtles and piranhas.

To get here, take S-train line C from the capital to Charlottenlund.

Klampenborg

Klampenborg, being only 20 minutes from Central Station on S-train line C, is one of the favourite spots for Copenhageners on family outings.

A few hundred metres east of Klampenborg station is Bellevue beach (see p60), a sandy stretch that gets packed with sunbathers in summer.

⊙ Sights

FREE Bakken   AMUSEMENT PARK

(Map p42; www.bakken.dk, in Danish; Dyrehavevej 62; admission free; ⊙varies, but generally 2-10pm or midnight, closed Sep-Mar) An 800m walk west from Klampenborg station is the 429-year-old Bakken, the world's oldest amusement park (it opened in the 16th century). A blue-collar version of Tivoli, it's a honky-tonk carnival of bumper cars, roller coasters, slot machines and beer halls. Multiride wristbands cost 239kr (219kr Monday to Friday from mid- to late August). See the website for opening times.

Dyrehaven   WALKING, CYCLING

Bakken is at the southern edge of Dyrehaven (more formally called Jægersborg Dyrehave), an expansive 1000-hectare area of beech trees and meadows crisscrossed by an alluring network of walking and cycling trails. Dyrehaven was established as a royal hunting ground in 1669 and has evolved into the capital's most popular picnicking area.

There are still about 2000 deer in the park, mostly fallow but also some red and Japanese sika deer. Among the red deer are a few rare white specimens, descendants of deer imported in 1737 from Germany, where they are now extinct.

Lyngby

The main sight of interest in the Lyngby area is Frilandsmuseet (Map p42; www.natmus.dk; Kongevejen 100; admission free; ⊙10am-5pm Tue-Sun late Apr-late Oct), a sprawling open-air museum of old countryside dwellings that have been gathered from sites around Denmark. Its 50-plus historic buildings are arranged in groupings that provide a sense of Danish rural life as it was in various regions and across different social strata.

Frilandsmuseet is a 10-minute signposted walk from Sorgenfri station, 25 minutes from Central Station on S-train line B. You can also take bus 184 or 191, both of which stop at the entrance.

Zealand

Best Places to Eat

Best Places to Stay

Why Go?

Denmark's largest island offers much more than the dazzle of Copenhagen. North of the city lie some of the country's finest beaches, quaintest fishing villages and vainest castles. Here you'll find Helsingør's hulking Kronborg Slot and Hillerød's sublimely romantic Frederiksborg Slot.

West of Copenhagen awaits history-steeped Roskilde, home to a World Heritage–listed cathedral, Scandinavia's top rock music festival and the superb Viking Ship Museum. History also comes to life at nearby Sagnlandet Lejre, an engrossing, hands-on archaeology site.

Further west stands the millennia-old Trelleborg ring fortress, while Zealand's southern assets include medieval Køge, fairy-tale hamlet Vallø and Næstved's hair-raising theme park.

Much of Zealand is easy to get around, and (bonus!) the Copenhagen Card allows free public transport and admission to many attractions.

When to Go

Between June and August are the best times to visit Zealand. The weather is at its warmest, the countryside is a luxuriant green, and the region's gorgeous north coast is at its most enticing. Tourist offices and attractions are in full swing, and world-class cultural events such as July's Roskilde Festival bring some of the world's top performers. The downside is that you won't be the only one soaking up the sun, sea and culture. Most Danes take their holiday in July, making coastal towns particularly crowded and accommodation scarce. Book ahead.

Outside of summer, May and September are your next best bets, with mild weather, fewer crowds, and most attractions open at full capacity.

ⓘ Getting There & Away

Most of northern Zealand can be reached from Copenhagen in less than an hour – quicker if you have your own transport. The Copenhagen Card (see p81) can be used for many bus or train trips in the area.

Frequent trains head northwards from Copenhagen, but take bus 388 from Klampenborg (the last stop on the C line of the S-train system) north to Helsingør for beautiful coastal views. Helsingør train station handles both DSB trains and the privately operated Lokalbanen, which runs a regional service in north Zealand.

The transportation system in the southern part of Zealand is also well linked to Copenhagen and just about all of it can be reached in an hour from the capital. This said, having your own transport is more important down south, since the destinations are more scattered than in the north and a good amount of the region's appeal lies in its pastoral scenery.

If you're travelling across the region between Køge and Korsør using your own transport, the rural Rte 150 makes an excellent alternative to zipping along on the E20 motorway.

ⓘ Getting Around

A joint zone fare system (24kr per zone travelled) embraces all Copenhagen buses, DSB/State Railway and S-trains in metropolitan Copenhagen, northern Zealand and as far south as Køge, as well as some privately operated railway routes in the area (within an approximately 40km radius of Copenhagen). It's possible to change between train and bus routes on the same ticket.

Depending on the number of zones crossed, it's often cheaper and more convenient to purchase a 24-hour ticket (all zones adult/child 12 to 15 years 130/65kr), or a seven-day FlexCard (all zones 590kr).

To reach most of the north coast you must switch trains in either Hillerød or Helsingør.

The main east–west train line between Copenhagen and Odense cuts across the central part of Zealand, servicing towns such as Sorø and Korsør. The main north–south route runs from Copenhagen to and from Nykøbing F on Falster, servicing the major southern towns of Køge and Vordingborg.

Many of the train routes in southern Zealand are privately run, and buses usually connect stations to towns and villages not serviced by train. For all public transport routes, timetables and prices, click onto the very useful www.rejseplan.dk.

ØRESUND COAST

This area is sometimes grandly referred to as the Danish Riviera, thanks to its expensive seaside mansions. However, it's a slightly misleading name – if you're dreaming of golden beaches, head for the north coast. The main attractions on north Zealand's eastern shore are two excellent museums, and the town of Helsingør, famous for its beast of a castle, Kronborg Slot.

The Øresund itself is the sound that separates Denmark from Sweden, just across the water.

Rungsted

If you're a fan of the fantastical, erotic, mordant writings of Karen Blixen (1885–1962), the coastal town of Rungsted holds a treat. Here you can visit Rungstedlund, Blixen's Danish estate, now a museum dedicated to her life and work. A little north of here is the Louisiana art gallery, see p81.

◉ Sights

Karen Blixen Museet   MUSEUM
(www.karen-blixen.dk; Rungsted Strandvej 111; adult/under 14yr 60kr/free; ⊙10am-5pm Tue-Sun May-Sep, 1-4pm Wed-Fri, 11am-4pm Sat & Sun Oct-Apr) Karen Blixen's former home in Rungsted is now the Karen Blixen museum. Fans of her writing will appreciate how it remains much the way she left it with photographs, Masai spears, paintings, shields and other mementoes of her time in Africa, such as the gramophone given to Blixen by her lover Denys Finch-Hatton. On her desk is the old Corona typewriter she used to write her novels.

One wing of the museum houses a library of Blixen's books, a cafe, bookshop and an audiovisual presentation on her life. The wooded grounds, set aside as a bird sanctuary, contain Blixen's grave, a simple stone slab inscribed with her name.

The museum is opposite the busy yacht harbour, 1.5km from the train station. Walk north up Stationsvej, turn right at the lights onto Rungstedvej and then, at its intersection with Rungsted Strandvej, walk south about 300m. See also the boxed text, p88.

ⓘ Getting There & Away

Trains to Rungsted run every 20 minutes from Copenhagen (84kr, 30 minutes) and Helsingør (60kr, 25 minutes).

ZEALAND RUNGSTED

Zealand Highlights

1 Are you in Denmark or the south of France? Ponder the question on the wide golden beach at **Hornbæk** (p97)

2 Snoop around the immense bastion **Kronborg Slot** (p88), setting for Shakespeare's *Hamlet*

3 Continue the castle odyssey at lakeside **Frederiksborg Slot** (p94), one of Denmark's finest historic buildings

4 Let your child run free with an axe at the Iron Age settlement at **Lejre** (p106)

5 Party hard at northern Europe's largest rock music festival in **Roskilde** (see the boxed text, p104)

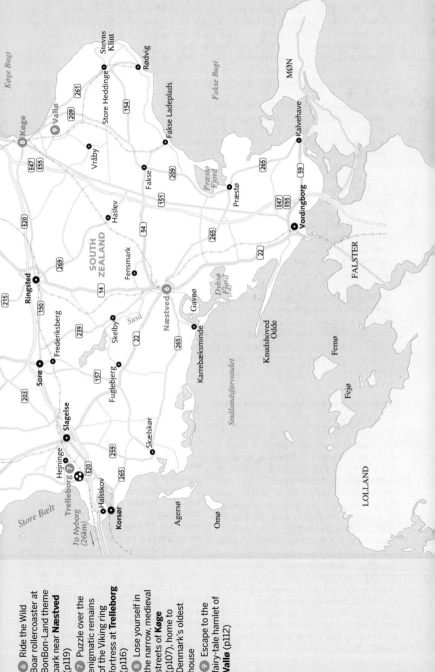

6 Ride the Wild Boar rollercoaster at BonBon-Land theme park near **Næstved** (p119)

7 Puzzle over the enigmatic remains of the Viking ring fortress at **Trelleborg** (p116)

8 Lose yourself in the narrow, medieval streets of **Køge** (p107), home to Denmark's oldest house

9 Escape to the fairy-tale hamlet of **Vallø** (p112)

OUT OF RUNGSTED

Karen Blixen (1885–1962) was born in Rungsted, a well-to-do community north of Copenhagen, as Karen Christenze Dinesen. Throughout her life, this unusual woman created an aura of eccentricity around herself, trying on different names, fictionalising her own life, and causing controversy with her 'decadent' writings.

In 1914, aged 28 and eager to escape the confines of her bourgeois family, she married her second cousin Baron Bror von Blixen-Finecke, after having a failed love affair with his twin brother Hans. It was a marriage of convenience – she wanted his title and he needed her money.

The couple moved to Kenya and started a coffee plantation, which Karen was left to manage. It was here that she was diagnosed with syphilis, contracted through the womanising baron (although it's possible that her ill health was caused by arsenic poisoning, taken as medicine for the syphilis she feared she had). The diagnosis was especially damaging psychologically since her father had committed suicide after contracting syphilis when Karen was 10 years old. Blixen came home to Denmark for medical treatment, then returned to Africa and divorced the baron in 1925.

She then lived with the great love of her life, Englishman Denys Finch-Hatton, for six years, until he died in a tragic plane crash in 1932. The couple were played by Meryl Streep and Robert Redford in the Oscar-winning film adaptation of *Out of Africa*, Blixen's autobiography. Soon after his death Blixen left Africa, returning to the family estate in Rungsted where she began to write. Denmark was slow to appreciate her, in part because she used an old-fashioned idiomatic style, wrote approvingly about the aristocracy and insisted on being addressed as 'Baroness' in a country bent on minimising class disparity.

Blixen's first book of short stories, *Seven Gothic Tales*, was published in New York in 1934 under the pseudonym Isak Dinesen. It was only after the book became immensely successful in the USA that Danish publishers took a serious interest.

After the commercial success of *Out of Africa* in both Danish and English, other books followed: *Winter's Tales* (1942), *The Angelic Avengers* (1944), *Last Tales* (1957), *Anecdotes of Destiny* (1958) and *Shadows on the Grass* (1960). Another Oscar-winning film, *Babette's Feast*, was based on her story about culinary artistry in small-town Denmark (see p311).

Helsingør

POP 46,280

The main sight at the busy port town of Helsingør (Elsinore) is imposing Kronborg Slot, a brute of a castle that dominates the narrowest point of the Øresund. It was made famous as Elsinore Castle in Shakespeare's *Hamlet,* although the intimate psychological nature of the play is a far cry from the military colossus squatting on the shore.

Helsingør is full of pedestrianised historic streets, just made for ambling along with an ice cream. They contain a delightful collection of half-timbered houses, Gothic churches and a medieval cloister, interspersed with interesting shops and good cafes.

Frequent ferries shuttle the short trip to and from Sweden, filled with Swedes on a mission to buy cheap (at least for them) Danish alcohol.

◉ Sights

⌜TOP⌝ CHOICE Kronborg Slot CASTLE

(www.ses.dk/en/SlotteOgHaver/Slotte/Kronborg; Kronborgvej; Royal Apartments, Casements & Chapel, Maritime Museum & Telegraph Tower adult/15-18yr/6-14yr 95/70/25kr; ⊙10.30am-5pm May-Sep, 11am-4pm Tue-Sun Apr & Oct, reduced hrs rest of year) The monstrous military bulk of Kronborg Slot is a Unesco World Heritage Site, and top of the town's sightseeing list. Despite the attention it has received as the setting of *Hamlet*, the castle's real function was far less romantic – it acted as a formidable tollhouse. Imagine sitting in the Øresund with the cannons of Kronborg aimed squarely at your creaking ship, and you can understand how wonderfully effective the castle was in its tax-gathering purpose.

The Danish king Erik of Pomerania demonstrated excellent business sense in the 1420s, when he built a small fortress, Krogen, at the narrowest part of the Øresund and then charged cargo ships one rose noble (a type of English gold coin) for sailing past. The 'sound dues' generated plenty of cash, enabling Frederik II to enlarge Krogen into Kronborg Slot in 1585.

Not long after the workmen had packed up tools, a devastating fire ravaged the castle in 1629, leaving nothing but the outer walls. The tireless builder-king Christian IV rebuilt Kronborg, preserving the castle's earlier Renaissance style and adding his own baroque touches, but soon afterwards disaster struck again. During the Danish-Swedish wars, the Swedes occupied Kronborg from 1658 to 1660, looting everything of value including its famous fountain.

Following the Swedish attack, Christian V bulked up Kronborg's defences, but the Danish royals gave up trying to make the castle a home. The building became a barracks from 1785 until 1924, when it became a museum (the Swedish government sportingly returning some looted items).

Although it costs to enter the interior, you can cross several swan-filled moats and walk into the dramatic courtyard free of charge, or make a circumnavigation of the castle's mighty sea barriers (open daily until sunset), a good picnic spot.

Royal Apartments

The Royal Apartments are rather empty today: the king's and queen's chambers, for example, have little in them but marble fireplaces, a few sticks of furniture, and some lavish ceiling paintings, although occasional modern-art exhibitions add an interesting dimension.

The most impressive room is the ballroom, the longest in Scandinavia when it was built in 1585. Banquets held here consisted of 65 courses, and each guest was given their own vomiting bucket. Seven of the tapestries that originally adorned the walls – in excellent condition, and with interesting explanations alongside – can be seen in the adjoining Little Hall.

Casements & Chapel

The chilly, low-ceilinged dungeon, which also served as storerooms and soldiers' quarters, stretches underneath a surprisingly large area of the castle. It's suitably dark and creepy, although you'll make better sense of its empty rooms if you read up on barracks life before heading downwards. Delights include nesting bats, and a statue of the Viking chief **Holger Danske** (Ogier the Dane), who, legend says, will wake and come to Denmark's aid in its hour of need.

The galleried chapel was the only part of Kronborg that escaped the flames in 1629, and gives a good impression of the castle's original appearance. Highlights include the gilt-covered altar and freakish faces decorating the pews.

Handels- og Søfartsmuseet

(Danish Maritime Museum; www.maritime-museum. dk) Tracing Denmark's maritime past and overseas colonies, Handels- og Søfartsmuseet, running round three whole sides of the courtyard, is worth a visit. This collection of model ships, paintings, nautical instruments and sea charts helps one to appreciate the impact of the sea on Danish culture and history. It also contains the world's oldest ship biscuit, c 1852 – which looks peculiarly edible.

ZEALAND HELSINGØR

TO BE OR NOT TO BE

Shakespeare's *Hamlet* (1602) is set in Kronborg Slot in Helsingør ('Elsinore'). Despite the vividness of the play, the Bard had never set foot in Denmark. It's possible that he gleaned details of the imposing new castle from a group of English players who performed in Helsingør in 1585, the year that Kronborg was completed. Shakespeare also included two actual Danish noblemen, Frederik Rosenkrantz and Knud Gyldenstierne (Guildenstern), who visited the English court in the 1590s.

Although the remaining characters are based on a story that was 800 years old in Shakespeare's time, audiences were utterly convinced of the play's authenticity. English merchants trading in Helsingør would visit the castle out of respect for Hamlet: so many visitors wanted to know where the indecisive Dane was buried that 'Hamlet's grave' was built in the grounds of Marienlyst Slot.

Performances of *Hamlet* take place in Kronborg's courtyard every August, from straight-up RSC versions to Chinese-opera interpretations – check www.hamletscenen. dk to see what's coming up.

Helsingør

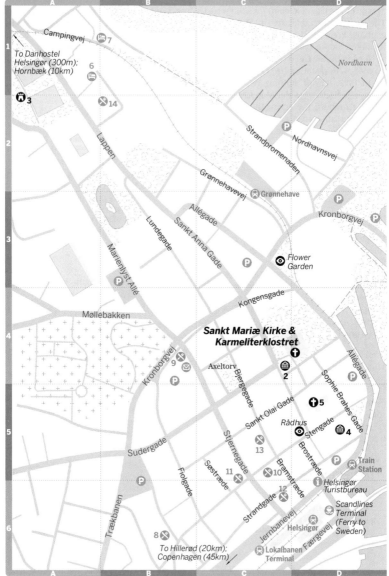

You can see the remains of the original Krogen fortress in the masonry of rooms 21 and 22; and it's worth the admission price to climb the winding staircase of the teetering **Telegraph Tower** for superb views.

**Sankt Mariæ Kirke &
Karmeliterklostret**　　　CHURCH, MONASTERY
(www.sctmariae.dk; Sankt Anna Gade 38; ⊙10am-3pm Tue-Sun) The medieval church of Sankt Mariæ Kirke contains some quite spiffy 15th-century frescoes. Alongside standard

Dieterich Buxtehude (1637–1707), a baroque composer who greatly influenced Bach; the frequent organ concerts are attended by aficionados.

Sankt Mariæ Kirke is attached to one of Scandinavia's best-preserved medieval monasteries, **Karmeliterklostret** (Carmelite monastery; ⊙tours 2pm Fri & Sat mid-Jun–mid-Sep), a soothing place of red brick and whitewash. Christian II's mistress, Dyveke (c 1490–1517), is thought to have been buried here.

Sankt Olai Domkirke   CATHEDRAL
(Sankt Anna Gade 12; admission free; ⊙10am-4pm May-Aug, 10am-2pm Sep-Apr) Surrounded by lime trees, Sankt Olai Domkirke is a handsome red-brick Gothic cathedral built in 1559. Unusual features include an over-the-top white-and-gold altarpiece (one of Denmark's largest at 12m high), an ominous black stone slab where the names of wrongdoers were written, and, wedged in an archway, an English cannonball fired en route to the Battle of Copenhagen (1801).

Helsingør Bymuseum   MUSEUM
(Sankt Anna Gade 36; adult/child 20kr/free; ⊙noon-4pm Tue-Fri & Sun, 10am-2pm Sat) One block north of the cathedral is Helsingør Bymuseum, built by the monks of the adjacent monastery in 1516 to serve as a

biblical scenes are bizarre faces from whose mouths spring frogs, foxes, bulls and rams, while in the southern aisle pipers and lute players burst from giant flowers.

There's also an ornate rococo gallery and a 17th-century organ, which was played by

sailors' hospital. There's a detailed model of 19th-century Helsingør, with an interesting 15-minute recording about the town's history in Danish, Swedish, German and English. There's also a hotchpotch of exhibits (old chemists' bottles, medieval pottery finds, 200 dolls) labelled mainly in Danish.

Museet Skibsklarerergaarden MUSEUM
(Strandgade 91; admission 30kr, entry by Danish guided tour only, on the hour; ⊙noon-4pm Tue-Fri, 10am-2pm Sat, last tour 1hr before closing) This higgledy-piggledy shipping agent's house is steeped in seafaring history: while the agent checked cargo and filled out paperwork in the office, ships' captains could stock up on supplies, have a meal, or catch forty winks in the attic. Unfortunately the 50-minute tours are in Danish only, but pop into the spicy-smelling 18th-century shop, and buy a beer brewed in the tiny backyard.

Danmarks Tekniske Museum MUSEUM
(www.tekniskmuseum.dk; Fabriksvej 25; adult/child 65kr/free; ⊙10am-5pm Tue-Sun) Southwest of the centre on an industrial estate, Danmarks Tekniske Museum displays innovative technological inventions from the late 19th and early 20th centuries: early gramophones, radios, motor vehicles and aeroplanes. The latter includes a 1906 Danish-built aeroplane that, it's claimed, was the first plane flown in Europe (it stayed airborne for 11 seconds!). The museum is a 15-minute ride away on bus 805, in the direction of Espergærde.

Marienlyst Slot HISTORIC BUILDING
(Marienlyst Allé 32; adult/child 30kr/free; ⊙noon-4pm Tue-Sun) About 1.5km northwest of town is Marienlyst Slot, a stately neoclassical manor house built in 1763, set back in a manicured garden ablaze with rhododendrons. Inside there's a small collection of silverware and 19th-century paintings of Helsingør and Hornbæk, including one on the 2nd floor that's half Venice and half Copenhagen.

'Hamlet's grave' can be found in the parkland behind the house, added because every good romantic garden should provoke melancholic thoughts; and as a tourist attraction for visiting English merchants convinced that Hamlet was real.

At the time of research, Marienlyst Slot was closed for restoration work.

The Hornbæk-bound train stops at Marienlyst station, 100m north of the manor house.

Hammermøllen HISTORIC BUILDING
(www.hammermollen.dk, in Danish; Bøssemagergade 21; adult/child 10/5kr; ⊙11am-5pm Thu & Fri, 10am-5pm Sat & Sun) If you don't have a pressing itinerary, consider cycling to Hammermøllen, about 5km west in Hellebæk. This picturesque old smithy was founded by Christian IV in 1765 to hammer out cannons for his battleships, and has also served as a copper mill and textile mill. Admire the thatched roof and waterwheels, and kick back with coffee and cake.

🛏 Sleeping

Marienlyst Hotel & Casino HOTEL €€
(☏49 21 40 00; www.marienlyst.dk; N Strandvej 2; s 950-1425kr, d 1150-1625kr; P @ 🖥 ≋) Helsingør's four-star hotel stretches along the seafront, and is practically a self-contained holiday centre, with two restaurants, bars, its own casino and a swimming pool. Rooms are tastefully neutral, with sleek white bathrooms; those with sea views cost around 175kr more.

Danhostel Helsingør HOSTEL €
(☏49 21 16 40; www.helsingorhostel.dk; Nordre Strandvej 24; dm 195kr, r without/with bathroom 350/475kr; P @ 🖥) This 180-bed hostel is based in a coastal manor house 2km northwest of town, on a little beach looking directly across to Sweden. The run-of-the-mill dorms have up to 10 beds and are in one of the smaller attached buildings. Facilities include a self-catering kitchen, small playground and outdoor ping-pong tables to keep kids amused. From Helsingør, bus 842 (24kr) will get you there.

**Helsingør Camping
Grønnehave** CAMPING GROUND, CABINS €
(☏49 28 49 50; www.helsingorcamping.dk; Strandalleen 2; camp site per person 60kr; ⊙year-round) It's a pleasant, low-key, two-star camping ground on the beach approximately 1.5km northwest of the town centre, Grønnehave, has a shop, laundry, and bike hire for 75kr per day. Cabins are also available (five-/six-person cabin 1300/1995kr per week). To get here, take bus 842.

🍴 Eating

There's a cluster of restaurants and beer gardens around the main square, Axeltorv. For coffee and cake, head for pedestrianised Stengade.

TOP CHOICE Rådmand Davids Hus   CAFE €

(Strandgade 70; mains 80kr; ☺10am-6pm Mon-Fri, to 5pm Sat) We love this popular cafe, with sunny staff, contained within a lopsided 17th-century half-timbered house. Traditional Danish food (nothing for vegetarians) is served up either in the cosy, crooked interior or the cobbled courtyard, bursting with greenery. The special is the 'shopping lunch' (79kr), typically a generous plate of salad, salmon pâté, and slices of lamb, cheese and homemade ryebread.

Madame Sprunck   INTERNATIONAL €€

(Stengade 48F; 2-course lunch/dinner 160/188kr; ☺lunch & dinner) Another great old building, with seating in a candlelit wooden interior or charming mustard-yellow courtyard. Food is a mixture of Danish, French and Mexican – everything from burgers to more sophisticated dishes such as steamed mussels in elderflower and white wine.

Café Vivaldi   INTERNATIONAL €€

(Stengade 9; sandwiches 89-99kr, dinner mains 129-199kr; ☺lunch & dinner) This popular, mock 'French bistro' cafe serves standard (albeit tasty) grub in a relaxed environment. The menu spans nachos, omelettes, salads and quiches to more substantial evening mains – steaks, burritos and pasta dishes. Live music adds to the buzz at weekends.

Møllers Conditori   BAKERY €

(Stengade 39; smørrebrød 55-65kr; ☺11.30am-5.30pm) Denmark's oldest *konditori* (bak-ery with cafe tables) has outdoor seats on bustling Stengade, a prime site for people-watching. Nibble on succulent pastries, fresh bread rolls or smørrebrød (open sandwiches) as you watch the passing crowds.

Slagter Baagø   DELI €

(Bjergegade 3; smørrebrød 14-38kr; ☺9am-5.30pm Tue-Thu, to 6pm Fri, to 2pm Sat) Self-caterers and picnickers can pick freshly prepared edibles from this deli.

There's a **Spar** (Lappen; ☺7.30am-6pm Mon-Thu, to 7pm Fri, 7to 2pm Sat, 8am-noon Sun) su-permarket near the camping ground, and a **Kvickly** (Stjernegade 25; ☺9am-8pm Mon-Fri, 8am-6pm Sat) supermarket and bakery west of Axeltorv.

ℹ Information

Danske Bank (Stengade 55) One of many banks and ATMs.

Helsingør Turistbureau (☎49 21 13 33; www.visitnordsjaelland.com; Havnepladsen 3; ☺10am-5pm Mon-Fri, to 2pm Sat & Sun late Jun-early Aug, reduced hrs rest of year)

Library (Allégade 2; ☺10am-9pm Mon-Fri, to 4pm Sat) Free internet access.

Post office (Stjernegade 25; ☺10am-5pm Mon-Fri, 10am-noon Sat) Inside the Kvickly supermarket building.

ℹ Getting There & Away

BOAT For information on ferries to Helsingborg in Sweden (person/car plus nine passengers 54/690kr return, 20 minutes), see p326.

ZEALAND HELSINGØR

THE WORLD ACCORDING TO TYCHO

It was on the island of Hven, in the sound between Denmark and Sweden, that the 16th-century Danish astronomer Tycho Brahe sought to collect evidence that the sun and moon revolved around the earth. Although he was wrong – and proven so by Johannes Kepler, his former assistant – Brahe's meticulous observations and calculations were still significant achievements and influenced Kepler's later findings. He was the first to measure planetary movement, and designed instrumentation light years more sophisticated than his predecessors.

While Brahe's mind may have been on the stars, his ambitions were decidedly worldly. Part of his nose was sliced off in a duel, reputedly over claims that his opponent was a better mathematician. He subsequently replaced the damaged organ with a copper one.

To prevent Brahe from being lured away from Denmark, King Frederik II gave Hven to the astronomer and financed the building of Uraniborg, an observatory, alchemical labo-ratory and castle. After falling out with Frederik's son Christian IV, Brahe closed down the observatory in 1597, and left Denmark for good two years later.

Unfortunately, Brahe's next appointment, as Imperial Mathematician to the Holy Roman Emperor, didn't last long – he died in Prague in 1601. It was long thought that his death was the result of holding in his urine for too long at a royal banquet, but recent investigations suggest that he may have died from mercury poisoning.

CAR Helsingør is 64km north of Copenhagen and 24km northeast of Hillerød. There's free parking throughout the city, including northeast of the tourist office, west of Kvickly supermarket and outside Kronborg Slot.

TRAIN Helsingør train station has two adjacent terminals: the DSB terminal for national trains and the smaller Lokalbanen terminal for the private railway that runs along the north coast.

Trains to Copenhagen (108kr, 45 minutes) run about three times hourly from early morning to around midnight. Trains to Hillerød (via Fredensborg 72kr, 30 minutes) run at least once hourly until around midnight.

The Lokalbanen train from Helsingør to Gilleleje (72kr, 40 minutes) via Hornbæk (36kr, 25 minutes) runs once to twice hourly until around midnight.

INLAND TOWNS

In the heart of Zealand lie Hillerød and Fredensborg, two small towns built around magnificent – and very different – royal residences. You're free to roam the ornate rooms and soaring towers of the castle at Hillerød, whereas the interior of the more modest palace at Fredensborg is only open in July the rest of the year, it's the beautiful lakeside gardens that are the main draw.

Hillerød

POP 30,350

Christian IV sure knew how to build a castle. Hillerød, 30km north of Copenhagen, is a pleasant modern market town, whose glorious palace elevates it to 'must visit' status. Frederiksborg Slot, sitting on a nest of islands in the middle of an attractive lake, is a vision of copper turrets and baroque gardens, and one of the most impressive attractions in the region.

Hillerød is also a transport hub for north Zealand, with train connections for the beaches on the north coast. The train station is about 500m from the town centre.

◉ Sights

TOP CHOICE Frederiksborg Slot   CASTLE
(www.frederiksborgmuseet.dk; Slotsgade 1; adult/student/6-15yr/family 60/50/15/120kr; ◷10am-5pm Apr-Oct, 11am-3pm Nov-Mar) Combining history, beauty and strength, the impressive Dutch Renaissance-styled Frederiksborg Slot spreads across three islets on the castle lake, Slotsø.

The oldest part of Frederiksborg Slot dates from the reign of Frederik II, after whom it is named. His son Christian IV was born here; most of the present structure was built by Christian in the early 17th century and can be seen as his homage to a place to which he had a deep attachment. Both kings used Frederiksborg as their royal seat; but after Hillerød suffered plague, fire and rampaging Swedes during the 17th century, the throne moved to quieter Fredensborg in the 18th century.

Frederiksborg Slot was ravaged by flames in 1859, and the royal family, unable to undertake the costly repairs, decided to give it up. Carlsberg beer baron JC Jacobsen spearheaded a drive to restore the castle as a national museum, a function it fulfils today.

The Interior

The sprawling castle has a magnificent interior boasting gilded ceilings, wall-sized tapestries and fine paintings, with 70 of its rooms open to the public. The **Slotskirken** (Coronation Chapel) is the most dazzling. It was spared serious fire damage and retains the original interior commissioned by Christian IV – a crazed confection of curling gold, pink-cheeked cherubs, and a silver pulpit and altarpiece. Danish monarchs were crowned in the chapel from 1671 to 1840, the perfect setting for such pomp and circumstance. You can hear the sound of the 17th century each Thursday between 1.30pm and 2pm, when the priceless **Compenius organ** (1610) is played, or at free concerts every Sunday at 5pm in July and August.

Also fairly intact is the **Audience Chamber**, an eye-boggling room containing trompe l'oeil details, a self-indulgent portrait of big-nosed Christian V posing as a Roman emperor, and best of all, a 17th-century elevator chair, which enabled the king to rise graciously through the floor!

Other rooms were restored to their original appearances in the 19th century. The richly embellished **Riddershalen** (Knights Hall), once the dining room, is particularly striking – check out the stucco friezes of deer, embedded with real antlers. Also impressive is the **Great Hall**, a vast ballroom complete with minstrels' gallery, fine tapestries and vivid ceiling paintings.

The rest of the 1st and 2nd floors contain the **Museum of National History**, a chronologically arranged portrait gallery of kings, noblemen and olden-day celebrities, interspersed with unusual pieces of furniture.

DENMARK'S MOST HAUNTED...

Esrum Kloster (www.esrum.dk; Klostergade, Esrum; adult/under 16yr 50kr/free; ☺10.30am-4.30pm Tue-Sun Apr-late Oct, 11am-4pm Thu-Sun mid-Oct–Apr), a monastery 15km north of Hillerød, has a juicy ghost story attached about the demonic Brother Rus, who was employed as the monastery's cook in the 16th century. Wicked old Rus served up decadent dishes and lashings of sinful wine to his fellow monks, in between chasing the serving wenches round the kitchen and having late-night chats with Satan.

Word of this evil-doing got back to the abbot, who had Brother Rus tortured to death on his own cooking grill (on view in the monastery today). A splatter of his blood has defied all attempts to wash it off, and the damned monk has been spotted wandering the monastery in the dead of night.

Bus 390R from Helsingør to Helsinge runs past the monastery.

It's a lot to digest in one go – you might be better off concentrating on the time periods that interest you.

On the 3rd floor is the **Moderne Samling** (Modern Collection), a large collection of 20th-century paintings and photography.

Slotshaven
The castle gardens lie to the north. The formal **baroque garden** (☺10am-sunset), visible from the castle windows and made up of perfect terraces and immaculately manicured yew and box, demonstrates that even nature must bend to a king's will. There's also a Romantic garden, **Indelukket**, where 18th-century rigidity melts into a wilder 19th-century notion of gardening. North again is the oak wood of **Lille Dyrehave**, which was planted to provide material for boat-building after the Danish fleet was confiscated by England in 1807. You could easily spend a pleasant hour's outing strolling through the three sections.

The Slotsø Ferry
From mid-May to mid-September, the little **Frederiksborg ferry** (adult/child 30/10kr) makes a 30-minute round-trip of the castle lake between 11am and 5pm Monday to Saturday, and between 1pm and 5pm on Sunday. It stops at three small piers: one on the edge of Torvet, one near the castle entrance and one by the baroque gardens.

🛏 Sleeping

Accommodation is scarce in Hillerød and fills up quickly even out of high season – book ahead. For a list of accommodation options, head to www.visitnordsjaelland.com.

Hillerød Camping CAMPING GROUND €
(☎48 26 48 54; www.hillerodcamping.dk; Blytækkervej 18; camp site per adult 82kr; ☺mid-Apr–mid-Oct)

This wonderful two-star camping ground is about a 20-minute walk directly south of the castle along Slangerupgade. You can really feel the love – free bike rental, bags of toys for children, a spotless kitchen, a cosy lounge with books and magazines, and even fresh flowers in the toilets.

Danhostel Hillerød HOSTEL €
(☎48 26 19 86; www.hillerodhostel.dk; Lejrskolevej 4; dm/s/d 180/390/420kr; @🛜) Although it's not very central – this lakeside hostel is 2.5km east of town – you can't complain about its facilities. The hostel is geared towards school groups: you'll find ping-pong, air hockey, badminton and pétanque, as well as bicycle (per hour/day 20/75kr) and canoe (per day 150kr) hire. Buses 301, 302 and 305 run from near the hostel to town.

Hotel Hillerød HOTEL €€
(☎48 24 08 00; www.hotelhillerod.dk; Milnersvej 41; s 620-1135kr; d 800-1340kr; 🅿@🛜) Each bathroom at this strangely designed modern bungalow hotel juts out into a kind of covered atrium – odd. Rooms are pleasant and entirely unmemorable in that Ikea-type of way. Sixty-two have superior facilities – flat-screen TVs and handy little kitchenettes. Hotel Hillerød is about 2km south of the castle. Bikes can be borrowed free of charge.

🍴 Eating

Café Vivaldi INTERNATIONAL €€
(Torvet 11; lunch 89-109kr, dinner mains 149-199kr; ☺lunch & dinner) Right in the centre of the sloping town square, this is the place to head on a sunny afternoon for people-watching. There's a good choice of light meals – nachos, wraps and salads, as well as more substantial offerings such as steaks.

Ristorante La Perla
ITALIAN €€

(www.laperla.dk; Torvet 1; 2/3 courses 169/189kr, pizzas 89-98kr; ☺lunch & dinner) La Perla's Sicilian chef serves up (mostly) genuine Italian food, and very tasty stuff it is. It's definitely more upmarket than your average pizzeria, yet the atmosphere is relaxed. In summer, you can dine in the cobblestone courtyard.

Thai 4 You
THAI €

(www.thai4you.dk; Østergade 22; mains 55-80kr; ☺lunch & dinner) East of Torvet, this authentic Thai restaurant has a long menu of favourites, including a tangy *tum yam* soup. If you want to test beers from local microbrewery Brøckshouse, there's a good selection here.

ℹ Information

Hillerød Turistbureau (☎48 24 26 26; www.visitnordsjaelland.com; Frederiksværksgade 2A; ☺10am-4.30pm Mon-Fri, to 2pm Sat late Jun-early Aug, 10am-4.30pm Mon-Fri May & Sep) A short walk from the castle entrance.

ℹ Getting There & Away

The S-train (E line) runs every 10 minutes between Copenhagen and Hillerød (108kr, 40 minutes).

Trains from Hillerød run eastward to Fredensborg (24kr, 10 minutes) and Helsingør (72kr, 30 minutes), north to Gilleleje (60kr, 30 minutes) and west to Tisvildeleje (60kr, 30 minutes); all services operate at least hourly.

Buses also link Hillerød with North Zealand towns but they are much slower than the train and cost just as much.

ℹ Getting Around

Buses 301 and 302 depart frequently from the train station and can drop you near the castle gate (24kr).

Fredensborg

POP 8375

Small, quiet Fredensborg *is* its royal palace, plus the wonderful palace gardens that stretch alongside Denmark's second-largest lake, Esrum Sø. The palace is only open to the public in July, but it's worth a day out here anyway for peaceful greenery, swimming, boating and fishing opportunities.

◉ Sights

Fredensborg Slot
PALACE

(www.ses.dk; Slotsgade 1; ☺Jul by guided tour only) The royal family's summer residence, Fredensborg Palace was built in 1720 by Frederik IV. Its name – 'Peace Palace' – commemorates the truce that Denmark had just achieved with its Scandinavian neighbours. The country-manor appearance reflects the more tranquil mood of that era, an abrupt contrast with the moat-encircled fortresses of Kronborg and Frederiksborg that preceded it.

The main Italian baroque mansion, with marble floors and a large central cupola, is not as impressive as some other Danish royal palaces, partly because of its spread-out design. The building's very...*neat,* but the palace is really made by its gardens, a blending of baroque formality and a more luxurian Romantic vision.

Fredensborg's interior can only be visited during July, when the royal family holidays elsewhere. Guided palace tours (adult/child 50/20kr) run every 15 minutes between 1pm and 4.30pm daily. Whenever the royal family is in residence, the building is flanked by smart Little-Tin-Soldier guards, with white-striped uniforms and bearskin hats. The changing of the guard is at noon daily.

The palace is about 1km from the train station, and well signposted.

Fredensborg Slotshave
GARDENS

The palace is surrounded by a huge area of garden and parkland (some parts with limited access). The **Palace Park**, open free to the public year-round, is a 120-hectare expanse of woodland, crossed by long riding avenues that radiate outwards from the palace. Wandering through tunnels of cool green leaves is particularly delightful on a hot summer's day. Its most unusual feature is **Normandsdalen**, west of the palace, a circular amphitheatre containing 70 life-sized statues of Norwegian and Faroese folk characters. The original small wooden dolls of these fishermen, farmers, soldiers and servants were carved by an 18th-century Norwegian postman, Jørgen Christensen Garnaas, who sent them to King Frederik V. Frederik liked them so much he had them made from sandstone.

The royal family jealously shield the Reserved Gardens from public eyes, except in July when you can visit the **Orangery and Herb Garden** (adult/child 50/20kr, joint ticket to palace & orangery 75/30kr) by guided tour between 1pm and 4.20pm.

Esrum Sø
LAKE, OUTDOORS

About 1km west of the palace gate along Skipperallé, you'll come to the lovely Esrum Sø, Denmark's second-largest lake at 17 sq km. A trail skirts around its shores, or you can explore the water by boat. You'll find a lakeside restaurant Skipperhuset (see following), as well as canoes and kayaks for hire. There's also a summer ferry service to Gribskov, a forested area with trails and picnic grounds on the western side of the lake.

🛏 Sleeping

Staff at the tourist office can book rooms in private homes, with doubles costing around 600kr including breakfast, plus a 25kr booking fee.

Danhostel Fredensborg HOSTEL €
(☏ 48 48 03 15; www.fredensborghostel.dk; Østrupvej 3; s 229-529kr, d 329-529kr; ☺Jan–mid-Dec; P ⊛) The hostel occupies a prime location just 300m south of Fredensborg Slot. There are no dorms here – most of its 88 beds are in double rooms (all with washbasin or bathroom). There's a large secluded garden, and a bread-baking service.

✖ Eating

Skipperhuset INTERNATIONAL €€
(www.skipperhuset.dk; Skipperallé 6; mains 88-168kr; ☺noon-5pm May-Oct) It's hard to imagine a more idyllic setting for alfresco dining than this restaurant on Esrum Sø. Fish is delicately prepared and topped with fresh seasonal vegetables, and there's usually a veggie option such as feta and spinach pancakes.

Ristorante Da Oscar ITALIAN €€
(www.daoscar.dk; Slotsgade 3A; pizzas 65-98kr, mains 185-220kr; ☺dinner Tue-Sun) Smart yet relaxed, Da Oscar serves decent Italian dishes in a garden setting. Tuck into pizza or pasta, or opt for interesting mains like veal with fennel-flavoured gorgonzola sauce, or grilled lamb with thyme, rosemary, sage, garlic and balsamic vinegar. As you may have gathered, vegetarians will struggle.

Café Under Kronen INTERNATIONAL €
(Jernbanegade 1; sandwiches 49-57kr) For quickie sandwiches, burgers, cake and ice cream, this round glass cafe is right outside the palace gates.

ℹ Information

Fredensborg Turistbureau (☏ 41 21 81 59; www.visitnordsjaelland.com; Dronning Ingrid Anlæg; ☺noon-4pm Mon-Fri Apr, 11am-4.30pm daily Jun-Aug, noon-4pm Sun-Fri May & Sep) Seasonal tourist bureau just outside the palace.

ℹ Getting There & Away

Fredensborg is midway between Hillerød (24kr, 10 minutes) and Helsingør (60kr, 20 minutes). Trains run about twice hourly from early morning.

NORTH COAST

Gorgeous white-sand beaches with shallow water and gentle waves line the northern Kattegat coast. Although the scattered small towns and villages only have a few thousand residents in winter, in summer the holiday homes fill and throngs of beach goers create a salubrious sunshine-and-icecream atmosphere.

Hornbæk

POP 3500

'Denmark's St Tropez!', shout the tourist brochures. There are two similarities: Hornbæk's Blue-Flag beach, a vast expanse of soft white sand, is just as beautiful as any you'll find in southern France; and it certainly attracts more than its fair share of foxy young socialites.

Danish artists first discovered the attractions of this little-known fishing village in the 19th century, with early tourists following hot on their heels. Thanks to some geographical peculiarities, Hornbæk enjoys more sunshine than anywhere in Denmark.

⊙ Sights & Activities

Hornbæk Beach BEACH
Hornbæk's gorgeous Blue-Flag beach is the best on the north coast and the town's main attraction. The sand is white, the air is scented with salt and wild roses, there's plenty of space for sunbathing, and in high summer lifeguards keep an eye on the water. The beach stretches out to either side of the harbour – even though it borders the town, it's pleasantly undeveloped, with all the commercial facilities on the other side of the dunes. The eastern side is where the kitesurfers and windsurfers hang out: you'll need your own gear to join them.

From the train station it's a five-minute walk – about 200m – directly north along Havnevej to the harbour. Climb the dunes to the left and you're on the beach.

Hornbæk Plantage WALKING
For an enjoyable nature stroll, Hornbæk Plantage, a public woodland that extends 3.5km along the coast east from Hornbæk, has

Hornbæk

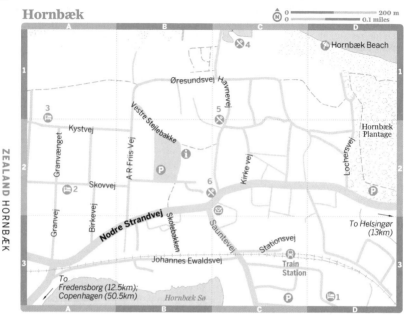

Hornbæk

Sleeping
1	Ewaldsgården Pension	D3
2	Hotel Hornbækhus	A2
3	Hotel Villa Strand	A2

Eating
4	Fiskehuset Hornbæk	C1
5	Hansens Café	C2
6	Restaurant Oliva	B2

numerous interconnecting trails branching out either side of Rte 237. One trail hugs the coast from Lochersvej in Hornbæk to the eastern end of the plantage. There are several areas along Nordre Strandvej (Rte 237) where you can park a car and start your wanderings. A free map *Vandreture i Statsskovene, Hornbæk Plantage* shows all the trails and is available from the tourist office.

🛏 Sleeping

The tourist office can book private single/double rooms from 300/500kr.

TOP CHOICE Ewaldsgården Pension GUESTHOUSE €€
(☑49 70 00 82; www.ewaldsgaarden.dk, in Danish; Johannes Ewaldsvej 5; s/d/f incl breakfast

550/850/1170kr; ⏱mid-Jun–mid-Aug; P@🤶) This 17th-century farmhouse pension is a delight, with a picture-perfect garden and a cosy mix of antiques and cottage-style furnishings. All 12 rooms have washbasins; showers and toilets are off the hall. There's also a simple guest kitchen. Ewaldsgården is a five-minute walk southeast of the train station.

Hotel Villa Strand HOTEL €€
(☑49 70 00 88; www.villastrand.dk; Kystvej 12; s 630-890kr, d 895-1420kr; ⏱Jun-Aug; P🤶) If this hotel was any closer to the sea, it would be floating towards Sweden. Rooms in the main building are large, with cool white decor, floorboards and a lofty air. There are smaller, cheaper, but still tasteful rooms (singles/doubles 630/895kr) in the garden annexe. All have bathrooms and breakfast includes kosher products.

Hotel Hornbækhus HOTEL €€
(☑49 70 01 69; www.hornbaekhus.com; Skovvej 7; s/d incl breakfast 1195/1395kr; P@🤶) Down another green lane full of flowers and birds, this is the grandest hotel in Hornbæk, with the feel of a stately home. Rooms are elegant and classically furnished, and some have their own balconies. Cheaper rooms with

shared bathrooms cost 725/825kr per single/double.

Hornbæk Camping

DCU CAMPING GROUND, CABINS €
(☎49 70 02 23; www.camping-hornbaek.dk, in Danish; Planetvej 4; camp site per person 72kr; ☺year-round) Nestling up to the woods of Hornbæk Plantage, this three-star camping ground is about 1.5km southeast of the centre, off Sauntevej. It has good facilities – smart bathrooms, huts for hire, and a playground and 'bouncy pillow' for kids.

✖ Eating

Hansens Café DANISH €€
(Havnevej 19; smørrebrød 76-85kr, dinner mains 174-218kr; ☺lunch Sun, dinner Thu-Tue) Hansens is in the town's oldest house, an earthen-roofed half-timbered building with a pleasant pub-like atmosphere. The menu changes daily but you can expect to find solid Danish grub such as *fiskefrikadeller* (fishballs) with homemade remoulade.

Fiskehuset Hornbæk SEAFOOD €
(Havnevej 32; fish & chips 50kr; ☺11am-8pm summer, reduced hrs rest of year) Hornbæk's humble harbourside gem is the Fiskehuset. Here you can dine like a lord, albeit outdoors with paper serviettes, on smoked cod's roe, cured herring, smoked mackerel, fresh prawns, *fiskefrikadeller,* mussel soup and all manner of wonderful, fresh, local seafood – for under 60kr.

Restaurant Oliva DANISH, ITALIAN €€
(www.oliva.dk in Danish; Havnevej 1; lunch 69-245kr, dinner mains 225-245kr; ☺lunch & dinner Tue-Sun) This upmarket restaurant serves meticulously prepared Danish and Italian-inspired dishes. You can nibble on grilled focaccia in the leafy patio garden at lunchtime, or dine on substantial mains such as Jersey steak or duck with rhubarb in the evening.

❶ Information

Danske Bank (Nordre Strandvej 350) In the town centre.
Hornbæk Turistbureau (☎49 70 47 47; www.hornbaek.dk; Vestre Stejlebakke 2A; ☺1-5pm Mon & Thu, 10am-3pm Tue, Wed & Fri, 10am-2pm Sat) Inside the library. To reach it take the walkway at the side of Danske Bank. The library offers free internet access.
Post office (Sauntevej 1; ☺noon-5pm Mon-Fri, 10am-1pm Sat) Inside the Super Brugsen supermarket.

❶ Getting There & Around

Trains connect Hornbæk with Helsingør (38kr, 25 minutes) and Gilleleje (38kr, 15 minutes) about twice hourly.
Hornbæk Cykeludlejning (☎20 78 03 43; Nordre Strandvej 315D; ☺9am-noon & 3-4pm Mon-Wed, to 5pm Thu, 10am-noon Sat & Sun) Rent bicycles for 75kr per day.

Gilleleje

POP 6490

Gilleleje, Zealand's northernmost town, has been a fishing village since the 14th century and retains a certain timeless character. During WWII, its fishing boats were used to smuggle thousands of Jews to neutral Sweden, but don't expect any such excitement today. Low-key charms include several beaches, an early morning harbourside auction, bustling fish restaurants, and a coastal walk to a small monument dedicated to Kierkegaard. Between Hornbæk and Gilleleje is Tegners Museum and Statuepark, devoted to one of Denmark's leading sculptors.

◎ Sights & Activities

Beaches BEACH
Although they aren't as long and golden as those at Hornbæk or Tisvildeleje, beaches surround the town. The one on the western side, a stretch of sand and stone, meets Blue-Flag standards and has lifeguards in summer.

Tegners Museum & Statuepark MUSEUM, MONUMENTS
(www.rudolphtegner.dk; Museumsvej 19, Villingerød; adult/under 12yr 50kr/free; ☺9.30am-5pm Tue-Sun Jun-Aug, noon-5pm Tue-Sun mid-Apr–May & Sep–mid-Oct) One of the first Danish sculptors to discover concrete, Rudolph Tegner (1873–1950) used the wild heathland midway between Gilleleje and Hornbæk as a backdrop for his monumental sculptures, made of plaster, clay, bronze and marble. This museum now displays more than 250 of Tegner's pieces, while the surrounding grounds showcase 14 of his monumental bronze sculptures. The museum also functions as a mausoleum – Tegner is buried in a chamber in the heart of the building. From Gilleleje, bus 362 runs past the museum.

Fyrhistorik Museum på Nakkehoved MUSEUM
(Fyrvejen 20; adult/child incl entry to the Gilleleje Museum 60kr/free; ☺11am-4pm Tue-Sun mid-Jun–mid-Sep, reduced hrs rest of year) The eastern

ZEALAND GILLELEJE

lighthouse is now the Fyrhistorik Museum på Nakkehoved, which traces the history of Danish lighthouses from the 16th century. You can get to the lighthouse on the coastal footpath or by turning north off Rte 237 onto Fyrvejen.

Gilleleje Museum   MUSEUM
(Vesterbrogade 56; adult/under 18yr incl entry to Fyrhistorik Museum på Nakkehoved 35kr/free; ⊘1-4pm Wed-Mon Jun-Aug, 1-4pm Wed-Fri, 10am-2pm Sat Sep-May) This museum on the western side of town traces Gilleleje's history from the Middle Ages to the advent of summer tourism. It includes a 19th-century fisherman's house.

Walking Trails   WALKING
Of the two coastal trails, the one to the west, which starts near the intersection of Nordre Strandvej and Vesterbrogade, leads 1.75km to a stone memorial dedicated to the Danish philosopher Søren Kierkegaard, who used to make visits to this coast.

The trail to the east begins just off Hovedgade and leads 2.5km to the site where two lighthouses with coal-burning beacons were erected in 1772.

Havtur   BOAT TOURS, FISHING
(☑28 95 39 58; www.havtur.dk in Danish & German) It operates a number of boat tours, including a return trip to Kronborg Slot (300kr), a sunset tour (125kr) and four-hour fishing expeditions (250kr). Contact Havtur directly for up-to-date sailing times and prices.

🛏️ Sleeping

There are no hostels or camping grounds in Gilleleje, but tourist office staff can book rooms in private homes for around 450/800kr for singles/doubles, plus a 35kr booking fee.

Gilleleje Badehotel   HOTEL €€
(☑48 30 13 47; www.gillelejebadehotel.dk; Hulsøvej 15; r incl breakfast 890-1390kr; P 🛜) Kierkegaard was a frequent guest at this luxurious beach hotel. The atmosphere is so richly nostalgic you half expect the hotel to be sepia-tinted, but instead a soothing egg-white colour scheme prevails. All the rooms are bright and sunlit and most have balconies with views of Sweden. Use of the sauna and steam is complimentary, though use of the Jacuzzi is a brow-raising 275kr. The hotel is 1km west of town.

🍴 Eating

Adamsen's Fisk   SEAFOOD €
(Gilleleje Havn; plaice & chips 65kr; ⊘11am-9pm, sushi bar 11am-8pm) This popular harbourside takeaway peddles fish, seafood and sides of chips and more salubrious salads. The fish and seafood are heavily battered, so delicate stomachs and waist-watchers may prefer the grilled options. After selecting your combo, you're given a token which flashes when your order is ready. For those who prefer their fish raw, Adamsen's has a sushi bar next door (10-piece sushi set 125kr).

Restaurant Brasseriet   SEAFOOD €€
(Nordre Havnevej 3; smørrebrød 55-108kr, dinner mains 158-268kr; ⊘lunch & dinner) By the harbour, Brasseriet offers open sandwiches of whitebait, herring, plaice, eel, salmon, shrimps and meatballs at lunchtime. The evening menu also has a good choice of fish dishes, including seafood pasta and sautéed plaice, plus meaty mains such as rib-eye steak and veal. Vegetarians may struggle.

Gilleleje Havn   FRENCH-DANISH €€
(Havnevej 14; lunch mains 88-168kr, dinner mains 119-258kr; ⊘lunch & dinner) Gilleleje Havn is an excellent modern option, with an open kitchen and innovative menu of French/Danish seafood, with the odd piece of chicken/steak among the fish dishes. There are good views over the harbour.

Rogeriet Bornholm   SMOKEHOUSE €
(Gilleleje Havn; fish 35kr; ⊘9am-4pm) Close to Adamsen's, this simple smokehouse sells inexpensive smoked fish by the piece.

ℹ️ Information

Tourist office (☑48 30 01 74; www.visitnordsjaelland.dk; Hovedgade 6F; ⊘10am-6pm Mon-Sat mid-Jun–Aug, 10am-4pm Mon-Fri Sep–mid-Jun) In the town centre, 200m east of the train station.

ℹ️ Getting There & Around

Trains run between Hillerød and Gilleleje (60kr, 30 minutes), and between Helsingør and Gilleleje (72kr, 45 minutes), about twice hourly on weekdays, hourly at weekends.

Tisvildeleje

Tisvildeleje is essentially a glorious sweep of golden-sand beach with a small seaside village attached. The beach is backed by hills and forests, threaded through with nature trails. You could easily spend several relaxing days here, sunbathing, swimming, strolling through the woods, and generally taking things very, very easy.

◉ Sights & Activities

Beach BEACH

The Blue-Flag beach, a kilometre-long stretch of pure white sand at the foot of the village, is why people come to Tisvildeleje. A shallow-sloping shore and lifeguards at the height of summer make it a favourite with families. There are changing rooms, toilets and an ice-cream kiosk at the edge of the large parking area. Other beaches are accessible a short walk away from town.

Forest Trails WALKING

From the car park, you can walk along the beach or on a dirt path through the woods, about 3km south to **Troldeskoven** (Witch Wood), an area of ancient trees that have been sculpted into haunting shapes by the wind.

Inland from the beach is **Tisvilde Hegn**, a windswept forest of twisted trees and heather-covered hills that extends southwest for more than 8km. Much of this enchanting forest was planted in the 18th century to stabilise sand drifts engulfing the area. Tisvilde Hegn has numerous trails, including one to **Asserbo Slotsruin**, the moat-encircled ruins of a 12th-century manor house and monastery, near the southern boundary of the forest. Trail maps are available free from the tourist office.

🏨 Sleeping & Eating

TOP CHOICE **Helenekilde Badehotel** HOTEL €€€

(☑48 70 70 01; www.helenekilde.com; Strandvej 25; d facing inland 1295kr, d with sea view 1595-2095kr; P 🛜) Like Tisvildeleje Strand, the interior of this enchanting beachfront hotel was designed by the ballet dancer Alexander Kolpin, who also co-owns both properties. The string of stylish, cosy communal areas feature beautiful furnishings, art and the odd vintage suitcase-turned-coffee table. Rooms are simple yet elegant, with 16 of them looking out over the waves. Dreamy sea views are also on tap at its casually elegant **restaurant** (mains 185-225kr; ⊘lunch & dinner mid-Jun–mid-Aug), which serves up honest, rustic Danish fare to the sound of crashing waves. The hotel is a five-minute walk along a leafy lane (signposted from the station).

Tisvildeleje Strand Hotel HOTEL €€

(☑48 70 71 19; www.strand-hotel.dk; Hovedgaden 75; r 850-1450kr; ⊘late Jun–mid-Aug; P 🛜) This one-time party hotel has reinvented itself as a more refined slumber spot, its neutral tones, art books and weathered antiques giving the place a chic 'Hamptons' vibe. Rooms are a soothing combo of coconut rug carpets, woollen throws and contemporary charcoal-hued bathrooms. The three rooms with shared bathroom are cheaper (850kr). The hotel **restaurant** (tapas 125kr, dinner buffet adult/child 295/150kr; ⊘lunch & dinner late Aug–mid-Aug) is well-known for its dinner 'grill' buffet, which includes succulent meats, dips, a variety of salads, and fresh seasonal fruit. Best of all, the hotel is within easy walking distance.

Danhostel Tisvildeleje HOSTEL, CAMPING GROUND €

(☑48 70 98 50; www.helene.dk; Bygmarken 30; camping per person 50kr, dm/s/d 150/470/490kr; ⊘year-round; P @ 🛜) One kilometre east of town, this modern hostel and camping ground shares the excellent facilities of the Sankt Helene holiday complex. The grounds cover 12 hectares and have walking trails, sports fields, playgrounds, farm animals, kids' activities and a nice restaurant, and are within walking distance of a sandy beach. The complex is accessible to people in wheelchairs. By train, get off at Godhavns station, one stop before Tisvildeleje: the hostel is a short walk north.

Bed & Breakfast

Hårlandsgård GUESTHOUSE €

(☑48 70 83 96; www.haarlandsgaard.dk, in Danish; Harlands Allé 12; s 400kr, d 490-600kr; P) This 18th-century farmhouse, about 1km from town near Godhavns station, has a sunny garden, comfy rooms, and an art gallery in the former stables. Breakfast is an extra 60kr. It's the house on the right-hand side of the first sharp turn of Harlands Allé.

Tisvildeleje Cafeen INTERNATIONAL €€

(Hovedgaden 55; lunch mains 110-125kr, dinner mains 165-225kr; ⊘lunch & dinner daily summer, Fri-Sun only rest of year) A popular spot, complete with alfresco summertime seating, this cafe dishes up a worldly menu spanning smørrebrød, burgers and salads, to gazpacho and *moules marinières* (mariners' mussels). It's one of the venues for the annual Tisvildeleje folk festival, and features live music and DJs on Friday and Saturday nights in summer.

Tisvildeleje has a good bakery (Hovedgaden 60; ⊙7am-6pm), and there's a grocery shop further up the street. A couple of kiosks, one in town and one at the beach car park, sell burgers, hot dogs, pizzas and ice cream.

ℹ Information

Tourist office (☑48 70 71 06; www.visitnord sjaelland.dk; Banevej 8; ⊙noon-5pm Mon-Fri, 10am-3pm Sat mid-Jun–Aug) Seasonal office based in Tisvildeleje train station.

ℹ Getting There & Around

Getting round the coast from Gilleleje to Tisvildeleje by public transport isn't as simple as it might be. From Gilleleje, catch bus 360R to Helsinge, then the train to Tisvildeleje (36kr, 55 minutes Monday to Saturday, 80 minutes Sunday). Services run half-hourly to hourly on weekdays, and hourly on weekends. Trains also run between Tisvildeleje and Hillerød (60kr, 30 minutes) every 30 to 60 minutes.

FJORD TOWNS

Roskilde Fjord slices its way over 30km inland. Several towns lie scattered around its shores, the best of which is undoubtedly Roskilde itself, an unmissable tourist spot with its fascinating Unesco-blessed cathedral, Viking artefacts and huge rock festival.

Roskilde

POP 47,115

In July, fans pour into town for the four-day Roskilde Festival, which vies with Glastonbury for the title of Europe's biggest rock festival. Anyone who's anyone on the international scene has played here – past crowds have grunged out to Nirvana, head-banged before Metallica and danced like idiots to the Arctic Monkeys.

If you're not a festival fan, pity the poor fools for their warm beer and toilet queues, and relish the town instead. Roskilde is justly famous for its superb Viking Ship Museum and striking cathedral, the burial site of Danish royalty.

The town itself came to prominence in the Viking Age, when it was the capital of Denmark. Harald Bluetooth built Zealand's first wooden-stave Christian church here in AD 980. It was replaced by a stone building in 1026 on the instructions of a woman named Estrid, whose husband was assassinated in the stave church after a heated chess match

(only in Scandinavia!). The foundations of the 11th-century stone church are beneath the floor of the present-day cathedral.

Medieval Roskilde was a thriving trade centre and the powerhouse of Danish Catholicism, big enough to support the country's grandest cathedral. The town began its decline when the capital moved to Copenhagen in the early 15th century, and its population shrank radically after the Reformation in 1536.

These days, Roskilde is a popular day trip from Copenhagen, a mere 30km away.

◉ Sights

| TOP | Viking Ship Museum | MUSEUM |
(www.vikingshipmuseum.com; Vindeboder 12; adult/under 18yr 100kr/free; ⊙10am-5pm late Jun-Aug, to 4pm rest of year) People with an interest in the Vikings will be wowed by the superb Viking Ships Museum, which displays five Viking ships discovered at the bottom of Roskilde Fjord. The museum is made up of two main sections – the Viking Ship Hall, where the boats themselves are kept; and Museumsø, where archaeological work takes place. There are free 45-minute guided tours in English daily at noon and 3pm from late June to the end of August; and at noon on weekends in May and early to late June.

Viking Ship Hall
Roskilde's Viking-era inhabitants were expecting trouble in the mid-11th century. Five clinker-built ships, all made between 1030 and 1042, were deliberately scuttled in a narrow channel 20km north of Roskilde, presumably to block an attacking army. Once they had been holed and sunk, a mass of stones was piled on top to create an underwater barrier.

In 1962, a coffer dam was built around the barrier and sea water was pumped out. Within four months, archaeologists were able to remove the mound of stones and excavate the ships, whose wooden hulks were in thousands of pieces. These ship fragments were painstakingly reassembled onto skeleton frames in the purpose-built Viking Ship Hall. This brutal-looking minimalist construction becomes something magical inside, where the ghostly boats seem to float once more on the waters of the fjord.

The ships, known as Skuldelev 1, 2, 3, 5 and 6, show off the range of the Viking shipwrights: there's an ocean-going trading vessel, a 30m warship for international raiding, a coastal trader, a 17m warship probably used around the Baltic, and a fishing boat. Carbon dating and dendrochronology have discovered further secrets, including their builders' geographical scope – Skuldelev 1, for example, was made in Norway, whereas Skuldelev 2 came from Dublin.

Interesting displays about the Viking Age put the boats into a historical context, and the basement cinema runs a 14-minute film (in Danish, English, French, German, Italian and Spanish) about the 1962 excavation. There's also a fascinating exhibition and film documenting the nail-biting 2007–08 voyage of the *Havhingsten fra Glendalough* from Roskilde to Dublin and back. Based on the 60-oared warship Skuldelev 2, it's the largest Viking ship reconstruction to date (an incredible 340 trees went into its creation).

Museumsø

On Museum Island, adjacent to the Viking Ship Hall, craftspeople use Viking-era techniques and tools to build replicas of Viking ships. *Ottar, Havhingsten fra Glendalough, Roar Ege, Helge Ask* and *Kraka Fyr* (reconstructions of Skuldelev 1, 2, 3, 5 and 6 respectively) are moored in the **harbour**, where you can really appreciate their light, flexible designs.

In summer, a shipwright, blacksmith, tar-burner, weaver, rope-maker and fletcher demonstrate their crafts. Children can join in the fun by striking coins and painting their own shields.

Museumsø also has an **archaeological workshop** (☺10am-5pm), where you can watch researchers from the National Museum analysing recent excavations.

Boat Trips

If you've always had an urge to leap aboard a longboat for a spot of light pillaging, join one of the museum's hour-long boat trips. **Traditional Nordic boats** are propelled across the water by *you* and the rest of your shipmates.

From late June to mid-August, 50-minute trips run daily at noon and 2pm, with extra trips most days at 11am, 3pm and 4pm. Reduced sailings also take place from May to late June and from mid-August to the end of September, weather dependent. Call ahead on ☎46 30 02 00 to confirm sailing times. Tickets (80kr) are additional to the main museum entry ticket.

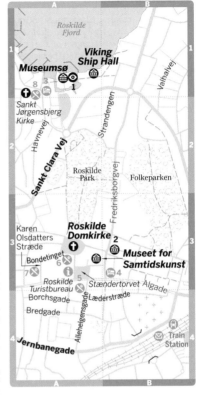

Roskilde

ROSKILDE ROCKS

Denmark's answer to Glastonbury and northern Europe's music festival heavyweight, Roskilde Festival (www.roskilde-festival.dk) is a four-day binge of bands and booze that rocks Roskilde every summer on the last weekend in June.

Since 1971, it has attracted the biggest and best international performers – some 170-plus rock, techno and world-music bands play on seven stages. The line-up in 2011 included Arctic Monkeys, Iron Maiden, Kings of Leon, PJ Harvey, Portishead and The Strokes... you get the picture! The promoters are astute at trend-spotting, so expect to see hot new bands who haven't yet come into the spotlight.

While the music is the main protagonist, there are plenty of other diversions, including a cinema, swimming lake and skatepark, plus yoga, dance workshops, art events and a naked run! Many people camp from the Sunday before the festival starts, spending four days 'warming up' for the festival proper. Stalls sell everything from tattoos to fast food but you may want to bring some food supplies as prices are high.

Tickets cost around 1830kr and can be purchased on the official festival website, which has a link to Billetlugen (www.billetlugen.dk). If lugging your own tent along seems bothersome, more expensive tickets (from 2390kr) are available that include a pre-pitched tent. There's a drunken-moron tradition of setting fire to tents at the end of the festival – beware.

Advance sales usually start in early December, but discounted 'early bird' tickets are sometimes available on the website months earlier. All 75,000-plus tickets are usually sold by June, so it pays to bag yours early.

Roskilde Domkirke   CATHEDRAL
(www.roskildedomkirke.dk; Domkirkepladsen; adult/10-18yr/under 10yr 60/20kr/free; ⊙9am-5pm Mon-Sat, 12.30-5pm Sun Apr-Sep, reduced hrs rest of year) Denmark's most amazing cathedral is Roskilde Domkirke, a designated Unesco World Heritage Site. It dates back to the 12th century, but has been added to so many times that it's now a superb showcase of 800 years' worth of Danish architecture. As the royal mausoleum, it contains the crypts of 37 Danish kings and queens – contemplating the remains of so many powerful historical figures is a moving memento mori. No fewer than 11 spectacular chapels and crypts sprout from the main body of the cathedral. No doubt every visitor will have their favourite: here are ours.

The chapel of King Christian IV, off the northern side of the cathedral, contains the builder king himself. His ocean-green coffin, surrounded by processing angels, is quite low-key for such an extravagant monarch. Most of the decoration in the chapel – vast, overly dramatic paintings of Christian's life surrounded by trompe l'oeil details – is actually from the 19th century, as the original sepulchre burned down a year before Christian's death. The only contemporary features are the chapel gates, so ornate they were said to have been created by the devil himself (although really the work of Christian's favourite metalsmith Caspar Fincke).

There are some fantastic 15th-century frescoes (the largest in Denmark) in the chapel of the Magi. It also contains the Renaissance sepulchres of Christian III and Frederik II, the most ornate in the cathedral. They look like antique temples, guarded by halberd-bearing soldiers. Another interesting feature of the chapel is the Royal Column, which shows the heights of visiting princes – from Christian I at a lofty 219.5cm down to titchy Christian VII at 164.1cm.

The neoclassical chapel of Frederik V whispers 'death' like no other part of the cathedral. You'll find 12 members of the royal family here, all interred in white alabaster sepulchres, surrounded by skulls, angels and weeping women.

The nave contains Christian IV's private box, and an intricate 17th-century pulpit (1610) made of marble, alabaster and sandstone by Copenhagen sculptor Hans Brokman. A killjoy dean disconnected the mechanism of the wonderful clock in the 18th century, annoyed that his parishioners paid more attention to it than to him, but today's church-people have relented. St George slays the dragon on the hour; the poor beast lets out a pitiful wheeze; and two ballad characters ting the bells.

Margrethe I's elegant sarcophagus and the shining golden altarpiece in the choir usually attract crowds of admirers. We prefer the wonderfully lively 15th-century choir-stall carvings: highlights from the New Testament line the northern side, and fearsome Old Testament tales adorn the south – Joseph being stuffed down a hole, Judith chopping off Holofernes' head, and Noah's family crammed into the ark...

Free concerts on the 16th-century baroque pipe organ are usually held at 8pm on Thursday in June, July and August. It's not unusual for the cathedral to be closed on Saturday for weddings, particularly in spring.

Museet for Samtidskunst MUSUEM
(Museum of Contemporary Art; www.samtidskunst. dk; Stændertorvet 3D; adult/student & under 18yr 40kr/free; ⊙11am-5pm Tue-Fri, noon-4pm Sat & Sun) Housed in the elegant 18th-century Roskilde Palace (built to be used by Christian VI whenever he was in town) is this surprisingly cutting-edge contemporary art space. Exhibitions lean towards new media, with often perplexing sound, video or performance installations by both Danish and international artists.

Roskilde Museum MUSEUM
(www.roskildemuseum.dk; Sankt Olsgade 18; adult/ child 25kr/free; ⊙11am-4pm) The well-presented Roskilde Museum covers Roskilde's history from the Stone Age through Harald Bluetooth's legacy to the contemporary 'rock age' of the Roskilde Festival. The exhibits have been arranged by two Danish artists, meaning that you get aesthetic pleasure along with an education.

⚡ Activities

You can hire kayaks for 175/300kr per two hours/day from Himmel & Hav (☑30 95 10 00; www.himmel-hav.dk, in Danish; Baunehøjvej 7; ⊙10am-sunset Apr-Sep), next door to Roskilde Camping.

🛏 Sleeping

Roskilde has limited accommodation for its size; being so close to Copenhagen, it's a popular day-trip destination. The tourist office books rooms in private homes for 450kr for doubles only, plus a 45kr booking fee.

Hotel Prindsen HOTEL €€
(☑46 30 91 00; www.prindsen.dk; Algade 13; s/d 1435/1535kr; P@⚟) First opened in 1695,

the centrally located Prindsen is Denmark's oldest hotel. It has a guest list that reads like a who's who of great Danes, from King Frederik VII to Hans Christian Andersen. The classically styled rooms are different sizes, but all have modern amenities and include breakfast. Deluxe rooms have sunken Jacuzzis and there's an in-house restaurant to boot. Rates drop on weekends and public holidays (singles/doubles 895/995kr).

Roskilde Camping CAMPING GROUND, CABINS €
(☑46 75 79 96; www.roskildecamping.dk; Baunehøjvej 7, Veddelev; camp site per person 80kr; ⊙Apr-Sep) Beautifully situated on the edge of Roskilde Fjord, 4km north of the Viking Ship Museum, this three-star camping ground is family-friendly with good facilities. There's a sandy Blue-Flag beach on the doorstep, and you can hire kayaks from Himmel & Hav next door. It's a 20-minute bus ride (24kr) by bus 603 from town.

Danhostel Roskilde HOSTEL €
(☑46 35 21 84; www.danhostel.dk/roskilde in Danish; Vindeboder 7; dm 180-250kr, s 425-525kr, d 450-650kr; ⊙year-round; P⚟) This modern hostel is right next door to the Viking Ship Museum. Each of the 40 large rooms has its own shower and toilet. Staff are friendly, although the mattress we slept on was frustratingly lop-sided. Wi-fi is an extra 20kr per hour (100kr per 24 hours).

Svogerslev Kro Hotel HOTEL €€
(☑46 38 30 05; www.svogerslevkro.dk; Svogerslev Hovedgade 45; s/d 725/950kr; P⚟) In a romantic red half-timbered building, this thatched inn is 4km west of town. Despite looking a little dowdy, the simply decorated rooms are homely and look onto the garden. There's a Danish/French restaurant, open daily for lunch and dinner. From Roskilde, it's a 20-minute ride on bus 602 (24kr).

🍴 Eating

Restaurant Mumm DANISH, INTERNATIONAL €€
(☑46 37 22 01; www.restaurantmumm.dk; Karen Olsdatters Stræde 9; 3/5/7 courses 435/535/635kr; ⊙dinner Mon-Sat) One of Roskilde's more exclusive dining destinations, Mumm takes Danish, French and Spanish influences and gives them a seriously creative twist. The result is nothing short of inspired, with dishes like fried catfish with pumpkin and liquorice, or silky cheesecake with blue cornflour and plums. Book ahead.

Store Børs
DANISH, INTERNATIONAL €€

(☑46 32 50 45; www.store-bors.dk, in Danish; Havnevej 43; lunch 85-158kr, dinner mains 218-278kr, 7-course tasting menu 495kr; ☺lunch & dinner Tue-Sat) Located down by the harbour, this melon-coloured cottage cooks up some of the town's finest food. The chefs smoke their own fish, use herbs from the restaurant garden, and create soulful evening gems such as fried mackerel with smoked potatoes, tarragon cream and sprouts. The lunch options offer simpler fare, including herring and cheese plates, carpaccio and beef tartar.

Raadhus-Kælderen
INTERNATIONAL €€

(www.raadhuskaelderen.dk; Stændertorvet; smørrebrød 42-108kr, dinner mains 168-328kr; ☺lunch & dinner Mon-Sat; ☎) Another reliable nosh spot is this atmospheric restaurant in the cellar of the old town hall (c 1430). Herring platters, salads, burgers and open sandwiches (including a gorgonzola and raw egg yolk number) feature on the lunch menu. The dinner menu is more ambitious, with dishes such as tomato soup with baked French goat cheese and a robust selection of grilled meats. Vegetarians may struggle, though.

Café Vivaldi
INTERNATIONAL €€

(Stændertorvet; salads 99kr, dinner mains 149-199kr; ☺lunch & dinner) Slap bang on the main square (cathedral views included), this modern faux-bistro is a good place to sit back and people-watch over abundant servings of tasty cafe grub. Edibles include soup, sandwiches, wraps, burgers and salads, as well as more substantial pasta and meat dishes. It's particularly handy on Sundays, when most of the town shuts down.

ℹ Information

Library (www.roskildebib.dk; Dronning Margrethes Vej 14; ☺10am-7pm Mon-Fri, 10am-2pm Sat year-round, also noon-4pm Sun mid-Sep–mid-Apr) Free internet access.

Nordea (Algade 4) One of several banks in the centre.

Post office (Jernbanegade 3; ☺10am-5.30pm Mon-Fri, 9am-1pm Sat) Next door to the train station.

Roskilde Turistbureau (☑46 31 65 65; www.visitroskilde.com; Stændertorvet 1; ☺10am-5pm Mon-Fri, to 2pm Sat Jul & Aug, reduced hrs rest of year) The tourist office provides information, as well as an accommodation booking service.

ℹ Getting There & Around

CAR If you're coming from Copenhagen by car, Rte 21 leads to Roskilde. Upon approaching the city, exit onto Rte 156, which leads into the centre. There is a large car park down by the Viking Ship Museum.

TRAIN Trains between Copenhagen and Roskilde are frequent (96kr, 25 minutes). Trains also run to Køge (48kr, 25 minutes) and Næstved (58kr, 42 minutes).

Lejre

The superb experimental archaeology centre outside Lejre (a tiny village about 8km southwest of Roskilde) is like nothing we've ever seen. Combine a visit to it with a trip to the palace, Ledreborg Slot, for a full day's outing.

◉ Sights

TOP CHOICE **Sagnlandet Lejre** HISTORIC RE-CREATION

(www.sagnlandet.dk; Slangealleen 2; adult/3-11yr 125/85kr; ☺10am-5pm late Jun–mid-Aug, 10am-4pm Tue-Fri, 11am-5pm Sat & Sun mid-Aug–mid-Sep, reduced hrs rest of year) The experimental archaeology centre 'Land of Legends' is an absolutely fascinating place. Here, enthusiastic re-enactors use ancient technology to test out various theories: How many people does it take to build a dolmen? What plants might have been used to dye clothing? And how do you stop the goats eating your reed roof?

The landscape at Lejre is just beautiful, with rolling hills and lake-filled hollows. A 3km-long path takes you past a Viking Age marketplace, prehistoric burial mounds, a dancing labyrinth, the Iron Age village 'Lethra', through fields of ancient crops, down to a sacrificial pool and over precarious staked-wood bridges.

Kids can let loose in the hands-on Fire Valley, paddling dug-out canoes, attempting to work a fire drill, baking biscuits and (ooh, it's hard not to wince) chopping up logs using primitive axes. Roaming aurochs and squelching, munching wild boar add to the fun.

Prices might look steep, but if you take a picnic and possibly some kids who don't mind losing a toe or two, you could easily spend most of the day here.

From Lejre train station, bus 233 will get you there.

DRAGSHOLM SLOT

Fancy a night in a culinary castle? Then pack your bag and your appetite and check in at Dragsholm Slot (✆59 65 33 00; www.dragsholm-slot.dk; Dragsholm Allé, Hørve; s/d from 1795/1995kr; ℗). Located at the edge of Zealand's fertile Lammefjorden (Denmark's most famous 'vegetable garden'), its medieval walls are home to Slotskøkkenet (The Castle Kitchen; 5/7 courses 650/800kr; ⊘dinner Tue-Sat late Jun-late Aug, Wed-Sat rest of Jun, reduced hrs rest of year), a New Nordic hot spot headed by ex-Noma chef Claus Henriksen. 'Locally sourced' is the catch-cry, from the area's prized carrots to herbs from the castle's own garden. The end result is deceptively simple, with sublime creations such as salads from the kitchen garden with oyster cream and juice of roasted peas. Upstairs, the more casual Spisehuset (2-/3-course lunch 195/245kr, 3-course dinner 345kr) offers cheaper, pared-back Nordic dishes using the same top-notch ingredients (think herb-marinated herring or hay-smoked salmon). Bookings are a must for Slotskøkkenet and recommended for Spisehuset.

Nosh aside, whitewashed Dragsholm is famed for its 800-year history, which includes the imprisonment of Roskilde's last Catholic bishop and the secret burial of a love-struck girl in the castle walls (eerily visible behind a plexiglass panel). While some rooms – spread across the castle and the nearby porter's lodge – feature contemporary styling, most ooze a distinguished baronial air, with anything from canopy beds to fleur-de-lis wallpaper and (in some cases) Jacuzzis. Add to this a string of Late Romantic salons and ballrooms and rambling fairy-tale gardens, and you'll soon be feeling like a well-fed noble. Check the website for dinner and accommodation packages (often cheaper than the official room rates), and request a room with field or garden views.

Dragsholm Slot is 91km west of Copenhagen via motorway 21. Getting here by public transport is very difficult.

Ledreborg Slot　　PALACE, GARDENS
(✆46 48 00 38; www.ledreborgslot.dk; Ledreborg Allé 2D; admission gardens 25kr, palace guided tour 2075kr, max 20 people; ⊘gardens 11am-4pm year-round, palace by guided tour only May-Sep) The grand manor house Ledreborg Slot is one of Denmark's finest rococo palaces. The stately home was built and decorated by Count Johan Ludvig Holstein in 1739: the count's descendants still live here, and the house's interior has barely changed in all that time. It's chock-full of curlicued furniture, gilded mirrors, chandeliers, oil paintings and wall tapestries. One of the most impressive rooms is the banquet room. You can also visit the family chapel, kitchens and – a house isn't a home without one – dungeon.

Outside are 80 hectares of gardens, recently restored to their full baroque glory; and in the woods you'll find the **Jungle Path**, a series of suspended walkways, ropes, ladders and installations. It's designed for children but is equally fun for adults.

❶ Getting There & Away

From Roskilde it's just a short train ride to Lejre station, where bus 233 continues to both Ledreborg Slot and Sagnlandet Lejre (24kr).

By car, from Roskilde take Ringstedvej (Rte 14), turn right on Rte 156 and then almost immediately turn left onto Ledreborg Allé. Follow the signs to Ledreborg, 6km away, where a long drive lined by old elm trees leads to the entrance. Sagnlandet Lejre is 2km further west along the same road.

SOUTHERN ZEALAND

While northern Zealand lays claim to most of the island's must-see sites, the island's south is not without its drawcards. You'll find Denmark's best preserved ring fortress at Trelleborg and its oldest half-timbered house in Køge. The region is also home to one of Denmark's most shamelessly charming enchanting hamlets, Vallø, as well as the soothing Suså River, a picture-perfect, kayak-friendly escape route.

Køge

POP 35,105

The country's largest town square sits at the heart of Køge, creating an open, relaxed feel straightaway. The main joy here is to wander the narrow cobbled streets containing

Denmark's best-preserved 17th- and 18th-century buildings. Add in a decent array of independent shops and tempting restaurants, and your maximum walking speed will be a lazy amble.

Køge is also a thriving fishing and trade centre. There are narrow beaches along the bay to the north and south of town, although you'll need to ignore the somewhat industrial backdrop of the modern commercial harbour.

In 1677 a vital naval engagement was fought in the waters off Køge. Known as the Battle of Køge Bay, it made a legend of Danish admiral Niels Juel, who resoundingly defeated the attacking Swedish navy.

⊙ Sights

Køge Museum   MUSEUM
(www.koegemuseum.dk, in Danish; Nørregade 4; adult/child 30kr/free; ⊙11am-5pm Tue-Sun Jun-Aug, 1-5pm Tue-Fri & Sun, 11am-3pm Sat Sep-May) Once a merchant's home, Køge Museum occupies a lovely half-timbered building dating from 1619.

As well as the expected furnishings, local-history artefacts and a large textile collection, there are two significant exhibits. One is the **Strøby Egede** grave from 4000 BC, containing the skeletons of eight children and adults – the only mass grave from that era to be found in Europe. The other is Denmark's biggest **coin-hoard**, a shining pile of 17th-century silver unearthed in the courtyard at Brogade 17 by two electricians. The 32kg pile is thought to have been stashed away during the Danish-Swedish wars.

In Hans Christian Andersen's day, a local inn was supposed to have had the words 'God, Oh God in Kjøge' scratched onto a windowpane. Failing to find the inscription, Andersen vandalised a window himself – writing smugly in his diary 'I wrote it, and now it is very legible'. The museum has the glass on show.

KØS   MUSEUM
(www.koes.dk; Nørregade 29; adult/18-24yr/under 18yr incl entry to the Køge Museum 50/20kr/free; ⊙10am-5pm Tue-Sun) Køge's Museum of Art in Public Spaces, Køge Skitsesamling is a unique entity, displaying not the artists' finished work, but the notes and scribblings, sketches, models and mock-ups that built

---

RINGSTED'S ROYAL CHURCH

Ringsted is mostly a modern town, with a bustling shopping centre but little in the way of tourist attractions. However, if you're passing through, it's worth stopping at the imposing **Sankt Bendts Kirke** (Sankt Bendtsgade 1; admission free; ⊙10am-5pm May–mid-Sep, 1-3pm rest of year), Scandinavia's oldest brick church. It was built in 1170 by Valdemar I, partly as a burial sanctuary for his father, Knud Lavard, and partly as a political act, to intertwine the influences of the Valdemar family and the Catholic Church.

Sankt Bendts' most interesting features are its magnificent 14th-century **frescoes**. These include a series depicting Erik IV (1216–50), whose short and turbulent reign saw him warring against his own family and the local peasantry, before he was assassinated on the orders of his brother Abel. The frescoes of Erik (known as 'Ploughpenny' for the despised tax he levied on ploughs) were painted in a doomed campaign to get the dead king canonised. They show Queen Agnes seated on a throne; on her left Ploughpenny's murderers stab the king with a spear, while on the right the king's corpse is retrieved from the sea by fishermen.

The church was a **royal burial place** for 150 years: flat stones in the aisle floor beneath the nave mark the graves of Denmark's early royals. An interesting find came from one of these tombs. Queen Dagmar (1186–1213), the first wife of Valdemar II, was a Bohemian princess revered by the Danes. In 1683, her tomb was opened and a small gold cross with finely detailed enamel work was discovered. Now known as the **Dagmar Cross**, it is thought to date from AD 1000. One side shows Christ with arms outstretched on the cross and the other side depicts him with the Virgin Mary, John the Baptist, St John and St Basil. The Byzantine-styled cross is now in the national museum in Copenhagen, with a replica on display in Sankt Bendts Kirke. Copies are traditionally worn by brides who marry in the church.

Note that the church is closed to visitors whenever there are weddings, a particularly common occurrence on Saturdays in April and May.

ZEALAND KØGE

Køge

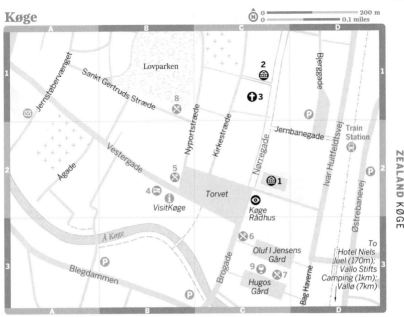

up into the final piece. It's fascinating, particularly for non-artists, to see the creative process deconstructed.

Sankt Nicolai Kirke   CHURCH
(Kirkestræde 31; admission free; ⏰10am-4pm Mon-Fri, noon-4pm Sun) Named after the patron saint of mariners, the Sankt Nicolai Kirke is two blocks north of Torvet.

On the upper eastern end of the church tower there's a little brick projection called Lygten, which was used to hang a burning lantern as a guide for sailors returning to the harbour. It was from the top of the church tower that Christian IV kept watch on his naval fleet as it successfully defended the town from Swedish invaders during the Battle of Køge Bay.

From July to early August, you can climb the 14th-century tower (adult/child 10/5kr; ⏰noon-4pm Mon-Fri), the oldest part of the church. Inside, features worth noting include the ornate 17th-century altar and pulpit, and the carved wooden gallery that raised Køge's nobility above the rabble.

Beaches & Harbour   BEACH
Early risers can watch the fishermen unload herring and eels at the working harbour. The yacht harbour lies 2km to the north,

Køge

◎ Sights
1 Køge Museum	C2
2 KØS	C1
3 Sankt Nicolai Kirke	C1

🛏 Sleeping
4 Centralhotellet	B2

🍴 Eating
5 Café Vivaldi	B2
6 Kant	C3
7 Sandwich Cafeen	C3
8 StigAnn	B1

🍷 Drinking
9 Hugos Vinkjælder	C3

and there are two beaches, lying north and south of the industrial harbour.

The large inlet Køge Bay, which looks as though someone has taken a huge bite out of Zealand's east coast, is well-known for the beaches at Solrød and Greve, 8km and 17km north of Køge respectively. They're a popular escape for the city-dwellers of Copenhagen, just a short ride away on the city's S-train.

KØGE: THE OLD & THE BEAUTIFUL

Storybook buildings pepper the streets of Køge, turning the clock back a few hundred years and firing up the imagination.

West of Torvet (Køge's main square), **Vestergade 7** dates from the 16th century, while **Vestergade 16** dates from 1644. The latter is a remarkably well-preserved merchant's house, featuring old hand-blown glass in the doors and intricately carved detail on the timbers.

Just off the northern edge of Torvet, **Kirkestræde 3** is the house built by Oluf Sandersen and his wife Margareta Jørgensdatter in 1638, the date recorded in the lettering above the gate. Half-timbered **Kirkestræde 13** dates from the 16th century – its twisting chimney pot was an advert to passers-by seeking a blacksmith. Another 17th-century house at **Kirkestræde 10** is now a kindergarten, while **Kirkestræde 20**, built in 1527, is the oldest half-timbered house in Denmark. Its 4m-by-5m dimensions housed a late-19th-century tanner, his wife and 10 children.

Handsome, red-timbered **Nørregade 31** dates back to 1612. South on Nørregade are more houses built in the early 17th century: **Nørregade 5** and **Nørregade 4**, the latter now home to the Køge Museum.

On the corner building at Torvet 2 is a marble **plaque** marked *Kiøge Huskors* (Kiøge and Kjøge are old spellings of Køge). It honours the victims of a witch-hunt in the 17th century, when 16 people were burned at the stake, including two residents of an earlier house on this site. Along the eastern side of Torvet is the yellow neoclassical **Køge Rådhus**, said to be the oldest functioning town hall in Denmark. At the back is a building erected in 1600 to serve as an inn for King Christian IV, when he travelled from his Copenhagen palace to visit his mother at Nykøbing Slot.

By the southeastern corner of Torvet, **Brogade 1** has housed a pharmacy on this site since 1660. Further south at **Brogade 7**, Oluf I Jensens Gård is a courtyard lined with a collection of typical 19th-century merchant buildings. **Brogade 19** is home to Hugos Gård, an even older courtyard. The wine bar Hugos Vinkjælder (see p111) contains a medieval brick-built cellar dating to 1300.

In the adjacent courtyard, at **Brogade 17**, workers unearthed a buried treasure in 1987 – an old wooden trunk filled with over 2000 17th-century silver coins, the largest coin-hoard ever found in Denmark. Some are on display at the Køge Museum. **Brogade 23** was built around 1638, its carved cherubs the work of famed 17th-century artist Abel Schrøder. Across the street, back towards Torvet, **Brogade 16** is famed as Køge's longest timber-framed house, erected in 1636 by the town's mayor.

🛏 Sleeping

The tourist office can book rooms in private homes for around 500kr per double; there's a 25kr booking fee.

Vallø Stifts Camping   CAMPING GROUND, CABINS €
(☎56 65 28 51; www.valloecamping.dk; Strandvejen 102; camp site per adult/child 72/40kr; ⊙Apr-Sep; @🛜) Technically part of Vallø, but actually only 1km from the centre of Køge, this lovely, leafy camping ground is inside a seaside nature reserve. It's ideal for families with young children – there are goats, mini-golf, table tennis, pétanque and playgrounds onsite, and a child-friendly beach just across the road. The camping ground also rents out basic four- to six-person wooden huts (per night 325kr to 565kr), as well as blankets, pillows and bed sheets.

Centralhotellet   HOTEL €€
(☎56 65 06 96; Vestergade 3; s/d without bathroom 420/795kr, with bathroom 595/895kr; P @) The aptly named Centralhotellet is adjacent to the tourist office. Charming owners Eva and Finn are slowly sprucing up the place, with a dozen very straightforward rooms above a small bar and in a separate wing at the back. Three of the doubles have bathrooms. Bike rental is also available (one/three days 80/200kr).

Hotel Niels Juel   HOTEL €€
(☎56 63 18 00; www.hotelnielsjuel.dk; Toldbodvej 20; s 775-1195kr, d 975-1395kr; P 🛜) Overlooking the harbour a couple of blocks south of the train station, this pleasant hotel/restaurant combo offers 51 well-furnished rooms in two colour schemes: maritime blue or warm-

and-earthy. All include phone, minibar and satellite TV, and all have been decorated with feng shui principles in mind! Wi-fi is an extra 50kr per 24 hours.

Danhostel Køge HOSTEL €
(🖂56 67 66 50; www.danhostel.dk/koege; Vamdrupvej 1; dm 200kr, s & d 380-480kr; ⊘yearround; 🅿@) In a quiet area 2km northwest of town, this friendly 116-bed hostel has small but cosy rooms, all with alarm clocks; those upstairs have velux windows with nice sky views. The more expensive rooms come with bathrooms. There's a laundry, small playground and breakfast buffet (50kr). To get here from Køge, catch bus 101A and get off at Norsvej, from where the hostel is an 850m walk.

✗ Eating

StigAnn INTERNATIONAL €€
(www.stigann.dk; Sankt Gertruds Stræd 2; lunch 65-110kr, dinner mains 195-255kr; ⊘lunch Fri & Sat, dinner Mon-Sat) One of Køge's best restaurants by far offers refined and ambitious Danish dishes with global twists – think smoked duck breast with marinated cranberry and walnut salad, or king prawns with a garlic and papaya chutney. Mains are mostly carnivorous.

Kant INTERNATIONAL €€
(Brogade 7; lunch 65-110kr, dinner mains 185-218kr; ⊘lunch daily, dinner Mon-Sat) Youthful Kant fuses a trendy bistro style with fresh, generous cafe standards like salads, club sandwiches and nachos. Slide onto the lipstick-red sofas for afternoon coffee and cake or tuck into the small but satisfying selection of dinner options, which might include fried mullet with sautéed spinach, mashed potatoes and a splash of lemon. There's a weekend brunch buffet (109kr), as well as alfresco courtyard seating in the warmer months.

Café Vivaldi INTERNATIONAL €€
(www.cafevivaldi.dk; Torvet 30; lunch 89-109kr, dinner mains 149-199kr; ⊘lunch & dinner) This chain 'bistro' is a safe bet for tasty, straightforward cafe grub like salads, sandwiches, burgers, burritos and more substantial meat and fish dishes. Order at the counter. There's seating right on the square and, at weekends, live music and a buzzing bar vibe.

Sandwich Cafeen SANDWICHES €
(Brogade 19; sandwiches 28-52kr, salads 32-44kr; ⊘10am-6pm Mon-Fri, to 3pm Sat) Situated in

Hugos Gård, this little shop probably sells the cheapest sandwiches in town. It also peddles salads and milkshakes. Take them away, or devour them at one of the few small tables in the courtyard.

There's a produce, cheese and flower market at Torvet on Wednesday and Saturday mornings.

🍷 Drinking

Hugos Vinkjælder WINE BAR
(Brogade 19; ⊘1-11pm Mon-Thu, to 2am Fri & Sat, to 6pm Sun) Hugos is a fantastic place, a dark and cosy little wine bar, curled up in a 14th-century cellar. The wine list is good, but it's the choice of almost 200 beers from around the world that really gives a rush of pleasure. It includes beers from several Danish microbreweries, including local outfit Bryghuset Braunstein. While you can't buy meals here, you're welcome to buy lunch from Sandwich Cafeen next door and eat it here. In summer, live jazz bands play in the courtyard around noon on Saturday.

ℹ Information

Library (www.koegebib.dk; Kirkestræde 18; ⊘10am-6pm Mon-Fri, to 2pm Sat) Free internet
Nordea (Torvet 14) Bank with ATMs.
Post office (Jernstøbervænget 2; ⊘10am-5.30pm Mon-Fri, 10am-1pm Sat)
VisitKøge (🖂56 67 60 01; www.visitkoege.com; Vestergade 1; ⊘9am-6pm Mon-Fri, 9am-3pm Sat) The tourist bureau is just off the town's main square.

ℹ Getting There & Away

BOAT BornholmerFærgen (🖂70 23 15 15; www.bornholmerfaergen.dk) Runs daily, year-round ferries between Køge and Rønne, on the Danish island of Bornholm. From Køge, the ferry departs at 12.30am, arriving in Rønne at 6am. From Rønne, the ferry leaves at 5pm, arriving in Køge at 10.30pm. A single fare costs 266/284/133kr per adult/adult cyclist/12-to-15-year-old. A car including five people costs 1532kr to 1550kr.
CAR Køge is 42km southwest of Copenhagen and 23km southeast of Roskilde. If you're coming by road take the E47/E55 from Copenhagen or Rte 6 from Roskilde and then pick up Rte 151 south into the centre of Køge.
TRAIN Køge is the southernmost station on greater Copenhagen's S-train network, at the end of the E line. Trains from Copenhagen (108kr, 40 minutes) run three to six times an hour. Køge is also on the train line between

Roskilde (48kr, 25 minutes) and Næstved (58kr, 40 minutes), with trains running to both towns approximately every half hour to hour.

ℹ Getting Around

You can hire bikes from Centralhotellet (p110) for 80kr per day, plus a 500kr deposit.

Car drivers can park in Torvet, but only for an hour; turn down Brogade, then follow Fændediget round for less-restricted free parking off Bag Haverne and north of the harbour.

Vallø

Tiny Vallø is a deeply romantic fairy-tale hamlet with cobblestone streets, a dozen mustard-yellow houses and an attractive moat-encircled Renaissance castle, Vallø Slot. Situated in the countryside about 7km south of Køge, Vallø makes a wonderful little excursion for those looking to get off the beaten track.

⊙ Sights

Vallø Slot   CASTLE, GARDENS
(www.valloe-stift.dk) Red-brick Vallø Slot ticks all the 'proper castle' boxes, with pointy turrets and a moat filled with lily pads and croaking frogs. Also like a proper castle, it's not open to riff-raff, ie the public. But you can walk in the beautiful woods and **gardens** (⊙8am-sunset) that extend from the castle building all the way to the sea.

Vallø Slot has a rather unusual history. On her birthday in 1737 Queen Sophie Magdalene, who owned the estate, established a foundation that turned the castle into a home for 'spinsters of noble birth'. Unmarried daughters of Danish royalty unable to live in their own castles were allowed to live at Vallø, supported by the foundation and government social programs. In the 1970s, bowing to changing public sentiments, the foundation amended its charter and declined to accept new residents. For now, the castle remains home solely to a handful of ageing blue-blooded women who took up residence before 1976.

The castle has retained its original 16th-century style, although much of it was rebuilt following a fire in 1893.

🛏 Sleeping & Eating

Vallø Slotskro   INN €€
(✏restaurant 56 26 62 66, inn 56 26 70 20; www.valloeslotskro.dk in Danish; Slotsgade 1; 3/4/5/6

courses 400/475/550/600kr; ⊙restaurant dinner Wed-Sat; P) Just outside the castle gate, this 200-year-old inn harbours an elegant restaurant of crisp white linen and decadent Franco-Danish dishes such as quail with foie gras and summer truffles. Alas, the inn's seven double rooms were closed for a revamp during our visit. Check the website for updates, as an overnight stay in Vallø makes for an enchanting retreat.

ℹ Getting There & Away

Take the train to Vallø station, two stops south of Køge, and from there it's an easy 1.25km stroll east down a tree-lined country road to the castle.

If you're travelling by road take Rte 209 south from Køge, turn right onto Billesborgvej and then left (south) onto Valløvej, which leads to Slotsgade.

There's a signposted cycle route from Køge that leads into Valløvej.

Sorø

POP 7805

Thick with old timber-framed houses and framed by peaceful lakes and woodlands, Sorø is a soulful, off-the-radar spot. It owes its existence to Sorø Akademi, an elite school for noblemen's sons established by Christian IV. The academy remains a prestigious school to this day; its grounds and lakeside park are open to the public, and make for an idyllic late-afternoon stroll.

During Denmark's 'Golden Age' (1800–50) of national romanticism, Sorø became a haunt for some of the country's most prominent cultural figures, including Bertel Thorvaldsen, NFS Grundtvig and Adam Oehlenschläger.

⊙ Sights & Activities

For a dose of vintage charm, slip into **Søgade**, a street that's lined with leaning half-timbered, mustard-yellow houses with red tiled roofs. You'll find it on the west side of the town's main square, Torvet.

Sorø Kirke   CHURCH
(admission free; ⊙10am-4pm Mon-Sat, noon-4pm Sun) Denmark's largest monastery church, and one of the country's oldest brick buildings, is the 12th-century Sorø Kirke, in the centre of the academy grounds. The Romanesque interior is simple and harmonious, brightened by **medieval frescoes** of blue, red, orange, green and white geometric pat-

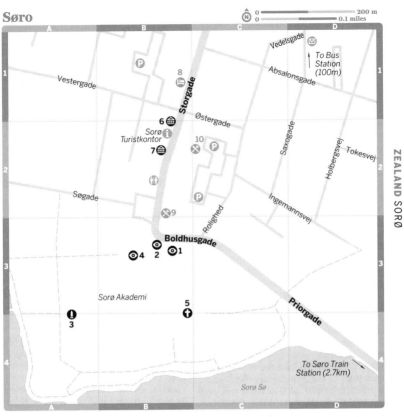

Søro

terns, shields and leaves, and lightened by a high 13th-century Gothic ceiling.

Bishop Absalon, a member of the influential Hvide family, was one of Denmark's most significant medieval statesmen. He established a Cistercian monastery in Sorø in 1161 and had this church built in the grounds to serve as a family mausoleum. Famous people who are buried here include the bishop, interred in a prime position directly behind the main altar. In a display cabinet to the right of the altar are the ivory crosier, gold-and-sapphire ring and silver chalice with which he was buried (extracted from his tomb in the 19th century).

Keeping Absalon company are kings Valdemar IV, Christopher II and Oluf III. Queen Margrethe I, the architect of the 1397 Kalmar Union, was buried here as well, but her remains were later transferred to Roskilde Domkirke. At the end of the left aisle is the marble sarcophagus of the great comic poet and playwright Ludvig Holberg.

The church's grand interior includes a 6m-high 16th-century crucifix by Odense sculptor Claus Berg, carved from a single piece of wood, and a beautifully detailed baroque altar and pulpit. The 16th-century **organ** is the centrepiece of the Sorø International Music Festival.

Sorø Akademi   HISTORIC BUILDINGS, GARDENS

After the Reformation, Frederik II decreed that Sorø's monastery should be turned into a school. In 1623, his successor, Christian IV, developed it into the Sorø Academy of Knights, an elite establishment dedicated to the education of the sons of the nobility. Lessons included the art of hunting, behaviour and manners – skills fitting to a noble diplomat.

Today its intake is a little less exclusive, but Sorø Akademi remains a prominent Danish school. The extensive grounds are owned by a private foundation (though the school itself is state-funded), and visitors are welcome to amble through them.

The southern end of Sorø's main street, Storgade, leads directly to the academy via Klosterporten, a medieval gate that once cloistered the monks from the outside world.

Other medieval monastery buildings were replaced with Renaissance structures – thought to be more conducive to learning – in the 17th century. Ridehuset, immediately west of Klosterporten, was built by Christian IV to stable the horses and dogs used for hunting. Boldhuset, just east of Klosterporten, also dates from the reign of Christian IV and now houses the library.

A statue of the great Danish playwright Ludvig Holberg (1684–1754), who rescued the school after a financial crisis forced it to close, can be found in the garden area in the western part of the grounds. Picturesque walking trails lead west from the statue down to Sorø Sø.

Vestsjællands Kunstmuseum   ART MUSEUM

(Art Museum of West Zealand; www.vestkunst.dk, in Danish; Storgade 9; adult/child 50kr/free; ⊙see website) At the time of research, Vestsjællands Kunstmuseum was due to reopen in autumn 2011 after a major refurbishment, including an award-winning extension by Copenhagen-based architects Lundgaard & Tranberg. The museum's booty spans 300 years of Danish art, with works running the gamut from medieval woodcarvings to wildly expressionist modern art. Check the website for updated opening times and changing exhibitions.

FREE Sorø Museum   MUSEUM

(www.aabne-samlinger.dk/SVM/soroe; Storgade 17; ⊙1am-4pm Tue-Thu & Sun, 11am-2pm Sat) The regional Sorø Museum is housed in a handsome half-timbered building dating from 1625. It contains rooms with period furnishings, from a peasant's quarters to the stylish living room of an aristocrat. There's also a grocery shop from 1880 and a room furnished with the personal belongings of the 19th-century poet BS Ingemann, who taught at Sorø Akademi. Most of the information is in Danish only.

☆ Festivals & Events

The Sorø International Music Festival (www.soroemusik.dk, in Danish) is held at Sorø Kirke, with classical concerts held mostly on Wednesday evening from late June to late August; tickets (75kr to 130kr) are available from the tourist office or at the venue 75 minutes before show time.

🛏 Sleeping

Sorø Camping   CAMPING GROUND, CABINS €

(☑57 83 02 02; www.soroecamping.dk; Udbyhøjvej 10; camp site per adult/child 79/40kr; ⊙Mar-Oct; P🐾) Three-star Sorø camping ground has a bucolic setting, on the edge of Pedersborg Sø northwest of town, about 150m north of Slagelsevej. There's a shop and laundry, two family bathrooms, toilets accessible to people in wheelchairs, baby goats, lollipop-making sessions, mini-golf and a 'bouncy pillow' to keep kids amused. Four- to six-person cabins and apartments (per night 450kr to 800kr) are also available. A 1km-long lakeside trail winds its way into town, or take bus 806 or 807. There are bicycles for hire and wi-fi access.

Hotel Postgaarden   HOTEL €€

(☑57 83 22 22; www.hotelpostgaarden.dk in Danish; Storgade 25; s/d 750/925kr; P@🐾) A good choice in the centre of town, this recently refurbished inn-style hotel boasts a 300-year history. Its 18 rooms may not be cutting-edge, but they're pleasant and comfortable. Some face the main pedestrianised street, while others look onto a quiet courtyard. There's a restaurant, wireless internet, and a web-connected computer located in the lobby.

LIFESTYLES OF THE RICH & VIKING

Denmark's richest Viking site is the 6th-century Viking manor house on the western shore of lake Tissø, between Slagelse and Kalundborg.

The most famous find (so far) is a massive solid-gold necklace, weighing 1.8kg. It's now displayed in Copenhagen's national museum, with a replica in Kalundborg museum. Over 10,000 items have been found since digs began in earnest in 1995, with the extent and high calibre of the finds causing real excitement. An abundance of Arabian and Nordic coins, beautifully cast silver brooches, animal-entwined bronze pendants, a golden hinge, a tuning-peg for a harp, and top-quality sword handles and stirrups, all dating from 500 to 1050 AD, are just some of the aristocratic treasures found.

The manor-house complex, four times the size of any other so far discovered, is thought to have been a royal estate, holiday home, hunting lodge, banquet house or cult centre (20 Thors' hammers have been found there), or possibly some combination of the above. The absence of any graves at the site leads archaeologists to believe that it wasn't a permanent dwelling-place.

Some experts think the site may have been the ancient seat of Viking kings. Artefacts from England, Ireland, Germany and Norway indicate that the manor house's visitors were heavily involved in military adventures and plundering – and therefore the elite of Viking society.

Getting here by public transport is difficult.

Danhostel Sorø   HOSTEL €
(☎57 84 92 00; www.kongskildefriluftsgaard.dk, in Danish; Skælskørvej 34; r 465kr; ☺year-round; ⓟ) This old lakeside watermill is set in a wonderful spot in the middle of a nature reserve, also known as Kongskilde Friluftsgård. On Rte 157, 9km southwest of town (take bus 615), it's a popular respite for hikers and cyclists – two national cycle routes, Nos 6 and 7, cross right at the inn. Hostel rooms (with washbasins) cost the same whether there's one occupant or four; they're fairly bog-standard and on the dim side, but with all this fresh air about, hopefully you won't spend much time indoors.

✖ Eating

Støvlet-Katrines Hus   FRENCH-DANISH €€€
(☎57 83 50 80; www.stovletkatrineshus.dk; Slagelsevej 63; 3-/5-course dinner 355/475kr; ☺lunch daily, dinner Mon-Sat) Originally built as a home for Christian VII's mistress, this atmospheric place is on the western edge of town. Today it's a grand gourmet restaurant, serving splendid French-influenced Scandi dishes such as grilled Norwegian lobster with rosehip compote, red currant, orange foam, malt and avocado cream. A wine selection matches each course. To get here from the centre of town, walk north along Storgade, turning left into Hauchsvej (which becomes Kongebrovej). The restaurant is at the end of the street (on the corner with Slagelsevej).

Ristorante Valencia   ITALIAN €€
(www.valencia.dk in Danish; Storgade 6; lunch meals 45-99kr, dinner mains 120-255kr; ☺lunch & dinner) This friendly Italian bistro-restaurant makes a great lunch stop, with a creamy interior cooled by breezy fans, and a view onto Torvet. Open sandwiches are big and beautifully presented, and there are one or two veggie choices. In the evening, there's a decent choice of Italian-, French- and Spanish-inspired meat and fish dishes.

There are several places to get cheap meals including a bakery and a takeaway pizzeria on Storgade. You can buy groceries at the **Super Best supermarket** (Storgade 28).

❶ Information

Library (Storgade 7; ☺2-7pm Mon, 10am-6pm Tue, Thu & Fri, 10am-7pm Wed, 10am-1pm Sat) Free internet access.

Nordea (Storgade 22) One of several banks in town.

Post office (Rådhusvej 6; ☺noon-5pm Mon-Fri, 10am-noon Sat)

Sorø Turistkontor (☎57 82 10 12; www.soroe. dk/cms/site.aspx?p=1504, in Danish; Storgade 15; ☺1-5pm Mon, 10am-5pm Tue-Fri, 10am-1pm Sat Jun-Aug, reduced hrs rest of year) Sorø's tourist office.

ℹ Getting There & Away

CAR Sorø is 15km east of Slagelse and 16km west of Ringsted via Rte 150 or the E20.

TRAIN Sorø train station is in Frederiksberg, 3km south of the town centre – buses 806 and 570 run from central Sorø to the train station at least half-hourly. Sorø is on the line between Copenhagen (89kr, 50 minutes) and Odense (164kr, 50 minutes), with trains running approximately every 30 to 60 minutes. Nearby towns on the same line include Slagelse (39kr, 10 minutes), Korsør (52kr, 20 minutes), Ringsted (39kr, 10 minutes) and Roskilde (49kr, 25 minutes).

Trelleborg

The best preserved of the four Viking ring fortresses in Denmark, Trelleborg is 7km west of Slagelse and 22km west of Sorø. Admittedly, Slagelse is rather uninspiring, so consider making Sorø your base if staying overnight. If you choose to stay in Slagelse, contact the Slagelse Turistbureau (☏70 25 22 06; www.visitsydvestsjaelland.dk) for accommodation options.

◉ Sights

TOP CHOICE Trelleborg ARCHAEOLOGICAL SITE
(www.vikingeborg.dk; Trelleborg Allé 4; adult/under 18yr 60kr/free; ⊙10am-5pm Tue-Sun Jun-Aug, 10am-4pm Tue-Sat Apr, May, Sep & Oct) History buffs will revel in visiting one of the most important Viking Age sites, while others may just enjoy strolling the site, which is in a deeply peaceful countryside setting at the confluence of two gurgling streams.

Museum

Before you head across the meadows to the fortress itself, visit the small but very informative museum, which explains how the fort was built, occupied and abandoned.

Displays contain weapons belonging to soldiers at the fort (spearheads, axes, arrowheads and shield bosses), as well as everyday items (pottery, bronze jewellery, locks and keys, combs and loom weights). There are also two skeletons from the graveyard.

The Fortress

Trelleborg was constructed as a circular fortress, built to a precise mathematical plan (see the boxed text, this page) and home to a garrison of around 500 soldiers, plus craftsmen and some women and children. Huge earthen banks, 17m wide and 6m high, formed a protective wall around the fort. Inside, two streets divided the circle into quarters, each containing four longhouses set around a courtyard. Two nearby streams gave the inhabitants boat access inland and out to the sea.

Trelleborg's impressive scale and strategic position, and the similarly designed forts at Fyrkat, Nonnebakken and Aggersborg, indicate a powerful 10th-century force at work, with immense manpower to command. Dendrochronology has shown that the trees for the palisade (which added an extra defensive layer to the earth banks) were cut down in AD 980, during the reign of Harald Bluetooth. One theory is that the forts were built by Harald after an uprising led by his son, Svein Forkbeard.

TRELLEBORG: VIKING PRECISION

While Vikings aren't usually associated with scientific sophistication in the popular imagination, Trelleborg's military origins are visible in its precise mathematical layout and use of the Roman foot (29.33cm) as a unit of measurement.

The Trelleborg compound consists of two wards that encompass about 7 hectares in all. The inner ward is embraced by a circular earthen rampart 6m high and 17m thick at its base. Four gates, one at each point of the compass, cut through the rampart. The ward is crossed by two streets, one east–west, the other north–south, which divide it into four symmetrical quadrants. In Viking times, each quadrant contained four long elliptical buildings surrounding a courtyard. Each of the 16 buildings was exactly 100 Roman feet long and contained a central hall and two smaller rooms.

An 18m-wide ditch ran around the exterior of the inner rampart; two bridges spanned the ditch, crossing over to the outer ward. This outer ward contained a cemetery holding about 135 graves and 15 buildings, each of which was 90 Roman feet long and lined up radially with its gable pointing towards the inner rampart. The buildings lying in the outer ward have no fireplaces, and so possibly functioned as storehouses.

A second earthen rampart separated the outer ward from the surrounding countryside.

THE GREAT BELT

The **Storebælts-forbindelsen** (Great Belt Fixed Link; www.storebaelt.dk; one-way toll motorcycle 115-220kr, small/medium/large car 115/220/335kr) is the stuff that engineers lust over. Spanning a whopping 18km, its combination of two bridges, island and tunnel allow the E20 motorway to connect Denmark's largest and third-largest islands, Zealand and Funen. It's an amazing piece of design and worth an admiring gasp. After all, the highest points in Denmark are the tops of the two 254m pylons on the East Bridge, which joins Zealand to Sprogø Island before carrying cars onwards over the West Bridge to Funen. The bridges look particularly stunning at night, glittering and twinkling against a black backdrop.

Three kilometres to the south on the Zealand side is **Korsør**, a one-time booming ferry town thanks to its position at the narrowest point between Zealand and Funen. The opening of the Storebælts-forbindelsen changed all that, turning the transport hub into another victim of progress. While the town itself has no major drawcards, it is home to the **Korsør By og Overfartsmuseum** (Korsør Town & Ferry Service Museum; www.byogoverfartsmuseet.dk, in Danish; Søbatteriet 3; adult/child 15/5kr; ⊙11am-4pm Tue-Sun Apr–mid-Dec), a museum dedicated to the ferries and icebreakers that traversed the Store Bælt over the past two centuries. (After all, everyone deserves a little love, right?)

Korsør's new train station is 3km north of town, by the Storebælt link. It's on the main line between Zealand and Funen, with trains running roughly every half hour to Copenhagen (124kr, one hour) and Odense (132kr, 30 minutes). Local buses 35 and 501 connect the train station to Korsør's town centre (26kr, 20 minutes).

Hints of big trouble are littered across Trelleborg. The fort was occupied for a very short space of time, before being abandoned around 990. There are signs of a large fire, and a **Viking graveyard** lying within the fort's outer defences contains two mass graves, both containing the bodies of men in their 20s and 30s.

Despite the passing of a millennium since its construction, the **circular earthen mound** is perfectly intact. Naturally, the wooden structures that once stood inside it have long since decayed, but the post holes and gable ends of the buildings have been filled with cement to show the outlines of the house foundations. You can walk up onto the grassy circular rampart and readily grasp the strikingly precise geometric design of the fortress. Grazing sheep imbue the scene with a timeless aura.

Reconstructions

Several Viking-era buildings have been reconstructed at the site, using authentic materials and methods. The most impressive is the **replica longhouse**, built in 1941 in Viking stave style. Sit quietly on one of the sleeping benches that line the walls, watching the swallows dart through the doorways and the smoke hole, and you half expect one of the fortress's former inhabitants to wander in.

Since it was built, archaeologists have changed their opinion on the external appearance of the longhouse. They now think that there was no outer gallery and that the roof was much lower – still, 10 out of 10 for effort.

A few reconstructed houses are clustered together to form '**Trelletorp**', a tiny Viking village, with besmocked interpreters doing chores of the period such as sharpening axes, chopping wood and baking bread. From June to August, there are often activities for children, such as archery demonstrations and pottery workshops.

ⓘ Getting There & Away

BUS & TRAIN Bus 312 runs from Slagelse to Trelleborg (26kr, 15 minutes) from Sunday to Friday. There are around seven buses per day, with the first leaving Slagelse at 7am and the last (to arrive within the museum's opening hours) at 2.56pm (June to August) and 1.56pm (April, May, September and October). Trains run frequently between Slagelse and Copenhagen (109kr, one hour).

CAR Driving from Slagelse, take Strandvejen to its end at the village of Hejninge and then follow the signs to Trelleborg, 1km further on.

TAXI From Slagelse, a taxi to the site costs about 190kr on weekdays, 220kr on weekends. To book one, call **Slagelse Taxa** (☑58 53 53 53).

Næstved & Around

POP 41,665

Drivers' hearts may sink as they enter Næstved, the largest settlement in the region, which at first glance appears to be nothing more than a mess of ring roads, slip roads and junctions. However, if you ditch the car and persevere to the pedestrianised heart, you'll discover a lively and cosy town dotted with medieval buildings (including two Gothic churches).

Næstved makes a convenient base from which to buzz in on some of Denmark's top family-oriented tourist attractions, all within a 10km radius – BonBon-Land theme park, the glassworks Holmegaard Glasværker and Næstved Zoo. More sedate types can explore the lakes and forests to the south and west, or join the happy throngs at seaside Karrebæksminde.

◉ Sights

NÆSTVED

Sankt Peders Kirke   CHURCH

(Sct Peders Kirkeplads; admission free; ⊘10am-3pm Mon-Fri) The large high-Gothic Sankt Peders Kirke features some notable 14th-century frescoes. One depicts Machiavellian King Valdemar IV and his queen Helvig kneeling before God. The Latin inscription

to the left of the king translates as: 'In 1375, the day before the feast of St Crispin, King Valdemar died, do not forget it'.

Sankt Mortens Kirke   CHURCH

(Kattebjerg 2; admission free; ⊘9am-1pm & 2-5pm Tue-Fri) Also built in brick, the smaller Sankt Mortens Kirke has a strikingly similar design to Sankt Peders Kirke, and is decorated inside with period frescoes. You can see examples from a renowned 17th-century family woodcarving workshop here – a pulpit, carved by Schröder senior, and the fabulously detailed 6m-high altar by his son, master craftsman Abel, covered in characteristic grimacing masks and stooping, moustached figures.

FREE Næstved Museum   MUSEUM

(www.naestved-museum.dk; Sct Peders Kirkeplads; ⊘10am-2pm Tue, Wed, Fri & Sat, to 6pm Thu, 1-4pm Sun) Næstved Museum is split over two buildings, in different parts of town.

Næstved's oldest building, **Helligåndshuset** (House of the Holy Ghost; Ringstedgade 4), was built in the 14th century as a religiously run hospital/orphanage/old people's home. Today it contains the museum's local history section. There's a roomful of finds from a Viking Age site at Vester Egesborg (10km south of Næstved), as well as 13th- and

Næstved

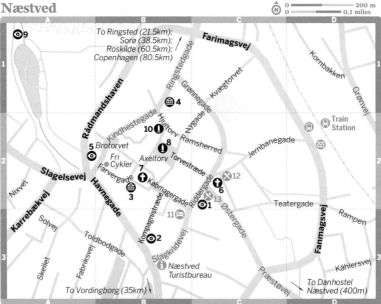

14th-century church carvings, exhibits on farming, trade and peasant life, some nicely presented old toys, and a section on the military in Næstved. Most of the information is in Danish, but the helpful museum staff will explain anything you can't translate.

Boderne (Sct Peders Kirkeplads), once a row of upmarket medieval flats, now displays ceramics and glass from two big craft workshops in the area: Kählers Keramiske Værksted and Holmegaard Glasværker.

Buildings & Monuments
HISTORIC BUILDINGS, MONUMENTS

The most stand-out medieval house is **Apostelhuset** (Riddergade 5), which takes its name from 13 exterior wooden braces separating the windows. Christ stands on the central brace, with six apostles on either side, each clutching their associated symbols or instruments of torture, and standing on the head of a gruesome monster. Dating from about 1510, they're among the oldest and best-preserved timber-frame carvings in Denmark.

The country's only remaining medieval guildhall, **Kompagnihuset** (Kompagnistræde), is a timber-framed building constructed in 1493. It gets its name from a later use – Christian IV gave it to a Spanish trading company to use as their headquarters.

Also with roots in the medieval period is the old town hall, **Rådhuskirken**, the brick and half-timbered building at the northwestern side of Sankt Peders Kirke.

Næstved

◉ Sights

The town's most novel curiosity is Denmark's smallest equestrian statue (Hjultorv). The tiny bronze, depicting Næstved's founder Peder Bodilsen, is only 42cm high and sits on top of a tall brick pedestal. In the adjoining square, Axeltorv, you'll find a rather curious sculpture by renowned artist Bjørn Nørgaard, entitled *Hanging Tits and Her Daughters from Rønnebæksholm*. According to Zealand folklore, 'Hanging Tits' was a giant hunter known for throwing her pendulous breasts over her shoulders while on the job.

AROUND NÆSTVED

BonBon-Land   AMUSEMENT PARK

(www.bonbonland.dk; Gartnervej 2, Holme Olstrup; admission high/low season 219/199kr, online tickets 175kr; ☺10am-7pm late Jun-early Aug, reduced hrs rest of year, closed late Oct–mid-Apr) One of Denmark's top five tourist attractions is the theme park BonBon-Land. Its biggest ride is the bonkers-looking Wild Boar rollercoaster, which sets off vertically before plunging into freefall, then looping-the-loop at speeds of up to 74km per hour. The other 60 or so amusements and rides are tamer, but your kids will love you for taking them there... especially when they hear about the sweets that shot the BonBon confectionary company to success – Dog Farts, Big Boobs and Seagull Plop.

BonBon-Land is about 7km east of Næstved: follow road 54, signposted to Rønnede. Trains to Holme Olstrup (32kr, 10 minutes) run every 30 to 60 minutes; the theme park is 300m from the station.

Holmegaard Park   GLASSWORKS

(www.holmegaardpark.dk, in Danish; Glasværksvej 54; adult/4-11yr/under 4yr 59/49kr/free; ☺science centre & candy store/workshop 10am-4pm Thu-Sun, shops 10am-6pm Mon-Fri, to 5pm Sat & Sun, brewhouse restaurant 10am-6pm Sun-Thu, to 9pm Fri & Sat) Anyone hypnotised by melting toffee-like glass can indulge at Holmegaard Glasværker, Denmark's principal glassworks. The company has turned the factory into a 'visitor experience' by adding attendant attractions – you can watch sweets and chocolates being made, sample beer from the on-site microbrewery, visit the Holmegaard shop or try your hand at glass-blowing (149kr). There's little in life more satisfying than producing your own lopsided masterpiece, but be warned: the glass takes two hours to cool, and the glass-blowing area closes two hours before main closing times, so it's a morning activity only. Access for people in wheelchairs is very good.

Holmegaard is at Fensmark, about 8km northeast of Næstved. Take road 54 out of town, following signs to Rønnede/Fensmark; the glassworks is well signposted. Bus 602 (32kr, 20 minutes) from Næstved stops 350m short of Holmegaard Glasværker.

Zoopark Sydsjælland   ZOO
(www.zoopark.dk in Danish; Ålestokvej 2; adult/3-11yr 95/55kr; ☺10am-6pm Mon, Wed, Fri & Sun, to 8pm Thu & Sat late Jun-early Aug, reduced hrs rest of year, closed mid-Oct–Easter) Kids will especially love this petting zoo, where visitors can get close to a cute cast of critters that include alpacas, does, kangaroos and American bison. Residents you won't be patting are the tigers, among them a majestic white tiger. You'll find the zoo southwest of Næstved, off the Karrebæksminde road.

Karrebæksminde   TOWN
Karrebæksminde, 10km southwest of Næstved, is the beach resort where stressed-out town-dwellers go to unwind. It's a pretty self-contained place, with harbours, hotels, camping grounds, restaurants, supermarkets and its own seasonal tourist office. Bus 603 (32kr, 20 minutes) runs there from Næstved.

🏃 Activities

🛶 Suså Kanoudlejning   CANOEING
(☎57 64 61 44; www.kanoudlejning.dk, in Danish; Slusehuset, Næsbyholm Allé 6) The calm waters of the Suså River make for good canoeing – you can paddle upstream through tranquil greenery for several days. Suså Kanoudlejning is a canoe-hire company tucked away in the large park just north of the centre. In July and early August, you can rent canoes for 370/660/830kr per one/two/three days Monday to Thursday, or 420/760/980kr Friday to Sunday. At other times phone their office for assistance. Make your booking at least a day in advance; and bring cash, as the company doesn't have credit card facilities.

There's a hostel for canoeists in Skelby, located halfway between Næstved and Sorø (see following).

🛏 Sleeping & Eating

The tourist office maintains a booklet of private rooms available for rent in the greater Næstved area, with singles from around 175kr, doubles from around 350kr.

Danhostel Næstved   HOSTEL €
(☎55 72 20 91; www.danhostelnaestved.dk; Præstøvej 65; dm 190-240kr, s/d with bathroom 495/545kr; ☺Feb-Nov; P☎) This hostel is based in a red-brick 1970s nunnery. You'll find modern rooms here, most with bathrooms, plus a laundry, small playground, life-size garden chess set and wi-fi. The hostel is 1km from the town centre: head south from the train station and then continue east along Præstøvej.

Depotet   HOSTEL €
(☎26 20 97 19; www.depotet-susaa.dk; Buen 18, Skelby; s/d 325/580kr; ☺May–mid-Sep; P@) Almost halfway between Næstved and Sorø this is a cheerful, homely little hostel set up for passing canoeists. It has a dock, cosy rooms, a warm and inviting lounge, a laundry and guest kitchen.

Hotel Kirstine   HOTEL €€
(☎55 77 47 00; www.hotelkirstine.dk; Købmagergade 20; s/d incl breakfast 845/1025kr; P@☎) The most charming place to stay is this romantic little hotel in the heart of Næstved. Crooked, cosy rooms roll out the red carpet, old furniture, cable TV and minibar (with complimentary drinks), while the downstairs lounge areas are supremely snug. Best of all is the hotel's **restaurant** (☺lunch & dinner), set in a glassed-in arcade and serving beautiful, seasonally inspired dishes like freshly caught brill with apples, radishes and chervil. If you're a nonsmoker, specifically ask for a nonsmoking room.

Café Oliver   INTERNATIONAL €€
(Jernbanegade 2; lunch 79-109kr, dinner mains 179-199kr; ☺lunch & dinner) On the sunny side of the street, trendy Oliver is the coolest spot to hang in Næstved. Perfect-looking blond, sunglassed people sit at the scattering of outdoor tables to enjoy coffee, a glass of wine or lunchtime sandwiches, burgers, salads and vegetable lasagne. Evening mains change with the seasons, but include dishes such as guinea fowl breast in a gorgonzola sauce.

Peperoncino Siciliano   ITALIAN €€
(Riddergade 1A; mains 129-230kr; ☺dinner) Weathered beams and dark brick walls lend a dim and cosy feel to this restaurant on one of Næstved's older streets. As you'd guess, this place specialises in Italian meals.

There's a small, rich, meat selection, and a longer list containing all the spaghetti, fettuccine and penne your mamma could feed you, including several veggie options.

❶ Information

Danske Bank (Hjultorv 18) One of several in the town centre.

Næstved Hovedbibliotek (Kvægtorvet 4-6; ⊘10am-7pm Mon-Thu, 10am-5pm Fri, 10am-2pm Sat) The central library, above the Kvickly supermarket, has free internet access.

Næstved Turistbureau (📌55 72 11 22; www.visitnaestved.com; Det Gule Pakhus, Havnen 1; ⊘9am-5pm Mon-Fri, to 1pm Sat mid-Jun–mid-Aug) Helpful staff.

Post office (⊘10am-5.30pm Mon-Fri, 10am-1pm Sat) By the train station.

❶ Getting There & Around

The bus and train stations are close together on Farimagsvej, opposite its intersection with Jernbanegade.

BICYCLE You can hire bicycles from **Fri Cykler** (Brotorvet 3; ⊘9am-5.30pm Mon-Thu, to 6pm Fri, to 2pm Sat) for 75/395kr per day/week, plus a 100kr deposit.

CAR The road system around Næstved (25km south of Ringsted and 28km north of Vordingborg) is fairly unpleasant for Denmark, as Rtes 14, 22, 54 and 265 all meet here in a disorientating tangle. Abandon the car as soon as possible (the car park outside Kvickly supermarket is central).

TRAIN Trains run about half-hourly from Copenhagen (100kr, one hour) and Roskilde (58kr, 35 minutes to one hour). There are also regular services to Vordingborg (48kr, 20 minutes), Køge (58kr, 40 minutes) and Ringsted (40kr, 20 minutes).

Vordingborg

POP 11,610

It's worth popping in to Vordingborg on your way to the southern islands, to saunter up the cosy pedestrian avenue Algade and climb the medieval Goose Tower.

If you've time, Knudshoved Odde peninsula is a short drive from town. Here you can find a few public parking spots with access to grassy lawns and very narrow rocky beaches, where you can swim if the temperature's right.

Vordingborg's large natural harbour and strategic location on the strait played an important role in Denmark's early history. It was the royal residence of Valdemar I, who reunited the Danish kingdom in 1157 after a period of civil war, and it continued to be a favoured residence of Valdemar's descendants.

◉ Sights

Gåsetårnet   HISTORIC BUILDING, RUIN

(Goose Tower; Slotsruinen 1; adult/under 18yr incl Sydsjællands Museum 45kr/free, tower only 30kr/free; ⊘10am-5pm Jun-Aug, 10am-4pm Tue-Sun Sep-May) The 14th-century Gåsetårnet, once part of a huge royal castle and fortress, is Scandinavia's best-preserved medieval tower and the only structure remaining from the Valdemar era. The name stems from 1365, when Valdemar IV placed a golden goose on top of the tower to express his scorn for the German Hanseatic League's declaration of war (Valdemar referred to the league as 'cackling geese'). The rest of the fortress, including seven other towers, has been demolished over the centuries but the 36m-high Gåsetårnet was spared because of its function as a navigational landmark. The tower's walls are an impressive 1m (3ft) thick in places, and you can climb the 107 steps for some pleasing views. Information boards are in Danish and German.

The fortress grounds, which have been turned into a park with walking paths, contain various brick and stone **foundation ruins** and a small **botanical garden** (admission free).

Sydsjællands Museum   MUSEUM

(adult/under 18yr 30kr/free; ⊘10am-5pm Jun-Aug, 10am-4pm Tue-Sun Sep-May) In addition, the fortress grounds hold the Sydsjællands Museum, southern Zealand's regional history museum. At the time of writing, the museum was set to close temporarily as construction of a new museum building was planned to commence. Its interesting collection includes Stone Age weaponry, plus the bones of elk, wild pigs, wolves and deer killed with the bone and flint arrows and harpoons. There are also sections on the Middle Ages and the Renaissance.

Vor Frue Kirke   CHURCH

(Kirketorvet; admission free; ⊘10am-3pm Mon-Fri Jun-Aug) Along the way, on the western side of Algade, is the brick-built Vor Frue Kirke, whose oldest section is a mid-15th-century nave. Inside are elegant frescoes, and a baroque altarpiece created in 1642 by master-carver Abel Schrøder.

🏃 Activities

Knudshoved Odde   WALKING

If you have your own transport, Knudshoved Odde, the narrow 18km-long peninsula west of Vordingborg, offers some hiking opportunities in an area known for its 'Bronze Age landscape'. A small herd of American buffalo roam the land, brought in by the Rosenfeldt family who own Knudshoved Odde. There's a car park (15kr) about halfway down the peninsula, where the trail begins.

🛌 Sleeping

There are a few private homes in the Vordingborg area with rooms for rent for around 200kr for singles and 400kr for doubles – the tourist office should be able to give you a list.

Danhostel Vordingborg   HOSTEL €

(☑55 36 08 00; www.danhostel.dk/vordingborg; Præstegårdsvej 18; dm/s/d without bathroom 150/250/400kr, s/d 350/500kr; ☺year-round; P🅿@) This 112-bed hostel, about 2km north of town, is in a peaceful rural area, surrounded by paths and lakes. Rooms are pleasant and facilities include a laundry.

Ore Strand Camping   CAMPING GROUND, CABINS €

(☑55 77 88 22; www.orestrandcamping.dk; Orevej 145; camp site per adult/child 70/35kr) The kitchen and toilets at this camping ground are on the dark and battered side, but the staff here are such sweeties, and the seafront location is so pleasant, that we would still recommend it. The beach has a Blue Flag award. The site is 2km southwest of town, and is well signposted.

Hotel Kong Valdemar   HOTEL €€

(☑55 34 30 95; www.hotelkongvaldemar.dk; Algade 101; s/d incl breakfast 675/875kr; P🅿🛜) Opposite Gåsetårnet in the town centre, this hotel has 60 bland rooms with bathroom and TV. The recently changed management plans to spruce up the place.

🍴 Eating

Babette   DANISH, INTERNATIONAL €€

(☑55 34 30 30; www.babette.dk, in Danish; Kildemarksvej 5; 3-/5-course menu 495/595kr; ☺lunch & dinner Wed-Fri, dinner Sat) If you're in the region it's definitely worth visiting Babette, 1km north of the centre, for a full gastronomic and aesthetic treat. The restaurant (named after the film *Babette's Feast*) is well known for its original pan-European cuisine, making use of local seasonal ingredients in sometimes unusual combinations – braised Duroc pork belly with fruit syrup, buckthorn and carrots, anyone? Culinary prowess aside, Babette is also blessed with a panoramic surf-and-turf vista. Book ahead.

Cafe Oscar   DANISH, INTERNATIONAL €€

(www.babette.dk in Danish; Nordhavnsvej 8; meals 68-195kr; ☺lunch & dinner Thu-Sun May, Tue-Sun Jun-Aug) Seasonal, affordable and snugly set in an old salting hut by the harbour, it's hard not to love Oscar. Run by the team from Babette (you're in capable hands!), its menu is reassuringly short, simple and fresh. Made-from-scratch salads, sandwiches and a gourmet burger spell lunch, while dinner usually offers a soup, pasta dish, meat and fish main... Oh, and that lip-smacking burger. More of a grazer? Opt for the plate of Danish cheese with olives and bread.

Café Piaf   INTERNATIONAL €

(Algade 85; sandwiches 60-80kr, tapas 95kr; ☺10.30am-5.30pm Mon & Tue, to 9pm Wed-Fri, to 3pm Sat) This friendly cafe, decorated with works by local artists, is a good central spot for salads, burgers, nachos and hearty steaks. There's a decent brunch for 95kr and homemade cake for that afternoon sugar fix.

ℹ Information

Nordea (Algade 78) One of several banks on Algade.

Post office (Rådhustorvet) In the Kvickly supermarket building, off Algade.

Vordingborg Turistkontor (☑55 34 11 11; www.visitvordingborg.dk; Slotsruinen 1) Inside the Sydsjællands Museum, next to the Goose Tower. At the time of research, the tourist office was set to move temporarily while construction of a new museum building commenced. Check the tourist office website for updates.

ℹ Getting There & Away

Vordingborg is 28km south of Næstved via Rte 22, and 13km from Møn via Rte 59.

By train, Vordingborg is around 75 minutes from Copenhagen (124kr) and 20 minutes from Næstved (48kr). If you're en route to Møn, you'll need to switch from the train to the bus at Vordingborg train station; see p125.

Møn, Falster & Lolland

Best Places to Eat

» Gourmet Gaarden (p127)

» Lolles Gård (p128)

» David's (p127)

» Klintholm Røgeri (p132)

» Schous Kød (p136)

Best Places to Stay

» Tohøjgaard Gæstgivern (p132)

» Bakkegaard Gæstgiveri (p131)

» Camping Møns Klint (p131)

» Liselund Ny Slot (p131)

» Hotel Nørrevang (p135)

Why Go?

Denmark's 'South Sea Islands' may lack the coconut palms and hula skirts usually associated with that phrase, but they *do* offer a fine glimpse of rural Scandinavian island life: rolling fields, sandy beaches and Neolithic tombs.

Møn deserves the most attention: it's perfectly sized, artistically spirited and home to something very unusual for Denmark – cliffs! Four churches exhibit wondrous medieval frescoes, from recognised masterpieces to primitive daubs. Add evocative beaches, enchanted forests and cosy guesthouses, and you've got the perfect island escape.

While less inspiring than Møn, Falster is famous for its beach, which lures Danish sun worshippers each (short) summer. Further west, Lolland's sprawl of farms and woods is punctuated with Maribo's small-town charm, as well as blockbuster attractions Lalandia waterpark and Knuthenborg Safari Park.

All three islands are easily accessed by road bridges from Southern Zealand.

When to Go

To catch a glimpse of Møn's rare orchids, head to the island between May and August. This is a good period in general, as many attractions and restaurants close or reduce their hours outside high season. Falster's famous beaches make July and August crowded, but if lazy beach days and lively bar nights are your thing, these are the months to go.

Across the islands, September is ideal, with relatively good weather and fewer crowds, especially at Lolland's family-focused drawcards.

Møn, Falster & Lolland Highlights

1 Track down prehistoric fossils in the gleaming chalk cliffs at **Møns Klint** (p130)

2 Channel your inner knight or maiden at the medieval-themed **Middelaldercentret** (p134), just outside Nykøbing F

3 Marvel at superb medieval frescoes inside Møn's **Elmelunde Kirke** (p130) and **Fanefjord Kirke** (p132)

4 Tan, splash and just kick back on the sand at **Marielyst** (p135), Falster's premier summer beach resort

5 Take a boat ride on the gorgeous **Søndersø** (p137)

in the picture-perfect town of Maribo

6 Monkey around at the drive-through **Knuthenborg Safari Park** (p139) at Bandholm

7 Make the kids squeal with glee at splash-happy theme park **Lalandia** (p139)

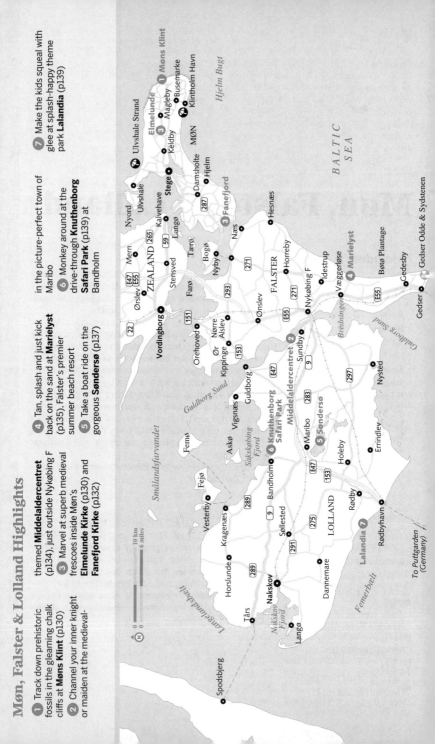

MØN

POP 9900

Expect to fall head over heels for Møn. By far the most magical of the south islands, its most famous drawcard is its spectacular white cliffs, Møns Klint. Soft, sweeping and crowned by deep-green forest, they're the stuff paintings are made of, which possibly explains the island's healthy headcount of artists.

Yet the inspiration doesn't end there, with beautiful beaches spanning sandy expanses to small secret coves, haunting Neolithic graves and medieval churches lined with some of Denmark's most vivid medieval frescoes.

Møn's rich clay soil draws potters to the area (look out for *'keramik'* signs along country roads), while its fields and coast inspire the island's handful of culinary must-tries.

So hit the pedal or get behind the wheel (Møn has no trains and the bus service is sketchy), and explore what is bound to become one of your favourite corners of Denmark.

Getting There & Away

Visitors need to take the train to Vordingborg in Southern Zealand then switch to a bus. Trains from Copenhagen to Vordingborg (124kr, 1¼ hours) leave at least hourly until around midnight.

Bus 660R (occasionally 664) from Vordingborg, in South Zealand, to Stege (48kr, 45 minutes), on Møn, connects with train arrivals, leaving Vordingborg about once an hour; there's a fuller service during weekday rush hours, and a lighter service on weekends.

Bus 750 runs between Stege and Nykøbing F (68kr, 55 minutes), on Falster, with around seven buses in either direction on weekdays only. This service does not run in summer.

Getting Around

Route 287, which cuts across the centre of the island from east to west, is Møn's main road. Numerous rural roads branch off it – they can be slow going but fun to explore.

BICYCLE

In Stege, bicycles can be rented at **Point S** (Storegade 91; per day 65kr; ⊘7.30am-5pm Mon-Fri, 9am-noon Sat). The camping ground in Ulvshale on Møn hires out bikes. Maps of cycling routes on Møns can be found at Møns Turistbureau.

BUS

Stege is the departure point for all buses on Møn. Fares depend on the number of zones travelled, with the highest fare between any two places on Møn being 32kr. Frequency of service varies with the day of the week and the season.

The most frequent service is bus 667, which goes from Stege to Klintholm Havn (32kr, 45 minutes) via Keldby, Elmelunde and Magleby.

To reach Møns Klint, alight at Magleby, from where the cliffs are a 6km walk east (wear comfy shoes). Bus 667 runs about hourly on weekdays and every couple of hours on weekends.

TAXI

For taxis, call **Møns Taxi** (⊠55 81 54 58).

Stege

POP 3825

Møn's main town and gateway, Stege is the island at its busiest. Its single narrow main street contains the island's main tourist office, a handful of good cafes, small independent shops, a cinema and (most importantly) a microbrewery. The island is so small that wherever you are, it's only a short drive back here to stock up on supplies.

During the Middle Ages, Stege was one of Denmark's wealthiest provincial towns, thanks to its lucrative herring industry. The entire town was fortified until 1534, when the castle walls were torn down – by citizens who supported a mutinous attacking army. Pieces of the rampart remain here and there, including near the camping ground.

◎ Sights & Activities

There's a signposted cycle path running between Stege and Møns Klint, and in the other direction from Stege to Bogø. Møns Turistbureau in Stege sells a Danish pamphlet called *Cykelture – Møn, Bogø & Nyord* (79kr), which maps out seven cycling trips, taking in the island's major sights.

Stege Kirke CHURCH

(Kirkepladsen 1; ⊘9am-5pm Tue-Sun) It looks as though a demented nine-year-old has been let loose inside Stege Kirke, built in the 13th century by one of the powerful Hvide family. The walls and ceiling are covered in endearingly naive 14th- and 15th-century frescoes in red and black paint: monkey-like faces sprout from branches, a hunter chases unidentifiable animals, and a sorrowful man is covered in big red blobs...measles? The church has a splendidly carved pulpit dating from 1630, featuring biblical reliefs, plus grotesque faces to remind the less virtuous of what's in store.

MØN, FALSTER & LOLLAND STEGE

Møn

Empiregården MUSEUM
(Storegade 75; adult/child incl entry to Museumsgården 45kr/free; ⊙10am-4pm Tue-Sun)
Part of Møn Museum, Empiregården covers local cultural history, with archaeological finds from the Stone Age to the Middle Ages (look out for Rasmus, the creepy skeleton), displays of 19th-century house interiors, toys, coins, pottery and a showcase dedicated to two unusual local men. Around a third is covered by English explanations.

Mølleporten HISTORIC BUILDING
Of the three medieval gates that once allowed entry into the town, Mølleporten (Mill Gate) on Storegade is the only one still standing. It's one of the best-preserved town gates in Denmark.

Møn Bolcher SWEETS FACTORY
(www.moenbolcher.dk; Kostervej 2; admission free; ⊙10am-4pm Mon-Fri, to 1pm Sat) Kids (and adult sweet tooths) may appreciate the Willy Wonka undertones of the Møn Bolcher sweets factory, where you can watch traditional boiled sweets being made.

🛏 Sleeping

The tourist office has a brochure with a list of B&Bs on the island. You're welcome to use the tourist office phone free of charge to book accommodation or you can pay 25kr to have the staff call for you. Singles/doubles in a private home average 300/400kr.

Motel Stege HOTEL €€
(☎55 81 35 35; www.motel-stege.dk; Provstestræde 4; s 500-650kr, d 575-750kr; P🛜) Owned by the same lovely couple behind Pension Elmehøj (p130), this is your best bet in central Stege. All 12 rooms are simple yet smart. Those in the main building have a mezzanine level (accessible by ladder), and sleep up to four. Rooms in the annexe have their own kitchenette, while all guests have access to a homely communal kitchen and dining area.

Møn

Added comforts include a washer, dryer, umbrellas and lockable bike garage.

🍴 Eating

TOP CHOICE Gourmet Gaarden DANISH €€

(☎55 81 42 67; Storegade 59; 2/3 courses 315/365kr; ☺dinner Tue-Sat, Fri & Sat only Jan, closed late Dec-Jan & Feb–mid-Mar) If you like your food seasonal, local and beautifully prepared by a chef who hails from one of Copenhagen's top restaurants, secure a table here. Henrik Bajer and his wife, Lina, are seriously passionate about Danish produce and flavours, and Henrik's simple yet sophisticated dishes allow the prime ingredients to shine; think slow-cooked veal, with obscenely fresh vegetables from Lammefjorden (Denmark's prime vegetable-growing area). Make room for the whimsical desserts, and always check the website for updated opening times and special culinary events.

David's INTERNATIONAL €€

(Storegade 11; lunches 76-140kr, 2-/3-course dinners 250/295kr; ☺10am-5pm Mon-Thu, 6-10pm Fri & Sat; 🛜) Another solid option, David's open kitchen prepares fabulous, contemporary cafe fare. Tuck into the celebrated Danish 'tapas' platter or opt for gems like the roll of smoked salmon and apples with trout mousse and green salad. House-made cakes keep gluttons happy, while coffee snobs will appreciate the real-deal espresso. Sunny days mean alfresco noshing in the courtyard.

Bryghuset Møn BREWERY €€

(www.bryghusetmoen.dk; Luffes Gård, Storegade 18; lunches 79-125kr, dinner mains 69-279kr; ☺lunch & dinner) There's a cafe inside Luffes Gård courtyard, serving burgers, omelettes, blini and sandwiches, and mostly meaty mains at night. But the chief draw is beer brewed in Stege's microbrewery. Go right through the courtyard to admire its shining copper vats.

There's a good bakery, **Guld Bageren** (Storegade 36; ☺5am-5pm Mon-Fri, 6am-2pm Sat, 6am-1pm Sun), and several large supermarkets. The most central supermarkets are **Netto** (Ved Stranden 32; ☺9am-8pm Mon-Fri, 8am-6pm Sat) and **Kiwi Mini Pris** (Storegade 46; ☺8am-10pm Mon-Fri, to 8pm Sat & Sun).

ℹ️ Information

Library (Møllebrøndstræde 12; ☺11am-5pm Mon & Tue, 1-7pm Wed, 11am-5pm Thu & Fri, 10am-2pm Sat) Free internet access.

Møns Turistbureau (☎55 86 04 00; www.visitvordingborg.dk; Storegade 2; ☺9.30am-4pm Mon-Fri, 9am-noon Sat; @) Has information about the entire island. Internet access costs 10kr per 15 minutes.

Nordea (Storegade 23; ☺10am-4pm Mon-Wed & Fri, to 5pm Thu) One of three banks in central Stege with an ATM.

Post office (Støvvasen 3; ☺11am-5pm Mon-Fri, 10am-noon Sat) Inside Super Brugsen supermarket.

Ulvshale & Nyord

Møn's best beach, **Ulvshale Strand**, sprawls along Ulvshale peninsula, 6km north of Stege. This pristine stretch of gently sloping white sand is created by pieces of cliff washing around the coast from Møns Klint. The beach is popular with windsurfers, has received its Blue Flag award (an international eco-label for the sustainable development of beaches and marinas) and is accessible to people in wheelchairs. It's easy to get to – the 'main road', Ulvshalevej, runs alongside – and it's edged by one of the few virgin woods left in Denmark (look out for adders). The forest extends to the end of the peninsula,

MØN, FALSTER & LOLLAND ULVSHALE & NYORD

Stege

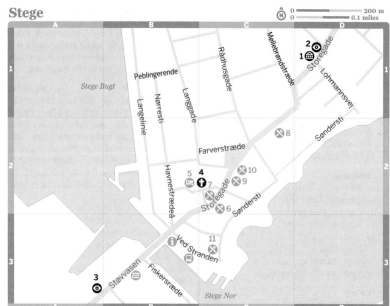

Stege

⊙ Sights
1	Empiregården	D1
2	Mølleporten	D1
3	Møn Bolcher	A3
4	Stege Kirke	C2

🛏 Sleeping
5	Motel Stege	B2

⊗ Eating
6	Bryghuset Møn	C2
7	David's	C2
8	Gourmet Gaarden	C2
9	Guld Bageren	C2
10	Kiwi Mini Pris	C2
11	Netto	C3

where there's a narrow bridge to the island of Nyord.

Nyord has only been connected to the Møn mainland since 1968. Its former isolation safeguarded it from development, and today the sole village (also named Nyord) is a perfect cluster of 19th-century thatched cottages, surrounded by idyllic gardens thick with roses, poppies, lupins and irises. Cars are banned (there's a car park outside), so the loudest sound is the chattering of

swallows. Much of the 5-sq-km island, particularly the east, is given over to marshland and salt meadows. There's a **bird-watching tower** (Map p126) about 1km west of the bridge – you can't miss it in this flat landscape. Birds include ospreys, kestrels, rough-legged hawks, snow buntings, ruffs, avocets, swans, black-tailed godwits, Arctic terns, curlews and various ducks.

🛏 Sleeping & Eating

Nyord B&B GUESTHOUSE €
(Map p126; ☎55 86 32 57; www.nyord-bb.dk; Aksvej 8, Nyord; r 400-650kr; ☺Apr-Oct; ⊚) If it's peace you're after, Nyord B&B has your name all over its farmhouse walls. Owned by affable ex-sailor Niels Andreasen and his family, it's snugly set in Møn's only car-free village, opposite the equally cosy Lolles Gård restaurant. The eight white rooms are simple, clean and comfortable, two with private bathroom and none with TV. Breakfast is an extra 75kr.

Lolles Gård DANISH €€
(Map p126; ☎55 81 86 81; www.lolles-gaard.dk; Hyldevej 1, Nyord; lunches 85-158kr, dinner mains 125-179kr; ☺lunch & dinner Easter–mid-Oct) Tucked away in Nyord, this criminally cosy restaurant is another must for foodies. Owner Anja Hansen proudly showcases

top-notch regional produce, from seafood and beef, to charcuterie, cheeses and vegetables. Seasonality and natural flavours define the menu, which might include Lolles Gård's famous fried eels with new potatoes and parsley sauce (285kr). Lighter lunch dishes include salads and homemade pies. Call ahead if dining in September as the restaurant sometimes closes in the evening.

Keldby

The Keldby area, about 5km east of Stege, is notable mainly for the superb frescoes in its roadside church. There's also a small farm museum a few kilometres south of Rte 287.

◎ Sights

TOP CHOICE Keldby Kirke   CHURCH
(Map p126; Rte 287; ☉8am-4.45pm) Some of Denmark's most splendid frescoes are splashed across the walls and ceiling of Keldby's 13th-century brick church. The oldest (1275) decorate the chancel walls. An impressive Judgment Day scene, where the saved join the saints and the damned descend into a devil-filled hell, dates from around 100 years later. It's a theme also visited by the 15th-century 'Elmelunde master' (see the boxed text, this page), whose cool-faced figures are found all over the soaring arches. There are too many wonderful scenes to describe here, but some quirky Elmelunde touches include Joseph making gruel for baby Jesus, and a warning against vanity – a monkey with a mirror.

Museumsgården   MUSEUM
(Map p126; Skullebjergvej 15; adult/under 18yr incl entry to Empiregården 45kr/free; ☉10am-4pm Tue-Sun mid-May–mid-Sep) A typical Møn farmhouse shelters this low-key museum, 3km south of Keldby. Its dim, musty-smelling rooms, centred around a courtyard, are decorated with 19th-century furniture, and there are hens and rabbits in the pretty grounds. You can pitch a tent (10kr) in the garden.

✖ Eating

Møn Is   ICE CREAM €
(Map p126; www.moen-is.dk, in Danish; Hovgårdsvej 4, Stege; 2 scoops 25kr; ☉11am-5pm daily summer, reduced hrs rest of year) Ice-cream makers often wax lyrically about 'fresh ingredients', but it doesn't get fresher than Møn Is, where you can blissfully lick in full view of the cows that made it all possible. Flavours include seasonal fruit sorbets and creamy stunners like crème caramel with macaroons. Although the farm's address is in Stege, it's actually 8km southeast of Stege (or 2km southeast of Kelbyville).

Elmelunde

Ancient fresco-filled churches are a recurring theme in this part of the world. Nevertheless, the church in this rural hamlet,

THE ELMELUNDE FRESCOES

Several of Møn's churches are covered in beautiful frescoes, so rich and abundant that the churches can be likened to medieval art galleries. These frescoes were a means of describing the Bible to illiterate peasants, and their cartoon-like clarity still gets the stories across today. Scenes run the gamut from light-hearted frolics in the Garden of Eden to depictions of grotesque demons and the yawning mouth of hell.

After visiting a couple of these churches, you may get a sense of déjà vu. This is because most of the loveliest 15th-century frescoes were painted by the same artist, whose exact identity is a mystery but who is known as Elmelundemesteren (the Elmelunde master) after the church of the same name. His people have calm emotionless faces, the artwork is given room to breathe by lots of balancing white space, and the master's palette is one of distinctive warm earth tones: russet, mustard, sienna, brick red, chestnut brown and pale aqua.

Møn's church frescoes, created by painting with watercolours on newly plastered, still-wet walls or ceilings, are some of the best-preserved in Denmark, although their survival is a lucky fluke. Lutheran ministers thought the frescoes too Catholic and whitewashed over them in the 17th century. Ironically, this preserved the medieval artwork from soiling and fading, thanks to a protective layer of dust that separated the frescoes from the whitewash. The whitewash wasn't removed until the 20th century, when the paintings were restored by artists under the auspices of Denmark's national museum.

halfway between Stege and Møns Klint, is the one after which the most renowned fresco painter was named. Bus 667 from Stege stops in front.

Elmelunde Kirke
CHURCH

(Map p126; Kirkebakken 41; ⊙8am-5pm May-Sep, to 4pm Oct-Apr) One of Denmark's oldest stone churches, Elmelunde Kirke dates back to 1080. The vaults were painted by the 'Elmelunde master', whose awesome frescoes span everything from the Creation to Christ in judgment. There's a splendid serpent in the Garden of Eden, with a snake-like body and human head; Herod's soldiers dressed in medieval armour; a devil leading the damned into the monstrous mouth of hell; and several hunting scenes, reminders of the shortness of human life. Go and gape. There's a service held each Sunday, after which the church is closed.

🛏 Sleeping & Eating

Pension Elmehøj
GUESTHOUSE €

(Map p126; ☑55 81 35 35; www.elmehoj.dk; Kirkebakken 39, Stege; s/d 315/420kr; ⊙closed Jan-Mar; ℗@🛜) Situated next door to Elmelunde Kirke, this pension has 24 pastel-hued bedrooms, all of which have shared toilets and showers. The somewhat institutional interiors are redeemed by the convenient guest kitchen, cosy TV lounge and lovely hosts (who also run Motel Stege, p126). There are discounts for stays of more than one night and children under 12 years of age stay for half-price. Wheelchair access is good and breakfast is an extra 55kr.

Møns Klint & Around

Sometimes it's a wonder that the whole island doesn't tilt eastwards with the sheer weight of visitors coming to admire the gleaming white cliffs of Møns Klint. In Denmark's rather dull flat landscape, these striking chalk cliffs, rising sharply above a jade-green sea, are worth putting on a postcard.

The main visitor area, Store Klint, has a car park (25kr), a GeoCenter and a decent cafe. Don't lose the car-park ticket – you need to blip the barcode to get out.

⊙ Sights & Activities

The Cliffs
LANDMARK

(Map p126) The 128m-high chalk cliffs are one of Denmark's most famous landmarks, although how long they'll be here is anyone's guess. In 2007 the country was shocked when, after the wettest winter since records began, two huge cliff-falls dumped well over half a million tonnes of chalk, clay and up-rooted beech trees into the sea. For the first time ever, the staircases that lead down the cliff face to the beaches below were closed for fear of more avalanches.

Years later, access is again possible in most places, including at Store Klint. Here, a near-vertical flight of wooden stairs leads down to the beach (unsuitable for swimming because of strong tides and rocks).

Strangely, the closer you get to the cliffs, the less white they become – up close, there are shades of orange, grey and purple, and layers of grey-black flint. Keep an eye out for peregrine falcons on the cliffs, the only place in Denmark where they nest.

At the bottom, keep your eyes peeled for Cretaceous-period fossils – we found a good handful of 65-million-year-old sea lilies, oysters and belemnites in a half-hour mooch. Take your chalky treasures to the GeoCenter to be identified by experts.

You can walk along the shoreline and then loop back up through a thick forest of wind-gnarled beech trees for a harder walk lasting about 1½ hours. You needn't limit your hiking to the coast: Klinteskoven (Klinte Forest), the woodland that extends 3km inland from the cliffs, has an extensive network of footpaths and horse trails.

TOP CHOICE GeoCenter Møns Klint
MUSEUM

(Map p126; www.moensklint.dk; Stengårdsvej 8; adult/3-11yr 115/70kr; ⊙10am-6pm late Jun-late Aug, to 5pm mid-Apr–late Jun & late Aug-Oct; 🛜) The impressive, high-tech GeoCenter Møns Klint, located at Store Klint, manages to make geology utterly engrossing. Imaginative displays (in Danish, German and English) explain how the cliffs were formed, show off an orderly fossil collection and bring alien-looking Cretaceous sea creatures to life. Kids absolutely love the inventive hands-on nature centre. There are also roaming experts to answer any questions. Ponder nature's craftiness at the smart upstairs cafe, which peddles coffee, cakes and open sandwiches. Access for people in wheelchairs is excellent.

Liselund
GARDEN

(Map p126) The ultimate romantic gift, the beautiful garden Liselund was built by Antoine de la Calmette in the late 1700s as a present for his wife (the name means 'Lise's

THE FABULOUS FLORA OF MØNS KLINT

Wild orchids are strewn throughout Klinteskoven, the woods behind Møns Klint. In fact there are 18 species, the greatest variety anywhere in Denmark, which all thrive thanks to the soil's high chalk content. Many of the flowers are rare, and all are protected. The pyramidal orchid (Anacamptis pyramidalis), with a mounded, multiblossomed pink head, and the dark red helleborine (Epipactis atrorubens), with an oval leaf, tall stem and numerous crimson flowers, are particularly beautiful. The best time to see them is from May to August.

You might notice that the leaves on the coastal beech trees are an unnaturally fresh green. Again, it's thanks to the chalky soil, which inhibits the trees' intake of iron and magnesium, elements that cause leaves to darken.

Grove'). Paths wind their way under spreading chestnut trees, by waterfalls, streams and ponds, up to a viewpoint on the sea cliffs, and past buildings designed to invoke exotic destinations – a Chinese pavilion with jingling bells, Greek 'ruins', an Egyptian pyramid. It's a blissful vision, disrupted occasionally by the raucous shriek of wandering peacocks.

The thatched manor house (bookings 55 81 21 78; tours 10.30am, 11am, 1.30pm & 2pm Tue-Sun) is open to visitors from May to October by guided tour only.

🛏 Sleeping & Eating

TOP CHOICE Bakkegaard Gæstgiveri   GUESTHOUSE €€

(Map p126; 55 81 93 01; www.bakkegaarden64.dk; Busenevej 64, Busene; s 420-470kr, d 620-820kr; P 🛜) Artists and the artistically inclined will adore this guesthouse, run by local painters Vivi Schlechter and Uffe Hofmann Andersen. Within walking distance of Møns Klint and set on peaceful grounds with sea views, its 12 cosy rooms are decorated by 13 local artists. The cultural theme continues with a small gallery and occasional art classes, while the in-house cafe serves mostly organic, local produce.

Camping Møns Klint   CAMPING GROUND €

(Map p126; 55 81 20 25; www.campingmoensklint. dk; Klintevej 544; sites per person 82kr; Apr-Oct; ◉🛜🏊) This massive, family-friendly, three-star site is about 3km northwest of Møns Klint. Despite its size, the hilly wooded layout gives a sense of privacy. The camping ground has impressive facilities: a 25m outdoor swimming pool, guest kitchen, coin laundry, tennis court, mini-golf, bike hire (100kr per day), boat hire (50kr per hour), internet cafe and a shop. In high summer there are guided kayak tours (350kr) and nature workshops in English, German and Danish.

Liselund Ny Slot   HISTORIC HOTEL €€

(Map p126; 55 81 20 81; www.liselundslot.dk; Langebjergvej 6; s/d incl breakfast 800/1200kr; P) If you require luxury, there are 17 rooms in this upmarket 19th-century manor house in the midst of Liselund. Whimsical touches include wall murals and the fact that each room is named after a Hans Christian Andersen fairy tale. There's also a summer cafe with suitably enchanting lawn seating.

Danhostel Møns Klint   HOSTEL €

(Map p126; 55 81 20 30; www.danhostel.dk/ moen; Langebjergvej 1; dm 165kr, r without bathroom 330kr; May-Aug; P🛜) With lots of shady trees and scurrying hares, this hostel has a pleasant lakeside location 3km northwest of Møns Klint. There are 29 rooms, cosy seating areas and plenty of kids' toys. From Stege, take bus 667.

Klintholm Havn

This sleepy one-road village wakes up in summer, when the large harbourside holiday resort throws open its doors, German tourist yachts mingle with the Klintholm fishing boats and sun-seekers flock to the long sandy beach. The eastern section is particularly pristine, with light grey sand backed by low dunes and the best surf. The safest swimming is on the stretch west of Klintholm.

A novel way to experience the white cliffs of Møns Klint is on a two-hour boat trip (21 40 41 81; www.sejlkutteren-discovery.dk, in Danish & German; adult/3-11yr 150/80kr) from Klintholm Havn, at 10am, noon, 2pm or 4pm in high season. People in wheelchairs can get aboard.

You can hire bicycles from the Spar supermarket (Thyravej 6; 7am-6pm) for 70kr per day.

🍴 Eating

Klintholm Røgeri
SMOKEHOUSE **€€**

(Map p126; Margrethevej 14; lunches/dinner buffets 98/148kr; ☺lunch & dinner summer; 🛜) For excellent value, walk 250m along the coastal road east of the fishing harbour to Klintholm Røgeri. At this smokehouse, you can buy fish by the piece and enjoy it at a picnic table. Alternatively, head into the white-on-white restaurant and tackle the lip-smacking buffet of grilled, smoked and marinated ocean treats.

Portofino
ITALIAN **€€**

(Thyravej 4A; pizzas 64-95kr, mains 129-158kr; ☺lunch & dinner daily mid-Jun–Aug, Sat & Sun only Easter-May & Sep–mid-Oct) It mightn't have the aesthetic charm of its namesake, but this simple restaurant does peddle some satisfying Italian dishes, including a just-like-Mamma's lasagne. If you're lucky, Tuscan owner Adriano might even serenade you on his electric keyboard.

Western Møn

You'll see more pheasants than people on the narrow country lanes at the western end of Møn: such tourist-free ruralism is very restful. There are a few worthwhile historic sights, but you'll need your own transport as public buses primarily serve Rte 287.

◉ Sights

ᴛᴏᴘ/ᴄʜᴏɪᴄᴇ Fanefjord Kirke
CHURCH

(Map p126; Fanefjordvej; ☺8am-6pm) This 13th-century church is adorned with superb, recently restored frescoes. The oldest, from 1350, depicts St Christopher carrying Christ across a ford, but most of the vaults are covered with a cartoon-like 'paupers' Bible' by the 'Elmelunde master' (see the boxed text, p129). Unique images include a gruesome one of Judas, with two devils pulling out his soul; Mary on doomsday, tipping the judgment scales in humanity's favour; and a gleeful horny-kneed demon listening to two women gossiping! You can see the master's signature (which resembles a stick man with rabbit ears) on an altar-facing rib in the northeastern vault.

Passage Graves
ARCHAEOLOGICAL SITES

(Map p126) There are an incredible 119 megalithic tombs on Møn, dating from 4000 to 1800 BC. Two of the best-known passage graves (jættestuer, or 'giants' rooms') are Kong Asgers Høj and Klekkende Høj, quite close to each other about 2km from the village of Røddinge.

Kong Asgers Høj (Kong Asgersvej) is northwest of Røddinge, just by the roadside. This is Denmark's largest passage grave, with a burial chamber 10m long and more than 2m wide. Bring a torch (flashlight) and watch your head.

Klekkende Høj, southeast of Røddinge, is the only double passage grave on Møn: two side-by-side entrances each lead to a 7m-long chamber. The grave is 400m away from a tiny car park through a farmer's field. The setting adds drama to the visit – it's an indescribable relief to crawl out of a cold tomb into a field of sunlight and waving corn.

Grønsalen
ARCHAEOLOGICAL SITE

(Map p126) A short walk down the road from Fanefjord Kirke (turn left out of the church driveway) is one of Denmark's longest megalithic barrows, Grønsalen. You can't go inside, but you can admire its scale – it's 102m long and surrounded by 145 huge blocks of sparkling, pinkish-coloured rock.

🛏️ Sleeping

ᴛᴏᴘ/ᴄʜᴏɪᴄᴇ Tohøjgaard Gæstgivern
GUESTHOUSE **€€**

(Map p126; 🖀55 81 60 67; www.tohoejgaard.com; Rytsebækvej 17, Hjelm; r 588-770kr; ☺Easter–mid-Sep; 🅿🛜) Book ahead to slumber at what has to be one of Denmark's most coveted guesthouses: an 1875 farmhouse surrounded by fields, a 4000-year-old burial mound and calming sea views. Six eclectic, individually themed guestrooms are a cosy combo of flea-market finds, books and fluffy bathrobes, while the welcome tray of organic local chocolates, seasonal fruit and juice is a sweet extra touch. At a communal table in the converted milking room, host Christine serves fabulous, Scandinavian dinners (two courses 210kr), using local produce and vegies and herbs straight from the garden. Best of all, nonguests can dine here too (book two days ahead). Check the website for low-season 'gourmet-weekend' packages too. The guesthouse lies 9.5km southwest of Stege; if you take public transport, you'll need to walk about 4km to get here.

Camping Vestmøn
CAMPING GROUND **€**

(Map p126; 🖀55 81 75 95; www.camping-vestmoen. dk; Hårbøllevej 87, Askeby; site per person 80kr; ☺May-early Sep) If you enjoy evening strolls on deserted beaches, you'll love this quiet, well-run camping ground directly on Hårbølle Strand. It's possible to rent bicycles (per day 50kr), the best way to experience western Møn's slow charm. Make sure to bring cash: credit cards are not accepted.

Bogø

The island of Bogø, west of Møn, is somewhere you pass through on the way to somewhere else. It's connected to Møn by a causeway, and to Zealand and Falster via the impressive Farø bridges.

Bicycles are not allowed on the Farø bridges, so cyclists need to take the summer-only **car ferry** (☎ 30 53 24 28; www.idas-venner. dk, in Danish; one way adult/4-14yr 25/15kr, car/bicycle 65/20kr; ☺mid-May–mid-Sep) that shuttles between southern Bogø and Stubbekøbing in Falster. Ferries run from Bogø hourly between 9.15am and 6.15pm, and from Stubbekøbing between 9am and 6pm.

FALSTER

POP 43,400

The southeastern coast of Falster is a summer haven where white-sand beaches act as a magnet for German and Danish holiday-makers. Marielyst in particular is a popular family seaside destination, with the emphasis on gentle activity holidays. A short drive away, Nykøbing's Middelaldercentret is another winner with the kids, where they can spend a pleasant half-day watching giant catapults being fired, cheering on jousting knights and exploring the medieval town.

You might fancy a car or bike ride through Falster's rather repetitive agricultural interior to the tip of the island, where Denmark's most southerly point is acknowledged by Sydstenen (The South Stone), a big rock with a bench in front of it.

ⓘ Getting There & Away

Nykøbing F is 128km southwest of Copenhagen. The north–south E55 highway goes directly through Nykøbing F, while Rte 9 connects Nykøbing F with Lolland via the Frederik IX bridge.

Trains leave Copenhagen hourly for Nykøbing F (154kr, two hours).

Buses leave just south of the train station. Buses 42, 43 and 741 run frequently to Marielyst (32kr, 25 minutes), particularly on weekdays.

For information on ferries from Gedser (26km south of Nykøbing F) to Rostock in Germany, see p326. Bus 740 runs to Gedser (32kr, 39 minutes), with around 24 daily services on

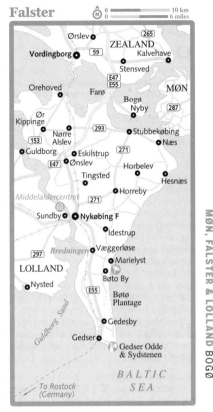

weekdays, 13 services on Saturdays and eight services on Sundays.

ⓘ Getting Around

From Nykøbing F train station it's a 25-minute bus ride to Marielyst (32kr). Buses are frequent, particularly on weekdays; catch bus 42, 43 or 741.

Bicycles can be hired from the Marielyst tourist information office for 60kr per day.

Nykøbing F

POP 16,465

Falster's only large town is sprawling Nykøbing F, which straggles over the Frederik IX bridge and onto the island of Lolland. The best thing about it is its Medieval Centre, complete with jousting knights, which makes a very entertaining family day out. Otherwise, Nykøbing F is predominantly a modern town with few tourist attractions.

The 'F', incidentally, stands for Falster and is used to differentiate the town from Denmark's two other Nykøbings.

Sights

Middelaldercentret
THEME PARK

(Medieval Centre; www.middelaldercentret.dk; Ved Hamborgskoven 2, Sundby L; adult/3-11yr/family 100/50/280kr; ☉10am-5pm late Jun–mid-Aug, to 4pm May-late Jun & mid-Aug–Sep, closed Mon May & Sep) This is the area's most popular attraction, which re-creates an early-15th-century medieval village – great fun, especially if you have kids. The site includes four brutal-looking siege engines (fired off at noon), a merchant's house with its own harbour and boats, a marketplace surrounded by craft workshops, and a cool playground with medieval-inspired play equipment.

Costumed interpreters weave cloth, cut shoe leather and hammer metal in the forge. A particularly good time to visit is during the knights' tournaments, which occur at 2pm daily from late June to mid-August (1.30pm Tuesday, Wednesday, Thursday, Saturday and Sunday outside those months).

The Medieval Centre is on the outskirts of Nykøbing F, across the bridge on Lolland. Bus 702 runs from Nykøbing F train station roughly hourly.

Museet Falsters Minder
MUSEUM

(Langgade 2; admission 30kr; ☉10am-4pm Mon-Sat Jun–mid-Aug, 11am-3pm Tue-Sat rest of year) This is a nicely presented local-history museum, occupying one of Nykøbing F's oldest houses. It includes costumes, toys, reconstructed 19th-century rooms, china and glass (look out for the bottle with the devil in the bottom!). Downstairs are older archaeological finds, including a Viking torque and arm rings. Most labelling is in Danish. One street over, the town's old water tower (www.kunst-vandtaarnet.dk, in Danish; Hollandsgård 20; adult/7-14yr 20/10kr; ☉10am-5pm Mon-Sat) is now home to changing exhibitions of contemporary art as well as great tower-top views. It's also home to a groovy little cafe (see opposite).

Guldborgsund Zoo
ZOO

(www.guldborgsundzoo.dk; Østre Allé 97; adult/3-11yr/family 70/35/150kr; ☉9am-5pm May-late Oct, 10am-4pm rest of year) You might consider taking the kids to this zoo/botanical gardens combo, located close to the hostel. Among its 80-odd species are marmosets, goats, kangaroos and tigers. There's a rainforest re-creation, shady gardens and more than 8000 species of summer flowers. We just wish the birds and monkeys had more space.

Sleeping

The tourist office keeps a list of rooms available in private homes; prices start at 300kr per person, with a 30kr booking fee.

Falster City Camping
CAMPING GROUND €

(☎54 85 45 45; www.fc-camp.dk, in Danish; Østre Allé 112; sites per person 75kr, small/large huts 160/230kr; ☉Easter-Sep; 🛜) A very nonurban city camping ground, this two-star place is down a quiet tree-lined lane, near the hostel and Nykøbing's excellent swimming pool. There are small red huts for rent, a playground with bouncy pillows, and free wi-fi. Bike hire costs 50kr per day.

Danhostel Nykøbing F
HOSTEL €

(☎54 85 66 99; www.danhostel.dk/nykoebingfalster; Østre Allé 110; dm 150kr, s 350-450kr, d 480-560kr; ☉mid-Jan–mid-Dec; P) Probably one of the few hostels in the world where you can hear the rusty belch of tigers, this modern 94-bed place is near the zoo, 1km east of the centre. An overhanging roof makes rooms quite dark, but all have bathrooms, and facilities include a washing machine and basement TV lounge. Take bus 42 (16kr) from Nykøbing F train station.

Hotel Falster
HOTEL €€

(☎54 85 93 93; www.hotel-falster.dk; Skovalléen 2; s/d 745/940kr; P@) This is a family-run place with 68 comfortable modern rooms and friendly management, although its location just off a busy main road is not appealing. The hotel's restaurant serves appetising dishes (mains 178kr to 225kr) such as whole roasted partridge, and smoked haunch of venison with cranberries.

Eating

Café Vandtårnet
CAFE €

(Hollandsgård 20; focaccias or sandwiches 40kr; ☉10am-5pm Mon-Sat) Channelling Copenhagen with its boldly coloured furniture, low-slung table lamps, and contemporary art, this cool, laid-back hang-out sits at the bottom of the town's old water tower. Tuck into delicious, made-on-site focaccias, muffins, biscuits and tarts, and wash it all down with the city's best coffee. Customers get a 50% discount to the gallery and lookout upstairs.

Czarens Hus
INTERNATIONAL €€

(Langgade 2; sandwiches 79-88kr, 2-/3-course dinner 275/325kr; ☉lunch Tue-Sat, dinner Wed-Sat)

Arguably Nykøbing's most upmarket option is this classic wood-panelled dining room. Its antique furnishings are original – from the days when it was a guesthouse (where tsar Peter the Great once stayed) 200 years ago. The steak specials are particularly filling.

17   CAFE €

(Torvet; sandwiches 45-48kr, salads 35-38kr; ☺11am-5.30pm Mon-Fri, to 2pm Sat) Beneath a smart black awning, this contemporary cafe peddles fresh, low-fuss grub like sandwiches and bagels, as well as ice cream, milkshakes and smoothies. Square-side seating makes it a popular summertime spot.

Restaurant Italy   ITALIAN €

(Langgade 23; pizzas 45-65kr; ☺lunch & dinner) A standard Italian restaurant, a block from Torvet, with large portions of freshly made pasta and large personal pizzas.

❶ Information

Torvet, the town centre, is a 10-minute walk west of the train station. **Nykøbing F Turistinformation** (☏51 21 25 08; www.visitlolland-falster. com; Langgade 2; ☺10am-5pm Mon-Thu, to 6pm Fri, to 2pm Sat) is located at the Museet Falsters Minder (p134). Free internet access is available at the **library** (Rosenvænget 17; ☺10am-7pm Mon-Thu, to 5pm Fri, to 2pm Sat), a few minutes' walk northeast of Torvet.

Marielyst

POP 780

With its glorious stretch of beach, Marielyst is one of Denmark's prime vacation areas. There are a holiday-tastic 6000 summer cottages here, and more being built all the time. Thankfully, the beach is long enough to absorb the crowds, and you should be able to find a relatively private patch of your own. For the most convenient parking, follow the main street until it dead-ends.

The town itself is one long, visually uninspiring strip of bucket-and-spade shops, bars, pizza places and ice-cream kiosks running perpendicularly down towards the beach. In high season, there are loads of different activities to try around Marielyst, from windsurfing classes to paintball.

✖ Activities

There's a hearty attempt to market Marielyst as a family-oriented 'activity town'. You can buy comprehensive activity packages from www.marielyst-adventure.dk (in Danish).

Aquasyd Dykker & Vandsportscenter   DIVING, KAYAKING

(www.aquasyd.dk, in Danish; Marielyst Strandvej 21; ☺2-5.30pm Mon, Tue, Thu & Fri, 10am-3pm Sat) Can arrange dives all over the south to submerged Stone Age villages and shipwrecks for around 375kr to 495kr, plus equipment hire. You can also go water-skiing, banana boating and sea kayaking – contact Aquasyd for details.

Surfcenter Falster   WINDSURFING

(☏23 60 30 26; www.surfcenterfalster.dk; Marielyst Strandpark 5) Located in a shop called Westwind adjoining the Fakta supermarket (beside the tourist office), Surfcenter Falster hires windsurfing equipment as well as offering windsurfing or kitesurfing classes for novices.

Superbowling   BOWLING

(www.superbowling.dk; Marielyst Strandpark 1; per hr from 140kr; ☺11am-10pm Sun-Thu, to midnight Fri & Sat Jul–mid-Aug, reduced hrs rest of year) Kids may enjoy Superbowling, a 10-lane bowling alley about 700m east of Marielyst centre, near the tourist office.

🛏 Sleeping

The tourist office can book summer houses (two-bedroom house from around 3500kr per week).

Hotel Nørrevang   HOTEL €€

(☏54 13 62 62; www.norrevang.dk; Marielyst Strandvej 32; s 870-945kr, d 1095-1195kr, cottages 1350kr, plus 400kr cleaning fee; P☎☀) Marielyst's most upmarket hotel offers smart, recently renovated rooms under a low-slung thatched roof. Standard rooms have bathroom, phone, satellite TV and free wireless internet. There are 54 cottages with kitchens that can accommodate four to six people, as well as an indoor pool with spa and water slide. The 'upmarket' restaurant is best avoided.

Marielyst Feriepark & Camping   CAMPING GROUND €

(☏70 20 79 99; www.marielyst-feriepark.dk, in Danish; Marielyst Strandvej 36; sites per adult/child 65kr/free; ☺Apr-Sep; @) This centrally located camping ground is off the main road. Hedges break up the pitches, but also make it feel slightly cramped.

✕ Eating

Many of Marielyst's eating places are closed for lunch and on Mondays out of the high

Marielyst

Marielyst

Activities, Courses & Tours

Sleeping

Eating

season. On the corner of Bøtøvej and Marielyst Strandvej you'll find several ice-cream and hot-dog kiosks.

Schous Kød   INTERNATIONAL €€
(Bøtøvej 12; mains 169-275kr; ⊙lunch & dinner) A short walk down Bøtøvej, Schous Kød offers a good alternative to junk food. It's attached to a busy butcher/deli, which might explain why the meals are traditional meaty affairs – think boeuf Béarnaise and lobster soup. Vegetarian options are limited but satisfying – tomato tart with mozzarella and mixed salad

when we visited. There's also a tasty, belt-busting lunch buffet (109kr) on weekends.

Larsen's Plads   INTERNATIONAL €€
(Marielyst Strandvej 53; pizzas 52-85kr, dinner buffets 159kr; ⊙lunch & dinner) 'My wife left me for my best friend. God, I miss him.' If you find that funny, there are plenty more jokes plastering the walls of idiosyncratic Larsen's Plads. It offers hearty beef, chicken and fish dishes, several vegetarian offerings, a big brunch (99kr) and takeaway pizzas. For fresh bread and smørrebrød, head to **Larsen's Bageri** (⊙6am-5pm; smørrebrød 22-45kr) across the road.

Tannhäuser   PIZZERIA €
(cnr Bøtøvej & Marielyst Strandvej; pizzas 47-70kr; ⊙lunch & dinner) This cheapie pizza place is a takeaway with tables, full of sunburned families on a budget. Other bad-for-you items on the menu include kebabs and burgers.

ℹ Information
Marielyst Turistbureau (☎54 13 62 98; www.visitmarielyst.com; Marielyst Strandpark 3; ⊙9am-4pm Mon-Fri, to 5pm Sat, 10am-2pm Sun; @) By the bowling alley on the outskirts of town. Internet access costs 15kr per half an hour.
Nordea (Marielyst Strandvej 54) ATM machine.

LOLLAND

POP 65,765

Lolland's flat farmland is enlivened by a smattering of family-friendly attractions – parents with their own transport should take the kids to see monkeys and tigers at Knuthenborg Safari Park, and to the vast, slide-filled waterpark of Lalandia. Far and away the most appealing of Lolland's towns is Maribo, nestled on the shores of a bird-filled lake: spend a few hours enjoying its relaxed, small-town charm.

Getting There & Around

The main east–west railway line runs between Nykøbing F and Nakskov (80kr, 45 minutes), with half-hourly to hourly trains during the week (hourly on weekends). The other railway line runs between Nykøbing F and the Rødby ferry (64kr, 22 minutes). Trains leave Rødbyhavn several times a day in conjunction with the ferry service from Puttgarden, Germany; most of the trains continue on from Nykøbing F to Copenhagen. For information about the ferry itself, see p326.

LangelandsFærgen (☎70 23 90 30; www.langelandsfaergen.dk) runs a car ferry between Tårs (in the far west of Lolland) and Spodsbjerg (in Langeland; adult/child/car with up to nine passengers 76/38/245kr per car) once an hour. Travel time is 45 minutes. See the website for up-to-date sailing times.

There's a direct ferry service to Puttgarden (Germany) from Rødbyhavn, a small harbourside town in the south. It provides the link in the inter-Europe E47 highway between Germany and Denmark.

Maribo

POP 5965

Maribo is easily the most agreeable of Lolland's towns, with a picture-perfect setting on the shores of a large inland lake, Søndersø. Its historic cathedral, thick beech woods, waterside walking paths and a few small museums are the main attractions – it's really a place for slow strolling, breathing deeply and letting all that tension slide away. The four-day **Maribo Jazz Festival** (www.maribojazz.dk) adds to the laid-back ambience on the third weekend in July.

◉ Sights & Activities

Maribo Domkirke   CATHEDRAL

(⏲9am-3pm Mon, 8am-8pm Tue-Sat, 8am-4pm Sun) Maribo's striking lakeside cathedral is strangely white and wide inside – its unusual appearance is caused by the nave and aisles being spanned by a single roof.

The cathedral, founded in the 15th century, was once part of a larger monastery/convent complex. Countess Leonora Christine,

MØN, FALSTER & LOLLAND MARIBO

Lolland

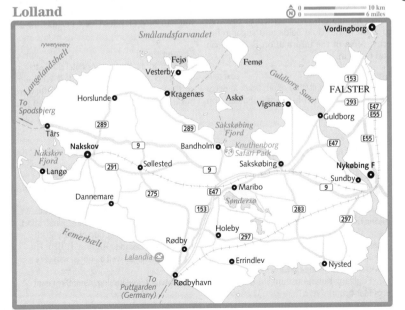

daughter of Christian IV, joined the convent in 1685 after she was released from a 22-year imprisonment in Copenhagen Castle. She lived the rest of her life here, editing the prison journals that record her tribulations – rat infestations, a flea-infested cell, a randy jailer and the vindictiveness of the queen, Sophia Amelia. Leonora Christine's crypt is in the cathedral, marked by a plainly lettered tombstone.

Frilandsmuseet Maribo　　OPEN-AIR MUSEUM
(www.museumlollandfalster.dk; Meinckesvej 5; adult/under 18yr incl admission to Stiftsmuseum Maribo 60kr/free; ⊙10am-4pm Tue-Sun May-Sep) A postcard-perfect outdoor museum, Frilandsmuseet Maribo is made up of buildings (farm, fire station, windmill, dairy, schoolhouse, smithy etc) plucked from elsewhere in Denmark. Old-fashioned games are scattered about the gardens – who could resist a round of Poke Out Palle's Eye? The museum is 1km from Torvet, close to the camping ground.

Stiftsmuseum Maribo　　MUSEUM
(www.museumlollandfalster.dk; Banegårdspladsen 5; adult/under 18yr incl admission to Frilandsmuseet Maribo 60kr/free; ⊙noon-4pm Wed-Sat) Beside Maribo's train station, this little museum contains Stone Age arrowheads, Viking combs, Iron Age glass-bead necklaces, and clothes, toys and furniture. Several rooms explore the experience of 18th-century Polish immigrants, who settled in the area to work in the cane fields and sugar refineries. Most of the information is in Danish and German.

Anemonen　　BOAT TOUR
(☑54 78 04 96; adult/child return ticket to Borgø 70/30kr) The good ship *Anemonen* sails on Maribo's rush-filled, island-dotted lake in summer. Some of the trips stop at Borgø, which hides the ruins of an 11th-century fortress destroyed by a medieval peasants' uprising. Trips run from the jetty outside the cathedral from mid-June to mid-September, at least once weekly (increasing to five times weekly from early July to mid-August). Contact the boat or tourist office for the latest sailing schedule.

🛏 Sleeping

The well-organised tourist office can book single/double rooms in private homes for around 300/500kr, plus a 25kr booking fee.

Maribo Sø Camping　　CAMPING GROUND, CABIN €
(☑54 78 00 71; www.maribo-camping.dk; Bangshavevej 25; sites per adult/child 76/40kr; ⊙Apr-late Oct; 🛜) This smart three-star camping ground has a prime position on Søndersø, with arresting views of the cathedral across the water. It's very well equipped, with shop, kitchen, laundry and TV lounge, and it's accessible to people in wheelchairs. The camping ground is 500m southwest of town.

Danhostel Maribo　　HOSTEL €
(☑54 78 33 14; www.maribo-vandrerhjem.dk; Søndre Blvd 82B; dm 130kr, s/d 350/400kr; ⊙Feb–mid-Dec; 🅿) About 2km southeast of Torvet, this modern hostel near Søndersø has 96 beds. There's a lakeside trail to town, and you can hire bicycles (85kr per day) to get you about.

Ebsens Hotel　　HOTEL €€
(☑54 78 10 44; www.ebsens-hotel.dk; Vestergade 32; s/d incl breakfast 595/795kr; 🅿@🛜) Rooms at Ebsens are small and straightforward, but it's a friendly family-run place and rela-

WORTH A TRIP

FUGLSANG KUNSTMUSEUM

Lolland's cultural cred received a much-needed boost with the opening of **Fuglsang Kunstmuseum** (www.fuglsangkunstmuseum.dk, in Danish; Nystedvej 71; adult/child 70kr/free; ⊙10am-5pm daily May-Aug, reduced hrs rest of year), considered one of Denmark's most comprehensive regional art museums. White, abstract and dramatically framed by Lolland's trademark green fields, its permanent collection spans Danish painting, illustration and sculpture from 1780 to today. Particularly impressive is its collection of early-20th-century works, among them Jais Nielsen's striking Futurist painting *Afgang!* (1918). The museum also hosts numerous annual temporary exhibitions, as well as housing a cafe and shop for a little cultural indulgence.

Fuglsang Kunstmuseum lies 4.5km south of the town of Sakskøbing, itself 9km east of Maribo.

tively good value, especially the four cheaper rooms without bathrooms. Two apartments with mini-kitchens are perfect for young families. While smoking is discouraged here, some guests do light up, which means that rooms can smell a little smoky. The hotel also has a lunch and dinner restaurant serving mostly Danish fare.

✗ Eating

Restaurant Svanen   INTERNATIONAL €€
(lunches 78-198kr; dinner mains 168-220kr; ⊘lunch & dinner) White-linen tables and a lakeside location befit Maribo's top restaurant, located inside Hotel Maribo Søpark. The simple lunch menu includes smørrebrød, a salad, a gourmet hamburger, omelette and fish. Dinner is a slightly more elaborate affair, with options spanning pepper-glazed steaks to steamed mussels in white wine with leek, garlic and parsley.

Panya Thai   THAI €€
(Vesterbrogade 55; mains 84-115kr; ⊘dinner) In a town plagued by uninspiring eateries, this tasty Thai restaurant is a good bet for a flavoursome feed. Dishes are reasonably authentic, and there are enough vegetarian dishes to keep herbivores happy.

❶ Information

The neoclassical 19th-century town hall, in the centre of the open town square, Torvet, contains **Maribo Turistbureau** (☑54 78 04 96; www. visitlolland-falster.com; Rådhuset, Torvet; ⊘9am-5pm Mon-Fri, 9.30am-1pm Sat Jun-Sep, reduced hrs rest of year), with information on all of Lolland, and on three tiny islands off its north coast: Askø, Fejø and Femø. The train/bus station is north of Torvet, about a five-minute walk via Jernbanegade.

Around Lolland

KNUTHENBORG SAFARI PARK

Drive-through **Knuthenborg Safari Park** (www.knuthenborg.dk; Knuthenborg Allé, Bandholm; adult/3-11yr 180/95kr; ⊘10am-6pm early Jul-early Aug, reduced hrs rest of year), 7km north of Maribo via Rte 289, is northern Europe's biggest safari park and one of Denmark's top attractions. Its collection of over 1200 wild animals includes free-roaming zebras, antelopes, giraffes, rhinoceroses, camels and other exotic creatures. The park occupies what was once Denmark's largest private estate and has an arboretum, aviary, a tiger forest (complete with free-roaming tigers) and a big adventure playground for your own little monkeys. The savannah is off limits to anyone not inside a vehicle. Just as well!

LALANDIA

As this **amusement park** (www.lalandia.dk; adult/under 12yr 160/100kr; ⊘waterpark 1-7pm) has Denmark's largest swimming area, Lalandia really undersells itself using the term waterpark. Sure it has indoor pools, outdoor pools, water slides, Jacuzzis and a wave machine, but there are also all kinds of other satellite attractions: a Blue Flag beach, golf simulator, bowling lanes, a fitness centre, pitch and field sports, restaurants, supermarket, the indoor playground Monky Tonky Land, and children's shows and discos. Most people come on an accommodation package, with a minimum two-night stay (from around 2250kr in high season). 'Residents' get in free to the waterpark and indoor playground, and enjoy priority hours. Lalandia is 5km northwest of the small port of Rødbyhavn, in the south of the island.

Bornholm

Includes »

Best Places to Eat

Best Places to Stay

Why Go?

The sunniest part of Denmark, Bornholm lies way out in the Baltic Sea, 200km east of Copenhagen. But it's not just (relatively) sunny skies that draw the hordes each year. Mother Nature was in a particularly good mood when creating this Baltic beauty, bestowing on it arresting chalk cliffs, soothing forests, bleach-white beaches and a pure, ethereal light that painters do their best to capture.

Humankind added the beguiling details, from medieval fortress ruins and thatched fishing villages, to the iconic *rundkirker* (round churches) and contemporary Bornholms Kunstmuseum (arts museum). The island's ceramic and glassware artisans are famed throughout Denmark, as are its historic smokehouses and ever-expanding league of food artisans. It's no wonder that seven out of 10 visitors to Bornholm return.

From October to April, many places close, so always do your homework (www.bornholm.info).

When to Go

Bornholm blooms from June to mid-September, with attractions, tourist offices, transport and cultural events operating at full steam. Long days and warmer weather are ideal for hiking, cycling and getting wet on Bornholm's beautiful beaches. On the food front, June plays host to Denmark's most famous one-day cook-off, Sol over Gudhjem.

Outside of these warmer months, the island slows down, with many attractions, restaurants and accommodation options reducing their hours or closing down for the season. Needless to say, prebook accommodation in the summer, especially in the most crowded month, July.

Getting There & Away

Bornholm can be reached by air, boat or a combination that couples the boat with a bus or train via Sweden.

AIR

Cimber Sterling (www.cimber.com) operates several flights a day between Copenhagen and Rønne. Book ahead for cheaper flights.

BOAT

BornholmerFærgens (www.bornholmerfaergen.dk) operates an overnight ferry service from Køge, 39km south of Copenhagen, to Bornholm. The ferry departs daily at 12.30am and arrives at 6am. The 266kr one-way fare for adults (cars cost 1532kr to 1550kr) is a good use of time as you travel while you sleep (a berth costs an extra 259kr). The downside is

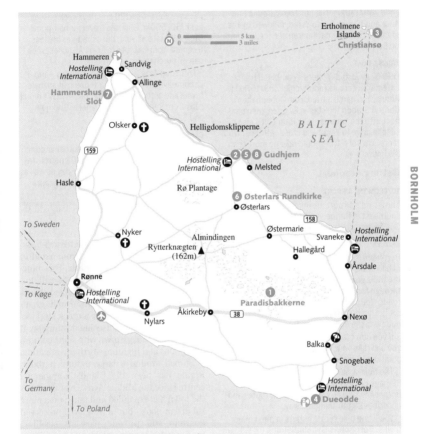

Bornholm Highlights

❶ Spot wild deer in the storybook woods of **Paradisbakkerne** (p146)

❷ Tuck into traditionally smoked fish in a Bornholm *røgeri*, or smokehouse, like the one in **Gudhjem** (p152)

❸ Time travel to the far-flung island fortress of **Christiansø** (p156) for a taste of cosy village life

❹ Wiggle the finest white sand between your toes on the sweeping beach at **Dueodde** (p146)

❺ Shop for one-off creations at the island's plethora of glass-blowers' and potters' studios, including **Baltic Sea Glass** (p150), one of the leading glass-blowing ateliers

❻ Hit the bike pedal from Gudhjem to the striking, whitewashed **Østerlars Rundkirke** (p153)

❼ Snoop around the clifftop ruins of **Hammershus Slot** (p155)

❽ Watch Denmark's top chefs battle it out at food fest heavyweight **Sol over Gudhjem** (p152)

the trip out to Køge, about 30 minutes by train south of Copenhagen.

For details on boats from Germany, Sweden and Poland, see p326.

BUS & BOAT

Graahundbus (www.graahundbus.dk, in Danish) runs buses several times daily between Copenhagen's Central Station and Ystad in Sweden, where it connects with a catamaran (adult/child 260/130kr). The bus takes around one hour and 10 minutes to Ystad, followed by the standard 1¼-hour catamaran service to Rønne on Bornholm.

TRAIN & BOAT

DSB (www.dsb.dk) offers a combined train/catamaran service (adult/child 303/167kr) to Rønne. You catch a train from Copenhagen's Central Station to Ystad in Sweden, then connect with the catamaran to Rønne. It's also possible to drive to Ystad and cross with a car from there. The total trip should take no more than 3½ hours.

Getting Around

TO/FROM THE AIRPORT

The island's airport, Bornholms Lufthavn, is 5km southeast of Rønne, on the road to Dueodde. Bus 3 connects the airport to Rønne.

BICYCLE

Bornholm is ideal for cycling, with over 230km of bike trails criss-crossing the island. Some of the trails go over former train routes, some slice through forests and others run alongside main roads. You can start right in Rønne, where bike routes fan out to Allinge, Gudhjem, Nexø, Dueodde and the Almindingen forest.

If you don't feel like pedalling the entire way, you can take your bike on public buses for an additional 24kr.

The tourist office in Rønne sells the handy 82-page English-language *Bicycle Routes on Bornholm* (129kr), which maps out routes and describes sights along the way.

You'll find bike rental outlets in most major towns. **Bornholms Cykeludlejning** (☺9.30am-5.30pm Mon-Fri, 9am-noon & 2-5.30pm Sat) is the handiest one, close to the Rønne ferry terminal and next door to the island's main tourist office.

Hire ranges from about 50kr to 75kr per day for three-speed bicycles; mountain bikes are 70kr to 90kr with costs reducing the longer you rent.

Biking Bornholm (www.biking.dk; Strandvejen 63, Allinge) offers package bicycle tours of the island from 3445kr per person including bus/ferry, cycle hire and transportation of your luggage.

BUS

Bornholms Amts Trafikselskab (BAT; www.bat.dk, in Danish) operates bus services on the island. Fares are based on a zone system, with the maximum fare being for five zones. Tickets cost 12kr per zone, and are valid for unlimited trips within one zone for 30 minutes. Another 15 minutes validity is added for each added zone. The multiride 'RaBATkort' ticket is good for 10 rides, can be used by more than one person, and will save you around 20 øre. Day/week passes cost 150/500kr. Children travel for half-price. Buses operate all year, but schedules are less frequent from October to April. All ticket types can be purchased on board.

From mid-May to late October, buses 7 and 8 circumnavigate the island, stopping at all major towns and settlements. Other buses make direct runs from Rønne to Nexø, Svaneke, Gudhjem and Sandvig.

CAR & MOTORCYCLE

Europcar (☎56 95 43 00; www.europcar.com; Nordre Kystvej 1, Rønne) is at the Q8 petrol station and rents cars from 500kr per day as well as scooters. It has another branch at the airport.

Rønne

POP 13,900

Rønne is Bornholm's largest settlement and the main harbour for ferries from Ystad in Sweden and Køge in Denmark. This functional little town has a number of small museums and an old quarter of cobbled streets flanked by pretty, single-storey dwellings. Although more of a place for a quick stopover than a compelling sightseeing destination, it is a pleasant enough town with some cultural attractions and nightlife worth investigating.

Spread around a large natural harbour, Rønne has been the island's commercial centre since the Middle Ages. Over the years the town has expanded and taken on a more suburban look, but a few well-preserved quarters still provide pleasant strolling, most notably the old neighbourhood west of Store Torv with its handsome period buildings and cobblestone streets. Two very pleasant streets with period buildings are the cobblestone Laksegade and Storegade.

◉ Sights & Activities

Bornholms Museum　　　MUSEUM
(www.bornholmsmuseum.dk; Sankt Mortensgade 29; adult/child incl entry to Hjorths Fabrik & Erichsens Gaard 70kr/free; ☺10am-5pm Jul & Aug, reduced hrs rest of year) Prehistoric finds including weapons, tools and jewellery are on show

Rønne

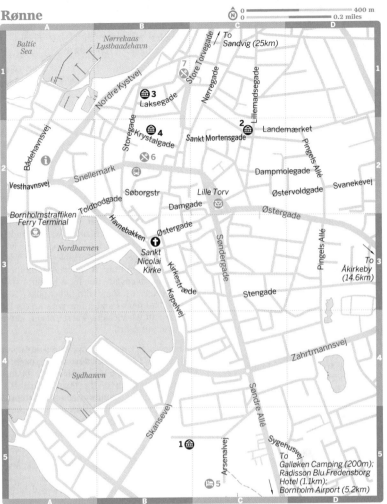

at this museum, which has a surprisingly large and varied collection of local history exhibits including some interesting Viking finds. A good maritime section is decked out like the interior of a ship and there's a hotchpotch of nature displays, antique toys, Roman coins, pottery and paintings.

Hjorths Fabrik MUSEUM, CERAMICS STUDIO
(www.bornholmsmuseum.dk/hjorths; Krystalgade 5; adult/child incl entry to Bornholms Museum & Erichsens Gaard 70kr/free; ⊙museum 10am-5pm daily Jul & Aug, reduced hrs rest of year, studio 10am-4pm Mon-Fri mid-May–late Oct) This ceramics

Rønne

◉ Sights

1 Bornholms Forsvarsmuseet	B5
2 Bornholms Museum	C2
3 Erichsens Gaard	B1
4 Hjorths Fabrik	B2
Kastellet	(see 1)

◉ Sleeping

5 Danhostel Rønne	C5

◉ Eating

6 Jensen's Bageri	B2
7 Poul B	B1

museum features a working studio, and watching the master artisans turn clay into beautifully moulded works of art is the real highlight. You'll find some delicate, locally made wares for sale in the shop in front (which is free to enter), much of it exquisite and at the upper end of the price scale. Some of it is made by the fourth generation of the Hjorth family, who once owned the museum.

Bornholms Forsvarsmuseum   MUSEUM
(Defence Museum; www.bornholmsforsvarsmu seum.dk, in Danish; Kastellet; adult/child 40kr/ free; ⊙10am-4pm Tue-Sat mid-May–Sep) A 17th-century citadel called Kastellet houses the Forsvarsmuseum, south of the town centre. The museum has extensive displays of guns, blades, bombs and military uniforms, but the historical context they are given is usually scant, although some brief explanatory notes in English are available from the ticket desk. There are especially large displays on the Nazi occupation of the island and on the bombing of Rønne and Nexø by the Soviets at the end of WWII.

Nylars Rundkirke   CHURCH
[TOP CHOICE]
(Kirkevej 17; ⊙7am-6pm) The attractive Nylars Rundkirke, built in 1150, is the most well-preserved and easily accessible round church in the Rønne area. Its central pillar is painted with wonderful 13th-century frescoes, the oldest in Bornholm, depicting scenes from the Creation myth, including Adam and Eve's expulsion from the Garden of Eden. The cylindrical nave has three storeys, the top one a watchman's gallery that served as a defence lookout in medieval times.

Inside the church, the front door is flanked by two of Bornholm's 40 rune stones (carved memorial stones that date back to the Viking era).

The church is about 8km from Rønne, on the road to Åkirkeby, and a 15-minute trip from Rønne on bus 6; alight at the bus stop near the Dagli Brugsen shop and turn north on Kirkevej for the 350m walk to the church. The cycle path between Rønne and Åkirkeby also passes the church.

Erichsens Gaard   MUSEUM, HISTORIC BUILDING
(www.bornholmsmuseer.dk/erichs; Laksegade 7; adult/child incl Bornholms Museum & Hjorths Fabrik 70kr/free; ⊙10am-5pm Jul & Aug, reduced hrs rest of year) Suitably nestled on a cute cobblestone street, this merchant's house from 1806 has been turned into a take-it-or-leave-it museum, complete with period furnishings.

🛏 Sleeping

The tourist office can book rooms (singles/doubles 225/400kr) in private homes in Rønne; there's no booking fee.

Skovly Hotel   B&B €€
(☑56 95 07 84; www.hotel-skovly.dk; Nyker Strandvej 40; s/d 555/850kr; ⊙r Mar-Sep, apt May-Sep; P) This picture-postcard farmhouse B&B, located in a protected forest, is 5km out of town but close to a wonderful beach. All rooms have their own entrance and terrace, and the three apartments (4500kr to 600kr per week), complete with kitchen, are especially ideal for families or groups wanting to self-cater.

Radisson Blu Fredensborg Hotel   HOTEL €€
(☑56 90 44 44; www.bornholmhotels.dk; Strandvejen 116; s/d 1075/1225kr; P@🛜) Perched on a pleasant knoll overlooking wave-pounded rocks at the southern end of Rønne, the Fredensborg has 72 comfortable rooms with classic 20th-century Scandi style (admittedly, some rooms are due for a revamp) – all with sea views, some with rather pokey '70s-style bathrooms and a few with access for people in wheelchairs. There's also a sauna and tennis court.

Galløkken Camping   CAMPING GROUND, CABINS €
(☑56 95 23 20; www.gallokken.dk; Strandvejen 4; adult/child per day 69/35kr; ⊙May-Aug; P) Just over 1km south of the town centre, this well-equipped, family-orientated camping ground also has basic but attractive four-bed wooden cabins (from 550kr per day) and bikes for rent (per day 70kr).

Danhostel Rønne   HOSTEL €
(☑56 95 13 40; www.danhostel-roenne.dk; Arsenalvej 12; dm/s/d 150/300/420kr; ⊙Apr–mid-Oct; P) The immaculately kept 140-bed hostel near Galløkken Camping is a secluded, whitewashed building with a neatly tended garden. It boasts typically small and tidy, if rather soulless, dorms.

🍴 Eating

There's a reasonable variety of restaurants and cafes in Rønne, including plenty of cheap fast-food places, but no real standout venues.

Poul B   DANISH €€
(www.restaurantpoulb.dk, in Danish; Store Torvegade 29; lunch meals 75-138kr, dinner mains 148-218kr; ⊙lunch & dinner; 🛜) Owned by artist Poul B, whose playful, childlike figures pimp the whitewashed wooden walls, this beach-chic cafe/restaurant is one of Rønne's better nosh

spots. Lunch options are simple and fresh (think smoked salmon sandwich with salad), while its locavore leanings shine through in a 'tapas plate' of Bornholm specialities. Dinner options are a little more ambitious, though some work better than others.

Jensen's Bageri　　　　BAKERY €
(Snellemark 41; mini pizza 15kr, pastries 10kr; ⊙6.30am-5.30pm Mon-Fri, to 1pm Sat) Opposite the main bus stop, this small bakery serves mini pizzas, sausage rolls and pastries to eat in or take away.

ℹ Information

Bornholms Centralsygehus (☑56 95 11 65; Sygehusvej 9) The island's hospital is at the southern end of town.

Nordeabank (Store Torv 18)

Post office (Lille Torv 18; ⊙10am-5pm Mon-Fri, 9.30am-noon Sat)

Public library (Pingels Allé; ⊙10am-7pm Mon & Tue, to 6pm Wed-Fri, to 2pm Sat) Offers free internet access.

Tourist office (Bornholms Velkomstcenter; ☑56 95 95 00; www.bornholm.info; Nordre Kystvej 3; ⊙9am-6pm Mon-Fri, 7.30am-6pm Sat, 9am-6pm Sun late Jun-early Aug, reduced hrs rest of year) A few minutes' walk from the harbour, this large friendly office has masses of information on all of Bornholm and Christiansø.

Åkirkeby

POP 2100

The inland town of Åkirkeby is a mix of old half-timbered houses and newer homes with less pull factor.

The tourist office, car park and a couple of simple eateries are at the eastern side of the church on Jernbanegade. The town square, post office and bank are 150m east of the tourist office.

⊙ Sights

NaturBornholm　　　　MUSEUM
(www.naturbornholm.dk; Grønningen 30; adult/5-11yr/under 5yr 95/50kr/free; ⊙10am-5pm Apr-Oct) This interactive museum offers a terrific geological and biological narrative of the island beginning from when it was just part of a large lump of cooling magma. The centre, designed by Henning Larsen (who also designed the Copenhagen Opera House and Copenhagen's Dansk Design Center), is one of the island's main attractions, especially for families. It is packed with interesting facts and lively interactive displays. Quite

appropriately, the centre is perched atop the ancient fault line where Bornholm's sandstone south is fused with its gneiss and granite north.

Aa Kirke　　　　CHURCH
(Nybyvej 2; ⊙10am-4pm Mon-Sat) The town takes its name from its main sight, the 12th-century Romanesque stone church Aa Kirke, occupying a knoll overlooking the surrounding farmland. The largest church on Bornholm, its crossroads location made it a convenient place of assembly for islanders. The interior houses a number of historic treasures, including a 13th-century baptismal font of carved sandstone depicting scenes of Christ and featuring runic script. The ornate pulpit and altar date from about 1600. For a 360-degree view of the town, climb the 22m-high bell tower, but watch your head on the low ceilings en route.

Vingården　　　　WINERY
(www.a7.dk, in Danish; Søndre Landevej 63, Pedersker; ⊙11am-5pm Jun-Sep, plus 11am-5pm Sun-Fri May & Oct) Yes, they really do make wine on Bornholm at Vingården. It's a fairly ordinary red, it has to be said, although that doesn't stop it fetching over 1000kr a bottle among collectors. The fruit brandies are a much better bet. Vingården lies 3km southeast of Åkirkeby.

✖ Eating

TOP CHOICE Kadeau　　　　MODERN DANISH €€€
(☑56 97 82 50; www.kadeau.dk; Baunevej 18; lunch meals 150-225kr, 3-/4-/5-/8-course dinner 450/550/575/800kr; ⊙Easter–mid-Oct) In recent years, Kadeau has firmly established itself as one of Denmark's most exciting and innovative destination restaurants. The menu is a confident, creative celebration of Nordic produce and foraged ingredients, including wild herbs from the adjacent beach and woods. Lunch options are limited but inspired (perhaps salted and baked cod with smoked cheese, cucumber malt Romaine lettuce and cherry vinegar), but the true tour de force is dinner, where dishes such as sugar-cured scallops in chamomile-infused milk, served with pickled celeriac, will have you swooning. Considering the calibre of food, service and views (over the Baltic), Kadeau is also great value for money. Take note that although Kadeau's address is in Åkirkeby, the restaurant is actually 8km southeast of the town, right on the beach. Bookings are essential.

Interior Woodlands

A fifth of Bornholm is wooded, making it the most forested county in Denmark. Beech, fir, spruce, hemlock and oak are dominant. There are three main areas, each laid out with walking trails (you can pick up free maps at tourist offices). A single bicycle trail connects them all.

Almindingen, the largest forest (2412 hectares), is in the centre of the island and can be reached by heading north from Åkirkeby. It's the site of Bornholm's highest point, the 162m hill **Rytterknægten**, which has a lookout tower called Kongemindet from where you can view the surrounding countryside.

Paradisbakkerne (Paradise Hills) contains wild deer and a trail that passes an ancient monolithic gravestone. It's 2km northwest of Nexø. **Rø Plantage**, about 5km southwest of Gudhjem, has a terrain of heather-covered hills and woodlands.

Dueodde

Dueodde, the southernmost point of Bornholm, is a vast stretch of breathtaking beach backed by deep green pine trees and expansive dunes. Its soft sand is so fine-grained that it was once used in hourglasses and ink blotters.

There's no real village at Dueodde – the bus stops at the end of the road where there's a hotel, a restaurant, a couple of food kiosks and a 'floating' pontoon footpath across the marsh to the beach. The only 'sight' is a **lighthouse** on the western side of the dunes; you can climb the 197 steps for a view of endless sand and sea.

The **beach** at Dueodde is a fantastic place for children: the water is generally calm and is shallow for about 100m out, after which it becomes deep enough for adults to swim. During July and August it can be a crowded trek for a couple of hundred metres along boardwalks to reach the beach, however. Once there, though, head left or right to discover your own wide-open spaces.

🛏 Sleeping

Dueodde Badehotel　　　APARTMENT €€
(☏56 95 85 66; www.dueodde-badehotel.dk; Sireneve 2; d per 3 nights 2184-3744kr, self-catering apt per 3 days 1760-3735kr; P🛜) These smart, modern Ikea-style apartments 150m from the beach have terraces or balconies overlooking the pleasant garden. Sleeping be-

tween two and five people, they're an especially good bet for families. The complex also offers double rooms, and those with terraces or balconies also feature a sofa and kitchenette. On-site perks include a coin laundry, tennis court and sauna.

**Dueodde Vandrerhjem
& Camping Ground**　　HOSTEL, CAMPING GROUND €
(☏20 14 68 49; info@dueodde.dk; Skrokkegårdsvejen 17; hostel s/d 225/375kr, camping per adult/child 67/37kr, tent 30-40kr; ☺May-Oct; P🛜) This is a modern beachside place a 10-minute walk east of the bus stop, or it can be reached by car from the main road. It also has pleasant, pine-clad cabins/apartments for rent at 3000kr per week for two persons. There's an indoor swimming pool.

🍴 Eating

There are a few kiosks selling ice cream, hot dogs and snacks at the end of the road opposite the bus stop.

**Dueodde Diner &
Steakhouse**　　　　　　　INTERNATIONAL €€
(Fyrvej 5; light meals 52-99kr, mains 99-179kr) You'll be whistling Dixie at this slice of Americana, complete with burgers, club sandwiches, nachos and steaks. As the name suggests, the menu is a mostly carnivorous beast.

Snogebæk

POP 736

A quaint seaside village with a pretty sweeping beach, Snogebæk makes a satisfying little detour if you are travelling by car or bike between Nexø and Dueodde. Right in town, **Kjærstrup Chocolate By Hand** (www.kjaerstrup.dk, in Danish; Hovedgade 9; ☺10am-5pm) keeps sweet tooths purring (and dentists wealthy) with its heavenly cocoa concoctions. Taste-test the sublimely flavoured ganaches and the Danish speciality *flødebolle* (the Danish version of chocolate snowballs with whipped sugary egg whites inside a crisp chocolate dome).

Down by the water, at the southern end of Havnevej and further along Hovedgade, you'll find a small cluster of shops selling clothes and quality, reasonably priced handblown glass. You'll also find a good **smokehouse** (Hovedgade 6; buffet 108kr; ☺noon-8pm) where you can get smoked fish, deli items and cold beer. Just to the right of it is another Bornholm foodie pit stop, **Boisen Is** (www.boisen-is.dk, in Danish; Hovedgade 4; 2 scoops 30kr;

HALLEGÅRD

It might be right off the tourist radar, but artisanal charcuterie **Hallegård** (☑56 47 02 47; www.hallegaard.dk, in Danish; Aspevej 3, Østermarie; tapas plate 80kr; ☉10am-7pm daily Jul, 11am-5pm Mon-Sat Aug, 11am-5pm Mon-Fri rest of year) is a darling of Danish locavores. Indeed, many of Copenhagen's top chefs procure their meats from this bucolic farmhouse, hidden away down a country lane 8km southwest of Svaneke. It's run by the affable Jørgen Toft Christensen, his wife Lis Frederiksen, and their family. Together they have built quite a reputation for both carnivorous concoctions, both traditional and modern. Among the classics is the 'Rita' sausage, made with pork, beef, cherry wine and dried onions. According to Jørgen's son-in-law, Christian, this is Hallegård's 'political sausage', named after a former minister of agriculture's wife, who offered the recipe and who still drops in for the odd 'quality control'.

In all, Hallegård produces around 30 types of charcuterie, some of which are smoked in traditional brick ovens. In the case of its cold smoked ham (a Bornholm 'prosciutto' of sorts), the smoking takes four to six months, with the hams stored in former WWII bunkers located nearby.

Peckish? The farmhouse deli/cafe offers a 'tapas' plate with a selection of its products, tailored to your taste buds. Pair it with a glass of the decent house wine (40kr) and you have one of Bornholm's most idiosyncratic, bargain feeds.

To get here from Svaneke, head southwest along Korshøje, turning right into Ibskervej at the 'T' intersection, then left into Lyrsbyvej (look out for the 'Gårdbutik' sign) and left again at Aspevej. Keep in mind that opening times in the low season can vary so it's a good idea to call ahead.

☉11am-7pm Jun-Aug), justifiably famous for its organic, made on-site, seasonally inspired ice cream.

The end of the road is a good site for spotting migratory ducks and other water birds. If you're feeling exploratory (or in need of burning some calories), follow the coastal footpath leading north along the beach.

Nexø

POP 3760

Nexø (Neksø) is Bornholm's second-largest town and like Rønne it makes up for its comparative lack of aesthetic charm with a bustling nature. It has a large modern harbour where fishing vessels unload their catch. The town and harbour were reconstructed after being destroyed by Soviet bombing in WWII. Despite taking a back seat to more touristy towns such as Gudhjem and Svaneke, Nexø has its fair share of picturesque buildings.

⊙ Sights & Activities

Nexø Museum   MUSEUM
(Havnen 2; adult/child incl entry to Martin Andersen Nexø's House 40/15kr; ☉10am-4pm Mon-Fri late May-late Oct, plus 10am-2pm Sat late Jun-late Aug) In a picturesque 1796 sandstone building opposite the waterfront, the modest yet en-

dearing Nexø Museum features intriguing exhibits on Nexø's history, including photos of Nexø before the bombs of WWII and wartime artefacts such as Nazi and Russian military helmets. Other curiosities include cannons, vintage toiletries and an old-school 150kg diving suit.

Martin Andersen Nexø's House   MUSEUM
(cnr Andersen Nexøvej & Ferskeøstræde; adult/child incl entry to Nexø Museum 40/15kr; ☉10am-4pm Mon-Fri, also 10am-2pm Sat Jul & Aug) Snoop around the childhood home of the author of *Pelle the Conqueror* (the book that inspired the 1988 Oscar-winning film). The house is in the southern part of town and displays photos of the author, along with some of his letters and other memorabilia.

Sommerfugle og Tropeland   NATURE RESERVE
(Butterfly Park & Tropical Land; www.sommer fugleparken.dk; Gammel Rønnevej 14; adult/child 75/65kr; ☉10am-5pm late Apr-late Oct) Just outside of Nexø is Sommerfugle og Tropeland, with jungle climates and over 1000 butterflies.

Balka   BEACH
Although Nexø's central waterfront is industrial, 2km south of town there's a popular

seaside area called Balka with a gently curving, white-sand beach.

🛏 Sleeping

Because the beaches on the outskirts are much more appealing, few people stay in Nexø proper.

Hotel Balka Søbad
HOTEL €€

(☎56 49 22 25; www.hotel-balkasoebad.dk; Vester Strandvej 25; r 570-780kr; ⊙late Apr-Sep; P@🛜🏊) Boasting its own bathing beach, this hotel has 106 commodious rooms in two-storey buildings. Rooms might recall the late '70s, but they're pleasant and clean, have at least two twin beds, a sofa bed, balcony and kitchenette; some even have a second bedroom. There's also a tennis court, bar and restaurant.

Hotel Balka Strand
HOTEL €€

(☎56 49 49 49; www.hotelbalkastrand.dk; Boulevarden 9; s 750-850kr, d 950-1050kr, apt per week 5950-7875kr; P🛜🏊) Only 200m from Balka's sandy beach, this hotel has double rooms and cheery apartments, all with modern decor. Extra perks include a sauna, pool, bar and restaurant.

🍴 Eating

Jantzens Fristelser
DANISH, INTERNATIONAL €€

(www.jantzensfristelser.dk; Havnen 4A; lunch meals 85-125kr, 2-/3-course dinner 335/380kr; ⊙lunch & dinner Mon-Sat, closed Sun & Mon Sep–mid-Dec) Servings may be a little 'petite' at times, but fans of high-quality, seasonal nosh will eat well at this waterside hot spot. Lunch is a simple but tasty affair, with options like house-smoked salmon with salad or fried herring with cider, herbs and apple. Evening brings a short, seasonal, elegant menu of more ambitious dishes (think guinea fowl breast stuffed with basil, sundried tomato and veal bacon). The owners are committed to using organic local produce where possible, though vegetarians will struggle.

Kvickly
SUPERMARKET €

(Købmagergade 12; ⊙9am-7pm Mon-Fri, 9am-4pm Sat, 10am-4pm Sun) If you want to pack a lunch for the beach, head to this supermarket near the bus stop in the town centre, which has a bakery and a deli section.

ℹ Information

There are banks on Torvet, the central square, just south of the tourist office.

Nexø-Dueodde Turistbureau (☎56 49 70 79; www.bornholm.info; Sdr Hammer 2G; ⊙10am-5pm Mon-Fri, also 9am-2pm Sat May-Aug) Opposite the main bus station, this helpful office has information on Nexø, Snogebæk, Svaneke and Dueodde.

Svaneke

POP 1100

Svaneke is a super-cute harbour town of red-tiled 19th-century buildings that has won international recognition for maintaining its historic character. Popular with yachters and landlubbing holidaymakers, its pretty harbourfront is lined with mustard-yellow half-timbered former merchants' houses, some of which have been turned into hotels and restaurants. Svaneke is also home to the island's most famous smokehouse and a notable microbrewery, both of which are highly recommended.

👁 Sights & Activities

Glastorvet
CRAFT STUDIOS

If you're interested in crafts, there are a number of pottery and handicraft shops dotted around town, and at Glastorvet in the town centre there's a workshop where you can watch glass being melted into orange glowing lumps and then blown into clear, elegant glassware.

Svaneke Kirke
CHURCH

You'll find some interesting period buildings near Svaneke Kirke, a few minutes' walk south of Svaneke Torv, the town square. The church, which has a rune stone, dates from 1350, although it was largely rebuilt during the 1880s.

Windmills
HISTORIC BUILDINGS

The easternmost town in Denmark, Svaneke is quite breezy and has a number of windmills. To the northwest of town you'll find an old post mill (a type of mill that turns in its entirety to face the wind) and a Dutch mill, as well as an unusual three-sided water tower designed by architect Jørn Utzon (of Sydney's Opera House fame). On the main road 3km south of Svaneke in the hamlet of Årsdale, there's a working windmill where grains are ground and sold.

🛏 Sleeping

Hotel Siemsens Gaard
HOTEL €€

(☎56 49 61 49; www.siemsens.dk; Havnebryggen 9; s 760-910kr, d 1125-1450kr; ⊙closed Jan & Feb; P@🛜) Although the straightforward rooms

Svaneke

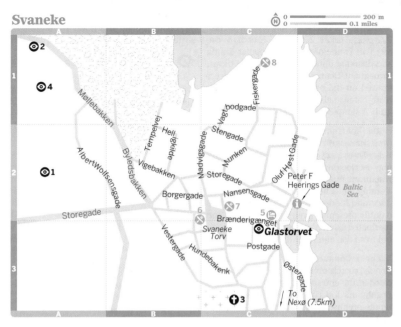

0 — 200 m
0 — 0.1 miles

Svaneke

at this harbourside hotel are a little dowdy, they are comfortable and equipped with fridge and bath (some doubles even have kitchenettes). Request a room in the old wing, a beautiful half-timbered building that dates from the mid-17th century. Service is friendly and guests can rent bikes for 70kr per day.

Hullehavn Camping CAMPING GROUND €
(☑56 49 63 63; www.hullehavn.dk in Danish; Sydskovvej 9; camping per adult/child 72/36kr; ☺mid-Apr–mid-Sep; @) Has the more natural setting of Svaneke's two camping grounds, including its own sandy beach. Three-star rating and just 400m south of Danhostel Svaneke.

Danhostel Svaneke HOSTEL €
(☑56 49 62 42; www.danhostel-svaneke.dk, in Danish; Reberbanevej 9; r 440-490kr; ☺Apr-Oct; P☎) A basic but modern low-roofed hostel, 1km south of the centre of Svaneke.

✕ Eating & Drinking

Røgeriet i Svaneke SMOKEHOUSE €€
(www.roegerietsvaneke.dk; Fiskergade 12; counter items 30-90kr; ☺9am-8.30pm mid-late Jul, to 7.30pm rest of Jul, to 6.30pm Jun & early Aug, reduced hrs rest of year) You'll find a fine selection of excellent, smoked fare at the long counter here, including wonderful smørrebrød (open sandwiches), great trout, salmon, herring, shrimp, fried fish cakes and tasty *frikadeller* (Danish meatballs). Chow inside with a view of the massive, blackened doors of the smoking ovens or at the outdoor picnic tables overlooking the old cannons. It's by the water at the end of Fiskergade, north of the town centre.

Bryghuset   PUB **€€**
(www.bryghuset-svaneke.dk; Torv 5; lunch 59-119kr,
2-/3-course dinner 209/259kr, ☺lunch & dinner) This is one of the most popular dining
and drinking options on the island, known
throughout Denmark for its excellent beers
brewed on the premises. If you haven't already eaten, it also serves decent, hearty pub
grub. A sampler of its three beers costs 45kr.

Hotel Siemsens Gaard   DANISH **€€**
(www.siemsens.dk; Havnebryggen 9; lunch 68-
198kr, dinner mains 198-258kr) With patio dining overlooking the harbour, this hotel's
restaurant makes an ideal lunch choice on
a sunny day. There is a focus on local produce, and it does good light lunches such as
daintily presented smørrebrød, smoked and
marinated salmon, and other more substantial fresh fish and meat dishes.

Svaneke Chokoladeri   CHOCOLATE **€**
(Torv 5; 3 chocolate truffles 30kr; ☺10am-5pm) Located at the entrance to Bryghuset is one of
Bornholm's top chocolatiers. Freshly made
on the premises, its sublime cocoa creations
include a zesty white chocolate, coconut and
lime truffle, as well as a very Bornholm *stout
øl* (stout beer) truffle.

Just off Torv you'll find a **Dagli Brugsen**
(☺8am-7pm Mon-Fri, to 3pm Sat & Sun) supermarket.

❶ Information
Nordeabank (Nansensgade 5)
Post office (Nansensgade 11) At the Dagli
Brugsen supermarket.
Svaneke Turistbureau (🖉56 49 70 79; Peter F
Heerings Gade 7; ☺10am-4pm Mon-Fri Jun-Aug)

Gudhjem & Melsted

POP 724

Gudhjem is arguably the most attractive of
all Bornholm's harbour towns. Its rambling
high street is crowned by a squat windmill
standing over half-timbered houses and
sloping streets that roll down to the pleasant harbourfront. Gudhjem is a good base
for exploring the rest of Bornholm; it has cycle paths, walking trails, convenient bus connections, reasonably priced places to stay, a
good range of restaurants and a boat service
to Christiansø.

It is also an enjoyable place to wander
about and soak up the harbourside atmosphere. The harbour was one of the settings

for the Oscar-winning film *Pelle the Conqueror,* based on the novel by Bornholm
writer Martin Andersen Nexø (see p147).

◉ Sights & Activities

Gudhjem's shoreline is rocky, though sunbathers will find a small sandy **beach** at
Melsted, 1km southeast. A 4km **bike path**
leads south from Gudhjem to the thick-
walled stoutly buttressed Østerlars Rundkirke (p153), the most impressive of the
island's round churches.

TOP CHOICE **Oluf Høst Museum**   ART MUSEUM
(www.ohmus.dk; Løkkegade 35; adult/child 75/35kr;
☺11am-5pm Tue-Sun Apr & May, 11am-5pm daily
Jun-Sep) This wonderful museum contains
the workshops and paintings of Oluf Høst
(1884–1966), one of Bornholm's best-known
artists. The museum occupies the home
where Oluf lived from 1929 until his death.
The beautiful back garden is home to a little
hut with paper, paints and pencils for kids
with a creative itch.

Baltic Sea Glass   GLASSWORKS, GALLERY
(www.balticseaglass.com; Melstedvej 47; ☺10am-
6pm Fri-Wed, to 7pm Thu) Wherever you travel
on Bornholm you will come across small
independent ceramicists' and glass-blowers'
studios. A couple of kilometres south of Gudhjem is one of the best: Baltic Sea Glass. It's
a large, modern workshop and showroom
with regularly changing exhibitions, as well
as a permanent display showcasing the work
of Maibritt Jönsson and Pete Hunner.

Gudhjem Glasrøgeri   GLASSWORKS
(Ejnar Mikkelsensvej 13A; ☺Easter-Oct) Watch
top-quality Bornholm glass being hand-
blown at Gudhjem Glasrøgeri at the dockside.

Gudhjem Museum   MUSEUM
(www.bornholmsmuseer.dk/gudhjem in Danish;
Stationsvej 1; adult/6-18yr/under 6yr 25/10kr/free;
☺10am-5pm Mon-Sat, 2-5pm Sun mid-May–mid-
Oct) In the handsome former train station
in the southern part of town, Gudhjem Museum features local history displays, temporary art exhibits and outdoor sculptures.

Walks   WALKING
A short five-minute climb up the heather-
covered hill, **Bokul** provides a fine view of
the town's red-tiled rooftops and out to sea.

From the hill at the southeastern end of
Gudhjem harbour you'll be rewarded with a
harbour view. You can continue along this

Gudhjem & Melsted

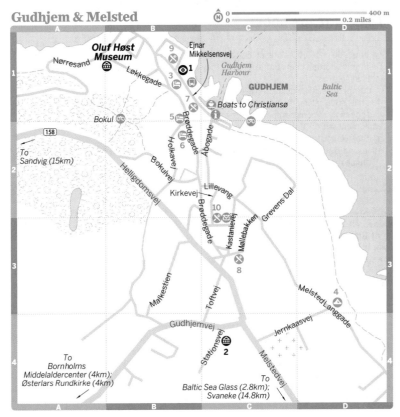

path that runs above the shoreline 1.5km southeast to Melsted, where there's a little sandy beach. It's a delightful nature trail, with swallows, nightingales and wildflowers.

🛏 Sleeping

Jantzens Hotel HOTEL €€
(☑56 48 50 17; www.jantzenshotel.dk; Brøddegade 33; s 700-725kr, d 1000-1200kr) One of the island's true charmers, Jantzens offers smallish but supremely cosy, stylish rooms in a handsome period building. Some rooms have sea views and the breakfast is one of Bornholm's best.

Therns Hotel HOTEL €€
(☑56 48 50 99; Brøddegade 31; s 600-750kr, d 630-1400kr; ☺Apr-Sep; 🐾) This reasonably priced and very central hotel (under the same management as the hostel) has 30 pleasant rooms, all with TV and some with handy kitchenettes. Breakfast costs an extra 70kr.

Gudhjem & Melsted

◎ Top Sights
Oluf Høst Museum.............................. B1

◎ Sights
1 Gudhjem Glasrøgeri B1
2 Gudhjem Museum C4

🛏 Sleeping
3 Danhostel Gudhjem........................... B1
4 Gudhjem Camping..............................D3
5 Jantzens Hotel B1
6 Therns Hotel B2

🍴 Eating
7 Café Klint.. B1
8 Gudhjem Mølle..................................C3
9 Gudhjem Rogeri B1
Karamel Kompagniet ....(see 5)
10 Super Spar C3

READY, STEADY, COOK!

Whet your appetite at Sol over Gudhjem (www.sogk.dk in Danish), Gudhjem's famous harbourside cook-off. Taking place on a Saturday afternoon in late June, it sees four of Denmark's hottest chefs battle it out as they use Bornholm produce to create their drool-inducing entries.

Competitive chefs aside, the event also features an appetising food market, with over 40 stalls showcasing the best of Danish produce and specialities, from herring to honey and cheeses. Various competitions means you might just walk away with new kitchen equipment, art or (better still) a free meal at one of Copenhagen's 'It' nosh spots. Best of all, the event is free! The competition usually starts at noon, so it's a good idea to head in at around 11am to get a good seat. After all, you'll want to taste-test the entries, right?

Check the website for festival dates and details.

Danhostel Gudhjem HOSTEL €

(☑56 48 50 35; www.danhostel-gudhjem.dk; Løkkegade 7; dm 200kr, s/d 350/450kr; ⊙year-round; P🛜) Right by the harbour, this hostel has cosy, bright six-bed dorms. The reception is at a small grocery shop on Løkkegade, about 75m northwest of the hostel. Mountain bikes can be hired for 90kr per day.

Sannes Familiecamping CAMPING GROUND, CABINS €

(☑56 48 52 11; www.familiecamping.dk; Melstedvej 39; camping per adult 55-90kr, child 30-60kr; ⊙Apr–mid-Sep; P) This lovely four-star site is right beside the beach but also boasts a sauna and solarium for when the weather doesn't deliver. It also rents out bicycles (one day/week from 65/250kr).

Gudhjem Camping CAMPING GROUND, CABINS €

(☑56 48 50 71; www.slettenscamping.dk; Melsted Langgade 36A; camping per adult/child 69/35kr; ⊙early May–mid-Sep; P) This is the nearest camping ground to town, a 15-minute walk south of Gudhjem harbour. Furnished four-person tents – complete with beds, kitchen and electricity – are available for 2195kr to 3550kr per week. Another option is the on-site furnished caravans, costing from 3095kr to 4765kr per week.

✗ Eating

Gudhjem Mølle DANISH, DELI €€

(Møllebakken 4C; light meals 65-179kr; ⊙10am-6pm daily Jun-Aug, 11am-5pm Thu-Sun Apr, May, Sep & Oct) Built in 1893, Denmark's biggest windmill now houses a gourmet cafe and provedore showcasing the island's produce. Nibble on freshly made sandwiches, tapas and cakes, many of them made using local produce. Take-home treats include Bornholm cheeses, sausages, honey and beer.

Café Klint INTERNATIONAL €€

(Ejnar Mikkelsensvej 20; light meals 35-118kr, dinner 108-188kr; ⊙Easter–mid-Oct) On a sunny day the patio here is the spot to kick back with a beer and a harbour view. Tasty edibles include salads, sandwiches, tapas and gutsy steaks. It's a popular summertime hang-out, with live music every night from mid-June to mid-August.

Gudhjem Rogeri SMOKEHOUSE €€

(www.smokedfish.dk; Gudhjem harbour; buffet 108kr; ⊙11am-8pm) This fine Bornholm smokehouse serves deli-style fish and salads – its speciality is the classic Sol over Gudhjem (Sun over Gudhjem; smoked herring with a raw egg yolk). There's both indoor and outdoor seating, some of it very challenging to get to (the upper floor is reached by a rope ladder!). July brings the occasional live folk, country or rock act.

Karamel Kompagniet SWEETS €

(Holkavej 17; ⊙10am-10pm Jul, to 6pm Jun & Aug, reduced hrs rest of year) Looking for all the world like the sweet factory in *Chitty Chitty Bang Bang* or a Willy Wonka franchise, you can see everything being made in shiny copper basins in this tiny sweet factory that turns out scrumptious caramels and chocolates.

Super Spar SUPERMARKET €

(Kirkevej; ⊙8am-9pm) This supermarket is just off Brøddegade.

ⓘ Information

There are toilets and showers at the harbour and a car park just northwest of it.

Gudhjem Turistbureau (☑56 48 52 10; mail@ntbook.dk; Åbogade 7; ⊙10am-4pm Jul & Aug, 1-4pm Mon-Sat Sep & Mar-Jun) Was at the library, just a block inland from the harbour, at the time of research, but was due to move to the harbour ferry building in 2012.

Post office (⊙10am-4.30pm Mon-Fri, to noon Sat) Inside the Super Spar grocery shop.

Around Gudhjem & Melsted

The area around Gudhjem harbours a number of cultural riches, including the island's impressive art museum, it's most striking round church, and an intriguing medieval re-creation. It's also where you'll find one of Bornholm's top two New Nordic restaurants.

◉ Sights

Østerlars Rundkirke   CHURCH
(Vietsvej 25; adult/under 10yr 10kr/free; ⊙9am-5pm Mon-Sat) The largest and most impressive of the island's round churches is Østerlars Rundkirke, which dates from 1150 (possibly even earlier) and is set amid wheat fields and half-timbered farmhouses. Bulky and thick-walled with seven weighty buttresses and an upper-level shooting gallery, this odd, striking building is unmistakeably a fortress. The roof was originally constructed with a flat top to serve as a battle platform, complete with a brick parapet but, because of the excessive weight this exerted on the church walls, the roof was eventually replaced with its present conical one.

The interior is largely whitewashed, although a swath of medieval frescoes has been uncovered and restored. There's a rune stone dating back to 1070 at the church entrance and a sundial above it.

A 4km cycle path to the church leads inland south from Gudhjem; the church can also be reached on either bus 1 or 9 from Gudhjem. From Rønne, catch bus 4.

Oluf Høst Museum   ART MUSEUM
(www.bornholms-kunstmuseum.dk; Helligdommen; adult/child 70kr/free; ⊙10am-5pm Jun-Aug, closed Mon Apr, May, Sep & Oct, reduced hrs rest of year) On a suitably inspiring spot overlooking sea, fields and (weather permitting) the distant isle of Christiansø, 100-year-old Bornholms Kunstmuseum, now housed in a svelte modern building echoing Louisiana (see the boxed text, p81), exhibits paintings by artists from the Bornholm School, including Olaf Rude, Oluf Høst and Edvard Weie, who painted during the first half of the 20th century. The art museum also has works by other Danish artists, most notably paintings of Bornholm by Skagen artist Michael Ancher. There's a cafe on-site. Buses stop in front of the museum (bus 2 from Rønne; bus 4 or 8 between Gudhjem and Sandvig).

Bornholms Middelaldercenter   OPEN-AIR MUSEUM
(Bornholm's Medieval Centre; www.bornholmsmiddelaldercenter.dk; Stangevej 1, Gudhjem; adult/3-6yr/under 3yr 125kr/40kr/free; ⊙10am-5pm Mon-Sat late Jun–mid-Aug, to 4pm Mon-Fri May-late Jun & mid-Aug–Sep) The 10.5-hectare Bornholms Middelaldercenter re-creates a medieval fort and village, and gives the Danes another chance to do what they love best: dressing up in period costume and hitting each other with rubber swords. They also operate a smithy, tend fields, grind wheat in a water mill and perform other chores of yore throughout the summer months. In July the activity schedule is beefed up to include falconry presentations, archery demonstrations and hands-on craft activities for children. From mid- to late

BORNHOLM AROUND GUDHJEM & MELSTED

ROUND CHURCHES

As the windmills are to Mykonos or the stone heads are to Easter Island, so are the four 12th-century round churches to Bornholm. The *rundkirker* (round churches) are the symbols of the island, immediately familiar to every Dane. Each was built with 2m-thick whitewashed walls and a black conical roof at a time when pirating Wends from eastern Germany were ravaging coastal areas throughout the Baltic Sea. They were designed not only as places of worship but also as refuges against enemy attacks – their upper storeys doubled as shooting galleries. They were also used as storehouses to protect valuable possessions and trading goods from being carried off by the pirates.

Each church was built about 2km inland, and all four are sited high enough on knolls to offer a lookout to the sea. These striking and utterly unique churches have a stern, ponderous appearance, more typical of a fortress than of a place of worship. All four churches are still used for Sunday services. You'll find them at Østerlars, Olsker, Nyker and Nylars.

July you'll also find a wonderfully atmospheric medieval market on-site.

The medieval centre is 500m north of Østerlars Rundkirke and can be reached by either bus 1 or 9 from Gudhjem.

Helligdomsklipperne PARK

Perhaps because Denmark hasn't much in the way of hills or lofty rocks, those it does have are almost revered. Such is the case with Helligdomsklipperne (Sanctuary Cliffs), where moderately high coastal cliffs of sharp granite rock attract sightseers. About 5km north of Gudhjem on the eastern side of the main coastal road, the Helligdomsklipperne area also has nature trails and an art museum.

🛏 Sleeping & Eating

TOP CHOICE Stammershalle Badehotel   HOTEL €€

(☎56 48 42 10; www.stammershalle-badehotel. dk; Sdr Strandvej 128, Rø; s 750kr, d 800-1000kr; P ๏) This has to be one of the island's most charismatic places to stay. Set in an imposing 19th-century bathing hotel overlooking a rocky part of the coast a few kilometres north of Gudhjem, it's a soothing blend of whitewashed timber and understated Cape Cod–esque chic. It's also home to one of Denmark's up-and-coming New Nordic restaurants, which means memorable meals are (quite literally) a few steps away from your room. Oh, and did we mention the dreamy views across the sea to Christiansø? Book ahead.

TOP CHOICE Lassens   MODERN DANISH €€

(☎56 48 42 10; www.stammershalle-badehotel. dk/lassen's-restaurant; Sdr Strandvej 128, Rø; 3 courses 395kr; ๏lunch Sun, dinner Tue-Sun, closed early Nov-early May) There are two restaurants foodies cannot afford to miss on Bornholm: Kadeau (p145) and up-and-coming Lassens, located at Stammershalle Badehotel. The latter nosh spot is home to young chef Daniel Kruse, 2011 recipient of the prestigious Roussillon Dessert Trophy and a former chef at two of Copenhagen's Michelin-starred A-listers. Savour pure, delicate compositions like smoked scallops with Icelandic *skyr* (strained yoghurt), dehydrated olives, truffle mayonnaise, parsley sauce and malt chips. Service is knowledgeable and personable, and the sea-and-sunset panorama as inspired as the kitchen's creations. Book ahead.

Sandvig & Allinge

POP 1725

Sandvig is a quiet little seaside hamlet with storybook older homes, many fringed by rose bushes and tidy flower gardens. It's fronted by a gorgeous sandy bay and borders a network of interesting walking trails (see p156).

Allinge, the larger and more developed half of the Allinge-Sandvig municipality, is 2km southeast of Sandvig. Although not as quaint as Sandvig, Allinge has the lion's share of commercial facilities, including banks, grocery shops and the area's tourist office.

Seven kilometres southeast of Sandvig, in the small village of Olsker, is the most slender of the island's four round churches. If you take the inland bus to Rønne, you can stop off en route to visit the church or catch a passing glimpse of it as you ride by.

🛏 Sleeping & Eating

Byskrivergaarden GUESTHOUSE €€

(☎56 48 08 86; www.byskrivergaarden.dk; Løsebækgade 3, Allinge; s/d 675/910kr; ๏May-Sep; P) This enchanting, white-walled, black-beamed converted farmhouse right on the water is our choice of places to stay in Allinge. The rooms (try to get the sea-facing not the road-facing ones) are smartly and simply decorated in a contemporary style. There's a pleasant garden, a large, cheerful breakfast room and kelp-filled rock pools nearby if you fancy taking a dip.

Hotel Romantik HOTEL, APARTMENT €€

(☎20 23 15 24; www.hotelromantik.dk, in Danish; Strandvejen 68, Sandvig; s/d without sea view 650/900kr, with sea view 800/1100kr, apt 1400-1600kr; ๏Apr-Oct; P@๏) One of the better options in Sandvig, the coast-hugging Romantik offers 17 simple, smart and comfortable hotel rooms, some with sea views. Even better are the 40 stylish apartments, which feature soothing natural tones, art-clad walls, suede lounges and modern kitchenettes. While some of the apartments also include Jacuzzis, all offer fabulous sea views. Wi-fi is available, but the reception is a little patchy in the apartments.

TOP CHOICE Nord Bornholms

Røgeri SMOKEHOUSE €€

(www.nbr.dk; Kæmpestranden 2, Allinge; buffet 172kr; ๏lunch & dinner) Several of Bornholm's best

DANIEL KRUSE – CHEF & BORNHOLM NATIVE

My favourite part of Bornholm...

...is the north coast. It's particularly diverse with its cliffs, beaches and forests. I'm a very visual person and my dishes are usually inspired by images. Once I have the forms and shapes in my head, I find the ingredients that not only fit the image, but that work wonderfully together. I use a lot of herbs from the island's forests and coast. My favourite is called *skovsyre* (forest acid). It's zesty, versatile and has a refreshing kick.

Food lovers on Bornholm shouldn't miss...

...eating at New Nordic restaurant Kadeau, or at one of Bornholm's famous *røgeri* (smokehouses). My favourite is Nord Bornholms Røgeri in Allinge. The guys there are genuinely passionate about the smoking process and the quality is wonderful. Stop for a local beer at Bryghuset in Svaneke, pick up local food products at provedore Gudhjem Mølle, and taste some amazing hams and sausages at Hallegård, a fantastic rural butcher near Østermarie. Then there's my restaurant, Lassens.

Beyond Bornholm, book a table at...

...Noma in Copenhagen. Not only is the food incredible, but the staff are intuitive and approachable. Another favourite of mine is Søllerød Kro, just north of Copenhagen. It's not so much New Nordic as French-Danish fusion. Just like at Noma, you know you're going to be taken good care of as soon as you walk through the door. They do lunch but go in the evening to get the full experience.

As told to Cristian Bonetto

chefs praise this smokehouse as the island's best. Not only does it serve a stunning buffet of locally smoked fish, salads and soup, but its waterside setting makes it the perfect spot to savour Bornholm's Baltic flavours.

Café Sommer　　　　　　　　CAFE €€
(Havnegade 19, Allinge; lunch 85-150kr, dinner mains 165-175kr; ☉lunch & dinner) Featuring a popular, harbour-facing terrace, Café Sommer's lunch grub includes salads, burgers and sandwiches, as well as great smørrebrød (three for 120kr including fried local salted herring with beets, onions and mustard). Dinner options are warming, mainly meaty meals like lamb cutlets with roast potatoes and herb butter.

ℹ Information

Allinge has the lion's share of commercial facilities, including banks, grocery shops and the area's tourist office.

Allinge Turistinformation (☑56 48 64 48; www.allinge.dk; Kirkegade 4, Allinge; ☉9am-4pm Mon-Fri, 11am-3pm Sat Jul, 9.30am-4pm Mon-Fri, 11am-3pm Sat Aug, reduced hrs May & Jun, closed rest of year) The area's tourist office.

Hammershus Slot

The impressive 13th-century ruins of Hammershus Slot, dramatically perched on top of a sea cliff, are the largest in Scandinavia. Construction probably began around 1250 under the archbishop of Lund, who wanted a fortress to protect his diocese against the Crown, engaged at the time in a power struggle with the Church. In the centuries that followed, the castle was enlarged, with the upper levels of the square tower added on during the mid-16th century.

Eventually, improvements in naval artillery left the fortress walls vulnerable to attack and in 1645 the castle temporarily fell to Swedish troops after a brief bombardment. Hammershus served as both military garrison and prison – King Christian IV's daughter, Leonora Christine, was imprisoned here on treason charges from 1660 to 1661.

In 1743 the Danish military abandoned Hammershus and many of the stones were carried away to be used as building materials elsewhere. Still, there's much to see and you shouldn't miss a stroll through these extensive fortress ruins. The grounds are always open and admission is free.

THERE BE TROLLS

As you travel around Bornholm you will almost certainly spot drawings and figures of the island's mascot: a disreputable-looking horned troll called Krølle Bølle who originated in stories told by local writer Ludvig Mahler to his son in the early 1940s. Usually depicted with a ready-smoked herring dangling from his fishing rod (a neat trick that, even for a troll), Krølle Bølle is said to live with his parents, Bobbasina and Bobbaraekus, beneath Langebjerg Hill, close to Hammershus Slot, appearing on the stroke of midnight when an owl hoots three times.

❶ Getting There & Away

There's an hourly bus (2 or 8) from Sandvig to Hammershus Slot, but the most enjoyable way to get here is via footpaths through the hills of Hammeren – a wonderful hour's hike. The well-trodden trail begins by the Sandvig Familie camping ground and the route is signposted.

If you're coming from Rønne, buses 2 and 7 make the trip to Hammershus Slot about once an hour.

Hammeren

Hammeren, the hammerhead-shaped crag of granite at the northern tip of Bornholm, is crisscrossed by walking trails leading through hillsides thick with purple heather. Some of the trails are inland, while others run along the coast. The whole area is a delight for people who enjoy nature walks.

For something a little more challenging, follow the trails between Sandvig and Hammershus Slot. The shortest route travels along the inland side of Hammeren and passes Hammer Sø, Bornholm's largest lake, and Opaløsen, a deep pond in an old rock quarry. A longer, more windswept route goes along the rocky outer rim of Hammeren, passes a lighthouse at Bornholm's northernmost point and continues south along the coast to Hammer Havn.

From Hammershus Slot there are walking trails heading south through another heather-clad landscape in a nature area called Slotslyngen, and east through public woodlands to Moseløkken granite quarry. Moseløkken is also the site of a small museum (www.bornholmsmuseer.dk/moseloekken,

in Danish; Moseløkkevej 4; adult/child 50/40kr; ⊘9am-4pm Mon-Fri Apr–mid-Oct) where you can see demonstrations of traditional rock-cutting techniques.

For a detailed map of the trails and terrain, pick up the free *Hammeren og Hammershus, Slotslyng* forestry brochure at any one of the island's tourist offices.

Christiansø

POP 100

If you think Bornholm is as remote as Denmark gets, you'd be wrong. Even further east, way out in the merciless Baltic, is tiny Christiansø, an intensely atmospheric 17th-century island fortress about 500m long and an hour's sail northeast of Bornholm. There is something of the Faroe Islands about Christiansø's landscape, with its rugged, moss-covered rocks, historic stone buildings and even hardier people. There is a real sense, too, that you are travelling back in time when you visit here, particularly if you stay overnight at the charming atmospheric Christiansø Gæstgiveriet and get to experience the island once most of the day-trippers have gone.

A seasonal fishing hamlet since the Middle Ages, Christiansø fell briefly into Swedish hands in 1658, after which Christian V turned it into an invincible naval fortress. Bastions and barracks were built; a church, school and prison followed.

Christiansø became the Danish Navy's forward position in the Baltic, serving to monitor Swedish trade routes and in less congenial days as a base for attacks on Sweden. By the 1850s, though, the island was no longer needed as a forward base against Sweden, and the navy withdrew. Those who wanted to stay on as fishermen were allowed to live as free tenants in the old cottages. Their offspring, and a few latter-day fisherfolk and artists, currently make up Christiansø's circa 100 residents. The entire island is an unspoiled reserve – there are no cats or dogs, no cars and no modern buildings – allowing the rich birdlife, including puffins, to prosper.

If the hectic pace of life on Christiansø is getting to you, try escaping to a smaller island, Frederiksø, by the footbridge.

Græsholm, the island to the northwest of Christiansø, is a wildlife refuge and an important breeding ground for guillemots, razorbills and other sea birds. It has to be one of the most remote places in Denmark and the locals protect its environment fiercely.

Together these three are known as the Ertholmene Islands, and they serve as spring breeding grounds for up to 2000 eider ducks. The ducks nest near coastal paths and all visitors should take care not to scare mothers away from their nests because predator gulls will quickly swoop and attack the unattended eggs. Conservation laws forbid the removal of any plants from this unique ecosystem.

◎ Sights & Activities

A leisurely walk of around an hour is all that's needed to explore both Christiansø and Frederiksø, making this a satisfying day trip.

Towers

The main sights are the two stone circular defence towers.

Lille Tårn   LANDMARK, MUSEUM

Lille Tårn (Little Tower) on Frederiksø dates from 1685 and is now the local history museum (adult/child 20/5kr; ⊙11am-4pm Mon-Fri, 11.30am-4pm Sat & Sun late Jun-Aug, 11.30am-4pm Mon-Sat, to 2pm Sun May-late Jun & Sep). The ground floor features fishing supplies, hand tools and ironworks; upstairs there are cannons, vintage furniture pieces, models and a display of local flora and fauna.

Store Tårn   LANDMARK

(Great Tower; adult/child 20/5kr; ⊙noon-4pm Jun-Aug) Christiansø's Store Tårn, built in 1684, is an impressive structure measuring a full 25m in diameter. The tower's 100-year-old lighthouse offers a splendid 360-degree view of the island; for 4kr you can climb to the top.

Walking

The main activity on Christiansø is the walk along the fortified stone walls and cannon-lined batteries that mark the island's perimeter. There are skerries (rocky islets) with nesting sea birds and a secluded swimming cove on Christiansø's eastern side.

🛏 Sleeping & Eating

Christiansø Gæstgiveriet   GUESTHOUSE €€

(☑56 46 20 15; www.christiansoekro.dk, in Danish; s/d 950/1050kr; ⊙closed late Dec-Jan; 🐝) Built in 1703 as the naval commander's residence, this is the island's only inn, with six simple rooms and a basic traditional Danish restaurant. Most of the rooms come with harbour views.

Christiansø Teltplads   CAMPING GROUND €

(☑24 42 12 22; www.christiansoeteltplads.dk; tent site 75-100kr) Camping is allowed in summer in a small field called the Duchess Battery at the northern end of Christiansø, but limited space means it can be difficult to book a site. Very basic four-person huts are also available (150kr to 400kr per night). The camping ground has a small kitchen for guests.

There's a small food store and snack shop beside Christiansø Gæstgiveriet.

❶ Getting There & Away

Christiansøfarten (☑56 48 51 76; www. bornholmexpress.dk; adult/6-14yr return Jul-early Aug 220/110kr, other times 200/100kr) operates passenger ferries to Christiansø from Gudhjem year-round and from Allinge from early May to mid-September.

A boat leaves Gudhjem at 10am daily (weekdays only in winter) and departs from Christiansø for the return trip at 2pm. Between mid-June and late August, boats also leave Gudhjem at 10.15am Monday to Friday, and 12.30pm daily.

A boat leaves Allinge at 12.30pm Monday to Friday between early May and mid-June and late August to mid-September. Between mid-June and late August, boats also leave Allinge at 10.45am daily and 1pm Tuesday to Thursday.

Dogs or other pets are forbidden on Christiansø island.

Funen

Best Places to Eat

» Simoncini (p167)

» Restaurant Rudolf Mathis (p171)

» Munkebo Kro (p171)

» Skovsgaard Café (p185)

» Restaurant Edith (p189)

Best Places to Stay

» Pension Vestergade 44 (p187)

» Hotel Ærø (p178)

» Rødkærgard B&B (p171)

» First Hotel Grand (p164)

Why Go?

Funen (Fyn) is a microcosm of the best of Denmark. Thatched farmhouses, picture-book coastal towns and Renaissance castles dot the island's patchwork quilt of fields and woods.

Its cultural and commercial centre is Hans Christian Andersen's birthplace, Odense. You can't miss the references to the author – sculptured trolls lounge on street corners, duckling-and-swan mobiles dangle in shop windows, lights at pedestrian crossings feature Andersen in silhouette. Odense offers plenty for families besides fairy tales: old steam engines, a first-rate zoo, imposing churches, art galleries and open-air museums.

The region's castles include the Renaissance masterpiece Egeskov Slot. At Ladby, you'll find Denmark's only Viking ship grave.

It's immensely pleasurable to hop between Funen's 90 islands. The loveliest is Ærø, with historic seafaring towns, although Langeland has its own unusual attractions, including Langelandsfort, a Cold War military installation.

When to Go

As elsewhere in Denmark, Funen really comes alive in the summer months. Odense hosts most of its festivals and cultural events from May to mid-August. Yachties descend on Funen's southern harbours from July onward, giving these towns an especially festive air.

Foodies will eat well year-round, although the local bounty from nearby farms and woods is at its best in early autumn.

To Århus
(74km)

JUTLAND

Æbelø

Fyns Hoved Korshavn
Hindsholm

Bogense 162

327

Fredericia 311 Otterup Mårhøj

Strib 317 Søndersø Viby
E20 Måle
Båring Munkebo
Middelfart Kerteminde
303 Stige 165
Nørre Åby 161 Seden Ladby 3
E20 Bullerup
Årup Korup Odense 2 6 Lange-
Vissenbjerg skov Ullerslev
Brandsø Bellinge 301
329 Nyborg
313 E20 315
Bågø Glamsbjerg Årslev Knudshoved
Åro 168 335 FUNEN 9 Ørbæk
Assens 43 Ringe 323
JUTLAND 328 8 163
Hårby Egeskov Slot 1 Kværndrup

Helnæs 329 Korinth Lundeborg
Svanninge Bakker Lohals
Bøjden Faaborg
Nordborg Bjørnø 44 Svendborg
Lyø Thurø
Avernakø Skarø Bregninge Trøense
ALS Fynshav Landet Valdemars Slot 305
8 Drejø Hjortø TÅSINGE
41 Skjoldnæs Søby Rudkøbing Tranekær
Fyr Strynø 9 Spodsbjerg
Sønderborg Mommark Ærøskøbing LANGELAND
Ærø 4 Lindelse
Marstal
Store Ristinge Humble
Rise
Marstal Bugt
Langelandsfort 5
GERMANY Gelting Bagenkop

Store Bælt

Romsø

Odense
Fjord

To Copenhagen
(90km)

Lille Bælt

Sund

Siø Sund

Marstal Bugt

Langelandsbælt

Funen Highlights

1 Cut loose at **Egeskov Slot** (p172), a splendid moat-encircled Renaissance castle with a garden full of mazes, museums and marvels

2 Explore the fairy-tale world of Hans Christian Andersen in **Odense**, at the excellent HC Andersens Hus (p160) museum and the children's cultural centre Fyrtøjet (p160)

3 Visit Denmark's only Viking Age ship grave, **Vikingemuseet Ladby** (p172), last resting place of a 10th-century chieftain

4 Sail away to one of the country's friendliest islands, gorgeous **Ærø** (p185), with undulating country lanes perfect for cycling

5 Don camouflage and descend into the bunkers and battleships at **Langelandsfort** (p184)

6 Be part of the lively nightlife scene in **Odense** (p168)

ODENSE

POP 166,300

Funen's 1000-year-old capital is a relaxed and cheerful small city that's a pleasure to explore by foot or bicycle. The city makes much ado about being the birthplace of Hans Christian Andersen, even though Andersen couldn't wait to flee the city after his poverty-stricken childhood for the glamour of Copenhagen.

Needless to say, there's a profusion of Andersen-related attractions, including museums dedicated to the man, sculptures of his most famous stories, and even fantastical street furniture, such as public benches with monsters' claws for legs.

Odense also offers a rich concentration of galleries and museums, an impressive cathedral with a saint's bones in the basement, a thriving cafe culture, a colourful Flower Festival in mid-August and, thanks in part to its student population, a lively bar and clubbing scene.

Odense translates as 'Odin's shrine', for the god of war, poetry and wisdom. Despite having no harbour, Odense was Denmark's largest provincial town by the middle of the 18th century. In 1800 it was finally linked to the sea by a large canal. The city went from strength to strength, becoming an important textile centre.

Odense is Funen's key transport hub.

⊙ Sights & Activities

HC Andersens Hus   MUSEUM

(www.museum.odense.dk; Bangs Boder 29; adult/under 18yr 60kr/free; ⊙10am-5pm daily late Jun-end Aug, reduced hrs rest of year) HC Andersens Hus lies amid the miniaturised streets of the old poor quarter, the 'City of Beggars'. The attraction incorporates Andersen's rather sparse birthplace. The museum extension surrounding the house contains a rich and thorough telling of Andersen's extraordinary life and times. It has good audiovisual material, including an audio clip of Shakespearean actor Sir Laurence Olivier wheeling out his finest chicken impressions in *It's Perfectly True*, a short tale of Chinese whispers in a henhouse.

There's also a reconstruction of Andersen's Copenhagen study, displays of his pen-and-ink sketches and paper cuttings, and a voluminous selection of his books, which have been translated into more than 170 languages from Azerbaijani to Zulu.

Fyrtøjet   MUSEUM

(www.fyrtoejet.com; Hans Jensens Stræde 21; admission 85kr; ⊙10am-4pm Jul-mid-Aug, 11am-3pm Tue-Sat mid-Aug-mid-Dec & Feb-Jun) Near the museum is the charming Fyrtøjet – Et Kulturhus For Børn (Tinderbox – A Cultural Centre for Children), where youngsters explore the world of Hans Christian Andersen through storytelling and music (in English as well as Danish from June to August). They can dress up as Andersen characters, have their face painted, act out stories and draw fairy-tale pictures in the art room. All materials are included in the admission price.

Odense Zoo   ZOO

(www.odensezoo.dk; Sønder Blvd 306; adult/3-11yr 160/85kr; ⊙10am-7pm Jul-mid-Aug, reduced hrs rest of year) Arguably Denmark's best zoo borders both banks of the river, 2km south of the city centre. The highlight is the zoo's new Kiwara area, a massive open area that aims to mimic the African savannah. You can feed giraffes or take in the views from the upper deck of the excellent visitor centre.

Elsewhere the animals generally have large enclosures and the zoo supports conservation and educational programmes. It's home to tigers, lions, giraffes, zebras, chimpanzees and African birds, and there's an 'oceanium' with penguins and – the zoo's biggest attraction – manatees. Children can also enjoy petting donkeys, a playground and lots of animal-related games.

Admission stops one hour before closing time; at certain periods, the zoo opens late on Thursday, Friday and Saturday – check the website for details.

Odense Åfart boats stop at the zoo during the peak season. City buses 11, 12, 31, 52, 81, 82 and S3 (17kr, 10 minutes) run there frequently, or you could walk or cycle along the 2km-long wooded riverside path that begins at Munke Mose.

HC Andersens Barndomshjem   MUSEUM

(Munkemøllestræde 3; adult/under 18yr 25kr/free; ⊙10am-4pm mid-Jun-mid-Aug, reduced hrs rest of year) In the city centre, HC Andersens Barndomshjem has a couple of rooms of mildly diverting exhibits in the small house where Andersen spent much of his childhood.

Brandts Klædefabrik   ARTS CENTRE

(www.brandts.dk; adult combined ticket 80kr, under 18yr free; ⊙10am-5pm Fri-Wed, noon-9pm Thu) The former textile mill on Brandts Passage has been converted into a sprawling cultural centre and cinema, with a photography museum, modern-art gallery and exhibition tracing the history of the Danish media. Bright and capacious, it holds around 25 changing exhibitions annually by artists from all over the world.

Museet for Fotokunst (Museum of Photographic Art; adult 30kr), dedicated to the photographic arts, has both permanent and temporary collections by national and international practitioners.

Kunsthallen Brandts (Art Gallery; adult 40kr), the modern-art gallery, has four large halls focusing on new trends in the visual arts. Thought-provoking and ever-changing displays include paintings, sculptures, installations and exhibits on Scandinavian design.

Danmarks Mediemuseum (Danish Media Museum; adult 30kr) traces the development of printing in Denmark over the last three centuries. One section covers lithography, engraving, bookbinding and paper-making; the other section concentrates on newspaper production. Commentary is mostly in Danish.

Fyns Kunstmuseum   ART GALLERY
(www.museum.odense.dk; Jernbanegade 13; adult/under 18yr 40kr/free; ⊙10am-4pm Tue-Sun) In a stately neoclassical building, Fyns Kunstmuseum has a serene atmosphere and contains a quality collection of Danish art from the 18th century to the present, chronologically arranged. Highlights include Gustava Emilie Grüner's cheerful *Portraegruppe Familien Leunbach* and HA Brendekilde's harrowing, powerful *Udslidt* ('Worn Out'), depicting a dead farm worker and distressed woman in a vast, flat field. Changing exhibitions are also staged.

Sankt Knuds Kirke   CHURCH
(www.odense-domkirke.dk; Klosterbakken 2; ⊙10am-5pm Apr-Oct, reduced hrs rest of year) Odense's imposing 14th-century Gothic cathedral reflects the city's medieval wealth and stature. The cathedral's most intriguing attraction lies in the chilly crypt, down an inconspicuous staircase to the right of the altar. You'll find a glass case containing the 900-year-old skeleton of Denmark's patron saint, King Canute (Knud) II, alongside the bones of his younger brother Benedikt. Both were killed by Jutland peasants during a revolt against taxes; legend holds that Knud was murdered whilst kneeling

in prayer. Although Knud was less than saintly, the pope canonised him in 1101 in a move to secure the Catholic Church in Denmark.

Two items of note in the cathedral's stark interior are a handsome rococo pulpit and an ornate gilded altar, dating from 1521. The altar is the crowning masterpiece of master woodcrafter Claus Berg, whose workshop was in Odense. An intricately detailed triptych, it stands 5m high and contains nearly 300 gilded, pink-cheeked figures.

FREE **Carl Nielsen Museet**   MUSEUM
(www.museum.odense.dk; Claus Bergs Gade 11; ⊙11am-3pm Wed-Sun) In Odense's concert hall, Carl Nielsen Museet details the career of the city's native son Carl Nielsen (1865–1931), Denmark's best-known composer.

Nielsen escaped a poor childhood by becoming a trumpet player in Odense's military band at the age of 14, before studying at the Copenhagen Conservatory. In 1888 his first orchestral work, *Suite for Strings,* was performed at the Tivoli concert hall to great acclaim. Nielsen's music includes six symphonies, several operas and numerous hymn tunes and popular songs.

The museum also details the life of sculptor Anne Marie Brodersen, with whom Nielsen had a tempestuous marriage. Displays include Brodersen's works and studio, and Nielsen's study and piano. At various points there are earphones to sample Nielsen's music.

Bymuseet Møntergården   MUSEUM
(www.museum.odense.dk; Overgade 48-50; adult/under 18yr 40kr/free; ⊙10am-4pm Tue-Sun) Odense's city museum is in a courtyard of half-timbered Renaissance houses. The 'Creative Man' exhibition on the ground floor focuses on Funen's very early cultural history, while upstairs there are nice Stone, Bronze, Iron and Viking Age finds, including a lur (a snaking bronze instrument sounding like a trombone).

Danmarks Jernbanemuseum   MUSEUM
(www.jernbanemuseum.dk; Dannebrogsgade 24; adult/5-13yr 80/40kr; ⊙10am-4pm) Clamber aboard a diverting collection of 19th-century locomotives at Danmarks Jernbanemuseum, located just behind the train station. The museum has about two dozen engines and wagons, including double-decker carriages and the Royal Saloon Car belonging to Christian IX, fully kitted out with every-

Odense

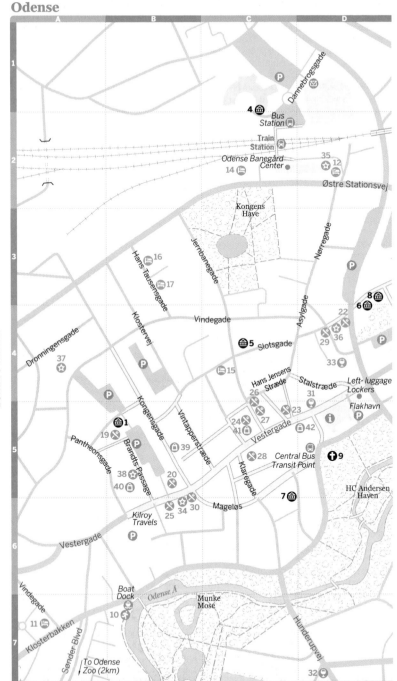

thing a king might need – even a writing desk. There's also a huge collection of Märklin model trains, and a separate exhibition about Denmark's ferries. Audiovisual explanations are provided in English, German and Danish.

Den Fynske Landsby   MUSEUM
(www.museum.odense.dk; Sejerskovvej 20; adult/under 18yr 60kr/free; ⏰10am-6pm daily Jul–mid-Aug, reduced hrs rest of yr) A delightful open-air museum, Den Fynske Landsby has relocated period houses from around Funen and laid them out to create a small country village, complete with barnyard animals, a duck pond, apple trees and flower gardens. Costumed 'peasants' tend to the geese, while children in knickerbockers play with hoops and sticks.

The museum is in a green zone 4km south of the city centre; city bus 42 (19kr, 25 minutes) runs nearby. The best way to get there, though, is by boat (May to mid-September only; see below).

Jernalderlandsbyen   MUSEUM
(www.jernalderlandsbyen.dk; Store Klaus 40, Næsby; adult/6-14yr 30/10kr; ⏰10am-4pm Sun-Fri Jul–mid-Aug, reduced hrs rest of yr) Slip back through the millennia at Jernalderlandsbyen, a smaller-scale (than Den Fynske Landsby) Iron Age village built using methods gleaned from archaeological finds. The village is 5km northwest of the city – take bus 91 or 191 (30kr, 10 minutes).

Odense Åfart Boat Trips   BOAT TOURS
(www.aafart.dk; adult/under 12yr return 75/55kr) The riverside Munke Mose park is an attractive place for a picnic, stroll or boat trip. From May to mid-September, Odense Åfart runs 35-minute river rides to the wooded Fruens Bøge area, where there's a 'nature playground' full of giant wooden toadstools and centipedes. From here, it's a 15-minute walk to Den Fynske Landsby. The boat stops at Odense Zoo en route.

On Saturday in high summer, the experience is enriched by live jazz music on board (booking advised). Trips leave Munke Mose on the hour from 10am to 5pm. People in nonmotorised wheelchairs can travel on the boats.

Independent or energetic types can paddle their own crafts in Munke Mose park, with rowing boats and swan-shaped pedalos (85kr per hour) for hire between 10am and 5pm, from May to mid-September.

FUNEN ODENSE

Odense

✦ Festivals & Events

Carl Nielsen Competition   MUSIC
(http://odensesymfoni.dk) This classical-music festival takes place at the concert house at the end of May to the beginning of June. Young professional musicians from all over the world compete playing the flute, organ violin or clarinet (one instrument is the focus each year).

Flower Festival   FLOWERS
(www.blomsterfestival.dk) For five days, in mid-August Odense is a riot of colour and scent during the Flower Festival. Shortly after this festival, the **Odense International Film Festival**, featuring short films, begins.

Culture Night   CULTURAL
(www.city-odense.dk) In early September the galleries, museums, arts venues and many shops open late or through the night for Odense's vibrant culture night.

🛏 Sleeping

Odense offers good-value and well-located budget and midrange accommodation but is less well served at the higher end. The large hotel chains in town generally don't inspire and in many cases are not very central.

The tourist office books rooms in private homes for around 370/500kr for singles/doubles.

CENTRAL ODENSE

TOP CHOICE **First Hotel Grand**   HOTEL €€€
(✆66 11 71 71; www.firsthotels.dk; Jernbanegade 18; s/d from 1200/1400kr; P@🛜) Odense's grand dame has had a skilfully done and much-needed facelift. It now boasts understatedly stylish, up-to-date rooms with desks, free wireless internet and comfy beds. The breakfast is excellent, with lots of seasonal and healthy options. The very central location can't be beaten. There's also a sauna, solarium and parking for 50kr per 24 hours.

Danhostel Odense City
HOSTEL €

(☑63 11 04 25; www.cityhostel.dk; Østre Stationsvej 31; dm/s/d 235/435/570kr; ⊙Feb–mid-Dec; @) This central, modern 140-bed hostel has accommodation in (extremely small) four- and six-bed dorms, each with its own bathroom. There's a guest kitchen, laundry facilities and a basement TV room with internet access (10kr per 15 minutes). The hostel is alongside the train and bus stations, perfect for early journeys but noisy at night.

Cabinn
HOTEL €€

(☑63 14 57 00; www.cabinn.com; Ostre Stationsvej 7-9; s/d/tr/q from 485/615/805/935kr; P @ ⊜ ☀) Right by the station, the Cabinn, part of this modern, spotless, no-frills and slightly institutional-feeling chain, makes an excellent fuss-free, midrange bet. The beds are narrow and the rooms lack charm but with free wi-fi and parking included, at these prices it's good value.

Hotel Domir
HOTEL €€

(☑66 12 14 27; www.domir.dk; Hans Tausensgade 19; s/tw/d/tr incl breakfast 575/650/700/800kr; P @ ⊜) One of the better midrange options, a short walk from the train station. Pleasant, good-value rooms, done out in simple white, all have phone, desk, TV and bathroom; some singles are cramped. There's free wi-fi and a computer in the lobby. The car park only holds six cars.

Ydes Hotel
HOTEL €€

(☑66 12 11 31; www.ydes.dk; Hans Tausensgade 11; s/tw/d/tr 475/610/795/920kr; P @) With the same family of owners as the Domir next door, Ydes has 26 smaller, spotlessly clean rooms. Rooms are similar, as are internet and parking conditions.

Ansgarhus Motel
MOTEL €€

(☑66 12 88 00; www.ansgarhus.dk; Kirkegårds Allé; s/d 445/575kr, without bathroom 450/550kr; P @ ⊜) A small, family-run place near the river and parkland with clean, welcoming rooms. Most have private bathrooms, but there are four singles that don't. Free wi-fi.

City Hotel
HOTEL €€

(☑66 12 12 58; www.city-hotel-odense.dk; Hans Mules Gade 5; s/d incl breakfast 725/1025kr; P @ ⊜) A comfortable modern hotel near HC Andersens Hus museum. Inoffensive rooms have settees and full amenities (satellite TV, alarm clock, hairdryer etc). Other pluses include wireless internet, a roof terrace with city views, a good breakfast,

friendly staff and a private car park. There's no restaurant, but guests get discounts at Den Gamle Kro (p167). The hotel also offers five comfortable, fully equipped apartments, ideal for self-catering families.

OTHER LOCALITIES

TOP CHOICE Billesgade B&B
B&B €€

(☑66 13 00 74; www.billesgade.dk; Billesgade 9; s/d incl breakfast from 375/440kr; P @ ☀) A very friendly, welcoming owner, spotless if no-frills rooms and a quiet location are all reasons to recommend this place a five-minute walk from the centre of town.

Danhostel Odense Kragsbjerggaard
HOSTEL €

(☑66 13 04 25; Kragsbjergvej 121; dm/s/d 245/435/570kr; ⊙Mar-Nov; P @) Kragsbjerggaard is an attractive hostel in an exclusive suburb 2km southeast of the centre. It's based in a historic manor house, built around a cobbled courtyard and garden. The renovated interior contains modern, mostly four-bed rooms all with washbasins. Dorm beds are available in high season. There's a washing machine and kitchen. Take city bus 61, 62, 63 or 64.

DCU Camping Odense
CAMPING GROUND €

(☑66 11 47 02; www.camping-odense.dk; Odensevej 102; adult/child/tent 72/36/20kr; @ ⊜ ☀) A neat three-star camping ground in a wooded area, with TV lounge, outdoor swimming pool, wireless internet access, shop and kids' amusements. There are several simple cabins for rent (450kr per night) with kitchenettes and shared bathrooms. The camping ground is 3.5km south of the city centre – take bus 22.

✗ Eating

The pedestrianised main street Vestergade contains several moderately priced restaurants and cafes, and there's a cluster of buzzing bars/bistros around Kongensgade and in Brandts Passage. Many stay open until at least midnight (often 2am or 3am on the weekend), but for drinking only. Kitchens stop taking food orders at 9pm or 10pm.

You'll find fast-food outlets all over the city, especially along Kongensgade. On Wednesday and Saturday morning there's a produce market along Claus Bergs Gade, the pedestrian street that runs south from the Odense Koncerthus. The train station contains a small grocery store that opens until midnight and a reasonable bakery with a sit-down section.

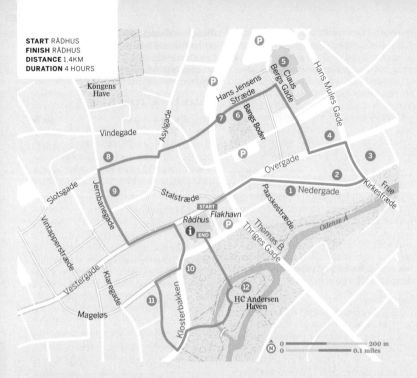

Walking Tour
Old Odense

Walking is the best way to explore the city. From the rådhus (town hall) head east on Vestergade, which becomes Overgade, then turn right onto ① **Nedergade**, a cobblestone street with leaning half-timbered houses and antique shops, including ② **Kramboden** (🕙10am-5.30pm Mon-Fri, 9am-1pm Sat), an old-world merchant's house selling toys and utensils from bygone days.

At the end of Nedergade, a left onto Frue Kirkestræde brings you to ③ **Vor Frue Kirke** (🕙10am-2pm Mon-Fri), traditionally the oldest church in Odense (records are hazy). Most of the interior dates to the 13th century.

From the church turn left back onto Overgade; you'll soon reach ④ **Bymuseet Møntergården**, the city museum. Turn right into Claus Bergs Gade, where you'll pass the city's only casino. Immediately north is the ⑤ **Odense Koncerthus**, with a museum dedicated to composer Carl Nielsen.

Just past the casino, turn left onto Ramsherred (which quickly becomes Hans Jensens Stræde) to reach ⑥ **HC Andersens Hus**,

Hans Christian Andersen's birthplace, and the children's centre ⑦ **Fyrtøjet**. The museum is in a pleasant neighbourhood of narrow cobbled streets and tiled houses.

Cross Thomas B Thriges Gade and follow Gravene to Slotsgade; ⑧ **Fyns Kunstmuseum**, Odense's notable fine arts museum, is on the corner of Jernbanegade. Turn left and follow Jernbanegade to Vestergade. Along the way you'll pass the site of ⑨ **Gråbrødre Kloster**, a medieval Franciscan monastery now a home for the elderly.

Reaching Vestergade, turn east back to the rådhus, then go south to ⑩ **Sankt Knuds Kirke**, Odense's intriguing cathedral. Opposite the cathedral, turn down Sankt Knuds Kirkestræde, then go south on Munkemøllestræde, where you'll pass ⑪ **HC Andersens Barndomshjem**, the writer's childhood home.

Loop back on Klosterbakken and take the path into ⑫ **HC Andersen Haven**, a riverside park with a prominent statue of the author. Walk north through the park to return to the rådhus.

TOP CHOICE **Simoncini** ITALIAN €€€

(✆66 17 92 95; www.simoncini.dk; Vestergade 70; mains 195kr, 3 courses without/with wine 375/700kr; ☺dinner Mon-Sat) Rustic, authentic Italian seasonal food created with flair and a solid appreciation of flavour is served at this cosy, welcoming place in an old Odense house. The first-rate homemade bread, fantastic pastas and flavoursome *secondi* (second courses) can be accompanied with well-paired wines.

Goma JAPANESE €€

(✆66 14 45 00; www.goma.nu; Jernbanegade 3; mains around 180kr, 6-piece sushi selections 159kr; ☺5.30pm-late Tue-Sat) Westernised but still excellent sushi is on offer at this hugely popular place right in the centre of town. It's justifiably popular, so book ahead at weekends.

Den Gamle Kro DANISH €€€

(www.den-gamle-kro.dk; Overgade 23; 2-course set meals 250kr, mains 200-350kr; ☺lunch & dinner) The atmospheric Gamle Kro spreads through several 17th-century houses, with a glass-roofed courtyard and medieval cellar. Traditional Danish (eg fillet of sole stuffed with salmon and spinach) and French (such as Chateaubriand or pork with Lyonnaise potatoes) recipes are mostly meat-based, but there's usually one vegie main. There's also a huge wine list.

Franck A FRENCH €€

(Jernbanegade 4; lunch 85kr, dinner mains 140-220kr; ☺10am-midnight Mon-Wed, 10am-late Thu-Sat, 9am-2pm Sun) Franck A does a bit of everything from brunch to lunch and dinner, with a dash of wine bar and sometimes at weekends a flourish of nightclub thrown in. Very popular for its outside dining in summer and swish atmosphere inside. It's a buzzy, lively spot with much to recommend it beyond the classic French-bistro fare.

Café Biografen EUROPEAN €€

(Brandts Passage 43; brunches 99kr, light mains 80-120kr; ☺11am-midnight) Ducks waddle around terrace tables at this cheerful place beside the Brandts Klædefabrik cultural centre. The cafe does a decent selection of baguettes, salads, quiches, burgers, tapas and tostadas, plus coffee, cakes and beer. Its varied clientele, from little old ladies to moody-looking artists, makes for great people-watching. Order at the bar.

Den Grimme Ælling BUFFET €€

(www.grimme-aelling.dk; Hans Jensens Stræde 1; lunch buffets 89kr, dinner buffets incl wine 265kr; ☺lunch & dinner) A charming restaurant in a cobbled lane, The Ugly Duckling specialises in varied, high-quality buffets. One area is set aside for cold ingredients – a rainbow of new potatoes, herring, olives, tomatoes, cucumber, sweet corn, pickled red cabbage and the like. Hot-plate items include fried plaice, succulent lumps of beef and plenty of sauces and gravies.

Kræz Night & Day INTERNATIONAL €€

(Gråbrødre Plads 6; mains 99-198kr; ☺10am-late) A night-time venue for live music, comedy, karaoke and lectures, this is also one for a summer's day – outdoor tables merge with those of several other restaurants around pedestrianised Gråbrødre Plads to form a convivial mass of diners. Food is bistro style – soup, Greek salad, burgers, Mexican platters, baked salmon etc – but served in monster portions and with tasty twists. A decadent weekend brunch includes chocolate brownies. Service can be slow when it's busy.

Froggy's Café INTERNATIONAL €€

(Vestergade 68; light mains 80-110kr; ☺11am-late) A good people-watching spot overlooking the main pedestrian street, Froggy's has an all-day menu of reasonably priced burgers, pastas, omelettes and salads. It's a late-opening nightspot on Friday and Saturday, when punters are shown the door at 5am. Sunday morning offers a restorative brunch (110kr).

Café Cuckoo's Nest EUROPEAN €€

(Vestergade 73; light lunches 70-95kr, dinner mains 130-190kr; ☺9am-late) A mid-priced place where you can go for breakfast and stay until the wee hours, Cuckoo's Nest does everything from scrambled eggs to cocktails. There's open courtyard seating, backgammon sets and occasional live blues and jazz. Vegetarians should double-check ingredients, as fish sometimes counts as a vegetable.

Odense Chokoladehus DELI €

(Nørregade 32; ☺10am-5pm Tue-Fri, to 1.30pm Sat) Happiness, it turns out, is a chocolate-and-praline-filled croissant, available here to go, along with other fixes of amazing artisan chocolate.

Joe & the Juice CAFE €

(Vestergade 20; ☺10am-5pm Mon-Sat; ☎) Freshly squeezed juices, decent coffee, plus light, healthy sandwiches and free wi-fi are all reasons to drop into this concession inside Magasin.

El Torito
MEXICAN €

(Vestergade 21; snacks 45-95kr; ⊘11am-9pm Mon-Sat, noon-9pm Sun) The Mexican restaurant El Torito has a little takeaway section at the back, where you can buy wraps, nachos and burritos.

Self-catering

Mamma's Deli
DELI €

(Klaregade 12; ⊘10am-5.30pm Mon-Thu, to 7pm Fri, to 3pm Sat) Attached to a pizza restaurant, this deli sells a wide choice of upmarket treats for picnickers – dried meats, cheese, marinated vegetables, strong coffee and freshly prepared panini.

Bazar Fyn
MIDDLE EASTERN €

(Thriges Plads 3-7; ⊘10am-6pm Tue-Sun) Odense's bazaar is about five minutes' walk from the train station. Barter for exotic Arabic cakes, Turkish bread, fresh figs, coconuts and spiced couscous.

♉ Drinking

The cafes around Brandts Passage and Vintapperstræde and the strip along Jernbanegade are good for an evening drink. Many stay open until 3am on Friday and Saturday.

Carlsens Kvarter
PUB

(Hunderupvej 19; ⊘11am-1am Mon-Sat, 1-7pm Sun; ⊚) A five-minute walk south of the city centre, Carlsens is an oasis for real ale and whisky drinkers. There's a great selection served by the knowledgeable landlord. With free wireless internet and a relaxed, friendly air, it makes an ideal neighbourhood-style bar to escape to if you want to avoid crowded music bars.

Bryggeriet Flakhaven
BREWERY

(Flakhaven; ⊘11.30am-10pm Mon-Sat, to 3pm Sun) Odense's microbrewery is attached to A Hereford Beefstouw restaurant.

Ryan's
PUB

(Fisketorvet 12) In the evening there's often live Irish folk music at this friendly Irish pub near the tourist bureau, with Guinness and Kilkenny on tap. It's popular with local university students and with footy fans when matches are showing on the big screens.

☆ Entertainment

Odense is a student town so the entertainment options, apart from the Odense Koncerthus, veer towards popular music in the widest sense of the term. It also has a lively club and late-night cafe scene.

Nightclubs

As elsewhere in Denmark, many of the cafes turn into nightclubs when the kitchen closes at weekends. There's also a lively selection of dedicated nightclubs. There are sometimes cover charges of around 75kr on Fridays and Saturdays in the larger clubs. The live-music cafes generally do not charge cover fees unless they are hosting a big name DJ or act.

Boogies
CLUB

(Nørregade 21; ⊘11pm-5am Thu-Sat) Boogies is a central and very popular dance spot, with a high proportion of student revellers.

Room
CLUB

(Brandts Passage 8; ⊘to 3am Fri & Sat) With affable staff and a sleek modern interior, this bistro also turns into a house-music nightspot on weekends.

Arkaden
CLUB

(Vestergade 68; ⊘8pm-5am Thu-Sat) This huge purpose-built place contains seven bars around a central square, with karaoke, live music and lots of dancing space.

Cinemas

BioCity
CINEMA

(Odense Banegård Center; adult/under 11yr 80/60kr) Denmark's largest cinema screen is inside the multiplex on the 2nd floor of the train station. For the program, see www.biobooking.dk.

Café Biografen
CINEMA

(www.cafebio.dk; Brandts Passage 43; admission 70kr) Located at Brandts Klædefabrik, this cafe shows first-run movies and art-house flicks.

Live Music

Dexter
JAZZ

(www.dexter.dk; Vindegade 65; admission usually 60kr; ⊘from 8pm Thu-Sat) The only dedicated jazz venue outside Copenhagen.

Odense Koncerthus
CONCERT VENUE

(www.odensesymfoni.dk; Claus Bergs Gade 9) Home of the Odense Symphony Orchestra. The classical-music programme commonly includes works by native son Carl Nielsen. Ticket prices vary according to the concert – anything from 80kr upward. The Koncerthus closes from mid-June to mid-August.

Brandts Klædefabrik
PERFORMING ARTS

(Brandts Passage) The open-air amphitheatre across from the arts complex hosts free summertime rock, jazz and blues concerts, usually on Saturday.

🛍 Shopping

Magasin
DEPARTMENT STORE

(Vestergade 20; ⊙10am-6pm Mon-Thu, to 8pm Fri, to 5pm Sat) The city's largest and smartest department store, Magasin stocks just about everything, from food delicacies to cosmetics and clothing.

Brandts Indoor
DESIGN

(Brandts Passage 27; ⊙11am-5.30pm Mon-Fri, to 2pm Sat) Brandts Indoor sells cool homegrown Danish-designed interiors classics. It's good souvenir- and present-hunting territory too, selling Viking-ship mobiles and copies of Hans Christian Andersen's paper cut-outs.

Antikvariatet
BOOKS

(Kongensgade 13; ⊙10am-5.30pm Mon-Fri, to 2pm Sat) Reasonably priced secondhand paperback novels.

GAD Bookshop
BOOKS

(Vestergade 37; ⊙9.30am-5.30pm Mon-Thu, to 7pm Fri, to 3pm Sat) Well stocked with English titles.

ℹ Information

The train station is in a large modern complex, the Odense Banegård Center, containing restaurants, shops, the public library and travel facilities. The tourist office is a short walk south from the train station. Most sights are within walking distance of the city centre.

Internet Access

Galaxy Net Café (Odense Banegård Center; per 30min/1hr 12/17kr; ⊙9am-1am) Handily placed on the 2nd floor of the train station.

Odense Central Library (Odense Banegård Center; ⊙10am-7pm Mon-Thu, to 4pm Fri, to 2pm Sat year-round, 10am-2pm Sun Oct-Mar) With free internet use and foreign-language newspapers.

Left Luggage

There are left-luggage lockers at the train station costing 30/40kr per 24 hours for small/large lockers.

Money

Plenty of banks along the main shopping street, Vestergade, have ATMs.

Nordea (Vestergade 64)

Post

Main post office (Dannebrogsgade 2; ⊙9am-6pm Mon-Fri, to 1pm Sat) North of the train station.

Tourist Information

Odense Tourist Bureau (☑66 12 75 20; www.visitodense.com; ⊙9.30am-6pm Mon-Fri, 11am-2pm Sat & Sun Jul & Aug, 9.30am-4.30pm Mon-Fri, 10am-1pm Sat Sep-Jun) In the town-hall building, about 650m from the train station.

Travel Agencies

Kilroy Travels (☑70 15 40 15; Vestergade 100; ⊙10am-5.30pm Mon-Fri) Specialises in youth and discount travel.

ℹ Getting There & Away

Odense is 44km northwest of Svendborg and 50km east of the bridge to Jutland.

Bus

Regional buses leave from Dannebrogsgade 6, at the rear of the train station. **Fynbus** (www.fynbus.dk) runs bus services from Odense to all major towns on Funen – see individual destinations for bus information.

Car & Motorcycle

Odense is connected to Nyborg by Rte 160 and the E20, to Kerteminde by Rte 165, to Jutland by the E20, to Faaborg by Rte 43 and to Svendborg by Rte 9.

Car-rental companies in town:

Avis (☑70 24 77 87; Rugaardsvej 3) Southeast of the city centre.

PS Biludlejning (☑66 14 00 00; Rugaardsvej 42) A competitive local option (from 425kr per day) if you don't need to drop the car in another town.

Train

There's a **ticket office** (⊙6.30am-8.15pm Mon-Fri, 8am-4.30pm Sat, 9am-8.15pm Sun) on the 2nd floor of the train station complex, and plenty of automatic machines.

Odense is accessible by the main railway line between Copenhagen (250kr, 1½ hours), Aarhus (217kr, 1¾ hours), Aalborg (335kr, three hours) and Esbjerg (197kr, two hours). Trains between Odense and Copenhagen stop at Nyborg (49kr, 20 minutes).

The only other train route in Funen is the hourly run between Odense and Svendborg (71kr, one hour).

ℹ Getting Around

Bicycle

Designed for pedal power, Odense is a delight to explore by bike, especially along the many riverside bike paths. The tourist office has a useful, free bike tour map and guide, *Going by Bike in Odense*. The city council also runs an extensive bike-share scheme but it's probably only worth using if you have credits with a local mobile-phone network, as you use phone credits to pay for the service. A simpler alternative is to rent bikes at **CSV Cykeludlejning** (☎63 75 39 64; Nedergade 36) for 60kr per day.

Alternatively, get a person with calves of steel to pedal you about. **Cycle-taxi tours** (☎28 12 75 13; www.pers-cykeltaxa.dk; ☉May-Oct) of the city centre cost a base rate of 40kr, plus 4kr per minute after that.

Boat

For boats from Munke Mose park in Odense to the zoo or Den Fynske Landsby, see p163.

Bus

In Odense, board city buses at the front and pay the driver (19kr) when you get off – exact change is recommended. The main transit point for city buses is in front of Sankt Knuds Kirke. All city buses except 71 also pass through the bus station behind the Odense Banegård Center.

Car & Motorcycle

Outside rush hour, driving in Odense is not difficult, but many central sights are on pedestrian streets. It's best to park your car and explore on foot.

Near the city centre, there's metered parking along the streets (come with lots of change). Spaces fill quickly, but there are substantial car parks around Brandts Klædefabrik, the Carl Nielsen Museet and by the train station. Parking costs around 13kr for one hour.

Taxi

Taxis are readily available at the train station, or you can order one by phoning **Odense Taxa** (☎66 15 44 15).

THE ARCHIPELAGO TRAIL

Denmark's latest long-distance walking trail – at 200km – snakes its way from west to east along the southern edges of Funen and across to Langeland. The final section spans the length of Ærø island to the southeast.

The trail is open to walkers and cyclists and takes in some of the most beautiful countryside in the region. It can be tackled in sections or attempted from start to finish.

Tourist offices in the region carry the seven-pamphlet series of free map guides or you can download PDF versions online at www.detsydfynskeoe hav.dk.

AROUND FUNEN

Woodlands and wheat fields claim most of Funen, with surprises hiding in the rural landscape – a Viking ship slumbering in an isolated mound, the fairy-tale castle Egeskov, an enigmatic 2000-year-old passage grave.

Funen's sleepy towns curl themselves around fortified mansions and medieval houses. Offshore, scattered islets are home to small communities – sometimes of people, sometimes just birds, rabbits and deer. Things liven up in Svendborg, the largest settlement outside Odense, whose bars and cafes are popular with visiting yachties.

Kerteminde

POP 5700

Beside the swift ebb and flow of tidal waters, small, sleepy Kerteminde has much to offer beyond its pleasant stretch of timbered houses, churches and town museums. The impressive aquarium, inviting sandy beaches and pleasing yacht-filled harbour with its working boat yards and chandleries make for pleasant diversions. Nearby, there's also the impressive collection of work by 'peasant painter' Johannes Larsen.

Kerteminde is also an ideal base from which to visit the superb Viking ship at Ladby, or to get away from it all on a boat trip to the uninhabited island of Romsø.

◉ Sights & Activities

Johannes Larsen Museet   ART MUSEUM
(www.johanneslarsenmuseet.dk; Møllebakken 14; adult/under 18yr 70kr/free; ☉10am-5pm Jun-Aug, reduced hrs rest of year) The vivid naturalistic paintings of wildlife and provincial Danish scenes that flowed from the brush of Johannes Larsen are on show in his former home north of town. Larsen (1867–1961) painted near obsessively from his studio here while his wife, Alhed, also an artist, captured the lush blooms of her greenhouse. There's an impressive purpose-built exhibition hall showcasing more of their work, alongside paintings by 50 other artists from the Fyn school. The tiny cafe at the end of the garden serves good light lunches.

Outside the main entrance is **Svanemøllen**, a windmill dating from 1853 with wooden cogs and wheels intact, bought by Johannes Larsen along with the house.

Parking spaces at the museum are only for people with disabilities. The nearest car park is at the corner of Hindsholmvej and Marinavejen.

Fjord & Bælt AQUARIUM
(www.fjord-baelt.dk; Margrethes Plads 1; adult/3-11yr 105/55kr; ⏲10am-5pm Feb-end Nov) Down by the harbour, this marine centre has aquariums, a 50m-tunnel under the harbour, and seals and porpoises. It's best to go at feeding times, usually around 11am and 2pm on weekdays, plus 12.30pm on weekends. Check the website for details of the boat, snorkelling and crab-catching competitions laid on in summer.

Romsø ISLAND
The wooded island of Romsø, whose only residents are deer, rabbits and birds, is a mere 30-minute boat ride from Kerteminde. You can walk a 3km coastal trail around the 109-hectare island or just soak up the solitude. Bring a picnic lunch – there are no facilities.

The **Romsø-Båden boat service** (☎23 43 63 04; www.romso.dk, in Danish; adult/under 12yr return 230/115kr) takes passengers to the island on Wednesday and Saturday from April to August, departing Kerteminde at 9am and Romsø at 2pm. Reservations are required.

Sleeping

TOP CHOICE **Rødkærgard B&B** B&B €€
(☎65 32 11 23; www.roedkaergaard.dk; Lille Vibyvej 49, Lille Viby; s/d/apt incl breakfast 300/440/675kr) If you have your own transport, try this lovely courtyarded farmhouse in the hamlet of Lille Viby, 3km west of Kerteminde off Rte 165. Rooms have old-fashioned homely decor, colour TVs and shared bathrooms, while apartments are self-contained, with kitchenettes, washing machines and tumble-driers.

Tornøes Hotel HOTEL €€
(☎65 32 16 05; www.tornoeshotel.dk; Strandgade 2; s/d 725/925kr; P@☎) Occupying a great harbourside spot in the town centre, this is a bright, cheerful place let down slightly by rooms that are chain-hotel bland. All have private bathroom and TV, and the hotel has a restaurant with a prime outlook over the fjord. There are often mini-holiday deals, and prices drop considerably out of season. Has wi-fi access.

Danhostel Kerteminde HOSTEL €
(☎65 32 39 29; www.dkhostel.dk; Skovvej 46; dm/r 175/520kr; ⏲Jan–mid-Dec; P) Nestled by a delightful wooded area, this hostel is a five-minute walk from a sandy beach and 15 minutes' walk south of town. The 30 rooms have a maximum of four beds, with showers and toilets. Dorm beds are available in high season. Accessible to people in wheelchairs.

Kerteminde Camping CAMPING GROUND €
(☎65 32 19 71; www.kertemindecamping.dk; Hindsholmvej 80; sites per person 78kr; ⏲Apr-Sep; @) A three-star camping ground, Kerteminde Camping is 1.5km north of town, close to the beach. Hedges divide the sites into long 'lanes' of caravans and tents.

Eating

TOP CHOICE **Restaurant Rudolf Mathis** SEAFOOD €€
(☎65 32 32 33; Dosseringen 13; lunch/dinner menus from 395/550kr; ⏲lunch & dinner Tue-Sun Mar-Dec) One of Funen's best seafood restaurants, occupying a commanding spot on the water south of Kerteminde harbour. This is classic seafood served in smart surroundings without fuss. Dishes might include fresh fish of the day cooked over an open wood fire, hand-dived scallops or lobster au gratin.

TOP CHOICE **Munkebo Kro** MODERN DANISH €€€
(☎65 97 40 30; www.thomaspasfall.dk; Fjordvej 56, Munkebo; lunch mains 98kr, dinner mains from 250kr; ⏲lunch & dinner) A 10-minute drive out of town in nearby Munkebo, this is one of the best classical restaurants on the island. There's an excellent wine list to match the finely wrought, high-end food made from the best local ingredients. Ideal for a romantic treat.

Restaurant Sejlklub EUROPEAN €€
(Marinavejen 2; lunch mains 80-100kr, dinner mains 149-199kr; ⏲lunch & dinner) For affordable waterfront dining, Restaurant Sejlklub at the yacht marina north of town offers Danish beef and seafood dishes. You can sit indoors or there's patio seating, ideal for a cold beer on a sunny afternoon.

Information

Kerteminde Turistbureau (☎65 32 11 21; www.visitkerteminde.dk; Hans Schacksvej 5; ⏲9am-5pm Mon-Fri, to 4pm Sat mid-Jun–Aug, 9am-4pm Mon-Fri, 9.30am-12.30pm Sat Sep–mid-Jun)

Post office (Hans Schacksvej 5) Shares a building with the tourist office.

ℹ Getting There & Away

Kerteminde is on Rte 165, 19km northwest of Nyborg and 21km northeast of Odense.

Buses 150 and 885 connect Kerteminde with Odense (45kr, 30 minutes). There's an hourly service to Nyborg (920; 45kr, 35 minutes).

Ladbyskibet & Vikingemuseet Ladby

Denmark's only Viking Age ship grave, also known as Ladbyskibet, is a captivating site. Around the year 925, a Viking chieftain was laid to rest in a splendid 21.5m warship, surrounded by weapons, jewellery, clothing, riding equipment, pots and pans, coins and a gaming board. The boat's hull was left imprinted in the earth, along with 2000 rivets, an anchor, iron curls from the ship's dragon-headed prow, and the grinning skulls of sacrificed dogs and horses.

The site of the find under a turfed-over mound gives an eerie sense of time and place. As soon as the automatic entrance doors into the burial mound hiss open, most people are awestruck by this compelling relic. The new museum **Vikingemuseet Ladby** (www.ostfynsmuseer.dk; Vikingevej 123; adult/under 18yr 50kr/free; ⏱10am-5pm Jun-Aug, reduced hrs rest of year) does a great job of telling what we know of the story. It displays finds from the grave and a reconstructed mock-up of the boat before it was interred, complete with slaughtered cattle, giving a vivid sense

of the scale and trouble taken over the burial of the chieftain.

ℹ Getting There & Away

Follow Rte 315 out of Kerteminde, towards Ullerslev. In Ladby village, 4km southwest, turn north onto Vikingevej, a one-lane road through fields that ends after 1.2km at the museum car park. The ship mound is a few minutes' walk along a field path.

Local bus 582 (24kr, five daily, Monday to Friday) makes the six-minute trip from Kerteminde to Ladby. Check the schedule with the bus driver, as the last return bus is typically around 4pm. You'll have to walk the Vikingevej section.

Egeskov Slot

Whatever you do, don't miss Egeskov Slot, aimed at families but with thrills for all. The castle opens until 11pm on Wednesday nights in July and early August, with a programme of evening concerts, falconry displays, ghost hunts and fireworks.

◉ Sights

Egeskov Slot   CASTLE
(www.egeskov.dk; Egeskovgade 18, Kværndrup; adult/4-12yr castle & grounds 195/105kr, grounds only 150/75kr; ⏱10am-7pm Jul–mid-Aug, to 5pm May, Jun & mid-Aug–Sep) Egeskov Slot is a magnificent example of the lavish constructions that sprang up during Denmark's 'Golden Age', complete with moat and drawbridge. It was built in 1554 on a foundation of thousands of upright oak trunks.

EXPLORING HINDSHOLM

To really lose yourself in rural relaxation, the remote Hindsholm peninsula, stretching north from Kerteminde, offers quiet roads and sleepy villages. The most fetching is **Viby**, at the southern end of the peninsula, which has a windmill and an early-Gothic church with frescoes.

Funen's largest (10m) single-chamber passage grave, dating from 200 BC, is further north in **Mårhøj**. Bring a torch (flashlight) and be prepared to crawl. The mound is easy to spot, in a farmer's field about five minutes' walk from the road.

At the northernmost tip is **Fyns Hoved**, an extension of the Hindsholm peninsula connected by a narrow causeway. You can walk to the edge of its 25m-high cliffs for views of the northern Funen coast and, on a clear day, Jutland and Zealand.

Exploring by car or bicycle are the best options. By car, Rte 315 runs the length of the peninsula from south to north. The looping cycle route from Kerteminde to Fyns Hoved makes a relaxed day-long tour.

It's possible, if time-consuming, to get to Hindsholm from Kerteminde by public transport on weekdays, via buses 481 (to Dalby) and then 483, which stops about 1km shy of Fyns Hoved (31kr). Ask at the Kerteminde tourist office for timetables.

Thirteen rooms plus the attic are open to visitors. As well as antique furnishings, grand period paintings, an abundance of hunting trophies (former owner Count Gregers Ahlefeldt-Laurvig-Bille was one of the main African big-game hunters of his day) and an old toy museum, the castle has two unique features.

Once located at Legoland, Titania's Palace is now in Rigborg's Room, on the 1st floor of Egeskov Slot. This jaw-dropping doll's house was created by English painter Sir Nevile Wilkinson, who filled it with miniature works of art over a 35-year period. You could study its marvels – including the world's smallest (working) organ, tiny glass decanters with removable stoppers, an illustrated Bible no bigger than a thumbnail – for hours.

Another oddity is the Wooden Man statue, which lies in the attic under the main turret. It's said that if he's moved, Egeskov will sink into the moat. To keep him sweet, the castle's owners bring him a bowl of rice pudding at Christmas time.

The Grounds
Designed in the 18th century, the castle's expansive 15-hectare park contains century-old privet hedges, free-roaming peacocks, a herd of deer, space-age sculptures and manicured English-style gardens. Visitor attractions include six museums: antique cars, antique motorcycles, ambulances and fire engines, agriculture, horse-drawn vehicles and a wartime grocery shop. There's also the cheesy Dracula's Crypt; a fabulous children's playground; a treetop walk with shaky bridges and push-button birdsong; a doll's-house exhibition; and four mazes, three of which are open to the public.

The castle grounds usually stay open an hour longer than the castle.

Egeskov by Night
On some Wednesdays in the main summer season, Egeskov opens its grounds to visitors in the evening. Simply bring your own picnic dinner and wait for the cannon to signal the fireworks show or take part in the special nocturnal events laid on, including cooking your own 'twistbread' on an open fire, taking part in various challenges or boarding the horse-drawn carriage for a tour of the grounds.

See the Egeskov Slot website for more details.

Sleeping & Eating

Just outside the gates there's a free camping ground for tents only. The plant shop will give you a toilet key for a 20kr deposit.

In the grounds are a couple of kiosks selling hot dogs and ice cream. More-substantial buffet-style fare is on offer at Cafe Jomfru Rigborg, as well as sandwiches, meatballs and pasta dishes.

Getting There & Away

Egeskov Slot is 2km west of Kværndrup on Rte 8, and is well signposted.

If you're in Nyborg or Faaborg, bus 920 (45kr, roughly hourly) runs 500m from the castle – ask the driver where to alight.

From Odense and Svendborg, it's simple between late June and mid-August, when bus 810 goes right to the front gate (weekends only mid-August to September). Otherwise take a train to Kværndrup station and catch the 920 bus mentioned above, or take a taxi.

Faaborg

POP 7200

The engaging little town of Faaborg retains hollyhock-trimmed houses from its 17th-century heyday, when it was home to one of Denmark's largest commercial fishing fleets. Holkegade, Adelgade and Tårngade are particularly pretty streets. If you're passing, it's worth stopping to stroll, enjoy some lunch or visit one of the small museums.

Sights

Faaborg Museum for Fynsk Malerkunst   ART MUSEUM
(www.faaborgmuseum.dk; Grønnegade 75; adult/under 18yr 60kr/free; ⊙10am-4pm Apr-Oct, reduced hrs rest of year) You'll find an important collection of Funen art, including works by Johannes Larsen, Peter Hansen, Jens Birkholm and Anna Syberg, and a flower-filled garden and cafe inside this handsome, imposing building. Kai Nielsen's original granite sculpture of the *Ymerbrønd* is also here.

Faaborg Arrest   MUSEUM
(Torvet; adult/under 18yr 40kr/free; ⊙10am-4pm mid-May–mid-Sep, reduced hrs rest of year) The strange little museum occupies the former prison cells in the town hall. Displays include a rogues' gallery of vagabonds from the 19th century, card sharps and army deserters, a selection of homemade tattooing

FUNEN FAABORG

Faaborg

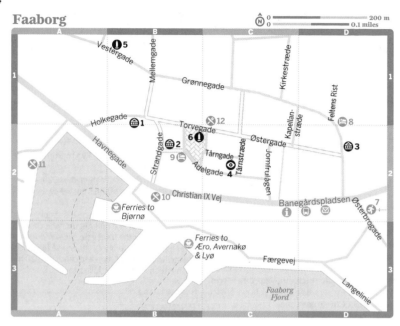

Faaborg

machines, and interesting interview snippets from former guards and prisoners.

Den Gamle Gaard   MUSEUM
(Holkegade 1; adult/under 18yr 50kr/free; ⏰10am-4pm daily mid-May–mid-Sep, 11am-3pm Sun mid-Sep–mid-Oct & Apr–mid-May) A well-presented museum, Den Gamle Gaard is in a timber-framed house that dates back to about 1725. The 22 rooms, arranged to show how a wealthy merchant lived in the early 19th century, are full of antique furniture, porcelain, toys, maritime objects and even a hearse carriage. One room contains personal items belonging to Riborg Voigt, a merchant's daughter with whom Hans Christian Andersen had a lifelong infatuation. Mementoes include one of Andersen's business cards with a lock of his hair sewn onto it.

Torvet   SQUARE
The main square, **Torvet**, features sculptor Kai Nielsen's striking bronze fountain **Ymerbrønd**, which caused a minor uproar on its unveiling. It depicts a Norse creation myth: the naked frost giant Ymir (from whose body the sky and earth were made) suckling at the udder of a cow.

Nearby, the recently refurbished **Klokketårnet** (Bell Tower; Tårnstræde; adult/under 18yr 12kr/free; ⏰11am-4.15pm Mon-Fri, 10am-1pm Sat & Sun mid-Jun–Aug) was once part of a medieval church. It's climbable in summer.

The medieval town gateway **Vesterport** (West Gate) was built in the 15th century to allow entry into Faaborg and is one of only two such gates remaining in Denmark.

Lyø, Avernakø & Bjørnø   ISLANDS
These three small islands offshore from Faaborg make pleasant day trips – bird-spotters in particular will enjoy the rich birdlife. There are primitive camping grounds if you're interested in staying overnight, or staff at Faaborg's tourist office can arrange stays with local families.

Lyø is the most 'heavily populated' and has the most to see: an old village with an unusual circular churchyard; the Klokkesten, a 1000-year-old dolmen that rings like a bell when struck; and several bathing beaches. You can hire bikes from the grocery store.

For information on getting to the islands, see p176.

✦ Activities

Intruders and criminals beware: in July and August a costumed night-watchman may sing comical night-watchman songs at you in Danish. If you care to join the night-watchman's walk, his rounds begin at Klokketårnet at 9pm.

The countryside north of Faaborg, Svanninge Bakker, has been dubbed – a little optimistically – the 'Funen Alps'. It's made up of rolling hills and woodland crossed with cycling and walking trails.

Syd Fyenske Veteranjernbane   TRAIN RIDE
(www.sfvj.dk; adult/4-12yr 60/30kr) This antique train makes summer runs from the old Faaborg train station northeast to Korinth. It departs at 1pm and 3.30pm Sunday from late June to August, and at 4pm and 7pm on Thursday from early July to early August. The return trip lasts 80 minutes. One carriage has a lift for people in wheelchairs.

🛏 Sleeping

The tourist office books rooms in private homes for around 375/500kr per single/double, plus a 30kr fee.

Hotel Faaborg   HOTEL €€
(✆62 61 02 45; www.hotelfaaborg.dk; Torvet; s/d incl breakfast 750/950kr; P@) In an old brick building, this small hotel with sweet courtyard garden has 10 double rooms, each with bathtub and TV. There's a bar and restaurant downstairs.

Hotel Faaborg Fjord   RESORT €€
(✆62 61 10 10; www.hotelfaaborgfjord.dk, in Danish; Svendborgvej 175; s/d incl breakfast 1295/1495kr; P@🛜🏊) This large purpose-built hotel

on the eastern outskirts of town has restful blue-painted chalet-style rooms, each with private balcony or terrace. Excellent amenities include a restaurant, pool, sauna, *pétanque,* volleyball pitch and wi-fi coverage. The sea is just across the road. Prices drop in summer.

Danhostel Faaborg   HOSTEL €
(✆62 61 12 03; www.danhostel.dk/faaborg; Grønnegade 71-73; dm/d 175/375kr; ⊙Apr-Oct) This is a simple, oh-so-cute 69-bed hostel, based in two handsome historic buildings – an old cinema and a half-timbered poorhouse, both full of sunshine and creaking woodwork. Dorm beds are available in high summer.

Faaborg Camping   CAMPING GROUND €
(✆62 61 77 94; www.faaborgcamping.dk; Odensevej 140; sites per adult/child 72/41kr; @🛜) The closest camping ground to Faaborg, about 2km north of town, has solar-heated water in the bathroom block, a shop, crazy golf, TV room, wi-fi internet access and bike hire (60kr per day).

🍴 Eating

Hæstrups Café   CAFE €
(Torvet 2; light lunches 50-90kr; ⊙10am-2am Jun-Aug, reduced hrs rest of year) The town's most popular spot for light meals and drinks, Hæstrups is in the thick of things on the square. The menu is standard Danish cafe fare – brunch, omelettes, salads, sandwiches, burgers and a few Mexican mains and steaks.

Det Hvide Pakhus   INTERNATIONAL €€
(www.dethvidepakhus.dk; Christian IX Vej 2; lunch mains 70-120kr, 1-/2-/3-/4-/5-course dinner menus 225/285/325/375/425kr; ⊙lunch & dinner Jun-Sep) Top spot for location, quality and value is The White Warehouse by the harbour. The fish-focused light lunches include herrings with onion, pan-fried plaice, and fried minced beef on toast with capers, beetroot, onions and egg yolk. In the evening, mains might include beef tenderloin with celeriac purée and red-wine sauce.

Faaborg Røgeri   SEAFOOD €
(Vestkaj; fish dishes 25-70kr; ⊙10am-9pm mid-Jun–Aug, reduced hrs rest of year) Nothing says 'Danish holiday' better than eating fishballs and remoulade from a paper plate in the salty-smelling harbourside sunshine.

ℹ️ Information

Jyske Bank (Østergade 36) One of several banks with ATMs.

Post office (Banegårdspladsen 4; ☉10am-5pm Mon-Fri, to noon Sat)

Tourist office (☎62 61 07 07; www.visit faaborg.dk; Banegårdspladsen 2a; ☉9am-5pm Mon-Sat Jun-Aug, 9am-4pm Mon-Fri, 10am-1pm Sat Sep-May) Has bike hire, cycling maps, fishing licences and phone cards.

ℹ️ Getting There & Away

Faaborg is 27km west of Svendborg and 37km south of Odense.

Boat

Aerøfærgerne A/S (☎62 52 40 00; www. aeroe-ferry.dk) runs daily ferries to Søby (adult/child aged four to 11 years/car/bicycle return 184/103/406/39kr, one hour), at the northwestern end of the island of Ærø. There are around five services per day on weekdays, and three or four on weekends. Drivers are advised to book ahead.

Ferries also run to the nearby islands of Bjørnø, Lyø and Avernakø. For Avernakø and Lyø, the small car ferry M/F *Faaborg II*, run by **Ø-Færgen** (☎62 61 23 07; www.oefaergen.dk, in Danish; adult/4-15yr return 115/80kr, bicycle/motorcycle 30/120kr), operates around five times daily from Faaborg, taking between 30 and 70 minutes. Visitors are discouraged from bringing cars. For Bjørnø, the passenger-only **M/S Lillebjørn** (☎20 29 80 50; www.bjoernoe -faergen.dk; adult/4-16yr return 56/28kr, bicycle 17kr) runs seven times daily Monday to Friday, four on Saturday, three Sunday. The trip takes 20 minutes.

Bus

Faaborg's bus station is on Banegårdspladsen, at the defunct train station on the southern side of town.

From Odense, buses 110, 141, 885 (68kr, 1¼ hours) run at least hourly to 11pm. From Svendborg, bus 930 (50kr, 40 minutes) runs at least hourly throughout the day.

Car & Motorcycle

Getting to Faaborg by car is straightforward: from the north, simply follow Rte 43. From Svendborg, Rte 44 leads directly west into Faaborg.

ℹ️ Getting Around

Bicycles can be hired at the tourist office for 60kr per day. There are sometimes boats for hire at the harbour for around 850kr per day, plus fuel – enquire at the tourist office.

Svendborg
POP 27,110

Hilly Svendborg is the region's largest town, a jolly place to be in summer when its cafes and bars fill up with holidaymaking yachties. Although it's predominantly a modern industrial settlement, it possesses several interesting historic buildings, a great natural-history museum and a first-rate hostel. Svendborg is a jumping-off point for the alluring islands beyond: Tåsinge, Langeland and Ærø.

Svendborg had grown into a busy port and shipbuilding centre by the 19th century, producing almost half of Denmark's wooden-hulled ships, and was the site of foundries, tanneries, tobacco-processing plants and mills. Today several shipyards continue to thrive, and more Danish boats are registered here than anywhere else outside Copenhagen.

◉ Sights & Activities

Naturama   MUSEUM

(www.naturama.dk; Dronningemaen 30; adult/under 18yr 100kr/free; ☉10am-4pm Tue-Sun mid-Jan–late Nov, to 5pm school holidays) Naturama natural-history museum is in an impressive spiral building with displays of stuffed animals and skeletons on three levels. Whale bones dominate the basement, Scandinavian mammals lurk on the middle floor, while birds from the tiny Pallas' leaf warbler to the golden eagle float on a balcony above it all. There's state-of-the-art sound and lighting, and regular film shows and a good hands-on section where you can stroke a mole, draw a wolf or dress up in skins.

[FREE] **Anne Hvides Gård**   MUSEUM

(Fruestræde 3; ☉11am-3pm Tue-Sun mid-Jun–mid-Aug) The oldest house in Svendborg, dating from 1560, is Anne Hvides Gård, a bumblebee-coloured structure that leans tipsily to one side. Its basic collection of local archaeological finds is labelled in Danish, but pop in if you're passing to see the strangest item: a 14th-century wooden statue of the four-faced god Svantevit.

Forsorgsmuseet Viebæltegård   MUSEUM

(www.svendborgmuseum.dk, in Danish; Grubbemøllevej 13; adult/under 18yr 40kr/free; ☉10am-4pm Tue-Sun May-Sep, 1-4pm Tue-Sun Oct-Apr) Forsorgsmuseet Viebæltegård is Denmark's only poorhouse and workhouse museum.

Svendborg

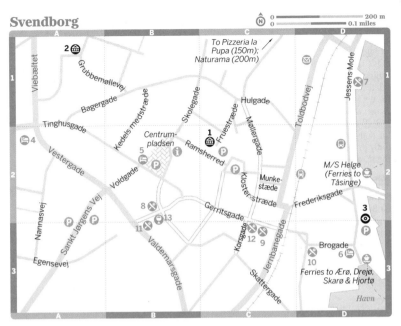

It's unusual – we'd certainly never seen a lice box before – and on Wednesday in high summer you can even sample poorhouse food. About a third of the information is in English.

Islands
ISLANDS

Three small islands, **Drejø**, **Skarø** and **Hjortø**, lie to the southwest of Svendborg and are pleasant escapes for those who dream of people-lite landscapes surrounded by lapping waves. They mainly attract yachties and ornithologists, drawn by large numbers of breeding sea birds. Camping is allowed at designated sites. Drejø has a restaurant and grocery shop, while Skarø has a small food shop and a snack bar. Car-free Hjortø has no facilities – bring a picnic. For information on getting to the islands, see p179.

Gorilla Park
ADVENTURE SPORTS

(www.gorillapark.dk, in Danish; adult/child 8-12yr/child 4-7yr 245/195/75kr; ☺10am-6pm Apr-end Oct) Release your inner primate and go ape at this adrenaline-fuelled high-ropes adventure park. White knuckles are guaranteed on the Tarzan swings, zipwires, high-rope scrambles, base jumping and stomaching-lurching BMX bridges. No climbing experience is necessary, although

a head for heights helps. Gorilla Park is about 5km north of Svendborg. Take route 44 out of town and then take a right onto Stagerupvej.

Svendborg

◉ Sights
1 Anne Hvides Gård	C2
2 Forsorgsmuseet Viebæltegård	A1
3 Maritimt Center Danmark	D2

⌂ Sleeping
4 Danhostel Svendborg	A2
5 Hotel Svendborg	B2
6 Hotel Ærø	D3

⊗ Eating
7 Bendixens Fiskehandel	D1
8 Café Under Uret	B2
9 Citronen	C3
Hotel Æro	(see 6)
10 Jette's Diner	D3
11 Kvickly	B3
12 Vintapperiet I Salig Simons Gard	C3

☺ Drinking
13 Børsen	B2
Hotel Ærø	(see 6)

Maritimt Center Danmark SAILING
(www.maritimt-center.dk; Havnepladsen 2; cruises adult/child from 270/170kr; ⊙Thu & Fri Jul & Aug) In high summer, the Maritimt Center Danmark runs **cruises** on the historic wooden sailing ship *Meta,* and there's often pirate-related fun for kids – contact the centre for details. Another vintage ship is the M/S *Helge,* which sails in Svendborg Sound – see p181. While you're down at the harbour, look for Sejlskibsbroen, a jetty lined with splendidly preserved sailing ships opposite where the Ærø ferry docks.

🛌 Sleeping

Svendborg and its surrounds have good B&Bs, many of which are listed in the *Funen and South Jutland B&B* brochure (found in tourist offices across Funen and South Jutland). The tourist office can book rooms for a 30kr fee. The nearest camping ground is on Tåsinge, on the southern side of Svendborg Sound; see p181.

TOP CHOICE Hotel Ærø HOTEL €€
(☎62 21 07 60; www.hotel-aeroe.dk, in Danish; Brogade 1; s/d incl breakfast 850/1025kr; P) The handsome mustard-and-white Ærø occupies an unbeatable harbourside position and has bags of atmosphere. The annexe of large, modern chalet-style rooms is light and airy. The 'British-colonial' style – big comfy wooden beds, mock mahogany desks and vaguely Chinese-looking lamps and wood floors – is restrained and relaxed. At busier times of the year the bar and restaurant underneath the bedrooms may disturb light sleepers.

Danhostel Svendborg HOSTEL €€
(☎62 21 66 99; www.danhostel-svendborg.dk; Vestergade 45; s/d/tr/q 490/520/540/560kr; P@🛜) This is an outstanding hostel, more like a hotel really, although it's not cheap. Basic but spotless two-, three- and four-bed rooms, each with a shower, toilet and satellite TV and wireless connectivity, are based in a renovated 19th-century iron foundry in the city centre. There are laundry facilities, a large kitchen, several lounge areas, vending machines, a trampoline and a coin-operated computer. The reception opens from at least 8am to 6pm (although it closes on Sunday afternoon), and there's good access for people in wheelchairs. The restaurant also serves a great-value breakfast and dinner.

Hotel Svendborg HOTEL €€€
(☎62 21 17 00; www.hotel-svendborg.dk; Centrumpladsen 1; s/d incl breakfast from 995/1225kr; P@🛜) Close to the centre of town, the Svendborg offers minimalist Scandinavian style – wooden floors and pale furniture – and a comfortable if no-frills stay. The 2nd-floor rooms have larger bathrooms, while the Scala rooms offer a notch more luxury, with pop art on the walls, tea-making facilities and flat-screen TVs with internet and wi-fi access.

The hotel is a member of the 'eco' Green Key scheme and offers good access for people in wheelchairs. Prices fall from mid-July to mid-August.

🍴 Eating

Citronen DANISH €€
(☎62 20 21 95; www.citronen.dk; Brogade 33; lunch mains 86-118kr, dinner mains 180-200kr; ⊙lunch & dinner Mon-Sat) Food made from fresh ingredients on the premises rather than taken from the catering truck is the appeal of Citronen. Light seafood lunches, such as tiger prawns in garlic and herbs with homemade bread and butter, or heartier dinner mains, such as steak in peppercorn sauce with potato pie, are typical. Save room so you can sample the deliciously sticky results of the dessert 'laboratory'.

Hotel Ærø DANISH €€
(☎62 21 07 60; Brogade 1; lunch mains 50-115kr; ⊙11am-9.30pm) Opposite the ferry terminal, the Ærø has a nautically themed, high-ceilinged dining room. Light lunches are unfussy Danish classics: minced fried beef on rye toast, eel with parsley sauce, potato and pickle, or fried plaice stuffed with prawns, asparagus and mushrooms in a lobster sauce. The food is prepared to a high standard and the cooks use fresh ingredients.

Vintapperiet I Salig Simons Gård WINE BAR €€
(☎62 22 34 48; www.vintapperierne.dk; Brogade 37; cheese/meat platters from 90kr; ⊙11am-5.30pm Mon-Sat) A good selection of wine and beer is the main idea here – great for stocking your picnic hamper – but it's also worth stopping and sampling the liquid delights with the deli cheese and meat platters.

Pizzeria la Pupa ITALIAN €€
(☎62 20 21 70; Møllergade 78; mains 70-200kr; ⊙lunch & dinner Mon-Sat, dinner Sun) Run by

an Italian family, this pizzeria and trattoria a short walk back from the harbour is a local favourite serving authentic, if generally standard Italian staples to eat in or take away. The pizzas are definitely the standout option.

Bendixens Fiskehandel SEAFOOD €
(✆62 21 18 75; Jessens Mole 2; snacks 55-65kr; ⊙shop 7am-6pm Mon-Fri, to 1pm Sat, grill 11am-8pm Mon-Sat) This bargain harbourside fish shop has an attached grill where you can buy fresh fish and seafood dishes – crab salad, smoked salmon, prawns, *fiskefrik-adelle* (fried fishballs) – to eat at a table outside.

Jette's Diner DINER €
(✆62 22 17 48; Kullinggade 1; mains 58-128kr; ⊙noon-9.30pm May-Aug, noon-9.30pm Tue-Sun Sep-Apr) A cut above the usual diner, this popular and relatively inexpensive place has a good choice of cafe food. Alongside salads and sandwiches, there's a Mexican selection and meat and vegie mains of the day. It's favoured by everyone, from workers nipping in for a beer to yachties from the nearby harbour.

Café Under Uret EUROPEAN €€
(✆62 21 83 08; www.under-uret.com, in Danish; Gerritsgade 50; lunch mains 65-85kr, dinner mains 150-170kr; ⊙9.30am-10pm Mon-Sat) This bistro's dim, candlelit interior is filled with wheat sheaves, comfy leather banquettes and easy-on-the-ear pop music, while outside tables catch the evening sun. Well-cooked, healthily huge brunches, sandwiches and burgers feature at lunch, while evening mains include chicken breast, beef and pasta.

Kvickly SUPERMARKET €
(Gerritsgade 33; ⊙9am-8pm Mon-Fri, 8am-5pm Sat) Self-caterers have this central supermarket, with a decent bakery.

🍷 Drinking & Entertainment

Hotel Ærø BAR €
(Brogade 1; ⊙to 11pm) The cosy bar at this hotel has a roaring fire in winter and serves a good range of Danish beer all year.

Børsen BAR €€
(Gerritsgade 31) Also a favourite with bright young things, Børsen opens late on Friday and Saturday night with DJs to provide the music.

ⓘ Information

Nordeabank (Centrumpladsen 8) One of many banks with ATMs.

Post office (Toldbodvej 13a)

Sydfyns Turistbureau (www.visitsydfyn.dk; Centrumpladsen 4; ⊙9.30am-6pm Mon-Fri, to 3pm Sat Jul & Aug, 9.30am-5pm Mon-Fri, to 12.30pm Sat Sep-Jun) Covers all of south Funen. Free internet access.

ⓘ Getting There & Away

Svendborg is the transit point between Odense and the southern Funen islands. It's 44km southeast of Odense on Rte 9 and 33km southwest of Nyborg on Rte 163.

Boat

Ferries to Ærøskøbing depart five times a day, the last at 10.30pm in summer. For more information, see p185.

For information on the M/S *Helge,* which sails between Svendborg and Tåsinge, see p181.

You can visit the islands of Drejø, Skarø and Hjortø on a day trip via small passenger-only ferries that leave from Svendborg's harbour. Detailed timetables are available at the Svendborg tourist office and at www.visitsvendborg.dk. The **Hjortø ferry** (✆40 97 95 18, 62 54 15 18; adult/2-14yr 75/50kr, bicycle 30kr) generally sails twice daily. The **Drejø & Skarø ferry** (✆62 21 02 62; adult/4-12yr return 90/55kr, bicycle 30kr) has three to five sailings daily (sailing time 30 to 75 minutes, depending on route).

Bus & Train

The bus and train stations are a few streets north of the ferry terminal.

There are frequent bus services between Svendborg and Faaborg (930 and 932, 50kr, 40 minutes), Rudkøbing (911, 912, 913, 44kr, 25 minutes) and other Funen towns.

Trains leave Odense for Svendborg about once an hour (70kr, one hour).

ⓘ Getting Around

Svendborg Cykeludlejning (✆62 20 77 41; www.svendborgcykeludlejning.dk; Jessens Mole 9B; ⊙9am-1pm Jun–mid-Aug) has 68 bikes for rent (adult 90kr per day). The Svendborg tourist office sells a good little booklet entitled *12 Biking Tours in South Funen & on Taasinge & Thurø* (15kr), outlining interesting bike rides around the area.

You need a parking disc for most parking spots in the town centre. The parking discs can be purchased from the Svendborg tourist office.

FUNEN SVENDBORG

Tåsinge

POP 6100

Tåsinge is the fourth-largest island in Funen, accessed by road bridges from Svendborg and Langeland. Its two main sights are both in the northeast: the pretty sea captains' village of Troense and the palatial 17th-century Valdemars Slot. The rest of the island is a mixture of woods, hedges and open fields, cut through by the main road, Rte 9.

◉ Sights

Troense   NEIGHBOURHOOD

Troense is a well-to-do seaside village with a small yachting harbour and quaint thatched houses: two particularly pretty streets are Grønnegade and Badstuen. The diverting **Søfartssamlingerne i Troense** (Strandgade 1; adult/under 18yr 30kr/free; ⊙10am-5pm Tue-Sun May-Sep), housed in the old village schoolhouse, is a kind of curiosity shop of items collected by globetrotting sailors and merchants of yore. It's an eclectic collection of paintings, photos, models, figureheads and items from all over the world.

Valdemars Slot   CASTLE

(www.valdemarsslot.dk; Slotsalléen 100; castle & hunting museum adult/4-12yr 85/40kr; castle & all museums 100/50kr; ⊙10am-5pm mid-Apr–late Oct) One of Christian IV's lavish palaces, Valdemars Slot was built for his son Valdemar Christian in 1644. Valdemar never actually lived here – he died on a Polish battlefield at the age of 34 – and the castle itself was badly damaged in the Danish–Swedish wars. It was gifted to the naval hero Niels Juel, who transformed it into the baroque mansion you see today. There's no admission charge to the grounds or sandy beach, just outside the southern gate.

The palatial interior is crammed with antique furniture and eccentricities – lavish Venetian glass, Chinese lamps, 17th-century Gobelin tapestries, a toilet hidden in a window frame, a secret ammo store, Niels Juel's sea chest pasted with engravings, and autographed photos of visiting celebs. In the attic is the grisly Jægt & Trofæmuseum, featuring ethnographical objects and animal trophies collected by hunter Boerge Hinsch and others.

Two other museums edge the large pond-filled courtyard. **Danmarks Legetøjsmuseum** (Denmark's Toy Museum; adult/4-12yr 40/20kr; ⊙10am-6pm Jul, to 5pm May, Jun, Aug & Sep) is an impressive private collection of vintage playthings, while **Danmarks Museum for Lystsejlads** (Denmark's Yachting Museum; adult/4-12yr 40/20kr; ⊙10am-6pm Jul, to 5pm Jun & Aug) contains a collection of 30 sleek, varnished sailboats.

About 1km southwest of the castle, look for the 400-year-old oak tree **Ambrosius Egen** along the northern side of the road. It's named after Ambrosius Stub, a romantic poet who worked at Valdemars Slot in about 1700 and who composed many of his verses beneath its shady branches.

You can get to Valdemars Slot by bus, but a better way is via M/S *Helge*, an old-style ferry that carries passengers from Svendborg to Valdemars Slot – see p181.

Bregninge   NEIGHBOURHOOD

The small village of Bregninge, on Rte 9, is home to Denmark's most visited church, the medieval **Bregninge Kirke**. Its attraction lies in the alluring panoramic views from the **church tower** (Kirkebakken 2A; adult/child 5/2kr; ⊙8am-9pm); at 72m, it's the highest point on the island.

Tåsinge Skipperhjem og Folkemindesamling (Kirkebakken 1; adult/under 15yr 40kr/free; ⊙10am-4pm Tue-Sun Jun-Aug), across the road from the church, is a local-history museum telling the story of Lieutenant Sixten Sparre and artist Elvira Madigan, Denmark's real-life Romeo and Juliet. Facing separation, the tragic lovers committed suicide in 1889. They are buried together on Tåsinge in the churchyard at Landet, 3km south of Bregninge, where brides still throw bouquets on their grave.

⊨ Sleeping & Eating

Bed-and-breakfast accommodation can be found in the booklet *Funen and South Jutland B&B*, or booked through the Svendborg tourist office. Troense has a bakery and minimarket. If you have your own transport, there's a Dagli'Brugsen supermarket at Vindeby, just over the bridge from Svendborg.

Hotel Troense   HOTEL €€

(✆62 22 54 12; www.hoteltroense.dk; Strandgade 5; s/d incl breakfast 795/1095kr; P) Perched above the harbour, Hotel Troense has 30 rooms divided between the main building (eight with sea views) and several modern blocks at the back (all twins with private seating areas in the garden). Its restaurant serves classic Danish smørrebrød at lunch (mains 60kr to 180kr) and traditional

French and Danish dishes for dinner (two-/three-course set menus 279/335kr), such as tournedos of red deer with red onion compote. There are several good meat-free options. The restaurant is open from noon to 9pm during high season, for dinner only the rest of the year.

Vindebyøre Camping CAMPING GROUND €
(☑62 22 54 00; www.vindebyoere.dk; Vindebyørevej 52; sites per adult/child 75/45kr; ☺Apr-Sep; @) This very well-kept three-star seaside facility right on the beach is the closest camping ground to Svendborg, located at the northern tip of Tåsinge, about 2km northeast of the Svendborg bridge. It's ideal for families, with two playgrounds and a child-friendly beach. There's a laundry, TV lounge, guest kitchen and internet cafe. The local ferry M/S *Helge* docks out front, and you can hire bicycles (75kr per day) and boats (600kr per day).

Valdemars Slot Café &
Restaurant DANISH €€€
(☑62 22 59 00; Slotsalléen 100; light lunch mains 65-99kr, dinner mains 155-245kr; ☺restaurant 11.30am-5pm Tue-Sun May-Sep) The cafe at Valdemars Slot serves snacks including hot dogs, ice cream and cake. For a more lavish hang-the-expense meal and atmosphere in spades, the romantic cellar restaurant serves Danish standards such as lunchtime smørrebrød, and French-influenced evening dishes (lobster bisque, foie gras terrine, beef and venison), with a high-quality wine list. From June to August the restaurant is open for dinner from 6pm to 10pm, Thursday to Saturday.

ℹ Getting There & Away

Route 9 connects Tåsinge with Svendborg on Funen, and Rudkøbing on Langeland. There are cycle paths running the entire way.

Buses run from Svendborg to Tåsinge, but the vintage ferry **M/S Helge** (☑62 23 30 85; www.mshelge.dk; ☺mid-May–mid-Sep) is much more fun. The boat leaves Svendborg harbour at 11am, 1.30pm, 3.30pm and 5.30pm from June to mid-August. It docks at Vindebyøre camping ground on the northern tip of Tåsinge, then at Christiansminde, a beach area east of Svendborg, before continuing to Troense and Valdemars Slot. Departures from Valdemars Slot are at 11.55am, 2.25pm, 4.25pm and 6.25pm. In May and late summer, *Helge* operates the three middle sailings only. Fares range from 30kr to 60kr one way (children aged between four and 11 half-price), depending on the distance. Bicycles (30kr) are allowed if there's space.

LANGELAND

Long thin Langeland is a dreamy stretch of green, connected by bridge to Tåsinge. Small farming villages and windmills dot the countryside, and everything moves at an unhurried pace.

Langeland's only large town, Rudkøbing, is unremarkable and the real attractions lie north at the wonderful Tickon sculpture park and south at the former military stronghold of Langelandsfort. This is good country for meandering exploration, birdwatching, visiting the island's scattered artists' studios and paddling in clear waters on the island's 28 small beaches.

ℹ Getting There & Away

Route 9 connects Langeland to Tåsinge, via the Langeland bridge.

There's a ferry service from Rudkøbing to Marstal on Ærø (see p185) and from Spodsbjerg to Tårs on Lolland (see p137).

Langeland

Buses 911, 912 and 913 make the 20km run from Svendborg to Rudkøbing (45kr, 25 minutes) at least hourly.

ⓘ Getting Around

Route 305 runs from Lohals to Bagenkop, nearly the full length of the island.

BICYCLE

There are asphalt cycle paths running from the Rudkøbing area north to Lohals, east to Spodsbjerg and south to Bagenkop. The tourist office in Rudkøbing sells a bicycle map of Langeland (30kr), and you can hire bikes from **Lapletten** (☑ 62 51 10 98; www.lapletten.dk; Engdraget 1), also in Rudkøbing, and from camping grounds elsewhere on the island.

BUS

Buses travel north to Lohals (50kr, 35 minutes) and south to Bagenkop (50kr, 30 minutes) at least once an hour on weekdays, about half as often on weekends. They connect all of Langeland's major villages en route.

Within Rudkøbing free green buses make a 50-minute loop around the city outskirts, going as far east as the Spodsbjerg harbour, about a dozen times a day on weekdays. All buses leave from the Rudkøbing bus station on Ringvejen.

A pass for unlimited one-day bus travel on Langeland and Ærø costs 170/85kr for adult/child – buy one at any bus station or ferry office.

Rudkøbing

POP 4700

Rudkøbing's tumbledown streets are pleasant enough for a brief meander. Rudkøbing is also a departure point for ferries to Ærø.

◉ Sights

Medieval Streets　　　　　NEIGHBOURHOOD

Just east of the harbour is a series of narrow medieval streets lined with tiny tilting houses. Combining three of the most interesting, **Ramsherred**, **Smedegade** and **Vinkældergade**, makes a fine 15-minute stroll.

HC Ørsted Statue　　　　　MONUMENT

Just near the end of Ramsherred is a **statue of HC Ørsted**, a local Danish physicist who proved that electricity flowing through wire will produce a magnetic field – and so electromagnets were born. Across the street is the old chemist's shop, Ørsted's birthplace.

Langelands Museum　　　　　MUSEUM

(☑ 63 51 10 10; Jens Winthersvej 12; adult/under 18yr 30kr/free; ⊙10am-4pm Mon-Thu, to 1pm Fri) Closed for renovations at the time of research, this small but interesting archaeological museum should have reopened by the time you read this. Among the finds on display are the skeleton of a Viking chieftain,

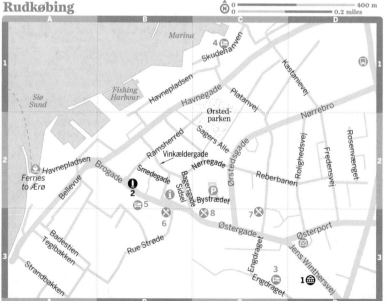

Rudkøbing

buried with his decapitated slave and excavated artefacts from Troldebjerg, the only Stone Age village discovered in Scandinavia, including an axe altar, a trepanned skull and a tooth showing signs of flint-drill dentistry.

🛏 Sleeping

Rudkøbing's accommodation choices aren't fantastic. Try the island's private rooms – the tourist office keeps a list – with doubles ranging from 400kr to 600kr.

Hotel Skandinavien   HOTEL €
(☑62 51 14 95; www.skanhotel.dk; Brogade 13; s/d 500/650kr; P@🤶) Right in the middle of Rudkøbing, opposite the church, the Skandinavien has been recently refurbished and offers basic but amenable rooms with TV – hostel rather than hotel quality. Wi-fi access.

**Danhostel Rudkøbing &
Camping**   CAMPING GROUND €
(☑62 51 18 30; www.rudkobing-camping.dk; Engdraget 11; sites per person 65kr, r 350kr; ⊙May-Sep) Langeland's only hostel is a 10-minute walk from Torvet, but it's a rather cheerless place, with very basic cabin accommodation. Tents can be plonked in the adjoining field.

**Danland Feriecenter & Hotel
Rudkøbing**   APARTMENT €€€
(☑62 51 46 00; www.danland.dk; Havnegade 21; 4-person apt 1772kr; P) Down by the modern marina, this holiday centre is part of the Danland empire. Many of the chalet-style apartments (all with bathroom, kitchen, TV and private balcony or terrace) have views over the water, and there's a restaurant, bar

and playground. Prices drop significantly out of season.

🍴 Eating

Thummelumsen   INTERNATIONAL €€
(www.thummelumsen.dk; Østergade 15; lunch mains 60-110kr, dinner mains 135-199kr) The pick of the high-street cafes/restaurants serving home-made light lunches, such as generously filled burgers, chilli, tortillas and meatballs with rye bread, and some fresh, flavour-packed evening fare, such as carpaccio and gazpacho.

Slagterpigerne   DELI €
(Torvet 6; sandwiches 30kr; ⊙9am-5pm Mon-Sat, to 1pm Sun) Self-caterers can buy takeaway smørrebrød at this butcher's shop.

Super Brugsen   SUPERMARKET €
(Ahlefeldtsgade 5; ⊙9am-6pm Mon-Fri, 8am-2pm Sat) The central supermarket has a cheapo cafe, serving meatballs, fried chicken and toasties. It opens earlier than anywhere else in town: join the throng for morning coffee. There's a good bakery inside the shop.

ℹ️ Information

Nordeabank (Østergade 39) One of three banks with ATMs.

Post office (Østerport 2A; ⊙11am-5pm Mon-Fri)

Tourist office (www.langeland.dk; Torvet 5; ⊙9am-5pm Mon-Fri, to 3pm Sat mid-Jun–Aug, 9.30am-4.30pm Mon-Fri, to 12.30pm Sat Sep–mid-Jun) Information on the entire island.

Northern Langeland

The main sight in Northern Langeland is Tranekær, a quiet village surrounding a medieval castle with artworks in the grounds. Lohals, at the island's northern tip, has camping grounds, hotels and beaches nearby, but it's not as charming as Tranekær and the southern beaches are better.

TRANEKÆR

The little village of Tranekær stretches between its church and the salmon-coloured 12th-century Tranekær Slot, Denmark's oldest inhabited building. The interior isn't open to the public, but the wooded grounds are home to the magical Tickon (Tranekær International Centre for Art & Nature; admission by honesty box 25kr), a collection of striking outdoor art installations. For the price of a hot dog, you can wander around the lake and arboretum, inhabited by a flighty herd

FUNEN NORTHERN LANGELAND

of red deer. There are surprises round every corner: a unicorn's horn sprouts in a glade, a blue-grey pool becomes a grass-sewn round of granite, a river of tree trunks floods down a hillside. There are 18 sculptures to enjoy, and all the fun of finding them in the 81-hectare landscape.

About 1km north is the castle's 19th-century wood-shingled windmill, **Tranekær Slotsmølle** (Lejbøllevej 3; adult/under 12yr 30kr/ free; ⊘10am-5pm Mon-Fri, 1-5pm Sun Jun–mid-Sep). Its wooden mechanics are still intact, and there's an exhibition on milling inside (in Danish and German).

🛏 Sleeping & Eating

Tranekær Gæstgivergaard B&B €€
(✆62 59 12 04; www.tranekaerkro.dk; Slotsgade 74; s/d incl breakfast750/950kr; 🅿) This village inn 200m south of the castle dates from 1802 and retains its period ambience. Most rooms have peaceful garden views and there's one lovely, bright family apartment. The highly rated restaurant (mains 230kr to 290kr) is strong on local seafood and game, such as venison, and always offers at least one vegetarian option. There are also good-value bed, breakfast and dinner packages.

Southern Langeland

Southern Langeland's pastoral landscape contains some gentle diversions. The island's favourite Blue Flag beach is at the little thatched seaside village of Ristinge. There are also several passage graves, a historic old manor-house museum and an unusual tourist attraction, Langelandsfort.

At the tip of Langeland, you might spy wild horses: two herds of Exmoor ponies have been introduced to keep the coastal meadows cropped. The area around Bagenkop also contains three excellent bird-watching sites connected by footpaths, and there's a coastal nature reserve, Tryggelev Nor, midway between Bagenkop and Ristinge.

Humble is the largest village in the area, with a bank and petrol station.

◉ Sights & Activities

Skovsgaard MUSEUM
(Kågårdsvej 12; adult/under 18yr 45kr/free; ⊘10am-5pm Mon-Fri, 11am-5pm Sun mid-May–Sep) If you've been touring Denmark's decadent palaces, it's refreshing to visit Skovsgaard. The kitchen cellars, pumproom, servants' dining room and housekeeper's room of the old manor house have been furnished with dummies and props, giving an interesting glimpse of how the lower half lived. The stables hold a carriage museum with 25 horse-drawn vehicles. There's also an organic food cafe – see p185.

Skovsgaard estate is off the main road, Rte 305, around 3km southeast of Lindelse.

Kong Humbles Grav MONUMENT
Langeland is full of megalithic monuments. The largest is Kong Humbles Grav, a few kilometres from Skovsgaard. Dating from about 3000 BC, the barrow is edged with 77 stones, extends 55m in length and has a single burial chamber. Legend holds that a king was buried here, although historians give little credence to the tale.

The dolmen is on private property, but visitors can walk there along a path that starts near the whitewashed church in Humble. Head northeast from the car park, which is just past the church, and bear left at the first intersection, following the trail past the farmhouses. The walk is about 1.5km each way.

Langelandsfort HISTORIC SITE
(www.ohavsmuseet.dk; Vognsbjergvej 4B; adult/ under 18yr 70kr/free; ⊘10am-5pm Mon-Fri, 11am-5pm Sat & Sun mid-May–Sep, reduced hrs rest of year) There are few better Danish examples of Cold War paranoia than Langelandsfort, built in 1953 to defend the western Baltic against the Russians. You can descend into various bunkers and command centres, board a claustrophobic U-boat, explore a minesweeper and peer inside two fighter planes (a Russian MiG-23 and an F-35 Draken). The solid grey masses of concrete, rusting barbed wire and camouflage-green emplacements and anti-aircraft guns are in startling contrast to the picnic-perfect countryside in which they are set.

The site is big – to see everything involves a walk of about 2km – and you'll need a couple of hours to look around. Admission stops one hour before closing time. The fort is just north of Bagenkop.

Surfcenter Langeland WINDSURFING
(✆62 57 20 40; kontakt@sc-langeland.dk; Østersøvej 6, Hesselbjerg) Beginners wanting to learn how to windsurf should contact Surfcenter Langeland based in Hesselbjerg, near Ristinge, which offers four-hour classes for 650kr per person (minimum four people). You can also hire sea kayaks (450kr

per day) and the brave can undertake kite-surfing courses.

🛏 Sleeping & Eating

Lindelse Kro
B&B €€

(☑62 57 24 03; www.lindelsekro.dk, in Danish; Langegade 21, Lindelse; s/d incl breakfast 595/795kr) Lindelse Kro has 10 rooms, all with bathroom and parking space outside, and mostly overlooking the garden. They're light and peaceful, if slightly old-fashioned. Attached is one of Langeland's top eating places (open from noon to 9pm), with meals made from fresh seasonal ingredients: light lunches (80kr to 120kr) of smørrebrød, omelette and smoked salmon terrine, and a luxury evening gourmet menu (two/three courses 319/369kr; dinner mains cost 180kr to 290kr). Both the accommodation and the restaurant are popular, so book ahead.

Humble Kro & Hotel
HOTEL €€

(☑62 57 11 34; www.humblekro.dk, in Danish; Ristingevej 2, Humble; s/d incl breakfast 595/860kr; 🅿) The nearest hotel to Ristinge beach is this one in Humble village. Simply decorated rooms all have bathrooms; the ones in the new wing are nicest. The restaurant has a lunch menu (mains 40kr to 80kr) of Funen *æggekage* (omelette), smørrebrød and homemade burgers, and serves heartier Danish fare (fresh fish, pork with parsley sauce, schnitzels, steak with fried egg, potato and beetroot) in the evening (108kr to 175kr).

Ristinge Camping & Feriecenter
CAMPING GROUND €

(☑62 57 13 29; www.ristinge.dk; Ristingevej 104, Ristinge; sites per person 88kr; ⊘Apr-Aug; @🐾) Within walking distance of the beach in Ristinge, this super three-star camping ground has a grocery shop, internet cafe, large swimming pool with waterslide, goats, grass tennis court, a good playground and a snack bar.

🔝 Skovsgaard Café
CAFE €

(☑62 57 24 60; Kågårdsvej 12; light lunches 60-99kr; ⊘10am-5pm Mon-Fri, 11am-5pm Sun mid-May–Sep) Run by the same people as Lindelse Kro, this bright, wood-floored, squeaky-clean organic cafe is at the entrance to the Skovsgaard estate and is our pick of lunch places on the island. It has a small menu of fresh-brewed coffee, homemade bread and cakes, salads, burgers and sandwiches. There's also a little garden with tables. Recommended.

ÆRØ

Of Funen's many islands, Ærø must be a contender for the loveliest. Quiet, rolling country roads, wheat fields, thatched houses, ancient passage graves and old windmills add to the isolation to give you the feeling of truly getting away from it all.

The island is rich in maritime history and crooked old houses, and is populated by some of the friendliest people in Denmark. Perhaps the only thing the island lacks, so far at least, is the range of foodie treats on offer in other Danish boltholes such as Bornholm.

The three main towns – Ærøskøbing, Marstal and Søby – are within perfect cycling distance of each other and campers who really want to get away from it all can take advantage of several primitive – and free – camping grounds (see the *Ærø* guide, available in the island's tourist offices, for details and locations of these sites).

In summer the place comes alive. There is a lively **jazz festival** (www.jazzisland.dk, in Danish) in late July/early August and it's a favourite yachtie destination, with 800 berths in its modern marinas – that's four times more moorings than hotel rooms. Commercial ferries leave from each of the three towns.

ℹ Getting There & Away

Ærøfærgerne A/S (☑62 52 40 00; www.aeroe-ferry.dk) runs year-round car ferries to Søby from Faaborg, to Ærøskøbing from Svendborg and to Marstal from Rudkøbing. All run about five times a day and take about an hour. A single ticket costs 118/72kr per adult/child (four to 11), 26kr per bike and 255kr per car. If you have a car it's a good idea to reserve, particularly on weekends and in summer. A ferry also runs between Søby and Fynshav (on Als) three times a day and takes 70 minutes.

ℹ Getting Around

BICYCLE

Cycling is the perfect way to enjoy Ærø, with three well-signposted cycle routes:
Route 91 begins at Marstal and continues up to Søby. Route 90 runs along the north of the island from Søby to Ærøskøbing. Route 92 runs from Ærøskøbing back to Marstal. The entire route is about 60km. Ærø's tourist offices sell an inexpensive English-language cycling map of the island, listing sights along the way.

You can rent bikes for around 60kr to 70kr per day across Ærø: in Ærøskøbing, at the hostel, camping ground, Hotel Ærøhus and at **Pilebækkens Cykelservice** (☑62 52 11 10; Pilebækken 11; ⊘9am-5pm Mon-Fri, to 1pm

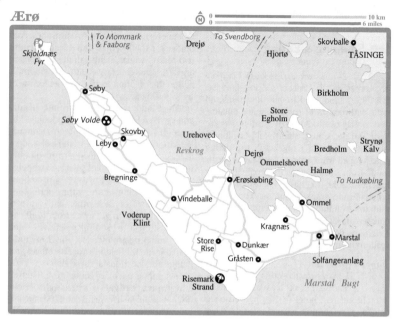

Ærø

Sat, plus 10am-1pm Sun Jul); in Marstal, at **Nørremarks Cykelforretning** (☑62 53 14 77; Møllevejen 77; ⊙10-11am Jul & Aug) in the harbour car park; and in Søby, at **Søby Cykelforretning** (☑62 58 18 42; Langebro 4A; ⊙9.30am-4.30pm Mon-Fri, plus 10am-12.30pm Sat early Jun-Aug & 10am-12.30pm Sun Jul).

BUS

Fyns Amt (☑63 53 10 10) operates buses 90, 91 and 92 from Marstal to Søby via Store Rise and Ærøskøbing. It runs hourly from 5.27am to 8.29pm on weekdays. Weekend buses are about half as frequent, with the first bus leaving Marstal at 8.24am. It takes about 50 minutes to get from one end of the island to the other. Fares range from 30kr to 50kr, depending on the distance. Passes for unlimited one-day bus travel on Ærø and Langeland (adult/child 170/85kr) are also available from bus stations or ferry offices.

Ærøskøbing

POP 980

A prosperous 17th-century merchants' town, Ærøskøbing has oodles of character. Cobblestone streets wind between crooked houses, each one different, although they're all cheerfully painted and gently skewed, with hand-blown glass windows, doorways full of bright hollyhocks, and half-hidden courtyards offering glimpses into private worlds.

Ærøskøbing has good accommodation options and makes an ideal base for a stay on Ærø.

☉ Sights & Activities

Hammerichs Hus   MUSEUM
(www.arremus.dk; Gyden 22; adult/under 18yr 30kr/free; ⊙noon-4pm Jun-mid-Sep) Our favourite of Ærøskøbing's museums, half-timbered Hammerichs Hus is the most gnarled, creaky hobbit-hole of a home imaginable. Its snug interior is full of antiques collected by sculptor Gunnar Hammerich: most impressive are the walls, lined with around 3000 beautiful 17th- and 18th-century Dutch tiles.

Flaske Peters Samling   MUSEUM
(www.arremus.dk; Smedegade 22; adult/under 18yr 40kr/free; ⊙10am-5pm mid-Jun-Jul, to 4pm Aug-mid-Oct & Apr-mid-Jun, reduced hrs rest of year) The former poorhouse displays Flaske Peters Samling, the life's work of ship's cook Peter Jacobsen – 'Bottle Peter' – who crafted 1700 ships-in-a-bottle. The fun perhaps lies less in the primitive folk-art ships and more with the characters – of leg-pulling Peter and his long-suffering wife.

Historic Streets   HISTORIC AREA
Wandering the timeless streets is like winding the clock back a century or two. The

oldest house, at Søndergade 36, dates to 1645. Other fine streets for strolling are Vestergade and Smedegade; there's a particularly charming house known as Dukkehuset (Doll's House) at Smedegade 37.

🛏 Sleeping

The tourist office has a list of B&Bs around the island costing about 400/550kr for singles/doubles. It can also book holiday cottages.

TOP CHOICE Pension Vestergade 44   B&B €€

(☑62 52 22 98; www.vestergade44.com; Østermarksvej 20; d incl breakfast 790kr; @) This delightful timbered house, built by a sea captain for his daughter and once owned by sculptor Gunnar Hammerich, is exquisitely decorated and crammed with heritage interest and period charm. The garden is a delight, the owner is welcoming and the breakfast of homemade jam and local eggs sets you up perfectly for the day. It's popular and with just six rooms, booking ahead is advised.

Tolbudhus   B&B €€

(☑62 52 18 11; www.toldbodhus.com; Brogade 8; s/d from 990/1250kr; without bathroom 750/890kr; P @) A close second to Pension Vestergade 44 for charm and warmth, this doll's house of a B&B with just four old-fashioned rooms also serves good breakfasts.

🌿 Ærøskøbing Camping   CAMPING GROUND €

(☑62 52 18 54; www.aeroecamp.dk; Sygehusvej 40B; sites per person 72kr, cabins from 125kr; ⊙May-Sep) Near a shallow beach 1km from the town centre, this camping ground has a three-star rating, which means a playground, TV room with wood-burning stove, laundry, shop and bikes to rent. The small, cute cabins are great, although no-frills. The camping ground is also a member of the Green Key eco scheme.

Harmoni Guesthouse   B&B €€

(☑62 52 1993; www.harmoni-aeroe.dk; Vejsnæs 2; s/d incl breakfast 445/645kr; @) Buddhas and other Eastern religious influences are part of the slightly hippieish 'mind, body, spirit' vibe at this relaxing, welcoming guesthouse. Relax in the grounds overlooking the sea or go for one of the massage or other alternative therapies on offer from your hosts. The guestrooms are not en suite.

Hotel Ærøhus   HOTEL €€€

(☑62 52 10 03; www.aeroehus.dk; Vestergade 38; s/d from 990/1250kr, without bathroom 600/800kr; P @) Close to the harbour, with comfortable, modernised double rooms in the beamed main building and a smart modern extension and garden annexe out the back. Facilities include a restaurant, and two tennis courts a five-minute walk from the hotel. Bicycle hire is 100kr per day.

🍴 Eating

Ærøskøbing Røgeri   SEAFOOD €

(Havnen 15; light mains 35-70kr; ⊙10am-8pm Jul & Aug, 11am-7pm Jun, 11am-5pm Apr, May & Sep) Ærøskøbing's smokehouse, adjacent to the harbour, serves cheap smoked fish and shrimp dishes in the garden or takeaway. Wash it down with some of the excellent ale from the island's Rise Bryggeri microbrewery.

Café Aroma   CAFE €€

(www.cafe-aroma.dk; Havnepladsen; light mains 40-99kr, dinner mains 140-198kr; ⊙11am-8pm mid-May–Sep) Decorated with film posters, a battered sofa, a barber's chair and old cinema seats, this attractive cafe opposite the tourist office offers inexpensive sandwiches, salads and burgers (including a vegetarian version) as well as scrummy homemade ice cream. The daily specials are usually worth a look. There's more space outside on the terrace.

Hotel Ærøhus   EUROPEAN €€

(☑62 52 10 03; Vestergade 38; lunch mains 100-130kr, 3-course dinner menus 415kr) The 'brasserie' here serves generous portions of pizza, burgers and steak. Inside the old-fashioned dining room, things are a touch more upmarket, with a full menu of Danish fish and meat dishes served alongside a reasonable wine list. Sample dishes include smoked venison haunch, steak with softly fried onions and pickle, and vegetable tart.

Ærøskøbing Bageri   BAKERY €

(Vestergade 62; sandwiches 30kr) The Ærøskøbing Bageri is a cut above even Denmark's high bakery standards for bread, sandwiches, bottles of locally brewed beer and some sensational pastries with delightful names such as Napoleon's Hat and Garbo.

Netto   SUPERMARKET €

(Vestre Allé 4; ⊙9am-7pm Mon-Fri, 8am-5pm Sat) By the harbour.

ℹ Information

Danske Bank (Vestergade 56)
Post office (Statene 8; ⊙noon-4.30pm Mon-Fri)
Ærøskøbing tourist office (☑62 52 13 00; www.visitaeroe.dk; Havnen 4; ⊙9am-4pm Mon-Fri Jun-Aug) Near the ferry terminal.

FUNEN ÆRØSKØBING

Marstal

POP 2340

Marstal, at the eastern end of Ærø, is steeped in maritime history and is the big draw on the island along with Ærøskøbing. In its 19th-century heyday, more than 300 merchant ships pulled into port annually. It's still a seafaring town with a busy shipyard, marina and excellent nautical museum. There's a reasonably good beach, half sandy and half rocky, 800m south of town.

The sea was such an integral part of people's lives that even the gravestones at the seamen's church on Kirkestræde are engraved with maritime epitaphs, the most frequently quoted being: 'Here lies Christen Hansen at anchor with his wife; he will not weigh until summoned by God.'

Appropriately enough, acclaimed author Carsten Jensen partly set his maritime epic *We, the Drowned* here. You can buy English-language versions of the novel at the museum and in the tourist offices. It's a great way to steep yourself in this sea dogs' home from home.

◉ Sights & Activities

Marstal Søfartsmuseum MUSEUM
(www.marmus.dk, in Danish; Prinsensgade 1; adult/under 18yr 50kr/free; ⊙9am-6pm Jul & Aug, to 5pm Jun, reduced hrs rest of year) If you don't know a barquentine from a brig, the absorbing nautical collection at Marstal Søfartsmuseum will make everything clear. It's stuffed full of ships' models, sea chests and sailors' souvenirs from around the world, a full-sized boat with seasickness-inducing moving background, and even some climbable rigging in the courtyard.

Havkayak KAYAKING
(☎50 21 94 60; www.havkajakcenter-marstal.dk, in Danish; Marstal Marina; ⊙Apr-Aug) A great way to explore the usually calm waters around the island, this school offers lessons, guided trips or just kayak hire for experienced paddlers.

🛏 Sleeping

Danhostel Marstal HOSTEL €
(☎62 53 39 50; www.marstalvandrerhjem.dk; Færgestræde 29; dm 150kr, s/d 500/550kr, without bathroom 325/375kr; ⊙mid-Apr–mid-Sep) Marstal has an adequate central 82-bed hostel, only 500m south of the ferry harbour and within walking distance of restaurants and the beach. A couple of rooms have sea views. Dorm rooms available in high season.

Hotel Marstal HOTEL €€
(☎62 53 13 52; www.hotelmarstal.dk, in Danish; Dronningestræde 1A; s/d incl breakfast from 895/995kr, without bathroom 495/625kr) Near the harbour, this family-run place has inexpensive and rather basic rooms in the old building. There are also 12 bright, modern, appealing ones with kitchenettes and bathrooms in the annexe. Sea views cost extra.

Marstal Camping CAMPING GROUND €
(☎63 52 63 69; www.marstalcamping.dk; Egehovedvej 1; sites per person 69kr; ⊙Apr-late Oct) Another seaside camping ground, it's behind the marina, 1km south of the harbour. There's a shop, TV room and laundry. The camping ground is also a member of the eco Green Key scheme.

🍴 Eating

At the ferry harbour there's a small food shop and a grill restaurant serving burgers, pizzas and other simple eats.

ENERGETIC ISLANDERS

'Ecofriendly' isn't just a buzzword on Ærø. With a strong record in renewable energy, the island entered into a competition in the 1990s to be recognised as Denmark's greenest island. It didn't win, but defeat spurred the ingenious islanders to even greater efforts.

Being green isn't easy, and despite efforts to become entirely energy self-sufficient by 2008, there's still some way to go.

Huge progress has been made, though, and during the summer months the island manages not to burn any fuel for its heating and energy needs. Three 100m-tall modern wind turbines produce half the island's electricity, and are owned by a collective of 500 locals. Look out for the windmills, swishing their elegantly featherlike blades high above Risemark Beach at the southern tip of the island.

Many of Ærø's homes are heated by district heating schemes using experimental biomass-burning and solar-heat-collecting farms, based just outside Marstal. There are also smaller solar plants in Ærøskøbing and Store Rise.

TOP CHOICE **Restaurant Edith** CAFE €€

(☑ 62 25 25 69; Kirkestræde 8; 3/4/6 courses 375/445/599kr; ◯6-11pm) Marstal now has a smart upmarket dining restaurant to call its own. The look is crisp and minimal – dark wood floors and crisp white linen – and the menu is small, just six dishes including starters, mains and desserts. The food is modern, inventive and playful: think veal risotto with pearl barley, fruit tart with candied fruit and sour cream, plus excellent local cheeses. There's a good wine list too.

Kongensgade 34 CAFE €€

(☑62 53 37 34; Kongensgade 34; lunch mains 40-120kr, dinner mains 70-130kr; ◯10am-11pm Jun-Sep, to 6pm Tue-Sun Oct-Dec & Feb-May) This cafe-delicatessen, near Marstal church, has a sharp modern look: jolly tablecloths, stripy wooden chairs and lime-green candles. It serves burgers, nachos and charcuterie platters at lunchtime, and a small menu oftraditional Danish meals, made from local produce, in the evening. Have a game of table football to work up an appetite.

Smageriet DELI €

(Kirkestræde 6; ◯Mon-Sat) Stop here for quality Italian ice creams, open sandwiches and deli treats for picnickers.

GuldBageren BAKERY €

(Prinsensgade 11; ◯6.15am-5.30pm Mon-Sat) This large bakery is near the museum.

Super Brugsen SUPERMARKET €

(cnr Kirkestræde & Skovgyden; ◯9am-6pm Mon-Thu, to 7pm Fri, to 4pm Sat) About 300m west of the ferry harbour.

ⓘ Information

Danske Bank (Prinsensgade 8) Located one block inland from the tourist office.

Marstal tourist office (☑62 52 13 00; www.visitaeroe.dk; Havnegade 5; ◯9am-4pm Mon-Fri Jun-Aug) A few minutes' walk south of the harbour.

Post office (Kongensgade 31A; ◯12.30-4.30pm Mon-Fri, 10am-noon Sat)

Søby

POP 598

The shipyard, fishing fleet and marina dominate the village of Søby. It has a few pretty thatched houses, but doesn't pack the same charm as Ærøskøbing.

◉ Sights & Activities

Skjoldnæs Fyr LIGHTHOUSE

(adult/4-12yr 5/2.50kr; ◯10am-4pm Mon-Fri) Best on a blustery day, Skjoldnæs Fyr is a 19th-century, granite-block lighthouse 5km from Søby, next to the golf course. You can climb the narrow stairway for exhilarating views of wind-tossed swallows and the sea. A few minutes' walk beyond the lighthouse is a pebble beach and bird breeding area.

Søbygård CASTLE

(Søbygaardsvej; adult/child 25/5kr; ◯10am-5pm Jun-Aug, 10.30am-4pm Apr & May, 11.30am-4pm Sep-mid-Oct) The earthen ramparts of Søby Volde, once part of a 12th-century fortress, hunch to one side of the main cross-island road, 3km south of Søby. Across the lane is 16th-century Søbygård, a compact manor house with a dry moat, haunted by a white lady. It stages art exhibitions, and classical concerts in August.

🛏 Sleeping & Eating

Skinner's B&B B&B €€

(☑63 52 70 11; Godthåb 13, Leby; www.skinnersbb.dk; s/d 300/500kr) Skinner's B&B sums up the Danish concept of *hygge* (cosiness) to the max. Four rooms – Charming Chicks, Ramblin' Roses, Coffee & Cream and Sea & Sand – are all cosily decorated by the crafty owner. Breakfast, with homemade jam and freshly laid eggs, is downstairs in the old stable.

Søby Camping CAMPING GROUND €

(☑62 58 14 70; www.soeby-camping.dk; Vitsø 10; sites per person 65kr) A friendly seaside two-star facility 1km west of town. Sites are protected by large hedges, there's a kiosk selling the basics, and a playground with giant bouncy cushions. It's open year-round, but it's a good idea to phone first between October and May.

Finn's Bageri BAKERY €

(Nørrebro 2; pizzas 50-60kr; ◯6.30am-6pm Jul & Aug, to 6pm Tue-Sun Sep-Jun) Søby's busy bakery, 200m south of the harbour, is a one-stop cake-and-gossip shop. There are indoor and outdoor tables for eating sandwiches, and 20 pizza varieties to eat in or take away.

There are a couple of fast-food kiosks near the harbour and a **Dagli'Brugsen** (Langebro 13; ◯8am-6pm) supermarket near the *kro* (inn).

ⓘ Information

Tourist office (☑62 52 13 00; www.visitaeroe.dk; ◯8am-4pm Mon-Thu, to 1pm Fri Jun-Aug) At the harbour.

FUNEN SØBY

Southern Jutland

Best Places to Eat

» Mormors Lille Café (p212)

» Sønderho Kro (p199)

» Otto & Ani's Fisk (p208)

» Sælhunden (p204)

» Café Ib Rehne Cairo (p213)

Best Places to Stay

» Hotel Koldingfjord (p192)

» Sønderho Kro (p199)

» Schackenborg Slotskro (p212)

» Weis Stue (p203)

» Danhostel Ribe (p206)

Why Go?

Southern Jutland gets its inspiration from a few different sources – from the North Sea, naturally, but also a little from the south. This is the only part of Denmark connected to mainland Europe (by a 68km-long border), and in some places you can feel the historic ties with Germany.

This is a region of salty offshore islands, understated royal palaces and character-filled historic towns, with unexpectedly modern treats in the form of edgy art and architecture, and offbeat design museums. The jewel in the crown is Ribe, the country's oldest town – this is historic Denmark at its most photogenic. The islands of Als, Fanø and Rømø have clear-cut appeal for beach-going holidaymakers, and bird-watchers also love this region. The tidal rhythms of the west-coast Wadden Sea bring an abundance of feathered friends (and their fanciers). An eclectic mix of royal-watchers, castle-collectors and design-enthusiasts may also be ticking must-sees off their list.

When to Go

If it's sunshine and beaches you're after, June to August is the obvious time to join the crowds on islands such as Rømø, Fanø and Als, and the region's biggest festival (Tønder Festival) farewells summer in style in late August.

A town such as Ribe charms at any time of year – December is especially delightful, with a Christmas market and festivities that make the atmosphere extra-*hyggelig* (cosy). The attractions of larger towns (Kolding, Esbjerg, Sønderborg, Tønder) are also year-round. Note that in spring (March to April) and autumn (September to October) there's some unique bird-watching to enjoy by the Wadden Sea.

Kolding

POP 57,200

Kolding is a picturesque and eminently likeable mid-sized town with a crowd-pleasing mix of old and new, wonderfully summed up in one of its major drawcards, the hill-top castle of Koldinghus. After a stroll through the old quarters at the town's heart, you can head to Trapholt to admire the modern furniture design that Denmark is renowned for. It's a winning combination.

◉ Sights

Koldinghus   CASTLE, MUSEUM
(www.koldinghus.dk; Markdanersgade 1; adult/child 70kr/free; ⊙10am-5pm) Koldinghus is the town's extravagant showpiece, with the requisite turbulent history. A fortress occupied the land in 1268, while parts of the castle

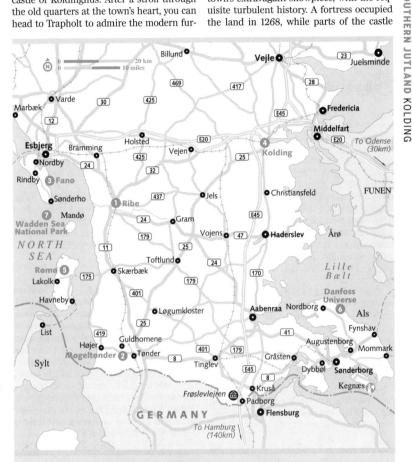

Southern Jutland Highlights

① Join the night-watchman on an evening walk through historic **Ribe** (p202)

② Dial the cuteness factor up to 11 in fairy-tale **Møgeltønder** (p211)

③ Head from modern, industrial Esbjerg to salty-dog **Fanø** (p198) in only 12 minutes

④ Envy **Kolding** (p191) its appealing mix of the old and the new

⑤ Check out the wind-driven blokarts and kite-buggies at Sønderstrand on **Rømø** (p207)

⑥ Wrap your head around the mind-bending exhibits and experiments of **Danfoss Universe** (p215)

⑦ See birds dance across the sky during the 'Sort Sol' in the new **Wadden Sea National Park** (p206)

MODERN ART MUSEUMS

Like your art modern and surrounded by cutting-edge architecture? As well as Kolding's superb Trapholt, in Jutland don't miss ARoS Aarhus Kunstmuseum (p217), Kunsten in Aalborg (p263), Silkeborg's Museum Jorn (p238), HEART and surrounds in Herning (see boxed text, p242) or Esbjerg Kunstmuseum (p195). And yes, take care when saying the word 'kunstmuseum'! If design-driven chairs are your thing, don't miss Trapholt or the water tower at Tønder Museum (p209).

you see today can be traced to the mid-15th century. The year of its most recent mishap was 1808 – at that time the castle was hosting Spanish soldiers during the Napoleonic Wars. Missing the Mediterranean summer, the soldiers lit a fire to restore some inner heat. This heat soon turned into an inferno, sending the castle up in a blaze of glory. The tower then spectacularly caught fire and collapsed through the Great Hall and onto the castle chapel. At the time, the Danish state was at war and bankrupt, and the prevailing school of thought was that the castle would be left in ruins.

If only they could see it now, shining like never before and supported internally by strikingly modern timber-and-steel structures. The interplay between old and new architectural styles is indeed a highlight, although there are good **displays**, too, including collections of historic paintings and silverware, and changing contemporary exhibits. Be sure to grab a floor plan to help find your way around. It's quite a climb to the top of the **tower** but you'll be rewarded with a panoramic view of the town.

TOP CHOICE Trapholt   ART GALLERY

(www.trapholt.dk; Æblehaven 23; adult/child 70kr/free; ☉10am-5pm Tue-Sun, to 8pm Wed) The Trapholt museum of modern art, applied art and furniture design is housed in an architectural wonder in a residential area on the northeastern outskirts of town. There are a couple of classics from the Skagen artists, vibrant modern pieces and a sculpture garden. Downstairs, the furniture collection has examples of covetable Danish chairs, with many fine examples by the likes of Hans Wegner, Arne Jacobsen and Verner Panton

(check out Jacobsen's wonderful Ant and Egg chairs).

One of the more intriguing exhibits is Jacobsen's prototype summerhouse, **Kubeflex** (the only one of its kind). It was designed by Jacobsen between 1969 and 1970 and involves cubic modules that were designed to be added to as the need arose. The house has been rebuilt in the garden and is open to the public at 1pm and 3pm daily (also at 11am on weekends). All in all, this is one of the most impressive museums in Jutland (and the view-enriched cafe and gift shop are also top-notch). Take bus 4 to get here.

Historic Buildings   HISTORIC BUILDINGS

The tourist office marks the town centre and the curvy streets sprawl out from here. The red-and-green half-timbered house close to the tourist office on Akseltorv is **Borchs Gård**, a decorative Renaissance building dating from 1595. The shopping strip of **Helligkorsgade**, just south of Akseltorv, is good for a stroll – cameras at the ready for Kolding's oldest house at **number 18**. It's an orange-coloured half-timbered affair built in 1589 with lots of wonky character, and the pocket of houses and small garden directly behind No 18 are fairy-tale stuff.

🛏 Sleeping

TOP CHOICE Hotel Koldingfjord   HOTEL €€€

(☎75 51 00 00; www.koldingfjord.dk; Fjordvej 154; s/d weekdays 1345/1645kr, summer & weekends 995/995kr; @🛜🏊) Play lord of the manor at this grand, castlelike estate (a former sanatorium) 7km east of the city, amid forest on Kolding Fjord (2km past Trapholt; take bus 4). It's a gorgeously restful spot, and the rooms are an ode to Scandi minimalism and design, with chairs direct from Trapholt and Bang & Olufsen TVs. It has an indoor pool, free bike rental, cafe, terrace and restaurant. Online 'hot rates' may be as low as 825kr per room.

Danhostel Kolding   HOTEL €

(☎75 50 91 40; www.danhostelkolding.dk; Ørnsborgvej 10; dm 180kr, s/d without bathroom 350/400kr, with bathroom 500/500kr; ☉Feb-Nov; @🛜) This top option is above a park about 1.5km north of the city centre (a 10-minute walk). There are pleasant rooms in the older-style main building, and a newer annexe boasting private bathrooms and a modern kitchen-dining area. It's deservedly popular with families and backpackers; bus 3 stops nearby.

Kolding

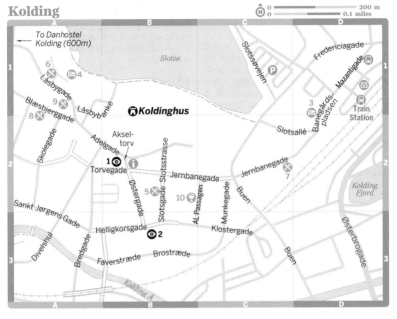

Kolding Byferie APARTMENT **€€**

(☑75 54 18 00; www.kolding-byferie.dk; Kedels-medgangen 2; d/f apt 950/1395kr; ☎) Built in the early 1990s but looking much newer, this central lakeside complex does family holidays in style. On offer are stylishly furnished apartments of various sizes (sleeping up to six) in funky-shaped buildings – triangular, circular, octagonal and star-shaped (great when admired from the Koldinghus tower). Linen and breakfast cost extra; residents get free entrance to the local swimming pool.

First Hotel Kolding HOTEL **€€**

(☑76 34 54 00; www.firsthotels.com; Banegårdsp-ladsen 7; d from 875kr; @☎) Opposite the train station, this hotel is bright, modern and style-driven, from the funky light fittings and pink ottomans in the lobby to the monochrome rooms and stylish ground-floor cafe. Online rates can drop to 550kr.

✗ Eating & Drinking

Den Blå Café INTERNATIONAL **€€**

(Slotsgade 4; lunch 68-118kr; dinner mains 98-198kr; ☺brunch, lunch & dinner) This casual all-day spot offers a large alfresco area and a menu of easy-pleasing favourites (burgers, pasta, salads, nachos). If the weather doesn't favour the great outdoors, get cosy in the cute

French-bistro interior. Good for a late-night drink, too.

Nicolai Biograf & Café ITALIAN **€€**

(Skolegade 2, entry on Blæsbjerggade; mains 70-125kr; ☺lunch & dinner) Inside a slickly renovated old school, the Nicolai has an art-house cinema alongside a cool cafe serving gourmet pizza and pasta. The weekend brunch buffet (148kr; from ·10am) is a hit with in-the-know locals.

Restaurant Le ASIAN €€
(Låsbygade 11; dinner buffet 135-155kr, mains 68-148kr; ⊘lunch & dinner) A well-priced, well-frequented jack-of-all-trades, this place has a menu full of decent Japanese, Thai, Vietnamese and Chinese dishes. There's a popular buffet of Asian and Danish specialities plus salad bar and fruit (sure, it sounds weird, but the price is right).

Kolding Smørrebrød SMØRREBRØD €
(Låsbygade 16; sandwiches from 28kr; ⊘from 10am Mon-Sat) Stop by to stock up on picnic supplies and to admire the artfully decorated smørrebrød (open sandwiches).

You'll Never Walk Alone Pub PUB
(AL Passagen 2; ⊘from 2pm Sun-Thu, noon Fri, 11am Sat) Quell any pangs of homesickness at this more-English-than-England pub (known in town simply as 'the English pub') in a passage between Jernbanegade and Klostergade. Outdoor seating, meals, live music and football matches on the big screen give this place an appeal beyond simply its 300-plus beers on the menu (including Danish microbrews).

Self-catering

Netto SUPERMARKET €
(Jernbanegade 48; ⊘9am-9pm Mon-Fri, 8am-7pm Sat) Central supermarket, close to the train station.

Market MARKET €
(⊘morning Tue & Fri) Sets up in front of the town hall on Akseltorv, selling fruit, veg and cheese.

🛍 Shopping

Kolding Storcenter MALL
(Skovvangen 42; ⊘Mon-Sat) This is an attraction of sorts for Kolding, the largest mall in Jutland and one of the largest in the country. There are over 120 shops (all the Danish high-street brands), plus restaurants and cinema. It's a few kilometres north of town; follow signs for Vejle to reach it.

❶ Information

Danske Bank (Jernbanegade 3)
Library (Slotssøvejen 4) Beautiful modern library with free internet.
Post office (Banegårdspladsen 8) Next to the train station.

Surfers Paradise (2nd fl, Jernbanegade 11; per hr 26kr; ⊘noon-8pm Mon-Sat) Internet cafe.
Tourist office (🖉76 33 21 00; www.visitkold ing.dk; Akseltorv 8; ⊘9am-5.30pm Mon-Fri, to 2pm Sat) Knowledgeable staff; good info on nearby activities.

❶ Getting There & Away

Kolding is 72km east of Esbjerg and 82km north of the German border. The E20 (which continues east to Funen) and the E45 connect Kolding with other major towns in Jutland. If you're travelling by road north to south, Rte 170 is a pleasant alternative to the E45.

There are regular train services from Kolding south to Padborg on the German border (109kr, one hour) and north all the way to Frederikshavn (319kr, 4½ hours), via Aarhus (154kr, 1½ hours) – both destinations may involve a change of trains in Fredericia. There's a second line west to Esbjerg (89kr, 50 minutes) or east to Odense (109kr, 40 minutes).

❶ Getting Around

BICYCLE For bike hire, visit **Kolding Cykelcenter** (Haderslevvej 7-9; per day/week 100/300kr), south of the centre.
BUS Buses leave from next to the train station.
CAR A ring road encircles the heart of town, with Ndr Ringvej and Slotssøvejen marking the northern and northeastern boundaries. There's parking off Slotssøvejen, opposite the library.

Esbjerg

POP 71,600

Esbjerg (pronounced *es*-be-air) has a touch of the 'wild frontier' about it – a new city (by Danish standards) that has grown big and affluent off the back of oil, fishing and trading. Its focus is to the west, to the oilfields of the North Sea, and its links to the UK mean it could well be your first introduction to Denmark.

First impressions do count, and if your first taste of Esbjerg is the sight of all those industrial plants, well, we wouldn't really blame you for giving it only a cursory glance en route to more glamorous Jutland destinations. True, with its grid layout and modern feel, Esbjerg lacks the cobblestone charm of Denmark's tourist meccas. But never judge a book by its cover. Esbjerg has some hidden gems, not least good bars, impressive art and a superb offshore island, Fanø, which is an easy 12-minute ferry ride away and offers picture-book charm in spades.

Esbjerg

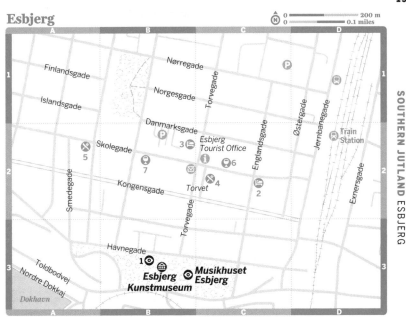

History

Esbjerg is both Denmark's youngest city and largest port, and it's the hub of the country's North Sea oil activities. Historically, Esbjerg owes its existence to the German invasion of Schleswig and Holstein in 1864, which forced Danish farmers to find another harbour from which to export goods to Britain. Thus, in 1868, the city of Esbjerg was created in what was then a desolate and far-flung corner of the country. In a relatively short time it has developed into a key industrial centre, growing into the nation's fifth-largest city.

◉ Sights & Activities

Musikhuset Esbjerg   ARCHITECTURE
(www.mhe.dk, in Danish; Havnegade 18) Famed Danish architect Jørn Utzon (he of the Sydney Opera House) designed Esbjerg's Music House together with his son, Jan. The performing arts centre opened in 1997 and is the city's main venue for music concerts, classical and otherwise.

Esbjerg Kunstmuseum   MUSEUM
(www.eskum.dk; Havnegade 20; adult/child 60kr/free; ⊙10am-4pm) Musikhuset Esbjerg is home to the small but eye-opening modern art collection of Esbjerg Kunstmuseum, which has notable works by Richard Mortensen, Robert

Jacobsen and Per Kirkeby – also look out for work from Svend Wiig Hansen (who created *Mennesket ved Havet*). In quite a magnificent display of openness (and a nod to restricted space), the Åbne Magasiner (Open Stores) downstairs allows you to look up and admire undisplayed works from the museum's collection. The other benefit to a visit is that from the museum it's easy to admire the angles and details (especially the mushroomlike columns) of the Utzons' architectural prowess.

Esbjerg Vandtårn
TOWER

(Havnegade 22; adult/child 15kr/free; ⊙10am-4pm daily Jun–mid–Sep, 10am-4pm Sat & Sun Apr–May & mid–Sep–Oct, closed Nov-Mar) Esbjerg self-consciously attempted to manufacture a medieval appearance in 1897 when town architect CH Clausen built Esbjerg Vandtårn, the water tower now conveniently (for tourists) located next door to Musikhuset Esbjerg. Climb up the impressive-looking tower to get your bearings and check out the sweeping port.

Fiskeri- og Søfartsmuseet
AQUARIUM

(www.fimus.dk; Tarphagevej 2; adult 90-115kr, child free; ⊙10am-6pm Jul-Aug, to 5pm Sep-Jun) For an up-close-and-personal look at North Sea marine life, head 4km northwest of the city centre to the saltwater aquarium at the Fisheries & Maritime Museum. Here you can see assorted local fish species getting along swimmingly, plus entertaining seals being fed at 11am and 2.30pm daily. The aquarium can be reached on buses 6 and 10; buses 1, 3 and 8 stop nearby.

Mennesket ved Havet
MONUMENT

(Hjertingvej) On the waterfront opposite Fiskeri- og Søfartsmuseet is Esbjerg's most interesting landmark, *Mennesket ved Havet* (Man Meets the Sea): four stark-white, 9m-high, stylised human figures, sitting rigid and staring out to sea. They were created by Danish sculptor Svend Wiig Hansen to commemorate the city's centennial in 1995 and they make a striking backdrop to holiday snaps.

Seal Safari
BOAT TRIPS

(adult/child/family 120/60/280kr; ⊙Esbjerg departures 11.20am & 2.20pm Mon-Thu, 11.20am Fri Jul-Aug) In July and August you can enjoy a 2½-hour sightseeing cruise around the harbour and into Ho Bugt (Ho Bay), with a chance of seeing seals in their natural habitat. Tours operate once or twice a day, Monday to Friday, and depart from the ferry harbour in Esbjerg (by the Fanø ferry); there is also the option to join the tour from Fanø (boats depart Nordby 40 minutes before the Esbjerg departure times listed here). Enquire at the tourist office for the latest schedule.

🛏 Sleeping

Staff at the tourist office can book private rooms and apartments (from 250kr per person per night) and holiday houses in Esbjerg and surrounds. Check details on the website www.visitesbjerg.dk.

Cab Inn Esbjerg
HOTEL €€

(🖉75 18 16 00; www.cabinn.com; Skolegade 14; s/d/tr from 545/675/835kr; @🛜) The best value in town is found here in this classy century-old building that's been thoroughly renovated and sits in a prime inner-city location. It's a hit with international and local visitors, who enjoy its good rates and light-filled rooms (with a bit more character than those of Cab Inn Aarhus), all with bathroom, kettle, phone and TV. Free parking, a decent breakfast buffet (60kr) and free wi-fi add up to a good deal.

🏠 Danhostel Esbjerg
HOSTEL €

(🖉75 12 42 58; www.esbjerg-danhostel.dk; Gammel Vardevej 80; dm 180kr, s/d without bathroom 350/400kr, with bathroom 500/600kr; @🛜) An excellent choice if you don't mind being out of the city centre. It's in a spiffy location – close to a sports stadium, swimming pool, park and cinema. The old building is lovely and the communal facilities typically top-notch; rooms in the new wing all have private bathroom. The hostel is 3km northwest of the city centre on bus 4.

🏠 Hotel Britannia
HOTEL €€€

(🖉75 13 01 11; www.britannia.dk; Torvet 24; s/d 1399/1599kr; @🛜) The town's largest and most business-oriented hotel has professional service, newly revamped rooms and good on-site eateries in a central location, but its rack rates are clearly pitched at expense-account business travellers. Summer rates (June to August) are much better value at 600/800kr per single/double.

Ådalens Camping
CAMPING GROUND, CABINS €

(🖉75 15 88 22; www.adal.dk; Gudenåvej 20; per adult/child/site 65/37/50kr; @🛜💦) This is kiddie-camping heaven, especially in peak season, with great facilities including a budgie-filled aviary, pet rabbits and sheep, playground, pool and mini-golf. Cabins (from 499/850kr low/high season) are also available at this large ground, about 7km northwest of the city centre – the turn-off is 3km past *Mennesket ved Havet*. Buses 1 and 7 stop 400m from the check-in area.

✕ Eating & Drinking

Dronning Louise   INTERNATIONAL €€
(Torvet 19; lunch 60-100kr, dinner mains 100-225kr; ☺brunch, lunch & dinner) The Queen Louise commands a great position on Torvet and entertains her loyal subjects with something-for-everyone panache: she's a cafe, restaurant, pub and even a nightclub (from midnight Friday and Saturday). There's also live music each Thursday. You can dine from the wonderfully broad all-day menu on the square, inside or in the rear courtyard. The brunch plates (from 80kr) offer serious bang for your buck, or try local boutique brews at the pub.

Sand's   TRADITIONAL DANISH €€
(Skolegade 60; lunch 45-169kr, dinner mains 139-229kr; ☺lunch & dinner Mon-Sat) The menu at this classy 100-year-old restaurant is an ode to old-school Danish favourites: lunchtime smørrebrød and herring platters, evening fish (try the *bakskuld,* a local fish not unlike a flounder) and plenty of classic *bøf* (beef).

Brasserie B   INTERNATIONAL €€
(Torvet 24; mains 138-225kr; ☺brunch, lunch & dinner) Hotel Britannia's restaurant has a wide-ranging menu of home-grown and international favourites, best enjoyed alfresco under the trees with a view to the town's main square. Any dish showcasing west-coast fish is a wise pick. Head downstairs afterwards to Underground (☺from 4pm Tue-Sat), an English-style pub with regular live music.

Industrien   CAFE €€
(Skolegade 27; burgers 109-159kr; ☺lunch Mon-Sat, dinner Mon-Sun) Skolegade is where to head to when you're thirsty; it has plenty of bars to choose from. Cool Industrien is a local favourite for its changing art exhibitions, live music, late, late hours (until 5am Friday and Saturday) and thumpin' burgers (of the beef, lamb, chicken or vegie persuasion – note the kitchen closes at 9pm).

Paddy Go Easy   PUB
(Skolegade 42) We like Paddy Go Easy for the real Irish accents behind (and often in front of) the bar, Kilkenny and Guinness on tap, and decent *craic* all round.

ℹ Information

Torvet, the city square, can be found where Skolegade and Torvegade intersect. The train and bus stations are about 300m east of Torvet, while the ferry terminal is 1km southwest.

Danske Bank (Torvet 18)

Krone Apoteket (Kongensgade 36; ☺24hr) A 24-hour pharmacy.

Library (Nørregade 19) Internet access.

Nordea (Kongensgade 48) Bank and ATM.

Post office (Torvet 20)

Tourist office (☎75 12 55 99; www.visitesbjerg.dk; Skolegade 33; ☺10am-5pm Mon-Fri, to 1pm Sat) On the corner of Torvet, the main square. Offers tourist information, maps and internet access.

ℹ Getting There & Away

Air

Esbjerg airport (EBJ; www.esbjerg-lufthavn.dk) is 10km east of the city centre, with daily connections to two other North Sea oil bases, Stavanger (Norway) and Aberdeen (Scotland).

Boat

For details of ferry services to/from Harwich in the UK, see the Transport chapter (p327). For information on boats for Fanø, see p199.

Bus

The bus station (local and long-distance) is on Jernbanegade, by the train station.

Thinggaard Express (www.expressbus.dk, in Danish) operates bus 980 from Esbjerg to Frederikshavn once or twice daily (340kr, five hours), calling at Viborg and Aalborg en route.

There's a useful bus connection (route 915X) that runs three times daily connecting Esbjerg with the southeast Jutland town of Sønderborg (177kr, 2½ hours), via Ribe.

Car

Esbjerg is 77km north of Tønder, 31km northwest of Ribe, 59km southwest of Billund and 92km west of the Funen-Jutland bridge.

If you're driving into Esbjerg, the E20 (the main expressway from the east) leads directly into the heart of the city and down to the ferry harbour. If you're coming from the south, Rte 24 merges with the E20 on the outskirts of the city. From the north, Rte 12 makes a beeline for the city, ending at the harbour.

The major car-rental agencies are in town, close to the train station. They also have booths at the airport, although advance reservations are required.

Train

Trains run twice-hourly during the day between Esbjerg and Copenhagen (347kr, three hours); there may be a change of train at Fredericia. There are regular services running south to Ribe (60kr, 35 minutes) and Tønder (100kr, 1½ hours); and east to Kolding (89kr, 45 minutes) and Aarhus (240kr, two hours).

ℹ️ Getting Around

Town bus 8 runs about once an hour between the bus station and the airport (26kr), as do long-distance buses 44 and 48. Bus 5 runs to the harbour (19kr) every 20 minutes.

Bikes can be hired from the office of **PJ Feriehusudlejning** (Hjertingvej 21; per day 50kr), about 2km from the city centre en route to *Mennesket ved Havet*. The tourist office has English-language brochures detailing suggested cycling itineraries.

Most city buses can be boarded at the train station. It's 19kr for a one-way ride, or 105kr for a 10-ride *klippekort* (multiuse ticket).

Parking is free in Esbjerg, but may have time limits. There's a convenient car park on Danmarksgade, but it has a two-hour limit; some unlimited parking is available in the car park on Nørregade, east of the library.

Taxis wait at the train station or can be called on ☎75 14 45 00.

Fanø

POP 3200

We think the intimate island of Fanø holds more charm than the larger, more-popular island of Rømø, further south. It may have something to do with the means of arrival (is it just us, or does a boat offer far more romance than a 10km-long causeway?). And this island backs it up with two traditional seafaring settlements full of idyllic thatch-roofed houses, blooming gardens and cobblestone streets lined with boutiques, cafes and galleries.

Beach-goers are blessed with wide, welcoming strips of sand on the exposed west coast, and a lively summer-season atmosphere. All this, and it's just 12 minutes from Esbjerg – too easy.

◉ Sights

Villages

Ferries from Esbjerg arrive at Nordby; the main villages of Nordby and Sønderho lie at each end of the 16km-long island. **Sønderho** in particular is one of Denmark's most charming villages. It dates from the 16th century and has more than a hint of Middle Earth to its jumble of low-level, half-timbered thatched houses.

The tourist office can provide brochures and maps outlining on-foot exploration of the two villages, pointing out the most historic buildings.

Museums

Nordby and Sønderho are home to a few low-key museums detailing Fanø's rich maritime history. Fanø's golden age peaked in the late 19th century, when it boasted the largest fleet outside Copenhagen; over a period of 150 years it was the site for the construction of more than 1000 vessels.

Nordby has a **maritime and costume museum**, and a **history museum**. Sønderho has an **art museum** and an original 17th-century **sea captain's house**. These are certainly interesting, but only if you have loads of time up your sleeve.

Beaches & Nature Reserve

Beaches   BEACHES

The west coast is nicely geared to family holidaymakers, with the bulk of the island's camping grounds. The best beaches are around **Rindby Strand** and **Fanø Bad** – the local bus drives along the sand and can drop you in prime beach territory. Further north is the vast sand spit that marks the northernmost tip, Søren Jessens Sand.

Fanø Klitplantage   NATURE RESERVE

Wildlife-watchers and nature-lovers will feel at home in the centre of the island where 1162 hectares make up the Fanø Klitplantage nature reserve. Take to the walking tracks and you'll find birds, deer and rabbits in abundance. Stop by the popular picnic site and forest playground near Pælebjerg.

🏃 Activities

If you're here on a day trip, it can be enjoyable to just wander around Nordby to soak up the charm, then jump on the bus to Sønderho, or hire a bike, visit the beach, take a boat trip (see p196) or see where the mood takes you – maybe to the local links golf course (the oldest golf course in Denmark; www.fanoe-golf-links.dk).

🛏️ Sleeping

There are seven camping grounds on Fanø, virtually all within a short walk of the coast. All are family-focused and most have cabins for rent. For more information, see www.visitfanoe.dk.

For information on booking summer holiday flats and houses (which typically sleep four to six people and are rented by the week), contact the tourist office. There are booking agents (www.fanohus.dk, www.fanoespecialisten.dk), but their websites are only in Danish and German.

TOP CHOICE Sønderho Kro

INN €€€

(☎75 16 40 09; www.sonderhokro.dk; Kropladsen 11, Sønderho; s 1100-1200kr, d 1300-1800kr) The loveliest place to stay on the island (and renowned around the country) is this thatched-roof slice of *hyggelig* heaven. It dates from 1722, and its 14 individually decorated rooms feature local antiques. The inn also has a notable gourmet restaurant (lunch 118kr to 178kr, dinner three/six courses 460/700kr), which showcases local and seasonal specialities, enjoyed inside or in the expansive garden.

TOP CHOICE Møllesti B&B

GUESTHOUSE €

(☎75 16 29 49; www.mollesti.dk; Møllesti 3, Nordby; s 300kr, d 450-500kr; ☺Jun-Aug or by arrangement) This B&B is hidden away in the atmospheric lanes of Nordby. It's home to four simple, stylish bedrooms sharing two bathrooms and a lovely kitchenette/lounge in a restored sea-captain's house from 1892. Prices are excellent. It can also open for guests on weekends outside of summer, but you'll need to arrange this in advance. Breakfast costs an additional 50kr; there's a two-night minimum stay.

Fanø Krogaard

INN €€

(☎76 66 01 66; www.fanoekrogaard.dk, in Danish; Langelinie 11, Nordby; d from 895kr) In operation since 1664, this charming old inn on the Nordby waterfront has cosy antique-filled rooms (plus more modern ones in a newer annexe) and an intimate atmosphere, plus a fabulous large terrace and long menu of local specialities, especially fishy favourites (lunch 74kr to 119kr, dinner mains 159kr to 219kr).

Feldberg Strand Camping

CAMPING GROUND, CABINS €

(☎75 16 24 90; www.feldbergcamping.dk; Kirkevejen 39, Rindby Strand; sites per adult/child 76/35kr; 🐾) This busy, well-positioned camping ground is a stone's throw from the beach (right by a supermarket and pizzeria) and gets very busy during the summer months.

✕ Eating & Drinking

As well as the inns serving food (reviewed under Sleeping), take a stroll along Nordby's Hovedgaden and Sønderho's Sønderland and you'll be tripping over appealing little eateries and sunny courtyard gardens.

There are supermarkets and bakeries in all the main villages on the island. The Nordby butcher, **Slagter Christiansen** (Ho-

vedgaden 17), is known throughout Denmark for his *Fanø skinke* (Fanø ham), a ham in the style of Italian parma. Heather honey is another local speciality. The **Fanø Bryghus** (www.fanoebryghus.dk, in Danish; Strandvejen 5, Nordby) is a microbrewery concocting well-respected beers – stop in to try a few at their on-site bar.

ℹ️ Information

The **tourist office** (☎70 26 42 00; www.visitfanoe.dk; Færgevej 1; ☺9am-5pm Mon-Fri, 10am-4pm Sat & Sun Jul-Aug, 10am-4pm Mon-Fri Sep-Jun) is close to the ferry dock in Nordby. The main street, Hovedgaden, begins just behind it – along here you'll find banks, stores and eateries.

ℹ️ Getting There & Around

It's expensive to take a car across to Fanø. If you're doing a day trip or overnight stay from Esbjerg, you're better off leaving your car on the mainland and hiring a bike or taking the bus once you reach the island.

FanøFærgen (www.fanoefaergen.dk; return adult/child 35/20kr) shuttles a car ferry between Esbjerg and Nordby, in Fanø's northeast, one to three times hourly from 5am to midnight. Sailing time is 12 minutes. It costs 280/390kr in low/high season to transport a car (return trip, including passengers), but only 35kr to transport a bike.

There's a local bus service (route 431) from the ferry dock that runs about once an hour, connecting Nordby with Fanø Bad (19kr), Rindby Strand (19kr) and Sønderho (26kr).

Bicycles can be hired from a number of places, including **Fanø Cykler** (www.fanoecykler.dk; per day 50kr) at Hovedgaden 96, Nordby and Kirkevejen 67, Rindby. Taxis can be reached on ☎75 16 62 00.

Ribe

POP 8200

The crooked cobblestone streets of Ribe (pronounced *ree*-buh) date from AD 869, making it Denmark's oldest town. It's easily one of the country's loveliest spots in which to stop and soak up some history. It's a delightfully compact chocolate-box confection of crooked half-timbered 16th-century houses, a sweetly meandering river and lush water meadows, all overseen by the nation's oldest cathedral. Such is the sense of living history that the entire 'old town' has been designated a preservation zone, with more than 100 buildings registered by the National Trust. Don't miss it.

Ribe

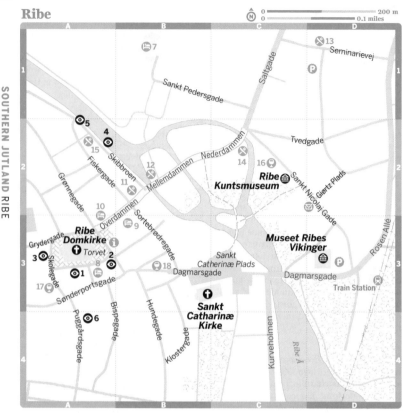

History

Founded around AD 700, Ribe evolved into a key post of the hailed Viking era. It began when the Apostle of the North, Ansgar, was given a parcel of land by the Danish king around 860 and permission to erect a church. It's not known when the church was built, but the earliest record of the existence of a bishop in Ribe is 948 – and bishops have cathedrals. During the Viking era, Ribe, linked to the sea by its river, flourished as a centre of trade between the Frankish empire and the Scandinavian states to the north.

In the 12th century the Valdemar dynasty fortified the town, building a castle and establishing Ribe as one of the king's Jutland residences.

The end of the medieval period saw Ribe enter its most torrid time. Two factors combined to send the town into 250 years of decline. A fire ripped through in 1580, and the relocation of the royal family to Copenhagen saw royal money leave the town. In turn the population diminished, and the bustling trade port turned into a struggling town with little regional importance or influence.

This economic downturn was something of a blessing – there was no finance available for building bigger and better houses, so the old town remained virtually untouched. In 1899 a tourist and conservation organisation (showing remarkable foresight) was established, and in 1963 the town council issued a preservation order covering the core of the old town. Their good sense has been well rewarded, with tourists flocking to soak up Ribe's old-world charm.

☉ Sights

Ribe Domkirke   CATHEDRAL
(Torvet; admission free; ☉10am-5pm May-Sep, 11am-4pm Apr & Oct, 11am-3pm Nov-Mar, from noon Sun year-round) Dominating Ribe's skyline is the impressive Ribe Cathedral, which dates

Ribe

⊚ Top Sights
Museet Ribes Vikinger	D3
Ribe Domkirke	A3
Ribe Kuntsmuseum	C2
Sankt Catharinæ Kirke	B3

⊚ Sights
1	Archaeological Excavations	A3
2	Den Gamle Rådhus	A3
3	Jacob A Riis House	A3
4	Johanne Dan	A2
5	Stormflodssøjlen	A2
6	Taarnborg	A4

🛏 Sleeping
7	Danhostel Ribe	B1
8	Den Gamle Arrest	A3
9	Hotel Dagmar	B3
10	Weis Stue	A3

🍴 Eating
11	Isvafeln	B2
12	Kolvig	B2
13	Kvickly Supermarket	D1
14	Postgaarden	C2
15	Sælhunden	A2
	Vægtkælderen	(see 9)
	Weis Stue	(see 10)

🍷 Drinking
16	Café Valdemar	C2
17	Ribe Bryghus	A3
18	Strygejernet	B3

notes to a folk song about Dagmar's death during childbirth.

The interior decor is a real hotchpotch of later influences. There's an organ with a facade designed by renowned 17th-century sculptor Jens Olufsen, a baptismal font from 1375, and an ornate pulpit created in 1597 by Odense sculptor Jens Asmussen. A mark on the pillar behind the pulpit shows where the flood of 1634 reached. You can find remains of paintings from the 16th century on the last two pillars on the northern side of the cathedral, while in the apse are modern-day frescoes, stained-glass windows and seven mosaics created in the 1980s by artist Carl-Henning Pedersen. The funky mosaics enliven the church and add a fascinating contrast to the more sombre features.

For a view over the countryside, climb the 248 steps (52m) up the **cathedral tower** (adult/child 10/5kr), which dates back to 1333. A survey of the surrounding marshland makes it easy to understand why the tower once doubled as a lookout station for floods.

In July and August you can join worthwhile guided tours of the cathedral (30kr); English-language tours are at 11am Monday and Thursday. Look out for summer classical-music concerts held here, too.

Historic Ribe HISTORIC NEIGHBOURHOOD
For a leisurely stroll that takes in some of Ribe's handsome half-timbered homes and ridiculously idyllic cobbled lanes, head along any of the streets radiating out from Torvet (note that the night-watchman walks cover much of this ground; see p202).

On Puggårdsgade is a privately owned 16th-century manor house, the charmingly skew-whiff **Taarnborg**, where no corner is 90 degrees. Next door at No 5 is a half-timbered house dating from 1550. From Grønnegade, narrow alleys lead down and across pretty Fiskergade to Skibbroen and the picturesque old harbour.

To help you appreciate the surrounds, drop by the tourist office and pick up a copy of the *Town Walk in Old Ribe* brochure (5kr); it's available in Danish, English, German, Dutch, Italian and French.

Also note the **archaeological excavations** going on by the cathedral; in 2011 the team uncovered a rune stone thought to date from around 1000 – you can view it at Museet Ribes Vikinger, and read about the progress of the excavations on information boards close to the site.

back to at least 948 (the earliest record of the existence of a bishop in Ribe) – making it the oldest in Denmark. The cathedral was largely rebuilt in 1150 when Ribe was at the heart of royal and government money, which in turn paved the way for some fine architectural structures.

The new cathedral was constructed primarily from tufa, a soft porous rock quarried near Cologne and shipped north along the Rhine. It took a century for the work to reach completion. Later additions included several Gothic features, but the core of the cathedral is decidedly Romanesque, a fine example of medieval Rhineland influences in architecture. One notable exterior feature is the original 'Cat's Head' door at the south portal of the transept, which boasts detailed relief-work including a triangular pediment portraying Valdemar II and Queen Dagmar positioned at the feet of Jesus and Mary. At noon and 3pm the cathedral bell plays the

DON'T MISS

NIGHT-WATCHMAN TOURS

One of the best free activities in Denmark is Ribe's 45-minute night-watchman tour (☉10pm May–mid-Sep, also 8pm Jun-Aug), which departs from out the front of Weis Stue, on Torvet, once or twice a night in the warmer months. Nowadays, it's a stroll through the town's historic streets, designed to entertain and educate visitors to Ribe, but the night-watchman's walk was originally born of necessity.

As early as the 14th century these watchmen made their nightly rounds in Ribe, ensuring the streets were safe for locals to walk. They were also charged with being on the lookout for fires or floods threatening the town. The job was abolished in Ribe in 1902, but reinstated in 1935 as a tourist attraction. Interesting factual titbits, singing and colourful stories of memorable Ribe citizens (in Danish and English) are just part of the act. Throw in narrow streets, pretty-as-a-picture houses and a late sundown, and it's a great (free) way to end a history-soaked day.

Riverfront Area   HISTORIC NEIGHBOURHOOD

Along the riverfront is Stormflodssøjlen (Skibbroen), a wooden flood column commemorating the numerous floods that have swept over Ribe. The ring at the top of the column indicates the water's depth during the record flood of 1634 (6m above normal!), which claimed hundreds of lives. Although these days a system of dikes affords low-lying Ribe somewhat more protection, residents are still subject to periodic flood evacuations.

Not far from here is *Johanne Dan,* an old sailing ship designed with a flat bottom that allowed it to navigate through the shallow waters of the Ribe Å; an onboard visit is usually only possible in conjunction with a guided tour (enquire at the tourist office).

Sankt Catharinæ Kirke   CHURCH

(Sankt Catharinæ Plads; ☉10am-noon & 2-4pm or 5pm) Founded by Spanish Black Friars in 1228, St Catharine's Church was originally built on reclaimed marshland, but it eventually collapsed. The present structure dates from the 15th century. Of the 13 churches built during the pre-Reformation period in Ribe, Sankt Catharinæ Kirke and Ribe Domkirke are the only survivors.

In 1536 the Reformation forced the friars to abandon Sankt Catharinæ Kirke and, in the years that followed, the compound served as an asylum for the mentally ill and a wartime field hospital, to name a couple of its incarnations. These days the abbey provides housing for the elderly.

In the 1920s Sankt Catharinæ Kirke was restored at tremendous cost (due to its still-faulty foundations) and was reconsecrated in 1934. In 2007 the church was again closed for extensive repairs. The interior boasts a delicately carved pulpit dating to 1591 and an ornate altarpiece created in 1650.

For a 5kr fee you can enter the tranquil cloister garden and enjoy a few minutes of contemplative silence.

Den Gamle Rådhus   HISTORIC BUILDING

(Von Støckens Plads; adult/child 15kr/free; ☉1-3pm Mon-Fri May & Sep, 1-3pm daily Jun-Aug) This is the oldest town hall (1496) in Denmark and was used as a courthouse until 2006 – these days it's a popular spot for civil weddings. As well as ceremonial artefacts, there's a collection of medieval weapons and the executioner's axe.

Ribe Kunstmuseum   ART GALLERY

(www.ribekunstmuseum.dk; Sankt Nicolaj Gade 10; adult/child 70kr/free; ☉10am-5pm daily Jul-Aug, 11am-4pm Tue-Sun Sep-Jun) An undeniable benefit of being the oldest town in the land is the opportunity to amass an impressive art collection. Ribe's newly restored art museum has been able to acquire some of Denmark's best works, including those by 19th-century 'Golden Age' painters. The singing birds outside present a glorious backdrop to collection pieces by big Danish names including Jens Juel, Nicolaj Abildgaard, Christoffer Wilhelm Eckersberg, Christen Købke and Michael Ancher, and the art gallery's garden area (open to all) is lovely.

It's also well worth exploring the very pretty area behind the art gallery, where paths pass over the river and lead either to St Catharine's Church or Nederdammen.

Museet Ribes Vikinger   MUSEUM

(www.ribesvikinger.dk; Odins Plads 1; adult/child 60kr/free; ☉10am-6pm Jul-Aug, to 4pm Sep-Jun, closed Mon Nov-Mar) To better come to grips with Ribe's Viking and medieval history, head along to see the informative displays of the Museum of Ribe's Vikings. Two rooms provide snapshots of the town in 800 and during medieval times in 1500. These portrayals are complemented by rare archaeological finds and good explanations, which add real substance to the tales.

Ribe VikingeCenter   VIKING OPEN-AIR MUSEUM
(www.ribevikingecenter.dk; Lustrupvej 4; adult/child 90/45kr; ⊙11am-5pm daily Jul-Aug, 10am-3.30pm Mon-Fri May-Jun & Sep-Oct) Embrace your inner Viking (well, let's leave aside the raping and pillaging part, shall we?) at Ribe Vikinge-Center, a much more hands-on experience than the museum. It attempts to re-create a slice of life in Viking-era Ribe using various reconstructions, including a 34m Fyrkat-style longhouse. The staff, dressed in period clothing, bake bread over open fires, demonstrate archery and Viking-era crafts such as pottery and leatherwork, and offer falconry shows and 'warrior training' (for kids, to learn to use a sword and shield). You'll no doubt learn more about Viking life than you could from a textbook. The centre is 3km south of town; bus 417 runs out here.

☞ Tours

Town Walks   WALKING
(adult/child 60kr/free; ⊙11.30am Mon-Fri Jul-Aug) As well as the very popular night-watchman tour (see the boxed text, p202), the tourist office also stages guided 90-minute town walks in high season. At the time of research these were being conducted in Danish and German only.

Ghost Walks   GHOST
(adult/child 50kr/free; ⊙9pm Wed Jul-Aug) The summertime ghost walks operated by (and departing from) Museet Ribes Vikinger show the town in a whole new light – listen out for tales of Maren Spliid, who was burned at the stake in 1641, the last victim of Denmark's witch-hunt persecutions. Walks are staged once a week, in Danish, German and English. Buy your ticket at the museum.

🛏 Sleeping

The tourist office distributes an annually updated brochure listing some 30 private homes in and around Ribe that rent great-value rooms and apartments – single/double rooms cost 300/400kr and apartments 450kr. Breakfast costs an additional 50kr to 75kr per person. You can see pictures of the accommodation online at www.visitribe.dk.

The tourist office can make a booking for a 30kr fee.

There are also very pleasant rooms for rent above the Sælhunden and Postgaarden eateries.

Weis Stue   GUESTHOUSE €
(☑75 42 07 00; www.weisstue.dk; Torvet 2; s/d with shared bathroom 395/495kr) This is the poorer, quirkier but no less charming sister to upmarket Hotel Dagmar. An ancient wooden-beamed house from 1600, it has small, crooked rooms above its restaurant, but they have lashings of character – creaking boards, sloping walls and low overhead beams. There are only eight rooms, and breakfast is taken at Hotel Dagmar.

🏠 Danhostel Ribe   HOSTEL €
(☑75 42 06 20; www.danhostel-ribe.dk; Sankt Pedersgade 16; dm 170kr, s/d from 340/380kr; ⊙reception 8am-noon & 4-6pm, until 8pm in summer; @奈) An ideal location, knowledgeable staff, sparkling rooms (all with bathroom) and impressive facilities make this a top-notch option suited to both backpackers and families. It rents out bikes and is a stone's throw from Ribe's historic centre; equally impressive is its commitment to the environment, from the Good Origin coffee in its vending machines to its promotion of sustainable travel in the Wadden Sea region.

STORK STALKING

In Denmark, Ribe is known as 'Storke-byen', the Stork Town, thanks to the graceful storks that once built their nests on top of its buildings – atop Den Gamle Rådhus in particular (where a stork nest still stands). A pair of storks usually arrived in late March or early April (the male first, the female shortly after), which was a welcome sign of spring for Ribe residents. The feathered pair would set up house and nest for the summer, hatching a young brood before migrating to Africa at the end of August. In recent years, however, things have changed. Blame global warming, changes to agricultural land use (resulting in fewer feeding opportunities) and/or strange local weather patterns – no storks have nested in Ribe since the early 2000s, although there are occasional sightings of storks passing through.

THE AMERICAN DREAM

Jacob A Riis (1849–1914), a local Ribe resident, was 21 when he lost his heart to the town's prettiest girl. Unfortunately, the girl was not as taken by young Jacob, so in 1870 he packed up his kit and headed west to the city of dreams, New York. Still heartbroken, he lived on the streets for seven years. This drew his attention to the inhumane slums that so many beaten New Yorkers called home. Combining his two potent passions, journalism and photography, he portrayed the poor through a series of graphic, moving slides that jolted a nation into action. His most acclaimed work was his first book printed in 1890, *How the Other Half Lives*, which depicted through vivid photographs and profound words the hopeless situation many immigrants faced in New York City during the late 19th century. Through such words, Riis, and close associate Theodore Roosevelt (then commissioner of police, later the USA's 26th president), helped clear the slums. Roosevelt remarked of Riis: 'I am tempted to call [him] the best American I ever knew'.

Riis was offered the post as mayor of New York but turned it down to pursue matters closer to the heart. Having directly helped well over a million people off the streets, he returned to Ribe to woo and marry the love of his life – completing the fairy tale in true Danish style. You can walk past his **former residence** (cnr Skolegade & Grydergade) in Ribe, and admire a statue of him in Badstuegade, by the river. To view some of his photographs, still heart-wrenching over 120 years later, visit the permanent free exhibition in the reception building of **Ribe Byferie** (Damvej 34; ⊙daily), a short walk southwest of Torvet.

Ribe Byferie APARTMENT €€
(☑79 88 79 88; www.ribe-byferie.dk; Damvej 34; apt for up to 4 people 945-1995kr; @🅟) This is a well-run 'village' of modern apartments in a quiet part of town, a short walk southwest of Torvet. The roomy self-catering apartments can sleep up to seven; families are catered to with a wellness centre, games room, bike and canoe hire, kids' club, playground and lovely barbecue area. Prices fluctuate with season; linen and breakfast cost extra.

Ribe Camping CAMPING GROUND, CABINS €
(☑75 41 07 77; www.ribecamping.dk; Farupvej 2; per adult/child/site 75/45/60kr; @🅟🅢) Just 1.5km north of the town lies this busy, well-equipped camping ground bursting with good cheer and excellent amenities; a summertime outdoor heated swimming pool, rental bikes and playground are all at your disposal. There are also some pretty swanky cabins for hire (with Jacuzzi!), from 550kr.

Den Gamle Arrest GUESTHOUSE €€
(☑75 42 37 00; www.dengamlearrest.dk; Torvet 11; d without bathroom 690-740kr, with bathroom 890-1090kr) You need to be creative when turning jail cells into hotel rooms, and the people behind the creation of these rooms can take a bow. This superbly positioned building served as a jail right up until 1989; now it allows guests to satisfy any 'lock-in' fantasy within bright, simple rooms that maximise space, with a mezzanine level holding table and chairs above a roll-away bed. Most rooms have a washbasin but share bathroom facilities.

Hotel Dagmar HOTEL €€
(☑75 42 00 33; www.hoteldagmar.dk; Torvet 1; s/d from 1045/1245kr; @🅟) Classy, central Hotel Dagmar is Denmark's oldest hotel (1581) and exudes all the charm you'd expect. There's a golden hue to the hallways and rooms, with old-world decor alongside tiling, artworks and antiques. It's pricey, but plenty of history and a bumper breakfast contribute to the experience; see the website for packages involving meals and accommodation.

✖ Eating

Sælhunden TRADITIONAL DANISH €€
(Skibbroen 13; lunch 75-135kr, dinner mains 120-235kr; ⊙lunch & dinner) Top choice is this handsome old black-and-white restaurant down by the waterfront, with outdoor seating by the *Johanne Dan* sailing ship. *Sælhund* means seal, so it's no surprise this place dedicates itself to serving the best seafood in town, usually in traditional Danish guises. Try the delicious *stjerneskud,* the house speciality (one fried and one steamed fillet of fish served on bread with prawns, caviar and dressing).

Weis Stue
TRADITIONAL DANISH €€

(Torvet 2; lunch 79-189kr, dinner mains 145-245kr; ⊗lunch & dinner) Don't come here looking for modern, could-be-anywhere cuisine. As befits the setting (one of Denmark's oldest inns, wonky and charming), the menu is a traditionalist's dream. The large meat-and-potatoes portions are full of northern European flavour (pepper pork medallions, Wiener schnitzel, grilled veal liver), best washed down with locally brewed beer. There's bags of atmosphere, plus a kids' menu, but little joy for vegetarians.

Vægterkælderen
DANISH €€

(Torvet 1; lunch 70-175kr, dinner mains 75-210kr; ⊗lunch & dinner) In summer you won't catch anyone down in the 'night-watchman's cellar' at Hotel Dagmar – they're all sitting out on the main square. The timber-heavy decor down here seems made for cold weather – soft leather banquettes and booths (a touch dated but very cosy). The menu runs from steamed mussels to quality steak, with the three-course set menu a good-value 248kr.

Postgaarden
CAFE €

(Nederdammen 36; meals 59-119kr; ⊗10am-8pm Mon-Sat, to 5pm Sun) Postgaarden has a wide range of Danish and international microbrews for sale in its delicatessen, and a changing selection of boutique (and sometimes obscure) brews on tap to accompany its cafe-style menu, best enjoyed in the photogenic courtyard. There's also a good array of picnic-worthy products on offer (ask about picnic baskets to go).

Kolvig
MODERN DANISH €€€

(Mellemdammen 13; lunch 68-145kr, dinner mains 195-235kr; ⊗lunch & dinner Mon-Sat) Kolvig's terrace overlooks the river, so alfresco dining is understandably popular and offers prime Ribe-watching. The menu is a good mix of traditional and modern; most interesting is the tapas plate of Wadden Sea flavours, including shrimp, salmon and marsh lamb.

Isvafeln
ICE CREAM €

(Overdammen 11; 2/3 scoops 20/25kr) Pizza places and ice-cream sellers aren't hard to find along the main drag. On a warm day, Isvafeln is swamped with holidaymakers devouring the great ice-cream flavours.

Kvickly
SUPERMARKET €

(Seminarievej; ⊗9am-8pm Mon-Fri, to 6pm Sat) Well placed for self-caterers staying at the hostel.

🍷 Drinking

Ribe Bryghus
BREWERY

(Skolegade 4B; ⊗10am-1pm Sat) Look out for this label's locally brewed beers at restaurants and bars around town, or pop into the brewery during its limited opening hours.

Café Valdemar
PUB

(Sankt Nicolaj Gade 6B; ⊗from 3pm Tue-Sat) The beach comes to Ribe! In the warmer months this place offers tropical outdoor furniture and a stretch of sand down to the gentle river, making it a perfect spot for lazy afternoon drinks. There's plenty of grass and a kids' play area, too. Look out for live music.

Strygejernet
PUB

(Dagmarsgade 1; ⊗from 3pm Tue-Sat) A small and cosy two-storey pub with a flat-iron triangular shape – it's a little slice of New York in Ribe. The top floor has just a handful of tables and looks out to the rådhus (town hall), or join the locals propping up the bar downstairs.

ⓘ Information

Danske Bank (Sanitarievej)

Library (Giørtz Plads) Close to the art museum, with free internet access.

Post office (Sankt Nicolaj Gade 12) Next to the art museum.

Tourist office (☑75 42 15 00; www.visitribe. dk; Torvet 3; ⊗9am-6pm Mon-Fri, 10am-5pm Sat, 10am-2pm Sun Jul-Aug, reduced hrs rest of year) Has an abundance of information on the town and surrounding areas, plus internet access. It offers the RibePas (adult/child 20/10kr) that grants the holder up to 20% discount at many museums and deals at local restaurants.

ⓘ Getting There & Away

Ribe is 31km south of Esbjerg via Rte 24 and 47km north of Tønder via Rte 11.

Trains from Ribe run hourly on weekdays and less frequently at weekends north to Esbjerg (60kr, 35 minutes), and south to Skærbæk for Rømø (28kr, 20 minutes) and Tønder (71kr, 65 minutes).

ⓘ Getting Around

Ribe is a tightly clustered town, so it's easy to explore. Everything, including the hostel and the train station, is within a 10-minute walk of Torvet, the central square that's dominated by the huge cathedral.

There's parking with a daytime two-hour limit around Torvet, a parking area with a three-hour limit at Museet Ribes Vikinger, and parking with no time limit at the end of Sankt Pedersgade near the hostel, and just north of the train station.

Bicycles can be hired from **Danhostel Ribe** (Sankt Pedersgade 16) and cost 75/130kr for one/two days.

Wadden Sea National Park

One of the five new national parks created in Denmark in the last few years is Nationalpark Vadehavet (Wadden Sea National Park; www.nationalparkvadehavet.dk). Stretching along Jutland's west coast from Ho Bugt (west of Esbjerg) to the German border, and incorporating the popular holiday islands of Rømø and Fanø, its marshlands provide food and rest for millions of migratory birds.

The Wadden Sea extends 450km, from west Jutland south and west to the Dutch island of Texel. Large parts of the Dutch and German Wadden Sea have been national parks for years; with the Danish area now also protected, this is one of the largest national parks in Europe. It is one of the most important areas for fish, birds and seals. Ten to 12 million waterbirds pass through the area on their way to/from their breeding grounds in northern Scandinavia, Siberia or Greenland. The birds forage in the sea's tidal flats, which are exposed twice every 24 hours.

🏌 Activities

VadehavsCentret ACTIVITY CENTRE, TOURS
(✆75 44 41 61; www.vadehavscentret.dk; Okholmvej 5, Vester Vedsted; adult/child 65/30kr; ⊙10am-4pm or 5pm mid-Feb–Oct) About 10km southwest of Ribe, VadehavsCentret is an information and activity centre reached by bus 412 from Ribe. There are exhibitions on the tides, flora and fauna of the national park, plus a regular tractor-bus running 6km across the tidal flats at low tide to the small outlying island of Mandø. It's possible to hire bikes to explore the island, and to stay at a local camping ground, apartments or *kro* (inns; see www.mandoetourist.dk).

VadehavsCentret also runs **tours** to explore different facets of the park – winter oyster-collecting seal-spotting and birdwatching, for example. One of the most popular options is to experience the 'Sort Sol' (Black Sun) in spring (approximate dates 20 March to 25 April) and autumn (15 September to 20 October). This describes the phenomena of large numbers of migrating starlings (up to a million) gathering in the marshes outside Ribe and Tønder. 'Sort Sol' takes place in the hours just after sunset, when the birds gather in large flocks and form huge formations in the sky before they decide on a location to roost for the night. The movements of the formations have been likened to a dance and the birds are so numerous that they seem to obliterate the sunset.

Ask at tourist offices on the west coast for ways to access the offerings of the park.

Naturcenter Tønnisgaard TOURS
(✆74 75 52 57; www.tonnisgaard.dk) Based on Rømø.

Sort Safari TOURS
(✆73 72 64 00; www.sortsafari.dk) Operates in the Tønder area.

Rømø

POP 700

Summer sees the large island of Rømø fill with tourists (predominantly German). This is hardly surprising given the entire west coast is one long, sandy beach that's prime happy-holiday turf, perfect for sun-bathing and sunset-watching or something more active. Rømø is connected to the mainland by a 10km causeway (with cycle lane). During the colder months it's a windswept sleeper with get-away-from-it-all charm that couldn't be more removed from its busy summer incarnation.

⊙ Sights

FREE **Kommandørgården** HOUSE
(Juvrevej 60, Toftum; ⊙10am-5pm Tue-Sun May-Sep, until 3pm Oct) Despite appearances it's not *all* about the beach on Rømø. Inland are thatched-roof houses nestled in scrubby pine woods, rolling grassland and the odd historic building. The handsome thatched Kommandørgården, 1.5km north of the causeway, is the preserved home of one of Rømø's 18th-century whaling captains. It stands as testimony to the prosperity that such men brought to the island through their whaling expeditions. It has Dutch tiles lining many walls and woodwork painted in rococo style (minimal labelling in English, however). In the barn is the skeleton of a sperm whale stranded on Rømø in 1996.

Rømø Kirke CHURCH
(Havnebyvej, Kirkeby) The 18th-century Rømø Kirke is on the main road in Kirkeby. It's not-

Rømø

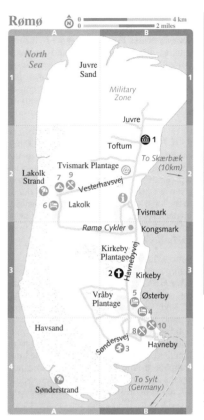

North Sea

Juvre Sand

Military Zone

Juvre

Toftum 1

Tvismark Plantage

Lakolk Strand 7 9

Vesterhavsvej

Lakolk 6

Tvismark

Rømø Cykler

Kongsmark

Kirkeby Plantage

2 Kirkeby

Havnebyvej

Vråby Plantage

5 Østerby

4

Havsand

8 10

Sønderstrand

Havneby 3

Søndervej

To Sylt (Germany)

To Skærbæk (10km)

Rømø

⊙ Sights
1 Kommandørgården.............................B2
2 Rømø Kirke B3

🏃 Activities, Courses & Tours
3 Dayz Rømø Golf & Wellness B4
  Kommandørgårdens
   Islændercenter ....(see 5)

🛏 Sleeping
4 Danhostel Rømø..................................B3
5 Hotel Kommandørgården...................B3
6 Hotel Lakolk Rømø A2
7 Lakolk Strand Camping A2

🍴 Eating
8 Brugsen Supermarket.........................B4
  Dayz Rømø Golf & Wellness .... (see 3)
  Holms Røgeri & Restaurant.......(see 10)
9 Lakolk Shopping Centre.....................A2
10 Otto & Ani's Fisk B4
  Ø.. (see 3)

ed for its unique Greenlandic gravestones (lining the northern wall of the churchyard), erected by sea captains and decorated with images of their boats and families.

🏃 Activities

Horse Riding

The beaches are perfect for an endless ride into the sunset.

Kommandørgårdens
Islændercenter   HORSE RIDING
(☏74 75 51 22; http://islander.kommandoer gaarden.dk, in Danish; Havnebyvej 201, Østerby) Based at Hotel Kommandørgården, it has a stable full of Icelandic horses and a range of rides to appeal to kids, beginners and more-experienced horse-folk, through forest and along the beach. A 3½-hour sunset tour costs 345/310kr for beginners/experienced riders, while a full-day tour to the north of Rømø costs 850kr.

Beach Activities

The long west-coast beach is divided into activity areas, with **windsurfing** a popular activity south of Lakolk. Most enthusiasts arrive with their own equipment, but if you come without, enquire at the tourist office about possibilities (at the time of research there were no places offering gear rental).

At the southwest corner of the island is **Sønderstrand**, a remarkable sight – full of cars, colour and land-based activities making great use of the air that blows in fresh from the North Sea. There's a small area for parking your car where the sealed road reaches the sand, or you can continue driving on the beach itself (north as far as Lakolk).

As the sealed road reaches Sønderstrand, to your left is an area dedicated to *strandsejlads,* aka land-yachts or blokarts (a three-wheeled go-kart that utilises a sail to capture the wind). To the right, it's all about *kitebug-gykørsel,* or buggies with attached parachutelike kites. Great speeds are reached, and it's quite a spectacle. If you want a crack at either, contact **Windriders** (☏22 85 50 15; www.windriders.dk, in Danish), which offers one-hour lessons from 250kr.

Walking

The inland section of Rømø has **walking trails** through heather moors and wooded areas, offering quiet hiking spots. There are three forest zones, each with a couple of

ⓘ THE LAY OF THE LAND

As you cross the causeway from the mainland, you continue straight to reach Lakolk, a large camping-ground-turned-village on the central west coast. It's also where you'll find the most popular beach – Lakolk Strand. Heading left (south) immediately after reaching Rømø takes you to Kongsmark, Havneby and the activity-rich **Sønderstrand** beach. If you head right (north) as you reach the island, you'll arrive at the historic centre, **Toftum** and **Juvre**. The far northern end of the island is a military zone (access prohibited).

kilometres of trails: **Tvismark Plantage**, along Vesterhavsvej, the main east-west road; **Kirkeby Plantage**, to the west of Kirkeby; and **Vråby Plantage**, a less-diverse area dominated by pines, about 1km further south.

Other Activities

Dayz Rømø Golf & Wellness SPA, ACTIVITY CENTRE
(☏74 75 56 55; www.dayz.dk; Vestergade 31, Havneby) This resort en route to Sønderstrand is home to a relaxation-inducing wellness spa (250kr for nonguests; no kids under 16); indoor swimming pool and fitness centre (adult/child 100/50kr); bowling alley (one hour 150kr); and a challenging links golf course (18 holes 300kr). Club and buggy hire are available.

🛏 Sleeping

The vast majority of accommodation is found in some 1600 summerhouses and apartments scattered around the island, which are usually rented by the week in the high season (outside this period there's usually a three-night minimum). Prices vary, depending on the season and the degree of luxury. The tourist office can provide a catalogue and handle the bookings.

Danhostel Rømø HOSTEL €
(☏74 75 51 88; www.danhostel.dk/romo; Lyngvejen 7, Østerby; dm 195kr, d with/without bathroom 450/350kr; ⓧmid-Mar–Oct) A picturesque red, thatched-roof complex that's well hidden off the main road and set among pines, but walking distance to a supermarket and bakery. The rooms (a few with bathroom) are basic but spick-and-span, and the outdoor areas beckon for a complete holiday wind-down.

Dayz Rømø Golf & Wellness RESORT €€€
(☏74 75 56 55; www.dayz.dk; Vestergade 31, Havneby; houses 1830-2960kr; 🐾🏊) A luxury-leaning, activity-rich playground for families enjoying the links golf course, wellness centre, gourmet restaurant and huge complex of two-bedroom, fully equipped houses (sleeping up to eight). There are plenty of weekly deals and golf/wellness packages.

Hotel Lakolk Rømø HOTEL €€
(☏74 75 51 45; www.hotel-lakolk.dk; Lakolk 150; s/d/f from 595/795/1195kr) Compared to the crowds of the camping ground, this hotel offers relative calm. It's pretty good value, too, given it's just a short walk over the dunes to the long, sandy beach. There are smallish, modern rooms on offer, some with kitchenette, plus apartments (three-day stay from 1695kr).

Lakolk Strand Camping CAMPING GROUND, CABINS €
(☏74 75 52 28; www.lakolkcamping.dk; Lakolk; site per adult/child 83/50kr; ⓧmid-Apr–Oct; @🐾) In high summer, the beachside camping ground and shopping centre at Lakolk is holiday heaven or hell, depending on your outlook. It's bursting at the seams with families praying for good weather; the huge camping ground is wall-to-wall with campervans and all the requisite facilities, including rental of on-site caravans and cabins.

Hotel Kommandørgården HOTEL, CAMPING GROUND €€
(☏74 75 51 22; www.kommandoergaarden.dk; Havnebyvej, Østerby; camping per adult/child/site 80/45/45kr, hotel s/d from 695/795kr, apt from 895kr; @🐾🏊) This astonishingly big complex has everything from camping and cabins to hotel rooms and apartments, and a restaurant and bar. Plus there are activities laid on thick, including a wellness centre, bike hire, kayaking, horse riding and indoor and outdoor swimming pools.

🍴 Eating

Havneby is the island's culinary hot spot, with a large Brugsen supermarket and good array of mostly family-oriented eateries. At Lakolk shopping centre there's a small supermarket and some casual refuelling spots including a bistro, summer nightclub, pizzeria, ice creamery and cafes.

Otto & Ani's Fisk SEAFOOD €
(Havnespladsen, Havneby; snacks & meals 35-195kr; ⓧ11am-8pm) This no-frills cafeteria is

right on the harbourside at Havneby, so the fish are as fresh as they come. Pull up a pew outside and feast on fish and chips (65kr) or a bread roll filled with Rømø shrimp (50kr). You can also buy fresh uncooked fish and seafood, and smoked fishy delicacies.

Holms Røgeri & Restaurant　SMOKEHOUSE **€€** (Nordre Havnevej 1, Havneby; lunch 52-128kr, dinner mains 79-198kr; ⊙lunch & dinner) It's hard to go past the lunchtime *fiskeplatte* at this fine smokehouse – a piscatorial pile-up of marinated herring, shrimps, smoked salmon, smoked mackerel and smoked halibut. At dinnertime the menu broadens to offer hefty steak options too.

Ø　DANISH **€€** (Vestergade 31, Havneby; lunch 59-105kr, dinner mains 149-189kr; ⊙lunch & dinner) Test your Danish pronunciation with the name of Dayz resort's restaurant (the letter means 'island'), home to one of Rømø's loveliest terraces. The lunch menu has Danish and international favourites (Caesar salad next to a herring plate), and the kitchen struts its stuff of an evening with its use of high-class Rømø produce (*marsklam,* or marsh lamb, fresh fish, local shrimps).

🛈 Information

Statoil (Juvrevej 3; per 30/60min 25/45kr; ⊙8am-5pm) Surprisingly, internet is offered at this petrol station, just as you reach Rømø via the causeway.

Tourist office (☑74 75 51 30; www.romo.dk; Havnebyvej 30, Tvismark; ⊙9am-5pm Mon-Sat, to 3pm Sun) Situated 1km south of the causeway; can arrange cottage rental.

🛈 Getting There & Away

Rømø is on Rte 175, about 14km west of Skærbæk. Bus 785 runs from Skærbæk to Havneby (34kr, 45 minutes) about hourly on weekdays, and less often at weekends. From Skærbæk there are hourly trains to Ribe (28kr, 20 minutes), Tønder (48kr, 30 minutes) and Esbjerg (58kr, 55 minutes).

The **SyltExpress** (www.syltfaehre.de) ferry operates between Havneby and the nearby German island of Sylt (car one way including passengers 339kr, adult return 74kr) several times a day; journey time is 45 minutes.

🛈 Getting Around

Roads allow cars to access the beaches at Lakolk and Sønderstrand, and you can drive up and down the west coast along the sand.

About 10 times a day on weekdays (considerably less on weekends), bus 785 makes a trip from Havneby up the east-coast road before pressing on to mainland Skærbæk (and vice versa). A number of these trips run via Lakolk.

If you don't have your own transport, the best option is to rent a bike from **Rømø Cykler** (www.romocykler.dk; Havnebyvej 74, Kongsmark; per day/week 60/360kr), as Rømø is as flat as a pancake and perfect for cycling.

Tønder

POP 7700

The record books say 1243 but talk to any local and they'll say the bloodlines run deeper into the past – so it's little wonder Tønder lays unofficial claim to the title of Denmark's oldest town. It's an inviting place that's had a rocky journey through serious flooding to German annexation; strong German links remain (not surprising, given Tønder's proximity to the border, just 4km south).

During the 16th century a series of dikes were erected to prevent the imminent threat of flooding. In doing so the town isolated itself from its sea-port connection and turned elsewhere for economic prosperity. Lace-making was introduced – an economic windfall that employed up to 12,000 workers during its peak in the 18th century. These days tourism adds a fair kick to the town – it's an eminently agreeable little place with drawcards out of proportion to its size.

◉ Sights

Tønder Museum　MUSEUM (Kongevej 51; adult/child 50kr/free; ⊙10am-5pm Jun-Aug, 10am-5pm Tue-Sun Sep-May) The multifaceted Tønder Museum has three components: first, **Kulturhistorie Tønder** housing a collection of delicate Tønder lace and decoratively painted furniture. In the adjacent

A WHALE OF A TIME

Between 1650 and 1850, many Rømø men worked as whalers off Greenland – this is still regarded as the golden age of the island. Skilled, confident and fearless fishermen from Rømø captained Dutch and German ships on dangerous voyages north to catch whales. Some returned rich, some didn't return at all. A trip to Rømø Kirke and Kommandørgården illustrates the sacrifice and rewards involved.

wing is **Kunstmuseet i Tønder**, full of Danish surrealist and modern art. Our favourite feature, however, is the 1902 **Vandtårnet** (water tower), which you can climb for sweeping views of the town and surrounding countryside (or take the lift up and walk down). On each of the tower's eight floors are the fabulous chair designs of locally born Hans Wegner, one of the most innovative and prolific of all Danish furniture designers. You will no doubt have seen his designs on your travels through Denmark – check out the Ox Chair on the 5th floor, the quirky Valet Chair on the 4th floor, and the Peacock and Wishbone chairs on the 2nd floor.

Historic Houses   HOUSES

To glimpse the past, head south from Torvet along Søndergade and turn right into **Uldgade**. The cobbled street has Tønder's best collection of unique gabled houses. On the main pedestrian street, **Drøhses Hus** (Storegade 14; adult/child 30kr/free; ⊙Apr-Dec) dates from 1672; it's been meticulously restored and is open to the public.

Kristkirken   CHURCH

(Torvet; ⊙10am-4pm Mon-Sat) The grand old Kristkirken on the northeastern side of Torvet dates back to 1592. Its opulent interior came courtesy of the town's rich cattle- and lace-merchants, who invested heavily between the late 17th and 18th centuries. The church interior boasts impressive carvings and paintings, including a rare baptismal font from 1350, an ornate pulpit from 1586 and a series of memorial tablets from around 1600. The 47.5m-high tower, part of an earlier church that stood on the same site, doubled as a navigational marker in the days when Tønder was connected to the sea.

Det Gamle Apotek   HISTORIC BUILDING

(The Old Pharmacy; Østergade 1; ⊙daily) Det Gamle Apotek, beside Torvet, has an elaborate 1671 baroque doorway flanked by two lions that stand guard over the old-fashioned interior and extensive gift-shop collection (everything you never thought you'd need, and then some).

✿ Festivals

Tønder Festival   MUSIC

(www.tf.dk) Growing in reputation and scale each year, the Tønder Festival takes place in the last week of August and draws some 20,000 attendees from all corners of the country. It's regarded as one of the best folk music festivals in Europe, with loads of Irish music and a friendly, fun atmosphere.

🛏 Sleeping

The tourist office can help arrange private-room accommodation in homes in the Tønder area, with prices around 300kr for a double. For something special, head to the old *kro* (inn) in Møgeltønder (p212).

Danhostel Tønder   HOSTEL €

(☑74 72 35 00; www.danhostel.dk/tonder; Sønderport 4; dm 160kr, s & d with bathroom 385kr; ⊙Feb–mid-Dec; @🖥) Cut from the same cloth as other southern Jutland Danhostels is a plain, low-slung brick building with plentiful rooms (all with bathroom), friendly staff, appealing communal areas and fresh, clean facilities. It's a few minutes' walk southeast of the town centre. The camping ground is next door.

Hostrups Hotel   HOTEL €

(☑74 72 21 29; www.hostrupshotel.dk; Søndergade 30; s/d from 380/490kr; 🖥) The low prices, then the worn carpet in the halls, may set off alarm bells, but there's no need – rooms here are fresh and bright. This pretty green-coloured hotel is opposite a small lake – try for a room that overlooks it.

Motel Apartments   HOTEL €

(☑74 72 37 60; www.motel-apartments.dk; Vestergade 87; s/d/apt 475/560/1000kr; 🖥) Another solid, well-priced option, this one is behind a facade that does it no favours. On offer are comfy rooms with kitchenette (and some with garden terrace). There are also apartment options for those seeking more space. Breakfast is an additional 60kr.

✕ Eating & Drinking

There are options around Torvet, including **Kloster Caféen** (Torvet 11), a cafe in Tønder's oldest house (from 1520 and boasting beautiful old tiles). The square is also home to a photogenic market selling fruit, vegetables and cheese on Tuesday and Friday mornings.

Victoria   INTERNATIONAL €€

(Storgade 9; mains 65-199kr; ⊙lunch & dinner) At the turn of the 19th century Tønder had a world-beating one bar for every 49 inhabitants. Only the Victoria kicks on now as a jack-of-all-trades pub/cafe/restaurant. It's a winner, with an all-ages crowd, old-world timber-rich decor and a good range of international and local beers. The menu is long, varied (burgers, burritos, pasta, sandwiches) and well priced; unless you order from the steak menu, mains come in under 110kr.

Café Engel CAFE €

(Gråbrødre Torv; sandwiches 39-119kr; ⏲10am-5pm Tue-Fri, 11am-4pm Sat) At the end of Uldgade, this place has a simple, streamlined interior, pretty seating on the square outside, and a small but tempting menu (cutely hand-drawn) of sandwiches (try one with salmon and homemade tzatziki).

Information

There are a couple of banks near Torvet, the central square.

Tourist office (☎74 72 12 20; www.visittonder.dk; Torvet 1; ⏲9am-5pm Mon-Fri, 10am-2pm Sat) Helpful office with information on the town and Møgeltønder.

Getting There & Around

BICYCLE **ToP Cykler** (Nørremarksvej 31) rents bikes for 70kr per day.

BUS Bus 266 runs regularly to Møgeltønder (19kr, 15 minutes).

CAR Tønder is on Rte 11, 4km north of the border with Germany and 77km south of Esbjerg.

TRAIN The train station is on the western side of town, about 1km from Torvet via Vestergade. Trains run hourly on weekdays and slightly less frequently at weekends to/from Ribe (71kr, 65 minutes) and Esbjerg (100kr, 1½ hours).

Møgeltønder

This little village is impossibly cute – if you could, you'd wrap it up and take it home for your grandmother. A royal castle, one of the most beautiful streets in Jutland and a church rich in frescoes are some of the joys to be found here.

Sights

Schackenborg CASTLE

(Schackenborgvej) On the eastern edge of town is Schackenborg, a small castle that was presented by the Crown to Field Marshal Hans Schack in 1661 following his victory over the Swedes in the battle of Nyborg. Eleven generations of Schacks lived there until 1978, when it was returned to the royal family.

In 1995 Queen Margrethe's youngest son, Prince Joachim, married Hong Kong–born Alexandra and the newlyweds made Schackenborg their primary residence. Joachim farms the surrounding land (he has a background in agriculture) and the couple have two sons, Princes Nikolai and Felix. The pair split in 2005, and in 2008 Joachim married Parisian-born Marie. The new couple welcomed a son, Prince Henrik, in 2008.

Anyhoo, you can see Schackenborg from the street, and while you can't join the inhabitants for a lazy brunch, the moat-surrounded grounds on the opposite side of the street have been turned into a small public park that you're free to enjoy. From mid-May to August there are in-demand guided tours of the **castle gardens** (adult/child 30/20kr) one or two afternoons a week (usually Tuesday and Thursday) – make enquiries regarding times and bookings with the Tønder tourist office.

ROYAL CONNECTIONS

Looking for more royal connections as you tour Jutland? As well as Schackenborg in Møgeltønder, head to Gråsten (boxed text, p214) and Marselisborg Palace in Aarhus (p225). And if you can't get there, check out all the royal castles in miniature plastic detail at Legoland (p246)!

Slotsgade STREET

Stroll along Slotsgade and soak up the market-village feel of this street with its immaculate, tightly packed houses. Look behind the houses and you'll notice that the blocks open into green fields – it's not a crammed market town at all, rather a purpose-built picturesque street.

Møgeltønder Kirke CHURCH

(Slotsgade 1; ⏲8am-4pm May-Sep, 9am-4pm Oct-Apr) At the western end of Slotsgade is Møgeltønder Kirke, a feast for the senses with its lavish interior. The Romanesque nave dates back to 1180 and the baptismal font is from 1200. The church has had many additions, however, as the Gothic choir vaults were built during the 13th century, the tower dates from about 1500 and the chapel on the northern side was added in 1763. The interior is rich in frescoes, gallery paintings and ceiling drawings. You'll also find here the oldest functioning church organ in Denmark, dating from 1679. The elaborately detailed gilt altar dates back to the 16th century. Note the 'countess' bower', a balcony with private seating for the Schack family, who owned the church from 1661 until 1970.

🛏 Sleeping & Eating

Schackenborg

Slotskro HOTEL, TRADITIONAL DANISH €€
(📞74 73 83 83; www.slotskro.dk; Slotsgade 42; s/d 1095/1345kr) With the palace as its neighbour and Prince Joachim as a part-owner, this classy old inn can claim tip-top royal connections. It has 25 rooms, at the inn and in three nearby houses; rooms are a little pricey but are elegant and well equipped. The Slotskro also has a fine reputation for traditional Danish cooking and makes a lovely spot for a lunch (108kr to 175kr) of salmon or herring, or the full-blown evening treatment (dinner mains 198kr to 268kr, or four-/six-course degustation menu 478/638kr).

Mormors Lille Café CAFE €
(Slotsgade 9; cakes 25-41kr, meals 98-141kr; ⊙11am-6pm summer) 'Grandma's little cafe' is perfectly in keeping with the village's character, cute as a button under its low, thatched roof, surrounded by outdoor tables and flowerbeds. Light meals may include quiche, sandwiches or herring, but it's the home-baked cakes (try the *lagkage,* or layer cake, a Danish favourite) and the delicate china teapots and coffeepots that really warm our heart.

❶ Getting There & Away

Møgeltønder is 5km west of Tønder via Rte 419. Bus 266 connects Tønder with Møgeltønder (19kr, 15 minutes) roughly hourly on weekdays, less frequently at weekends.

Sønderborg

POP 27,200

Sønderborg, nestled on both sides of the Als Sund (Als Sound), nurtures a modern ambience despite its medieval origins. In 1169 Valdemar I (the Great) erected a castle fortress along the waterfront and the town has since spread out from there, with fishing as the economic mainstay.

To some degree the town has shaped Denmark, acting as the battleground for two wars against Germany in the middle of the 19th century. In 1864, during the battle of Dybbøl, Danish forces gathered here while a bombardment of 80,000 German shells paved the way for the German occupation of Jutland for some 60 years. After WWI the region once again became Danish soil. Reconstruction of the city since that fateful war has led to its modern feel and a

bombardment of another kind – the annual descent of German and Danish holidaymakers. There's not as much English spoken in these parts; understandably, German is the second language for many.

◉ Sights & Activities

Sønderborg Slot CASTLE
(Sønderbro 1) Sønderborg Castle dates back to about 1170, when a stronghold was built on the site; later bastions were added for further fortification. Between 1532 and 1549 the castle was used to hold the deposed king, Christian II; rather than be confined to the dungeon he was free to stroll the grounds and enjoy the royal chambers. In the late 16th century the fortified castle was turned into a royal residence; the castle took on its baroque appearance during further restorations in 1718. During the German occupation it was used as a German barracks.

In 1568 under the reign of Queen Dorothea, widow of King Christian III, Denmark's first Lutheran **chapel** was constructed. The chapel still stands today, and rates as one of Europe's oldest preserved royal chapels.

Nowadays the castle houses a **museum of regional history** (adult/child 60kr/free; ⊙daily Apr-Oct, Tue-Sun Nov-Mar), with exhibits on the wars of 1848 and 1864 as well as paintings from the Danish 'Golden Age' and insight into the political history of the region.

In previous years, the castle has hosted summertime **ghost tours**. At the time of research the tours were not operating, but make enquiries at the tourist office.

There's a small, sandy **beach** right in town by the southern side of the castle.

Historiecenter Dybbøl Banke MUSEUM
(www.museum-sonderjylland.dk; Dybbøl Banke 16; adult 60-90kr, child 30-45kr; ⊙10am-5pm Apr-Oct) On 18 April 1864 the German army steamrolled the Danes and took control of southern Jutland until the end of WWI. Danish men were forced to fight for Germany in WWI on both fronts. On the western edge of town, the Dybbøl Banke history centre gives an informative glimpse into the bloody war of 1864, with demonstrations and storytelling. Although it offers typically high-quality displays of a very important time, if you're not Danish, German or have no interest in military history, it can probably be skipped. Bus 1 runs out here from town.

FRØSLEVLEJREN

The town of Padborg (population 4500), right by the German border, is the site of Frøslevlejren (Frøslev Camp), an internment camp opened near the end of WWII following negotiations with Germany to keep Danish POWs in Denmark (despite this agreement, 1600 Danish patriots were deported to concentration camps in Germany). During its nine months in operation, Frøslev held 12,000 prisoners.

Frøslevlejrens Museum (www.froeslevlejrensmuseum.dk, in Danish; Lejrvej 83; admission free; ⊙9am-4pm Tue-Fri, 10am-5pm Sat & Sun Feb-Nov) tells fascinating stories of the Danish Resistance movement and daily prison life at Frøslev. If you've visited other German-run wartime camps, you're in for a surprise here. A shining light in the German POW camps, Frøslev had ample food, no torture and no executions (prisoners were even allowed one visitor per month). The only real horror was the threat of deportation across the border. Interestingly, when the war ended and the prisoners were released, the camp's name was changed to Faarhuslejren; the new inmates were suspected Nazi collaborators.

Frøslevlejren is on the northwestern outskirts of Padborg, 1km west of the E45 (take exit 76). There are no buses – without your own wheels you'll need to walk or take a cab the 4km from Padborg train station.

Dybbøl Mølle   LANDMARK
(Dybbøl Banke 7; adult 25-45kr, child 12-30kr; ⊙daily mid-Apr–Oct) The Dybbøl windmill has been bombed twice and now stands as a national symbol. The exhibits here cover the mill's history and explain the symbolism of the site.

Town Walks   WALKING
For self-guided wanderings in the city, the tourist office publishes glossy English-language brochures detailing various architectural periods such as old Sønderborg, with buildings from the Middle Ages and the Renaissance; the city's art nouveau treasures; or modern features.

🛏 Sleeping

Danhostel Sønderborg City   HOSTEL €
(☏74 42 31 12; www.sonderborgdanhostel.dk; Kærvej 70; dm 175kr, s/d with bathroom 435/580kr; @🖢🛜) A 15-minute walk north of the town centre, this modern hostel is built around lovely garden areas, complete with outdoor furniture and barbecues. All rooms have bathroom. It's a classy place for a budget bed – note that beds in dorms are only offered from June to August. Town bus 6 stops nearby.

Hotel Sønderborg Garni   HOTEL €€
(☏74 42 34 33; www.hotelsoenderborg.dk; Kongevej 96; s/d from 650/850kr; 🛜) Friendly service and a prime location in an upmarket residential neighbourhood soften the slightly spooky appearance of this small hotel (complete with turret). The 1904 building has 18 rooms, all different (the cheapest singles are tiny but comfy) and with a homely, relaxed feel.

Sønderborg Camping   CAMPING GROUND €
(☏74 42 41 89; www.sonderborgcamping.dk in Danish; Ringgade 7; per adult/child/site 75/30/25kr; ⊙Apr-Sep) Set in an idyllic position next to the yacht marina, and a lovely 10-minute walk into town along the waterfront. It's a family-friendly, amenity-rich place where sites are in high demand come summer – book ahead. Cabins and caravans can be hired.

🍴 Eating & Drinking

You'll find a good selection of eateries down by the harbour (on Havnegade) and on Rådhustorvet.

Café Ib Rehne Cairo   INTERNATIONAL €€
(Rådhustorvet 4; meals 67-165kr; ⊙brunch, lunch & dinner) The story behind this venue's name is probably more interesting than the food on offer: Ib Rehne was a veteran Danish correspondent, stationed in Cairo for a spell. His well-known sign-off, 'Ib Rehne, Cairo,' has become the moniker of this all-day cafe-bar. Still, Ib himself seems to bear little relation to the fresh decor and crowd-pleasing menu. The alfresco tables on the square get a workout from brunch-time, but there's also a loungey area inside, perfect for evening cocktails.

Brøggeriet   INTERNATIONAL, BREWERY €€
(Rådhustorvet 6; meals 65-145kr; ⊙brunch, lunch & dinner) There's not a whole lot to differentiate Brøggeriet from its neighbour (Ib Rehne

WORTH A TRIP

GRÅSTEN PALACE

For three weeks each summer the sleepy town of Gråsten (population 4200) is abuzz as Queen Margrethe and Prince Henrik (and usually the extended family) head for some R&R at their summer residence. When they're not visiting, the lovely palace gardens are open to the public; it makes a good half-day trip from Sønderborg, 15km away.

Gråsten Palace (www.ses.dk; Slotsgade) is on the banks of the lake, Slotssø. It was originally built in the middle of the 16th century but destroyed by fire in 1603. It was rebuilt, only to be ravaged by fire again in 1757; in 1842 the main building you see today was constructed, and in 1935 the rights to the castle were handed to the royal family.

When the HRHs aren't in town you can visit the **palace gardens** (⊘from 7.30am year-round) to envy the green fingers behind this abundance of flora. Queen Ingrid designed the garden and drew on English influences in landscaping. Seasonal closing times vary from 4.30pm in winter to 8pm in summer.

The only part of the palace open to the public is the richly adorned **chapel** (⊘11am-2pm Wed, 10am-noon Sat, 2-4pm Sun Apr-Oct), built between 1699 and 1702 and the only section of the old castle to survive the fire of 1757.

Just down the road from the palace, **Den Gamle Kro** (Slotsgade 6; lunch 72-135kr, dinner mains 98-145kr; ⊘lunch & dinner Mon-Sat) dates from 1747 and has a traditional lunchtime menu of smørrebrød (open sandwiches), herring and the like, plus some fine cake options.

Gråsten's helpful **tourist office** (Kongevej 71) is at the train station, 1km south of the castle. Trains run to Gråsten from Kolding (124kr, 1¼ hours) and continue on to Sønderborg (48kr, 15 minutes). Bus 10 and 915X also operate between Gråsten and Sønderborg (48kr).

Cairo) – same alfresco tables, all-day options etc. The reason for stopping by is to try the boutique beer brewed on-site – try the '1864' pilsner or the brown ale named after Sønderborg's most famous one-time resident, deposed king Christian II.

OX-EN Steakhouse   STEAKHOUSE €€€
(Brogade 2; mains 138-239kr; ⊘dinner Mon-Sat) Prime Australian steaks have found themselves halfway across the globe to be salivated over (and paired with New World wines) at this chic, busy harbour restaurant. If you don't get your kicks from lavastone-grilled meat, there are a few nonsteak concessions on the menu.

❶ Information

Sønderborg spreads along both sides of the Als Sund, joined by two bridges. The town centre and Sønderborg Slot are to the east, on the island of Als. The Dybbøl area and the train station are on the western side (part of mainland Jutland).

Banks, pharmacies and other services can be found on the pedestrian street Perlegade, immediately north of Rådhustorvet.

Post office (Rådhustorvet 1)

Tourist office (☑74 42 35 55; www.visitson derborg.com; Rådhustorvet 7; ⊘10am-5pm Mon-Fri, 10am-1pm Sat) On the main square.

❶ Getting There & Around

Sønderborg is 30km northeast of the German border crossing at Kruså, via Rte 8. It's connected by trains to Kolding (125kr, 1½ hours) and the rest of Jutland and northern Germany (many destinations involve a change of trains in Tinglev). The train station is on the western side of town, by the modern Alsion building. Town bus 1 connects the train station with the east-side bus station (on Jernbanegade, a block east of Perlegade).

At the time of research, the closest bike-rental place was in Vollerup, 5km out of town; enquire at the tourist office to see if there's somewhere closer.

Als

The island of Als, separated from Jutland by the thin Als Sund, is relatively untouched by large-scale tourism and provides visitors with a snapshot of the laid-back Danish country lifestyle. It's a good region for lazy drives or cycling (bus schedules can be erratic). Down south is where the best beaches lie (nice and sheltered – locals recommend Kegnæs); up the east coast you'll encounter engaging little villages. And camping grounds are everywhere, heaving in summer with Danes and Germans.

Information and maps for the area can be obtained from the Sønderborg tourist office. For island-hoppers there are ferries connecting Fynshav on Als' east coast to Søby on the island of Ærø (see www.aeroe-ferry.com), or to Bøjden on Funen (www.faergen.dk).

◉ Sights

Augustenborg Slot   CASTLE
(Slotsallé) Augustenborg, 10km northeast of Sønderborg along Rte 8, is one of Als' more easily accessible and interesting villages. Spend an afternoon wandering around the lush gardens (including sculpture park) of the grand yellow-and-white Augustenborg Slot – you'll be following in the footsteps of Hans Christian Andersen, who sought peace and tranquillity here.

The castle now serves as a psychiatric hospital. There is a small exhibition in the gatehouse, and the lavish palace chapel (follow the signs for 'Slotskirken') is open to the public in summer. Bus 13 regularly connects Sønderborg with Augustenborg.

TOP CHOICE Danfoss Universe   SCIENCE PARK
(www.danfossuniverse.com; Mads Patent Vej 1, Nordborg; adult/child 175/150kr; ⊙daily mid-Apr–Oct) Als' big-ticket drawcard is Danfoss Universe, off Rte 405 en route north to Nordborg. Danfoss is a Danish-based global company involved in refrigeration, air-conditioning and heating, and this place has been set up as an 'exploration park for the curious', and a very popular attraction for families and schools.

There are more than 200 attractions enabling you to discover how nature and technology work. But education while you're on holidays? Well, yes. It's all well-designed, superinteractive fun and will stop the kids bothering you with questions you can't answer (How does a fridge work? Where does wind come from?). Heck, you might even learn something yourself.

The park is about 30km north of Sønderborg; bus 13 will get you there.

Central Jutland

Best Places to Eat

» Kähler Spisesalon (p229)

» Nordiske Spisehus (p229)

» Klassisk 65 Bistro & Vinbar (p228)

» Molskroen (p235)

» Hotel Julsø (p244)

Best Places to Stay

» Niels Bugges Hotel (p255)

» Hotel Guldsmeden (p227)

» Hotel Legoland (p247)

» Danhostel Silkeborg (p240)

» Hotel Randers (p251)

Why Go?

Easily the largest and most varied of all Danish regions, central Jutland encompasses dramatically different features, from the calm beaches of the sheltered east coast to the wild and woolly west coast, battered by North Sea winds. Lying in between, offering visual stimulation among the flatness, are the rolling hills and beech forests of the Lake District.

The real beauty of this region is that you can skip between themes depending on your mood. Fancy some world-class art and top-notch restaurants? Aarhus, Jutland's main city and Denmark's second-largest metropolis, will provide. How about Viking history? Set sail for Hobro. Religious history? Off to Jelling. Want to explore the great outdoors? Head for Rold Skov or Silkeborg. Are you really up to tackling nature's forces? Let loose on the waters of Hvide Sande. And OK, you've suppressed that inner child long enough – make a beeline for plastic-fantastic Legoland, and beware the accompanying pangs of childhood nostalgia.

When to Go

Warm weather is the key to enjoying much of this region – the beaches, theme parks, music festivals, activities – but Aarhus holds year-round appeal. Its museums, cafes and stores will entertain you in all weather, but the city's bars are in fact quieter in summer, when Aarhus University has its break and students head for home or on holidays.

The star attraction in this region, Legoland, is open daily from May to August and most days in April, September and October. It's closed from November to March.

AARHUS

POP 250,000

Sure, Aarhus (*oar*-hus) may be Denmark's second-largest city, but it feels more like a relaxed and friendly big town, a little bashful in the shadow of its more glamorous, attention-seeking big sister, Copenhagen.

Regular visitors will notice Aarhus' growing confidence. The stunning art museum, ARoS, is a prime example of the city demanding to be noticed. Further evidence can be found in the redevelopment of the Å river through town (once buried under concrete but now flowing again in the public eye), and the boulevard of sleek restaurants that has sprung up alongside it (from the school of obvious names, that would be called Åboulevarden). Latest developments are happening dockside, with Nordhavnen, a new harbourfront suburb, being built, full of impressive architectural designs for offices and apartments. The city's sizable student population continues to enliven Aarhus' parks and cobblestone streets (and fill its impressive number of bars). Savvy travellers are coming to appreciate the city's charms.

The train station (Aarhus Hovedbanegård) marks the south side of the city centre. A pedestrian shopping street extends 850m from the station to Aarhus Domkirke (the cathedral) in the heart of the old city.

History

Due to its central seaside location, Aarhus has always been a busy trading town. Its name comes from Aros, meaning 'place at the river's mouth'. Excavations from the mid-1960s suggest the city was founded around 900.

Medieval times were Aarhus' most turbulent, as the town was wedged in the middle of feuding neighbouring states. King Sweyn II of Denmark and King Magnus of Norway engaged in a major battle off Aarhus in 1043, and just a few years later, in 1050, Aarhus was ravaged by the Norwegian warrior king Harald Hardrada. Prosperity was kept in check over the following centuries by raids from rival Vikings and attacks by fearsome Wend pirates.

Stability then ensued until the 1500s and it was during this time that Aarhus flourished as a centre of trade, art and religion. Its natural asset, a large, protected harbour, drew attention from far and wide and in the process turned Aarhus into one of Jutland's most important transport and trading hubs.

The university has a tale of its own, as Aarhus established it against the wishes of the national government in 1928. By the time it was ready in 1933 the government had changed its tune and was in full support. Nowadays it's a cornerstone of the vibrant life of the city; there are around 40,000 students living in Aarhus, studying at the uni and various other higher education establishments.

◉ Sights

TOP CHOICE ARoS Aarhus Kunstmuseum   ART MUSEUM

(www.aros.dk; Aros Allé 2; adult/child 100kr/free; ◷10am-5pm Tue-Sun, to 10pm Wed) The towering, cubist, red-brick walls of Aarhus' showpiece art museum look rather uninspiring from the outside, but inside it's nine floors of sweeping curves, soaring spaces and white walls. Intriguingly, the museum's main theme is Dante's *The Divine Comedy;* the entrance is on level 4, and from there you either descend into Hell or climb towards Heaven. Hell is De 9 Rum (The 9 Spaces), on the bottom floor, painted black and home to some moody installation pieces; Heaven is the spectacular Your Rainbow Panorama, a 360-degree rooftop walkway offering technicolour views of the city through its glass panes in various shades of the rainbow. The walkway, opened in May 2011, is the brainchild of Danish-Icelandic artist Olafur Eliasson, famed for big, conceptual pieces such as *The Weather Project* at London's Tate Modern in 2003, and the *New York City Waterfalls* in 2008.

AARHUS VS ÅRHUS

On 1 January 2011, the city of Århus reverted to the old spelling of its name: Aarhus. The letter å was officially introduced to the Danish alphabet in 1948 and represents the sound 'aa', pronounced as the 'a' in the English 'walk', but it is not commonly used in names of people or towns. It has been argued that the new spelling will help strengthen the city's international profile, help private enterprise and make it easier to access Aarhus on the internet. We follow the new spelling, but be aware that you may still encounter Århus on a number of signs, maps etc.

Central Jutland Highlights

1 View the Aarhus rooftops through rose-coloured glass atop **ARoS Aarhus Kunstmuseum** (p217)

2 Explore the other sights of **Aarhus** (p217), then eat superbly and drink plentifully while sampling the nightlife

3 Revel in the great outdoors on a gentle canoe trip in the **Lake District** (p238)

4 Marvel at microcosmic Miniland at **Legoland** (p246) before jumping on a few rides

5 Enjoy the wind in your hair – and sails – while learning to windsurf on the wild **west coast** (p256)

6 Feel the weight of history at **Jelling** (p244), the spiritual home of the Danish royal family

7 Hop between beaches, theme parks and animal parks in the prime family-holiday territory of **Djursland** (p234)

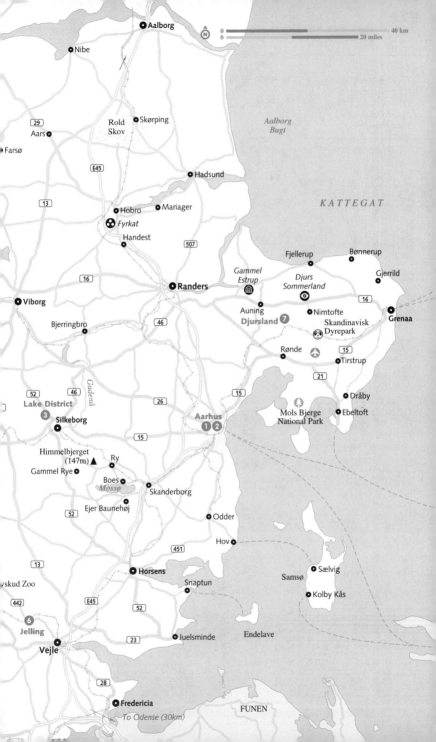

Aarhus

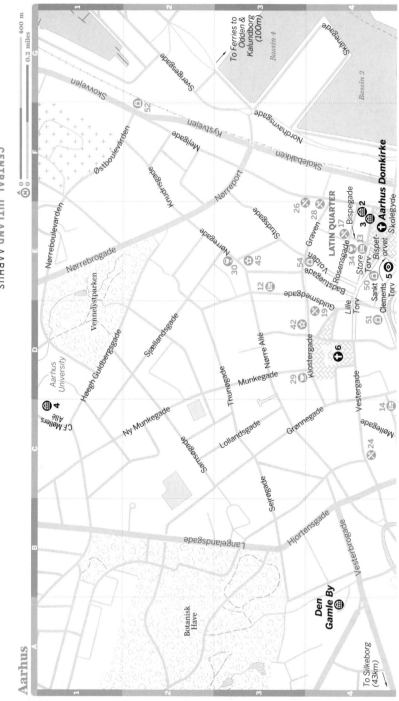

400 m
0.2 miles

To Ferries to Odden & Kalundborg (100m)

Bassin 4

Bassin 2

Skibbrogade

Nordhavnsgade

Sverigesgade

Skovvejen

Kystvejen

Mejlgade

Skolebakken

Østboulevarden

Nørreboulevarden

Nørreport

Nørrebrogade

Knudrisgade

Studsgade

Nørregade

Vennelystparken

Aarhus University

Høegh Guldbergsgade

Sjællandsgade

CF Møllers Allé

Ny Munkegade

Thunøgade

Munkegade

Nørre Allé

Samsøgade

Lollandsgade

Grønnegade

Sejrøgade

Langelandsgade

Hjortensgade

Vesterbrogade

Botanisk Have

Den Gamle By

To Silkeborg (43km)

Vestergade

Møllegade

LATIN QUARTER

Graven

Bispegade

Volden

Rosensgade

Badstuegade

Guldsmedgade

Klostergade

Store Torv

Sankt Clements Torv

Bispet-orvet

Skolegyde

Aarhus Domkirke

26
28
17
13
34
54
50
51
30
45
12
19
42
29
24
14
52
2
3
5
6
4

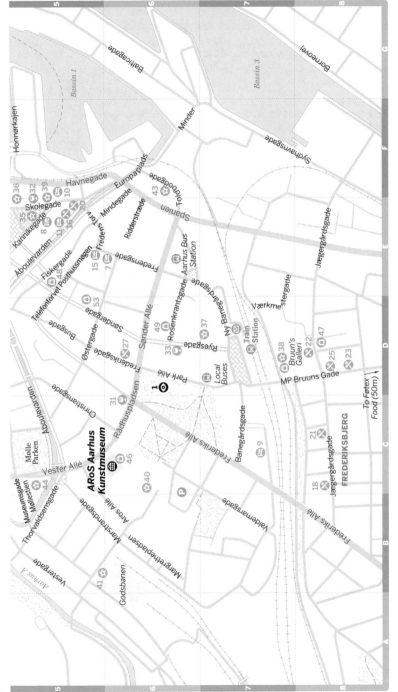

Aarhus

Opened in 2004, ARoS has a wonderful selection of Golden Age works, as well as examples of Danish modernism from 1900 to 1960, and an abundance of arresting and vivid contemporary art. Perhaps the most compelling piece is Ron Mueck's **Boy** on level 1, an astoundingly lifelike, oversized (5m-high) sculpture of a crouching boy.

The museum stages some fabulously varied special exhibitions – check what's on when you're in town (it could be anything from vintage racing cars to Frank Gehry's architectural vision). ARoS also houses a great gift shop and large, light-filled cafe on level 4 (free entry), and a restaurant on level 8.

Den Gamle By OPEN-AIR MUSEUM

(The Old Town; www.dengamleby.dk; Viborgvej 2; adult 50-125kr, child free; ☉daily) The Danes' seemingly limitless enthusiasm for dressing up and re-creating history reaches its zenith at Den Gamle By. It's an engaging and picturesque open-air museum of 75 half-timbered houses brought here from all corners of Denmark and reconstructed as a provincial town, complete with a functioning bakery and craftspeople practising their trade.

Re-created neighbourhoods from 1927 and 1974 are the latest additions – the TV and hi-fi store stocking authentic 1970s gear is quite a trip (yes, the prices are real!). Also in this new area are the **Danish Poster Museum**, with some fabulous retro pieces, and the Gallery of Decorative Arts, showcasing silverware, porcelain and clocks.

You can take a horse-drawn wagon ride (adult/child 40/30kr) around the site, and then visit each building and shop to see what life was all about. There are activities for visitors throughout the year, especially in the peak summer period and in the lead-up to Christmas – check the website for more information. Kids are very well catered for (the Toy Museum is a hit). The site includes picnic spots, plus a busy cafeteria.

Den Gamle By is about 1.5km west of the city centre (a 20-minute walk from the train station); buses 3A, 4A, 11, 15 and 19 can take you there. There's a detailed schedule of opening hours and admission prices (set according to the activity going on in the museum) outlined on the website. Outside of opening hours you can stroll the cobbled streets for free.

Botanisk Have   GARDENS
The Botanical Gardens occupy the high ground above Den Gamle By and can be reached through an exit from Den Gamle By or directly from Vesterbrogade. Redevelopment is taking place here, with an architecturally arresting new greenhouse expected to open in mid- to late 2012.

Moesgård   MUSEUM, OUTDOORS
Visit Moesgård, 10km south of the city centre, for its glorious beech woods and the trails threading through them towards sandy beaches. Visit for the well-presented history exhibits from the Stone Age to the Viking era at the Moesgård Museum (www.moesmus.dk;

Moesgård Allé 20; adult/child 60kr/free; ☺10am-5pm Apr-Sep, 10am-4pm Tue-Sun Oct-Mar). But above all else, visit Moesgård for the museum's most dramatic exhibit: the 2000-year-old Grauballe Man (Grauballemanden) whose astonishingly well-preserved body was found in 1952 at the village of Grauballe, 35km west of Aarhus.

The superb display on the Grauballe Man is part history lesson, part *CSI: Crime Scene Investigation* episode. Was he a sacrifice to Iron Age fertility gods, an executed prisoner perhaps, or simply a victim of murder? Either way, the broken leg and the gaping neck wound suggest his death, sometime around 290 BC (give or take 50 years), was a horribly violent one. His body and skin, tanned and preserved by the unique chemical and biological qualities of the peat bog in which he was found, are remarkably intact, right down to his hair and fingernails (and even the remains of his final meal – a herb-filled porridge – in his stomach).

Away from the death and violence, there's an enjoyable walking trail, dubbed the 'Prehistoric Trackway' (Oldtidsstien), leading from behind the museum across fields of wildflowers, past grazing sheep and through woods down to Moesgård Strand, one of Aarhus' best sandy beaches. The trail, marked by white stones, passes reconstructed historic sights including burial sites and an Iron Age house. Before heading off, pick up a brochure and map at the museum. You can walk one way and catch a bus from the beach back to the city centre, or follow the trail both ways as a 4km round trip.

CENTRAL JUTLAND AARHUS

AARHUS IN...

Two Days

Start by mixing the old with the new at Aarhus' two big-ticket attractions – **ARoS** for cutting-edge art and architecture, and **Den Gamle By** for a charming taste of yesteryear. Alfresco dinner and drinks along Åboulevarden offers you the chance to sample the local nightlife and indulge in prime people-watching. Next day, visit the **Moesgård Museum** to pay your respects to the remarkable Grauballe Man, then return to town to visit the **cathedral** and poke around the Latin Quarter, where you'll have no trouble finding a cool spot to refuel or listen to some live tunes.

Four Days

Follow the two-day itinerary, and on the third day grab a **free city bike** and venture further afield, south to **Marselisborg**, or north to **Risskov**. Take your swimsuit if it's warm enough. Later, check out the boutiques and restaurants of the **Frederiksbjerg** neighbourhood. On day four, consider jumping on a train or bus and checking out the waterways of **Silkeborg** or the beaches or funparks of **Djursland**.

Bus 18 from Aarhus terminates at the museum, and runs half-hourly during the day (hourly on Sundays). Bus 31 runs in summer and terminates at Moesgård Strand. If you have your own wheels, it's a lovely drive through forest to reach the museum – take Strandvejen south and follow the signs.

Note, too, that an exciting new building is being constructed at Moesgård for the display of the collections; it is expected to open in mid-2014.

Aarhus Domkirke
CATHEDRAL

(www.aarhus-domkirke.dk; Bispetorv; admission free; ◎9.30am-4pm Mon-Sat May-Sep, 10am-3pm Mon-Sat Oct-Apr) With a lofty nave spanning nearly 100m in length, Aarhus Domkirke is Denmark's longest church. The original Romanesque chapel at the eastern end dates from the 12th century, while most of the rest of the church is 15th-century Gothic.

Like other Danish churches, the cathedral was once richly decorated with frescoes that served to convey biblical parables to unschooled peasants. After the Reformation in 1536, church authorities, who felt the frescoes smacked too much of Roman Catholicism, had them all whitewashed, but many have now been uncovered and restored. They range from fairy-tale paintings of St George slaying a dragon to scenes of hellfire.

A highlight of the cathedral is the ornate, five-panel gilt altarpiece made in Lübeck by the renowned woodcarver Bernt Notke in the 15th century. In its centre panel, to the left of the Madonna and child, is a gaunt St Clement, to whom Aarhus Domkirke was dedicated.

Other items worthy of special attention are the bronze baptismal font dating from 1481, the finely carved Renaissance pulpit created in 1588, the magnificent baroque pipe organ made in 1730, the large votive ship from the 18th century, and the baroque sepulchre in the Marselis family chapel.

Vor Frue Kirke
CHURCH

(Frue Kirkeplads; admission free; ◎10am-2pm Mon-Fri, 10am-noon Sat Sep-Apr, 10am-4pm Mon-Fri, 10am-2pm Sat May-Aug) Set back from Vestergade, Vor Frue Kirke (Church of Our Lady) is like a Russian *matryoshka* (nesting doll), opening to reveal multiple layers beneath the surface. It was here that the original Aarhus cathedral was erected shortly after 1060 when King Sweyn II, bent on weakening the power of the archbishop who led the

Danish church, divided Denmark into eight separate dioceses, one of which was Aarhus. The cathedral was constructed from rough stone and travertine, and stood until about 1240, when it was replaced by the current Vor Frue Kirke.

Built of red brick, the church has a largely whitewashed interior although the chancel features a few exposed frescoes depicting the coats of arms of wealthy families from the 14th century. There's also a detailed triptych altar carved by Claus Berg in 1530. The main treasure, however, is in the church basement – the vaulted crypt of the original cathedral (the oldest surviving church interior in Denmark). Entered via the stairs beneath the chancel, the musty, atmospheric crypt was uncovered by chance in 1955 during a restoration by the national museum.

Vor Frue Kirke has yet another chapel, this one exhibiting early 16th-century frescoes. It can be entered through the garden courtyard – take the left door.

While you're in this part of town, be sure to wander down nearby Møllestien, easily Aarhus' prettiest street – all cobblestones, colourful cottages, climbing roses and flowering hollyhocks.

Kvindemuseet
MUSEUM

(Women's Museum; www.kvindemuseet.dk; Domkirkeplads 5; adult/child 45kr/free; ◎10am-4pm Tue-Sun, to 8pm Wed, also Mon Jul-Aug) Denmark is today a model for equality between the sexes, but this hasn't always been the case. In a fresh and engaging exhibition inside the old town hall, the museum charts women's lives in Denmark and their hard-won achievements. It's pretty inspiring stuff, but it's not just one for the chicks – families will love the hands-on kids' exhibits in the 'History of Childhood' section. There's also a lovely cafe here.

Besættelsesmuseet
MUSEUM

(www.besaettelsesmuseet.dk; Mathilde Fibigers Have 2; adult/child 30kr/free; ◎11am-4pm Tue-Sun Jun-Aug, 11am-4pm Tue, Sat & Sun Sep-May) For those interested in the German Occupation of Denmark during WWII, the small Occupation Museum is inside the building that the Germans once used to interrogate and house prisoners (the entrance is just behind Kvindemuseet). It has well-presented displays of military equipment, Nazi and Danish propaganda, and insights into everyday life during the war. Labels are in Danish – be sure to ask for the explanatory guide in English when you enter.

FREE **Vikingemuseum** MUSEUM
(Sankt Clements Torv 6; ⊙10am-4pm Mon-Fri, to 5.30pm Thu) There's more than the expected vaults in the basement of Nordea bank, a stone's throw from the cathedral. In the mid-1960s this site was excavated and impressive artefacts from the Viking era were unearthed. Exhibits include a skeleton, a reconstructed house, 1000-year-old carpentry tools and pottery, and photos of the excavation. It's accessible only during the bank's opening hours – enter the bank and take the staircase to the left.

Aarhus Rådhus ARCHITECTURE
(Rådhuspladsen) Aarhus' controversial town hall was designed by renowned architect Arne Jacobsen, a pioneer of Danish modernism, and completed in 1942. It's clad in Norwegian marble and has a distinctive grey appearance. Jacobsen also designed many of the interiors (along with Verner Panton) – it's worth a look inside.

In July and August, **VisitAarhus** (www.visitaarhus.com) arranges a weekly tour (50kr) of the town hall (in Danish and English). It also offers the opportunity to climb the tower here, twice a week (40kr). Schedules vary; see the website for information.

University Campus UNIVERSITY, MUSEUMS
The characteristic yellow-brick buildings of Aarhus University are gathered in and around Universitetsparken (University Park), north of the city centre. In July and August, **VisitAarhus** (www.visitaarhus.com) arranges a weekly, two-hour tour (75kr) of the campus, in English.

There are two museums in Universitetsparken, open to the public. Buses to the university include routes 1A, 12, 13, 14 and 18 (alight at Nørrebrogade).

Naturhistorisk Museum (www.naturhisto riskmuseum.dk, in Danish; Wilhelm Meyers Allé 210; adult/child 50kr/free; ⊙10am-4pm Sat-Thu, 10am-2pm Fri) delves into the evolution of the Danish landscape since the Ice Age, and has a comprehensive collection of stuffed birds and animals from all corners of the globe.

Steno Museet (www.stenomuseet.dk; CF Møllers Allé 1100; adult/child 30kr/free; ⊙9am-4pm Tue-Fri, 11am-4pm Sat & Sun) showcases the history of science and medicine (more interesting than it sounds), and features a medicinal herb garden and small planetarium.

CENTRAL JUTLAND AARHUS

Marselisborg OUTDOORS, PALACE
A green belt begins 2km south of the city centre and runs nearly 10km south, hugging the coast – it's a great place for hiking and cycling. It's divided into three sections, with the northern end known as Marselisborg, the midsection Moesgård and the southern end Fløjstrup – names taken from the former estates of which they were once part.

Landmark features on the northern tip of the woodland are the Tivoli Friheden amusement park, Jysk Væddeløbsbane (a horse-trotting track) and Atletion (a sports complex encompassing various stadiums).

Marselisborg Palace & Park (Kongevejen 100) is a summer home of the royal family, and when they're not in residence the public is able to explore the English-style grounds and rose garden (free admission). When the blue-bloods are here on vacation, you can watch the changing of the guard at noon from a vantage point on the road. The palace can be reached by bus 19.

A further 1.5km southeast of the palace is **Dyrehaven** (Deer Park) which, as the name suggests, has an abundance of deer (along with wild boar). The wooded park makes for a relaxing stroll on a sunny day.

Tivoli Friheden AMUSEMENT PARK
(www.friheden.dk; Skovbrynet; adult/child 75/55kr; ⊙mid-Apr–Sep) Neither as big nor as fabulous as Copenhagen's major drawcard, Aarhus' Tivoli is still a fun, wholesome family attraction, full of childhood favourites – dodgem cars and a Ferris wheel – as well as newer, faster rides. It's a good way to break up the cultural bombardment if museums are

ℹ️ AARHUS FOR KIDS

Aarhus – and indeed all of Jutland – is an incredibly family-friendly place to travel (see p30 for more on exploring Denmark with kids in tow). Entry to most museums is free for kids, and you won't have to minimise your time in culture-vulture places lest your offspring start climbing the walls – almost every attraction has factored kids into its audience, with displays and activities designed especially to keep them entertained. And then there are places designed *solely* with families in mind – Tivoli Friheden in Aarhus, for example, but also parks in Djursland, Randers and, of course, Legoland, although the plastic-fantastic world is 100km from Aarhus and might be a bit too far to consider as a day trip.

Other factors point to a relatively stress-free experience: many hotels have family rooms (Danhostel Aarhus, Cab Inn Aarhus and Aarhus City Apartments are good options); many restaurants have a *børnemenu* (children's menu); the outdoors is gentle and the beaches calm; and you can hire kids' bikes or seats from Bikes 4 Rent (see p234). Go forth and multiply!

wearing a little thin. You can buy a multi-ride pass (adult/child 205/185kr, including admission) and go hard, or pay for each ride individually.

The park is at the northern edge of Marselisborg woods and can be reached on bus 16. It has a complex schedule of hours (daily until as late as 11pm in peak summer, weekends only until 7pm at other times), so check the website.

🏃 Activities

The easiest and most enjoyable way for visitors to experience the great outdoors surrounding Aarhus is on foot or by bike, and the best hiking and cycling can be found along the green belt south of the city.

Beaches

If the weather's good and you're keen to get sand in your shorts, popular family-friendly beaches lie on the town's outskirts and feature clean, calm (but often cool) waters. The best-loved spots to the north are the traditional sea baths known as Den Per-

manente, in Risskov not far from the hostel. Bellevue, a little further north of Den Permanente (about 4km north of the city centre), is also popular; buses 17 and 20 will get you there.

Otherwise head south to Moesgård Strand, about 7km from the centre on bus 31. Den Permanente tends to draw a younger crowd; families head to Moesgård.

Ice-Skating

If you're here in the cooler months, rug up and get your skates on – from December to March, Bispetorvet (the square next to the cathedral) is transformed into a free ice-skating rink (skate rental 40kr).

🗣️ Tours

Outside of the peak summer months, you're left to your own devices.

Guided City Walks   WALKING
(☑87 31 50 10; www.visitaarhus.com; 1/2hr tour 50/75kr) In July and August, VisitAarhus offers a limited schedule of guided walks, taking in various sights according to themes (eg the city's history or architecture). Starting times and rendezvous points vary, so it's best to make enquiries before you travel or when you arrive.

Aarhus City Sightseeing   BUS
(☑52 14 66 05; www.citysightseeing.dk; 1-/2-day ticket adult 125/150kr, child 65/75kr) Over a six-week period from late June to early/mid-August, this company operates a hop-on, hop-off double-decker bus over two routes and 12 stops throughout the city. The departure point is on Park Allé, in front of the town hall.

🎭 Festivals & Events

Spot Festival   MUSIC
(www.spotfestival.dk) This annual event (May/early June) showcases up-and-coming Danish and Nordic talent, with most forms of popular music evident in and around Musikhuset (p231).

Sculpture by the Sea   CULTURAL
(www.sculpturebythesea.dk) This month-long festival transforms the city's southern beach-front into an outdoor gallery, with around 65 sculptures from both Danish and foreign artists displayed beside (and in) the water. It's held biennially (June in odd-numbered years).

NorthSide Festival
MUSIC

(www.northside.dk) A new music festival getting a big reputation (in 2011 many claimed its line-up beat that of the Roskilde Festival), NorthSide is held centrally, in mid-June.

Aarhus Jazz Festival
MUSIC

(www.jazzfest.dk) This week-long jazz celebration is held in mid-July, with big-name local and international acts doing their thing in various theatres, cafes and town squares.

Viking Moot
CULTURAL

(www.moesmus.dk) A Viking-style market is held at Moesgård Strand in late July. There are crafts, food and equestrian events, plus Vikings of all nationalities competing to outfight each other.

Aarhus Festival
CULTURAL

(www.aarhusfestival.com) The city dons its shiniest party gear at the end of August, when this festival transforms the town for 10 days, celebrating music, food, short film, theatre, visual arts and outdoor events for all ages (many of which are free). Events take place all over the city.

🛏 Sleeping

Denmark's second-biggest city doesn't have a huge range of accommodation. If you're after something special, avoid the bland chains and book early to snare a room at one of the boutique hotels.

The Accommodation section of the VisitAarhus (www.visitaarhus.com) website lists rooms in private homes, as well as private apartments for rent. Many of these are central and well priced.

Note that where parking is indicated in reviews below, it is rarely free.

TOP CHOICE Hotel Guldsmeden   BOUTIQUE HOTEL €€

(☎86 13 45 50; www.hotelguldsmeden.dk; Guldsmedgade 40; s/d without bathroom 775/975kr, with bathroom 1195/1325kr; @🛜) A top pick for its warm staff, French Colonial–style rooms with Persian rugs on hardwood floors, four-poster beds with soft white linen, a pretty garden oasis and a generally relaxed, stylish ambience. There's brilliant attention to detail too: breakfasts (included in price) are mainly organic, and the hotel has its own organic toiletries range. *Guldsmed* means both goldsmith and dragonfly in Danish – look for sweet use of the dragonfly motif in the decor.

Villa Provence
BOUTIQUE HOTEL €€

(☎86 18 24 00; www.villaprovence.dk; Fredens Torv 12; s/d/ste from 1095/1295/2200kr; P🛜) Elegant rooms (individually decorated in Provençal country style) for a mature, well-heeled crowd. The suites are large and lovely; standard rooms are smaller but with the same attention to detail – all have flat-screen TVs, French linen and original French movie posters. Besides the gourmet breakfast, our favourite feature might just be the courtyard, replete with flowering pot plants and fairy-lit lime trees.

Hotel Ferdinand
BOUTIQUE HOTEL €€

(☎87 32 14 44; www.hotelferdinand.dk, in Danish; Åboulevarden 28; d studio/ste from 1150/1300kr; 🛜) Ferdinand is in the centre of the Åboulevarden action, with a cracking French brasserie downstairs. There are eight suites above the restaurant (all large and luxurious); in the building next door are five slick studio apartments, with full kitchen, washing machine and balconies overlooking Åboulevarden.

Møllestien Cottages
COTTAGES €€

(☎86 13 06 32; www.house-in-aarhus.com; Møllestien 49 & 51; d 800-900kr) On Aarhus' prettiest street, a local ceramicist rents out two neighbouring cottages – small, homely places with courtyard, kitchen, lounge and bathroom (the cheaper of the two is more rustic); be warned that the staircases to the upstairs bedrooms are *steep*. Book early for a totally enchanting experience; one-night stays cost an extra 300kr.

Havnhotellet
HOTEL €

(www.havnehotellet.dk; Marselisborg Havnevej 20; r incl breakfast 550kr; P🛜) These great-value rooms at the marina are straight off the Ikea production line – fresh and functional, and attractive too. All booking is done online (hence no phone number), and check-in is via a computer. The hotel is about 1.5km south of the centre (off Strandvejen; catch bus 5A or 19) and walking distance to Marselisborg; at your doorstep is a handful of restaurants (and free parking). Tip: choose a room on the 1st floor (1.sal), as ground-floor rooms lack privacy. The price drops to 500kr for second and subsequent nights.

Danhostel Aarhus
HOSTEL €

(☎86 21 21 20; www.aarhus-danhostel.dk; Marienlundsvej 10, Risskov; dm 200kr, r with/without bathroom from 570/456kr; ⊘reception 8am-noon

& 4-8pm; (P@?) The main building here is as pretty as a picture: a large octagonal room that was a dancehall in a previous life and now serves as the breakfast room. Accommodation is bright and basic, and for most of the year room rates apply whether there are one or four people in the room. The hostel is 3km north of the city centre, in lovely green woods close by Den Permanente beach. With your own vehicle, follow Havnegade/Kystvejen north; or catch bus 5A, 7 or 20 and then it's a 300m walk east along Marienlundsvej. Breakfast is 59kr; parking is free.

Cab Inn Aarhus   HOTEL €€

(86 75 70 00; www.cabinn.com; Kannikegade 14; s/d/tr/f from 485/615/805/935kr; P@?) 'Sleep cheap in luxury' is this hotel chain's motto and hey, it's all relative. Cheap? By Scandi big-city standards, sure. Luxury? Well, it's a stretch, but the small, functional rooms (based on ships' cabins, hence the name) are bright and amenity-loaded for the price (all with wi-fi, bathroom, kettle, phone and TV). The location is top-notch, with Åboulevarden and the cathedral at your doorstep. Breakfast costs 60kr.

City Hotel Oasia   HOTEL €€

(86 13 45 87; www.hoteloasia.dk; Kriegersvej 27; d weekdays/weekend 1195/975kr; P@?) Clearly a subscriber to the minimalist school of design, Oasia offers bright modern rooms full of clean lines and the best of Scandinavian fittings (Hästens beds, Bang & Olufsen TVs, designer chairs). It's well placed for the train station.

Hotel Royal   HOTEL €€€

(86 12 00 11; www.hotelroyal.dk; Store Torv 4; s/d 1495/1850kr; P?) If you've come to expect restrained Scandi style in your top-end Danish hotels, prepare to be surprised. From the over-the-top entrance portico to the chandelier-lit reception area and incredible murals, the Royal seems a little, well, gaudy in parts. But fun, too – we love the fish-tank reception desk and the rich colour schemes. The rooms are appropriately lavish (check out the blingy white-and-gold bathrooms).

City Sleep-In   HOSTEL €

(86 19 20 55; www.citysleep-in.dk; Havnegade 20; dm 170kr, tw with/without bathroom 500/440kr; reception 8-11am & 4-9pm; @?) The most central budget option has small, basic rooms – you'll be more drawn to the communal areas, such as the pretty courtyard

or 1st-floor TV room. There's helpful staff, a global feel and decent amenities (free wi-fi, lockers, kitchen, pool table, laundry). The doubles are pricey, however – if you need to rent bed linen (50kr) and a towel (20kr), you might want to start looking at the cheaper midrange hotels. Breakfast is 65kr.

Blommehaven

Camping   CAMPING GROUND, CABINS €

(86 27 02 07; www.blommehaven.dk; Ørneredevej 35, Højbjerg; per adult/child/site 75/46/45kr; late Mar-late Oct; P@) It's a big beachside camping ground 6km south of the city centre, in the scenic Marselisborg woods en route to Moesgård. It's got loads of family-oriented facilities, plus simple cabins (625kr). If you're driving, follow Strandvejen south; otherwise, take bus 18 or (in summer) 31.

Aarhus City Apartments   APARTMENTS €€

(86 27 51 30; www.hotelaca.dk; Fredensgade 18; d r/studio/apt from 799/969/1169kr; P?) Good for families and long-stayers, this charcoal-coloured three-storey apartment block is home to modern rooms, studios and apartments. All have kitchens (kitchenettes in the rooms), cable TV and wi-fi. There's no reception, so you need to book ahead and arrange to be met. Short stays are penalised with high prices – stay a minimum of three nights to get the rates we've listed.

Eating

Away from the same-same feeling you may get when perusing the restaurants and cafes lining Åboulevarden, fertile hunting grounds come dinnertime include the Latin Quarter (good for bistro-style cafes); Skolegade and its extension, Mejlgade (the latter home to some excellent budget options); and the cool Frederiksbjerg neighbourhood, south of the train station (centred on MP Bruuns Gade and Jægergårdsgade).

Where phone numbers are listed for reviews, booking is a good idea.

TOP CHOICE Klassisk 65 Bistro

& Vinbar   FRENCH-DANISH €€

(86 13 12 21; Jægergårdsgade 65; mains 135-205kr, Sunday brunch buffet 185kr; dinner daily, brunch Sun) Heavy on rustic, shabby-chic charm, this tightly packed place is all about carefully mismatched furniture and crockery, and shelves laden with wine. The locals flock for the much-prized *hyggelig* (cosy) atmosphere, generous spirit and value for

money. The kitchen puts a Danish spin on French country cooking, and the three-course menu of the day is perfect at 280kr.

TOP CHOICE **Nordisk Spisehus** MODERN DANISH €€€
(☎86 17 70 99; www.nordisskspisehus.dk; MP Bruuns Gade 31; mains 220kr, weekend brunch buffet 149kr; ☺lunch Mon-Fri, dinner nightly, brunch Sat & Sun) From the team behind the acclaimed Malling & Schmidt comes this more-affordable, in-town option, with a three-course menu that's a bargain 300kr. This simple, elegant restaurant serves regional delicacies such as local free-range veal, Nordic cheeses and fjord mussels. We recommend the home-smoked salmon, which is given an extra last-minute hay-smoking beneath a glass cloche at your table.

TOP CHOICE **Kähler Spisesalon** MODERN DANISH €€
(MP Bruuns Gade 33; weekend brunch buffet 130kr, 3-course dinner menu 275kr; ☺breakfast, lunch & dinner) A gorgeous interior welcomes you to this new kid on the block, filled with plants, lamps, mirrors and covetable ceramics (made by Kähler, a 170-year-old ceramic company with a handy store down the road, at No 41). It's a great choice at any time of the day, for its cheap weekday breakfast buffet (55kr), excellent coffee or artful reinterpretation of the classic smørrebrød (open sandwich).

Malling & Schmidt MODERN DANISH €€€
(☎86 17 70 88; www.mallingschmidt.dk; Grenåvej 127; 3/5/8 courses 350/695/995kr; ☺dinner Tue-Sat) Aarhus' culinary A-lister is home to respected chef Thorsten Schmidt and his inspired takes on Nordic ingredients. In a new location about 4km north of the city centre, Schmidt and his team create dishes where the emphasis is on seasonal and local produce: a summertime three-course 'Taste of the North' menu might start with lobster, then move to ox from the forest, finishing with summer berries. Book ahead.

Oli Nico INTERNATIONAL €
(Mejlgade 35; classic dishes 50-105kr, 2-/3-course menu 85/115kr; ☺lunch & dinner) You may need to fight for one of the sought-after tables at Oli Nico, a small deli-restaurant with a menu of classic dishes at astoundingly good prices (*moules-frites* for 60kr, rib-eye steak for 105kr – both with homemade chips!). The daily-changing three-course menu may be Aarhus' best-kept secret.

Globen Flakket INTERNATIONAL €€
(Åboulevarden 18; dinner mains 116-195kr; ☺breakfast, lunch & dinner) Pitching to a broad demographic, this upbeat riverside venue is a decent option at any hour. As well as a classic-hits menu of burgers, pasta etc, loads of good-value buffet options draw in the punters (weekday breakfast/lunch buffet 30/92kr, weekend brunch 102kr, afternoon cake buffet 28kr, Friday and Saturday dinner buffet 148kr).

LYNfabrikken CAFE €
(www.lynfabrikken.dk; Vestergade 49B; meals 27-98kr; ☺9am-6pm Mon-Sat; 🛜) This is more than just a place where creative types come to pop open their Macs. On the 3rd floor of this design studio is a humming cafe serving joyous brunch or tapas plates (a little taste of everything you like), or there's coffee and cake to go with your free wi-fi. Head inside the courtyard and climb the stairs.

Sct Oluf FRENCH €
(Mejlgade 33; lunch 45kr, 2-/3-course dinner menu 135/145kr; ☺lunch & dinner) The price is right and the portions generous at this rustic brasserie. There are no à la carte offerings, just a simple, French-inspired concept: a starter, a main (usually a choice between meat or fish), and dessert or cheese, all focused on fresh, in-season offerings.

Brasserie Ferdinand FRENCH €€
(☎87 32 14 44; www.hotelferdinand.dk; Åboulevarden 28; lunch 95-235kr, dinner mains 135-235kr; ☺lunch & dinner Mon-Sat) Local, seasonal, organic produce informs the Franco-Danish dishes at this chic, canalside brasserie. The four-course menu (375kr) is good value, while pan-fried foie gras and classic beef tartare are dependable menu staples.

Raadhuus Kafeen TRADITIONAL DANISH €€
(Sønder Allé 3; smørrebrød 69-105kr, dinner mains 115-195kr; ☺lunch & dinner) Sleek riverside spots are all well and good, but what if you want to look at a menu and really know you're in Denmark? This classic wood-panelled dining room is the place – a taste of old-school Danish cuisine from the herring plate to *Pariserbøf* (cooked beef tartare) to 101 lunchtime smørrebrød options.

Forlæns & Baglæns TAPAS €€
(Jægergårdsgade 23; tapas dishes 94-135kr; ☺lunch & dinner Tue-Sat) It can be tough to snare a table at this little hot spot, which dishes up tapas and cocktails. Sit among the

colourful light fittings dangling from the ceiling and choose between tempting morsels such as Spanish meatballs or grilled tiger prawns.

Casablanca
CAFE €€

(Rosensgade 12; meals 90-155kr; ⊙breakfast, lunch & dinner Mon-Sat) This hidden Latin Quarter gem offers oodles of Continental charm.

Café Svej
DANISH €€

(Åboulevarden 22; dinner mains 158-195kr; ⊙breakfast, lunch & dinner) Among the homogenous Åboulevarden options, Svej differentiates with a menu of traditional Danish specialities.

Self-Catering

Supermarkets are generally open from 9am to 8pm or 9pm Monday to Friday, and 8am to 6pm or 7pm Saturday. Bakeries inside supermarkets start selling their wares from 7am. Sunday opening hours are confusing – some supermarkets open on either the first or last Sunday of the month (or both).

You will find two outlets of Føtex Food, at MP Bruuns Gade 55 and Guldsmedsgade 3. The **Kvickly** (MP Bruuns Gade) shopping centre, inside Bruun's Galleri, is accessible from the train station.

Fresh-Produce Market
FOOD MARKET €

(Ingerslev Blvd; ⊙8am-2pm Wed & Sat) In our favourite Aarhus neighbourhood of Frederiksbjerg, this colourful farmers market sells fruit and veg, flowers, fish, cheese etc.

🍸 Drinking

Aarhus' large student contingent guarantees the bars fill up from Thursday onwards. There are a few streets lined with wall-to-wall drinking dens: Åboulevarden is full of chic restaurant-bars and a more savvy, fashionable crowd. A few similar places have spilled into nearby Skolegade, alongside intimate boozers and dive bars; Frederiksgade gives you more boisterous English/Irish pubs than you can poke a pint at, all attempting to woo students with discounted beer (25kr for a pint of Carlsberg) and schedules of live music, jam sessions, televised sports, quiz competitions (generally in English) and karaoke. A number of places mentioned under Eating are also decent drinking spots.

Strandbaren
BAR

(www.strandbaren2011.dk, in Danish; Dagmar Petersens Gade 101; ⊙from 11am Thu-Sun May-Sep)

Plonk shipping containers and a whole heap of sand on a harbourfront spot and voila – a beach bar. This chilled-out bar in the Nordhavnen area (northeast of the cathedral and beyond the ferry port) offers food, drink, flirting and a variety of (weather-dependent) activities and events: beach volleyball; zumba, yoga and tango lessons; concerts etc. Check hours and location on the website, as it may change from year to year (due to harbour redevelopment and shiny new apartments being built out this way). You'll need a car or bike to reach it.

Løve's Bog- & Vincafé
BAR-CAFE

(Nørregade 32; ⊙9am-6pm Mon-Wed, 9am-midnight Thu-Fri, 10am-midnight Sat, 10am-5pm Sun) This snug 'book and wine cafe' is full of book-lined shelves and old furniture, and a reading/laptopping clientele. Poetry readings and jazz bands may make an appearance, and the short, simple menu will refuel further study.

Sigfred's Kaffebar
COFFEE BAR

(Ryesgade 28; ⊙Mon-Sat) Sigfred's has quite possibly the best coffee in Jutland, brewed by expert baristas and sipped by ever-faithful regulars. Accompaniments include flaky pastries and Italian-inspired panini.

Under Masken
BAR

(Bispegade 3; ⊙noon-2am) The ethnic masks lining the walls and ceiling may leer and scowl but the real natives in this convivial little basement pub are friendly. The eclectic decor even extends to the fish tanks, decorated with sculptures, and the mood is relaxed and unpretentious. Note – no food is served.

Sidebar
BAR

(Skolegade 21; ⊙from 4pm Mon-Sat) A huge cocktail selection, a smooth lounge bar with DJs, and a late-night kitchen (food available to midnight) make this a bar worth knowing about.

Café Gemmestedet
BAR-CAFE

(Gammel Munkegade 1; ⊙10am-late) A cosy jumble of chandeliers, candles, board games and piano, this bohemian cafe-bar is known for its kookily named cocktails ('When Katherine grew up and still wished for a horse', anyone?). There's also tasty Turkish-influenced grub and semiregular live jazz.

Sherlock Holmes Pub
PUB

(www.sherlock-holmes.dk; Frederiksgade 76D; ⊙from noon or 1pm) This is a real English rainy-day pub (perfect for Danish weather then), dim and cosy and with an array of live music, karaoke, televised football and a Thursday-night jam session. You can pop next door to the **Golden Lion** for a good dose of English pub grub, too. Not far along the street are popular Irish pubs: **Tir na Nog**, at No 40, and **Waxies** at No 16.

☆ Entertainment

Live Music

Aarhus is considered Denmark's music capital, so aside from the diverse offerings of Musikhuset Aarhus and the live-music events of club venues such as Train, it's not hard to track down quality music being played in more intimate venues. Look for summertime outdoor concerts too, in venues such as Tivoli Friheden amusement park (p225); festivals also are a boon to live-music lovers.

Websites for the following may be in Danish but the events calendars should be easy enough to follow.

Musikhuset Aarhus   LIVE MUSIC
(www.musikhusetaarhus.dk; Thomas Jensens Allé) You're bound to find something that appeals in Aarhus' Music House, a large, glass-fronted venue that hosts a range of events, from art-house films to piano concerts and jazz performances (many of them free) in its large, light-filled foyer. The formal offerings in the concert halls cut a broad swathe through the arts, from Damien Rice to *Rigoletto*, performances from Den Kongelige Ballet (the Royal Danish Ballet) to percussion supremos Stomp, or an evening of flamenco dance.

Radar   LIVE MUSIC
(www.musikcafeen.dk, in Danish; Godsbanen, Skovgaardsgade 3-5; ☉live music Wed-Sat) Radar is the new name for what was formerly known as Musikcaféen, which in 2012 moved from its 33-year home on Mejlgade to a new location inside the Godsbanen freight yard, a new cultural hub for the city (see www.godsbanen.dk). Musikcaféen offered a peek into Aarhus' alternative scene with a wide range of music (including rock, techno, jazz and world music); Radar seems set to continue that tradition.

VoxHall & Atlas   LIVE MUSIC
(www.voxhall.dk, www.atlasaarhus.dk, in Danish; Vester Allé 15) VoxHall is another established live-music locale (capacity 700) hosting an eclectic range of acts. Attached is the new and more-intimate Atlas (capacity 300), specialising in folk, jazz and world-music performers.

Fatter Eskil   LIVE MUSIC
(www.fattereskil.dk, in Danish; Skolegade 25; ☉Tue-Sat) Has live music every night – often cover bands – with a mixed bag of pop, rock, soul, blues and jazz.

Nightclubs

Train   LIVE MUSIC, CLUB
(www.train.dk; Toldbodgade 6; ☉nightclub from about 11.30pm Fri & Sat) Aarhus' premier club, Train is first and foremost a concert venue, with shows a couple of nights a week. Some well-established international names have played here over the years. Train opens as a nightclub as well, on Friday and Saturday nights, with room for up to 1600 party people and a serious DJ line-up. You need to be 21 to enter the club on Friday, 23 on Saturday; admission price varies. The complex also incorporates restaurant **Perron** (Platform), and **Kupé** (Compartment), a funky lounge club.

Social Club   CLUB
(www.socialclub.dk; Klostergade 34; admission 20-40kr, free with student card before 2am; ☉from 11pm Thu, midnight Fri & Sat) Completely focused on the student crowd, and attracting them in droves, this club is a packed and sweaty dance affair; cheap shots, two-for-one drink offers and other social lubricants help the night along.

Theatre

Aarhus Teater   THEATRE
(www.aarhusteater.dk, in Danish; Bispetorv) This is a suitably theatrical building dating from 1900, embellished with gargoyles and other extravagant decor. Performances are largely in Danish, but musical and dance productions are also occasionally staged. The box office is across the road from the theatre, at Skolegade 9.

Cinema

Cinema tickets cost from 65kr to 80kr – it's cheaper to see a daytime session. The website www.kino.dk (in Danish) has screen times.

BioCity Aarhus   CINEMA
(Sankt Knuds Torv 15) Shows Hollywood and local productions, just off Ryesgade.

Cinemaxx CINEMA
(MP Bruuns Gade 25) Inside Bruun's Galleri shopping centre (you can enter via the train station); screens the latest blockbusters alongside smaller local films.

Øst for Paradis CINEMA
(www.paradisbio.dk, in Danish; Paradisgade 7-9) Art-house cinema in northern reaches of the Latin Quarter. Show films in original language, with Danish subtitles.

🔒 Shopping

The shopping is excellent, but you may be surprised by the limited opening hours in Denmark's second city. Many stores are closed by mid-afternoon on Saturdays; Sunday trading is permitted on the first Sunday of the month, but not all shops open.

Shopping Areas

Søndergade, the 850m-long busy pedestrian street (known as Ryesgade at its starting point opposite the train station), is lined with largely mainstream shopping and chain stores (Danish and international).

The Latin Quarter is a cobblestone, largely pedestrianised area offering original finds in cool fashion and design boutiques. Check out Badstuegade and Volden, and west along Vestergade.

Frederiksbjerg has more eclectic clothing and design stores, including some retro stores and artisan studios. Stroll Bruuns Gade, Sankt Pauls Kirkeplads and Jægergårdsgade.

Department Stores

Central department stores offer everything from cosmetics to fashion to homewares, including big-name Danish brands (Lego toys, Royal Copenhagen porcelain, Holmegaard glass etc). Be sure to ask about paperwork for VAT refunds. Stores include Magasin du Nord (Immervad 2) and Salling (Søndergade 27).

Boutiques

ARoS Aarhus Kunstmuseum BOOKS, GIFTS
(Aros Allé 2) The art museum's gift shop has an extensive range of art books, homewares, accessories and nifty knick-knacks.

Decorate Shop HOMEWARES
(Jægergårdsgade 100) Decorate encourages you to do just that, with fun and colourful homewares, including ceramics, linen and toys, from established and up-and-coming designers.

Georg Jensen DESIGN
(www.georgjensen.com; Søndergade 1) Exquisite silverware and jewellery from the Danish master; next door is Georg Jensen Damask, selling classic linen pieces for the kitchen, dining room and bedroom.

HAY DESIGN
(www.hay.dk; Rosenkrantzgade 24) Well-chosen examples of the latest Danish furniture as well as fabulous designer homewares, textiles and rugs.

Kristian F Møller BOOKS
(Store Torv 5) Well-priced English-language books and a range of travel guides.

Paustian DESIGN
(www.paustian.dk, in Danish; Skovvejen 2) A shrine to the best of Danish (and international) design. Prepare to desire everything that couldn't possibly fit in your suitcase…

Summerbird Chocolaterie FOOD
(Volden 31) Exquisite choc-shop in the Latin Quarter. The pretty packaging makes these a classy souvenir for someone back home.

ℹ️ Information

The AarhusCard (p225) offers discounts to sights and entertainment venues, and free transport.

Emergency

Police/ambulance (📞112)
Police station (📞87 31 14 48; Ridderstræde 1; ◔24hr)

Internet Access

Gate 58 (Vestergade 58B, 1st fl; per hr 18-28kr; ◔10am-midnight Mon-Fri, noon-midnight Sat & Sun)
Hovedbiblioteket (www.aakb.dk; Møllegade 1; ◔Mon-Sat) Get online for free at the main public library, off Vester Allé.

Left Luggage

Coin-operated lockers are available at the train and bus stations; a small/large locker costs 20/40kr for a 24-hour period.

Library

Hovedbiblioteket (www.aakb.dk; Møllegade 1; ◔Mon-Sat) Read international newspapersas well as use the internet for free.

Medical Services

Aarhus Universitetshospital (📞87 31 50 50; www.aarhussygehus.dk; Nørrebrogade 44) Hospital with a 24-hour emergency ward; call before arriving.

After-hours medical assistance (☑70 11 31 31; ☺4pm-8am Mon-Fri, all day Sat & Sun)

Løve Apotek (Store Torv 5; ☺24hr) Convenient pharmacy.

Money

There are banks and ATMs all over town, with a good concentration along the pedestrianised shopping strip (Ryesgade/Søndergade) and around the cathedral.

Forex (Ryesgade 28) Foreign exchange close to the train station.

Nordea (Sankt Clements Torv 6) Near Aarhus Domkirke.

Sydbank (Banegårdspladsen 1) At the front of the train station.

Post

Post office (Banegårdspladsen 1A; ☺10am-6pm Mon-Fri, 10am-1pm Sat) Next to the train station.

Tourist Information

In 2011, VisitAarhus took the unusual step of closing its central tourist office. With changing travel trends, VisitAarhus now aims to reach travellers in traditional and nontraditional ways, via its website (www.visitaarhus.com), phone line (☑87 31 50 10), mobile info booths in peak periods, and touch-screen computers at many of the town's attractions, transport hubs and accommodation providers.

There will be apps to come, and social media pages to follow for up-to-date info (see 'This is why I love Aarhus' on Facebook; follow Visit Aarhus on Twitter). It's an interesting experiment – we're not completely convinced this will cover the needs of all visitors.

ℹ Getting There & Away

Air

Aarhus airport (AAR; www.aar.dk), also known as Tirstrup airport, is 45km northeast of the city.

Scandinavian Airlines (SAS) and Cimber Sterling have numerous daily flights to/from Copenhagen; there are also regular direct connections to Stockholm, Helsinki and Oslo. Ryanair has daily connections to/from London (Stansted), and less-frequent services to Oslo and Malaga.

Boat

Kattegat-ruten (☑38 11 12 22; www.kattegat -ruten.dk) Operates ferries between Aarhus and Kalundborg on Zealand (one-way adult/ child/car 180/90/375kr, 2¾ hours, up to three sailings daily). Rates for car passage include passengers.

Mols-Linien (☑70 10 14 18; www.mols-linien. dk) Operates high-speed ferries between Aarhus and Odden in north Zealand (one-way adult/child/car 349/174/775kr, 70 minutes,

minimum five sailings daily). Rates for car passage include passengers.

Bus

All long-distance buses stop at Aarhus bus station *(rutebilstation)* on Fredensgade, 300m northeast of the train station. From Aarhus you can reach most Jutland towns of note on the **X-bus** (www.xbus.dk, in Danish) network.

Abildskou (☑70 21 08 88; www.abildskou. dk) Express bus line 888 runs up to nine times daily between Aarhus and Copenhagen's Valby station (290kr, three hours), with connections to Copenhagen airport. Students and seniors travel for 140kr Monday to Thursday.

Car & Motorcycle

The main highways to Aarhus are the E45 from the north and south, and Rte 15 from the west. The E45 doesn't make it into the city itself – take exits 46 to 50.

Train

Inside the train station *(hovedbanegård)* you'll find the **ticket office** (☺6.10am-6.30pm Mon-Thu, 6.10am-7pm Fri, 8am-5pm Sat, 10am-7pm Sun) with its orderly ticket-queuing system: red for internal journeys, green for international. For internal journeys, skip the queues by using one of the ticket machines (instructions available in English; credit cards accepted). Friday trains are always busy, and it's strongly advised to reserve a seat (30kr) for long journeys.

Trains to Copenhagen (one way 347kr, three to 3½ hours), via Odense (217kr, 1¾ hours), leave Aarhus roughly half-hourly.

Other frequent services are Aalborg (175kr, 1½ hours), Frederikshavn (228kr, 2¾ hours; may involve a change of train in Aalborg), Grenaa (78kr, 1¼ hours) and Silkeborg (66kr, 50 minutes).

ℹ Getting Around

To/From the Airport

AARHUS A bus service (route 925X) connects Aarhus with the airport at Tirstrup (95kr, 50 minutes). Buses depart from the front of the train station (close to the post office) and the changeable schedule is geared to meet all incoming and outgoing flights – phone ☑86 12 86 22 for up-to-date information. A taxi between the airport and the city centre will set you back a hefty 650kr.

BILLUND Aarhus is connected by bus with the large airport at Billund, about 80km southwest and a 1½-hour bus ride away (180kr).

Bicycle

Look out for free **Aarhusbycykel** (www.aarhus bycykel.dk) city bikes, available from various spots around the city from April to October (these can often be tricky to find – download a map from the website before you travel, or ask at your accommodation). There are a few bikes close to the Subway store opposite the train station, and some outside the town hall. You need to put a 20kr coin into the slot to obtain the bike (refunded when you return it).

If you're visiting from November to March, or you want a better-quality bike for a lengthy period, **Bikes 4 Rent** (☎20 26 10 20; www. bikes4rent.dk; Skanderborgvej 107; 1 day/ 2 days/1 week 75/140/245kr) can help out with a good range of bikes and accessories. The store is 2.5km southwest of the train station.

Bus

Aarhus has an extensive, efficient local bus network. Most in-town buses stop close to the train station on Park Allé. You get on via the back or middle doors of the bus and buy your ticket from the machine (20kr, allowing up to two hours' travel), then exit at the front of the bus. You can also buy a good-value *klippekort* ticket, valid for 10 rides, for 120kr. Information on tickets, routes and schedules is available from the bus station on Fredensgade, via the website www. midttrafik.dk (largely in Danish) or by dialling ☎86 12 86 22.

Car & Motorcycle

A car is convenient for getting to sights such as Moesgård on the city outskirts, although the city centre is best explored on foot.

PARKING There's paid undercover parking in municipal car parks, including one near Musikhuset Aarhus and at Bruun's Galleri shopping centre. Such car parks generally charge by the hour. There are also numerous *billetautomat* (parking meters) along city streets. You'll usually need to pay for street parking from 9am to 7pm Monday to Friday and 9am to 4pm Saturday (outside those hours parking is generally free of charge. Parking costs 12/15kr for the first/second hour, and 20kr per hour after that. Press a button on the *billetautomat* for English instructions.

RENTAL All the major players (Europcar, Bud-get, Hertz, Sixt and Avis) have car-rental desks at Aarhus airport. In town, **Europcar**

ON YOUR BIKE

OK, so you've found yourself a *bycykel* and are looking to explore. Good two-wheeled trips (not too taxing, mind):

» South to **Marselisborg**, taking in the palace and park. Stop off to refuel at the marina en route.

» North to the university museums, or further north to **Risskov** to check out the pretty woodlands and beach.

(☎89 33 11 11; Sønder Allé 35) has a central office across from the bus station.

Taxi

Taxis are readily available at the train station and at a rank by the cathedral; you can also flag one on the street or order one by phone (☎89 48 48 48). All taxis have a meter – expect to pay up to 100kr for destinations within the inner city.

DJURSLAND

Djursland, the large peninsula northeast of Aarhus (Jutland's 'nose'), is prime summer-holiday territory for hordes of beach-going Danish, Swedish and German families. The area's standout towns are Ebeltoft and Grenaa. Sprawling Grenaa (connected by ferry to Varberg in Sweden) is the larger of the two and the surrounding beaches are better, but Ebeltoft has more charm. There are some top-notch sandy beaches all over the peninsula (particularly in the north, at Fjellerup, Bønnerup and Gjerrild, and just south of Grenaa), while family-focused, land-based activities range from historic manor houses to animal parks, shark pools and a hugely popular funpark.

Djursland's public-transport connections with Aarhus are excellent. If you have your own set of wheels, Rte 15 heads out of Aarhus towards Ebeltoft (via Rte 21) and on to Grenaa – but with a little time up your sleeve we recommend you take the rural back roads.

Ebeltoft

POP 7600

Ebeltoft has all the ingredients you need for a great summer getaway. Cobblestone streets lined with pretty half-timbered houses, white-sand beaches and a classic warship attract large numbers of ice-cream-eating holidaymakers.

The tourist office, the *Fregatten Jylland* and the harbour are along Strandvejen. From the harbour walk a block east on Jernbanegade to reach Adelgade, the main shopping street. Torvet, the town square, is at the southern end of Adelgade.

◉ Sights & Activities

Fregatten Jylland   OLD WARSHIP
(www.fregatten-jylland.dk; SA Jensens Vej 4; adult/child 110/80kr; ☺daily mid-Feb–Nov) *Fregatten Jylland* has quite a presence. From bow to

stern the frigate is 71m, making it the longest wooden ship in the world. It played an instrumental role in Denmark's navy in the 19th century; today it's been restored for visitors – step inside and experience the life of a crew member.

Glasmuseet Ebeltoft MUSEUM

(www.glasmuseet.dk; Strandvejen 8; adult/child 85kr/free; ☉daily Apr-Oct, Tue-Sun Nov-Mar) Contemporary glass art is beautifully showcased at the typically sleek Glasmuseet Ebeltoft. If you're brave enough to try getting something home in one piece, you'll love the shop here, which sells stunning vases, bowls and candleholders (many of them produced by glass-blowers working their magic on-site).

FREE Museum Østjylland – Ebeltoft MUSEUM

(Torvet; ☉daily May-Sep, Sat & Sun Oct-Mar) The diminutive old town hall, built in 1789, has a half-timbered, chocolate-box appearance and is now home to local history exhibits. It's a popular spot for weddings.

From here, head north along cobbled Adelgade, easily one of the loveliest main streets in Jutland, lined with pastel-coloured cafes and stores and pretty courtyards.

Beaches BEACHES

Ebeltoft sits on a calm, protected bay fringed with white-sand beaches; you'll find a nice stretch right along Ndr Strandvej, the coastal road that leads north from the town centre.

Ree Park – Ebeltoft Safari SAFARI PARK

(www.reepark.dk; Stubbe Søvej 15; adult/child 140/80kr; ☉from 10am daily mid-Apr–late Oct) The latest addition to Djursland's multitude of family-focused parks houses an impressive collection of animals from all corners of the globe, with Africa taking more than the lion's share (pun intended). Visitors can pay extra to ride a camel (30kr) or take a Land Rover tour through the 'African savannah' (40kr); there are plenty of animal feedings throughout the day. The park is about 8km north of Ebeltoft via Rte 2; there are no buses out this way.

🍴 Sleeping & Eating

Danhostel Ebeltoft HOSTEL €

(☎86 34 20 53; www.ebeltoft-danhostel.dk; Egedalsvej 5; s/d/tr/q 400/450/495/550kr; @🤙) A map and your own set of wheels are almost compulsory to find this hostel, perched above the town (3km by road, or about a 25-minute walk). But it's worth the trip, with hotel-standard accommodation (all rooms with bathroom and TV) and some cool design features. Breakfast is 60kr.

Ebeltoft Strand Camping CAMPING GROUND, CABINS €

(☎86 34 12 14; www.ebeltoftstrandcamping.dk; Ndr Strandvej 23; per adult/child/site 90/50/50kr; @🤙🛏) The first camping ground you'll see, on your right as you enter town, has plenty of good sites backing onto a beach. It's well geared for family fun, with pool, playgrounds and mini-golf to entertain.

Hotel Ebeltoft Strand HOTEL €€

(☎86 34 33 00; www.ebeltoftstrand.dk; Ndr Strandvej 3; standard s/d 925/1125kr; 🤙🛏) In a plumb position on the beachfront and close to the tourist office, this large hotel offers good facilities (restaurant, heated indoor pool) and a range of price options, from no-frills budget (double 800kr) to 'deluxe' (double 1275kr) rooms.

Molskroen FRENCH-DANISH €€€

(☎86 36 22 00; www.molskroen.dk, in Danish; Hovedgaden 16, Femmøller Strand; lunch mains 125-205kr, 3-/4-course dinner menu 465/560kr; ☉lunch & dinner) For something special, hang the expense and make your way 6km northwest of town to this acclaimed *kro* (inn). Sample the chef's award-winning French-inspired creations as part of an eight-course degustation menu for 725kr, or a five small-course lunch for 395kr. If you can't travel far after all that exquisite food, there are equally impressive rooms here, with beautiful, design-heavy doubles starting at 1580kr.

Glascaféen CAFE €

(Strandvejen 8; mains 59-109kr; ☉lunch) You don't need to pay the entry price at Glasmuseet Ebeltoft just to enter its small, sleek cafe overlooking the water. There's a short, simple menu of sandwiches, salads and *fiske-frikadeller* (fishballs), and the homemade *lagkage* (layer cake) is itself a work of art.

❶ Information

Tourist office (☎86 34 14 00; www.visitdjursland.com; SA Jensens Vej; ☉9am-5pm Mon-Fri, 10am-4pm Sat & Sun mid-Jun–mid-Aug, 9am-4.30pm Mon-Fri, 10am-1pm Sat mid-Aug–mid-Jun) Off Strandvejen, next to *Fregatten Jylland*.

❶ Getting There & Around

Ebeltoft is on Rte 21, 54km east of Aarhus and 35km southwest of Grenaa.

MOLS BJERGE NATIONAL PARK

One of the five new national parks created in Denmark in the last few years, **Mols Bjerge National Park** (www.nationalparkmolsbjerge.dk) covers 180 sq km of Djursland forests, moors and open grasslands as well as lakes, coastal areas and the sea. It encompasses the town of Ebeltoft and nearby villages, and is named after the best-known natural feature of the region, Mols Bjerge (Mols Hills – rising to all of 137m).

The Ebeltoft tourist office can give you the necessary literature if you're interested in exploring the park. A dedicated information centre is likely to be built in the not-too-distant future, and will probably be in the vicinity of Kalø (south of Rønde), where you can explore typical park highlights such as forest, an 18th-century manor and ruins of a 14th-century castle.

BICYCLE Bicycles can be hired from **Bikefever** (Havnevej 10a) or at the Danhostel.

BOAT Mols-Linien (☑70 10 14 18; www.mols-linien.dk) operates a high-speed car ferry between Ebeltoft and Odden in north Zealand at least four times daily. The service takes 45 minutes and one-way fares cost adult/child/car 349/174/775kr; the rate for car passage includes up to nine passengers.

BUS Bus 123 runs between Aarhus and Ebeltoft (72kr, 1¼ hours). Bus 351 has regular services between Ebeltoft and Grenaa (48kr, one hour).

Grenaa

POP 14,300

A purpose-built harbour complete with (captive) sharks, a historic old town and 7km of fine, sandy beaches are the defining attractions of this town. The old town, radiating out from Torvet, is the economic and shopping hub of the district. It's about 3km west of the harbour, where the waterfront is peopled by shark-fanciers and Sweden-bound ferry-goers.

◉ Sights & Activities

Beaches BEACH

Grenaa's 7km of Blue Flag–winning beach runs south out of town and is where it's at on hot days; this area is known for its child-friendly shallow waters. To get here just follow the coast south from the harbour. If you want to be surrounded by holidaymakers, the northern end of the beach is always a hive of activity, but as you run south it becomes a little more private.

Kattegatcentret OCEANARIUM

(www.kattegatcentret.dk; Færgevej 4; adult/child 155/85kr; ☺10am-4pm or 5pm) If you fancy being just inches from a shark and in total control, you'll love the glass tunnel at Katte-gatcentret, where the focus is on surrounding sea life. Call ahead or check the website to ensure you're around for a shark-feeding session – a good way to see just why sharks are at the top of the food chain. There is also a seal pool (and feeding sessions), and a kid-friendly touch pool. Check the website for winter closing dates.

FREE Museum Østjylland – Grenaa MUSEUM

(Søndergade 1; ☺11am-4pm Mon-Fri, noon-3pm Sat & Sun Jun-Aug, 1-4pm Tue-Fri, noon-3pm Sun Sep-May) This eye-catching green-and-gold merchant's house, just south of Torvet, houses artefacts that have been discovered in the region and includes plenty of model boats to keep the budding builder entertained.

Grenaa Kirke CHURCH

(Torvet; ☺Mon-Fri) The Gothic-style parts of this church, in the same neighbourhood as the museum, date back to the 14th century.

🛏 Sleeping & Eating

The tourist office maintains a list of private homes in the area that rent rooms from around 300kr per person. It also has information on beachside holiday cottages (usually rented by the week).

Grenaa Strand Camping CAMPING GROUND, CABINS €

(☑86 32 17 18; www.grenaastrandcamping.dk; Fuglsangvej 58; per adult/child/site 82/60/100kr; ☺Apr–mid-Sep; @🛜🏊) A super option if your visit to Grenaa is all about the beach, this site is in pole beachside position a few kilometres south of town. Loads of high-season activities for kids plus a swimming pool (with waterslide) will keep everyone happy. Cabins and on-site caravans are well priced; there's also a minimarket and summertime cafe.

Danhostel Grenaa
HOSTEL €

(☑86 32 66 22; www.danhostelgrenaa.dk; Ydesvej 4; dm/s/d 300/400/500kr; ☎) A little removed from the action (about halfway between the town centre and the harbour), but offering modern, high-quality rooms (all with bathroom) in a green area by a sports stadium.

Hotel Grenaa Havlund
HOTEL €€

(☑86 32 26 77; www.hotelgrenaahavlund.dk; Kystvej 1; s/d from 695/895kr; ☎) This sunny little beachfront hotel offers simple, comfy rooms.

Restaurant Skakkes Holm
SEAFOOD €€

(Lystbådehavnen; dinner buffet incl drinks adult/child 229/68kr; ☺dinner) Over a footbridge by Kattegatcentret is the marina, a pleasant little place to explore and home to a few eating options. Of an evening you'll find hungry folks loading their plates from the impressive buffet at Restaurant Skakkes Holm. Given the surroundings, it's only fitting that the emphasis here is on fish.

ℹ Information

Tourist office (☑87 58 12 00; www.visit djursland.com; Torvet 1; ☺9am-5pm Mon-Fri, 9.30am-2pm Sat mid-Jun–mid-Aug, 9am-4.30pm Mon-Fri, 10am-2pm Sat mid-Aug–mid-Jun) Opposite the cathedral in the main square.

ℹ Getting There & Around

BICYCLE Bicycles can be hired from **Viggo Jensen** (Strandgade 14) near the harbour.

BOAT Stena Line (www.stenaline.com) connects Grenaa with Varberg, Sweden; see p326.

BUS Bus 122 and train services run throughout the day between Aarhus and Grenaa (78kr, 1¼ to 1½ hours); the train is sightly faster than the bus, but the prices are the same. In Grenaa, buses and trains leave from the station at Stationsplads, a short walk from Torvet.

Bus 351 has regular services between Ebeltoft and Grenaa (48kr, one hour).

CAR Grenaa is 63km northeast of Aarhus on Rte 15 and 57km east of Randers along Rte 16.

Around Djursland

Gammel Estrup
HOUSE, MUSEUM

(www.gammelestrup.dk; Randersvej 2, Auning; manor & museums adult/child 85kr/free; ☺10am-5pm daily Apr-Oct, 10am-3pm Tue-Sun Nov-Mar, closed Jan) On the outskirts of Auning, 33km west of Grenaa, is the magnificent manor house Gammel Estrup, where two museums, exquisite gardens and an aura of Danish gentility await.

The moat-encircled manor house that is home to **Herregårdsmuseet** (the Manor Museum), has been preserved and presented in much the same way as it was in the 17th century, with spacious rooms, antique furniture, elaborate tapestries, historic portraits, glorious views and creaking floorboards that tell a thousand stories. Unless you're a farmer, the **Dansk Landbrugsmuseum** (Danish Agricultural Museum) may hold less appeal, but its exhibits are of the same high quality and tell the story of Danish farming. There's a mammoth collection of old farm equipment plus gardens full of orchards and vegetables.

To get to Gammel Estrup, take bus 212 or 214 from Randers. If you're driving, take Rte 16 between Grenaa and Randers.

Djurs Sommerland
AMUSEMENT PARK

(www.djurssommerland.dk; Randersvej 17, Nimtofte; admission 199-225kr; ☺from 10am daily mid-Jun–mid-Aug, also open select days in May, Sep & Oct) If you're travelling with hyperactive kids, let them drag you to one of Djursland's biggest drawcards, Djurs Sommerland. It's a much-hyped amusement park with arguably the best outdoor rides in Jutland (more than 60) and a waterpark, with pools and waterslides for all ages. Your wallet may feel the sting, however, when you realise that everyone over the age of three pays the same entrance fee; once this is paid, though, you're free to play to your heart's content. Closing hours vary (from 5pm to 9pm); check the website to confirm opening days and hours.

The park lies 20km west of Grenaa in Nimtofte. Plenty of bus options will get you there – from Aarhus take bus 121, 122 or 123; from Randers or Grenaa take bus 214.

Skandinavisk Dyrepark
SAFARI PARK

(www.skandinaviskdyrepark.dk; Nødagervej 67B, Nødagervej; adult/child 155/85kr; ☺10am-5pm or 6pm May-Oct) Animals in captivity can be a tad confronting for sentimental adults. Still, if you were to be a caged bear, this is where you would want to be, alongside other Nordic species. The biggest attraction here is the impressive polar bear facility; other star performers include brown bears, moose, musk ox and wolves. Fallow deer, reindeer and goats can be fed by hand.

To reach the park, follow the signs from Kolind or from Rte 15, 2km north of Tirstrup. Bus 120 runs between Aarhus and Grenaa and stops near the park.

THE LAKE DISTRICT

One of Jutland's most prized areas is the Lake District (Søhøjlandet), as it gently dazzles with hills, forests and lakes not found anywhere else in Denmark. This region is home to Denmark's longest river (the Gudenå; 160km), Jutland's biggest lake (Mossø) and Denmark's highest point, Møllehøj (a smidge under 171m, bless its cotton socks). In many countries, visiting the land's highest/longest/biggest anything would probably mean gobsmacking scenery and grasping for superlatives. Not in Denmark! Instead of craning your neck at sky-reaching peaks, here you can marvel over the gentle nature, neat and tame, and the superbly pretty scenery.

Silkeborg

POP 42,700

In a country of supreme flatness, the modern town of Silkeborg is something of a black sheep, surrounded as it is by hills, sitting on an expansive lake and spaciously laid out. Modern-art lovers and history boffins will find cause to stop here, but nature lovers have the most to celebrate. It's Silkeborg's surrounding landscapes that draw plenty of tourists – not thrill-seekers but rather families and outdoorsy folk drawn to the lush forests and waterways that are perfect for gentle cycling, rambling and, especially, canoeing.

◉ Sights

Silkeborg Museum   MUSEUM

(www.silkeborgmuseum.dk; Hovedgårdsvej 7; adult/child 50kr/free; ◎10am-5pm daily May–mid-Oct, noon-4pm Sat & Sun mid-Oct–Apr) Here you can check out the amazingly well-preserved body of the **Tollund Man**, the central (albeit leathery) star in an otherwise sweet but predictable collection. The well-preserved face of the Tollund Man is hypnotic in its detail, right down to the stubble on his chin. Like the Grauballe Man at Aarhus' Moesgård Museum, the life (and death) of the Tollund Man remains a mystery. His intact remains were found in the outskirts of Silkeborg in 1950, and have been radiocarbon dated to around 350 BC. The autopsy suggests he had been hanged, yet he was placed as though lying asleep with only a leather hat over his face and a thin leather noose around his neck. Was he an executed prisoner, or a sacrifice to the gods? That's the big unanswered question, but the accompanying displays aren't as engrossing as those at Moesgård.

Museum Jorn   ART MUSEUM

(www.museumjorn.dk; Gudenåvej 7; adult/child 70kr/free; ◎10am-5pm Tue-Sun Apr-Oct, noon-4pm Tue-Fri, 10am-5pm Sat & Sun Nov-Mar) Fresh from a major renovation, Museum Jorn (formerly Silkeborg Kunstmuseum) contains some striking work, such as the large ceramic walls by Jean Dubuffet and Pierre Alechinsky that greet visitors at the entrance. It displays many of the works of native son Asger Jorn and other modern artists, including Max Ernst, Le Corbusier and Danish artists from the influential CoBrA group. It's 1km south of the town centre.

KunstCentret Silkeborg Bad   ART MUSEUM

(Art Centre Silkeborg Baths; www.silkeborgbad.dk; Gjessøvej 40; adult/child 60kr/free; ◎10am-5pm Tue-Sun May-Sep, noon-4pm Tue-Fri, 11am-5pm Sat & Sun Oct-Apr) This former spa dates from 1883 and is now a beautiful, modern art space, with permanent works and changing exhibitions of art, sculpture, ceramics, glassware, design and architecture, surrounded by parkland (always open) featuring contemporary sculpture. It's about 2km southwest of town; local bus 17 runs out here.

Aqua   AQUARIUM

(www.visitaqua.dk, in Danish; Vejlsøvej 55; adult/child 115/60kr; ◎from 10am daily Jan-Nov) Situated 2km south of the town centre is Aqua, an entertaining aquarium and exhibition centre built into several outdoor lakes. It explores the ecosystems of the surrounding area, with lots of touch tanks and fishy creatures, cute otters and fishing birds among the imaginative displays. Closing times vary from 4pm to 6pm.

Indelukket   PARK

(Åhave Allé) Don't miss a stroll through Indelukket, a picturesque riverside park – follow Åhavevej south about 1km from the tourist office to reach it. There's a kiosk here, as well as minigolf, a marina and an open-air stage. If you're on foot, it's the desired route to get to Museum Jorn, the camping ground and points further south.

🏃 Activities

The tourist office has oodles of information on the following activities and more (including options such as golf, horse riding and fishing).

Boat Trips

The **Hjejlen** (☎86 82 07 66; www.hjejlen.com; Havnen), the world's oldest operating paddle steamer, has been faithfully plying the waters of the Lake District since it was first launched in 1861. These days the boat shuttles tourists from Silkeborg to the foot of Himmelbjerget during the summer season (10am and 2pm daily, July to mid-August). The operators have other boats regularly plying the same route during this period, and from May to September. The route (adult one way/return 80/115kr, 1¼ hours, up to seven services daily) takes in a wealth of river and lake scenery and is one of the most popular outings in the Lake District. It also makes stops at Indelukket park and Aqua aquarium.

Canoeing

In the warmer months (May to September) the tourist office promotes popular self-guided canoe tours that take you through some magnificent countryside. Tour options range from two to five days and are outlined on the tourist office website.

As the name suggests, the five-day **Family Tour** (two adults plus two children from 3195kr) is ideal for kids. It takes you along a route from Tørring north to Silkeborg, staying in camping grounds where your tent is pre-erected for you. Tents and cooking gear are all sorted – you just need to bring a sleeping bag and mattress, and food. The Family Tour is available from mid-June to the end of August; shorter options are also possible.

Pioneer Tours are a more challenging option, for those who like getting back to nature and sleeping at primitive tent sites along the way. If you're a softie who prefers a real bed at the end of the day, **Luxury Tours** have accommodation and meals arranged at atmospheric old inns.

Alternatively, you can plan your own tour and consult the region's various canoe hirers for the finer details – they are a wealth of information and will rent canoes by the hour (100kr) or day (380kr) and help with transport of gear to the chosen departure point, if necessary. If you don't have your own camping gear, you should also enquire about tent rental (usually possible if you arrange it a few days in advance).

If all you have is a day, recommended options are the 24km round-trip across the lakes east to Himmelbjerget (a harder, more exposed route), or a gentler option travelling with the currents north from Silke-borg to Kongensbro (and taking the bus back to town). Make enquiries with **Silkeborg Kanocenter** (☎86 80 30 03; www.silke borgkanocenter.dk, in Danish; Østergade 36). You can also hire motor boats here (per hour/day 180/850kr) if the exertion of canoeing doesn't appeal.

Hiking & Cycling

The tourist office has plenty of brochures on hiking and cycling routes – a worthwhile purchase is either *12 beautiful bicycle tours* or *12 lovely walks in the Lakelands*, each priced at 40kr.

The beech forest of **Nordskoven** is criss-crossed with hiking and bike trails. To reach Nordskoven head south down Åhavevej from the tourist office, then go left over the old railway bridge near the hostel.

The track of the old railway from Silkeborg to Horsens is now an excellent walking and cycling trail of about 50km or so. The **Hærvej** (www.haervej.dk), the Old Military Road, passes through the region (west of Silkeborg). This is a 250km historic route from the German border north to Viborg along the backbone of Denmark; it's been converted into a cycling, hiking and horse-riding trail.

For bike rental, see p242.

Swimming

For an idyllic (if crowded) lakeside swimming spot, head to Almindsø. Head south of town on Frederiksberggade and take a left at the roundabout in the direction of Horsens. The swimming area is signposted on your right after 2km; there are bathing jetties, change rooms and a kiosk here.

✯✮ Festivals & Events

Riverboat Jazz Festival   MUSIC
(www.riverboat.dk) There's something about Scandis and jazz. They love it, and Silkeborg has embraced it with the five-day Riverboat Jazz Festival, held in late June. It's not quite New Orleans but you can buy a ticket and take a cruise down the river, or stroll the streets and take advantage of the free jazz.

🛏 Sleeping

Budget and midrange choices in town are limited, making B&B accommodation an especially good option. The tourist office publishes a B&B booklet, with singles/doubles costing around 250/500kr; for a 50kr fee, the office will book a room for you.

Silkeborg

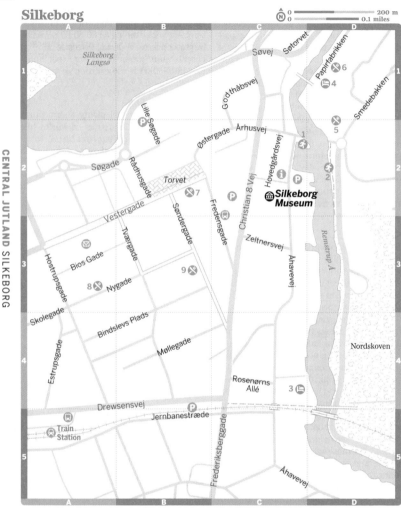

Danhostel Silkeborg HOSTEL €
(☎86 82 36 42; www.danhostel-silkeborg.dk; Åhavevej 55; dm 250kr, r with shared/private bathroom 470/670kr; ☺Mar-Nov; @) The superb riverbank location, modern facilities and lack of budget alternatives in town make this hostel very popular, so book ahead. Once here, enjoy the outdoor tables and homely communal areas alongside cyclists, families and Euro-backpackers. The dorms are available June to August; breakfast costs 65kr.

Gammel Skovridergaard HOTEL €€€
(☎87 22 55 00; www.glskov.dk; Marienlundsvej 36; s/d 1225/1550kr, weekends & summer 775/1150kr; @☎) This magnificent former manor farm is now a hotel and conference centre with oodles of charm and an idyllic location close to lakes and forests, yet only 2km south of the town centre (en route to Aqua). The grounds are superb, and the rooms and facilities are excellent.

Silkeborg

⊙ Top Sights

⊕ Activities, Courses & Tours

🛏 Sleeping

⊗ Eating

Radisson Blu Hotel HOTEL €€
(☎88 82 22 22; www.radissonblu.com/hotel-silke
borg; Papirfabrikken 12; r 995-1595kr; 📶) This
polished performer lives in the redeveloped
paper factory that was once the backbone
of the local economy. It's right on the river,
among a clutch of restaurants, and the designer rooms are smaller than expected but
comfy and well equipped. Weekend rates are
cheaper than midweek.

**Gudenåens
Camping** CAMPING GROUND, CABINS €
(☎86 82 22 01; www.gudenaaenscamping.dk; Vejlsøvej 7; per adult/child/site 79/42/60kr; @📶) Follow the signs for Aqua to find this tree-filled
riverside park, about 2km south of the town
centre (just south of Indelukket). Cabins
and caravans are available for hire (only by
the week in high season), and staff can set
you up with bikes and canoes. Local bus 10
runs down this way.

🍴 Eating & Drinking

There are two places you need to know
about when scouting for eating (and drinking) options in Silkeborg: the reinvigorated
Papirfabrikken (the old paper factory) and
the fast food and international cuisines
found on Nygade. End-of-week nightlife
venues cluster around the corner of Nygade
and Hostrupsgade.

The tourist office can provide information about microbreweries and farm shops
(*gårdbutikker*) in the region.

Café Evald INTERNATIONAL €€
(Papirfabrikken 10B; mains 89-199kr; ⊘breakfast,
lunch & dinner) In among the family restaurants, cinema and cafe-bars of Papirfabrikken is bustling Evald, wooing patrons
with a crowd-pleasing menu. Sit at a riverside table, order a beer from the local Grauballe Bryghus (brewery) and try the 'tapas'
plate – a sampler plate comprising five
small tastes of seasonal favourites.

**Restaurant Gastronomisk
Institut** EUROPEAN €€€
(☎86 82 40 97; Søndergade 20; dinner mains
199-255kr; ⊘lunch & dinner Tue-Sat) The ambitious name creates high expectations, and
this place delivers, with changing menus
highlighting seasonal produce. Its summertime three-course 'North Sea' dinner menu
(369kr) runs from crayfish tail to monkfish
and on to sorbet of seasonal fruits. Bookings
are recommended if you plan to come here
in the evening.

Café 1.Række CAFE €
(Papirfabrikken 80; sandwiches 32-58kr; ⊘lunch)
The name means first row, and (appropriately enough) this large modern space
is part of the Jysk Musik & Teaterhus.
There's a great waterside terrace, while inside smartly dressed tables and plenty of
plant life accompany a short, smørrebrød-
focused menu. Look out for good-value fish
buffets (199kr) three or four nights a week
in summer.

Okkels Is ICE CREAM €
(Nygade 26E) Excellent homemade Italian-
style ice cream.

Føtex SUPERMARKET €
(Torvet 4; ⊘9am-8pm Mon-Fri, 8am-6pm Sat)
Central supermarket with on-site bakery
and cafe.

ⓘ Information

Banks and other services are found along the
main shopping strip, Vestergade.

Library (Hostrupsgade 41) For accessing the
internet.

Post office (Bios Gade) Small, central branch,
one block behind Vestergade.

Tourist office (☎86 82 19 11; www.visitsilke
borg.dk; Åhavevej 2A; ⊘9.30am-5.30pm Mon-
Fri, 10am-2pm Sat Jul-Aug, 9.30am-4pm Mon-
Fri, 10am-1pm Sat Apr-Jun & Sep, 10am-3pm
Mon-Fri Oct-Mar) Well-stocked office; faces the
river, next to the museum.

ℹ Getting There & Around

Silkeborg is 37km south of Viborg on Rte 52 and 43km west of Aarhus on Rte 15. Half-hourly trains connect Silkeborg with Aarhus (66kr, 50 minutes) via Ry (34kr, 15 minutes).

Bikes can be hired from **Silkeborg Kayak og Cykel Udlejning** (www.skcu.dk; Åhave Allé 7; mountain bike per day 125kr).

Ry

POP 5550

Mellow, more-rural Ry lies in the heart of the Lake District. It has a pretty duck-filled harbour area, where you'll find tourist boats to Himmelbjerget, canoe hire, a kiosk and a marina. There's also an assortment of activities around town to keep you busy, and quaint villages perfect for discovering.

🏃 Activities

Ask at Ry's tourist office for leaflets detailing walking and cycling options.

Hiking

One of the best hikes from Ry is the two-hour, 7km walk west to Himmelbjerget (see opposite). The starting point for the hike is the dirt road that begins off Rodelundvej, about 400m south of the Ry bridge. The signposted path leads to the Himmelbjerget boat dock before climbing the hill to the tower. A nice idea is to hike out and catch a boat back to Ry or on to Silkeborg.

Cycling

Cycling is a great way to explore the low-key charms of the local area. For ideas for a cycling itinerary, check out the boxed text, p243.

WORTH A TRIP

HERNING & THE HEART OF ART

If you're a fan of modern art, chances are you've heard of Italian conceptual artist Piero Manzoni (1933–63). What you may not know is that the biggest public collection of his work is not in Milan, but on the eastern fringe of Herning (population 46,300), a regional textile centre 40km west of Silkeborg. You'll find Manzoni's work, and that of visionaries such as Mario Merz and Man Ray, at **HEART** (www.heartmus.dk; Birk Centerpark 8; adult/child 75kr/free; ☺10am-5pm Tue-Sun, to 10pm Thu), Herning's striking contemporary-art museum. Designed by US architect Steven Holl, its shirtlike crumpled walls and sleeve-inspired roof honour the collection's founder, Danish shirt manufacturer and passionate art collector Aage Damgaard (1917–91). In the summers of 1960 and 1961, Damgaard invited Manzoni to indulge his creative spirit in Herning. The result was a string of masterpieces and the forging of Herning's Manzoni legacy. But HEART doesn't stop at 20th-century conceptual art, with several world-class exhibitions of contemporary art staged annually.

Across the street, the **Carl-Henning Pedersen and Else Alfelt Museum** (www.chpeamuseum.dk, in Danish; Birk Centerpark 1; adult/child 40kr/free; ☺10am-5pm Tue-Sun) showcases the riotously colourful paintings, watercolours, mosaics, ceramics and sculptures of artists Carl-Henning Pedersen (1913–2007) and Else Alfelt (1910–74); there's a large sculpture park beyond the museum. Next door to HEART stands Danish architect Jørn Utzon's 1970-designed **Prototype House** (closed to the public), while further south you'll stumble across artist Ingvar Cronhammar's ominous **Elia**. Attracting lightning, shooting random flames of gas, and looking straight off a *Dr Who* set, it's northern Europe's largest sculpture.

HEART and its neighbours aside, another reason you might be heading to Herning is for an event at **Boxen Arena** (www.mch.dk; Kaj Zartows Vej 7), a slick new indoor sporting arena and concert venue hosting big-name touring acts – in 2011, these included George Michael, Red Hot Chili Peppers, Britney Spears and Bob Dylan (surprisingly, some of these acts were not performing in Copenhagen, only in Herning).

You might consider Herning a day trip from Silkeborg, easily reached by train (one way 58kr, 40 minutes). For the museums, alight at Birk Centerpark station (not Herning station), from where the sights are a short walk. Boxen Arena is south of the city, off Hwy 15 (take the train to Herning Messecenter).

TOURING AROUND RY

This is a lovely area for a country drive or cycle, exploring small villages and enjoying the scenery. If you're cycling, be aware that this area isn't flat as a pancake like elsewhere in Denmark!

Set out from Ry westbound on Rte 445 to **Gammel Rye** (5km away). Take a breather at an old *kro* (inn) or at the 1872 Dutch-style **windmill** (Møllestien 5), now a museum of wooden shoe making.

From Gammel Rye it's another 4km to reach **Øm Kloster Museum** (Munkevej 8, Emborg; adult/child 40kr/free; ⊙10am-4pm Tue-Sun). Øm is the ruins of a medieval monastery, where glass-topped tombs reveal the 750-year-old bones of Bishop Elafsen of Aarhus and many of his abbots.

Continue east from Øm and after 3km you'll reach pretty-as-a-picture **Boes**, a tiny hamlet with picturesque thatch-roofed houses and vivid flower gardens.

From Boes it's about 4km back to Ry, making your round-trip 16km. But if you have the stamina to add another 12km, it's worth exploring further, to the eastern shores of **Mossø** (Jutland's largest lake) and the lovely lakeside summerhouses beyond **Alken** (follow the signs for Fuldbro Mølle). Head back to Alken when it's time to return to Ry and cycle via Svejstrup, rather than take the busier main road.

Ry Cykel CYCLING

(☑86 89 14 91; Parallelvej 9B) Ry Cykel is 1.5km east of the train station, towards Skanderborg. Bikes can be rented here for 75kr per day.

Canoeing

Ry Kanofart CANOEING

(☑86 89 11 67; www.kanoferie.dk, in Danish; Kyhnsvej 20; ⊙May–mid-Sep) If you want to explore the surrounding lakes and rivers, Ry Kanofart has canoes for hire, costing 100/380kr per hour/day. As with the operators in Silkeborg, staff here can help you plan lengthy river trips on the Gudenå.

Boat Trips

Hjejlen Boat Company BOATING

(☑86 82 07 66; www.hjejlen.com; return adult/child 75/40kr) Schedules three or four boats daily from Ry to Himmelbjerget, operating June to August (and weekends in May and September), leaving Ry at 10.15am, 12.15pm and 2.15pm, and sailing from Himmelbjerget one hour later. You need to book a day in advance.

Climbing

Denmark's tallest tree used to stand in a forest outside Ry. Then a storm blew it down and enterprising locals converted it into an impressive **climbing pole** measuring 44m in height. Enquire at the Ry tourist office about scaling the pole to enjoy a bird's-eye view of the area.

🛏 Sleeping

Ry Park Hotel HOTEL €€

(☑86 89 19 11; www.ryparkhotel.dk; Kyhnsvej 2; s/d from 790/990kr; @🛜🏊) There are two room categories at this, Ry's only, hotel – the newly renovated rooms are a better bet. It's a large, pleasant-enough place, popular for conferences and weddings, and it can help arrange canoeing and cycling in the surrounding countryside. There's also a small indoor pool and a good on-site restaurant.

Birkhede Camping CAMPING GROUND, MOTEL €

(☑86 89 13 55; www.birkhede.dk, in Danish; Lyngvej 14; per adult/child/site 79/49/70kr, motel d 625kr; ⊙late Apr–mid-Sep; 🏊) You really need your own transport to get to this park (3.5km by road from Ry township), but once here you may not want to leave. There's a swimming pool and waterslide, playground and lakeshore, plus canoe and bike rental, all in a green and woodsy setting.

🍴 Eating

There are a few takeaway options and Italian restaurants on Skanderborgvej, or pack up a picnic lunch for your hike or ride. **Le Gâteau** (Klostervej 12; ⊙from 7am daily), a bakery opposite the train station, is a good place to start; there's also a large Kvickly supermarket not far back from the harbour.

Le Saison INTERNATIONAL €€

(Kyhnsvej 2; lunch 98-128kr, dinner mains 168-288kr; ⊙lunch & dinner) Easily Ry's fanciest dining option, this shiny outfit is attached to Ry

Park Hotel and has a comprehensive menu of classics.

ℹ️ Information

Tourist office (☎86 69 66 00; www.visit skanderborg.com; Klostervej 3; ☉7am-4pm Mon-Fri, 10am-noon Sat) Very helpful office at the train station.

ℹ️ Getting There & Around

Ry is on Rte 445, 20km southeast of Silkeborg and 35km west of Aarhus. Half-hourly trains connect Ry with Silkeborg (34kr, 15 minutes) and Aarhus (54kr, 30 minutes).

For bike hire, see p243.

Himmelbjerget

There's something quite endearing about a country that will name one of its highest points Himmelbjerget (meaning 'sky mountain'), especially when that peak only hits 147m. It's a mere hillock to non-Danes, but it does afford charming vistas of the surrounding forests and lakes and is a popular tourist spot. While the scenery is indeed sweet, the money-grabbing and tacky souvenir stalls do detract a little from the commune with nature.

First up, it costs 10kr to park your vehicle here. Once you've completed the brief pilgrimage from the car park to the mountaintop, you could climb the 25m tower (another 10kr) for a fine 360-degree view of the lakes and countryside, but the view from outside the tower seems just as good (the tower is open daily May to mid-September).

There are a number of interesting memorials in the vicinity, plus marked hiking trails in the woodland area. One trail leads 1km from the tower down to the lakeshore where boats from Ry and Silkeborg dock.

At the dock you'll find **Hotel Julsø** (snacks & meals 60-245kr), a gorgeous old *kro* (inn) with a truly lovely panorama.

There are a handful of nondescript kiosks and cafes surrounding the car park. There's also **Hotel Himmelbjerget**, an old chalet-style hotel that is scheduled to be replaced by a new 70-room hotel and wellness centre (expected sometime in 2013).

ℹ️ Getting There & Away

Himmelbjerget is a 10-minute drive west of Ry on Rte 445. It can also be reached by a pleasant 7km hike from Ry, or by a scenic boat ride from either Ry or Silkeborg – see those sections for details.

THE INTERIOR

The landscape of Jutland's interior ranges from hilly woodland up the middle to rolling fields in the east. Industry is prominent throughout the area, and indeed there are plenty of medium-sized towns that are pleasant enough places to while away a day if you find yourself in the neighbourhood, but are not particularly worth going out of your way for (no offence to the towns themselves, mind, but we're talking about the likes of Fredericia, Vejle, Horsens, Skive and Holstebro).

Our advice is pretty straightforward – with limited holiday time, head to the towns with the most visitor appeal, be it in the form of Viking relics, historic churches or theme parks.

Jelling

POP 3250

A sleepy town with a big history, Jelling is revered as the birthplace of Christianity in Denmark, the monarchy and all that is

---

THE HILLS ARE ALIVE...

Skanderborg (population 18,250) is a rather humdrum town about 15km southeast of Ry and 30km west of Aarhus; its standout feature is its lovely lakeside setting. It is best known in Denmark for the annual **Skanderborg Festival** (www.smukfest.dk), which bills itself as Denmark's most beautiful festival due to its gorgeous location among beech forest in the Lake District. It's second only to Roskilde in terms of scale, but has a reputation of being considerably more chilled and, well, tree-hugging than the Zealand behemoth – a special feature is the Sunday-morning concert performed by the Aarhus Philharmonic Orchestra.

The festival takes place during the second weekend in August in Dyrehaven, parkland a couple of kilometres east of the town, and attracts up to 40,000 people with an entertaining mix of (mostly Danish) rock and pop artists, with a few big international acts too.

truly Danish. The town served as the royal seat of King Gorm during the Vikings' most dominant era; Gorm the Old was the first in a millennium-long chain of Danish monarchs that continues unbroken to this day. The site of Gorm's ancient castle remains a mystery, but other vestiges of his reign can still be found at Jelling Kirke. People come to pay homage at the church, inspect the two nearby rune stones and climb the burial mounds. The area became a Unesco World Heritage Site in 1994.

◉ Sights

Jelling Kirke CHURCH

(www.jellingkirke.dk, in Danish; Vejlevej; admission free; ⊙church from 8am Mon-Sat, 12.30pm Sun, closes 4-6pm, grounds open 24hr) Jelling Kirke, erected in about 1100, is one of Denmark's most significant historical sites. Inside this small whitewashed church you'll find some vividly restored 12th-century frescoes that are among the oldest in Denmark. The main attractions, however, are the two well-preserved rune stones just outside the church door.

The smaller stone was erected in the early 10th century by Gorm the Old in honour of his wife. The larger one, raised by Gorm's son, Harald Bluetooth, is adorned with the oldest representation of Christ found in Scandinavia. It reads:

> King Harald ordered this monument to be made in memory of Gorm his father and Thyra his mother, the Harald who won for himself all Denmark and Norway and made the Danes Christians.

Harald Bluetooth did, in fact, succeed in routing the Swedes from Denmark and began the peaceful conversion of the Danish people from the pagan religion celebrated by his father to Christianity. The larger stone, commonly dubbed 'Denmark's baptismal certificate', not only represents the advent of Christianity but also bids a royal farewell to the ancient gods of prehistoric Denmark. One side of the stone, which depicts a snake coiled around a mythological creature, is thought to symbolise this change of faith.

Two huge burial mounds flank Jelling Kirke. The barrow to the north was long believed to contain the bones of Gorm and his queen, Thyra, but when it was excavated in 1820 no human remains were found. In 1861 Frederik VII oversaw the excavation of the southern mound but, again, only a few objects were found with no mortal remains among them.

In the 1970s a team of archaeologists dug beneath Jelling Kirke itself and hit pay dirt. They found the remains of three earlier wooden churches; the oldest is thought to have been erected by Harald Bluetooth. A burial chamber was also unearthed at this time and human bones and gold jewellery were discovered. The jewellery was consistent with pieces that had been found earlier in the northern burial mound.

Archaeologists now believe that the skeletal remains found beneath the church are those of Gorm, who had originally been buried in the northern mound but was later reinterred by his son. Presumably Harald Bluetooth, out of respect, moved his parents' remains from pagan soil to a Christian place of honour within the church. The bones of Queen Thyra have yet to be found.

From 2008 to 2011, the Jelling Project (http://jelling.natmus.dk), led by the National Museum, has been further investigating Jelling's monuments with the aim of better understanding the transition from paganism to Christianity and the establishment of Danish royal power in the Viking Age. Read about the archaeological excavations and findings on its website.

FREE Kongernes Jelling MUSEUM

(Royal Jelling; www.kongernesjelling.dk; Gormsgade 23; ⊙10am-5pm Tue-Sun Jun-Aug, noon-4pm Tue-Sun Sep-May) Kongernes Jelling, opposite the church, is an enthralling modern museum providing further insight into the town's magnificent monuments and its importance in Danish royal history. An enlarged coloured version of the larger rune stone helps visitors understand the meaning behind it, while a family tree shows the direct line of descent from Gorm the Old to present-day Queen Margrethe II.

Givskud Zoo & Lion Park ZOO, SAFARI PARK

(www.givskudzoo.dk; Løveparkvej 3, Givskud; adult/child 160/95kr; ⊙from 10am daily mid-Apr–late Oct) It's a decent leap from Christianity to lions (or is it?), but if you're in the area and in need of a fun family distraction, Givskud Zoo & Lion Park, 8km northwest of Jelling, can provide. It's an entertaining safari park with plenty of African animals, and you explore from the comfort of your own car or in the park-run safari buses (30kr). Walking trails will take you past elephant and gorilla enclosures; for littlies there's also a petting

BLUETOOTH TRIVIA

Today the term 'Bluetooth' is used to describe the wireless transportation of electronic data between computers, mobile phones etc. It is in fact named after 10th-century Harald Bluetooth, who was known for his unification of previously warring tribes from Denmark and Norway (including the then-Danish territory of Skåne in Sweden, which is where Bluetooth technology was developed by Swedish company Ericsson). Bluetooth was likewise intended to unify different technologies. The Bluetooth logo merges Nordic rune symbols. So now you know...

zoo. Closing times vary (from 4pm to 8pm). Bus 211 runs regularly to the zoo from Vejle, via Jelling. There's a Danhostel in the park's immediate vicinity.

🛏️ Sleeping & Eating

You're not exactly spoiled for choice in Jelling. Options are better in the larger town of Vejle, 10km southeast – or, better yet, in Billund (about 20km west).

Jelling Camping　　　CAMPING GROUND, CABINS €
(☑75 87 16 53; www.jellingcamping.dk; Mølvangvej 55; per adult/child/site 70/40/40kr; ☺Apr-Sep; ☒) In the holiday period you'll be surrounded by happy families taking advantage of this park's proximity to Givskud Zoo and Legoland; the park caters to them beautifully with a summertime pool, playgrounds, cafe and bike rental. You can hire well-priced on-site tents, caravans and cabins, too. It's 1km west of Jelling Kirke.

Byens Café　　　　　CAFE €€
(Møllegade 10; meals 88-149kr; ☺10am-10pm) The smart new Byens Hus (Town's House) is home to the local library, a cinema, gallery and a spacious, airy cafe serving quality all-day dishes (brunch plate, sandwiches, burgers, spareribs with coleslaw). Inside you'll see the big copper vats of the local microbrewery, Jelling Bryggeri, and can sample the wares (try Kong Haralds Pilsener).

Jelling Kro　　　TRADITIONAL DANISH €€
(Gormsgade 16; lunch 89-98kr, dinner mains 98-198kr; ☺lunch & dinner Tue-Sun) In a 1780 bright-yellow building bristling with character, this country inn serves up traditional meat-heavy Danish fare.

ℹ️ Information

Jelling Kirke is in the centre of town, a two-minute walk due north from the train station along Stationsvej.

Tourist office (☑75 87 13 01; www.visitjelling. dk; Gormsgade 23; ☺10am-5pm Tue-Sun Jun-Aug, noon-4pm Tue-Sun Sep-May) Part of the Kongernes Jelling museum, directly opposite the church.

ℹ️ Getting There & Away

Jelling is 10km northwest of Vejle on Rte 442. From Vejle trains run at least hourly on weekdays, slightly less frequently at weekends (28kr, 15 minutes). Bus 211 covers the same ground for the same price.

Billund & Legoland

POP 6150

Legoland is so geared to families you might feel a little, well, underdressed if you visit without your own set of excited ankle-biters; but don't let that stop you from embracing your inner child and allocating the park some generous time in your itinerary.

Mind-blowing Lego models and the happy-family magic associated with great theme parks have transformed Legoland into Denmark's most visited tourist attraction outside of Copenhagen. It's a great day outing (you'll need at least a day), and sits smack-bang in the middle of Jutland, 1km north of the town of Billund.

☉ Sights & Activities

Legoland　　　　　AMUSEMENT PARK
If you're 'of a certain age', the paramount attraction of Legoland is **Miniland** – the 20 million plastic Lego blocks snapped together to create miniature cities and replicate global icons. You can't help but marvel at the brilliant Lilliputian models of the Kennedy Space Centre, Amsterdam, Bergen or a Scottish castle, and you'll no doubt vow to head home and drag your Lego out of storage to see what masterpiece you can create (surely it's not that hard?). In Miniland you can also do some advance sightseeing of **Danish landmarks** including Copenhagen's Nyhavn, Ribe, Skagen or the royal palace of Amalienborg. Or take a trip in miniboats past landmarks such as the Statue of Liberty, the Acropolis and an Egyptian temple. The

LEGOLAND PRACTICALITIES

Legoland (www.legoland.dk; adult/child 279/249kr; ⊙from 10am Apr-Oct, closing time between 6pm and 9pm, closed Nov-Mar) is no doubt the reason you're in Billund. To maximise your time, consider buying your tickets online before you visit and avoid the queues (you can also buy tickets at most accommodation in the town). Note that adult tickets are for those aged 13 and over; infants under two years are admitted free. Seniors aged 65 and over pay 249kr. To enable a cheaper second day at the park, visit a ticket booth with your ticket and pay an additional 99kr.

Inside Legoland you'll find a bank, ATMs, lockers, a baby room, pushchair rental and almost anything else you might need. Do we need to mention there's a huge, busy Lego shop?

Also worth knowing – and not well publicised – is that the park opens its gates about a half-hour before the rides close, and no ticket is necessary to enter. Rides normally close one or two hours before the park itself (check the website), so with a bit of luck you could end up with 2½ hours to browse and check out Miniland for free.

For visitors to Legoland with their own wheels, you can avoid the 50kr charged for parking at the car parks directly opposite Legoland's entrance. If you're prepared to walk a little there is plenty more (free) parking.

reconstructions are on a scale of 1:20 to 1:40 and the attention to detail is incredible. The park's largest piece, a model of **Mt Rushmore** with the four US presients, was built with a staggering 1.5 million Lego bricks. (The smallest piece? A Miniland dove, built of four small white bricks.)

New to the park is the **Star Wars** area of Miniland, where 1.5 million bricks have been used to re-create seven detailed scenes from the six *Star Wars* movies. The four-legged robotic walkers rendered in Lego are quite something, as is the miniature Tatooine cantina scene.

Be sure to pick up a park map to assist with further exploration. The park is divided into themed areas, including Legoredo Town, a Wild West area; Knights' Kingdom, where a medieval castle awaits; Pirate Land, which hosts ships and sword-play; and Duplo Land, with plenty of safe, simple rides and activities for the little 'uns.

Legoland's smorgasbord of rides and activities is mostly geared to pre-teens and wholesome family fun. For wilder rides suited to older kids, Legoland compares unfavourably to somewhere such as Copenhagen's Tivoli. Still, adrenalin-junkies should seek out **X-treme Racers**, a roller coaster that cranks up to a speed of 60km/h, then head to the nearby **Power Builder** to defy gravity on a Terminatorlike robotic arm.

For some downtime stop by **Atlantis**, an aquarium built around Lego models of divers and submersibles. For the chilled park-goer there are rides aplenty to keep the

blood pressure down, from merry-go-rounds to a tranquil train ride. Once the entrance fee is paid, all rides are free – the only exception is the **Statoil Driving School** (55kr), which lets kids aged seven to 13 obtain their driving licences and puts them out onto the 'open road' (that is, the open Lego road).

FREE **Lalandia** WATERPARK, ENTERTAINMENT COMPLEX (www.lalandia.dk; Ellehammers Allé) Adding to the extreme family-friendly focus of Billund is the new Lalandia, a showy entertainment complex that's more like Vegas for kids (there's also a Lalandia in southern Lolland). This roofed complex (where the sky is always blue and temperature warm) houses the **Aquadome waterpark** (adult/child 210/160kr), **Monky Tonky indoor playground** (admission 50kr), games, minigolf, tenpin bowling, sports activities, kids concerts and a handful of restaurants and shops. There's also an associated estate of holiday houses for rent ('residents' access the Aquadome and Monky Tonky for free) – see the website for more.

🛏 Sleeping

Billund hotels are generally quite pricey, but they're all busy catering to a market focused firmly on family fun (colourful decor, playrooms, peak-summer activities etc). Advance bookings are highly recommended.

TOP CHOICE **Hotel Legoland** HOTEL €€€ (☎75 33 12 44; www.hotellegoland.dk; Aastvej 10; standard s/d/f 1805/2210/3220kr, themed rooms 4120kr; @🖘) Lego figures greet you at the door and a copy of a Lego *Mona Lisa* hangs near the reception area. There's amazing kid-friendly detail here, and plenty of space for grown-ups as well as Lego-filled playrooms. Double rooms are fairly standard, though of high quality. Where this place shines is in the family rooms, and the utterly fabulous knight-, princess- and pirate-themed rooms. Rates include breakfast buffet and park admission.

TOP CHOICE **Legoland Village** HOSTEL **€€**

(☑75 33 27 77; www.legoland-village.dk; Ellehammers Allé; s/d/f low season 595/695/975kr, high season 825/925/1135kr; @ 🤝) Once a regular Danhostel but now tarted up and billed as a 'five-star family hostel', this place is beside the camping ground. It offers bright, large rooms sleeping up to five, all with bathroom, wi-fi, TV and Lego for the kids to play with. You'll need to bring your own linen, or pay extra to hire it (60kr per person). Breakfast is included in the price, and there are guest kitchen facilities. Look for smile-inducing Lego-themed details everywhere, from the key chains to the hooks behind the doors.

Billund FDM Camping CAMPING GROUND, CABINS **€**

(☑75 33 15 21; www.billundcamping.dk; Ellehammers Allé; per adult/child/site 83/45/60kr; @ 🤝) This busy year-round park is loaded to the gills with kid-friendly facilities – play-grounds, petting zoo, mini-golf and even summertime pony rides. The ground is well maintained, including the small but well-equipped chalets (sleeping five, 675kr to 885kr); there's a restaurant on-site (shared with Legoland Village).

Zleep Hotel HOTEL **€**

(☑24 61 06 35; www.zleephotels.com; Billund Airport; d 299-799kr; @ 🤝) If you can do without the frills, bright Zleep (part of an expanding chain) is right by the airport terminal and offers simple, comfy rooms sleeping up to four, all with bathroom and TV. Advance online bookings bring the best rates; breakfast costs an additional 69kr. There's also bike rental here – handy for covering the 2km to Legoland.

Hotel Propellen HOTEL **€€**

(☑75 33 81 33; www.propellen.dk; Nordmarksvej 3; s/d/f 1148/1298/1598kr; @ 🤝 ⛲) Compared to other places in town, Propellen has a grown-up feel, but still caters to families with its indoor pool, playroom and playground. Adults will enjoy the sauna, Jacuzzis and restaurant.

✖ Eating

There are offerings within Legoland and inside Lalandia, and eateries attached to the hotels, or you can head into the township of

---

PLASTIC FANTASTIC

Ever thought that you're only one good idea away from a million big ones? Well, Ole Kirk Christiansen probably didn't, but that's all it took. A carpenter by trade, when business was slow during a Depression-era slump in 1932 he turned his tools to making wooden toys in Billund. Christiansen came up with the business name Lego, a contraction of *leg godt*, meaning 'play well' in Danish (in a beautiful piece of symmetry, it was later realised that *lego* can mean 'I put together' in Latin). What followed was a heart-warming story showing that 'from little things big things grow'. By the late 1940s Lego became the first Danish company to acquire a plastics-injection moulding machine for toy production and began making interlocking plastic blocks called 'binding bricks' – the forerunner of today's Lego blocks.

Every rags to riches story has its tragedy, however, and this one is no exception. In 1960 the wooden-toy warehouse went up in flames. Lego decided to focus production on its plastic toys instead, an idea that proved to be the cornerstone of the company's success. Lego blocks soon became the most popular children's toy in Europe – in 2000 *Fortune* magazine named the Lego brick 'toy of the century'.

If you believe the official literature, on average every person on the planet has 75 Lego bricks – and seven Lego boxes are sold every second (in the lead-up to Christmas that changes to nearly 28 boxes per second!). Even in the age of technology, Lego goes hand in hand with growing up: one foot in front of the other, one block on top of the other. The company (but not the theme park) is still owned by Ole Kirk's descendants; primary concept and development work takes place at the Billund headquarters, where the company employs around 120 designers.

Billund itself, which has a big supermarket, plenty of pizzerias and a few other options.

Within the park there are loads of picnic spots, plus restaurants and outlets selling the usual takeaway fare. The names of these simple eateries – Sandwich Supreme, Donut Bakery, Chicken Delight, Pizza Slice – should cause you no confusion over what they serve. For sit-down fare you can head to the Family Buffet (adult/child 159/88kr) or Pizza & Pasta house (mains 89kr to 149kr), or try the spare ribs at the Saloon. From the park you can also access the Legoland Hotel Restaurant.

Legoland Hotel Restaurant   BUFFET €€€
(☑75 33 12 44; Aastvej 10; mains 150-250kr; ☺lunch & dinner) A large, light-filled place with a comprehensive kids' menu. The buffet lunch (adult/child 198/119kr) and dinner (248/119kr) represent pretty decent value, and kids (adults, too) will love the potatoes shaped like Lego bricks. An à la carte menu is also offered. In high season it can be worth booking a table.

La Famille Café & Bistro   BUFFET €€
(Ellehammers Allé 2; buffet adult/child 168/84kr; ☺dinner) At the camping ground/hostel is this more-economical option with a good-value evening carvery buffet. We also like the 'self-prepared lunchboxes' offered here (adult/child 60/30kr), plus there are takeaway meals.

❶ Information

Legoland Holidays (☑96 23 47 95; www.legolandholidays.dk) Official agency that can organise accommodation packages.

Tourist office (☑79 72 72 99; www.visitbillund.dk; Rådhuscentret 16; ☺9am-3pm Mon-Fri, 10am-2pm Sat) In Billund township, south of Legoland off Grindstedvej.

❶ Getting There & Away

Air

Billund airport (BLL; www.billundairport.dk) sits almost right outside Legoland's gate, serving not only Legoland but most of Jutland. Because of its central location, it has grown into Denmark's second-busiest airport.

There's a comprehensive schedule of direct flights from Billund to various Scandinavian and European cities. Scandi low-cost airline **Cimber Sterling** (www.cimber.com) has a base at Billund and offers flights to Danish holiday destinations such as Mallorca and Malaga, as well as to London (Gatwick) and Dublin. **Ryanair** (www.ryanair.com) connects Billund with Barcelona, Edinburgh, London (Stansted), Milan, Rome and more.

Bus

There's no train service to Billund. If you're travelling by train, the most common route is to get off at Vejle and catch a bus from there. Bus 43 runs between Vejle and Billund airport (61kr, 30 minutes); bus 143 runs a slower route from Vejle and stops at Legoland (61kr, 40 minutes), Billund town centre and the airport.

Buses run up to 10 times daily between Billund and Aarhus (180kr, 1½ hours). Other buses run to the airport from major Jutland towns including Esbjerg, Ribe and Kolding.

Car

Billund is on Rte 28, 59km northeast of Esbjerg and 28km west of Vejle.

The big international car-rental agencies have offices at the airport.

❶ Getting Around

The tourist office arranges bike rental for 80kr per day.

Most local buses stop at Billund town centre, Legoland and the airport. A summertime shuttle bus (July to mid-August) connects the accommodation and attractions of Billund with the town centre and airport.

Randers

POP 60,700

Randers' appeal lies partly in its impressive old town and partly in its most flaunted attraction – a triple-domed zoo that mesmerises families and wildlife-enthusiasts alike. Industrial pursuits are still the heartbeat of the city but there's also history and culture if you know where to look. Randers doesn't feature strongly on the traveller's radar, but if you have the time and an interest in diverse subject matter (from Elvis to tropical animals), it's worth a visit.

◉ Sights & Activities

Randers Regnskov   ZOO
(www.regnskoven.dk; Tørvebryggen 11; adult/child 165/95kr; ☺10am-4pm or 6pm daily) The city's most visited attraction is this dome-enclosed tropical zoo ('*regnskov*' means rainforest), where the temperature is always a humid 20°C to 30°C (dress accordingly). Trails within the sultry domes pass through enclosures housing crocodiles, monkeys, pythons, iguanas, orchids, hibiscus and other rainforest flora and fauna. The South American dome is a standout (the others represent Africa and Asia), as waterfalls and an abundance of wildlife engulf you. It

Randers

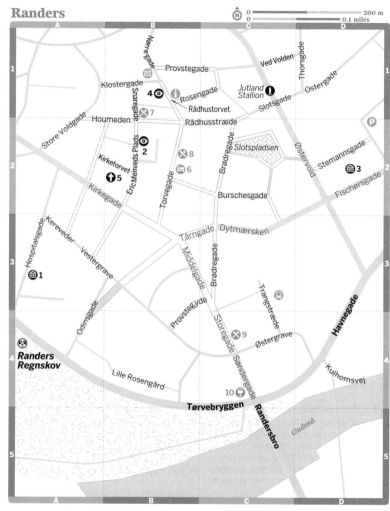

is astounding how well-done this ecosphere is, considering it's on the wrong side of the equator.

Graceland Randers   MUSEUM, ENTERTAINMENT COMPLEX
(www.elvispresley.dk; Graceland Randers Vej 3; ⊙10am-6pm) If everything else sounds too highbrow, 2km southeast of the town centre is the **Elvis Presley Museum** (adult/child 95/65kr), housed in a replica Graceland mansion (double the size of the original) that opened in 2011. True, you don't expect to find a shrine to the King in regional

Denmark, but one mad-keen local fan has proved his dedication in building this showcase for his personal collection of memorabilia (though we think the admission fee is way too steep). Check out the rare photo of a star-struck crown princess (now queen) Margrethe II meeting Elvis in Hollywood in 1960. At the kitschy complex there's an Elvis shop, American diner and mini movie theatre. Thankyouverymuch.

Danish Design Museum   MUSEUM
(Hospitalsgade 13; adult/child 50kr/free; ⊙11am-4pm Thu-Sun) In no way connected to Copen-

Randers

◎ Top Sights
Randers Regnskov A4

◎ Sights
1 Danish Design Museum A3
2 Helligåndshuset....................................B2
3 Kulturhuset..D2
   Museum Østjylland.....................(see 3)
4 Paaskesønnernes Gård......................B1
5 Sankt Mortens Kirke...........................B2

🛏 Sleeping
6 Hotel Randers B2

🍴 Eating
7 Café Borgen B1
8 Café Mathisen......................................B2
9 Niels Ebbesens Spisehus...................C4

🍸 Drinking
10 Tante Olga..C4

hagen's fine showcases, this small museum exhibits one local's eclectic personal collection. There are old stereos, lamps, posters, ceramics and scooters; the highlight is the collection of Kay Bojesen–designed wooden toys.

Historic Buildings   HISTORIC NEIGHBOURHOOD
By far the most interesting part of Randers is its central area, a real hotchpotch of architecture with some antique gems alongside more-modern eyesores. Hunt down the pearls, and the stories behind them, with the *Star Route* brochure, free from the tourist office. It outlines a self-guided tour around town, highlighting the likes of the late 15th-century **Paaskesønnernes Gård** (Rådhustorvet 7); **Helligåndshuset** (Eric Menveds Plads), once part of a medieval monastery; and the imposing red medieval **Sankt Mortens Kirke** (Kirketorvet).

FREE **Kulturhuset**   MUSEUM
(Stemannsgade 2) The modern Kulturhuset houses the town's library alongside **Museum Østjylland** (☺10am-4pm Tue-Sun), which comprises two sections, one dedicated to cultural history, the other to art. There's a good collection of Danish artworks from 1800 to the present – the *Cosmic Room* glass installation by Faroese artist Tróndur Patursson is well worth checking out.

🛏 Sleeping

There's not a great deal of accommodation in town; many families visit Randers Regnskov from nearby holiday hot spots such as Djursland. The tourist office can arrange accommodation in private homes.

TOP CHOICE **Hotel Randers**   HOTEL €€
(☑86 42 34 22; www.hotel-randers.dk; Torvegade 11; s/d/ste from 795/975/1375kr; 🐾) This is an old-world, art deco treasure. It was built in 1856, refurbished in the 1920s and has retained its unique style thanks to the owner, one 80-something Fru Mathisen who lives at the hotel Howard Hughes–style. The decor is rich and individualised – if you can afford to upgrade to an 'antique room' you can live the high life for a night.

Danhostel Randers   HOSTEL €
(☑86 42 50 44; www.danhostelranders.dk; Gethersvej 1; dm from 196kr, s/d without bathroom 378/428kr, with bathroom 515/540kr; @🐾) A cheerful, modern spot on the edge of a park, 12 minutes' walk northwest of the town centre. There are rooms with and without bathroom, plus the necessities (laundry, kitchen) and the added extras (pool table, table tennis).

Hotel Kronjylland   HOTEL €€
(☑86 41 43 33; www.hotelkronjylland.dk; Vestergade 51; d weekday/weekend from 749/1079kr; @🐾) This smart hotel close to the train station (a 10-minute walk west of town) caters to both business folk and holidaymakers. The crisp decor and efficient service are impressive; rates vary according to room standard and demand.

🍴 Eating & Drinking

Café Borgen   CAFE €
(Houmeden 10; light meals 39-67kr; ☺brunch, lunch & dinner) Offers a little slice of Euro-life, with Parisian-style outdoor seating and a low-lit interior. Home to rich coffee and lazy lunches, it then morphs into an inviting spot for late-night drinks.

Café Mathisen   INTERNATIONAL €€
(Torvegade 11; lunch 75-128kr, dinner mains 145-258kr; ☺lunch & dinner Mon-Sat) Part of the delightful Hotel Randers, the Mathisen has elegant black-and-white decor that brings to mind the art deco era. Lunch offerings are light and simple, and it's not too fancy to put a burger next to braised veal with truffle on the dinner menu.

Niels Ebbesens
Spisehus
TRADITIONAL DANISH €€

(Storegade 13; lunch 59-109kr, dinner mains 179-259kr; ⊘lunch & dinner) You can't miss this photogenic restaurant – red, three-storey and half-timbered, built in 1643. As befits the history-filled building, the restaurant's menu is Danish food at its most traditional – lunch on herring, or go for *peberbøf* (pepper steak) or *svinemørbrad* (pork tenderloins).

Tante Olga
BAR

(Søndergade 6; ⊘Thu-Sat night) This club-bar is an institution in town – live music, stand-up comedy, beer- and/or whisky-tasting, jazz nights and plenty of local colour. Head along to see what's happening.

❶ Information

The train station is west of the city centre. It's a 12-minute walk from there via Vestergade to Rådhustorvet, the central square.

Tourist office (☑86 42 44 77; www.visitrand ers.com; Rådhustorvet 4; ⊘10am-5pm Mon-Fri, 10am-2pm Sat Apr-Oct, 10am-5pm Mon-Fri Nov-Mar) Has plenty of good local information; offers bike hire.

❶ Getting There & Around

Randers is 76km south of Aalborg and 36km north of Aarhus on the E45, and 41km east of Viborg on Rte 16. All trains between Aarhus (60kr, 30 minutes) and Aalborg (100kr, 50 minutes) stop here, at the station on Jernbanegade, just west of the city centre. The bus terminal is off Dytmærsken.

Hobro

POP 11,500

Hobro's biggest asset is Fyrkat, a recently discovered 10th-century Viking ring fortress. The town itself is pleasant enough, lying at the mouth of the Mariager Fjord, but there's little historical and visual enchantment due to the town's history of fires. Nowadays Hobro primarily acts as a service town to the surrounding farms.

◎ Sights

Fyrkat
VIKING SITE

(Fyrkatvej; adult/child incl entry to Vikingecenter Fyrkat 60kr/free; ⊘noon-5pm May-Sep) Although it's smaller than the better-known Trelleborg in Southern Zealand, the 1000-year-old Fyrkat fortress south of Hobro so closely resembles Trelleborg that both are presumed to have been built by the Viking king mastermind Harald Bluetooth around 980.

When archaeologists discovered the fortress in 1950 they realised its importance and excavated the area over the following decade. Fyrkat was found to be a military stronghold used to monitor 'traffic' movement throughout Jutland. Evidence indicates that 800 Vikings and their families lived within the fort; the site is thought to have been abandoned when it was destroyed by fire just after its completion.

Today, as you walk out onto the grass-covered circular ramparts, you can almost envisage the Viking warriors roaming the fortress. Absorb the fort's impressive symmetrical design and marvel at the four cuts in its earthen walls, formerly imposing gates that faced the four points of the compass. Within the rampart walls the fortress was divided into four quadrants, each with a central courtyard surrounded by four symmetrical buildings, which housed the inhabitants of Fyrkat. Stone foundation blocks show the outline of these elongated buildings. Cows grazing in the fields add a timeless backdrop to it all.

Although no structures remain standing in the ramparts, just outside is a replica Viking house built of oak timbers utilising a stave-style construction technique. At the entrance to Fyrkat there are some period farm buildings, including a 200-year-old working water mill.

Fyrkat is 3km southwest of Hobro's town centre via Fyrkatvej; a taxi ride from the train station costs about 100kr. If the weather is good, stop at the Vikingecenter Fyrkat and walk the last kilometre to the fortress site. There is no bus service.

Vikingecenter Fyrkat
VIKING OPEN-AIR MUSEUM

(Fyrkatvej; adult/child incl entry to Fyrkat 60kr/free; ⊘10am-4pm May, 10am-5pm Jun-Aug, 10am-3pm Sep) Complementing Fyrkat fortress is a Viking-style farmstead 1km north along Fyrkatvej. Archaeologists believe such farms existed around the fortress walls, supplying encamped Vikings with fresh produce.

The complex took more than a decade to erect, using only materials and tools authentic to the period; the 33m longhouse is particularly impressive. Costumed interpreters provide demonstrations of silverwork, archery, breadmaking, music and other Viking crafts. Many of these folk are volunteers who come to Fyrkat every year for a week or so to live as the Vikings did:

sleeping in the longhouse, mastering the crafts etc. They'll be happy to answer any questions you might have.

Hobro Museum MUSEUM
(Vestergade 21; adult/child 30kr/free; ⊙noon-5pm May-Sep) Round out your trip by checking out some excavated items of interest from Fyrkat and a detailed history of Hobro at the Hobro Museum, in an 1821 merchant's house.

Festivals & Events

Fyrkatspillet CULTURAL
(www.fyrkatspillet.dk, in Danish) Fyrkat annually hosts a play put on by a local amateur theatre troupe, Fyrkatspillet, over a two-week period in late May/early June. Although performed in Danish, the general theme is easy to follow (sword-wielding Viking warriors, damsels, conflicts and resolutions). Enquire after tickets with the Hobro tourist office or check the troupe's website.

Sleeping & Eating

The tourist office has a list of rooms in private homes.

Hotel Amerika HOTEL €€
(☎98 54 42 00; www.hotelamerika.dk; Amerikavej 48; s/d from 825/1075kr; @🛜) This hotel feels like a country retreat, thanks to its forest location and spacious grounds. The rooms are classically furnished and equipped with all the necessities. The restaurant is equally refined. It's 2.5km east of town.

Danhostel Hobro HOSTEL €
(☎98 52 18 47; www.danhostelhobro.dk; Amerikavej 24; dm/s/d 200/375/450kr; @) A large modern hostel often bustling with school groups; all rooms have bathrooms. It's about 1.5km east of town.

Restaurant Bies Bryghus DANISH, MICROBREWERY €
(Adelgade 26; lunch 88-124kr, dinner mains 148-218kr; ⊙lunch & dinner Tue-Sun) In a cobbled courtyard tucked off the main pedestrian street, this old brewery (founded 1841) has been reborn as a bright microbrewery-restaurant serving up hearty treats, from lunchtime smørrebrød to evening steaks with Béarnaise sauce, with its beers.

Information

The train station lies on the western edge of the town. To reach the centre walk 1km east along Jernbanegade, using the church tower as your central reference. The pedestrian street, Adelgade, is home to banks, supermarkets and assorted services.

Tourist office (☎70 27 13 77; www.visitmariagerfjord.dk; Søndre Kajgade 10; ⊙daily Jun-Aug, reduced hours rest of year) At the small, sweet harbour, with cafes as neighbours. Offers bike rental (good for reaching Fyrkat).

Getting There & Away

Rte 180 runs straight through Hobro, connecting it with Randers 27km to the southeast, and Aalborg 49km to the north. The speedier E45 runs along the outskirts of Hobro, connecting with the same cities.

Hobro is on the main Frederikshavn–Aarhus railway line. Trains run about twice hourly to Randers (40kr, 15 minutes) and Aalborg (81kr, 40 minutes).

Rebild Bakker & Rold Skov

The heart-warming story of Rebild Bakker (the Rebild Hills) dates back to 1912, when a group of Danish-Americans presented 200 hectares of (previously privately owned) forest to the Danish government on the proviso that it would remain in a natural state, be open to all visitors and be accessible to Danish-Americans for the celebration of US holidays.

This act of goodwill inspired the Danish forest service to acquire adjacent woodland and collectively the 80-sq-km area is now known as **Rold Skov** (Rold Forest; Denmark's largest). The area has good walks (and mountain-biking trails) that take you through rolling heather-covered hills, while its woods contain European aspen, beech and oak trees.

Sights

Lincoln Log Cabin MUSEUM
(adult/child 20kr/free; ⊙daily Jun-Aug) Modelled on the log cabin that US president Abraham Lincoln grew up in, this cabin contains bits of Americana as seen through Danish eyes, plus displays on Danish emigration to the USA. It's just west of the car park at the start of the park's trails.

Spillemandsmuseet MUSEUM
(Fiddlers' Museum; adult/child 25kr/free; ⊙daily May-Sep, Sun Oct-Apr) At the far end of the car park, this simple regional museum focuses on some quirky aspects of country life: guns and traps, and fiddles and folk music.

🏃 Activities

Walking

There are numerous walking trails criss-crossing the park. One pleasant 4km route begins in a sheep meadow west of the car park. It goes past Tophuset, a small century-old thatched house that was built by the first caretakers; the Lincoln Log Cabin; a large glacial boulder called Cimbrerstenen, sculpted in the form of a Cimbrian bull's head by Anders Bundgaard; a hollow where the 4 July celebrations are held; and Sønderland, the park's highest hill (102m). It's a particularly lovely area in summer and autumn, when the heather adds a purple tinge to the hillsides.

Mountain Biking

No, your eyes don't deceive you – these mountains (of sorts) are a magnet for mountain-bikers, and there are 23km of bike tracks throughout the park. See Getting Around for bike rentals.

🎉 Festivals & Events

The **Rebild Festival** (www.rebildfesten.dk) is an annual 4 July celebration (held since 1912) that is the biggest outside the USA. Singing, dancing, country music and US guest-speakers are in abundance. The festival's popularity has waned over the decades, particularly among the younger generation, and attendances have dropped from one-time highs of 10,000 to around 4000. International guests tend to stay in Aalborg.

🛏️ Sleeping & Eating

Rebild Bakker is a pretty sleepy, albeit scenic, place. Unless there's a festival in full swing, this is more a place for a day trip and a picnic. Still, if you're keen to stay overnight, there are decent options.

Danhostel Rebild   HOSTEL €
(☑98 39 13 40; www.danhostel.dk/rebild; Rebildvej 23; dm/s/d 250/395/450kr; @🛜) Supremely photogenic underneath its thatched roof, this hostel is of a typically high standard. Rooms are in an annexe behind the old main building and all have their own bathroom; staff can help arrange bike hire.

Rold StorKro   HOTEL €€
(☑98 37 51 00; www.rold.dk; Vaelderskoven 13; hikers s/d 395/495kr, standard s/d 895/1095kr; @🛜🏊) Some 2km past the park entrance, off Rte 180 to Hobro, is this classic inn. Accommodation includes simple 'hikers' rooms' with shared bathroom, or regular modernised rooms (pretty pricey). Facilities are good, including an indoor swimming pool and large minigolf course. The best feature is the **Panorama Restaurant** (lunch 55-155kr; dinner mains 158-235kr), which offers a forested outlook and a traditional menu – fresh and smoked venison (farmed on the property) is the house speciality.

ℹ️ Information

Tourist office (☑99 88 90 00; www.visit rebild.dk; KulturStationen, Sverriggårdsvej 4; ⊙9am-4pm Mon-Fri, 9am-noon Sat) Superhelpful office opposite the train station at Skørping, 3km east of Rebild Bakker. It has loads of info and maps of the area and makes a good first port of call. Note that there are plans to move the tourist office to a new facility closer to the park itself, possibly in 2013.

ℹ️ Getting There & Away

Rte 180 runs through the Rold Skov forest, connecting Rebild Bakker with Hobro, 23km to the south.

Trains running between Aalborg (54kr, 25 minutes) and Aarhus (144kr, 1¼ hours) stop in Skørping, from where it's 3km west to Rebild Bakker. Bus 104 runs between Skørping and Rebild Bakker (18kr) hourly on weekdays, less often at weekends. By train you can also easily reach nearby towns such as Hobro (36kr, 20 minutes) and Randers (71kr, 40 minutes).

ℹ️ Getting Around

Rold Skov Cykler (☑98 39 11 72; Jyllandsgade 23) Bikes and info on mountain biking can be arranged at Rold Skov Cykler in Skørping; city/ mountain bikes cost 150/250kr per day.

Viborg

POP 35,900

Rich in religious history and bordering two idyllic lakes, Viborg is a superbly romantic getaway. During its holiest period (just prior to the Reformation), 25 churches lined the streets. Nowadays, however, only two can be found in the town centre. The Viborg cathedral is part of a charming old centre perfect for wandering.

👁️ Sights & Activities

Viborg Domkirke   CATHEDRAL
(Sankt Mogens Gade 4; admission by donation; ⊙11am-4pm Mon-Sat, noon-4pm Sun Apr-Sep, closes 3pm Oct-Mar) The striking, twin-towered Viborg Domkirke is equally impressive in-

side and out, with exquisite **frescoes** painted over five years (1908–13) by artist Joakim Skovgaard evocatively portraying the story of the Protestant bible. In 1876 the cathedral was almost entirely rebuilt, becoming the largest granite church in Scandinavia, an enduring claim to fame. The crypt is all that survives from its birth date, 1100.

Of the paintings inside, two are especially notable: God creating women (on the left as you enter), and the 12 Apostles and four evangelists with St Paul replacing Judas (the centrepiece on the roof). There is a 10kr booklet for sale at the church that details the biblical story behind each of the 51 paintings and is a worthwhile investment. The impressive exterior features the massive walls and semicircular arches common to Norman-style buildings. You can climb the south tower (free) during the church's opening hours to enjoy scenic town views.

Skovgaard Museet   ART MUSEUM
(www.skovgaardmuseet.dk; Domkirkestræde 4; adult/child 50kr/free; ⊙10am-5pm Tue-Sun Jun-Aug, 11am-4pm Tue-Sun Sep-May) Just outside the cathedral, this art museum highlights further work of cathedral-artist Joakim Skovgaard, among other artists and changing exhibitions.

Historic Quarter   HISTORIC NEIGHBOURHOOD
The old part of town lies just to the north and west of the cathedral; the tourist office has excellent printouts, including English-language versions, which describe walks around the town with historical and cultural themes. **Sankt Mogens Gade** has a charming pocket of homes from the mid-16th century, including Den Hauchske Gård at No 7, Villadsens Gård at No 9A, and Den Gamle Præstegård at No 11.

Viborg Stiftsmuseum   MUSEUM
(Hjultorvet 4; adult/child 40kr/free; ⊙11am-5pm Tue-Sun mid-Jun–Aug, 1-4pm Tue-Fri, 11am-5pm Sat & Sun Sep–mid-Jun) This local history museum tells the story of Viborg's rich religious past.

Margrethe I   BOAT TRIPS
(adult/child 50/30kr; ⊙2pm mid-May–Aug) Jump on board the *Margrethe I* in summer for a one-hour cruise on and soak up the sun – and Viborg – from out on the lakes. There are additional tours from mid-June; the boat departs from outside Golf Salonen on Randersvej. From mid-May to September, you can also rent canoes and rowboats from the park kiosk for lake exploration (45/70kr for 30/60 minutes).

🛏 Sleeping

🔝 **Niels Bugges Hotel**   BOUTIQUE HOTEL €€
(☎86 63 80 11; www.nielsbuggeskro.dk; Egeskovvej 26, Hald Ege; s/d without bathroom 570/790kr, d/ste with bathroom 1250/1450kr; 🅿) We adore this place, an old inn set amid forest on the outskirts of town (take Rte 13 south, then Rte 12 west and take the first road on your right). It's a real destination hotel, where design and cuisine are taken seriously and the result is something special. Rooms are superbly decorated in farmhouse chic, all florals, patchworks and antiques; and the library, outdoor areas and sky-blue on-site restaurant, Skov (meaning 'forest'), had us begging to either move in or recruit their decorator.

The owners also have the nearby, lakeside **Niels Bugges Kro** (Ravnsbjergvej 69, Dollerup), an inn with a more traditional restaurant, plus an annexe in the countryside with yet more beautiful accommodation. Bus 53 runs out this way.

Oasen Viborg   BOUTIQUE HOTEL €€
(☎86 62 14 25; www.oasenviborg.dk; Nørregade 13; s/d 350/500kr, with private bathroom 450/650kr; 🅿) Oasen is an inviting complex of central rooms and apartments, beautifully bridging the gap between hostels and pricey business hotels. Some rooms have shared bathroom, but all have cable TV and free wi-fi, plus kitchen access. Breakfast (75kr) is taken in a sweet little 'cafe' in the garden.

Danhostel Viborg   HOSTEL €
(☎86 67 17 81; www.danhostel.dk/viborg; Vinkelvej 36; dm 150kr, d with/without bathroom 460/390kr; ⊙mid-Jan–Nov; @🅿) This well-run place feels like a country escape, 3km from town in green surrounds and backed by botanic gardens down to the lakeshore. Take a walk or enjoy the table tennis and giant chess set in the garden. Rooms are top-notch, too (most with bathroom). Local bus 5 runs out here but stops short of the hostel. Note that the town's camping ground is next door.

🍴 Eating

Café Morville   INTERNATIONAL €€
(Hjultorvet; mains 65-185kr; ⊙brunch, lunch & dinner Mon-Sat, lunch Sun) One of those chic all-day cafes that seem compulsory in Danish towns. You can park yourself on the leather banquettes for a mid-morning coffee or late-night drink and everything in between, from brunch plates to burgers.

Brygger Bauers Grotter INTERNATIONAL €€€

(Sankt Mathias Gade 61; lunch 69-145kr, dinner mains 205-285kr; ⊗lunch & dinner Tue-Sat) Follow the candlelit passageway for a polished dining experience inside vaulted 'cave rooms' that date back more than 100 years. The atmosphere comes at a premium – lunch on the terrace is cheaper and more casual. You can also enter from Domkirkestræde, behind the cathedral.

Tortilla Flats MEXICAN €€

(Sankt Mikkelsgade 2; mains 95-140kr; ⊗dinner Tue-Sun) A fun place with California-leaning Mexican options, including menu joy for vegetarians.

🛈 Information

The post office, banks and other services can be found on Sankt Mathias Gade.

Tourist office (☑87 87 88 88; www.visitviborg. dk; Nytorv 9; ⊗9am-5pm Mon-Fri, 9am-2pm Sat Jun-Aug, reduced hours rest of year, closed Sat Nov-Feb) Clued up on the area, with good brochures and maps. Also offers bike hire (100kr per day).

🛈 Getting There & Away

Viborg is 66km northwest of Aarhus on Rte 26 and 41km west of Randers on Rte 16. Trains to/from Aarhus (124kr, 1¼ hours) run half-hourly on weekdays, less frequently at weekends. The train station is about 1km southwest of the tourist office.

CENTRAL WEST COAST

The sweeping, windswept coastline of the central west is dotted with an array of summer towns catering primarily to German summer tourists. The coast's most flaunted area is Holmsland Klit, the thin neck of sand and dunes stretching nearly 35km from north to south and separating the North Sea from Ringkøbing Fjord. Windsurfers flock to Hvide Sande as its reputation for the best wind conditions in Denmark spreads.

Hvide Sande

POP 3200

Hvide Sande (the name means 'white sands') owes its existence to the wind. Wind caused the sand migration that forced the construction of a lock here in 1931 to assure a North Sea passage for the port of Ringkøbing. And wind continues to be the big drawcard for the large number of tourists who come here for windsurfing.

Aside from the wind, it's all about the fish. Hvide Sande has a busy deep-sea fishing harbour, with trawlers, fish-processing factories and an early-morning fish auction. There's also a small fishing museum/aquarium adjacent to the tourist office. Ask at the tourist office about fishing trips with local anglers, and the fish auctions (held weekly in summer for tourists).

🏃 Activities

Westwind WINDSURFING, KITESURFING

(☑97 31 25 99; www.westwind.dk, in Danish; ⊗May-Oct) A consistent, howling westerly coupled with both an invitingly safe lake in Ringkøbing Fjord and the wild North Sea around Hvide Sande make this area ideal for windsurfers of all skill levels.

Westwind has two bases on the outskirts of Hvide Sande (one in the north, the other just south). The company offers instruction (in English, German or Danish) in surfing, windsurfing, kitesurfing and stand-up paddle surfing, plus gear rental, including kayaks. A three-hour introductory windsurfing course costs 400kr; a nine-hour course (in three three-hour blocks) costs 995kr – and they guarantee you can windsurf after those nine hours. A two-hour introduction to kitesurfing/stand-up paddle surfing costs 290/350kr.

Kabel Park WATERSKIING, WAKEBOARDING

(☑30 29 26 26; www.kabelpark.dk; Gytjevej; ⊗mid-Apr–Oct) Next to the northern branch of Westwind (in what's labelled the 'Aqua Sports Zone') is this entertaining place, where waterskiers and wakeboarders are pulled by cable rope-tow along an 800m-long course, complete with jump-ramps for the experienced. If you're keen to get involved there's a two-hour intro course for novices (395kr), otherwise one/two hours on the course costs 270/370kr, including wetsuit and skis or wakeboard. It's also pretty cool to watch the antics – there's a cafe here for that purpose.

Vinterlejegaard Ridecenter HORSE RIDING

(☑75 28 22 77; www.vinterlejegaard.dk, in Danish; Vesterledvej 9) Hvide Sande is perfect for glorious rides at sunrise and as the sun sets over the water (well, providing it's not *too* windy). Contact this riding centre for details; it's about 8km south of Hvide Sande and offers one-hour beach rides for beginners to experienced rides for 175kr.

🛏 Sleeping

The tourist office rents out a number of sexy state-of-the-art houseboats, as well as summer cottages and rooms in private homes (the houseboats and cottages are generally rented by the week in summer).

Danhostel Hvide Sande   HOSTEL €
(☑97 31 21 05; www.hvidesande.dk/danhostel; Numitvej 5; dm 130kr, s/d without bathroom 250/300kr, with bathroom 380/395kr; ⊙Feb–mid-Dec; @🐼) Tucked away from the madness in a side street on the northern side of the channel, this typically high-quality hostel offers clean, no-frills rooms (many with bathroom) and access to the nearby sports centre with which it's affiliated.

Hvide Sande Sømandshjem & Hotel   HOTEL €€
(☑97 31 10 33; www.hssh.dk; Bredgade 5; s/d/f 745/945/1145kr; @🐼) The only hotel in town has lovely fresh rooms in an old seamen's home down at the bustling harbour. There's a well-priced on-site cafeteria.

Hvide Sande Camping   CAMPING GROUND, CABINS €
(☑97 31 12 18; www.hvidesandecamping.dk, in Danish; Karen Brandsvej 70; per adult/child/site 74/40/40kr; ⊙Apr-Oct) If you're here for the windsurfing, this is the camping ground for you. It's on the southern side of town, across the road from the Westwind operation, and offers good facilities including cabins and bike hire.

🍴 Eating

Down at the harbour there's a supermarket and no shortage of cafes, ice-creameries and bakeries competing for holidaymakers' appetites.

Edgar Madsen   SEAFOOD €
(Metheasvej 11) A proud and long-standing purveyor of all things fishy. Build your own picnic – fish-filled bread rolls sell for a bargain 30kr.

Restaurant Under Broen   SEAFOOD €€
(1 fl, Toldbodgade 20; lunch 78-138kr, dinner mains 118-218kr; ⊙lunch & dinner) Given the prime harbourside location of this elegant dining room, and the fishing boats moored just metres away, it doesn't take a brainiac to know the menu will feature superfresh fish options. The downstairs Cafe Marina has simpler fare at cheaper prices.

ℹ Information

Tourist office (☑70 22 70 01; www.visitvest.dk; Nørregade 2; ⊙9am-5pm Mon-Fri, 10am-2pm Sat & Sun) On the northern side of the channel.

ℹ Getting There & Away

Hvide Sande is on Rte 181. Bus 58 runs between Hvide Sande and Ringkøbing station (34kr, 30 minutes) roughly hourly on weekdays, less frequently at weekends.

Ringkøbing
POP 9700

Pretty, fjordside Ringkøbing is a pleasant, if unremarkable, place acting as a service centre for the surrounding beachside communities. It nurtures the strongest hold on the past of any town on the central west coast, and makes a decent base if you're interested in more than just beach-going.

Ringkøbing was once a prominent North Sea port, until shifting sands caused the mouth of the fjord to slowly migrate south and threatened to cut off the town's lifeline

CENTRAL JUTLAND RINGKØBING

ACTION HOLIDAY HOT SPOTS

In the market for a destination that allows for more than just strolling and window-shopping? Here are our picks for Jutland's best places to enjoy an adventure holiday.

» **Lake District** (p238) – for superb canoeing down the Gudenå

» **Hvide Sande** (p256) – feel the wind in your hair, and in your windsurfing or kitesurfing sails

» **Klitmøller** (p280) – water-based activities that take advantage of the raging winds (surfing and windsurfing)

» **Rebild Bakker** (p253) – walking and mountain-biking (yes, you read that right, mountains!) in Denmark's largest forest

» **Rømø** (p207) – create new land-speed records on kitebuggies and blokarts

to the sea. In 1931 the town acquired a constant North Sea passage when a lock was built at Hvide Sande. Today the port is not a big player in exports, and the town is surrounded by industry, namely windmills.

Sights

Historic Buildings
HISTORIC BUILDINGS

From the tourist office, pick up the English-language brochure detailing the town's historic buildings. Hotel Ringkjøbing, right by the tourist office, has a timber-framed wing dating from 1601; the church northwest of the hotel dates from medieval times and has a sundial from 1728 on its western buttress. The marina is another good spot for aimless wandering, where old fishermen's huts contrast with modern development; to reach it, head down Vestre Strandgade from Torvet.

Ringkøbing Museum
MUSEUM

(Herningvej 4; adult/child 40kr/free; ⊙11am-5pm Mon-Fri, 10am-1pm Sat Jul & Aug, reduced hours rest of year) The most interesting exhibitions at this museum, east of Torvet, feature displays on the ill-fated Greenland expedition (1906–08) led by local explorer Ludvig Mylius-Erichsen.

Sleeping

Campers should head 9km west to the camping grounds around Søndervig on Rte 181.

Danhostel Ringkøbing
HOSTEL €

(☎97 32 24 55; www.rofi.dk; Kirkevej 28; dm 200kr, s/d 350/400kr, with private bathroom 425/475kr; @🖥🛜) This is up there with the best of them – it has a great socialising/relaxing area, a modern layout, activities in abundance (it's in a sports centre), and large, light-filled rooms (most with bathroom and TV). Families will love the on-site bowling alley, playground and mini-golf. The drawback: the hostel is neither terribly easy to find, nor accessible by local bus. It's 1.5km northeast of the train station, via Holstebrovej.

Hotel Ringkjøbing
HOTEL €€

(☎97 32 00 11; www.hotel-ringkobing.dk; Torvet 18; s/d 950/1095kr; 🛜) Dating to 1601 and located in a prime position on the main square, this hotel has loads of yesteryear charm. The rooms (above the restaurant and in a couple of neighbouring buildings) are a mixed bag in terms of decor and appeal, so ask to see a couple.

Eating

Café & Restaurant Kræs
DANISH €€

(Ved Fjorden 2B; lunch 72-165kr, dinner mains 155-245kr; ⊙lunch & dinner Mon-Sat) As well as a boutique that sells wine, coffee and chocolates, this handsome modern restaurant at the marina has a small but well-crafted menu featuring plenty of local specialities (lots of fish). Try the lunchtime *fiskefrikadeller* or savoury pancakes. If the menu here doesn't hold much appeal, there are good alternatives in the neighbourhood.

The Watchman's Pub
TRADITIONAL DANISH €€

(Torvet 18; lunch 79-129kr, dinner mains 139-199kr; ⊙lunch & dinner) This cosy restaurant, in Hotel Ringkjøbing, is great for people-watching from its alfresco tables on Torvet, plus it has a comprehensive menu of old-school Danish favourites, from herring platters to fried plaice by way of *fiskefrikadeller*.

Information

Tourist office (☎70 22 70 01; www.visitvest. dk; Torvet; ⊙10am-5pm Mon-Fri, 9.30am-1pm Sat) Centrally placed; can help arrange local accommodation, from rooms to beach houses.

Getting There & Around

Ringkøbing is on Rte 15, 46km west of Herning and 9km east of the North Sea. By rail it's between Esbjerg (100kr, 1¾ hours) and Struer (61kr, one hour).

Bus 58 runs to Hvide Sande from Ringkøbing station (34kr, 30 minutes) about hourly on weekdays, less frequently at weekends.

Northern Jutland

Includes »

Best Places to Eat

» Klitmøller Røgeri (p280)

» Mortens Kro (p264)

» Jensens Fiskerestaurant (p270)

» Skagens Museum Cafe (p274)

» Ruths Hotel (p274)

Best Places to Stay

» Villa Vendel (p278)

» Villa Rosa (p264)

» Aahøj (p270)

» Badepension Marienlund (p273)

Why Go?

Northern Jutland, split from the rest of Jutland by the Limfjord, will enthral you with its magnificent light, and intimidate and beautiful barren landscapes of shifting sands. The region is promoted as 'Lysets Land', or the Land of Light, and if you witness the soft blue nuances by the water as day turns into night, you'll understand how the name came about (and begin to comprehend the region's appeal to artists).

But it's not just painters who flock here. Windsurfers and beach-goers make a beeline for the north the minute the weather turns kind. Families head off to the zoos, aquariums and funparks, and seafood-lovers rejoice in the fresh-off-the-boat catch.

The area's most coveted tourist destination is Skagen, at Denmark's northern tip. It's both a civilised place of chichi restaurants and art museums, and a wild place where nature calls the shots – which sums up the entire region, really.

When to Go

Summer is prime time to visit the north. The beaches, theme parks, festivals and activities are in full swing in July and August, when accommodation prices hit their peak.

That said, Aalborg has year-round attractions, and there's some appeal to the notion of rugging up and braving the cooler weather someplace such as Skagen, where you can admire the turbulent tides and shifting sands without the summer crowds and high-season prices. Winter is better for the Danish art of *hygge* (cosiness), after all.

Aalborg

POP 103,600

Things are on the way up for Aalborg, Denmark's fourth-largest city. It sits at the narrowest point of the Limfjord (the long body of water that slices Jutland in two), and recent developments have seen the waterfront become the focal point of the town. A concerted effort has been made to rejuvenate the central industrial areas and turn neglected spaces into something far more appealing, and authorities are wooing tourists with free city bikes and a free summertime city-circle bus.

Traditionally Aalborg has flown under the traveller's radar, but that could easily change. There are enough low-key diversions here to occupy a few days for most visitors, from architecture fans to families, party animals to history boffins.

Sights & Activities

Utzon Center   ARCHITECTURE
(www.utzoncenter.dk; Slotspladsen 4; adult/child 60kr/free; ⊙10am-5pm Tue-Sun) An impressive 700-sq-metre design and architecture space, the Utzon Center, with its distinctive silver roofscape, sits pretty on the waterfront. It bills itself as 'a dynamic and experimental centre of culture and knowledge' and is the last building designed by celebrated Danish architect, Jørn Utzon (1918–2008). Utzon famously designed the Sydney Opera House; he grew up in Aalborg and died shortly after the eponymous centre was finished. It hosts a changing program of exhibitions on architecture, design and art; there's also a high-quality restaurant here. Note that a ticket allows free same-day entrance to Kunsten art museum.

Waterfront   LANDMARK
The Aalborg waterfront promenade, between Limfjordsbroen and the Utzon Center, is a good example of urban regeneration, taking what was a scruffy dockside area and opening it up to locals. Here you'll find restaurants, a park, playground, basketball courts and moored boats (including an old ice-breaker) serving as restaurants and bars. One of the nicest features is the brand-new

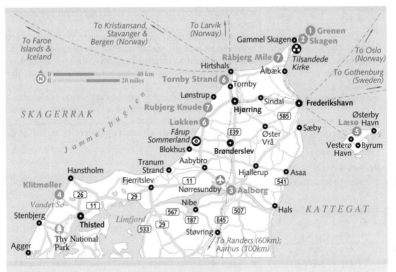

Northern Jutland Highlights

❶ Stand in the meeting place of two seas at Denmark's northernmost point, **Grenen** (p271)

❷ Find inspiration in the treasured artworks of **Skagens Museum** (p271)

❸ Discover the new, improved appeal of **Aalborg** (p260)

❹ Let the wind take you places at **Klitmøller** (p280)

❺ Step back in time on low-key **Læsø** (p269)

❻ Loll about on lovely **Løkken beach** (p278) or **Tornby Strand** (p276)

❼ Play amid Mother Nature's sandcastles at **Rubjerg Knude** (p279) and **Råbjerg Mile** (p275)

Aalborg Havnebad (⊙10am-6pm Jul-Aug), the outdoor pool that enables you to take a dip in the Limfjord.

The mid-16th-century **Aalborghus Slot** (Slotspladsen), nearby, is more an administrative office than a castle but there's a small **dungeon** (admission free; ⊙8am-3pm Mon-Fri May-Oct) you can visit.

Nordkraft   CULTURAL CENTRE
(www.nordkraft.dk; Kjellerups Torv) Another new development in Aalborg, this power station–turned–cultural centre is home to a theatre, concert hall, art-house cinema, art gallery, fitness centre, plus a couple of eateries. It's big and well done but still finding its feet – there's ongoing development in the area to revitalise this once-neglected part of town. The tourist office is here, so it's worth popping in to see what's happening.

Budolfi Domkirke   CATHEDRAL
(Algade 40; ⊙9am-4pm Mon-Fri, to 2pm Sat Jun-Aug, 9am-3pm Mon-Fri, to noon Sat Sep-May) This 12th-century cathedral marks the centre of the old town and its elegant carillon can be heard every hour, on the hour. Its white-washed interior creates an almost Mediterranean ambience.

As you enter the cathedral from Algade, look up at the foyer ceiling to see colourful frescoes from around 1500. The interior boasts some beautifully carved items, including a gilded baroque altar and a richly detailed pulpit. Look out for free summer concerts in the cathedral.

Aalborg Historiske Museum   MUSEUM
(Algade 48; adult/child 30kr/free, free Tue; ⊙10am-5pm Tue-Sun) A block west of Budolfi Domkirke is the Aalborg history museum, with artefacts from prehistory to the present and furnishings and interiors that hint at the wealth Aalborg's merchants enjoyed during the Renaissance.

Gråbrødrekloster Museet   MUSEUM
(Algade 19; ⊙10am-5pm Tue-Sun) This underground museum allows you to step off one of Aalborg's busiest shopping streets to explore the life of a Franciscan friary in medieval times. Entry is via an elevator outside Salling department store on Algade; the museum is free to enter, but you pay to ride the elevator (30kr).

Helligåndsklostret   MONASTERY
(CW Obels Plads; adult/child 50kr/free; ⊙guided tours in English 2pm Tue Jul–mid-Aug) An alley between the Aalborg Historiske Museum and post office leads to the rambling Monastery of the Holy Ghost, which dates from 1431 and is home to some fascinating frescoes. The interior can only be visited on a guided tour.

Historic Buildings   HISTORIC BUILDINGS
Aalborg has lost chunks of its historical quaintness to industrial and commercial development, but the centre contains enough ancient half-timbered buildings to give you an idea of the kind of affluence its Renaissance merchants enjoyed.

East of Budolfi Domkirke are three noteworthy buildings: the baroque-style **old town hall** (c 1762), at the corner of Østerågade and Gammel Torv; the five-storey **Jens Bangs Stenhus** (c 1624) at Østerågade 9; and **Jørgen Olufsens House** (c 1616) at Østerågade 25. The latter two are lovely Renaissance buildings – Jens Bang's house was built by a well-heeled merchant and now functions as a pharmacy; Jørgen Olufsen's house was built by a wealthy mayor and now operates as a cosy Irish pub.

In addition, the neighbourhood of half-timbered houses around **Vor Frue Kirke** (Peder Barkes Gade) is worth seeing, particularly the cobbled L-shaped street of Hjelmerstald. Halfway down the street is **Langes Gård** (Hjelmerstad 15), a photogenic courtyard full of sculptures and ceramics.

Ask at the tourist office for the English-language *Good Old Aalborg* booklet, which maps out two walking tours and provides details of buildings and sights along the way.

FREE **Lindholm Høje**   VIKING SITE
(⊙dawn-dusk) The Limfjord was a kind of Viking motorway providing easy, speedy access to the Atlantic for longboat raiding

---

ⓘ AALBORG CARD

If you're in town for a couple of days, the Aalborg Card may be worth considering – it gives free entry to most of the sights, plus free parking (at Kennedy Arkaden, southeast of the train station) and free use of public transport. A 24-hour pass costs adult/child 179/89kr, a 72-hour pass is 299/149kr. It's particularly worthwhile if you plan to visit expensive sights such as the zoo; buy it from the tourist office.

Aalborg

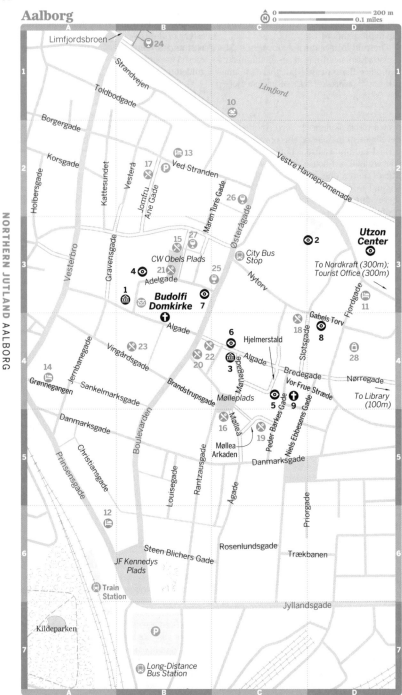

Aalborg

parties. It's not surprising, then, that the most important piece of Aalborg's historical heritage is a predominantly Viking one.

The atmospheric Lindholm Høje is a Viking burial ground where nearly 700 graves from the Iron Age and Viking Age are strewn around a hilltop pasture ringed by a wall of beech trees. Many of the Viking graves are marked by stones placed in the oval outline of a Viking ship, with two larger end stones as stem and stern. At the end of the Viking era the whole area was buried under drifting sand and thus preserved until modern times.

The **Lindholm Høje Museet** (Vendilavej 11; adult/child 60kr/free; ⊙10am-5pm daily Apr-Oct, 10am-4pm Tue-Sun Nov-Mar) adjoins the site and explains its history, and has displays on archaeological finds made during its excavation. Huge murals behind the exhibits speculate on how the people of Lindholm lived.

Lindholm Høje is 15 minutes north of central Aalborg via bus 2. With your own wheels, head north from the centre over Limfjordsbroen to Nørresundby, and follow the signs, taking Lindholmsvej north.

Kunsten   ART MUSEUM
(www.kunsten.dk; Kong Christians Allé 50; adult/child 60kr/free; ⊙10am-5pm Tue-Sun) A strikingly modular marble building designed by Finnish architect Alvar Aalto houses this regional museum of modern and contemporary art. Its light-filled interior houses a fine collection of predominantly Danish art, including works by JF Willumsen, Asger Jorn and Richard Mortensen.

To get there take the tunnel beneath the train station, which emerges into **Kildeparken**, a green space with statues and water fountains. Go directly through the park, cross Vesterbro and continue through a wooded area to the museum, a 10-minute walk in all. Alternatively, take bus 15. Note that a ticket to Kunsten allows free same-day entrance to the Utzon Center.

Aalborg Zoo   ZOO
(www.aalborg-zoo.dk; Mølleparkvej 63; adult/child 160/95kr; ⊙from 10am year-round) Teeming with feathered, furry and four-legged friends, it's no surprise this zoo is one of Denmark's most popular. Some 1200 animals call it home, including tigers, zebras, elephants, giraffes, chimpanzees, penguins and polar bears. It's southwest of the city and can be reached by bus S3 or 11; closing times vary, from 3pm in winter, to 8pm in July.

⌖ Tours

Over a six-week period from late June to early/mid-August, **Sightseeing Bus** (www.sightseeingbussen.dk; adult/child 60kr/free; ⊙departures 11am & 1pm), a double-decker sightseeing bus, departs from Gabels Torv (in front of Friis shopping centre) for a 90-minute tour of greater Aalborg, with commentary in Danish and English.

⭐ Festivals

Each year in late May, Aalborg kicks up its heels hosting the **Aalborg Carnival** (www.karnevaliaalborg.dk), the biggest Carnival celebrations in northern Europe, when up to 100,000 participants and spectators shake their maracas and paint the town red. Festivities include a street parade, kids' carnival and live music.

🛌 Sleeping

With few exceptions, Aalborg's hotel scene is lacklustre. The city is crying out for a boutique crash-pad to woo the city-breakers. The tourist office can book budget rooms in private homes.

TOP CHOICE Villa Rosa   GUESTHOUSE €€

(☎98 12 13 38; www.villarosa.dk; Grønnegangen 4; r & apt 500-800kr; 🅿🛜) Easily the most interesting option in town, so the reasonable rates and central location are added bonuses. Book early to snare one of only six theatrically decorated rooms over three floors (no lift) at this late-19th-century villa. The three small self-contained apartments are the standout bargain here – the English Room is especially lovely. Three rooms share a large bathroom and guest kitchen.

Cab Inn Aalborg   BUDGET HOTEL €€

(☎96 20 30 00; www.cabinn.com; Fjordgade 20; s/d/tr from 485/615/805kr; @🛜) The cheap, reliable Cab Inn chain recently added Aalborg to its portfolio with this large, modern, centrally located hotel across the road from the Utzon Center and neighbouring the new Friis shopping centre. All 239 rooms have TV and bathroom, but there's little room for cat-swinging in the cheaper rooms.

First Slotshotel Aalborg   HOTEL €€

(☎98 10 14 00; www.firsthotels.com; Rendsburggade 5; d from 846kr; 🅿@🛜) Some of the newly renovated rooms at this smart fjordside hotel near the Utzon Center have water views, and the free parking is a bonus, as is the central location. Online rates can drop to 570kr, making it a relative bargain.

Danhostel Aalborg   HOSTEL €

(☎98 11 60 44; www.bbbb.dk; Skydebanevej 50; dm/d from 196/436kr; 🅿@🛜) The hostel is handy for boating activities on the fjord

(you can hire canoes and kayaks here) but it's hardly central. The surrounds are green and the accommodation is simple (all rooms with bathroom); dorm beds are available in summer. There's an adjoining camping ground with budget cabins. It's in the marina area about 3km west of the town centre; take bus 13.

Prinsen Hotel   HOTEL €€

(☎98 13 37 33; www.prinsen-hotel.dk; Prinsengade 14; s/d from 545/745kr; 🅿@🛜) Modern, simple rooms (some are rather small) and a location that's close to the train and bus stations make this a decent option – the downside is that it's a lengthy walk to the waterfront action.

Radisson Blu Limfjord Hotel   HOTEL €€€

(☎98 16 43 33; www.radissonblu.com/hotel-aalborg; Ved Stranden 14; r weekdays/weekend 1525/1125kr; 🅿🛜) It may be considered the flashest place in town, but the rack rates are high for what you get – make sure you get a discount, online or otherwise.

🍴 Eating

Mortens Kro   FRANCO-DANISH €€€

(☎98 12 48 60; www.mortenskro.dk; Mølleå 2-6, Mølleå Arkaden; 3-/5-/7-course menu 498/698/898kr; ☺dinner Mon-Sat) Hands down both the best and priciest place to eat in town, Mortens Kro is owned by celebrity chef Morten Nielsen. It's a stylish, well-hidden setting for inventive Franco-Danish fare that showcases seasonal local produce – home-smoked trout, poached flounder, blueberry meringue gateau. This place is always hot, so an advance booking is a good idea. Mølleå Arkaden is accessed from Peder Barkes Gade 40A or Mølleplads.

Friis Modern Steakhouse   STEAKHOUSE €€

(Friis shopping centre; lunch 75-125kr, dinner mains 125-298kr; ☺lunch & dinner Mon-Sat) Yes, it's inside a shopping centre (enter from Nørregade), but this bright, classy eatery gives you a chance to sample chef Morten Nielsen's wares at manageable prices. Locally farmed steak (118kr at lunchtime) comes with a choice of sauces and potato options; there's a three-course dinner menu for 248kr.

Café KlosterTorvet   CAFE-BAR €

(CW Obels Plads 4; meals 39-81kr; ☺lunch & dinner) It's a funky, laid-back cafe-bar with a studenty feel, thanks largely to its cheap meals (baguettes, lasagne and the like), strong coffee, well-priced boozy drinks and backgammon-playing clientele.

Penny Lane
DELI, CAFE €

(Boulevarden 1; sandwiches & salads 75-78kr; ⊗brunch & lunch Mon-Sat) Heavenly delicatessen offering its own freshly baked bread, local cheeses and cured meats for fine picnicking, plus there's an in-house cafe offering a standout brunch platter (99kr) or snack-worthy sandwiches, quiche and tarts.

Pingvin Tapas & Vincafé
INTERNATIONAL €€€

(Adelgade 12; plate of 4/6/8 tapas 178/218/248kr; ⊗lunch & dinner Mon-Sat) This chic restaurant-bar offers a selection of 30 'tapas' (it's not so much a place to order dishes to share, but more an individual tasting-plate approach). Enjoy taste sensations such as lamb tagine, duck confit or grilled swordfish. There's an excellent global wine list.

Schak Nielsen
FISH €

(Algade 23; mains around 32kr; ⊗lunch Mon-Sat) This fishmonger sells a range of fishy morsels, from sushi to fish and chips. It's cheap and cheerful, quelling hunger pangs on a budget.

CaféMinisteriet
CAFE, BAR €€

(Mølleplads; mains 75-175kr; ⊗brunch, lunch & dinner) A fashionable crowd enjoys generous portions of classic cafe fare (burgers, sandwiches, salads and so on), preferably on the fab summer terrace. The cafe becomes a popular drinking spot of an evening.

Cox Orange
INTERNATIONAL €€

(Jomfru Ane Gade 23; lunch 75-98kr, dinner 159-228kr; ⊗lunch & dinner) Bringing an air of sophistication to a sometimes-seedy strip, Cox Orange serves up a meat-heavy menu (steaks and burgers) outdoors or in its brick-lined interior.

Self-Catering

Føtex
SUPERMARKET €

(Slotsgade 8; ⊗9am-8pm Mon-Fri, 8am-6pm Sat)

SuperBrugsen
SUPERMARKET €

(Vingårdsgade 10; ⊗9am-8pm Mon-Fri, to 5pm Sat)

Drinking

If it's a flirt, a drink or loud repetitive beats in the form of thumping techno, Euro-rock or house music you're after, trawl Jomfru Ane Gade, Aalborg's take-no-prisoners party street, jammed solid with bars. The venues themselves are pretty homogenous, so it's best to explore until you hear your kind of music or spy your type of crowd. Things are pretty tame early in the week (when the crowd of middle-agers dining along the strip may take you by surprise), but things get rowdy later in the week.

You won't have trouble finding somewhere to whet your whistle along Jomfru Ane Gade, so we've listed a few places away from the main strip that you might not track down on your own.

[TOP CHOICE] Den Fede Ælling
CAFE, BAR

(Strandvejen 12C; ⊗from noon Tue-Sun) The Fat Duckling is a fabulous 'fjordbar' and cafe under Limfjordsbroen, set on a funky converted houseboat. It serves meals (the changing three-course dinner menu is 295kr) and cocktails either inside or on the top deck; service is perhaps not its greatest strength, so sit back and enjoy the panorama over Aalborg.

Irish House
PUB

(Østerågade 25) It's almost too beautiful a setting in which to get sloshed. Inside a 17th-century building loaded with timber carvings and stained glass, this cheerful pub offers live music Thursday to Saturday, cheap pub grub and a big range of beers.

Søgaards Bryghus
MICROBREWERY

(CW Obels Plads 4) Every Danish town worth its salt now has a microbrewery, and Aalborg's is a cracker. With a swank interior, loads of outdoor seating and a long menu of beer accompaniments, you could easily lose an afternoon here sampling the different brews.

Duus Vinkjælder
RESTAURANT, BAR

(Østerågade 9) A superb way to cap off the evening is with a glass of wine at this romantic 300-year-old candlelit wine cellar under Jens Bangs Stenhus. If you can't hear your lover's sweet nothings over your rumbling tum, there's plenty of traditional Danish food on offer.

ℹ Information

Aalborg spreads along both sides of the Limfjord, with its two sections linked by bridge and tunnel. The business, shopping and dining hub and most traveller amenities are on the southern side.

Emergency
Police/ambulance (☎112)
Police station (☎96 30 14 48; Jyllandsgade 27) East of the train station.

Internet Access

Library (Rendsburggade 2) Free internet; enter from Nørregade.

Laundry

Møntvask (cnr Christiansgade & Rantzausgade) Coin laundry.

Medical Services

Aalborg Sygehus Syd (☑99 32 11 11; Hobrovej 18-22) Hospital about 2km south of town.

Budolfi Apotek (cnr Vesterbro & Algade; ⊘24hr) A 24-hour pharmacy.

Money

Forex (Ved Stranden 22; ⊘9am-6pm Mon-Fri, 10am-3pm Sat) Foreign exchange.

Jyske Bank (Nytorv 1)

Nordea (Algade 41)

Post

Post office (Algade 42; ⊘9.30am-6pm Mon-Fri, to 1pm Sat)

Tourist Information

Det Danske Udvandrerarkiv (The Danish Emigration Archives; ☑99 31 42 20; www.emiarch. dk; Arkivstræde 1; ⊘9am-4pm Mon-Thu, to 2pm Fri) Behind Vor Frue Kirke; keeps records of Danish emigration history and helps foreigners of Danish descent trace their roots.

Tourist office (☑99 31 75 00; www.visitaal borg.com; Nordkraft, Kjellerups Torv; ⊘10am-4.30pm or 5.30pm Mon-Fri, to 1pm Sat) It's a small, noncentral office inside Nordkraft, but in summer it has roving info booths.

❶ Getting There & Away

Air

Aalborg airport (airport code AAL; www.aal.dk) is 6.5km northwest of the city centre. There are direct connections with Copenhagen, and flights to/from Oslo and Amsterdam. **Norwegian** (www.norwegian.com) has daily connections with London (Gatwick).

Bus

Long-distance buses stop at the bus station south of JF Kennedys Plads (behind the Kennedy Arkaden shopping centre), near the train station. From Aalborg you can reach most Jutland towns of note on the **X-bus network** (www.xbus.dk, in Danish).

Express bus line 888, operated by **Abildskou** (☑70 21 08 88; www.abildskou.dk), runs twice daily from Aalborg to Copenhagen's Valby station (330kr, 5½ hours, three hours).

Thinggaard Express (www.expressbus.dk) operates bus 980 from Esbjerg to Frederikshavn once or twice daily, calling at Viborg and Aalborg en route.

Car & Motorcycle

Aalborg is 117km north of Aarhus and 65km southwest of Frederikshavn. The E45 bypasses the city centre, tunnelling under the Limfjord, while Rte 180 (which links up with the E45 both north and south of the city) leads into the centre.

To get to Lindholm Høje, or points north of the centre, take Rte 180 (Vesterbro), which crosses Limfjordsbroen.

Train

Trains run about hourly north to Frederikshavn (99kr, 1¼ hours), where there are onward connections to Skagen (from Aalborg 135kr, two hours), and south to Aarhus (175kr, 1½ hours) or to Copenhagen (388kr, 4½ to five hours).

❶ Getting Around

To/From the Airport

Town buses 2A, 2B and 22 run frequently between the city centre and the airport (18kr).

Bicycle

FREE BICYCLES Free city bikes (www.aalborg bycyklen.dk) are available from various spots around town from April to October. You put a 20kr coin into the slot to obtain the bike, which is refunded when you return it.

RENTAL Bikes can be hired from **Munk's Eftf** (www.munk-aalborg.dk; Løkkegade 25; per day/week 80/400kr).

Bus

For about eight weeks in peak summer (late June to late August) there is a free City Circle bus running half-hourly from 10am to 5.30pm (until 1.30pm on Saturday and Sunday). The circuit takes in major sights such as the zoo, Kunsten and the waterfront.

Almost all city buses leave from south of JF Kennedys Plads and pass the city-centre stops on Østerågade and Nytorv, near Burger King. The standard local bus fare is 18kr; you can also buy a good-value *klippekort*, valid for 10 rides, for 118kr, or a 24-hour turistkort valid for all transport in northern Jutland (adult/child 134/67kr, available May to August). Information on tickets, routes and schedules is available at the helpful **Nordjyllands Trafikselskab** (www. nordjyllandstrafikselskab.dk, in Danish) office at the bus station near JF Kennedys Plads, or by dialling ☑98 11 11 11.

Car

Car-rental companies Hertz, Avis and Europcar have booths at the airport or in town.

Apart from a few one-way streets, Aalborg is easy to travel around by car. There's free (but time-restricted) parking along many side streets, and metered parking in the city centre. There are also several large commercial car parks, including at Ved Stranden 11 (opposite the Radisson hotel), at Kennedy Arkaden (enter from Østre Allé), and under the Friis shopping centre (enter from Nyhavnsgade). These aren't cheap (up to 16kr per hour, maximum 160kr for a 24-hour period).

Taxi

You can order a **taxi** (☏98 10 10 10), or just pick one from the rank at the train station.

Frederikshavn

POP 23,300

A transport hub rather than a compelling destination, Frederikshavn shuffles more than three million people through its port each year, making it Jutland's busiest international ferry terminal. The majority of visitors are Scandinavians raiding Denmark's supplies of relatively cheap booze and meat. The town itself lacks the historical glamour of its coastal neighbours but can successfully entertain you for a few hours with its feature attraction, Bangsbo – still, Skagen or even Sæby make for more appealing overnight options.

☉ Sights

Bangsbo   MUSEUM, COUNTRY ESTATE

It's well worth exploring the Bangsbo area, 3km from the centre on the southern edge of town. The main drawcard is **Bangsbo Museum** (www.bangsbo.com; Dronning Margrethes Vej 6; adult/child 50kr/free; ☉weekdays year-round, Sat & Sun Jun-Aug), an old country estate with an interesting mix of exhibits. The manor house displays antique furnishings and collectibles, while the old farm buildings house ship figureheads, military paraphernalia and exhibits on the Danish Resistance during WWII. The most intriguing exhibit is the Ellingå ship, the reconstructed remains of a 12th-century Viking-style merchant ship that was dug up from a nearby streambed. Bus 3 from central Frederikshavn stops near the entrance to the museum, from where it's an enjoyable 500m walk through the woods to the museum. The adjoining **Bangsbo Botaniske Have** (Botanic Gardens) has a deer park and is a pleasant place to stroll or picnic.

Bangsbo Fort (Understedvej 21; adult/child 50kr/free; ☉10am-4pm Mon-Fri Jun-Sep), about 800m over the wooded ridge from the gardens, is an atmospheric WWII bunker complex housing some big guns and com-

Fredrikshavn

manding wonderful views across to Frederikshavn and out to sea.

Krudttårnet   TOWER

(Kragholmen; adult/child 15kr/free; ☉10am-4pm Tue-Fri, 11am-4pm Sat & Sun Jun-Aug) If you're waiting for a train it's an ideal time to climb the whitewashed gunpowder tower, a remnant of the 17th-century citadel that once protected the port. Various pieces of artillery are on display at the top.

🛏 Sleeping

Danhostel Frederikshavn City   HOSTEL €

(☏98 42 14 75; www.danhostelfrederikshavn.dk; Læsøgade 18; dm/s/d 200/500/550kr; @🛜) Frederikshavn's brand-new hostel is perfectly positioned behind the tourist office, with a supermarket and cafe-bar as neighbours. It's busy with ferry passengers enjoying the fresh new facilities (all rooms have a bathroom). Communal areas are top-notch, as is the courtyard garden with barbecue. Breakfast costs 60kr.

Hotel Herman Bang　　　　HOTEL €€
(☑98 42 21 66; www.hermanbang.dk, in Danish; Tordenskjoldsgade 3; standard s/d from 795/945kr; ☎) The midpriced rooms here are bright and comfortable, and the most expensive are huge, new and luxurious. The cheapest ('standard' rooms) are poor value – you're better off at the hotel's newly decorated, budget annex, **Herman Bang Bed & Breakfast** (Skolegade 2; s/d with shared bathroom 400/500kr, with bathroom & breakfast 500/600kr). The hotel has an upmarket spa and American-style diner.

TopCamp Frederikshavn Nordstrand　　CAMPING GROUND, CABINS €
(☑98 42 93 50; www.nordstrand-camping.dk; Apholmenvej 40; site incl 2 adults 240-330kr; ☺Apr-Sep; ☎☎☎) Found 4km north of town (walking distance to Frederikshavn's best beach, Palme Stranden) this huge park is chockers with summertime fun and family-friendly facilities. It also has cabins and caravans. Take bus 4.

✗ Eating

Karma Sushi & Cocktails　　JAPANESE €€
(Lodsgade 10; 8-piece signature sushi 125-165kr; ☺dinner Tue-Sat) When hunger strikes, head for the eastern end of Lodsgade, where there are oodles of eating options. The standout is good-looking Karma, an oasis of calm and elegance among the bustling Mexican-Italian buffets – but its enticingly fresh sushi morsels don't come cheap.

Møllehuset　　DANISH €€
(Skovalléen 45; lunch 95-195kr, dinner 185-225kr; ☺lunch daily, dinner Tue-Sat) This handsome old *kro* (inn) from the mid-18th-century is in a pretty setting in the Bangsbo area, and the small menu has plenty of appeal in the form of tapas tasters, cheese platters and fresh fish.

❶ Information

An overhead walkway leads from the ferry terminals to the tourist office, which sits at the edge of the central commercial district. The train station and the adjacent bus terminal are a 10-minute walk north of the ferry terminal. Danmarksgade is the pedestrian shopping strip, with banks and other services.
Library (Parallelvej 16) Free internet.

Post office (Skippergade 27) Beside the train station.
Tourist office (☑98 42 32 66; www.visitfrederikshavn.dk; Skandiatorv 1; ☺9am-4pm Mon-Fri, 10am-1pm Sat) Over the walkway from the ferry terminal, it offers the low-down on the town and surrounds.

❶ Getting There & Around

BICYCLE Ask at the tourist office about the free town bikes for rent, available from mid-April to September. The key to the bike also grants free admission to the town's major attractions.

BOAT **Stena Line** (www.stenaline.com) connects Frederikshavn with Gothenburg (Sweden) and Oslo (Norway); for information, see p326.

BUS Bus routes in northern Jutland extend as far afield as Hirtshals, Hjørring and Løkken. **Thinggaard Express** (www.expressbus.dk) operates bus 980 from Frederikshavn to Esbjerg once or twice daily (340kr, five hours), calling at Viborg and Aalborg en route.

CAR Frederikshavn is 65km northeast of Aalborg on the E45 and 41km south of Skagen on Rte 40.

TRAIN Frederikshavn is the northern terminus of Danske Statsbaner (DSB) train lines (the national rail network); however, a private train line operates hourly trains north to Skagen (54kr, 35 minutes). DSB trains depart about hourly south to Aalborg (99kr, 1¼ hour) and Aarhus (228kr, 2¾ hours).

Sæby
POP 8900

While Skagen is the inspiration behind world-renowned Scandinavian artists, Sæby could well be called the spiritual home (or at least the holiday house) of Danish literature. The pretty town was the inspiration behind Herman Bang's *Sommerglæder* (Summer Pleasure) and Henrik Ibsen's renowned work *Fruen fra havet* (The Lady from the Sea). In summer, Sæby's harbour and old town are packed with ice-cream-toting holidaymakers. It's a sleeper compared with Skagen further up the road, but it has plenty of charm.

◉ Sights & Activities

Sæby Museum　　MUSEUM
(Algade 1-3; adult/child 40kr/free; ☺Tue-Fri year-round, also Sat & Sun Jun-Aug) Just north of the tourist office is the town museum, occupying a charming 17th-century timber-frame house. Expect to see an amber collection, a 1920s classroom and a classically furnished Victorian sitting room.

LOVELY LÆSØ

The appeal of Læsø (population 2000) lies in its ability to stay firmly entrenched in the past. It may be an island just 28km off the coast of Frederikshavn, but it seems 100 years in arrears. It's home to small farms, sandy beaches, heathlands, dunes, much-loved traditions and charming small communities.

Fittingly, legend has it that Queen Margrethe I was saved from a shipwreck off Læsø in the 14th century and rewarded her rescuers with a stunning dress, giving them the right to adapt it as an island costume. Although such regional customs had largely disappeared elsewhere in Denmark by the 19th century, Læsø women wore their traditional island dress daily until just after WWII; today the costume is still worn on special occasions.

Another island tradition continues in the making of Læsø salt. At one time an island export, salt is now sold in small souvenir bags and is respected for its medicinal qualities as well as its gourmet potential. On the island you can visit the saltworks, and take a salt bath at Læsø Kur (www.saltkur.dk), a wellness centre inside a former church.

Læsø is free of large resort hotels and attracts visitors looking for a low-key holiday. The island has a few small towns (Vesterø Havn, Byrum and Østerby Havn), a couple of medieval churches, and a smattering of museums (including a seaweed-roofed farm museum). South of the main island is Rønnerne, an area of tidal wetlands with extensive seaside meadows and heathland, impressive birdlife and unique flora and fauna.

Day trips to Læsø

A good way to experience Læsø is by doing a day trip from Frederikshavn, landing at Vesterø Havn. There are five options – all outlined on the ferry company's website (www.laesoe-line.dk) and costing between 220kr and 350kr for the day, including return ferry passage (if you're staying on the island you can also join the tours and pay a lesser charge).

» Option 1: 4½-hour bus tour of the island, taking in the major sights
» Option 2: self-guided cycling tour of the island, including cycle hire and lunch
» Option 3: a boat trip from Vesterø Havn to investigate a seal colony
» Option 4: learn about the flora and fauna of southerly Rønnerne with a ranger
» Option 5: visit Læsø Kur

Check the complex schedules for these tours, and make bookings, online.

Staying on Læsø

The island's tourist office near the ferry port can organise holiday cottages around the island; if you're visiting in July and August, book accommodation in advance. The larger hotels have on-site restaurants (and dinner, bed and breakfast packages), plus there's no shortage of cafes, particularly in Vesterø Havn.

A great planning website is www.laesoe-booking.dk.

Information

The tourist office (☑98 49 92 42; www.laesoe-tourist.dk; Vesterø Havnegade 17; ◷9am-3pm Mon-Fri, to 2pm Sat & Sun Jun-Aug, shorter hrs rest of year) is 300m east of the ferry terminal in Vesterø Havn.

Transport

Færgeselskabet Læsø (☑98 49 90 22; www.laesoe-line.dk; return adult/child Jul & Aug 215/105kr, Sep-Jun 135/55kr) sails three to eight times daily year-round between Læsø and Frederikshavn (1½ hours).

A free public bus runs between the villages of Vesterø Havn, Byrum and Østerby Havn; it operates in connection with ferry departure and arrival times.

Bicycles can be rented from Jarvis Cykler (Vesterø Havnegade 29; per day 75kr), close to the ferry terminal. The tourist office has cycling maps outlining various routes.

Algade
HISTORIC BUILDINGS

The town's living history beats the museum, and you can soak it up on a walk along the town's oldest street, Algade, which is lined with gardens, half-timbered houses and a handful of artists' studios and craft shops. At Algade 7 you'll pass the former home of Adda Ravnkilde (1862–83), who wrote three powerful novels regarding female artists in a male-dominated domain and then tragically took her life at the age of 21.

Sæby Klosterkirke
CHURCH

(Strandgade 5; ☉8am-6pm Mon-Sat, 9am-4pm Sun Apr-Oct, 8am-4pm Mon-Sat, 9am-noon Sun Nov-Mar) Amble along Algade and you'll reach Sæby Klosterkirke, all that remains of a four-winged Carmelite monastery dating from 1470. Its visually imposing exterior is coupled with an interior that boasts beautiful frescoes from the Middle Ages and a 16th-century pulpit and canopy.

Harbour
HARBOUR

From the church you can readily access the harbour (take the path marked 'Kirkestien'), with both an older and modernised section and plenty of fish restaurants. For those disappointed with the physical size of the Little Mermaid in Copenhagen, Sæby's symbol of protection, **the Lady from the Sea statue**, has presence *and* stature. It's based on Henrik Ibsen's play of the same name, which he wrote after a summer spent walking along the beach and up into the woods around Sæby.

🛏 Sleeping

TOP CHOICE Aahøj
GUESTHOUSE €€

(☏98 46 11 27; www.aahoj.dk; Hans Aabelsvej 1; s/d from 525/625kr) Easily the top pick in town, for its intimate atmosphere (nine homely rooms in an elegant 1896 villa) and central location. The sunroom is the perfect spot in which to enjoy breakfast, while the idyllic riverside garden beckons for a lazy afternoon with a book. There's a minimum two-night stay in July.

Sæby Fritidscenter-Danhostel
HOSTEL €

(☏98 46 36 50; www.saebyfritidscenter.dk; Sæbygaardvej 32; dm 135kr, s/d with shared bathroom 255/300kr, with bathroom from 410/420kr; @🖧🖰) This excellent hostel is around 1.5km west of the town centre, at a large sports centre and with plenty of open space. Facilities are of the usual high standard, and there's a choice of rooms – the cheapest have shared bathrooms, while the A++ rooms (560kr) have bathroom, balcony, TV and fridge. There are also sweet, simple cottages (sleeping five) for hire.

🍴 Eating

Jensens Fiskerestaurant
FISH €€

(☏98 46 11 56; Havnen; buffet lunch/dinner 129/189kr; ☉lunch & dinner Apr-Sep) In the harbour area, restaurants woo you with tables overloaded with fresh shrimp bounty and assorted fishy treats. Upstairs at Jensens is a smart, light-filled restaurant offering buffet or à la carte offerings (the buffets are the best value-for-money); downstairs is a more casual cafe/takeaway serving well-priced fish and chips (60kr) to a beer-drinking, sun-seeking crowd. Reservations for the restaurant are a good idea.

Frøken Madsen's Spisehus
DANISH €€€

(☏98 40 80 36; Pindborggade 1; dinner mains 189-299kr; ☉lunch Sat & Sun, dinner Wed-Sun) Frøken Madsen serves up an international menu alongside plenty of Danish favourites in a cosy old building a block back from the main street. Sure, it's cute inside, but on a warm evening you can't go wrong with a table on the flower-filled garden terrace above the small river. Dinner mains of high-quality imported beef are on the pricey side – a surer bet is the weekend lunch buffet (99kr) or the Friday-night dinner buffet (169kr); book ahead.

ℹ Information

The **tourist office** (☏98 46 12 44; www.visit saeby.dk; Krystalgade 3; ☉9am-5pm Mon-Sat, 10am-1pm Sun Jul–mid-Aug, 9am-4pm Mon-Fri, 10am-1pm Sat mid-Aug–Jun) is in the middle of town. Nearby is the main shopping street, Vestergade.

ℹ Getting There & Away

Sæby is 12km south of Frederikshavn on Rte 180. There is no train line here but the hourly route 73 bus between Aalborg and Frederikshavn stops at Sæby (27kr from Frederikshavn, 25 minutes).

The Sæby bus station is 300m southwest of the town centre (take Stationsvej off Grønnegade).

Skagen

POP 8500

With its rich art, fresh seafood, photogenic neighbourhoods and classic characters, Skagen (pronounced Skain) is an utterly delicious slice of Denmark.

In the mid-19th century, artists flocked here, charmed by the radiant light's impact on the ruggedly beautiful landscape. Now tourists flock, drawn by an intoxicating combination of busy working harbour, long sandy beaches and buzzing holiday atmosphere. The town gets packed in summer but maintains its charm, especially in the intimate, older neighbourhoods, filled with distinctive yellow houses framed by white-picket fences and red-tiled roofs. Catering to the tourist influx are numerous museums, arts and craft galleries, bike-rental outlets, ice-creameries and harbourside restaurants serving fish fresh off the boats. Come and see why half the Danish population lights up whenever the town's name is mentioned.

⊙ Sights & Activities

Ask at the tourist office for a copy of the English-language *Strolling in Skagen* brochure, which gives great information about the town.

The closest beach to town is accessed from Østre Strandvej; east-coast beaches are sheltered and good for families, the west coast is wilder.

TOP
CHOICE Skagens Museum ART GALLERY

(www.skagensmuseum.dk; Brøndumsvej 4; adult/child 80kr/free; ⊙10am-5pm daily May-Aug, Tue-Sun Sep-Apr) Artists discovered Skagen's luminous light and its colourful, wind-blasted heath-and-dune landscape in the mid-19th century, and fixed eagerly on the romantic imagery of the area's fishing life that had earned the people of Skagen a hard living for centuries. Painters such as PS Krøyer and Anna and Michael Ancher followed the contemporary fashion of painting *en plein air* (out of doors), often regardless of the weather. Their work established a vivid figurative style of painting that became known internationally as the 'Skagen School'.

This wonderful gallery showcases the outstanding art that was produced here between 1870 and 1930, much of it kitchen-sink portraits of the lives and deaths of those in the fishing community. PS Krøyer's work is quite incredible, particularly his efforts to 'paint the light'. He was particularly transfixed by the 'blue hour', the transition between day and night, when the sky and the sea seem to merge into each other in the same shade of blue.

Overall, the paintings here evoke a sense of place and demonstrate a real community of artists in Skagen who worked and played together. The gallery also houses the former dining room of the Brøndums Hotel, onetime hang-out of many of the Skagen artists. The portrait-filled room was moved in its entirety in 1946 from the hotel across the road.

Grenen LANDMARK

Appropriately enough for such a neat and ordered country, Denmark doesn't end untidily at its most northerly point, but on a neat finger of sand just a few metres wide. You can actually paddle at its tip, where the waters of the Kattegat and Skagerrak clash, and you can put one foot in each sea – but not too far. Bathing here is forbidden because of the ferocious tidal currents and often-angry seas.

The tip is the culmination of a long, curving sweep of sand at Grenen, about 3km northeast of Skagen along Rte 40. Where the road ends there's a car park (12kr per hour), excellent restaurant and small art gallery. From the car park the 30-minute walk up the long, sweeping stretch of sand passes the grave of writer Holger Drachmann (1846–1908).

The tractor-pulled bus, the Sandormen (adult/child return 25/15kr; ⊙Apr-Oct), can take you out to the point if it's raining or if time is

---

JUTLAND'S BEST BEACHES

It's true, the water's never going to be as warm as the Med, but Denmark has long coastal stretches of appealing white sand. Following are some of our fave Jutland beach-going spots:

» southern Als (p214)
» western Fanø (p198)
» Grenaa (p236)
» Løkken (p277)
» Moesgård Strand (Aarhus; p226)
» western Rømø (p206)
» Skagen (p271)
» Tornby Strand (Hirtshals; p276)

Skagen

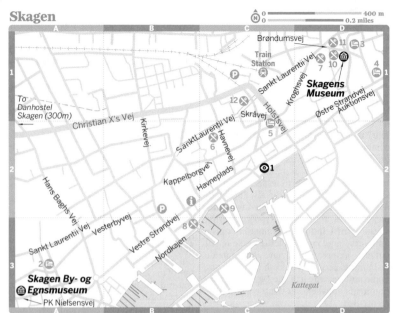

Skagen

not on your side; it leaves from the car park at Grenen from 9.30am daily, and runs regularly all day, according to demand.

In high summer, bus 99 runs between Skagen station and Grenen (18kr).

Gammel Skagen BEACH

There's a touch of Cape Cod in refined Gammel Skagen (Old Skagen, also known as Højen). Renowned for its gorgeous sunsets, upmarket hotels and well-heeled summer residents, it's a fine place to head late in the afternoon. It was a fishing hamlet before sandstorms ravaged this windswept area and forced many of its inhabitants to move to Skagen on the more protected east coast. It's a pleasant bike ride 4km west of Skagen: just head towards Frederikshavn and turn right at Højensvej, which takes you to the waterfront.

Skagen By- og Egnsmuseum MUSEUM

(www.skagen-bymus.dk; PK Nielsenvej 8; adult/child 50kr/free; ⊙daily Jun-Sep, Mon-Fri Oct-May) Evocatively presented, this open-air museum, 200m southwest of the harbour, depicts Skagen's maritime history and gives an insight into the traditional fishing community that so transfixed the Skagen artists (but without the romanticism!).

Tilsandede Kirke CHURCH RUINS

The Tilsandede Kirke (Buried Church) was erected during the late 14th century and was once the biggest church in the region, but in time it fell victim to a sand drift that began in the 17th century and became progressively worse – so much so that churchgoers eventually had to dig their way into God's sacred building. In 1795 the relentless sand drift broke the will of the congregation and the church was closed. The main part of the church was torn down in 1810 but the white-washed tower (adult/child 10/5kr; ☺Jun-Aug) still stands. It was used as a navigational tool for sailors back in the early days.

The photogenic church tower and the surrounding area comprise part of Skagen Klitplantage, a nature reserve. It's about 5km south of Skagen and well signposted from Rte 40. The nicest way to get here is by bike; take Gammel Landevej from Skagen.

Skagen Odde Naturcenter
MUSEUM

(www.skagen-natur.dk, in Danish; Bøjlevejen 66; adult/child 65/30kr; ☺10am-4pm Mon-Fri, 11am-4pm Sat & Sun May-Oct) In a beautiful Utzon-designed building on the northern outskirts of town, this centre gives an insight into the natural elements that surround Skagen and make it unique (the shifting sands, the luminous light, the raging winds, the clashing waters). It's a little pricey but well done, and there's plenty of interactive kid-friendly fun (particularly the remote-controlled model boats).

Festivals

Since 1971 the Skagen Festival (www.skagen festival.dk) has seen the town packed with performers, buskers and appreciative visitors, and acts encompassing rock to folk music. It's held on the first weekend of July; book accommodation well in advance.

Sleeping

The tourist office can book rooms (doubles 375kr to 425kr plus 75kr booking fee) in private homes, or help with securing a holiday cottage for a week-long stay. You'll need to book ahead for summer visits, when hotel accommodation can be scarce (and at its highest rate; outside July to August most prices drop).

Badepension Marienlund
GUESTHOUSE €€

(☎98 44 13 20; www.marienlund.dk; Fabriciusvej 8; s/d low season 480/770kr, high season 610/1015kr; ☺mid-Mar–Oct; 🛜) A cosy atmosphere, idyllic garden and attractive lounge and breakfast areas make Marienlund a top option. There are only 14 rooms, all light, white and simply furnished, and it's almost a child-free zone,

so makes for an appealing romantic retreat. It's in a residential neighbourhood west of the centre; bikes are available for rent.

Finns Hotel Pension
GUESTHOUSE €€

(☎98 45 01 55; www.finnshotelpension.dk; Østre Strandvej 63; s 525-775kr, d 750-975kr; ☺mid-Apr–Oct) This place is a feast for the senses, inside and out. Gay-friendly, TV-free and adults-only (no kids under 15), Finns is a stone's throw from the beach and housed in a 'log cabin' built as a holiday house for a Norwegian count in 1923. Inside are six individually decorated rooms and no end of art, photos, antiques and memorabilia. Accommodating hosts will cook dinner for guests (275kr for two courses) and you can make yourself at home in the library or garden.

Danhostel Skagen
HOSTEL €

(☎98 44 22 00; www.danhostelskagen.dk; Rolighedsvej 2; dm 150kr, s/d high season 500/600kr; ☺Mar-Nov; @🛜) Always a hive of activity, this hostel is modern, functional and spick-and-span. It's decent value for families or groups, but prices for a double are quite steep in high season (600kr, with or without a bathroom), plus there's the added charges for linen and breakfast. It's 1km towards Frederikshavn from the Skagen train station (if you're coming by train, get off at Frederikshavnsvej).

Grenen Camping
CAMPING GROUND, CABINS €

(☎98 44 25 46; www.grenencamping.dk; Fyrvej 16; sites incl 2 adults 220-310kr; ☺mid-Apr–mid-Sep; @🛜) This busy, well-organised place is in an ideal seaside location on the outskirts of town towards Grenen. There's plenty of tree cover and excellent facilities, including cabins (available only by the week in July) and bikes for hire.

FISHY BUSINESS

They say the early bird catches the worm but if you want to catch the heartbeat of this fishing community, head down to the fish auctions (Auktionsvej 10; ☺from 7am Mon-Fri) at the port when the boats return with their catch. The theatre of it all is infectious, as the auctioneers and buyers go toe-to-toe in rapid Danish. The fishermen have harsh, weather-beaten faces and some fantastic yarns up their sleeves.

Brøndums Hotel
HOTEL €€

(☎98 44 15 55; www.broendums-hotel.dk; Anchersvej 3; s/d with shared bathroom 850/1350kr) This charming hotel is steeped in history – it had close associations with the Skagen artists in its heyday. There have been recent renovations to bring the decor up to date, but prices are high given bathrooms are still shared. There's a cheaper annex nearby with more rooms (some with bathroom). The hotel's breakfast buffet is something special; there's an excellent on-site restaurant. Open year-round.

Hotel Plesner
BOUTIQUE HOTEL €€

(☎98 44 68 44; www.hotelplesner.dk; Holstvej 8; 895-1695kr; ☎) It has 16 fresh, petite double rooms; with designer touches throughout, including a great garden lounge.

Ruths Hotel
HOTEL €€€

(☎98 44 11 24; www.ruths-hotel.dk; Hans Ruths Vej 1, Gammel Skagen; r from 1725kr; ☺Feb-Dec; ☎☒) One of Denmark's grand bathing hotels in Gammel Skagen, with acclaimed restaurant, a wellness centre and stylish modern-meets-traditional decor.

✗ Eating & Drinking

Perhaps a dozen seafood shacks line the harbour selling fresh seafood to devour inside, outside or takeaway. Freshly caught prawns/shrimp *(rejer)* are the favourite fare, costing around 100kr for a generous helping. Havnevej, the road connecting the harbour and the town centre, has a cluster of eateries and bars (including that puzzling Danish entity, the Italian-Mexican restaurant). At Havneplads things get a little seedier (well, as seedy as Denmark gets), with some late-opening summertime nightclubs.

It's a good idea to make dinner reservations in summer, when the town is heaving.

TOP CHOICE Skagens Museum Cafe
CAFE €

(Brøndumsvej 4; lunch 60-95kr; ☺lunch) For morning/afternoon tea in a magical garden setting, head to the summertime cafe at Skagens Museum, serving a super spread of delicious home-baked cakes and tarts for 35kr to 45kr a pop. Note: you don't need to pay the museum's admission charge if you're just visiting the cafe.

Ruths Hotel
FRENCH €€

(☎98 44 11 24; Hans Ruths Vej 1, Gammel Skagen; restaurant 3/4/5 courses 650/750/950kr, brasserie mains 145-195kr; ☺brasserie lunch & dinner) The formal, fine-dining restaurant at Ruths (open for dinner three to five nights a week from April to September) is run by one of Denmark's finest French chefs, Michelin-starred Michel Michaud. If your holiday dollar won't stretch that far, Ruths Brasserie has a big outdoor terrace and an all-day menu of classic French dishes making great use of local produce (try the home-smoked salmon or fish soup, or go old-school with steak tartar or escargot). The brasserie's bakery starts selling its delectable pastries from 7.30am.

Pakhuset
SEAFOOD €€

(☎98 44 20 00; Rødspættevej 6; cafe mains 160-235kr, 3-/4-course restaurant menu 350/390kr) Two harbourside options are worthy contenders for the best in town – best for seafood, atmosphere and late-night drinks (often accompanied by live music). The discerning seafood-lover will feel at home upstairs at Pakhuset (open dinner only), where dishes are meticulously prepared and served on white linen. Downstairs is Pakhuset's more relaxed cafe (open for lunch and dinner), with easier-on-the-wallet prices and meals such as fish soup or steamed mussels. We give Pakhuset the nod over its rival, Skagen Fiskerestaurant, solely for the cheerful wooden ship mastheads it displays inside.

Skagen Fiskerestaurant
SEAFOOD €€

(☎98 44 35 44; Fiskehuskaj 13; cafe mains 87-235kr, 3-course restaurant menu incl wine from 525kr) The other contender for the town's favourite restaurant, this dockside place has the same approach as Pakhuset – more-casual downstairs fare at lunch and dinner (*fiskefrikadeller,* fishballs, or fresh-off-the-boat prawns you peel yourself), and a smarter upstairs area for fancy-pants dining. Downstairs is rustic and fun (you know it doesn't take itself too seriously when the floor is covered in sand).

Brøndums Hotel
FRENCH, DANISH €€€

((☎98 44 10 55; Anchersvej 3; lunch 75-145kr, dinner mains 185-345kr; ☺lunch & dinner) French cuisine is the main influence on the otherwise classic Danish dishes, with more of that local seafood on offer. Meals are served in the old-world ambience of the dining room – it has a special-occasion feel, but you can just as easily pop in for classic lunchtime smørrebrød or afternoon coffee and cake. In the warmer months, there's also a picture-perfect garden for alfresco dining, and a fun 1st-floor 'champagne terrace'.

Jakobs Café & Bar
INTERNATIONAL **€€**

(Havnevej 4A; lunch 79-185kr, dinner mains 185-255kr; ☺brunch, lunch & dinner) The terrace of this relaxed cafe-bar is primed for people-watching, and the comprehensive menu has universal favourites such as burgers, Caesar salad, *moules-frites* and steaks. On long summer nights the place is generally heaving with young Danes enjoying a few warm-up drinks; there's live music on weekends.

Karma Sushi
SUSHI **€**

(Sankt Laurentii Vej 15; 8-piece sushi box 89-99kr) All that fresh fish is put to good use at this takeaway spot (kitchen closes 8pm); large hand rolls are OK value at 69kr.

Self-Catering

SuperBrugsen
SUPERMARKET

(Sankt Laurentii Vej 28; ☺9am-7pm Mon-Fri, to 4pm Sat) Has an in-house bakery open from 7.30am. It opens daily in summer, with longer hours (until 8pm).

Slagter Munch
BUTCHER, DELICATESSEN

(Sankt Laurentii Vej 1) The queues out the door attest to this butcher's reputation for award-winning *skinke* (ham) and sausages. There's also a selection of picnic-worthy salads and deli produce for sale.

ⓘ Information

Sankt Laurentii Vej, the main street, runs almost the entire length of this long, thin town and is never more than five minutes' walk from the waterfront. The train station is on Sankt Laurentii Vej, 100m north of the pedestrianised town centre.

Danske Bank (Havnevej 1)

Library (Christian X's Vej) At the new Kappelborg 'Kulturhus', also home to a cinema. It offers free internet.

Nordjyske Bank (Sankt Laurentii Vej 39)

Post office (Sankt Laurentii Vej 28) Inside the SuperBrugsen supermarket.

Tourist office (☏98 44 13 77; www.skagen. dk; Vestre Strandvej 10; ☺9am-4pm Mon-Sat, 10am-2pm Sun Jul-Aug, 9.30am-4pm Mon-Fri, to 1pm Sat Sep-Jun) In front of the harbour, the well-stocked tourist office has loads of info on regional sights, attractions and activities.

ⓘ Getting There & Away

BUS The summertime bus 99 connects Skagen with other northern towns and attractions (see p277).

CAR Skagen is 41km north of Frederikshavn on Rte 40 and 49km northeast of Hirtshals via Rtes 597 and 40.

TRAIN There are private trains to Frederikshavn about once an hour (54kr, 35 minutes).

ⓘ Getting Around

BICYCLE The best way to get around is by bike, and loads of places offer rental. **Skagen Cykeludlejning** (www.skagencykeludlejning. dk; Banegårdspladsen; per day/week 80/325kr) is adjacent to the train station and has a wide range of bikes. It has a second outlet close to the harbour, at Fiskergangen 10.

CAR Parking is at a premium in summer – there's paid parking (12kr per hour) beside and in front of the tourist office, and beside the train station.

TAXI Taxis (☏98 43 34 34) are available at the station.

Råbjerg Mile

Denmark's largest expanse of drifting sand dunes, Råbjerg Mile is an amazing natural phenomenon. These undulating, 40m-high hills are fun to explore and almost big enough to lose yourself in. The dunes were formed on the west coast during the great sand drift of the 16th century and have purposefully been left in a migratory state (moving towards the forest at a rate of 15m per year). The dunes leave a low, moist layer of sand behind, stretching westwards to Skagerrak.

Råbjerg Mile is 16km southwest of Skagen, signposted off Rte 40 on the road to Kandestederne. It's about 4km from Hulsig station, on the Frederikshavn–Skagen train line.

Hirtshals

POP 6200

Beloved by discount-hungry Norwegians and largely inhabited by hardened Hirtshals seamen, this modern town makes a reasonable base for sightseeing, but its looks certainly won't take your breath away. It has ferry connections to points further north (way north, such as Iceland, the Faroe Islands and Norway); beaches and an impressive show of sea life may add to the appeal.

ⓞ Sights & Activities

Nordsøen Oceanarium
AQUARIUM

(www.nordsoenoceanarium.dk; Willemoesvej 2; adult/child 150/80kr; ☺9am-6pm Jul-Aug, 10am-4pm or 5pm Sep-Jun) If you've always wondered what lurks beneath, just head to the impressive North Sea Oceanarium, home to the largest aquarium in northern Europe. Here, 4.5 million litres of seawater is the home of thousands of elegantly balletic North Sea mackerel and herring in a huge, four-storey tank. Every day at 1pm a diver enters the tank to feed the marine life (in July and August there's an additional feeding at 4pm). The seal pool outside comes alive during feeding time at 11am and 3pm daily. Touch pools and playgrounds make this a good family excursion.

By car the E39 passes close to the aquarium (signposted); if you're coming by train from Hjørring, get off at Lilleheden station, from where it's a five-minute walk.

Tornby Strand
BEACH

If all you're after is a long stretch of untouched white sand, Tornby Strand delivers it in spades (and buckets), 5km south of Hirtshals. As the sand is compact enough to drive on, many park next to the breakers. Hiking is possible among the high mounded dunes and into the coastal woodlands that back the southern side of the beach.

Tornby Strand can be reached from Hirtshals via Rte 55 and Tornby Strandvej. The village here has a summer camping ground and a handful of sleeping and eating options.

Sleeping & Eating

Danhostel Hirtshals
HOSTEL €

(☎98 94 12 48; www.danhostelhirtshals.dk; Kystvejen 53; dm 150kr, d with/without bathroom 570/520kr; ☺Mar-Oct; @🛜) This is a good budget option, 1km southwest of the train station, with helpful staff and the usual high-standard Danhostel facilities. Its best feature is its location, across the road from a beach. Dorm beds are available July to mid-September.

Hotel Hirtshals
HOTEL €€

(☎98 94 20 77; www.hotelhirtshals.dk; Havnegade 2; d hotel/motel from 895/695kr; 🛜) On the main square above the fishing harbour, Hotel Hirtshals has bright, comfortable rooms with steepled ceilings – try for one with a sea view. It's in the best position for enjoying the town's restaurants and is heavily peopled by ferry-going Norwegians. In the older annex are cheaper, no-frills motel rooms (no TV or phone, but with bathroom).

Hirtshals Kro
FISH €€

(Havnegade; lunch 55-189kr, dinner 95-198kr; ☺lunch & dinner) The best spot in town for a meal, with loads of character with its low ceilings, wooden beams and assorted fishing memorabilia. There's a large outdoor terrace, plus an intimate bar where Norwegians are known to overindulge in the cheap Danish beer (it's all relative!).

ℹ️ Information

The main pedestrian street is Nørregade, west of the train station. The seaward end of Nørregade opens out into Den Grønne Plads (The Green Square), which overlooks the fishing harbour. There are banks and services in the area.

The **tourist office** (☎98 94 22 20; www.visithirtshals.dk; Dalsagervej 1; ☺9am-4pm Mon-Fri, to noon Sat) is part of a new 'Velkomstcenter' (Welcome Centre), 2.5km southeast of the train station off the E39 (to Aalborg), catering to motorists fresh off the Norwegian ferries.

ℹ️ Getting There & Around

BOAT The following international ferries use Hirtshals as their main port (for more info, see p326 and p326).

Color Line (www.colorline.com) Service to/from the Norwegian ports of Kristiansand and Larvik.

Fjordline (www.fjordline.com) Fast catamaran to Kristiansand from mid-April to mid-September, plus year-round ferry to Stavanger and Bergen.

Smyril Line (www.smyrilline.com) Weekly departures to the Faroe Islands and Iceland.

BUS Summer bus 99 (see opposite) stops at Nordsøen Oceanarium, Tornby Strand and Hirtshals station.

CAR Hirtshals is 49km southwest of Skagen via Rtes 597 and 40, and 41km northwest of Frederikshavn via the E39 and Rte 35.

TRAIN Hirtshals' train station is on Havnegade, west of the ferry terminals. A private railway connects Hirtshals with Hjørring at least hourly (27kr, 20 minutes). At Hjørring you can connect with a DSB train to Aalborg, Frederikshavn or destinations further south.

Hjørring
POP 24,800

That the inland town of Hjørring has few hotels speaks volumes – the holiday action is going on elsewhere, at the surrounding seaside towns. Still, if you don't have your own wheels, Hjørring may be an OK base, given its good transport connections. And it's a handsome service town, far more atmospheric than Hirtshals, with medieval churches, street sculptures, and some good eating and shopping opportunities.

SUMMER BUSES

The Danish train system doesn't extend to northwest Jutland. If you're holidaying in the area in summer and don't have your own transport, you may come to rely on 'Toppen af Denmark' (Top of Denmark) – the number 99 bus that runs from the top tip of Jutland (Grenen) along the northwest coast, taking in Skagen, Gammel Skagen, Hirtshals, Tornby Strand, Hjørring, Lønstrup, Løkken, Fårup Sommerland (where it connects with bus 200E to Aalborg) and Blokhus. Naturally, it also does the route in reverse.

The service runs only for about six weeks (the height of the summer season) from late June/early July to mid-August. Pick up a timetable or call ✆98 11 11 11; the website for Nordjyllands Trafikselskab (NT; North Jutland Transport Association; www.nordjyllands trafikselskab.dk) is in Danish, but timetables are easy enough to access (just look for 'Sommerbusser').

If you're using Hjørring as a base, the attractive midrange Hotel Phønix (✆98 92 54 55; www.phoenix-hjoerring.dk; Jernbanegade 6; s/d 795/895kr; ☞) is a better choice than the out-of-town hostel, thanks to its position close to the train and bus stations.

ℹ Information

Hjørring's old town is around its main square, Springvandspladsen, and runs north up to Sankt Olai Plads, which is bordered by three medieval churches. Springvandspladsen is a five-minute walk north of the train station along Jernbanegade; stroll 200m further north on the pedestrian walk Strømgade to reach Sankt Olai Plads.

The tourist office (✆72 33 48 78; www. visithjoerring.dk; Østergade 30; ☺10am-6pm Mon-Fri, to 1pm Sat) is at the library, inside the new Metropol shopping centre.

ℹ Getting There & Away

BUS Hjørring is well served by regional buses operated by Nordjyllands Trafikselskab (NT; North Jutland Transport Association; www. nordjyllandstrafikselskab.dk, in Danish), with services to many parts of northern Jutland. The bus station is across the road from the train station, accessed from Asylgade.

CAR Hjørring is 35km west of Frederikshavn on Rte 35 and 17km south of Hirtshals on Rte 55 or the E39.

TRAIN Hjørring is on the Aarhus–Frederikshavn DSB train line and is also the terminus of a short private train line to Hirtshals. Destinations by train:

Aalborg (81kr, 45 minutes)

Aarhus (208kr, 2¼ hours)

Frederikshavn (54kr, 30 minutes)

Hirtshals (27kr, 20 minutes)

Skagen (63kr, 1½ hours) Change trains at Frederikshavn.

Løkken

POP 1600

A generation of Danish holidaymakers may raise an eyebrow when they read this, but Løkken is now an appealing holiday spot for all ages. It was once the renowned summer habitat of teenage party-animals, but has matured considerably since those heady days and now draws a tamer crowd.

The former fishing town's biggest drawcard is its wide, sandy beach, and the requisite shops, ice-creameries and cafes welcome the summer bombardment. Colder months see the town go into hibernation.

◉ Sights & Activities

Fårup Sommerland   AMUSEMENT PARK
(www.faarupsommerland.dk; Pirupvejen, Blokhus; admission 205-230kr; ☺from 10am daily mid-Jun–mid-Aug, also open select days in May & early Sep) In the top five most-visited Danish attractions, this wholesome (and pricey) amusement park caters to holidaying families in search of distractions – of which there are plenty, from a wooden roller coaster to kiddie-safe rides and a huge waterpark with wave pool and waterslides. Everyone over the age of three pays the same entrance fee; it may be worth visiting just in the afternoon, when the entry price drops to 130kr to 160kr (depending on the time of year). Closing hours vary (from 5pm to 9pm); check the website to confirm opening days and hours.

The park is on the outskirts of Blokhus, about 15km south of Løkken. Such is its popularity, frequent summer buses run here from Aalborg (bus 200E), Frederikshavn (bus 89) and Skagen (bus 99, via Hirtshals, Hjørring and Løkken).

Løkken Beach
BEACH

Go looking for your own (free) beachside fun at Løkken's lovely long strand, lined with neat rows of white wooden beach huts and a few stout little fishing vessels (interestingly, these 450-plus beach huts are stored inland during winter). Check out the kitesurfers taking advantage of west-coast winds (BYO gear).

Museums
MUSEUMS

(⊙limited hrs Jun-Aug) The charming little **Løkken Museum** (Nørregade 12; adult/child 10kr/free) and **Kystfiskerimuseet** (Coastal Fishing Museum; Ndr Strandvej; adult/child 10kr/free), perched above the beach, tell the story of Løkken seagoing.

🛏 Sleeping

The tourist office has loads of holiday houses on its books, usually rented out weekly in high season. Hotels and apartments are also generally geared to long-stayers rather than overnighters passing through; the tourist office has details of private rooms for rent.

TOP CHOICE Villa Vendel
GUESTHOUSE €€

(☑98 99 14 56; www.villavendel.dk; Harald Fischers Vej 12; r 400-660kr, apt 675-950kr; 🛜) East of Torvet is this delightful option, a member of the Small Elegant Hotels group (an apt description), with five rooms (four with shared bathroom) and five apartments (two apartments are at the guesthouse address, others are elsewhere in town). There's a classy old-world feel with wooden floors and neutral decor, plus a guest kitchen, a courtyard for alfresco breakfast (60kr) and a large garden. Friendly owners, plenty of local info, great-value prices and year-round opening make for an impressive package.

Løkken Campingcenter & Hytteby
CAMPING GROUND, CABINS €

(☑98 99 17 67; www.loekken-hytteby.dk, in Danish; Søndergade 69; per adult/child/site 95/35/25kr; ⊙mid-Apr–Aug) This is very much a summer family playground, with all the requisite facilities and outdoor play areas. It's a couple of hundred metres to both town and beach. Cabins are available on a weekly basis.

🍴 Eating

You'll have no problems finding a place to eat on Torvet, bursting with alfresco tables and relaxed holidaymakers. While you're here, pop into the nightmare of every visitor to a dentist, **Bolcheriet** (Torvet 1; ⊙daily Jul, Wed-Sun Feb-Jun & Aug-Dec), a Willy Wonka world where you can see boiled lollies being made (and of course purchase the sweet stuff).

Peter Baadsmand
PUB, RESTAURANT €€

(Sdr Strandvej 4; lunch 59-129kr, dinner 2-/3-course menu 249/279kr; ⊙lunch & dinner) This salty-dog pub is just short of the beach and worth a visit for its ye-olde fishing interior. The front bar is an old rowing boat, and there are the requisite lanterns, ropes, beams and fishing paraphernalia to add atmosphere. The food is good honest fare, and the place turns into a club later on, with live music and/or a disco.

Løkken Fiske-Restaurant
FISH €€

(Nørregade 9; lunch 55-79kr, dinner mains 178-249kr; ⊙lunch & dinner) Just off Torvet and offering a taste of the coast, this restaurant serves up good-value lunches of fish and chips or herring on rye bread, or more up-market dinnertime options, including lobster tail and Greenland halibut. The evening fish buffet (174kr) is a piscatorial treat.

ℹ Information

The super-helpful **tourist office** (☑98 99 10 09; www.loekken.dk; Møstingsvej 3; ⊙10am-4pm Mon-Sat Jul-Aug, 10am-3pm Mon, Tue, Thu & Fri, 9am-noon Sat Sep-May) is behind Torvet. It has a wealth of knowledge on the area and can book hotels and summerhouses. It also has bike rental.

ℹ Getting There & Away

Løkken is on Rte 55, 18km southwest of Hjørring. Bus 71 runs hourly on weekdays (less frequently on weekends) between Løkken and Hjørring (36kr, 30 minutes), and Løkken and Aalborg (72kr, 70 minutes). Løkken is also on the summertime bus 99 route (see p277).

Hanstholm
POP 2400

Despite its interesting wartime museum and status as the northern boundary of one of Denmark's new national parks, modern Hanstholm is a charmless place – thanks largely to the fact that a small, lacklustre shopping centre serves as the town's heart. The town's star appears to be on the wane, with ferries that once used its large harbour now preferring another northern town (Hirtshals).

RUBJERG KNUDE

About 13km north of Løkken (en route to the town of Lønstrup) is Rubjerg Knude, an area of sand dunes that show just how Mother Nature calls the shots on this wind-whipped coast. Rubjerg Knude Fyr (lighthouse) stood 200m inland when it opened in 1900, some 60m above sea level. Over time the sea moved closer, and by the late 1960s the lighthouse had to be closed because frequent heavy sand drifts were making its light near-impossible to see from the sea. In 1980 it opened as a museum with exhibitions about the migrating sands, but had to close in 2002 as the sand drift was burying the museum buildings. Today it attracts tourists as a photogenic landmark and curiosity, partly submerged in sand. It is expected that the lighthouse will fall into the sea in the coming decade or so, due to coastal erosion. There's good information online at www.rubjergknude.dk.

To reach Rubjerg Knude, take Rte 55 northeast from Løkken and turn left after about 6km, onto Lønstrupvej (signposted). It's quite a walk from the car park to the lighthouse. Two kilometres south of the car park, Strandfogedgården (adult/child 40kr/free; ⏰11am-5pm mid-Jun–mid-Sep) houses an exhibition on the lighthouse and the geology of the region. Summer bus 99 passes through the area.

🅞 Sights

Viewpoint   VIEWPOINT

Hanstholm's impressive commercial harbour was completed in 1967; since then the town has developed into one of Denmark's largest fishing ports and prominent industrial centres. There's a good viewpoint over the harbour at the end of Helshagevej (follow the signs for 'Havneudsigt'). Up here you'll find Brasserie Pyten (lunch 84-138kr), an impressive cafe with sweeping views. It's open for lunch and afternoon tea from April to September.

MuseumsCenter Hanstholm   MUSEUM

(www.museumscenterhanstholm.dk; Molevej 29; adult/child 60/25kr; ⏰10am-5pm Jun-Aug, to 4pm Feb-May & Sep-Oct) Hanstholm was a key player in the German occupation of Denmark and this impressive museum is based around a German bunker. Hitler used this as part of his 'Atlantic Wall' system, a series of fortifications that spread from Kirkenes in Norway to the Pyrenees. Along with the bunker you can visit the Documentation Centre, which outlines this period in more detail and provides an insight into the way of life for locals under Hitler's rule. The museum is 300m west of the town centre and well signposted.

🍽 Sleeping & Eating

Eating options are limited. There's a cafe at the museum, lunch options at Brasserie Pynten (see above), and dinner at the hotel. Alternatively, head to Klitmøller.

Hotel Hanstholm   HOTEL €€

(☎97 96 10 44; www.hotelhanstholm.dk, in Danish; Christian Hansens Vej 2; s/d 795/1145kr; @🛜🏊) A smart option, inland from the harbour and close to the town 'centre' (aka shopping centre). Rooms are of a high standard and facilities are laid on thick, including indoor pool, sauna and on-site restaurant (dinner mains 148kr to 218kr).

ℹ Information

The summertime **tourist office** (☎97 92 19 00; www.visitthy.dk; Tårnevej 21; ⏰noon-5pm Mon-Fri, 11am-2pm Sat late Jun-Aug) is at the local lighthouse dating from 1843 (which you can climb, for 10kr).

ℹ Getting There & Away

By road, Hanstholm is at the terminus of Rtes 181, 26 and 29. Thisted, 21km to the south via Rte 26, has the nearest train station. Buses 90 and 322 regularly connect Thisted and Hanstholm (27kr, 40 minutes); bus 322 runs via Klitmøller.

Klitmøller

POP 800

Klitmøller's windy ways and curving waves have transformed the small fishing village into one of Europe's premier surfing destinations, known colloquially as 'Cold Hawaii'. It's a small holiday settlement of summerhouses, where wetsuit-clad surfers roam the streets and outdoorsy folk get around on bikes, seemingly oblivious to the cracking wind.

THY NATIONAL PARK

One of the five new national parks created in Denmark in the last few years, Thy National Park (www.nationalpark thy.dk) stretches 55km south along the North Sea coast from Hanstholm to Agger Tange, covering an area of 244 sq km of coastline, dunes, lakes, pine forest and moors. There are plenty of windswept, wide-open spaces to access: marked hiking, cycling and horse-riding trails, bird-watching opportunities, plus a good dose of history too, in fishing hamlets and WWII-era German bunkers.

Local tourist offices will help with information on activities within the park, or check out www.visitthy.dk. If you're in the area, there's a small park information centre (open April to October) in the coastal settlement of Stenbjerg, off Rte 181 halfway between Agger and Klitmøller. Bus 313 runs from Thisted (which has a train station) to Stenbjerg.

Klitmøller hosts a PWA (Professional Windsurfing Association) world cup event each September.

🏃 Activities

Don't despair if you're not world-championship windsurfing material. In addition to the challenging waves of the North Sea, Vandet Sø, a few kilometres east of Klitmøller, is a popular windsurfing lake, with conditions suitable for all levels.

Westwind Klitmøller   WINDSURFING, KITESURFING
(☑97 97 56 56; http://klitmoller.westwind.dk; Ørhagevej 150) Westwind is by the beach and has enthusiastic surfers keen to show you the ropes of windsurfing, kitesurfing, surfing and stand-up paddle surfing (in English, German or Danish). A three-hour introductory windsurfing course costs 400kr, or six hours is 799kr – and they guarantee you'll be able to windsurf after the course. A 4½-hour introduction to kitesurfing costs 899kr. For those who know what they're doing, gear rental is available.

Cold Hawaii Surf Camp   SURFING
(☑29 10 88 73; www.coldhawaiisurfcamp.com; Ørhagevej 151) This new company, established by an Israeli with a fine surfing pedigree, offers surfing lessons (from 190kr for 90 minutes), plus surf camps and board/wetsuit rental. It also runs a hostel in town (dorm beds 199kr).

🛏 Sleeping & Eating

At the time of research, Klitmøller Gammel Kro & Badehotel (www.klitmollerbadehotel. dk; Krovej 15) was closed for extensive renovations, with plans for new holiday apartments on the property. Check the website for updates.

You might also consider a cheap dorm bed through Cold Hawaii Surf Camp.

Nystrup Camping   CAMPING GROUND, CABINS €
(☑97 97 52 49; www.nystrupcampingklitmoller. dk, in Danish; Trøjborgvej 22; per adult/child/site 79/free/30-60kr; @🐾) Populated by windblown types and littered with surfing kit, this popular ground has plenty of trees for shelter and decent facilities including horse riding, bike hire and playground. It also has a minimarket and cafe.

⌐TOP CHOICE⌐ Klitmøller Røgeri   FISH €
(Ørhagevej 152; meals 47-88kr; ☺lunch & dinner May-Sep) Offers a sensational selection of fresh and smoked seafood not far from the beach – grab some fish and chips (65kr) or a baguette stuffed with prawns and watch the water acrobatics in full swing.

Fiskerestaurant Niels Juel   FISH €€
(Ørhagevej 150; fish buffet 149kr; ☺dinner Tue-Sun May-Sep) The large terrace of this elevated restaurant – whitewashed under a thatched roof – is the best spot to watch the surfing action. The good-value fish buffet heaves with herrings, prawns and salmon. Downstairs from the restaurant is a casual all-day cafe-bar with draught beer and fast food.

ℹ Getting There & Away

Klitmøller is 11km southwest of Hanstholm on Rte 181, and 18km northwest of Thisted on Rte 557. Bus 322 runs frequently between the three towns; Thisted has a rail connection for journeys south.

Understand
Denmark

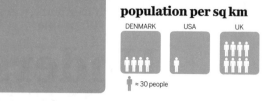

population per sq km

DENMARK   USA   UK

👤 ≈ 30 people

Denmark Today

Happiness & Harmony?

The Danes are, overwhelmingly, a happy bunch. If you believe those contentment surveys and liveability lists, Denmark is one of the happiest nations on earth with some of the best quality of life.

It's not hard to see why: despite the bumps of the Global Financial Crisis, it has among the highest per-capita GDP in the European Union and unemployment is relatively low. Education is free, and its social-welfare programs are the envy of many.

But there is more to the Danes' contentment. Stroll around Copenhagen or almost any Danish town and you'll experience some of the most harmonious civic spaces anywhere.

Look a bit closer, however, and – as in a Hans Christian Andersen fable – you'll find a darker side, too. As with other European nations, there's been a gradual shift to the political right in this famously liberal nation. Concern has grown over immigration – particularly from Muslim countries – and an erosion of traditional values.

For all the talk of assimilation and the comprehensive state effort to achieve it, racial, cultural and religious fault lines and prejudices remain. This challenge to tolerance has unnerved many Danes, while many of them avoid confronting their underlying resentment towards non-European newcomers.

> » Population: 5.56 million
>
> » Area: 43,098 sq km
>
> » Coastline: 7314km
>
> » Highest point: Møllehøj 171m
>
> » Unemployment: 4.2%
>
> » GDP per capita: $36,600

Politics & Economics

After a decade of conservative rule and with a sluggish economy due to the Global Financial Crisis, Denmark's political pendulum has again moved left. In the 2011 elections, a new, centre-left coalition took government after a close election fought largely over which side was better equipped to steer the Danish economy out of its malaise. The new

Top Icons

» **Queen Margrethe** The much-loved monarch

» **Dannebrog** The Danish flag

» **Hans Christian Andersen** The master storyteller

» **Vikings** More than just marauders

» **Lego** The plastic brick that changed childhoods

» **Hygge** Cosiness and contentment

Top Tunes

» **'Wonderful Copenhagen'** (Danny Kaye) Don't pretend you haven't been singing this to yourself since you got here

» **'Barbie Girl'** (Aqua) Contender for most annoying song ever

population distribution
(%)

Urban   Rural

if Denmark were 100 people

80 would be Lutheran   4 would be Muslim
15 would be no   1 would be other
denomination

---

government is led by Social Democrat Helle Thorning-Schmidt, the country's first female prime minister. Thorning-Schmidt's party pledged to roll back some of the tough immigration laws of the previous government and increase public spending to stimulate the economy, to be largely funded through tax rises on high earners and banks.

Despite the country's reputation as one of the world's most highly taxed nations, a significant majority of Danish voters believes that their tax rates are fair, and that the public services they get in return are worth it.

Sustainability

As well as their admirable attitudes to civic duties (voter turnout at parliamentary elections is around 87%; there is relatively low tax evasion), Danes go about their business with a green conscience.

While some Western governments continue to debate the veracity of climate-change science (I'm looking at you, Australia and the USA), Denmark gets on with (sustainable) business. Wind power generates 20% of Denmark's energy supply, and the country is a market leader in wind-power technology, exporting many wind turbines. The country is aiming for complete independence from fossil fuels by 2050, while the city of Copenhagen has pledged to go carbon-neutral by 2025. Islands compete for the title of 'most green' – Samsø is officially a zero-emissions island, with all of its energy generated by wind and solar power.

> Income tax rates are complex, but equate to about 30% for low-income earners, 36% for mid-income earners, 45% for high-income earners. The value added tax (VAT) is 25%.

> The Kingdom of Denmark also comprises Greenland and the Faroe Islands, both of which have autonomous self-rule.

Mythbusting

» **'Fly on the Wings of Love'** (Olsen Brothers) Super-proud 2000 Eurovision winner

» **'Played-A-Live (The Bongo Song)'** (Safri Duo) Huge percussive club hit

» **'Fascination'** (Alphabeat) Sugary, feel-good pop

» Not all Danes are blond.

» With a bit of insider knowledge, Denmark is no more expensive than other Western European countries.

» Yes it's liberal (it was the first country in the world to legalise pornography, in 1969), but that doesn't mean the population is randy and sex-mad.

History

Despite its small size, Denmark has been a major player in the shaping of the region. Proof of this can be seen with the martial and globetrotting prowess of the Vikings, the cultural contributions of the Danish Renaissance monarchs, the philosophers and writers of 19th-century Copenhagen, and the scientists and doctors of the 20th century.

Stone Age villagers buried their dead in dolmen, a type of grave monument comprising upright stones and topped by a large capstone; features still common to Denmark's meadows.

DOLMEN

Of Stone, Bronze & Iron

Humans first trod the earth and dug the region's flint tens of thousands of years ago as retreating glaciers let lichen and mosses grow, attracting herds of reindeer. Permanent settlements sprang up in about 12,000 BC.

Stone Age culture relied primarily on hunting, but as the climate gradually warmed these hunters resettled near the sea, subsisting on fish, sea birds and seals. Small-scale agriculture followed and villages developed around the fields.

Around 1800 BC the first artisans began fashioning weapons, tools, jewellery and finely crafted works of art in the new metal, bronze, traded from as far away as Crete and Mycenae.

Locally available iron then led to superior ploughs, so permitting larger-scale agricultural communities. Present-day Denmark's linguistic and cultural roots date to the late Iron Age arrival of the Danes, a tribe thought to have migrated south from Sweden about AD 500.

At the dawn of the 9th century, the territory of present-day Denmark was on the perimeter of Europe, but Charlemagne (r 768–814) extended the power of the Franks northward to present-day northern Germany. Hoping to ward off a Frankish invasion, Godfred, king of Jutland, reinforced an impressive earthen rampart called the Danevirke. However, the raiding Franks breached the rampart, bringing Christianity to Denmark at sword point.

TIMELINE	c 12,000 BC	c 4000 BC	c 1800 BC
	The first permanent settlements are established on Jutland and the nearby Baltic islands.	People begin to grow more food crops. The advent of agriculture sees woods cleared by slash-and-burn and grain is sown in the resulting ash.	Bronze introduced to Denmark, giving rise to skilled artisans who fashion weapons, tools, jewellery and works of art. Trade routes to the south bring the supply of bronze.

The Vikings

The image of bearded thugs wearing horned helmets, jumping from a longship and raping and pillaging their way through early Christendom is what many people summon up when they hear the word Viking.

Some of these Northmen (as they were known in Britain, one of their favoured pillaging spots) undoubtedly did go in for pillage and slaughter as well as slave trading, robbery and the murder of clergy.

But the real history of the Scandinavian seafarers from Norway, Denmark and Sweden that came to be known as Vikings is more complex than the simple image presented by many of the horrified accounts of the era, and a great deal of myth-making since.

The Viking era spanned a couple of centuries and took on a different character through the decades. Although unrecorded raids had probably been occurring for decades, the start of the Viking Age is generally dated from AD 793, when Nordic Vikings ransacked Lindisfarne Monastery, off the coast of Northumbria in northeastern England. Survivors described the Vikings' sleek square-rigged vessels as 'dragons flying in the air' and the raiders as 'terrifying heathens'.

Early Viking raiders often targeted churches and monasteries for their wealth of gold and jewels. Books and other precious but perishable cultural artefacts were just some of the raids' collateral damage. Roughing up monks – who wrote the history of the age – hardly endeared the Vikings to posterity.

The Vikings were initially adventurous opportunists who took advantage of the region's turmoil and unstable political status quo but in time their campaigns evolved from piratical forays into organised expeditions that established far-flung colonies overseas. The Vikings' challenge to Europe's kings and chieftains, with their decades of lightning raids, did much to enhance their notoriety.

Battle and bloodlust was not their only talent. The Vikings were successful traders, extraordinary mariners and insatiable explorers whose exploits took them to Byzantium, Russia, North Africa, even as far as the Caspian Sea and Baghdad. They also established settlements in Iceland, Greenland and Newfoundland.

They settled too, in several places including Northern France and the British Isles, proving to be able farmers. They were also shrewd political players establishing their own kingdoms and intermarrying with local nobles or squeezing protection money from local kings (their hated Danelaw in England being a good example).

Even the historically pivotal 1066 Battle of Hastings can be thought of not as a battle between England and France, but essentially a fight between two leaders descended from this Nordic stock (William and Harold).

So fearsome were the Vikings that the English introduced a special prayer into church services: 'From the fury of the Northmen, good Lord, deliver us'.

Just for the record, Vikings didn't have horned, or winged, helmets (sorry!). Nor did they celebrate slaughter by drinking mead from cups made of skulls, another popular myth. Happily, they did rejoice in some storybook names, including Erik Bloodaxe and Sweyn Forkbeard.

c AD 500

Arrival of the Danes in the late Iron Age. This tribe, thought to have migrated south from Sweden, forms present-day Denmark's linguistic and cultural roots.

793

The first documented raid at Lindisfarne on northeastern England by Danish Vikings.

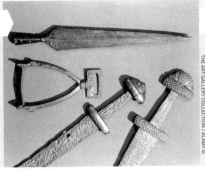

» Viking stirrup and weapons

DENMARK'S BOG BODIES

The people of Iron Age Denmark left little evidence and precious little by way of written records of themselves. Some extraordinary discoveries in the last couple of centuries offer tantalising insights into this culture.

Drainage and peat cutting in Denmark's bogs has yielded hundreds of often amazingly well-preserved bodies of men, women and children mostly from the Iron Age (the early centuries BC and AD).

Many of the bodies are also compelling historical who- and why-dunnits. Burial was unusual (cremation was common at the time) and some appear to have been ritually killed, perhaps due to the supernatural power the Iron Age people are thought to have attributed to the bogs.

If it was ritual killing, were these people victims or willing participants? The Windeby Girl, for example, found in 1950 in Germany, aged about 14, had her hair carefully cropped, suggesting some kind of ritual. Others may have simply been waylaid, murdered and dumped.

The Grauballe Man (p223) certainly died a nasty death that suggests a brutal execution, a subject brilliantly illustrated in the display near Aarhus, a history and a forensics conundrum.

The most famous body of all is that of the Tollund Man (see p238) in Silkeborg, whose head is extraordinarily preserved right down to the stubble on his chin. He died, aged in his 30s, naked but for the beautifully plaited leather noose used to strangle him and the leather cap he has worn for 2000 years. It frames an utterly serene face.

Settlement and assimilation was one reason for a decline in raiding and fighting. The Jelling Stone (p244) of Harald I (Bluetooth) that still stands in the churchyard in Jelling is the document of an even more important factor: the embrace in the 10th century of Christianity in Scandinavia and thus closer cultural ties and a degree (very relatively speaking) of 'civilisation'.

As well as Jelling, other fascinating Viking heritage worth seeking out in Denmark includes the Nationalmuseet in Copenhagen (p43), the Viking ring fortress at Trelleborg (p116) and (if you'd like to see 'real' live Vikings hit each other with rubber swords, and let's face it who doesn't?), the Ribe Vikingecenter (p203).

Perhaps the best way to get a feel for the technical supremacy, bravery and hardihood of the Vikings is to experience their longships first hand at the Roskilde Viking Ship Museum (p102).

950–985	985–1014	1066	1137–1157
King Harald I (Bluetooth), son of Gorm the Old, unifies Denmark. He spearheads the conversion of Danes to Christianity from his court at Jelling.	During the reigns of Harald Bluetooth's son Sweyn Forkbeard and grandsons Harald II and Canute the Great, England is conquered and a short-lived Anglo-Danish kingdom formed.	The defeat of Norwegian Vikings by Harold II of England at the Battle of Stamford Bridge heralds the end of the Viking Era.	Civil strife, assassinations, plots and general skulduggery continues until Valdemar, son of Knud Lavard, takes the throne in 1157, introducing progressive policies in the Jyske Lov (Jutland Code).

A Unified Denmark (Sort Of)

By the early 9th century Jutland (and parts of southern Norway) were more or less united under a single king. In the late 9th century unification of the territories that make up modern-day Denmark inched forwards when warriors led by the Norwegian chieftain Hardegon conquered the Jutland peninsula; Hardegon then began to extend his power base across the rest of Denmark's territory.

The current Danish monarchy traces its roots back to Gorm the Old, Hardegon's son, who reigned in the early 10th century from Jelling in central Jutland. His son, Harald Bluetooth, who ruled for 35 years, concluded the conquest of Denmark as well as completing Denmark's adoption of Christianity, partly to appease his powerful Frankish neighbours to the south who, a century earlier, had sent the missionary Ansgar to build churches in the Danish towns of Ribe and Hedeby.

Harald Bluetooth's son Sweyn (Svend) Forkbeard (r 987–1014) and grandsons Harald II (r 1014–18) and Canute the Great (r 1019–35) conquered England establishing a short-lived Anglo-Danish kingdom over much of the British Isles. Canute the Great was the first true Danish king to sit on the throne of England, reigning in much the same manner as an English king except that he employed Scandinavian soldiers to maintain his command.

When Canute's son Hardecanute died, the balance of power shifted to the English heirs of Alfred the Great, although many of the Danes who had settled in England elected to stay on.

Unsuccessful attempts by the Danes to reclaim England followed and the defeat of the Norwegian Vikings by Harold II of England at the Battle of Stamford Bridge in 1066 heralded the end of the Viking era.

The Bloody Middle Ages

Internal strife, plots, counter plots and assassinations involving rival nobles, wealthy landowners and corrupt church leaders blighted the early medieval era – just look at the blood-soaked timeline from 1086 to 1157.

King Valdemar I eventually united a war-weary country and enacted Denmark's first written laws, known as the Jyske Lov (Jutland Code). His successors enacted other laws that were quite progressive for their time: no imprisonment without just cause, an annual assembly of the *hof* (national council), and the first supreme court.

Margrethe, who had assumed de facto control of the Crown after her young son Oluf died in 1387, became the official head of state and Denmark's first ruling queen. The next year Swedish nobles sought Margrethe's assistance in a rebellion against their unpopular German-born

Key Viking sights

» Lindholm Høje
» Roskilde longships
» Ladbyskibet Nationalmuseet

Denmark is the oldest monarchy in Europe.

MONARCHY

1219	1363	1375–87
The Dannebrog (Danish flag; today the oldest national flag in the world) is raised for the first time, its creation supposedly divinely provided and firing the Danes to victory in Estonia under Valdemar II.	Norway's King Haakon marries Margrethe, daughter of the Danish king Valdemar IV, who is to become an influential and powerful queen.	Five-year-old Oluf becomes king of Denmark following the death of Valdemar IV, and five years later also becomes Norwegian king. His mother assumes de facto control on his death.

OJPHOTOS / ALAMY ©

» Dannebrog (Danish flag)

king. The Swedes hailed Margrethe as their regent, and in turn she sent Danish troops to Sweden, securing victory over the king's forces.

A decade later Margrethe established a formal alliance between Denmark, Norway and Sweden known as the Kalmar Union, to counter the powerful German-based Hanseatic League that had come to dominate regional trade.

In 1410 King Erik of Pomerania, Margrethe's grandson, staged an unsuccessful attack on the Hanseatic League, which sapped the Kalmar Union's vitality. This, together with Erik's penchant for appointing Danes to public office in Sweden and Norway, soured relations with aristocrats in those countries. In 1438 the Swedish council withdrew from the union, whereupon the Danish nobility deposed Erik.

Erik's successor, King Christopher III, made amends by pledging to keep the administrations of the three countries separate. However, the union continued to be a rocky one, and in 1523 the Swedes elected their own king, Gustav Vasa. The Kalmar Union was permanently dissolved, but Norway would remain under Danish rule for another three centuries.

> Learn everything you ever wanted to know about a millennium of Danish monarchy at www.danske konger.dk.

The Lutheran Reformation & Civil War

The monarchy and Catholic Church played out a pivotal power struggle during the Danish Reformation. Caught in the middle of this religious and political foment was King Frederik I who over some 10 years went from promising to fight heresy against Catholicism to inviting Lutheran preachers to Denmark. When Frederik died, the lack of a clear successor left the country in civil war.

The following year (1534) Hanseatic mercenaries from Lübeck (now in Germany) invaded southern Jutland and Zealand. By and large the Lübeckers were welcomed as liberators by peasants and members of the middle class, who were in revolt against the nobility.

Alarmed by the revolt, a coalition of aristocrats and Catholic bishops crowned the Lutheran Christian III as king. Still, the rebellion raged on. In Jutland, manor houses were set ablaze and the peasants made advances against the armies of the aristocracy.

Christian's general, Rantzau, took control, cutting Lübeck off from the sea and marching northward through Jutland, brutally smashing peasant bands. Rantzau's troops besieged Copenhagen, where merchants supported the uprising and welcomed the prospect of becoming a Hanseatic stronghold. Cut off from the outside world, Copenhagen's citizens suffered starvation and epidemics before surrendering after a year in 1536.

Christian III quickly consolidated his power, offering leniency to the merchants and Copenhagen burghers who had revolted in exchange for their allegiance. Catholic bishops, on the other hand, were arrested and

> The Order of the Elephant was instituted by King Christian 1 in the 1470s to celebrate the battle elephants of the Christian crusades.

1396–1439	1534	1588–1648
Reign of King Erik of Pomerania, Margrethe's grandson, stages an unsuccessful attack on the Hanseatic League, which exhausts the resources of the Kalmar Union. The Danish nobility depose Erik in 1439.	Following King Frederick I's death, Hanseatic mercenaries from Lübeck (now in Germany) invade southern Jutland and Zealand. Danish peasants and members of the middle class welcome the invaders.	The early prosperous and peaceful years of Christian IV's long reign end in 1625 when Christian attempts to neutralise Swedish expansion by beginning the Thirty Years' War. Denmark suffers crippling losses.

» Christian IV's Rosenborg Slot

monasteries, churches and other ecclesiastical estates became the property of the Crown.

Thus the Danish Lutheran Church became the only state-sanctioned denomination and was placed under the direct control of the king. Buoyed by a treasury enriched by confiscated Church properties, the monarchy emerged from the civil war stronger than ever.

War & Absolute Monarchy

A period of peace marked the early reign of Christian IV who then embarked on what became the ruinous Thirty Years' War. The aim of the war was to neutralise Swedish expansion; its outcome for Denmark was morale- and coffer-sapping losses.

Seeing a chance for revenge against Sweden, following its troubled occupation of Poland, Christian IV's successor, Frederik III, once again declared war in 1657. For the Danes, ill-prepared for battle, it was a tremendous miscalculation.

Sweden's King Gustave led his troops back from Poland through Germany and into Jutland, plundering his way north. During 1657–58 – the most severe winter in Danish history – King Gustave marched his soldiers across the frozen seas of the Lille Bælt between Fredericia and the island of Funen. King Gustave's uncanny success unnerved the Danes and he proceeded without serious resistance across the Store Bælt to Lolland and then on to Falster.

The Swedish king had barely made it across the frozen waters of the Storstrømmen to Zealand when the thawing ice broke away behind him, precariously separating him and his advance detachment from the rest of his forces. However, the Danes failed to recognise their sudden advantage; instead of capturing the Swedish king, they sued for peace and agreed to yet another disastrous treaty.

In 1658 Denmark signed the humiliating Treaty of Roskilde, ceding a third of its territory, including the island of Bornholm and all territories on the Swedish mainland. Only Bornholm, which eventually staged a bloody revolt against the Swedes, would again fly the Danish flag.

Absolute monarchy returned in 1660, when King Frederik III cunningly convened a gathering of nobles, placed them under siege, and forced them to nullify their powers of council. Frederik declared his right of absolute rule, declaring the king the highest head on earth, above all human laws and inferior to God alone.

In the following decades the now all-powerful monarchy rebuilt the military and continued to pick fruitless fights with Sweden. Peace of a sort eventually descended and for much of the 18th century the Danes and Swedes managed to coexist without serious hostilities.

A polar bear was included in the Danish coat of arms in the 1660s to symbolise the country's claim of sovereignty over Greenland.

So concentrated were royal powers that Frederik III's successor had to place the crown upon his own head during the church service – nobody else was deemed worthy.

1658	1660-5	1675–1720	1784
Denmark signs the Treaty of Roskilde, the most lamented humiliation in its history, losing a third of its territory, including the island of Bornholm and all territories on the Swedish mainland.	King Frederik III establishes absolute monarchy. He introduces an absolutist constitution called the Kongeloven (Royal Act), which becomes the law of the land for most of the following two centuries.	The monarchy rebuilds the military and fights three more wars with Sweden (1675–79, 1699–1700 and 1709–20), without regaining its lost territories. A period of relative peace follows.	The young Crown Prince Frederik VI assumes control, brings progressive landowners into government and introduces a sweeping series of reforms improving rights for the masses.

Revolution

By the turn of the 19th century, Denmark's trading prowess was worrying Britain, by now the world's pre-eminent sea power. When Denmark signed a pact of armed neutrality with Sweden, Prussia and Russia, Britain's navy attacked Copenhagen in 1801, heavily damaging the Danish fleet and forcing Denmark to withdraw from the pact.

When Napoleon fell in 1814, the Swedes, then allied with Britain, successfully demanded that Denmark, an ally of France, cede Norway to them.

Denmark managed to avoid further conflicts and actually profited from the war trade until 1807, when a new treaty between France and Russia once again drew the Danes closer to the conflict.

Wary of Napoleon's growing influence in the Baltic, Britain feared that Denmark might support France. Despite Denmark's neutrality, the British fleet unleashed a devastating surprise bombardment on Copenhagen, setting much of the city ablaze, destroying its naval yards and confiscating the entire Danish fleet.

Although the unprovoked attack was unpopular enough back home to have been roundly criticised by the British parliament, Britain nonetheless kept the Danish fleet. The British then offered the Danes an alliance – they unsurprisingly refused the offer and instead joined the continental alliance against Britain, who retaliated by blockading both Danish and Norwegian waters, causing poverty in Denmark and famine in Norway.

Despite the disastrous early years of the 19th century, by the 1830s Denmark was flourishing again, economically and culturally. Philosopher Søren Kierkegaard, theologian Nikolaj Frederik Severin Grundtvig and writer Hans Christian Andersen emerged as prominent figures. Sculptor Bertel Thorvaldsen bestowed his grand neoclassical statues on Copenhagen, and Christoffer Wilhelm Eckersberg introduced the Danish school of art.

Democracy

When revolution swept Europe in the spring of 1848, Denmark's new political parties, which had arisen from the debating chambers of the new provincial assemblies, waxed with the waning power of the monarchy. The new Danish king, Frederik VII, under pressure from the new liberal party, abolished the absolute monarchy and drew up a democratic constitution, establishing a parliament with two chambers, Folketing and Landsting, whose members were elected by popular vote.

Although the king retained a limited voice, parliament took control of legislative powers. The constitution also established an independent judiciary and guaranteed the rights of free speech, religion and assembly. Denmark had changed overnight from a virtual dictatorship to one of the most democratic countries in Europe.

When Denmark's new constitution threatened to incorporate the border duchy of Schleswig, linguistically and culturally German, as an inte-

Late 18th century	1800–01	1846–49	1901
Feudal obligations of the peasantry abolished. Large tracts of land are broken up and redistributed to the landless. Education is made compulsory for all children under the age of 14.	Denmark signs a pact of armed neutrality with Sweden, Prussia and Russia. In response Britain's navy attacks Copenhagen, battering the Danish fleet and forcing Denmark to leave the pact.	Political ferment sweeps Europe; two growing Danish factions (farmers and liberals) join forces to form a liberal party in 1846. The Danish constitution is enacted in 1849 and absolute monarchy abolished.	The Venstrereformparti (Left Reform Party) sweeps to power and embarks on an ambitious social reform program, including amending the constitution to give women the right to vote.

DENMARK'S FINEST HOUR

Soon after taking full control of the country during WWII, in October 1943, Denmark's Nazi occupiers planned, as elsewhere in the parts of Europe they occupied, to round up Jewish Danes, with the aim of deporting them to their deaths in the concentration camps. The Danish resistance had other ideas and in an extraordinarily well co-ordinated operation smuggled some 7200 Jews – about 90% of those left in Denmark – into neutral Sweden.

gral part of Denmark, the German population in the duchy allied with neighbouring Holstein, sparking years of unrest.

In 1864 the Prussian prime minister, Otto von Bismarck, declared war on a militarily weak Denmark and captured Schleswig. Further eroding Denmark's sovereignty, it raised doubts about Denmark's survival as a nation.

In the wake of that defeat, a conservative government took and retained power until the end of the century. The conservatives oversaw a number of economic advances: extending the railway throughout the country and rapid industrialisation that established large-scale shipbuilding, brewing and sugar-refining industries.

The 20th Century

Denmark declared neutrality at the outbreak of WWII, but Germany, threatened by the growing Allied presence in Norway, coveted coastal bases in northern Jutland and in April 1940 seized key Danish strategic defences and occupied the country.

The Danes, managing to retain a degree of autonomy, trod a thin line, running domestic affairs under close Nazi supervision until August 1943 when the Germans took outright control. A Danish resistance movement quickly mushroomed.

Although the island of Bornholm was heavily bombarded by Soviet forces, the rest of Denmark emerged from WWII relatively unscathed.

The Social Democrats led a comprehensive social-welfare state in postwar Denmark and the cradle-to-grave medical care, education and public assistance was established. As the economy grew and the labour market increased, women entered the workforce in unprecedented numbers and household incomes reached new heights.

In the 1960s, a rebellion by young people, disillusioned with growing materialism, the nuclear arms race and an authoritarian educational system, took hold in the larger cities. The movement came to a head in Copenhagen in 1971, when protesters tore down the fence of an abandoned military base at the east side of Christianshavn and turned the site into

In recognition of its actions in saving its Jewish population, Denmark is remembered as one of the Righteous Among the Nations at the Yad Vashem Holocaust Memorial in Jerusalem.

1943	1953	1973	2000
In a hastily planned operation, the Danish resistance successfully smuggles some 7200 Jews into Sweden on hearing of Nazi plans to round them up and transport them to its European concentration camps.	Danish constitution is amended to allow a female monarch, paving the way for Margrethe II to become monarch, Denmark's first female monarch since the 14th century.	Denmark joins the European Community (now the European Union).	Reaching the limits of their tolerance for the extent of the European project, Denmark votes against adopting the new European currency, the euro.

a commune, the 'free state of Christiania'. Thousands of people flocked here, and the government let Christiania stand as a 'social experiment' that survives to this day.

Denmark's external relationships were not without their troubles either. It joined the European Community, the predecessor of the EU, in 1973, but has been rather more hesitant about the subsequent expansion of the EU's powers. Denmark rejected the 1992 Maastricht Treaty (which set the terms for much greater economic and political cooperation) as well as the adoption of the euro.

Meanwhile, Denmark maintained its leadership stance for socially liberal policies, including same-sex marriage (instituted in 1989) and aggressive implementation of alternative energy sources.

In the late 1990s and early 2000s, the government was a coalition of the centre-right Venstre party and the Conservative People's Party, sometimes also calling on the support of the generally nationalist right-wing Danish People's Party (DPP). This new power structure led Denmark to impose some of the toughest immigration laws in Europe in 2002, including restrictions on marriage between Danes and foreigners.

> In 2000 Denmark resoundingly rejected the adoption of the euro by a referendum.

> A History of Denmark by Palle Lauring is a well-written excursion through the lives and times of the Danish people.

Modern Times

The last decade has been turbulent – by Danish standards anyway – in the social and political realms.

As in other European nations, the political right has been resurgent in this famously liberal nation. It's been reflected in a growing concern over immigration – particularly from Muslim countries – and an erosion of traditional values.

The cultural and religious challenge posed by immigration was put into relief in 2006. Denmark found itself in the unfamiliar role of villain in the eyes of many Muslims, and became the focus of violent demonstrations all around the world, following the publication of cartoons depicting the prophet Mohammed – a deep taboo for many Muslims but an issue of freedom of speech for liberal news editors – in the *Jyllands-Posten* newspaper.

The rise of the right-wing DPP, which has become an influential minority party in the Danish parliament, is instructive. The traditionalist, antimulticultural DPP supports, among other things, the monarchy, the national church, strong defence, law and order.

In practical terms, the DPP's participation contributed to Denmark's joining the USA, UK and other allies in the 2003 Iraq War and Denmark's commitment to maintain its role in Afghanistan.

By 2010, the political pendulum began swinging to the left again as discontent over the country's stuttering economic performance grew. In September 2011, parliamentary elections saw a new, centre-left coalition take over after a closely fought election. See p282 for more details.

2004

Crown Prince Frederik weds Australian-born Mary Elizabeth Donaldson in a fairy-tale ceremony watched by millions of people around the world.

2005–06

Denmark becomes a villain to many Muslims, and the focus of violent demonstrations following the publication of cartoons depicting the prophet Mohammed in *Jyllands-Posten*.

» Crown Prince Frederik and Crown Princess Mary

Danish Design

Is there a more design-conscious nation than Denmark, or a more design-obsessed capital than Copenhagen? Sure, the Italians like a nice sofa and the French have their frocks, but in Denmark design excellence runs deeper than that.

One of the country's most inspirational qualities is its love and mastery of the applied arts. Along with its Scandinavian neighbours, Denmark has had a massive influence on the way the world builds its public and private spaces, and on the way it designs interiors, furniture and homewares. Since the 1950s Danish designers have blazed trails in these fields, much of their output defined by cool clean lines, graceful shapes and streamlined accessibility.

Architecture

In the second half of the 20th century a number of Danish architects introduced new designs. The most influential was Jørn Utzon, who designed the world-famous Sydney Opera House, constructed in the 1960s.

Copenhagen X (www.cphx.dk) is a brilliant source of information about new architecture, innovation and urban development in the capital. It's website offers downloadable maps with bike routes and podwalks for archi-buffs.

CAPITAL DRAMA

Functional, humanistic, organic and sympathetic are all adjectives that might be used to describe the defining features of classic postwar Danish architecture, best embodied in the work of architects such as Jørn Utzon and Arne Jacobsen. Their usually restrained take on modernism has been superseded since the 1990s, often by a much bolder, brasher, even aggressive type of building.

Here is a handful of Copenhagen's most dramatic modern buildings.

» **Radisson Blu Royal Hotel** (Arne Jacobsen) Not content with merely creating a building, Jacobsen designed every item in the hotel, down to the door handles and cutlery, and including the famous Egg and Swan chairs. Room 606 remains entirely as it was on opening day in 1960.

» **The Black Diamond** (Schmidt, Hammer & Lassen) Located next to the waterfront, Copenhagen's monolithic library extension in black granite and smoked glass, completed in 1999, makes a strikingly modern statement.

» **Operaen** (Henning Larsen) It seems to be the rule that any large commissioned public building must be marked by the word 'controversial' and the opera house (completed 2005) is no exception. Its squat exterior still divides opinion, although the marble and maple-wood interior is a triumph.

» **Arken** (Søren Robert Lund) This remarkable contemporary art museum is renowned for the building that houses it (completed 1996, extensions in 2008 and 2009). Its nautical ship shape is inspired by its beachfront location.

» **Royal Danish Playhouse** (Lundgaard & Tranberg) The Skuespilhuset (completed 2008) faces Operaen and has an elegant glass-house design, including a projected upper floor of coloured glass that hosts alfresco dining.

DESIGN WEEK

He's known for incorporating elements as wide-reaching as Maya, Japanese and Islamic into traditional Danish design.

In Jutland you can admire the designs of Jørn Utzon in Esbjerg and Skagen, but the best place to visit is the Utzon Center in Aalborg. This impressive design and architecture space was the last building designed by the celebrated architect before his death in 2008.

Other notable contemporary Danish architects include Johan von Spreckelsen, who designed the huge cubelike La Grande Arche in Paris, and Arne Jacobsen, an innovator in international modernism who pioneered Danish interpretations of the Bauhaus style. Check out Jacobsen's Radisson Blu Royal Hotel in Copenhagen, the functionalist town hall he designed for Aarhus (with interiors by Hans Wegner), and his Kubeflex prototype summerhouse at Kolding's Trapholt museum.

Furniture & Interiors

As befits one of the great design cities of the world, Copenhagen stages a biennial design event, Copenhagen Design Week (www.copenhagendesignweek.com), in late August/early September in odd-numbered years.

As wonderful as Danish design-focused stores, museums, hotels and restaurants are (and my word they are wonderful), the very best place to see Danish design is in its natural environment: a Danish home. To the Danes, good design is not just for museums and institutions; they live with it and use it every day. And they're quietly patriotic too, preferring Danish brands over imports.

Visit a Danish home and you'll invariably find a Bang & Olufsen stereo and/or TV in the living room, Poul Henningsen lamps hanging from the ceiling, Arne Jacobsen or Hans Wegner chairs in the dining room, and the table set with Royal Copenhagen dinner sets, Georg Jensen cutlery and Bodum glassware.

Modern Danish furniture focuses on a practical style and the principle that its design should be tailored to the comfort of the user. This smooth, unadorned style traces its roots to Kaare Klint (1888–1954), an architect who founded the furniture design department at the Royal Academy of Fine Arts in Copenhagen. He spent much of his career studying the human form and modified a number of chair designs for added functionality.

In 1949 one of Klint's contemporaries, Hans Wegner (1914–2007), created the Round Chair. Its fluid, curving lines made it an instant classic and a model for many furniture designers to follow, as well as helping

THE ROOTS OF MODERN DANISH DESIGN

'Modern Danish design stems from an era in the 1950s when there was a remarkable confluence of talented designers and also manufacturers who were interested in design and fed up with traditional dark, heavy furniture.

'It was an ideal time for Denmark: in a small country it is easier for talented people to find and work with each other, and while much of the rest of Europe had until recently lain in ruins, Denmark had remained relatively untouched. The fact that industrialisation came quite late to Denmark also meant that it had retained much of its tradition of craftsmanship. The care for detail and the love of simplicity were at the heart of the movement.

'Much of the innovation taking place today is away from interiors and furniture in the fields of industrial and agricultural design, although there's a lot going on in design generally. Some of the new young designers are still influenced by the heroes of the 1950s, but many are going in their own crazy directions. Danish design is a lot less provincial today; designers travel more and bring more influences to bear on their work.

'Although the styles might be changing, I think there's still very much a focus on the experience of the end-user, which has always been an important strength.'

Birgitta Capetillo, design consultant

FOUR LEGS GOOD: CLASSIC DANISH CHAIRS

Labouring with an almost fetishistic obsession, the great Danish designers such as Arne Jacobsen could spend long, angst-ridden months, even years, perfecting a single chair. Still, the results made the world sit up straight; in the 1950s *Time Magazine* even devoted a cover to the phenomenon. There are dozens to choose from, but some of the classics follow.

» **The Round Chair** (Hans Wegner) In 1950 US *Interiors* magazine put the chair on its cover, calling it 'the world's most beautiful chair'. It became known simply as 'the Chair', and began making high-profile appearances such as the televised 1961 presidential debates between Nixon and Kennedy.

» **The Ant Chair** (Jacobsen) Perhaps the most (in)famous chair in the world, thanks to the 1960s Lewis Morley photograph of call girl Christine Keeler (from the British Profumo Affair) sitting on one.

» **The Egg Chair** (Jacobsen) This represents the essence of jetsetting 1950s modernity. Jacobsen designed the Egg Chair for the Radisson Blu Royal Hotel.

» **The Panton Chair** (Verner Panton) After helping with Jacobsen's Ant Chair, Panton went on to do great things in plastic, the most iconic being his Panton Chair.

» **Nxt Chair** (Peter Karpf) Beech plywood moulded into angular planes is the defining characteristic of this striking design, which took 30 years to reach production. It helped spawn the Voxia line, which is still going strong.

establish the first successful overseas export market for Danish furniture. A wonderful array of Wegner-designed chairs is displayed in the Tønder Museum in the designer's home town (see p209).

A decade after Wegner's Round Chair, architect Arne Jacobsen created the Ant, a form of chair designed to be mass-produced, which became the model for the stacking chairs now found in schools and cafeterias worldwide. Jacobsen also designed the Egg and the Swan; both are rounded, uncomplicated upholstered chairs with revolving seats perched on pedestal stands.

Danish design prevails in stylish lamps as well. The country's best-known lamp designer was Poul Henningsen (1894–1967), who emphasised the need for lighting to be soft, for the shade to cast a pleasant shadow and for the light bulb to be blocked from direct view. His PH5 lamp created in 1958 remains one of the most popular hanging lamps sold in Denmark today.

The clean lines of industrial design are also evident in the avant-garde sound systems and televisions produced by Bang & Olufsen; and in Danish silver and cutlery design generally. The father of modern Danish silverwork was the sculptor and silversmith Georg Jensen (1866–1935), who artistically incorporated curvilinear designs; his namesake company is still a leader in the field.

INDEX: is a Danish-based nonprofit organisation that works to promote design and design processes that have the capacity to improve the lives of people worldwide. Read more about its inspiring work at www.index award.dk.

Outdoor Activities

Denmark is a nation with close ties to the sea. Its 406 islands (about 70 of them inhabited), and its coastline stretching 7314km, ensure that no place in Denmark is more than 52km from the beach.

Having been cooped up for most of the winter, Denmark comes alive in summer, shaking off winter's grey blanket to catch a Scandi tan. Although small, the country has some great diversity for activities, from island-hopping cycling adventures to canoeing through the Lake District. The sea, never far away, offers fishing, sailing, windsurfing and beach going, while the national parks and hiking trails offer walkers a chance to stretch their legs. And everywhere, the cycling opportunities are outstanding.

Cycling

Denmark is a superb country for cyclists, with more than 12,000km of signposted cycle routes and relatively quiet country roads that wend through an attractive, gently undulating landscape.

As well as the Danes' use of cycling as a widespread means of commuting, you'll also see locals (and tourists) enjoying increasingly popular cycling holidays. The big draw for touring cyclists are the 11 national routes (see the table, p298), which are in excellent condition, but there are also oodles of regional and local routes to get you pedalling. The routes are well suited to recreational cyclists, including families with children.

Danish cyclists enjoy rights that, in most other countries, are reserved for motorists. There are bicycle lanes along major city roads and through central areas, road signs are posted for bicycle traffic, and bicycle racks can be found at grocery shops, museums, train stations and many other public places. Drivers are so accommodating to cyclists in this country that cycling is an almost surreal experience.

When touring the country by bike, accommodation is easy to find, be it at a small country inn or camping ground. One advantage of Denmark's small scale is that you're never far from a bed and a hot shower.

For quality rental bikes, Copenhagen and Aarhus are your best starting points. For general information on bicycle transport, see p327.

'TIS THE SEASON

If you're thinking about visiting Denmark to partake of the outdoors, it's worth bearing in mind a few things. There's an old joke that Denmark has two winters – a green one and a white one – but that is rather unkind. While it's true the weather can be fickle, the summer season most reliably runs from mid-June to mid-August. That's when there are enough travellers around to ensure regular departures of boat cruises or frequent schedules of windsurfing classes etc, and hence there's a wider range of activity options during this two-month window. Depending on weather and demand, however, many operators may open in May and remain open until mid/late September.

And in winter…? Denmark is *not* a destination for winter-sports enthusiasts. The country's highest post is a trifling 171m. That's not to say that Danes don't love (or excel at) snowbound activity – it's just that many of them head north to Norway to engage in it.

OUTDOOR ACTIVITIES SWIMMING

CYCLING BORNHOLM

Out in the Baltic, magical Bornholm is ideal for exploring by bike. More than 230km of bike trails cover main roads, extensive forests, former train routes and fine sandy beaches. There's a multitude of picturesque coastal hamlets and medieval round churches, and the excellent local food and drink are a great reward for pedalling.

Consider burning some calories on the 24km Gourmet Route from Gudhjem to Østermarie and on to Svaneke, cycling via factories producing chocolates, toffees and sweets; smokehouses; farm shops; a dairy; and a microbrewery. Pick up route information from the tourist office in Rønne or bike-hire outlets.

Cycling Routes

Signs along cycling routes are blue, with a white bike symbol.
» National routes: white route number in a red square. North–south routes have uneven numbers; east–west routes are even.
» Regional routes: white route number on a blue background, with numbers 16 to 99.
» Local routes: white route number on a blue background, with numbers 100 to 999.

The table on p298 outlines Denmark's 11 national cycling routes.

Planning & Resources

The best way to tour Denmark by bike is by grabbing a map and planning it yourself. Tours, not surprisingly, are also available and are well run although they tend to be rather pricey.

The best map for planning is the *Cycling Map of Denmark* (25kr), a 1:500,000-scale map that shows all the national routes. (Note that it's great for general planning, but not detailed enough to use on the trail.) Each county produces its own detailed 1:100,000 cycle touring maps; many of them come complete with booklets detailing accommodation, sights and other local information, making it easy to self-plan your tour. These maps are in Danish, German and English, cost around 129kr, and are readily available at tourist offices or online via the Danish cycling federation, Dansk Cyklist Forbund (its shop is at http://shop.dcf.dk).

Websites

Cycle Guide DK (http://cycleguide.dk) Copenhagen-focused, but with good advice on safety issues, and cycling culture and etiquette.
Dansk Cyklist Forbund (www.dcf.dk, some in Danish) Website of the Danish Cycling Federation.
Visit Denmark (www.visitdenmark.com/cycling) Loads of useful information on its cycling-dedicated pages.

Swimming

Although the water temperature would worry even brass monkeys most of the year, enjoyable seaside swimming can be had in the warmer months (July and August). Generally speaking the Baltic waters will be a degree or two warmer than those of the North Sea. The quality of the beaches is outstanding as the majority have clean water, silky sand and plenty of room. If you're swimming on the west coast of Jutland, caution needs to be taken with currents and undertows, otherwise the waters are generally calm and child-friendly.

Aside from the miles of beaches, the vast majority of towns have a family-focused aqua centre with heated pool (look for the *svømmehal*, or swimming hall). These are getting larger and more grandiose, offering

The Cycling Embassy of Denmark (www.cycling-embassy.dk) has a great range of information and some cool stats too – for example, in Denmark, 16% of all trips are by bike. Nine out of 10 Danes own a bicycle; 45% of all Danish children cycle to school.

DENMARK'S CYCLING ROUTES

ROUTE NO	ROUTE NAME	DISTANCE	DESCRIPTION
1	Vestkystruten (West Coast Route)	560km (70% sealed)	Begins in Rudbøl (near Møgeltønder, by the German border) and runs to Skagen along the windswept west coast of Jutland, taking in sandy beaches, tidal flats and dunes. You'll have to contend with winds! See also www.northsea-cycle.com.
2	Diagonalruten (Diagonal Route)	420km (80% sealed)	Begins in the north Jutland fishing port of Hanstholm and runs southeast across central Jutland to Ebeltoft. The Elbeltoft–Odden ferry allows you to pick up the route again through northern Zealand to Copenhagen.
3	Hærvejsruten (Hærvej Route)	450km (78% sealed)	Heads from Skagen along the backbone of Jutland all the way to Padborg on the German border. From Viborg it follows the Hærvej, or Old Military Road. See also www.haervej.dk.
4	Øst-Vest Ruten (East-West Route)	310km (90% sealed)	Runs from Søndervig on the west Jutland coast east to Aarhus, then by ferry across to Kalundborg, and east across Zealand to finish in Copenhagen.
5	Østkystruten (East Coast Route)	650km (90% sealed)	The longest route begins in Skagen and runs the length of Jutland, hugging the capes and headlands of the east coast to finish at Sønderborg.
6	Englandsruten (England Route)	330km (92% sealed)	Begins at the ferry terminal in Esbjerg (with ferries to/from England's Harwich, hence the route's name) and runs east through Funen and Zealand to finish in Copenhagen. Note: cyclists are not permitted on the 18km Storebælt bridge linking Funen and Zealand; you will need to take a train across.

pools of Olympic proportions plus plenty of other ways to wrinkle your skin (waterslides, Jacuzzis, saunas, kids' play area, day spas).

Watersports

The wild winds of Jutland's west coast have gained plenty of attention from windsurfers and kitesurfers, and the consistently good conditions attract many European enthusiasts to Klitmøller and Hvide Sande.

Not only do these towns hold numerous contests each year, but they boast great terrain for all skill levels. Experts can carve up the wild North Sea breakers, while beginners can master the basics on the inland fjords.

At both Klitmøller and Hvide Sande, outfits offer gear rental and lessons in windsurfing and kitesurfing. There are other watersports on offer, too – surfing, and stand-up paddle surfing. At Hvide Sande there's also a cool water-skiing course, which skiers navigate using cable rope-tows.

Sailing

Denmark's varied 7314km of coastline and 406 islands are made for sailing, something the Danes embrace enthusiastically. The island-speckled, sheltered cruising area between Jutland's east coast and Sweden is very popular. The mixture of sea, calmer inshore waters and still fjords, combined with scores of pretty, cobbled and often historic harbours makes sailing a perfect way to explore the country. Yachts

ROUTE NO	ROUTE NAME	DISTANCE	DESCRIPTION
7	I Hvidernes Fodspor (In the Footsteps of the Whites)	240km (90% sealed)	A family-friendly route that begins at Odden in northwest Zealand and travels south through north Falster and Lolland to end at Rødbyhavn.
8	Grænseruten (Border Route)	360km (95% sealed)	Also known as the South Sea Route, this trail sweeps across southern Denmark and requires a couple of island hops. It begins in Rudbøl, traverses Jutland to Als, crosses to southern Funen, Langeland, Lolland, Falster and ends at Møns Klint. See also www.grenzroute.com.
9	Øresundsruten (Øresund Route)	290km (92% sealed)	This route has links with Sweden and Germany thanks to ferry connections at its start (Helsingør) and end (Gedser) points. It follows the east coast of Zealand before tracking south through Møn and Falster.
10	Bornholm Rundt (Around Bornholm)	105km (90% sealed)	Bornholm is an idyllic island encircled by a popular cycling route. The distances between sights and villages are very cyclist-friendly.
12*	Limfjordsruten (Limfjord Route)	610km (90% sealed)	The newest national route hugs both sides of the Limfjord in northern Jutland, from the Kattegat to the North Sea. Ferry and bridge 'shortcuts' across the fjord are possible. See also www.visitlimfjorden.com.

*Note: there is no route 11.

and motorboats equipped with all the necessary safety, living and navigational equipment can be hired – prices vary considerably by season and size of craft.

Charter a yacht through Scancharter (www.scancharter.com) or JIM Søferie (www.jim-soeferie.dk). The latter website also has a few tour suggestions, while www.visitdenmark.com/sailing and www.archipelago.nu offer good sailing overviews.

If hiring your own craft sounds too much like hard work, major towns along Funen's southern coast offer sailing cruises around the islands of the South Funen Archipelago.

Canoeing & Kayaking

Canoeists and kayakers will be equally at home paddling the extensive coastline and fjords or the rivers and lakes. White water is about the only thing that's missing in mountain-free Denmark.

The country's best canoeing and kayaking can be experienced along the rivers Gudenå (in Jutland) and Suså (in Zealand). The idyllic forests and gentle waterways of central Jutland's prized Lake District are perfect for cycling, rambling and, especially, canoeing – multiday canoeing-and-camping adventures are possible here. You can hire canoes and equipment in Silkeborg. The lakes are generally undemanding

Check the eco credentials before you hit the beach courtesy of Blue Flag (www.blueflag.org). It's an organisation that works towards sustainable development of beaches and marinas through strict criteria.

TOP BEACHES

Our authors have travelled the length and breadth of Denmark to give you their favourite spots to take a dip.

Copenhagen (Islands Brygge) Not technically a beach, but slap-bang in Copenhagen's main canal, this designer outdoor pool comes with downtown views and delectable eye candy.

Zealand (Tisvildeleje) Sandbars, shallows and chic hotels on Zealand's north coast 'riviera'.

Møn, Falster & Lolland (Marielyst, Falster) Endless sandy beaches and a family-friendly holiday vibe.

Bornholm (Dueodde) Soft endless sand, epic skies and a Nordic forest backdrop.

Funen (Drejø, Skarø and Hjortø) Tiny islands southwest of Svendborg make great escapes for wild swimming away from the crowds. Lapping waves and seabirds may be your only company.

Southern Jutland (Rømø) Miles of west-coast emptiness, plus hair-raising speed-machine activities down south.

Central Jutland (Hvide Sande) Colourful wind- and kitesurfers harnessing the North Sea wind.

Northern Jutland (Skagen) Wild winds and shifting sands to the west, calm family-friendly waters to the east, and everywhere are the blue hues that inspired artists.

as far as water conditions go, although some previous experience is an advantage.

Canoeing the small coves, bays and peninsulas of several Danish fjords is also an option, including Limfjorden in northern Jutland and the fjords of Zealand: Roskilde Fjord, Holbæk Fjord and Isefjord.

The Hærvej (www.haervej.dk), the Old Military Road, is a 250km historic route from the German border north to Viborg. It's been converted into a popular, well-maintained cycling, hiking and horse-riding trail; the website has information about facilities along the route.

Walking

There's not much wilderness in wee Denmark (especially in comparison to its larger, more mountain-endowed neighbours), and walking and hiking is not as widespread a phenomenon as cycling. But rambling is popular nonetheless, and the tourist authorities are trying to raise the profile of the activity – check out www.visitdenmark.com/walking for a primer.

All the local tourist offices will be able to point you in the direction of a local area with walking trails. In Jutland, there are some picturesque trails through the Rebild Bakker and Mols Bjerge national parks, and the Lake District; in southern Funen, the Archipelago Trail (p170) is a beauty.

Fishing

All that coastline means great fishing, and fishing enthusiasts can opt for river and lake fishing, or angling in the rolling North Sea or the calmer Baltic. Everything you need to know (including licensing requirements) is at www.visitdenmark.com/angling.

Food & Drink

Not so long ago, Denmark would have been among the last places on earth recommended for food-lovers to visit. Today, gourmands are worshipping at the altar of New Nordic cuisine, and Copenhagen is seen as an essential destination for anyone interested in food and food trends (but can they land a reservation at Noma?).

The Danish capital is home to the world's number-one restaurant (Noma, taking top spot in the S.Pellegrino World's 50 Best Restaurants rankings in both 2010 and 2011); the best young chef (Rasmus Kofoed, gold medallist at the 2011 chef Olympics, the Bocuse d'Or); and more Michelin-starred restaurants per capita (10) than any other city. Word is spreading: Denmark has produce to be proud of, and chefs with the training and skills to make the most of it.

Two high-calibre food festivals are Copenhagen Cooking (www. copenhagencooking.dk), held annually in the second half of August, and Denmark's biggest chef competition, Sol Over Gudhjem (www.solover gudhjemkonkurrence.dk, in Danish), held on Bornholm in June.

New Nordic Cuisine

So what's taken the Danish capital from its humdrum pork-and-potatoes tradition to culinary dynamo, and what exactly is New Nordic cuisine?

Chief responsibility for the spotlight now shining Copenhagen's way lies with the city's young chefs, many of whom have apprenticed with some of the most influential chefs in the world.

These young guns have taken their experience and combined it with a passion for Denmark's raw ingredients – its excellent pork products, beef, game, seafood, root vegetables, wild berries – and a reverence for

For the authors' picks of the best restaurants in each region, turn to the introductory page of each regional chapter. For information on travelling and dining with kids in tow, check out p34.

ESSENTIAL DANISH FOOD & DRINK

» **New Nordic flavours** Sample creations inspired by the culinary movement that has everyone talking, in one of Copenhagen's hottest restaurants (book ahead).

» **Smørrebrød** Rye bread topped with anything from beef tartar to egg and shrimp, the open sandwich is Denmark's most famous culinary export.

» **Sild** Smoked, cured, pickled or fried, herring is a local staple and best washed down with generous serves of akvavit (alcoholic spirit, commonly made with potatoes and spiced with caraway).

» **Kanelsnegl** A calorific delight, the 'cinnamon snail' is a sweet, buttery pastry, sometimes laced with chocolate.

» **Akvavit** Denmark's best-loved spirit is caraway-spiced akvavit from Aalborg, drunk straight down as a shot, followed by a chaser of øl (beer).

» **Beer** Carlsberg may dominate, but Denmark's expanding battalion of microbreweries includes Ølfabrikken (in Roskilde), Amager Bryghus (Copenhagen) and Mikkeller (brewed at different breweries).

the seasons. They have then cast their net wider, to encompass ingredients from the wider Nordic region – produce that is unique to, or thrives in, the often-extreme Nordic climates, landscapes and waters (such as Greenlandic musk ox, horse mussels from the Faroe Islands, obscure berries from Finland, truffles grown on the Swedish island of Gotland).

Taken to extremes, this means Noma's owner-chef René Redzepi eschews all nonindigenous produce in his creations (no olive oil, for example, and no tomatoes). He plays with modest, often-overlooked ingredients (pulses and grains) and consults food historians, digging up long-lost traditions. Famously, he also forages in the wilderness for herbs and plants. Ingredients are skilfully prepared using traditional techniques (curing, smoking, pickling and preserving) alongside contemporary experimentation.

What is also interesting is the spirit of community among Danish chefs and restaurateurs. Many of the chefs leading the hottest new restaurants have done a stint at Noma, and in the spirit of Danish niceness, they continue to support, sample and promote the collective output (of chefs, sommeliers, boutique and organic producers, festival organisers and so on).

It would be misleading to say, however, that the entire Danish nation was in the grip of a fervent foodie revolution. It isn't. Rather, things are changing slowly but surely, in the normal Danish way.

Danes are gradually waking up to the fact that they have a fantastic array of seasonal produce at their disposal. As happened in England at around the turn of the millenium, Denmark is undergoing a resurgence of interest in the traditional food culture – chefs are rediscovering old recipes with a renewed sense of pride in the country's culinary heritage. Some menus have waved goodbye to could-be-anywhere cuisine and are embracing local dishes – perhaps with a modern reinterpretation, or better utilisation of local and/or seasonal produce.

The day after Noma won the title of world's best restaurant in 2010, 100,000 people attempted to make a table reservation. The restaurant does around 75 covers a day, five days a week. In other words: landing a reservation is the equivalent of winning the food lovers' lottery.

Danish Staples & Specialities

The intriguing dishes from Noma's menu are clearly *not* the dishes eaten daily by the average Dane. The majority of Danes tuck into hearty dishes of meat and potatoes. Here's a brief summary of what makes up traditional Danish food.

Meat

Traditional meat-based dishes include *frikadeller* – fried minced-pork meatballs, commonly served with boiled potatoes and red cabbage (*fiske-*

RENÉ REDZEPI & NEW NORDIC CUISINE

In 2010 and 2011, René Redzepi's Copenhagen restaurant, Noma, topped the list of S Pellegrino World's 50 Best Restaurants, bringing global attention to Copenhagen dining like never before. Here René gives us a primer.

Nordic cuisine is about... A sense of time and place, purity, nature, commitment, patience and determination. I find inspiration in Nordic landscapes, memories, and conversations between growers, colleagues and people living in nature.

A lesser-known local ingredient... Is sea arrow-grass, a plant we pick on the shores of Zealand. It's succulent and tastes like coriander.

My Macedonian heritage... Helps me see different contexts for local produce and cooking techniques. For many native Danes, certain foods and methods had only been seen in one specific light.

Foodies in Copenhagen shouldn't miss... Eating traditional Danish smørrebrød at Schønnemann and fresh fish at Kødbyens Fiskebar.

As told to Cristian Bonetto

A MATTER OF TASTE

The Danes' usually unimpeachable good taste reveals its 'quirkier' side in some of their most popular foodstuffs:

» Pickled herring in curry sauce – Is this the most disturbing food combination ever? (It actually works surprisingly well.)

» Salt liquorice – Do you eat it, or leave it out for the slugs?

» Remoulade – A tart celery-based mayonnaise that Danes dollop on everything, given half a chance.

» *Stegt flæsk med persille sovs* – A dish of pork fat, and only fat, in parsley sauce. Mmmm.

» *Peberod* – Or 'horseradish', which the Danes cook to accompany meat, fish and everything else.

frikadeller are made from fish). Pork *(flæsk* or *svinekød)* is ubiquitous: *flæskesteg* is roast pork, usually with crackling, served with potatoes and cabbage; *mørbradbøf* is pork tenderloin.

Beef *(bøf or okse)* is popular, ranging from cheaper comfort-food dishes using mince to expensive cuts of steak (often with Béarnaise sauce to accompany). *Hakkebøf* is a dish of minced-beef burger, usually covered with fried onions and served with boiled potatoes, brown sauce and beets. Finding its way back onto menus is *pariserbøf,* a rare beef patty topped with capers, raw egg yolk, beets, onions and horseradish (it tastes a little better than it sounds).

Fish & Seafood

With all that coastline, it stands to reason there'll be excellent fish. Herring *(sild)* is a staple. Salmon *(laks)* is common – *gravad laks* is cured or salted salmon marinated in dill and served with a sweet mustard sauce. *Stegt rødspætte* is fried, breaded plaice, usually served with parsley potatoes, while *kogt torsk* is poached cod, usually with mustard sauce and served with boiled potatoes. Another dish finding its way back onto menus around the country is the delicious *stjerneskud* – literally it means 'shooting star' and usually consists of one steamed and one fried fish fillet (often plaice), with a little smoked salmon, shrimp and caviar, on a piece of bread.

The Danes are great fish smokers; you'll find smokehouses preserving herring, eel, shrimp and other seafood all around the coast of the country. The most renowned are on Bornholm. Fresh shrimp *(rejer)* and lobster *(hummer)* are utterly delicious – a great place to eat them fresh off the boat is by the docks in Skagen.

Smørrebrod

Sushi and sandwiches have changed the way Danes snack just as they have elsewhere in the Western world, but the locals still hold a place in their heart for the traditional lunchtime Danish open sandwich, or smørrebrød. The basic smørrebrød is a slice of rye bread topped, for example, with roast beef, tiny shrimps, pickled herring, liver pâté, or fried fish fillet, and finished with a variety of garnishes (the final sculptured product often looks too good to eat).

Smørrebrød is served in many restaurants and cafes (at lunchtime), although it's cheapest in bakeries or specialised smørrebrød takeaway shops found near train stations and office buildings. Try to pronounce smørrebrød as 'smuhr-bruth', but don't feel bad if your pronunciation doesn't match a native Dane's (it never will).

Apart from Copenhagen, another first-rate destination for foodies is Bornholm – home to excellent smokehouses, fantastic organic produce, a brace of fine-dining restaurants and scores of local specialities and treats, from caramel to micro-brewed beer.

DINNER WITH DANES

Two agencies offer visitors the chance to spend an evening in the home of locals, sampling traditional Danish food and learning about Denmark straight from the horse's mouth. The host families are mainly in Copenhagen (although Dine with the Danes can help with destinations further afield), and the agencies usually attempt to match you with people of similar ages and interests. The price is around 400/200kr per adult/child aged eight to 14, for two to three courses. If you're interested, fill in an online request a week or so in advance.

Contact the following:

Dine with the Danes (www.dinewiththedanes.dk)
Meet the Danes (www.meetthedanes.dk)

In the laws of Danish smørrebrød, smoked salmon is always served on white bread, herring on rye bread.

Koldt Bord

Another distinctively Danish presentation is the *koldt bord* (cold table), a buffet-style spread of cold foods – such as cold sliced meats, smoked fish, cheeses, vegetables, salads, condiments, breads and crackers – plus usually a few hot dishes such as *frikadeller,* and breaded, fried fish (usually plaice). The cornerstone of the *koldt bord* though is herring, which comes in pickled, marinated and curried versions.

Pastries

In Denmark the sweet pastry known elsewhere in the world as a 'Danish pastry' is called *wienerbrød* ('Viennese bread', ironically), and nearly every second street corner has a *bageri* (bakery) with varieties. As legend has it, the naming of the pastry can be traced to a Danish baker who moved to Austria in the 18th century, where he perfected the treats of flaky, butter-laden pastry. True to their collective sweet tooth, Danes eat them for breakfast.

Claus Meyer is a superstar on the Danish food front – he is a TV chef, food educator, co-founder of Noma restaurant, cookbook author, gastro-entrepreneur and much more. His website (www.clausmeyer.dk) outlines the fascinating manifesto for New Nordic cuisine.

Hot Dogs

Traditionally, the favourite fast food is a *pølse* (hot dog) from one of the wagons dotted around town – all churning out precisely the same frankfurters, buns and dressings. Late at night, after a couple of beers, we have to admit that a hot dog covered with fake mustard and ketchup can be damned hard to resist.

Danish Dining Diary

Working through the typical Danish food day, for breakfast *(morgenmad)* Danes surprise foreign visitors by serving pastries, breads, cheeses and cold meats, often all together in one calorific, metabolism-slowing orgy of sugar, dairy produce and carbohydrates. Some may take the muesli-and-yoghurt route.

For Danes, lunch *(frokost)* may be smørrebrød, or these days just as likely a tray of takeaway sushi or a regular sandwich. Dinner *(aftensmad* or *middag)* is the main meal of the day. For most it will be pasta, pizza or some arrangement of meat and veg, unless guests are invited, in which case the latest celebrity-chef cookbook may be consulted. In the past, Danes haven't embraced the notion of eating out, except for special occasions. That is changing, particularly in the cities and among the younger generations.

Where to Eat & Drink

Many Danish chefs are creating fresh, original, seasonal and, above all, local food worth travelling for. In rural areas, there are several historic castle and manor-house hotels – such as Dragsholms Slot and Søllerød Kro on Zealand – where locally sourced, seasonal produce is being used by accomplished chefs to spectacular effect. In the larger cities, options span mod-Scandi hot spots to hip restaurant-bar combos to historic eateries dishing up smørrebrød, herring and akvavit.

But despite all the recent noises, you *can* eat badly in Denmark, particularly in the provinces, where dry schnitzels, rubbery pizzas and inauthentic pasta remain the chief outsourced foodstuff for the masses. To help avoid such disappointment, here are a few tips: in coastal areas, look for a traditional *røgeri* (smokehouse), where you can get great, inexpensive seafood. In many villages, you can often find classic Danish home cooking in a traditional *kro* (inn). Also, hit a *bageri* (bakery) – the Danes are master bakers, especially when it comes to *rugbrød* (rye bread).

Wherever you dine, be aware that kitchens close relatively early in Denmark compared with other European countries, so aim to eat before 10pm (9pm in smaller towns). For many restaurants and cafes, the closure of the kitchen signals a move into 'bar mode', with drinks available until late (along with live music or a DJ in some venues). Note too, that in the bigger cities, some places shut for a few weeks in July and/or August.

As you drive around rural areas in the summer months, keep an eye out for roadside stalls selling fresh farm produce (usually with an honesty-box system in place). *Jordbær* are strawberries, *kirsebær* are cherries, *ærter* are peas, and *kartofler* are potatoes.

Cheap Eats

Dining out can be expensive in Denmark, particularly the gourmet places that tend to be more costly than comparable restaurants in Paris and London. If you're kroner-conscious, look out for special, pared-back lunch menus, available at several of the most-sought-after restaurants. Alcohol is also spectacularly costly in these kinds of places, and Danes do not generally bring their own alcohol. Midrange dining options can also be expensive (you can easily spend 200kr on a humdrum cafe meal) so shop around and check out menus on display. It's worth bearing in

---

READING MENUS

Many restaurants will offer a menu in English – but here's a rundown of some common terms.

spisekort or menu	menu
børnemenu	children's menu
dagens ret	daily special
retter	dishes, courses
forretter	starters, appetisers
hovedretter	main dishes
desserter	desserts
ost	cheese
mad	food
drikke	drink
tag selv buffet	self-serve buffet
udvalg af	assorted/selection of
morgenmad	breakfast
frokost	lunch
middag or aftensmad	dinner

As well as à la carte offerings, many cafes and restaurants offer good-value fixed menus of two, three or four selected courses. Look for '2-retter menu' or '3-retter menu'.

BRUNCH

Danes rarely eat breakfast out. They do, however, embrace brunch in a big way. Many cafes and restaurants put on lavish buffets on weekends, from about 10am to 2pm (the price is about 120kr to 150kr and generally includes nonalcoholic drinks); on weekdays, loads of eateries offer a 'brunch plate' (brunch tallerken) on their menu, served from 10am through lunch. These are often-creative samplings of brunch classics: muesli and yoghurt, cold cuts, bread and cheese, something sweet (pastry or pancakes), all on one plate and offering a little slice of brunch heaven. We love 'em!

mind that drinks in general are expensive when eating out – a soft drink or coffee could easily be priced around 40kr.

Aside from the aforementioned smokehouses and bakeries, for cheaper food there are a few options. Thai and Chinese restaurants are common, but rarely authentic. Mediterranean buffets and Italian restaurants serving standard pizza-and-pasta fare can be well priced – there seems to have been an explosion of restaurants serving Italian-Mexican fare (huh?). Simple Greek, Lebanese and Turkish eateries selling inexpensive shawarma (a filling pitta-bread sandwich of shaved meat) are another favourite alternative to the fast-food chains (which are actually not so ubiquitous as elsewhere in Europe). You can also find a cheap, if not particularly healthy, munch at one of the aforementioned pølsevogn (the wheeled carts that sell a variety of hot dogs).

Acclaimed 'gypsy brewer' Mikkel Borg Bjergsø travels to the world's most legendary breweries to create one-of-a-kind beers. At Mikkeller, his basement bar in Copenhagen, you can enjoy craft-brewed beers on tap and a range of speciality beers. See www.mikkeller.dk.

Breakfast

Hotels and hostels will put on an invariably impressive breakfast buffet including pastries, breads, cheeses and cold meats, plus fruit, juice, cereal, yoghurt, boiled eggs, and possibly some hot dishes (scrambled eggs, bacon, sausage). Midrange and top-end hotels usually include breakfast in their rates; budget hotels and hostels charge around 60kr per person. If you're staying somewhere where breakfast isn't offered, your best bet is to go to a bakery. Note that most large supermarkets have an in-house bakery that opens earlier than the supermarket itself (generally around 7.30am). For later risers, try a brunch buffet or brunch plate at a restaurant or cafe.

Vegetarians & Vegans

Despite the countrywide adoration of all things pork, vegetarians should be able to get by comfortably throughout Denmark (although in smaller towns the options will be limited). Danish cafes commonly serve a variety of salads, and vegetarians can often find something suitable at the smørrebrød counter. Most restaurants will have at least one veg-friendly dish on the menu, or can whip something up if requested.

Tipping

A service charge is included in your restaurant bill and Danes do not normally tip. However, rounding up the bill is not uncommon when the service has been particularly good.

Drinks

The Danes are enthusiastic drinkers, and not just of their world-famous domestic beers. Beer (øl), wine (vin) and spirits are served in most restaurants and cafes. They can also be purchased at grocery shops during normal shopping hours. Prices are quite reasonable compared with those in other Scandinavian countries (but may not compare favourably with home).

Beer

Danes are prodigious producers and consumers of beer. Carlsberg Breweries, based in Copenhagen, markets the Carlsberg and Tuborg labels and is one of the world's largest brewery groups. It's also the largest exporter of beer in Europe. Danes themselves down an average of around 90 litres of beer per person annually, ranking them in the top 10 of the world's greatest beer drinkers.

The best-selling beers in Denmark are pilsners, a lager with an alcohol content of 4.6%, but there are scores of other beers to choose from. These range from light beers with an alcohol content of 1.7% to hearty stouts that kick in at 8%. You'll find the percentage of alcohol listed on the bottle label. Here's a short list of beer terms:

» *øl* – beer
» *pilsner* – lager
» *lyst øl* – light beer
» *lagerøl* – dark lager
» *fadøl* – draught
» *porter* – stout

Bored with a liquid diet of pilsner and more pilsner from the two big Danish brewers, in the last decade Danes have developed a growing taste for microbrews and craft beers, and there are now more than 120 small breweries dotted around the country. Any Danish town worth its salt now has its own *bryghus* (brewery), and these are often innovators producing a wide variety of beer styles.

Many bars and pubs proudly list their boutique bottled offerings and changing draught beers, with obscure local drops getting a run next to the better-known brands. Various bars and stores cater to the more discerning beer-drinker. And the country's largest beer festival, **Ølfestival** (beerfestival.dk, in Danish), held in mid- to late May in Copenhagen, draws crowds of over 13,000 thirsty attendees.

Wine

The Danes are also enthusiastic when it comes to the consumption of wine too (there are even a couple of vineyards in Denmark now). Over the last 30 years Danes have moved away from their favourite tipple of beer, to wine. They favour red wine (75%) over white (25%) and consumption is still increasing. Traditional Danish cuisine tends to favour heavyweight reds, although sharp Rieslings go well with vinegary

A few important customs: make eye contact with everyone during a toast. And before you leave the table, *always* thank your host or hostess for any food or drink, even if it's just a cup of coffee.

FOOD & DRINK DRINKS

CHRISTMAS IN DENMARK

Not surprisingly, the Danes do Christmas (*jul*) with an abundance of *hygge* (cosiness) – candles, festive decorations and twinkling lights hold the wintry darkness at bay. The biggest festivities are on Christmas Eve – the centrepiece of the traditional dinner with family is roast duck or goose, served with red cabbage and potatoes. Gifts are given and songs are sung around the Christmas tree.

Another Christmas Eve tradition is rice pudding, eaten warm after the meal. Hidden inside the rice pudding is a single whole almond – the person who finds the almond in his or her bowl gets a prize (eg a sweet made of marzipan). And of course, there are traditional Christmas sweets, including *brunekager* and *pebernødder* (spice cookies) and *klejner* (deep-fried knotted dough). *Æbleskiver* are small, spherical pancakes traditionally served with *gløgg* (mulled wine) during Advent. Other Christmas-time drinks include beers brewed for the season and akvavit.

On 25 December, the leftovers make for an excellent *koldt bord* lunch.

PANTS ON BOTTLES

Most soft drinks and nondraught beers, are sold in bottles (glass or plastic) – you pay a refundable deposit (the *pant*) on top of the price, and you get the *pant* as a cash refund when returning empty bottles to a supermarket with a reverse vending machine. That 1.50kr per small bottle won't make you rich, but it will help the environment.

The Scandinavian Kitchen, by Danish chef and media personality Camilla Plum, outlines 100 essential Scandi ingredients and 200 recipes. Plum is a household name in Denmark; she runs an organic farm north of Copenhagen that's open to visitors on Saturdays. See www.fuglebjerg gaard.dk.

herring dishes. One wine producer is everywhere man Claus Meyer – on the tiny island of Lilleø (between Zealand and Lolland), he is involved in the production of Arwen white wine (a blend of grape varietals), named after René Redzepi's daughter.

Unlike the other Scandinavian countries, the Danish government does not hold a monopoly on alcohol sales; in fact, wine tends to be one of the best-value products you can buy in Danish supermarkets. As with the British, the Danes' preference for New World wines has grown dramatically in recent years.

Common wine terms used in Denmark include *hvidvin* (white wine), *rødvin* (red wine), *mousserende* (sparkling wine) and *husets vin* (house wine). *Gløgg* is a mulled wine that's a favourite speciality during the Christmas season, served with almonds and raisins.

Akvavit

The most popular spirit in Denmark is the Aalborg-produced akvavit. There are several dozen types, the most common of which is made from potatoes and spiced with caraway seeds. In Denmark akvavit is not sipped but is swallowed straight down as a shot, usually followed by a chaser of beer.

Literature & Film

Like so many Danish forays onto the world stage, Denmark's contribution to Western culture has been in inverse proportion to its size.

Literature

The Golden Age

The first half of the 19th century has been characterised as the 'Golden Age', as the country flourished economically and culturally. Among the writers of that period were two superstars of the Danish literary legacy: Hans Christian Andersen (1805–75), whose fairy tales have been translated into more languages than any other book except the Bible; and noted philosopher and theologian Søren Kierkegaard (1813–55), considered the father of existentialism.

Once upon a Time...

For the Danes, Hans Christian Andersen is Shakespeare, Goethe and Dickens rolled into one. That may sound a little excessive for a writer of fairy tales, but Andersen was more than that. As well as single-handedly revolutionising children's literature, he wrote novels, plays and several fascinating travel books. Stories such as *The Little Mermaid*, *The Emperor's New Clothes* and *The Ugly Duckling* have been translated into over 170 languages and are embedded in the global literary consciousness like few others.

Andersen infused his animals, plants and inanimate objects with a magical humanity. His antagonists are not witches or trolls, but human foibles such as indifference and vanity, and it's often his child characters who see the world most clearly. The result is a gentleness that crosses borders and generations. His work is said to have influenced Charles Dickens, Oscar Wilde and innumerable modern-day authors.

Andersen was born in Odense in 1805, the son of a cobbler and a washerwoman. In his autobiographies he mythologised his childhood as poor but idyllic. His father died when Andersen was 11, and Andersen left for Copenhagen soon after, an uneducated 14-year-old on a classic fairy-tale mission: to make his fortune in the big city. He tried and failed at various occupations until he eventually found success with his writing, initially his poems and plays, and then his first volume of short stories.

His later success and accompanying wealth were some compensation for what was an otherwise troubled life. Andersen was a neurotic, sexually ambivalent, highly strung hypochondriac. It may go some way to explaining why he was such a restless nomad to the last. Andersen's collected works (156 in all) include poems, novels, travel books, dramatic pieces and three autobiographies. He died of liver cancer in 1875 and is buried in Copenhagen's Assistens Kirkegård.

How to tackle Kierkegaard's works? Consider starting with *Kierkegaard*, by Michael Watts, which gives a short biography of the philosopher's life and family, plus tips and ideas on how to read and analyse his complex work.

Hans Christian Andersen Sites

» Den Gamle Gaard, Faaborg

» Fyrtøjet, Odense

» HC Andersens Barndomshjem, Odense

» HC Andersens Hus, Odense

TOP DANISH READS

» *The Complete Fairy Tales* by Hans Christian Andersen – the most famous Danish book in the world

» *Either/Or* by Søren Kierkegaard – the first great work of the father of existentialism

» *Miss Smilla's Feeling for Snow* by Peter Høeg – a worldwide hit set largely in Copenhagen's Christianshavn neighbourhood

» *Silence in October* by Jens Christian Grøndahl – an engaging meditation on the dissolution of a marriage

» *We, the Drowned* by Carsten Jensen – an epic tale of sailors from the seafaring town of Marstal on Ærø, published in 2006 (in English in 2010); voted the best Danish novel of the past 25 years

20th-Century Literature
Prize-winning Prose

Around 1870 a trend towards realism emerged, focusing on contemporary issues. One of the leading figures of this movement, Henrik Pontoppidan, won a Nobel Prize for Literature (shared with compatriot Karl Gjellerup) in 1917 for 'his authentic descriptions of present-day life in Denmark'.

In 1944 another Dane, Johannes Vilhelm Jensen, won the Nobel Prize in Literature, and in 1999 Jensen's *The Fall of the King* was acclaimed as the best Danish novel of the 20th century. It is a historical novel, published in three parts from 1900 to 1901, centred around King Christian II.

International Acclaim

The most famous Danish writer of the 20th century, Karen Blixen (1885–1962) started her career with *Seven Gothic Tales,* published in New York under the pen name Isak Dinesen. She is best known for *Out of Africa,* the memoirs of her farm life in Kenya, written in 1937; it was made into an Oscar-winning movie (1985). You can visit her Danish estate (p88), now a museum dedicated to her life and work.

One of Denmark's leading contemporary novelists is Peter Høeg, whose works focus on nonconformist characters on the margins of society. In 1992 he published the global hit *Miss Smilla's Feeling for Snow* (published as *Smilla's Sense of Snow* in the USA and made into a movie in 1997), a suspense mystery about a Danish-Greenlandic woman living in Copenhagen.

Recent Trends
Nordic Noir

The hugely popular genre of Scandinavian crime fiction seems dominated by authors from Sweden (Henning Mankell and Stieg Larsson) and Norway (Jo Nesbø), while Denmark has been busying itself with acclaimed television crime dramas, including International Emmy award-winning series such as *The Protectors, The Eagle, The Killing* and *Unit One.*

There are noteworthy Danish authors contributing to the genre, including Jussi Adler-Olsen, whose star is on the rise (he won the 2011 Glass Key award). The first of his series dealing with the intriguing Department Q was published in English in 2011 – in the UK with the title *Mercy*, in the US as *The Keeper of Lost Causes.*

Can't get enough Nordic noir? Google 'Glass Key award' to learn about the recipients of this literary award, given annually to a crime novel by

The best TV crime drama out of Denmark in recent times is the moody whodunit *The Killing* (in Danish, known as *Forbrydelsen*), dark and intensely gripping as the plot slowly unravels. A US version was made, but get the original on DVD and prepare to be hooked.

an author from the Nordic countries. The award is named after the novel *The Glass Key* by US crime writer Dashiell Hammett.

Film

An Early Cinematic Hero

Denmark's best-known director of the early 20th century was Carl Theodor Dreyer (1889–1968). He's best known for the 1928 French masterpiece *La Passion de Jeanne d'Arc,* a ground-breaking silent film acclaimed for its rich visual textures and innovative use of close-ups – some have called it 'transcendental cinema'.

Academy Success

It wasn't until the 1980s that Danish directors attracted a broader international audience, with a swag of trophies to prove it.

In 1988 *Babette's Feast* (1987), directed by Gabriel Axel, won the Academy Award for Best Foreign Film. The movie was an adaptation of a story written by Karen Blixen, whose novel *Out of Africa* had been turned into an Oscar-winning Hollywood movie just three years earlier. *Babette's Feast* is set in a rugged west-coast village in 1871 and shows the impact of a French housekeeper on two pious sisters; it sets the gold standard for food movies to follow.

Remarkably, just a year later, a Danish film again won Best Foreign Film at the Academy Awards (as well as the Cannes Film Festival's Palme d'Or): *Pelle the Conqueror* is directed by Bille August and adapted from Martin Andersen Nexø's book about the harsh life of an immigrant in 19th-century Denmark.

In 2011 another Danish film won the Oscar for Best Foreign Film: *In a Better World,* directed by Susanne Bier. This contemplative drama has a storyline that begins with playground bullying and takes in infidelity, bereavement, evil warlords and revenge – a plot engineered by Bier to question the cosy stereotype of her homeland.

Directors of Note

Denmark has produced some high-profile directors, many of whom have crossed over from local Danish-language films to big Hollywood productions.

Bille August – Known for his literary adaptations: *Pelle the Conqueror* (1988); *The House of the Spirits* (1993), based on the novel by Chilean writer Isabel Allende; *Smilla's Sense of Snow* (1997), from the bestseller by Peter Høeg; *Les Miserables* (1998), adapted from Victor Hugo's classic tale.

Carl Theodor Dreyer's *La Passion de Jeanne d'Arc* was named the most influential film of all time in a list of the 'Essential 100' published by the Toronto International Film Festival in 2010.

LITERATURE & FILM FILM

TOP DANISH FILMS

» *Pelle the Conqueror* (1988) – director: Bille August

» *Babette's Feast* (1987) – director: Gabriel Axel

» *In a Better World* (2010) – director: Susanne Bier

» *Italian for Beginners* (2000) – director: Lone Scherfig

» *The Idiots* (1998) – director: Lars von Trier

» *After the Wedding* (2006) – director: Susanne Bier

» *Smilla's Sense of Snow* (1997) – director: Bille August; adapted from the book, *Miss Smilla's Feeling for Snow*

» *Breaking the Waves* (1996) – director: Lars von Trier

» *Festen* (The Celebration; 1998) – director: Thomas Vinterberg

» *Qivitoq* (1956) – director: Erik Balling

WEBSITES

Susanne Bier – One of Denmark's leading directors, she has made a name for herself internationally with respected local films *Brothers* (remade into an American production with the same name), *After the Wedding* (2006) and *In a Better World* (2010).

Lone Scherfig – Scherfig's romantic comedy *Italian for Beginners* (2000) dealt with diverse but damaged Danes learning the language of love and became an international hit. She also directed the dark comedy *Wilbur Wants to Kill Himself* (2002), a Danish-Scottish co-production. Recent acclaim has come for the UK film *An Education* (2009).

Thomas Vinterberg – Cofounder of the Dogme95 movement, he conceived, wrote and directed the first of the Dogme movies, *Festen* (The Celebration; 1998), to wide acclaim. Subsequent films flopped, but the bleak *Submarino* (2010) may indicate a return to form.

Nicholas Winding Refn – Famous for directing the gritty and violent *Pusher* trilogy, which explores the criminal underworld of Copenhagen. His latest film, the US 'art-house noir' *Drive*, won him the Best Director award at the 2011 Cannes Film Festival.

And then there's Lars von Trier, who warrants his own section...

Lars von Trier & Dogme95

Two excellent websites for film buffs belong to Det Danske Filminstitut (The Danish Film Institute; www.dfi. dk) and Zentropa (www.zentropa. dk), Lars von Trier's immensely influential film production company.

Whether he's depicting the apocalypse in *Melancholia* (2011), framing female genital mutilation in the polarising *Antichrist* (2009) or sympathising with Hitler in comments made at the Cannes Film Festival in 2011, there is little doubt that the leading Danish director and screenwriter of the 21st century remains Lars von Trier, who continues to live up to his label as the film world's *enfant terrible*.

Von Trier's better-known films include the melodrama *Breaking the Waves* (1996), which featured Emily Watson and took the Cannes Film Festival's Grand Prix; *Dancer in the Dark* (2000), a musical starring Icelandic pop singer Björk and Catherine Deneuve, which won Cannes' Palme d'Or in 2000; and the frequently difficult and experimental *Dogville* (2003), starring Nicole Kidman.

Von Trier is a cofounder of Dogme95, sometimes dubbed the 'vow of chastity'. This artistic manifesto pledged a minimalist approach to filmmaking using only hand-held cameras, shooting on location with natural light and rejecting the use of special effects and pre-recorded music. It attracted both ardent fans and widespread dismissal, but its impact and influence on modern cinema cannot be underestimated.

Survival Guide

Directory
A–Z

Accommodation

High standards of comfort and convenience are the norm in Denmark whether you're camping, hostelling or staying in a guesthouse or hotel, although nothing is that cheap.

Hotels outside Copenhagen offer less variety, however, and a few brands tend to dominate. It means truly cheap hotels are virtually unknown, while dazzling boutique or luxury hotels are not that common outside the capital. If you're looking for something a little more special than a chain hotel room it's well worthwhile thinking about staying in a castle, historic manor house or farm.

Camping grounds, hostels and homestay bed and breakfast accommodation offer excellent standards and are good ways to secure comfort on a budget, while self-catering flats and cottages can make appealing and cost-effective alternatives for groups planning to stay in one place for a while.

Staff at local tourist offices provide lists of local accommodation and may be able to arrange bookings. Fees may apply. During July and August it's advisable to book ahead. Even camping grounds can fill up.

Some hotels and restaurants are also members of the Green Key eco accreditation scheme (www.green-key.org), in which they aim to cut their use of energy, chemicals and use of non-renewable resources.

The price ranges quoted in the sleeping reviews in the On the Road chapters are for double rooms and are presented as follows:

€ under 600kr (including camping grounds and dorm beds)
€€ from 600kr to 1500kr
€€€ more than 1500kr

Camping

With 500 registered sites, Denmark is well set up for campers, although many are open only in the summer months, while others operate from spring to autumn. About 100 stay open year-round and some offer low-season rates.

You'll need a pass for stays at all camping grounds. A Camping Card International will do, or you can buy a Danish carnet at the first camping ground you visit or from tourist offices. The cost for an annual pass is 100kr; it covers all accompanied children aged under 18.

The per-night charge to pitch a tent or park a caravan typically ranges from 55kr to 70kr for each adult and about half that for each child. In summer, some places also tack on a surcharge of 30kr to 40kr per tent/caravan.

IT'S IN THE STARS...

Camping grounds in Denmark are rated by the Danish Camping Board using a star system. Some examples are as follows.

» **One star**: running water, toilets, at least one shower and at least one electricity outlet for shavers.

» **Two stars**: at least one shower for every 25 sites, kitchen with hot water tap and hotplates, playground for children, location within 2km of a grocery shop.

» **Three stars**: hot water in the washbasins, communal lounge, large play area for children, nursing rooms, sinks or washing machines for laundry, location within 1km of a grocery shop. Four- and five-star ratings indicate further upgraded facilities.

» Hostels, too, are categorised by a star system (one to five). A one-star hostel will be pretty basic, two stars will get you luggage storage and a small shop, while four- and five-star facilities have TV lounges and a minimum of 75% of rooms with shower and toilet.

Many Danish camping grounds also rent simple cabins (and/or on-site caravans) sleeping four to six people, often with cooking facilities, though rarely with bed linen and blankets – bring your own sleeping bag or pay to hire them. Toilet and shower facilities are usually shared with other campers. Many cabins are only available by the week during the summer months, starting at about 2400kr per week.

Backpackers and cyclists, note: even if a camping ground is signposted as fully booked for motorists, sometimes there are sites for light-travelling campers.

Throughout Denmark camping is restricted to established camping grounds or private land with the owner's permission. You risk a fine camping in a car or caravan at the beach or in a car park.

See www.danishcamp sites.dk and www.dk-camp. dk for further details.

Farm Stays

A great way to get a feel for rural Denmark is on a farm stay, which can simply mean bed and breakfast accommodation or actually working on the land or helping out with other farm activities. An excellent starting point is **Landsforeningen for Landboturisme** (www.bonde gaardsferie.dk), which books stays on more than 110 farms throughout Denmark. There's an interesting variety of farmhouses, ranging from modern homes to traditional straw-roofed, timber-framed places. The cost, including breakfast, averages around 350kr per person per day (half-price for children under 12 years old). The options also include self-contained flats and small rural houses that can accommodate up to six people and cost around 2500kr to 4500kr per week.

Although it's best to plan in advance, if you're cycling or driving around Denmark you may well come across

PRACTICALITIES

» **Weights and measures**: Denmark uses the metric system. Fruit is often sold by the piece (*stykke* or 'stk').

» **Numbering**: a comma indicates a decimal point; points indicate thousands. So 12,345.67 in English would be written 12.345,67 in Denmark.

» **Newspapers and magazines**: *Jyllands-Posten* and *Politiken* are the leading Danish-language newspapers (of some 50 nationwide). Danish news in English is available in the *Copenhagen Post* (www.cphpost.dk), published weekly. Other English-language publications available include the *International Herald Tribune, Guardian, Wall Street Journal, Financial Times, Economist* and *Time*.

» **Radio**: Radio Danmark International at 1062MHz (five-minute news briefs in English at 10.30am, 5.05pm and 10pm Monday to Friday). Other stations play a mix of Danish-language news and cultural programming, and music. BBC radio is available via shortwave.

» **TV**: Danish TV broadcasts local and international programmes, with English-language programmes usually presented in English with Danish subtitles. International cable channels such as CNN and BBC World are available in many hotels.

farmhouses displaying *værelse* (room) signs.

Homestay Bed & Breakfast

Much like many British bed and breakfast places, homestays can be a great way to see the countryside and meet local people. Rates vary widely but average about 400/450kr for singles/doubles. In most cases, breakfast is available for around 60kr extra per person. Sleeping arrangements vary from staying in your host's house or in adjoining accommodation.

Staff at many tourist offices can help with bookings, or see **Dansk Bed & Breakfast** (☑39 61 04 05; www.bed andbreakfast.dk).

Hostels

Some 100 hostels make up the **Danhostel association** (☑33 31 36 12; www.danhostel. dk), which is affiliated with Hostelling International (HI).

Danish hostels appeal to guests in all age categories

and are oriented as much towards families and groups as to budget travellers by offering bedrooms as well as dorms in many instances. Typical costs are 150kr to 240kr per person for dorm beds. For private rooms, expect to pay 300kr to 650kr per single, 300kr to 700kr per double, and between 50kr and 60kr per each additional person in larger rooms.

In dorms, typically you can expect single bunk-style beds. Blankets and pillows are provided, but you'll have to bring or hire (typically between 45kr and 65kr per stay) your own sheets. All Danish hostels provide an all-you-can-eat breakfast costing around 60kr, and many also provide dinner (around 90kr). Most hostels also have guest kitchens with pots and pans.

Advance reservations are advised, particularly in summer. In a few places, reception closes as early as 6pm. In most hostels the reception office is closed, and the phone not answered, between noon and 4pm.

Between May and September, hostels can get crowded with children on school excursions. Most Danish hostels close for at least part of the low season.

Hotels

Hotels can be found in the centre of all major Danish cities and towns. This book considers hotel rooms costing under 600kr (double with bathroom) to be in the budget category, 600kr to 1500kr per night midrange and over 1500kr top-end, though these are 'rack rates' and specials are often available.

Although the cheapest places are fairly spartan, Danish hotels are rarely seedy or unsafe. Interestingly, standard top-end hotels generally cost only about a third more than budget hotels, particularly if you use weekend rates or other hotel discount schemes.

A *kro*, a name that implies a country inn but is more commonly the Danish version of a motel, is typically found along major motorways near the outskirts of town. A *kro* tends to be cheaper and simpler than a hotel.

Both hotels and *kros* usually include an all-you-can-eat breakfast, which can vary from a simple meal of bread, cheese and coffee to a generous full-table buffet.

The **Danske Kroer & Hoteller** (☎75 64 87 00; www.krohotel.com) group offers 'cheques' valid at more than 100 accommodation options. The cheques can be purchased at Danish tourist offices and travel agencies, and cost from around 750kr for one night in a double room to 1700kr and upwards for two nights in a room for two adults and two children; all rooms include private facilities and breakfast. Note that there are blackout periods, while at other times there's a surcharge of up to 400kr.

Manor Houses

Denmark is simply stuffed with castles and manor houses, many of them offering atmospheric accommodation set in beautiful grounds. **Danske Slotte & Herregaarde** (☎86 60 38 44; www.slotte-herregaarde.dk) books rooms in more than 50 manor houses and small castles around Denmark. Singles range from 600kr to 1800kr, doubles range from 700kr to 2300kr, including breakfast. Brochures are available by mail and at larger tourist offices in Denmark.

Rental Accommodation

Many seaside resort areas are filled with cottages and flats. These are generally booked by the week and

Climate

Copenhagen

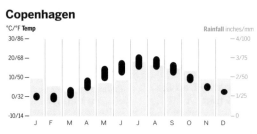

Esbjerg

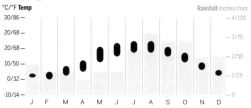

Fano

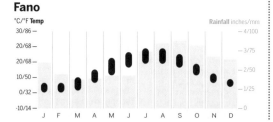

require reservations. Rates vary greatly, depending on the type of accommodation and the season, but generally they're cheaper than hotels.

DanCenter (☑70 13 00 00; www.dancenter.dk) handles holiday cottage bookings nationwide. Many tourist offices can also help make reservations. Alternatively try Novasol (☑70 42 44 24; www.novasol.dk/), which organises self-catering options in cottages and summer houses.

Business Hours

Office hours are generally 9am to 4pm Monday to Friday. Most banks open 9.30am to 4pm Monday to Friday (to 6pm on Thursday), though opening hours can be longer at airports and major train stations.

Shops are typically open from 9.30am to 5.30pm on weekdays (7pm on Friday) and to 2pm on Saturday. Shops are permitted to open on the first Sunday of the month, and Sundays in December, though many choose not to.

Restaurants and cafes tend to open from 11am to 11pm or midnight, and bars and nightclubs until 1am Monday to Wednesday and until 3am or 5am Thursday to Saturday.

Post offices are open from 9am or 10am to 5pm or 5.30pm Monday to Friday, and until noon or 1pm on Saturday.

Hours are not listed in reviews unless they differ from the standard opening times.

Customs Regulations

One litre of spirits and 200 cigarettes can be brought into Denmark duty-free if you're coming from outside the EU. Those coming from an EU country are allowed to bring in 3200 cigarettes and 10L of spirits.

Electricity

Denmark uses the Europlug, which has two round plugs and operates on 230V (volts) and 50Hz (cycles) AC. Visitors may also come across a three-plug version.

230V/50Hz

230V/50Hz

Discount Cards

Copenhagen Card (24/72hr adult 229/459kr, child 115/225kr) Provides access to all major sites in the city and the wider

region plus unlimited travel on buses and trains in Copenhagen and throughout North Zealand. The card is available at Central Station, tourist offices and some hotels. Some of the other major cities, for example, Aarhus and Aalborg, offer something similar.

Student Identity Card (ISIC; www.isic.org) An ID-style photo card with discounts on many forms of transport and reduced admission to some museums and sights.

Embassies & Consulates

The following embassies and consulates are in and around Copenhagen:

Australia (☑70 26 36 76; Dampfærgevej 26, Copenhagen)

Canada (☑33 48 32 00; Kristen Bernikows Gade 1, Copenhagen)

Finland (☑33 13 42 14; Sankt Annæ Plads 24, Copenhagen)

France (☑33 67 10 00; Kongens Nytorv 4, Copenhagen)

Germany (☑35 45 99 00; Stockholmsgade 57, Copenhagen)

Iceland (☑33 18 10 50; Strandgade 89, Copenhagen)

Ireland (☑35 42 32 00; Østbanegade 21, Copenhagen)

Netherlands (☑33 70 72 00; Toldbodgade 33, Copenhagen)

Norway (☑33 14 01 24; Amaliegade 39, Copenhagen)

Sweden (☑33 36 03 70; Sankt Annæ Plads 15A, Copenhagen)

UK (☑35 44 52 00; Kastelsvej 40, Copenhagen)

USA (☑33 41 71 00; Dag Hammarskjölds Allé 24, Copenhagen)

Food

Denmark, and Copenhagen in particular, has become Scandinavia's culinary powerhouse, boasting plenty of Michelin stars in the capital and many more excellent new places throughout the country. For in-depth information about local cuisine, see p301.

Eating categories in the reviews use the price of a main course as a rough estimate. For places where smørrebrød or set menus predominate, we have gone with the cost of a full meal.

Price ranges for main courses in the reviews in the On the Road chapters are as follows:

€ under 100kr
€€ from 100kr to 200kr
€€€ more than 200kr

Gay & Lesbian Travellers

Given Denmark's high degree of tolerance for alternative lifestyles of all sorts, it's hardly surprising that Denmark is a popular destination for gay and lesbian travellers. Copenhagen in particular has an active gay community and lots of nightlife options, but you'll find gay and lesbian venues in other cities as well.

For general info, contact **Landsforeningen for Bøsser og Lesbiske** (LBL, Danish National Association for Gays & Lesbians; www.lbl.dk).

A useful website for travellers with visitor information and listings in English is www.copenhagen-gay-life.dk.

The main gay and lesbian festival of the year is the **Copenhagen Pride Parade** (aka Mermaid Pride Parade; www.copenhagenpride.dk), a big Mardi Gras–like bash that takes place in Copenhagen on a Saturday in August. There's also the gay and lesbian film festival **Mix Copenhagen** (www.mixcopenhagen. dk), held each October.

Health

Denmark is a relatively healthy place and travellers shouldn't need to take any unusual health precautions.

Prevention is the key to staying healthy while abroad.

See your dentist before a long trip. Carry a spare pair of contact lenses or glasses, and take your optical prescription with you. Bring medications in their original, clearly labelled, containers. A signed and dated letter from your physician describing your medical conditions and medications, including generic names, is also a good idea.

Insurance

If you're an EU citizen, the European Health Insurance Card (which replaced the E111 form in 2006) covers you for most medical care but not for nonemergencies or for emergency repatriation home. Apply online via your government health department's website. Citizens from other countries should find out if there is a reciprocal arrangement for free medical access in Denmark. Make sure your health insurance covers you for the worst possible scenario, such as an accident requiring an emergency flight home.

Recommended Vaccinations

There are no specific vaccination requirements for entry to Denmark, other than against yellow fever if you're coming from an affected area.

Availability & Cost of Health Care

Good health care is readily available and for minor ailments pharmacists can give valuable advice and sell over-the-counter medication. They can also advise when more specialised help is required and point you in the right direction. Matas is the largest (nondispensing) chemist chain in Denmark with more than 200 outlets.

Infectious Diseases

Tickborne encephalitis is spread by tick bites. It is a serious infection of the brain and vaccination is advised

for those in risk areas who are unable to avoid tick bites (such as campers, forestry workers and hikers). Two doses of vaccine will give a year's protection, three doses up to three years'.

Heat Exhaustion & Hypothermia

Denmark has a fairly mild climate year-round and visitors are not at excessive risk from either of these conditions. It is surprisingly easy, however, to become overexposed to the sun in a temperate climate, even on a cloudy day, and to become dangerously cold in mild, damp weather if out cycling or hiking.

Heat exhaustion occurs following excessive fluid loss with inadequate replacement of fluids and salt. Symptoms include headache, dizziness and tiredness. Dehydration is already happening by the time you feel thirsty – aim to drink sufficient water to produce pale, diluted urine.

Acute hypothermia follows a sudden drop of temperature over a short time. Hypothermia starts with shivering, loss of judgment and clumsiness. Unless rewarming occurs, the sufferer deteriorates into apathy, confusion and coma. Prevent further heat loss by seeking shelter, warm dry clothing, hot sweet drinks and shared bodily warmth.

Insurance

A travel insurance policy to cover theft, loss and medical problems is a good idea, but policies vary widely in terms, conditions and requirements on you, the policy holder. Be sure to read the fine print. For example, some policies specifically exclude 'dangerous activities', which can include motorcycling.

Check that the policy covers ambulances or an emergency flight home. Travellers from the EU must carry a European Health Insurance

Card to be covered for emergency medical treatment.

Worldwide travel insurance is available at www.lonelyplanet.com/travel_services. You can buy, extend and claim online anytime – even if you're already on the road.

Legal Matters

Authorities are very strict about drink driving, and even a couple of drinks can put you over the legal limit of 0.05% blood-alcohol level. Drivers detected under the influence of alcohol are liable to receive stiff penalties and a possible prison sentence.

Always treat drugs with a great deal of caution. In Denmark all forms of cannabis are officially illegal.

If you are arrested for any punishable offence in Denmark, you can be held for up to 24 hours before appearing in court. You have the right to know the charges against you and the right to a lawyer, and you are not obliged to answer police questions before speaking to the lawyer. If you don't know of a lawyer, the police will provide a list. You can get free legal advice on your rights from **EU Legal Aid** (☎33 14 41 40).

Maps

Excellent maps of Denmark's larger cities can be picked up free from tourist offices, and include the cities of Copenhagen, Odense, Aarhus and Aalborg. Staff at the tourist offices in smaller cities and towns can generally provide simpler maps that are suitable for local sightseeing.

The quality foldout, colour *Map of Denmark – ferry guide & attractions* is a good road map and comes free at Denmark's overseas tourist offices. Car rental agencies usually also have good, free maps.

Those maps will suit most travellers' needs, but for exploring back roads, nooks and crannies you may also want to pick up the detailed road map of Denmark published by Kort-og Matrikelstyrelsen in a handy atlas format and labelled *Færdselskort 1:200,000 Danmark*. It's readily found in Danish bookshops.

Money

Although Denmark is an EU member nation, Denmark's citizens rejected adopting the euro in a referendum in 2000. Denmark's own currency, the krone, is most often written with the symbol DKK in international money markets, Dkr in northern Europe and kr within Denmark. Throughout this guide we've used kr.

One krone is divided into 100 øre. There are 50 øre, one krone, two kroner, five kroner, 10 kroner and 20 kroner coins. Notes come in denominations of 50, 100, 200, 500 and 1000 kroner.

The krone is pegged to the euro, so its value relative to other currencies fluctuates with that of its neighbours to the south.

See p14 for exchange rates and information about costs.

ATMs

Most banks in Denmark have automated teller machines (ATMs) that give cash advances on Visa and Master-Card credit cards as well as Cirrus and Plus bank cards. Although ATMs are accessible outside normal banking hours, not all are open 24 hours; particularly outside of Copenhagen, many Danish ATMs shut down for some part of the night, often from around 1am to 6am.

Typically you'll get a good rate when withdrawing money directly from a Danish ATM, but keep in mind that your home bank may charge you a fee for international transactions or for using another bank's ATM – check before you leave.

Cash

Foreign-exchange booths at Copenhagen airport are open to meet all scheduled incoming flights. If you're on an international ferry to Denmark, you can not only exchange US dollars and local currencies to Danish kroner on board but, if you buy a meal or use one of the shops, regardless of the currency you pay in, many will give you change in Danish kroner upon request. ATMs are also available at the airport.

Danish banks will convert a wide range of currencies including the US dollar, euro, UK pound, Canadian dollar, Swiss franc, Australian dollar, Japanese yen and kroner from

INTERNET ACCESS

With the proliferation of wi-fi, and most locals carrying laptops and/or smartphones, the old-fashioned internet cafe seems to be a dying breed in Denmark. There may be a couple catering to gamers and to laptop-less travellers in the major cities, but public libraries are your best bet in midsized and small towns. Libraries offer computers with free internet access (though access policies vary and you may need to book in advance). Libraries also offer free wi-fi, as do many cafes.

Wi-fi is common in hotels and hostels (indicated in this book using the 🛜 icon) and is often included in the rates. Some hostels and hotels will offer a computer for guests to use, free or for a small charge (indicated in our reviews with the @ symbol).

Norway and Sweden. Banks seldom accept foreign coins.

A few banks, especially in Copenhagen, have 24-hour machines that change major foreign currencies into Danish kroner.

Credit Cards

Credit cards such as Visa and MasterCard (also known as Access or Euro-card) are widely accepted in Denmark. American Express and Diners Club are occasionally accepted.

In many places (hotels, petrol stations, restaurants, stores) a surcharge may be imposed on foreign cards (up to 3.75%). If there is a surcharge, it must be advertised (eg on the menu, at reception).

If a card is lost or stolen, inform the issuing company as soon as possible. The following numbers are Copenhagen phone numbers:

AmEx (☑70 207 20)
Diners Club (☑36 73 73 73)
MasterCard (☑80 01 60 98)
Visa (☑80 01 02 77)

Tipping

Restaurant bills and taxi fares include service charges in the quoted prices. Further tipping is unnecessary (staff are in any case generally well paid in Denmark), although rounding up the bill is not uncommon when service has been especially good.

Travellers Cheques

The main benefit of travellers cheques and preloaded cash cards is that they can provide protection from theft. Large companies such as American Express and Thomas Cook generally offer efficient replacement policies.

Keep a record of the cheque numbers and those you have used so you can replace lost cheques if need be. Keep this information separate from the cheques themselves, along with the emergency phone number in case cheques need to be replaced.

Public Holidays

Many Danes take their main work holiday during the first three weeks of July, but there are numerous other holidays as well.

Banks and most businesses close on public holidays and transport schedules are commonly reduced.

New Year's Day (Nytårsdag) 1 January

Maundy Thursday (Skærtorsdag) Thursday before Easter

Good Friday (Langfredag) Friday before Easter

Easter Day (Påskedag) Sunday in March or April

Easter Monday (2.påskedag) day after Easter

Common Prayer Day (Stor Bededag) fourth Friday after Easter

Ascension Day (Kristi Himmelfartsdag) sixth Thursday after Easter

Whitsunday (Pinsedag) seventh Sunday after Easter

Whitmonday (2.pinsedag) seventh Monday after Easter

Constitution Day (Grundlovsdag) 5 June

Christmas Eve (Juleaften) 24 December (from noon)

Christmas Day (Juledag) 25 December

Boxing Day (2.juledag) 26 December

School Holidays

In addition to the public holidays noted above, schools generally close as follows:

Winter holidays a week in February or March

Easter holidays a week around Easter time

Summer holidays around 20 June to around 10 August

Autumn holidays a week in mid-October

Christmas and New Year two weeks

Telephone

Denmark has an efficient phone system, and payphones abound in busy public places such as train stations and shopping areas.

You have a choice of using either cardphones or coin phones, although cardphones are coming to predominate. Coin phones take all Danish coins in denominations of 1kr to 20kr but won't return change from larger coins.

Denmark's *Yellow Pages* is also on the internet at www.degulesider.dk. You can use the website to search for business, government and residential details; find the English version by looking at the bottom of the website. Note that the letters æ, ø and å are placed at the end of the Danish alphabet, and so come after z in the hard copy of telephone directories.

Mobile Phones

Denmark uses the worldwide GSM network, so you shouldn't have any problem getting your phone to work here. As befits a techno-

---

VAT REFUNDS

The value-added tax (VAT; called MOMS in Danish) on all goods and services in Denmark is 25%. Citizens from countries outside the EU can claim a VAT refund on goods as they leave the EU (as long as they spend a minimum of 300kr per shop, and the shop participates in one of the refund schemes). Get the shop to fill in a refund form, then present it, together with your passport, receipts and purchases, at the airport upon departure.

savvy Scandinavian country, many locals carry a mobile phone – but they also know how to use them politely, and judiciously. Please follow their custom. If you want to use your mobile phone from your home country while you're away, a good way to avoid steep overseas call charges is to use services that create local numbers for you, family and friends to dial, but which divert to your mobile. **Rebtel** (www.rebtel. com) is one such service.

Danish mobile service providers, which offer cheap, local pay-as-you-go SIM cards (which should be cheaper than using your own phone on roaming), include the following:

TDC-mobil (tdc.dk)
Telenor (www.telenor.dk)
Telia (telia.dk)

Phone Codes

All telephone numbers in Denmark have eight digits; there are no area codes. This means that all eight digits must be dialled, even when making calls in the same city.

For local directory assistance dial 118. For overseas enquiries, including for rates and reverse charge (collect) calls, dial 113.

The country code for Denmark is 45. To call Denmark from another country, dial the international access code for the country you're in followed by 45 and the local eight-digit number.

The international access code in Denmark is 00. To make direct international calls from Denmark, dial 00 followed by the country code for the country you're calling, the area code, then the local number.

Phonecards

If you're going to be making many calls, consider using a debit phonecard (*telekort*), sold in denominations of 30kr, 50kr and 100kr. These cards, sold at post offices and many kiosks, are used

for making both local and international calls.

Cardphones work out slightly cheaper than coin phones because you pay for the exact amount of time you speak; an LCD screen shows how much time is left on the card. It's possible to replace an expiring card with a new card without breaking the call. Cardphones have information in English detailing their use as well as the location of the nearest place that sells phonecards.

Time

Time in Denmark is normally one hour ahead of GMT/UTC, the same as in neighbouring European countries. When it's noon in Denmark, it's 11am in London, 6am in New York and Toronto, 3am in Los Angeles, 9pm in Sydney and 11pm in Auckland.

Clocks are moved forward one hour for daylight-saving time from the last Sunday in March to the last Sunday in October. Denmark uses the 24-hour clock system and all timetables and business hours are posted accordingly. *Klokken*, which means o'clock, is abbreviated as kl (kl 19.30 is 7.30pm).

Dates are written with the day followed by the month, thus 3/6 means 3 June and 6/3 means 6 March.

Tourist Information

Denmark is extremely well served with tourist offices at major transit points – see local listings. Important websites for visitors to Denmark include www.denmark. dk and www.visitdenmark. com. Regional tourist offices include the following:

Bornholm (www.bornholm. info)
Copenhagen (www.visit copenhagen.dk)
East Jutland (www.visiteast jutland.com)

Funen (www.visitfyn.dk)
Northern & Central Jutland (www.visitnordjylland.dk)
Southern Jutland (www. sydjylland.com)
West Jutland (www.visit vest.dk)
Zealand, Møn, Falster & Lolland (www.visiteast denmark.com)

Travellers with Disabilities

Denmark is improving access to buildings, transport and even forestry areas and beaches all the time, although accessibility is still not ubiquitous, making forward planning essential. On the website www.visitden mark.com, click Visitor, and then 'Accessible Denmark' under 'Inspiration' to reach a useful series of links including local disability guides, features offering ideas for accessible destinations, detailed transport information and a directory of useful organisations.

Most Danish tourist literature, such as the Danish Tourist Board's hotel guide, the camping association listings and the hostel booklet, indicates which establishments have rooms accessible to people in wheelchairs and facilities.

Once in Denmark, disabled travellers who have specific questions can contact **Dansk Handicap Forbund** (http://dhf-net.dk).

Visas

Citizens of the USA, Canada, Australia and New Zealand need a valid passport to enter Denmark, but they don't need a visa for tourist stays of less than three months. In addition, no entry visa is needed by citizens of EU and Scandinavian countries.

Citizens of many African, South American, Asian and former Soviet bloc countries do require a visa. The Danish

Immigration Service publishes a list of countries whose citizens require a visa at its website at www.nyidanmark.dk/en-us/coming_to_dk/visa/visa.htm

If you're in the country and have questions on visa extensions or visas in general, contact the Danish Immigration Service: **Udlændingeservice** (www.nyidanmark.dk).

Women Travellers

Women travellers are less likely to encounter problems in Denmark than in most other countries. However, use common sense when it comes to potentially dangerous situations such as hitching and walking alone in cities at night.

Dial ☎112 for rape crisis assistance or in other emergencies.

Center for Information om Kvinde-og Kønsforskning (Kvinfo, Danish Centre for Information on Gender, Equality and Ethnicity; www.kvinfo.dk) is an information resource for women.

In Aarhus, contact the **Kvindemuseet i Danmark** (Womens Museum in Denmark; www.womensmuseum.dk), which has exhibits both historic and topical. There's also a cafe (admission free).

Transport

Getting to Denmark is simple. The capital, Copenhagen, has worldwide air links, and some carriers fly into regional airports around the small nation. Train, road and bridge links exist to Germany and Sweden, and there are ferry connections to/from several countries.

Once you get to Denmark, transport stays hassle-free. Most journeys by train, car or bus are so short, you can reach regional destinations before your next meal.

Flights, tours and rail tickets can be booked online at www.lonelyplanet.com/bookings.

GETTING THERE & AWAY

Entering the Country

If you're arriving by air, there are no forms to fill out in advance as long as you're from a country that doesn't require a visa (for visa information see p321). If you're from a country that does require a visa, immigration officials may give you marginally more scrutiny. Also, if you're arriving in Denmark from a non-EU or non-Schengen country, expect your papers to be checked carefully.

If you're arriving by ferry, particularly from a neighbouring country, passports are not usually checked.

Passport

All travellers – other than citizens of Norway, Iceland, Sweden and Finland – require a valid passport to enter Denmark. For entry into the Schengen area, you must have a passport valid for three months beyond your proposed departure date.

Air

Airports

The majority of overseas flights into Denmark land at **Copenhagen International Airport** (www.cph.dk) in Kastrup, about 9km southeast of central Copenhagen (see p79 for airport information).

A number of international flights, mostly those coming from other Nordic countries or the UK, land at smaller regional airports:

Aalborg (www.aal.dk) Serves northern Jutland.

Aarhus (www.aar.dk) Serves east Jutland.

Billund (www.bll.dk) Denmark's second-largest airport; serves central Jutland (and is minutes from Legoland).

Esbjerg (www.esbjerg-lufthavn.dk) Serves west Jutland.

Karup (www.karup-lufthavn.dk) Serves central Jutland.

Sønderborg (www.sonderborg-lufthavn.dk) Serves south Jutland.

Airlines

Dozens of international airlines fly to/from Danish airports; the airport websites have up-to-date information on all the relevant carriers.

Airlines that use Denmark as their primary base:

CLIMATE CHANGE & TRAVEL

Every form of transport that relies on carbon-based fuel generates CO_2, the main cause of human-induced climate change. Modern travel is dependent on aeroplanes, which might use less fuel per kilometre per person than most cars but travel much greater distances. The altitude at which aircraft emit gases (including CO_2) and particles also contributes to their climate change impact.

Many websites offer 'carbon calculators' that allow people to estimate the carbon emissions generated by their journey and, for those who wish to do so, to offset the impact of the greenhouse gases emitted with contributions to portfolios of climate-friendly initiatives throughout the world. Lonely Planet offsets the carbon footprint of all staff and author travel.

BUS FARES FROM COPENHAGEN

TO	ONE-WAY FARE	DURATION	FREQUENCY
Amsterdam	449kr	13½hr	daily
Berlin	304kr	7½hr	1-2 daily
London	759kr	20hr	4 weekly
Oslo	385kr	9hr	most days
Paris	664kr	17½hr	1-2 daily
Stockholm	385kr	9¾hr	most days

Cimber Sterling (www.cimber.com)

Scandinavian Airlines (SAS; www.flysas.com) The flag carrier of Denmark (and Norway and Sweden).

Land

Denmark's only land crossing is with Germany, although the bridge over the Øresund from Sweden functions in the same way.

Bicycle

You can carry your bicycle into Denmark aboard a boat, plane or train.

Ferries Boats into Denmark are all well equipped for passengers with bicycles, usually for a nominal fee.

Flights Bicycles can travel by air, but airline baggage regulations seem to be in constant flux and their approach can be very inconsistent. If you intend to travel with your bike, check with the airline well in advance, preferably before you pay for your ticket.

Trains You will generally need to buy a ticket to transport your bike on a train to Denmark, and in peak times reserve a place for it.

Bus

Copenhagen is well connected to the rest of Europe by bus daily (or near daily). Major Jutland cities also have links – from Norway south via Hirtshals ferry port to Aalborg and Aarhus.

The most extensive European bus network is maintained by **Eurolines** (www.eurolines.com), a consortium of bus operators that stretches from Helsinki to Lisbon and Glasgow to Athens. For Eurolines passengers, there's a 10% discount for young people aged 12 to 25, seniors over 60, and holders of valid student cards. Children aged four to 11 pay 50% of the adult fare; those aged three and under pay 20%. Return fares for all age groups are about 10% to 15% less than two one-way fares. Advance reservations are advised.

Note that there may be a supplement (20kr to 70kr, depending on the journey duration) for travel in high season (July and August, and from mid-December to early January).

Sample destinations and fares from Copenhagen are shown in the table, p324.

Not under the Eurolines umbrella, **Abildskou** (www.abildskou.dk) links Aarhus and Berlin (one way 510kr, nine hours, daily) with stops in Kolding and Vejle (Denmark) and Flensburg and Neumünster (Germany) en route. There is an option to connect to services to Hamburg (city and airport; 360kr, five to six hours).

Car & Motorcycle

Requirements for bringing your own vehicle into Denmark are: a valid driver's license, certificate of registration and nationality plate, and proof of third-party insurance.

GERMANY

The E45 motorway is the main road link with Germany, although there are several smaller crossings. The E45 runs north through Jutland from the German border to Frederikshavn. With a bridge linking the Jutland peninsula to the island of Funen, and a toll bridge (the 18km Storebæltsbroen, or Great Belt Bridge) from Funen to Zealand, it's possible to drive all the way from mainland Europe to Copenhagen (and on to Sweden).

BRIDGING THE GAP

With the bridge-tunnel connection between Denmark and Sweden such a success, now there are plans for a similar link between the German island of Fehmarn and the Danish island of Lolland. Planning is underway, with debate continuing on whether to close the 19km Fehmarn Belt with a bridge or tunnel; that decision is expected sometime in 2012, with a tunnel the likely outcome.

Whatever option is decided, it is hoped that construction will begin in 2014, and that the connection will be operating in 2020, considerably shortening travel time between Hamburg and Copenhagen. Read about the project at www.femern.com.

RIDESHARING

If you want to find passengers to share fuel costs, try www.carpooling.co.uk, which has an international search option.

There are also international car ferries to Danish islands. See p326 for more information.

NORWAY
Unless you fancy a road trip through southern Sweden to cross the Øresund Bridge, car ferries are still the most efficient (and often the most enjoyable) way to arrive from Norway. See p326 for more information.

SWEDEN
The remarkable 16km Øresunds Bron (Øresund Bridge) joins Copenhagen with Malmö, Sweden, via the E20 motorway. It's actually a combination of tunnel beneath the sea, artificial island (Peberholm), and a suspension bridge catering for cars and trains. The toll station is situated on the Swedish side. You can pay by cash (at the manned stations), credit/pay cards (automatic stations) and credit token (automatic passage). Read more at www.oresundsbron.com.

There is also the option of car ferries, including Gothenburg–Frederikshavn, Varberg–Grenaa, and Helsingborg–Helsingør. See p326 for more information.

UK
You could take the Channel Tunnel to the continent then make your way northeast through France, Belgium and Germany to Denmark. An alternative is to take the car ferry from Harwich to Esbjerg. See p327 for more.

Train
The Danish state railway, **Danske Statsbaner** (DSB;

70 13 14 15; www.dsb.dk) can provide schedule and fare information.

All Eurail, Inter-Rail and Scanrail tickets are valid on the DSB. That said, it's hard to get your money's worth on a rail pass if you're travelling most of the time in tiny Denmark, although a pass may make sense if you're visiting other countries as well. There's a dizzying variety of passes, depending on where you reside and where you're going to travel. For a basic rundown, see the boxed text, below.

A great reference for Europe-wide rail travel is the website **The Man In Seat 61** (www.seat61.com).

See p329 for more about travelling on trains within Denmark.

RAIL PASSES

In addition to the websites listed below, details about rail passes can be found at www.railpass.com. And remember, if you buy a rail pass, read the small print.

InterRail Passes
InterRail (www.interrailnet.com) passes are available to people who have lived in Europe for six months or more. They can be bought at most major stations and student travel outlets, as well as online.

InterRail has a **Global Pass** encompassing 30 countries that comes in five versions, ranging from five days of travel in 10 days to a full month's travel. Prices depend on age and class of travel. For an adult travelling in 2nd class for one month, the price is €619. There are differing prices for children (aged four to 11), youths (12 to 25 years) and seniors (over 60). Children aged three and under travel for free.

The InterRail **one-country pass** for Denmark can be used for three, four, six or eight days during a one-month period. An eight-day adult pass, travelling 2nd class, costs €235.

Eurail Passes
Eurail (www.eurail.com) passes are for those who've been in Europe for less than six months and the passes are supposed to be bought outside Europe. They're available from leading travel agencies and online.

Eurail Global Passes are good for travel in 22 European countries (not including the UK); forget it if you intend to travel a lot in Denmark. Passes are valid for 10 or 15 days within a two-month period, 15 or 21 consecutive days, or for one, two or three months.

The **Eurail Select Pass** provides between five and 15 days of unlimited travel within a two-month period in three to five bordering countries in Europe.

Eurail also offers a **Denmark one-country pass**, a **two-country regional pass** (covering Denmark and Sweden, or Denmark and Germany) and a **Scandinavia Rail Pass** (valid for travel in Norway, Sweden, Finland and Denmark). For these passes, you choose from between three and 10 days' train travel in a one- or two-month period. The adult seven-day national pass (valid for one month) costs €142.

THE ESSENTIAL TRANSPORT WEBSITE

For getting around in Denmark, the essential website is www.rejseplanen.dk. This excellent resource allows you to enter your start and end point, date and preferred time of travel, and will then give you the best travel option, which may involve walking or taking a bus or train. Bus routes are linked, travel times are given, and fares listed. You can also compare travel times and costs (and even carbon emissions) for public transport versus driving your own vehicle. You can't travel without it!

Sea

Ferry connections are possible between Denmark and Norway, Sweden, Germany, Poland (via Sweden), Iceland, the Faroe Islands and the UK.

Fares on these ships vary wildly, by season and by day of the week. The highest prices tend to occur on summer weekends and the lowest on winter weekdays. Discounts are often available, including for return tickets, car and passengers, holders of rail passes or student cards, and seniors. Child fares are usually half of the adult fares.

If travelling in peak times, in particular if you are bringing along a vehicle, you should always make reservations well in advance – this is doubly true in summer and on weekends. Taking a bicycle incurs a small additional fee.

Faroe Islands & Iceland

Smyril Line (www.smyril line.com) Makes the return journey from the northern Jutland port of Hirtshals to the Faroe Island capital of Tórshavn at least once a week year-round (one-way sailing time: 37 hours). The adult high-season one-way fare is 505kr plus cabin berth (from 360kr). From April to October the journey extends to Seyðisfjörður (Iceland) on a circuitous,

week-long route that calls in twice at Tórshavn (once north-bound, once south-bound). Cruise packages are available.

Germany

BornholmerFærgen (www. bornholmerfaergen.dk) From April to October, it sails from Sassnitz to Rønne (on Bornholm; 3½ hours, three to eight services weekly). The adult high-season one-way fare is 210kr.

Scandlines (www.scandlines. de) Operates to the southern Danish islands: Puttgarden–Rødbyhavn (on Lolland; 85kr in high season, 45 minutes, every half-hour); Rostock–Gedser (on Falster; 100kr in high season, 1¾ hours, nine times daily).

SyltExpress (www.syltfae hre.de) Operates between Havneby (on west-coast Rømø) and the German island of Sylt (45 minutes) several times a day, year-round. Adult high-season one-way fare is 74kr.

Norway

Color Line (www.colorline. com) Connects Kristiansand–Hirtshals (3¼ hours) and Larvik–Hirtshals (3¾ hours) a couple of times daily, year-round. Adult high-season one-way fare is from 500kr on both routes.

DFDS Seaways (www. dfdsseaways.com) Connects Oslo with Copenhagen daily (16½ hours). The adult high-

season one-way fare is from 1100kr.

Fjordline (www.fjordline.com) Runs a fast catamaran on the Kristiansand–Hirtshals route (one way from 289kr in high season, 2¼ hours) two or three times daily from mid-April to mid-September. Fjordline also runs additional year-round ferry connections from Bergen to Hirtshals via Stavanger (the Bergen–Hirtshals journey time is 20 hours, while the Stavanger–Hirtshals is 11½ hours). The adult high-season one-way fare costs from 279kr on both of these routes.

Stena Line (www.stenaline. com) Connects Oslo and Frederikshavn daily during July to August, and six times a week the rest of the year. Sailing time varies, from 8½ hours to 13 hours. Adult high-season one-way fare is 215kr.

Poland

Polferries (www.polferries. com) Connects Świnoujście with Ystad in southern Sweden daily (7¾ hours); from Ystad there is a connecting bus service to Copenhagen via the Øresund Bridge for foot passengers; those in cars receive a pass for passage across the bridge. Note that from Ystad there are regular ferries to Bornholm. The adult high-season one-way fare is 520kr.

Sweden

BornholmerFærgen (www. bornholmerfaergen.dk) Runs frequently (up to eight times daily) between Ystad and Rønne (Bornholm; fast ferry 1¼ hours, regular ferry 2½ hours). Adult high-season one-way fare is 181kr.

Scandlines (www.scand lines.de) Makes the 20-minute journey from Helsingborg to Helsingør dozens of times daily (up to four sailings every hour). Adult high-season one-way fare is 28kr.

Stena Line (www.stenaline. com) Operates two popular routes: Gothenburg–Frederikshavn (300kr in high season, fast ferry two hours, regular ferry 3½ hours) and Varberg–Grenaa (205kr in high season, 4¼ hours to 5¼ hours).

UK

DFDS Seaways (www.dfds seaways.com) Connects Harwich with Esbjerg (17 hours) with up to four sailings per week in either direction. Adult high-season one-way fare is from £60, plus cabin (from £135).

GETTING AROUND

Air

Denmark's small size and efficient train network mean that domestic air traffic is limited, usually to business travellers and people connecting from international flights through Copenhagen. Still, domestic carriers offer frequent services between Copenhagen and a few of the more distant corners of the country.

Cimber Sterling (www. cimber.com) Has flights connecting Copenhagen with regional airports at Aalborg, Aarhus, Billund, Bornholm, Karup and Sønderborg. It also flies between Billund and Bornholm.

Scandinavian Airlines (SAS; www.flysas.com) Connects Copenhagen with Aarhus and Aalborg.

Bicycle

It's easy to travel with a bike anywhere in Denmark, even when you're not riding it, as bicycles can readily be taken on ferries and trains for a modest fee. Be aware on trains that reservations should be made at least three hours prior to departure because bikes generally travel in a separate section of the train.

Cyclists here are very well catered for, and there are excellent cycling routes throughout the country (for more information, see p296).

Always lock up your bike, especially if you're travelling with an expensive model, as bike theft is not uncommon, particularly in larger cities.

Hire

Rest assured, you'll be able to hire a bike in almost every Danish town and village. Some tourist offices, hostels and camping grounds rent them out, and some bike shops provide a hire service. A few upmarket hotels have free bikes for guest use, while the largest cities (Copenhagen, Aarhus, Odense, Aalborg) have a free *bycykler* (town bike) scheme. Helmets are not compulsory for cyclists in Denmark.

If you're renting, prices average around 80/350kr per day/week for something basic. Note that helmets are generally not included with hired bicycles.

Boat

There's an extensive network of ferries linking Denmark's many islands. See listings in the destination chapters for details.

Bus

Long-distance buses run a distant second to trains. Still, some cross-country bus routes work out to about 25% cheaper than trains.

Daily express buses include connections between Copenhagen and Aarhus (290kr, three hours) and Copenhagen and Aalborg (330kr, 5½ hours) – full timetables and the Jutland cities served are at www. abildskou.dk.

There's also a daily express bus between the Jutland port cities of Frederikshavn and Esbjerg (340kr, five hours), which runs via Aalborg. See www.express bus.dk or listings in the destination chapters for details.

Car & Motorcycle

Denmark is an excellent destination for a driving holiday. Roads are high quality and usually well signposted. Except during rush hour, traffic is quite light, even in major cities. One thing to be aware of is the large number of cyclists – they often have the right of way. It is particularly important that you check cycle lanes before turning right.

Access to and from Danish motorways is straightforward: roads leading out of town centres are named after the main city that they lead to (eg the road heading out of Odense to Faaborg is called Faaborgvej). Petrol stations, with toilets, baby-changing facilities and minimarkets, are at 50km intervals on motorways.

Denmark's extensive ferry network carries motor vehicles at reasonable rates. Fares for cars average three times the passenger rate. It's wise for drivers to make ferry reservations in advance, even

CAMPERVANNING

Camper vans are an excellent and increasingly popular way to tour Denmark and most camping grounds are well set up for their use. Although your camper van can be your home away from home – an eating, sleeping and entertainment centre – note that free camping, such as in motorway rest areas, is illegal in Denmark.

ROAD DISTANCES (KM)

	Aalborg	Copenhagen	Esbjerg	Frederikshavn	Grenaa	Helsingør	Kalundborg	Kolding	Næstved	Nyborg	Odense	Ringkøbing	Rødby	Skagen	Thisted	Tønder	Viborg	Århus (Aarhus)
Aalborg	---																	
Copenhagen	402	---																
Esbjerg	216	298	---															
Frederikshavn	65	465	278	---														
Grenaa	136	367	216	193	---													
Helsingør	443	47	339	506	408	---												
Kalundborg	345	103	241	408	310	139	---											
Kolding	199	230	72	261	164	271	173	---										
Næstved	342	85	238	405	307	125	71	152	---									
Nyborg	274	228	170	337	239	169	71	102	68	---								
Odense	243	165	139	306	208	206	108	71	105	37	---							
Ringkøbing	174	336	81	236	188	377	279	115	276	208	177	---						
Rødby	410	181	306	473	375	221	176	238	105	136	173	344	---					
Skagen	105	505	319	41	233	546	448	302	445	377	346	277	513	---				
Thisted	90	399	185	138	186	440	342	196	339	271	240	123	407	172	---			
Tønder	284	315	77	347	249	356	258	86	255	187	156	148	323	387	252	---		
Viborg	80	323	136	142	100	354	266	119	263	195	164	94	331	183	87	205	---	
Århus (Aarhus)	112	304	153	171	63	345	ferry	101	244	176	145	127	312	212	153	186	66	---

if it's only a couple of hours ahead of time. On weekends and holidays, ferries on prime crossings can be completely booked. See destination chapters for more information on car ferries.

There's brief but useful information on the English-language pages of www.trafikken.dk. The hotline 1888 has automated traffic information (traffic conditions, road works, detours); alas, it's only in Danish.

Driving Licence

Short-term visitors may hire a car with only their home country's driving licence (so long as the licence is written in Roman script; if not, an international driving licence is necessary).

Fuel

Leaded and unleaded petrol and diesel fuel are available. Although prices fluctuate in keeping with international oil prices, prices at the time of research were around 12kr per litre.

In towns, petrol stations may be open until 10pm or midnight, but there are some 24-hour services. In rural areas, many stations close in the early evening and don't open at all on weekends. Some have unstaffed 24-hour automatic pumps operated with credit cards.

Hire

Rental cars are relatively expensive in Denmark, but a little research can mean big savings. Walk-in rates start at about 650kr per day for a small car, althoug h naturally the per-day rates drop the longer you rent.

You may get the best deal on a car rental by booking with an international rental agency before you arrive. Be sure to ask about promotional rates, pre-pay schemes etc. Ensure you get a deal covering unlimited kilometres.

Avis, Budget, Europcar and Hertz are among the largest operators in Denmark, with offices in major cities, airports and other ports of entry. There are very few local budget operators. If you'll be using a rental car for a while, you might consider hiring your car in cheaper Germany and either return it there afterwards, or negotiate a slightly more expensive one-way deal.

Rental companies' weekend rates, when available, offer real savings. For about 1000kr, you can hire a small car from Friday afternoon to Monday morning, including VAT and insurance. These deals may have restrictions on the amount of kilometres included (often around 300km) – request a plan that includes unlimited kilometres if you'll need it.

Road Rules

» Drive on the right-hand side of the road.

» Cars and motorcycles must have dipped headlights on at all times.

» Drivers are required to carry a warning triangle in case of breakdown.

» Seat belt use is mandatory. Children under 135cm must be secured with approved child restraint appropriate to the child's age, size and weight.

» Motorcycle riders (but not cyclists) must wear helmets.

» Speed limits: 50km/h in towns and built-up areas, 80km/h on major roads, up to 130km/h on motorways. Maximum speed for vehicles with trailers: 80km/h. Speeding fines can be severe.

» Using a hand-held mobile phone while driving is illegal; hands-free use is permitted.

» It's illegal to drive with a blood-alcohol concentration of 0.05% or more.

» Use of a parking disc (P-skive) is usually required – this is a device that looks like a clock, which you place on the dashboard of your car to indicate the time you arrived at a car-parking space. Discs are often available from petrol stations and tourist offices.

» Motorways have emergency telephones every 2km interval, indicated by arrows on marker posts. From other telephones, dial ☏112 for emergencies.

Tolls

There are two toll routes in Denmark:

» The 18km motorway bridge across the **Store-bælt** (Great Belt) linking Funen and Zealand (www.storebaelt.dk). Casual one-way passage for a regular car/motorcycle is 220/115kr. For customer service, phone ☏70 15 10 15.

» The 16km motorway bridge/tunnel across the **Øresund** between Denmark and Sweden (www.oresundbron.com). Casual one-way passage for a regular car/motorcycle is 295/165kr. For customer service, phone ☏70 23 90 60.

Hitching

Hitching is never entirely safe anywhere in the world and we don't recommend it. Travellers who decide to hitch should understand that they are taking a small but potentially serious risk.

At any rate, hitching is not a common practice in Denmark and generally not a very rewarding one. It's also illegal on motorways.

For more info on the ins and outs of hitching, check out www.digihitch.com.

Local Transport

Bus

Nearly every town in Denmark supports a network of local buses, which circulate around the town centre and also connect it with outlying areas. In smaller towns, the local bus terminal is often adjacent to the train station and/or long-distance bus terminal.

Fares are around 18kr to 26kr per ride. A *klippekort* can be useful – this is a type of multiple-use transport ticket, often providing 10 rides at a discounted rate to the regular ticket price (they can be used by more than one person).

Taxi

Taxis are generally readily available for hire in city centres, near major shopping centres and at train stations. If you see a taxi with a lit *fri* sign (or a green light), you can wave it down, or you can phone for a taxi instead – hotels and tourist offices have numbers for local companies. Tipping is included in the fare.

Train

Denmark has a very reliable train system with reasonable fares and frequent services. The network extends to most corners of the country, with the exception of the southern islands and a pocket of northwestern Jutland. In these areas, a good network of local buses connects towns.

Most long-distance trains on major routes operate at least hourly throughout the day. **DSB** (☏70 13 14 15; www.dsb.dk) runs virtually all trains in Denmark. Types of DSB trains include the following:

InterCity (IC) Ultramodern comforts, cushioned seats, reading lights, headphone jacks, play areas for children.

InterCityLyn (ICL) On certain well-travelled routes. Same facilities as InterCity, but with fewer stops.

Regionaltog Regional trains; reservations generally not accepted.

S-tog The combined urban and suburban rail network of Greater Copenhagen.

Fares & Discounts

Standard train fares work out to be a fraction over 1kr per kilometre, with the highest fare possible between any two points in Denmark topping out at around 450kr (Copenhagen to Skagen). The reservation fee for seats is 30kr. Note that the 'Stillezone' on trains is a quiet zone.

A **DSB 1** (1st-class ticket) generally costs about 50% more than the standard fare. DSB1 tickets give an automatic seat guarantee on IC or ICL services.

TIP!

Nearly all Danish train stations have left-luggage lockers (from 20kr for 24 hours).

Discounts include the following:

Children (under 12) Travel free if they are with an adult travelling on a standard ticket (each adult can take two children free).

Children (aged under 15) Half the adult fare.

Group *'Minigruppe'* offers 20% discount for groups of three to seven people travelling on the same ticket (minimum two adults); there are also *'gruppebillet'* rebates for eight or more adults travelling together (contact DSB to access these).

Orange Discounted tickets (as low as 99kr for lengthy journeys – Copenhagen–Aarhus, for example) – although the number of tickets available at that price is limited. To find the cheapest fares, you should buy your ticket well in advance (up to two months before your travel date), travel outside peak hours, and travel Monday to Thursday or on a Saturday.

Seniors (65 and over) A 25% discount on Friday and Sunday and 50% discount on other days.

Youth (aged 16 to 25) Can buy a DSB WildCard (youth card) valid for one year for 185kr; it allows a 25% discount on Friday and Sunday and a 50% discount on other days.

Train Passes

For details of rail passes that can be used in Denmark (some of which should be bought before you arrive in the country), see the boxed text, p325.

Language

WANT MORE?

For in-depth language information and handy phrases, check out Lonely Planet's *Scandinavian Phrasebook*. You'll find it at **shop.lonelyplanet.com**, or you can buy Lonely Planet's iPhone phrasebooks at the Apple App Store.

As a member of the Scandinavian or North Germanic language family, Danish is closely related to Swedish and Norwegian. With about 5.5 million speakers, it's the official language of Denmark and has co-official status – alongside Greenlandic and Faroese respectively – in Greenland and the Faroese Islands. Until 1944 it was also the official language of Iceland and today is taught in schools there as the first foreign language. Danish is also a minority language in the area of Schleswig-Holstein in northern Germany, where it has some 30,000 speakers.

Most of the sounds in Danish have equivalents in English, and by reading our coloured pronunciation guides as if they were English, you're sure to be understood. There are short and long versions of each vowel, and additional 'combined vowels' or diphthongs. Consonants can be 'swallowed' and even omitted completely, creating (together with vowels) a glottal stop or *stød* steudh which sounds rather like the Cockney pronunciation of the 'tt' in 'bottle'. Note that ai is pronounced as in 'aisle', aw as in 'saw', eu as the 'u' in 'nurse', ew as the 'ee' in 'see' with rounded lips, ow as in 'how', dh as the 'th' in 'that', and r is trilled. The stressed syllables are in italics in our pronunciation guides. Polite and informal forms are indicated with 'pol' and 'inf' respectively.

BASICS

Hello.	*Goddag.*	go·*da*
Goodbye.	*Farvel.*	faar·*vel*
Yes./No.	*Ja./Nej.*	ya/nai
Please.	*Vær så venlig.*	ver saw *ven*·lee
Thank you.	*Tak.*	taak
You're welcome.	*Selv tak.*	sel taak
Excuse me.	*Undskyld mig.*	*awn*·skewl mai
Sorry.	*Undskyld.*	*awn*·skewl

How are you?		
Hvordan går det?		vor·*dan* gawr dey
Good, thanks.		
Godt, tak.		got taak
What's your name?		
Hvad hedder		va *hey*·dha
De/du? (pol/inf)		dee/doo
My name is ...		
Mit navn er ...		mit nown ir ...
Do you speak English?		
Taler De/du		*ta*·la dee/doo
engelsk? (pol/inf)		*eng*·elsk
I don't understand.		
Jeg forstår ikke.		yai for·*stawr i*·ke

ACCOMMODATION

Where's a ...?	*Hvor er der ...?*	vor ir deyr ...
campsite	*en camping-plads*	in *kaam*·ping·plas
guesthouse	*et gæstehus*	it *ges*·te·hoos
hotel	*et hotel*	it hoh·*tel*
youth hostel	*et ungdoms-herberg*	it *awng*·doms·heyr·beyrg

Do you have a ... room?	*Har I et ... værelse?*	haar ee it ... *verl*·se
single	*enkelt*	*eng*·kelt
double	*dobbelt*	*do*·belt

How much is it per ...?	Hvor meget koster det per ...?	vor maa·yet kos·ta dey peyr ...
night	nat	nat
person	person	per·sohn

DIRECTIONS

Where's the ...?
Hvor er ...?   vor ir ...

What's the address?
Hvad er adressen?   va ir a·draa·sen

Can you show me (on the map)?
Kan De/du vise mig   kan dee/doo vee·se mai
det (på kortet)? (pol/inf)   dey (paw kor·tet)

How far (away) is it?
Hvor langt (væk) er det?   vor laangt (vek) ir dey

How do I get there?
Hvordan kommer   vor·dan ko·ma
jeg derhen?   yai deyr·hen

Turn ...	Drej ...	drai ...
at the corner	ved hjørnet	vi yeur·nedh
at the traffic lights	ved trafik-lyset	vi traa·feek·lew·set
left	til venstre	til vens·tre
right	til højre	til hoy·re

It's ...	Det er ...	dey ir ...
behind ...	bag ...	ba ...
far (away)	langt (væk)	laangt (vek)
in front of ...	foran ...	fo·ran ...
left	til venstre	til vens·tre
near (to ...)	nær (ved ...)	ner (vi ...)
next to ...	ved siden af ...	vi see·dhen a ...
on the corner	på hjørnet	paw yeur·net
opposite ...	på modsate side af ...	paw mohdh·sa·te see·dhe a ...
right	til højre	til hoy·re
straight ahead	lige ud	li·e oodh

Signs	
Indgang	Entrance
Udgang	Exit
Åben	Open
Lukket	Closed
Forbudt	Prohibited
Toilet	Toilets
Herrer	Men
Damer	Women

EATING & DRINKING

What would you recommend?
Hvad kan De/du   va kan dee/doo
anbefale? (pol/inf)   an·bey·fa·le

What's the local speciality?
Hvad er den lokale   va ir den loh·ka·le
specialitet?   spey·sha·lee·teyt

Do you have vegetarian food?
Har I vegetarmad?   haar ee vey·ge·taar·madh

Cheers!
Skål!   skawl

I'd like (the) ..., please.	Jeg vil gerne have ..., tak.	yai vil gir·ne ha ... taak
bill	regningen	rai·ning·en
drink list	vinkortet	veen·kor·tet
menu	menuen	me·new·en
that dish	den ret	den ret

Could you prepare a meal without ...?	Kan I lave et måltid uden ...?	kan ee la·ve it mawl·teedh oo·dhen ...
butter	smør	smeur
eggs	æg	eg
meat stock	kød-boullion	keudh·boo·lee·yong

Key Words

bar	bar	baar
bottle	flaske	flas·ke
breakfast	morgenmad	morn·madh
cafe	café	ka·fey
children's menu	børne-menu	beur·ne·mey·new
cold	kold	kol
cup	kop	kop
daily special	dagens ret	da·ens rat
dinner	middag	mi·da
drink	drink	drink
food	mad	madh
fork	gaffel	gaa·fel
glass	glas	glas
hot	varm	vaarm
knife	kniv	kneev
lunch	frokost	froh·kost
market	marked	maar·kedh
menu	menu/spisekort	me·new/spee·se·kort
plate	tallerken	ta·ler·ken
restaurant	restaurant	res·toh·rang

snack	mellemmåltid	me·lem·mawl·teedh
spoon	ske	skey
teaspoon	teske	tey·skey
with	med	me
without	uden	oo·dhen

Meat & Fish

beef	oksekød	ok·se·keudh
chicken	hønsekød	heun·se·keudh
cod	torsk	torsk
eel	ål	orl
fish	fisk	fisk
herring	sild	seel
lamb	lammekød	la·me·keudh
lobster	hummer	haw·ma
meat	kød	keudh
mutton	fårekød	faw·re·keudh
pork	svinekød	svee·ne·keudh
salmon	laks	laks
seafood	skaldyr	skal·dewr
steak	engelsk bøf	eng·elsk beuf
trout	forel/ørred	foh·rel/eur·redh
tuna	tunfisk	toon·fisk
veal	kalvekød	kal·ve·keudh

Fruit & Vegetables

apple	æble	eb·le
apricot	abrikos	a·bree·kohs
banana	banan	ba·nan
beans	bønner	beu·na
cabbage	kål	kawl
carrots	gulerødder	goo·le·reu·dha
cauliflower	blomkål	blom·kawl
cherry	kirsebær	keer·se·ber
corn	majs	mais
cucumber	agurk	a·goork
fruit	frugt	frawgt
leek	porre	po·re
lemon	citron	see·trohn
mushroom	champignon	sham·peen·yong
nuts	nødder	neu·dha
onion	løg	loy
orange	appelsin	a·pel·seen
peach	fersken	fers·ken
peanut	jordnød	jor·neudh
pear	pære	pe·re

Question Words

How?	Hvordan?	vor·dan
What?	Hvad?	va
When?	Hvornår?	vor·nawr
Where?	Hvor?	vor
Who?	Hvem?	vem
Why?	Hvorfor?	vor·for

peas	ærter	er·ta
pineapple	ananas	a·na·nas
plum	blomme	blo·me
potato	kartoffel	ka·to·fel
spinach	spinat	spee·nat
strawberry	jordbær	jor·ber
vegetable	grønsag	greun·saa
watermelon	vandmelon	van·mey·lon

Other

bread	brød	breudh
butter	smør	smeur
cake	kage	ka·e
cheese	ost	awst
cream	fløde	fleu·dhe
egg	æg	eg
garlic	hvidløg	veedh·loy
honey	honning	ho·ning
ice	is	ees
jam	syltetøj	sewl·te·toy
noodles	nudler	noodh·la
pepper	peber	pey·wa
rice	ris	rees
salad	salat	sa·lat
soup	suppe	saw·pe
sugar	sukker	saw·ka

Drinks

beer	øl	eul
buttermilk	kærnemælk	ker·ne·melk
coffee	kaffe	ka·fe
(orange) juice	(appelsin-) juice	(aa·pel·seen·) joos
lemonade	citronvand	see·trohn·van
milk	mælk	melk
mineral water	mineralvand/ danskvand	mee·ne·ral·van/ dansk·van
red wine	rødvin	reudh·veen

soft drink	*sodavand*	soh·da·van
sparkling wine	*mousserende vin*	moo·sey·ra·ne veen
tea	*te*	tey
water	*vand*	van
white wine	*hvidvin*	veedh·veen

EMERGENCIES

Help!	*Hjælp!*	yelp
Go away!	*Gå væk!*	gaw vek
Call ...!	*Ring efter ...!*	ring ef·ta ...
a doctor	*en læge*	in le·ye
the police	*politiet*	poh·lee·tee·et

It's an emergency!
Det er et nødstilfælde! dey ir it neudhs·til·fe·le

I'm lost.
Jeg er faret vild. yai ir faa·ret veel

I'm sick.
Jeg er syg. yai ir sew

It hurts here.
Det gør ondt her. dey geur awnt heyr

I'm allergic to (antibiotics).
Jeg er allergisk over for (antibiotika). yai ir a·ler·geesk o·va for (an·tee·bee·oh·tee·ka)

Where's the toilet?
Hvor er toilettet? vor ir toy·le·tet

Numbers		
1	*en*	in
2	*to*	toh
3	*tre*	trey
4	*fire*	feer
5	*fem*	fem
6	*seks*	seks
7	*syv*	sew
8	*otte*	aw·te
9	*ni*	nee
10	*ti*	tee
20	*tyve*	tew·ve
30	*tredive*	traadh·ve
40	*fyrre*	fewr·re
50	*halvtreds*	hal·tres
60	*tres*	tres
70	*halvfjerds*	hal·fyers
80	*firs*	feers
90	*halvfems*	hal·fems
100	*hundrede*	hoon·re·dhe
1000	*tusind*	too·sen

SHOPPING & SERVICES

Where's the ...?	*Hvor er ...?*	vor ir ...
ATM	*der en hæve-automat*	deyr in he·ve-ow·toh·mat
bank	*der en bank*	deyr in baank
local internet cafe	*den lokale internet café*	den loh·ka·le in·ta·net ka·fey
nearest public phone	*den nærmeste telefonboks*	den ner·mes·te te·le·fohn·boks
post office	*der et postkontor*	deyr it post·kon·tohr
public toilet	*der et offentligt toilet*	deyr it o·fent·leet toy·let
tourist office	*turist-kontoret*	too·reest·kon·toh·ret

I'm looking for ...
Jeg leder efter ... yai li·dha ef·ta ...

Can I have a look?
Må jeg se? maw yai sey

Do you have any others?
Har I andre? haar ee aan·dre

How much is it?
Hvor meget koster det? vor maa·yet kos·ta dey

That's too expensive.
Det er for dyrt. dey ir for dewrt

What's your lowest price?
Hvad er jeres laveste pris? va ir ye·res la·ve·ste prees

There's a mistake in the bill. (restaurant/shop)
Der er en fejl i regningen/kvitteringen. deyr ir in fail ee rai·ning·en/kvee·tey·ring·en

TIME & DATES

What time is it?
Hvad er klokken? va ir klo·ken

It's (two) o'clock.
Klokken er (to). klo·ken ir (toh)

Half past (one).
Halv (to). (lit: half two) hal (toh)

At what time ...?
Hvad tid ...? va teedh ...

At ...
Klokken ... klo·ken ...

am (morning)	*om morgenen*	om mor·nen
pm (afternoon)	*om eftermiddagen*	om ef·taa·mi·da·en
pm (evening)	*om aftenen*	om aaft·nen
yesterday	*i går*	ee gawr
today	*i dag*	ee da
tomorrow	*i morgen*	ee morn

Road Signs

Ensrettet	One Way
Indkørsel Forbudt	No Entry
Motorvej	Freeway
Omkørsel	Detour
Parkering Forbudt	No Parking
Selvbetjening	Self Service
Vejarbejde	Roadworks
Vigepligt	Give Way

Monday	mandag	man·da
Tuesday	tirsdag	teers·da
Wednesday	onsdag	awns·da
Thursday	torsdag	tors·da
Friday	fredag	fre·da
Saturday	lørdag	leur·da
Sunday	søndag	seun·da

January	januar	ya·noo·ar
February	februar	feb·roo·ar
March	marts	maarts
April	april	a·preel
May	maj	mai
June	juni	yoo·nee
July	juli	yoo·lee
August	august	ow·gawst
September	september	sip·tem·ba
October	oktober	ohk·toh·ba
November	november	noh·vem·ba
December	december	dey·sem·ba

TRANSPORT

Public Transport

Is this the ... to (Aarhus)?	Er dette ... til (Århus)?	ir dey·te ... til (awr·hoos)
boat	båden	baw·dhen
bus	bussen	boo·sen
plane	flyet	flew·et
train	toget	taw·et

What time's the ... bus?	Hvad tid er den ... bus?	va teedh ir den ... boos
first	første	feurs·te
last	sidste	sees·te
next	næste	nes·te

One ... ticket (to Odense), please.	En ... billet (til Odense), tak.	in ... bee·let (til oh·dhen·se) taak
one-way	enkelt	eng·kelt
return	retur	rey·toor

At what time does (the train) arrive/leave?
Hvornår ankommer/   vor·nawr an·ko·ma/
afgår (toget)?   ow·gawr (taw·et)

Does it stop at (Østerport)?
Stopper den/det på   sto·pa den/dey paw
(Østerport)?   (eus·ta·port)

What's the next station/stop?
Hvad er næste station/   va ir nes·te sta·shohn/
stoppested?   sto·pe·stedh

Please tell me when we get to (Roskilde).
Sig venligst til når vi   see ven·leest til nawr vee
kommer til (Roskilde).   ko·ma til (ros·kee·le)

Please take me to (this address).
Vær venlig at køre mig   ver ven·lee at keu·re mai
til (denne adresse).   til (de·ne a·draa·se)

Please stop here.
Venligst stop her.   ven·leest stop heyr

Driving & Cycling

I'd like to hire a ...	Jeg vil gerne leje en ...	yai vil gir·ne lai·ye in ...
bicycle	cykel	sew·kel
car	bil	beel
motorbike	motor-cykel	moh·tor·sew·kel

air	luft	lawft
oil	olie	ohl·ye
park (car)	parkere	paar·key·ra
petrol	benzin	ben·seen
service station	benzin-station	ben·seen·sta·shohn
tyres	dæk	dek

Is this the road to (Kronborg Slot)?
Fører denne vej til   feu·ra de·ne vai til
(Kronborg Slot)?   (krohn·borg slot)

Can I get there by bicycle?
Kan jeg cykle derhen?   kan yai sewk·le deyr·hen

I need a mechanic.
Jeg har brug for en   yai haar broo for in
mekaniker.   mi·ka·ni·ka

I've run out of petrol.
Jeg er løbet tør for   yai ir leu·bet teur for
benzin.   ben·seen

I have a flat tyre.
Jeg er punkteret.   yai ir pawng·tey·ret

GLOSSARY

Note that the Danish letters æ, ø and å fall at the end of the alphabet. For words and phrases on food and drink, see p305.

akvavit – schnapps
allé – avenue
amt – county
apotek – pharmacy, chemist

bad – bath, bathroom
bageri – bakery
bakke – hill
banegård – train station
bibliotek – library
billet – ticket (P-billet means parking ticket required)
billetautomat – automated parking-ticket dispenser
Blue Flag award – eco-label for the sustainable development of beaches and marinas
bro – bridge
bryggeri – brewery
bugt – bay
by – town
børnemenu – children's menu

campingplads – camping ground
cykel – bicycle

dag – day
dagens ret – dish of the day
dansk – Danish
domkirke – cathedral
DSB – Danske Statsbaner (Danish State Railway), Denmark's national railway
dyrepark – animal park, zoo
døgn – 24-hour period

Fyn – Funen
fyr – lighthouse
færge – ferry
færgehavn – ferry harbour

gade – street
gammel, gamle – old
gård – courtyard, farm

hav – sea, ocean
have – garden
havn – harbour

helligdage – public holidays
hus – house
hverdage – weekdays (ie, Monday to Friday)
hygge – to make cosy (verb), cosiness (noun)
hyggelig – cosy (adjective)
hytte – hut, cabin

IC – intercity train
IR – inter-regional train

jernbane – railway
Jylland – Jutland

kart – map
keramik – ceramic, pottery
kirke – church
kirkegård – churchyard, cemetery
klint – cliff
klippekort – type of multiple-use transport ticket
klit – dune, sand hill
kloster – monastery
konditori – bakery with cafe tables
kort – card
kro – inn
kunst – art
køkken – kitchen
køreplan – timetable

lufthavn – airport
lystbådehavn – marina

mad – food
magasin – department store
morgenmad – breakfast
museet – museum
møntvask – coin laundry

nat – night
nord – north
ny – new

og – and

plads – place, square
plantage – plantation, tree farm, woods
P-skive – parking disc (device you place on car dashboard

to indicate the time you arrived at a parking space)
pris – price

retter – dishes, courses
rundkirke – fortified round church, found on Bornholm
rutebilstation – bus station (for long-distance buses)
røgeri – fish smokehouse
rådhus – town hall, city hall

samling – collection, usually of art
Sjælland – Zealand
skov – forest, woods
slagter – butcher
slot – castle
smørrebrød – open sandwich
sti – path, walkway
strand – beach, shoreline
stykke – piece (eg of fruit)
sund – sound
svømmehal – swimming pool
syd – south
sø – lake

teater – theatre
tog – train
torv, torvet – square, marketplace
turistkontor – tourist office
tårn – tower

udsigt – view, viewpoint
uge – week

vandrerhjem – youth and family hostel
vej – street, road
vest – west
værelse – room (to rent);

wienerbrød – Danish pastry, literally 'Vienna bread'

ø – island, usually attached as a suffix to the proper name
øl – beer
øst – east

å – river
år – year

behind the scenes

SEND US YOUR FEEDBACK

We love to hear from travellers – your comments keep us on our toes and help make our books better. Our well-travelled team reads every word on what you loved or loathed about this book. Although we cannot reply individually to postal submissions, we always guarantee that your feedback goes straight to the appropriate authors, in time for the next edition. Each person who sends us information is thanked in the next edition – the most useful submissions are rewarded with a selection of digital PDF chapters.

Visit **lonelyplanet.com/contact** to submit your updates and suggestions or to ask for help. Our award-winning website also features inspirational travel stories, news and discussions.

Note: We may edit, reproduce and incorporate your comments in Lonely Planet products such as guidebooks, websites and digital products, so let us know if you don't want your comments reproduced or your name acknowledged. For a copy of our privacy policy visit lonelyplanet.com/privacy.

OUR READERS

Many thanks to the travellers who used the last edition and wrote to us with helpful hints, useful advice and interesting anecdotes:

G Borchorst, Rowena Cahill,Marta Fernández, Ines Freier, Edward Arturo Haeusler, Kathrine Hansen, Mike Honings, Gary Kauffman, Jesper Klausholm, Jens Højlund Lauridsen, Henrik Madsen, Mick Mandrup, Annemarie Oorthuizen, Despoina Papadopoulou, Brian Quinn, Louisa Radice, Morag Reynish, Rolf Richardson, Ander Schroeder, Alex Smith, Vic Sofras, Mikkel Sönnichsen, TJ van de Ven, Arie van Oosterwijk, Bart vd Nieuwenhuizen, Guy Voets, Stephen Ziguras

AUTHOR THANKS

Carolyn Bain

Heartfelt gratitude goes to my Danish family, the Østergaards, who always welcome me back into the fold so warmly. A stellar support cast helped make this trip so memorable: Sally O'Brien and William and Fiona Reeve provided fine company at Noma; Graham Harris made Legoland so much fun; Karin Vidstrup Monk critiqued coffee with me in

Aarhus. To Poul Nielsen, much appreciation for hospitality in Hald Ege. To Cristian Bonetto, bouquets for making me laugh during write-up and for sterling work. Finally, *tusind tak* to the countless Danes who graciously shared their expertise, including Tina Jensen, Peter Jacobsen, Marie-Louise Munter and Christian Holmsted Olesen.

Cristian Bonetto

A sincere *tak* to all those who offered their expert insights on everything from Danish art, design and food, to the best spots to ride a bike. Special thanks to Vivi Schlechter, Henrik Bajer, Daniel Kruse, Tue Hesselberg Foged, as well as Mads and Mikkel Marschall. On the home front, huge thanks to my co-authors Carolyn Bain and Andrew Stone.

Andrew Stone

To Michael and Lissen, who were the reason I visited the country in the first place, thanks yet again for the amazing hospitality. And don't you ever dream of leaving the castle. My research on the ground was made much easier by the assistance of the various helpful tourist offices, not to mention locals who went out of the way to share their tips and insights. *Tusind tak.*

ACKNOWLEDGMENTS

Climate map data adapted from Peel MC, Finlayson BL & McMahon TA (2007) 'Updated World Map of the Köppen-Geiger Climate Classification', *Hydrology and Earth System Sciences*, 11, 163344.

Cover photograph: Nyhavn canal, Copenhagen; Massimo Borchi/Corbis

Many of the images in this guide are available for licensing from Lonely Planet Images: www.lonelyplanetimages.com.

This Book

This 6th edition of Lonely Planet's *Denmark* was researched and written by Carolyn Bain, Cristian Bonetto and Andrew Stone. The 5th edition was researched and written by Andrew Stone, Carolyn Bain, Michael Booth and Fran Parnell, and the 4th by Andrew Bender, Sally O'Brien, Andrew Stone, Rick Starey and Michael Grosberg. The 1st, 2nd and 3rd editions were researched and written by Glenda Bednure and Ned Friary. This guidebook was commissioned in Lonely Planet's London office, and produced by the following:

Commissioning Editors Katie O'Connell, Glenn van der Knijff
Coordinating Editor Evan Jones
Coordinating Cartographer Jolyon Philcox
Coordinating Layout Designer Wendy Wright
Managing Editors Barbara Delissen, Brigitte Ellemor, Martine Power, Kirsten Rawlings
Managing Cartographer Amanda Sierp
Managing Layout Designers Chris Girdler, Jane Hart
Assisting Editors Janet Austin, Kim Hutchins, Kate Kiely, Anne Mulvaney, Gabrielle Stefanos
Assisting Cartographers Enes Basic, Jennifer Johnson
Assisting Layout Designer Joseph Spanti
Cover Research Liz Abbott
Internal Image Research Sabrina Dalbesio
Language Content Annelies Mertens

Thanks to Helen Christinis, Ryan Evans, Yvonne Kirk, Trent Paton, Susan Paterson, John Taufa, Branislava Vladisavljevic, Gerald Walker, Juan Winata

NOTES

NOTES

how to use this book

These symbols will help you find the listings you want:

◉	Sights	👉	Tours	🍷	Drinking
🏄	Beaches	🎊	Festivals & Events	☆	Entertainment
🏃	Activities	🛏	Sleeping	🔒	Shopping
🎓	Courses	🍴	Eating	❶	Information/Transport

Look out for these icons:

TOP CHOICE	Our author's recommendation
FREE	No payment required
🌿	A green or sustainable option

Our authors have nominated these places as demonstrating a strong commitment to sustainability – for example by supporting local communities and producers, operating in an environmentally friendly way, or supporting conservation projects.

These symbols give you the vital information for each listing:

📞	Telephone Numbers	📶	Wi-Fi Access	🚌	Bus
🕐	Opening Hours	🏊	Swimming Pool	⛴	Ferry
🅿	Parking	🥗	Vegetarian Selection	Ⓜ	Metro
⊖	Nonsmoking	📋	English-Language Menu	Ⓢ	Subway
❄	Air-Conditioning	👪	Family-Friendly	⊖	London Tube
@	Internet Access	🐾	Pet-Friendly	🚊	Tram
				🚆	Train

Reviews are organised by author preference.

Map Legend

Sights
- 🏖 Beach
- 🔵 Buddhist
- 🏰 Castle
- ✝ Christian
- 🕉 Hindu
- ☪ Islamic
- ✡ Jewish
- ❶ Monument
- 🏛 Museum/Gallery
- 🔲 Ruin
- 🍇 Winery/Vineyard
- 🐾 Zoo
- ◉ Other Sight

Activities, Courses & Tours
- 🤿 Diving/Snorkelling
- 🛶 Canoeing/Kayaking
- ⛷ Skiing
- 🏄 Surfing
- 🏊 Swimming/Pool
- 🚶 Walking
- 🏄 Windsurfing
- ➕ Other Activity/Course/Tour

Sleeping
- 🛏 Sleeping
- ⛺ Camping

Eating
- 🍴 Eating

Drinking
- ☕ Drinking
- ☕ Cafe

Entertainment
- 🎭 Entertainment

Shopping
- 🔒 Shopping

Information
- 📮 Post Office
- ❶ Tourist Information

Transport
- ✈ Airport
- ⊗ Border Crossing
- 🚌 Bus
- 🚡 Cable Car/Funicular
- 🚲 Cycling
- ⛴ Ferry
- Ⓜ Metro
- 🚝 Monorail
- 🅿 Parking
- Ⓢ S-Bahn
- 🚕 Taxi
- 🚉 Train/Railway
- 🚊 Tram
- ⊖ Tube Station
- Ⓤ U-Bahn
- • Other Transport

Routes
- Tollway
- Freeway
- Primary
- Secondary
- Tertiary
- Lane
- Unsealed Road
- Plaza/Mall
- Steps
-)≈≈(Tunnel
- Pedestrian Overpass
- Walking Tour
- Walking Tour Detour
- Path

Boundaries
- International
- State/Province
- Disputed
- Regional/Suburb
- Marine Park
- Cliff
- Wall

Population
- 🔴 Capital (National)
- ◉ Capital (State/Province)
- ● City/Large Town
- • Town/Village

Geographic
- 🏠 Hut/Shelter
- 💡 Lighthouse
- 👁 Lookout
- ▲ Mountain/Volcano
- 🌴 Oasis
- 🌳 Park
-)(Pass
- 🏕 Picnic Area
- 💧 Waterfall

Hydrography
- River/Creek
- Intermittent River
- Swamp/Mangrove
- Reef
- Canal
- Water
- Dry/Salt/Intermittent Lake
- Glacier

Areas
- Beach/Desert
- +++ Cemetery (Christian)
- ××× Cemetery (Other)
- Park/Forest
- Sportsground
- Sight (Building)
- Top Sight (Building)

OUR STORY

A beat-up old car, a few dollars in the pocket and a sense of adventure. In 1972 that's all Tony and Maureen Wheeler needed for the trip of a lifetime – across Europe and Asia overland to Australia. It took several months, and at the end – broke but inspired – they sat at their kitchen table writing and stapling together their first travel guide, *Across Asia on the Cheap*. Within a week they'd sold 1500 copies. Lonely Planet was born.

Today, Lonely Planet has offices in Melbourne, London and Oakland, with more than 600 staff and writers. We share Tony's belief that 'a great guidebook should do three things: inform, educate and amuse'.

OUR WRITERS

Carolyn Bain

Coordinating author, Southern Jutland, Central Jutland, Northern Jutland As a teenager, Melbourne-born Carolyn spent a year living smack in the heart of Jutland, and today speaks (often mangled) Danish with a *jysk* (Jutlandish) accent, according to those who know such things. Since her year among the Danes, Carolyn has frequently returned to dose up on history, hospitality and *hygge*, and she drops in while updating guidebooks to various parts of northern Europe (including Sweden and Estonia). She also covered Jutland for the previous edition of this title. As with every Denmark visit, on this trip she was in heaven revisiting favourite haunts such as Skagen and Ribe, coveting designer chairs, rummaging in flea markets and lingering over brunch plates.

Read more about Carolyn Bain at:
lonelyplanet.com/members/carolynbain

Cristian Bonetto

Copenhagen; Zealand; Møn, Falster & Lolland; Bornholm As a fan of modernist furniture, locavore menus, and cycle-toned bodies, Cristian's lust for Denmark was fate. Since his first visit in 2003, the reformed soap scribe has developed a chronic obsession with the country's enlightened attitudes and creative edge. His musings on all things Danish have appeared in Lonely Planet's *Copenhagen Encounter* and *Scandinavia* guides, as well as in numerous magazines across the globe. When he's not nibbling on wood sorrel, peddling across Møn, or downloading Alphabeat songs, chances are you'll find Cristian cool-hunting in his other favourite haunts – New York, Naples and his beloved hometown, Melbourne.

Read more about Cristian Bonetto at:
lonelyplanet.com/members/cristianbonetto

Andrew Stone

Funen, History, Directory Journalist and author Andrew first visited Denmark in the late 1990s to see friends who had settled there and has been back almost every year since for work and pleasure. In his time he has explored most of the country while researching the previous two editions of this title as well as three editions of Lonely Planet's *Scandinavia*.

Read more about Andrew Stone at:
lonelyplanet.com/members/andrewstone

Published by Lonely Planet Publications Pty Ltd
ABN 36 005 607 983
6th edition – May 2012
ISBN 978 1 74179 281 2
© Lonely Planet 2012   Photographs © as indicated 2012
10 9 8 7 6 5 4 3 2 1
Printed in China